AMERICA IN THE AGE OF THE TITANS

SEAN DENNIS CASHMAN

AMERICA IN THE AGE
OF THE TITANS

The Progressive Era and
World War I

NEW YORK UNIVERSITY PRESS

NEW YORK & LONDON

Library of Congress Cataloging-in-Publication Data
Cashman, Sean Dennis.
America in the age of the titans : the Progressive Era and World
War I / Sean Dennis Cashman.
p.   cm.
Bibliography: p.
Includes index.
ISBN 0-8147-1410-2   ISBN 0-8147-1411-0 (pbk.)
1. United States—History—1901–1920.   2. World War, 1914–1918—
United States.   3. Progressivism (United States politics)
I. Title.
E741.C27 1988
973.91—dc19   87-31563
CIP

New York University Press books are Smythe-sewn
and printed on permanent durable acid-free paper.

Book design by Ken Venezio

For
Peter and Maria Diamandopoulos

Contents

·ℱ·

Illustrations

·❦·

Preface

·ⱻ·

THIS BOOK is intended as a general, interdisciplinary history of
the United States from the accession of Theodore Roosevelt
to the presidency in 1901 to the rout of Woodrow Wilson's foreign policy in 1920. It charts the course of domestic politics and
foreign policies, and tells something of the stories of industrial
and economic, social and cultural history. These were heroic years
for the United States. Not only were the tremendous processes
of industrialization, immigration, and urbanization begun in the
Gilded Age of 1865–1901, largely accomplished in the early years
of the century, but equally significant developments occurred in
politics, transportation and communication, culture, and world
affairs. The profound achievements of the Progressive Era of 1901–
17 were set against the dramatic advent of World War I and the
Russian Revolution.

The book is a work of synthesis, based partly on primary
sources, partly on recent scholarship. It is complemented by a
sequel on America in the period 1920–41. However, certain subjects are treated thematically in a single chapter. Hence the story

of architecture is told in this volume, while the story of black America is told in the companion volume. The book aims at a clear presentation of essential facts and a synthesis of academic interpretation, and places some emphasis on the personalities of the principal actors.

I began this book at the invitation of Colin Jones, who offered constructive advice about structure, composition, and detail. My research was facilitated by two travel grants provided by the University of Manchester, England, where I used to teach in the Department of American Studies. The support and encouragement of my Manchester colleagues, notably Professor Peter Marshall, were most appreciated. The book was completed in March 1987 while I was teaching at New York University as visiting professor in history. The invitation to teach at NYU came from Professors Carl Prince and David Reimers, formerly, and respectively, chairman, and director of graduate studies, in the history department. The new chairman, Professor Thomas Bender, and director of graduate studies, Professor Robert Scally, as well as the director of undergraduate studies, Professor Fred Shult, and their most considerate administrator, Lynn Anderson, indefatigably steered me through the hazards of a new university while the manuscript was being completed. I thank them for the invitation and, also, my colleagues at Manchester for the generous way they allowed me to accept it.

While wanting to give appropriate weight to political history, both Colin Jones and I also wanted to emphasize major developments in social and cultural history, including inventions, transportation, and the arts. Even so, *America in the Age of the Titans* is not a complete history. It does not treat such important subjects as philosophy, education, sports, and music. I wrote, and we rejected, separate chapters on cities and industrial organization.

Without the assistance and participation of several friends and colleagues my task would have been far harder. Iain Halliday undertook preliminary work, locating material, synthesizing previous scholarship, and writing drafts on Progressivism, architecture, and the arts. The extent and variety of his work were much appreciated. Daniel Couzens both found material and prepared draft sections on the subjects of inventions and radio. Chris Hasson provided a detailed account of workers and labor organizations. In every case my friends' help prepared the ground for what had to be done.

Two other colleagues provided useful, critical scrutiny of my work. Dr. J. A. Thompson of Cambridge and Princeton universities, and an eminent authority on Progressivism, read the chapters on Roosevelt, the Progressives, and Wilson. He offered valuable advice about how to explain the progressive movement and corrected various minor errors as well as providing stimulating ideas on presentation. Dr. Daniel Cornford, formerly of the Universities of California at Santa Barbara, San Francisco, and Manchester, and an expert on labor history, read the material on workers and labor organization. He had vigorous arguments to make about what exactly should be included and what rejected, and what extra scholarship had to be done.

I also owe much to the sustained support of my mother, Margaret Cashman, and my good friend Kenneth McArthur throughout the long writing of this book and its sequel.

The book is partly intended as a tribute to journalist and editor Mark Sullivan whose six volume history of America from the turn of the century to the 1920s, collectively entitled *Our Times,* provides a mine of information on such varied subjects as Theodore Roosevelt's personality and politics, pure food and drugs, new spelling, and Woodrow Wilson's war strategies. Mark Sullivan's interpretations make it a useful complement to the considerable professional achievements of political, social, and economic historians who have been working on the same period in more recent times and I have drawn from his work. In order to make *America in the Age of the Titans* and its prequel, *America in the Gilded Age,* truly self-contained, I chose to repeat a modicum of thematic material on such subjects as inventions, industry, progressivism, monopolies, architecture, movies, and imperialism in both books.

The illustrations were found in the Museum of Modern Art, the Whitney Museum of American Art, and, principally, in the

Prints and Photographs Division of the Library of Congress. Ms. Mary Ison, head of the reference section, and Ms. Maya Felaca were most helpful in advising on the selection of illustrations. Mrs. Eileen Grimes typed the manuscript. Ms. Caroline Sutton typed most of the voluminous correspondence. Paul Sturm prepared the index. My thanks to them for their labor.

Note on the English Presentation of Chinese Names

In the past few years what amounts to a linguistic revolution has been accomplished in the new preferred English presentation of Chinese names and place names. We are all now aware that Beijing is a more accurate rendering of the name of the Chinese capital than the traditional Peking. We have become familiar with such new forms as the Liaodong Peninsula instead of Liaotung, of Guangzhou Bay instead of Kwangchow Bay, of Weihai instead of Wei-hai-Wei, of Heilongjiang instead of Heilungkiang, and of Shandong instead of Shantung. However, some of the revisions are more striking. The dowager empress whom we formerly knew as Tz'u-hsi should now be known as Cixi, and the Manchu dynasty as the Qing Dynasty. Port Arthur is now known as Lushun, Jehol is known as Rehe, and Dairen as Dalian, and the Pescadores as the Penghu Islands or the Penghus, or Penghu Liedao. However, I thought it better, for the time being at any rate, to preserve traditional English spelling on the grounds that these forms were those current at the time of the period covered in this book and that to introduce the new versions with substantive explanations in the text might, at this particular juncture, be more confusing to students. In the future, of course, the new versions may become more widely used and understood.

Introduction

·🟎·

T HE UNITED STATES in the opening years of the twentieth century experienced an age of titans. The most significant were
the three political giants of twentieth-century America, Presidents Theodore Roosevelt (1901–9), Woodrow Wilson (1913–21),
and, after an interval, Franklin Delano Roosevelt (1933–45).

For twenty years after the turn of the century the Republican
TR and the Democrat Woodrow Wilson proved themselves dynamic leaders who dominated American politics. In every presidential election between 1900 and 1916 at least one of them stood
as a candidate and in 1912, two. In the next election of 1920 the
major issue was the controversy over Woodrow Wilson's foreign
policy. People differed greatly in their response to the kind of
personality TR and Wilson showed but no one doubted its forcefulness and the way they had reshaped American society and politics. Later, Franklin Delano Roosevelt's impact was even deeper
and more wide-ranging; his, still controversial, but generally acknowledged position as one of the greatest of all presidents, a
leader to compare with Washington and Lincoln, is supported by
his unique contribution. The only man to be elected president

four times, he led the United States through the tragedy of the Great Depression, proposed the New Deal—the most wide-ranging legislative program ever—and then led America and its allies to the point of victory in World War II.

In his work, *The Progressive Presidents,* historian John Blum finds that Theodore Roosevelt and Wilson set their mark on American government and on domestic and foreign policies as the first progressive presidents; and that in the 1930s Franklin Roosevelt continued and expanded their form of presidential leadership, using his power to improve the quality of social life for many Americans and mobilize the United States for a pivotal role in world affairs.

During the administration of all three, the great questions of political reform related to the location and use of power in the United States, to the relationship between the power of private individuals and groups—businessmen and corporate entities in particular—and the growing power of the federal government; and within that government, to the changing balance of power among the legislative, the judicial, and the executive branch which was increasingly the strongest.

We might characterize Theodore Roosevelt, Woodrow Wilson, and Franklin Roosevelt as energetic and strong presidents who believed in using the office to achieve social and economic reforms and to frame an intelligent and responsive foreign policy.

At first glance 1901 does not seem a decisive date in American history, representing any major turning point, as does 1776 or 1861. The United States was still in the midst of some notable transitions. The American Industrial Revolution that surged forward after the Civil War had already made the United States the dominant industrial power in the world and it was now in the midst of a phase of concentration in industry and manufacturing in the great merger movement of 1897–1903. The wave of new immigration from central, southern, and eastern Europe had already exceeded immigration from northwest Europe in 1896 and was breaking in annual waves of about a million until checked, first by World War I and then by the restrictive immigration acts of 1921 and 1924. The erosion of black civil rights in the South was a gradual process beginning in 1890 and continuing well past the first mass exodus of blacks from South to North in the Great Migration that started in 1915. Furthermore, many of the outstanding inventions that were to transform society in the twentieth century were creations of the nineteenth, including the telephone (1876); phonograph (1877); electric light (1879); motor car (1893); motion picture (1896); and wireless telegraphy (1896).

Yet the turn of the century was decisive for the United States. In 1898 it had just fought and won its first overseas war and acquired an overseas empire, including the Philippines, Guam, Puerto Rico, and the right to intervene in Cuba. In 1901 the great merger movement scored its most signal victories—the creation of the United States Steel Corporation and the Northern Securities Company (a railway consolidation). And the dynamic Theodore Roosevelt became president after the assassination of William McKinley. Here was a nation of considerable domestic and international achievements, and much future potential, poised in a period of renewed prosperity to play a still more decisive role in world affairs.

Theodore Roosevelt turned the sights of government toward a modicum of social reform to redress the conditions that had provoked the agrarian revolt and labor protests of the 1890s. Woodrow Wilson brought the program of progressive reform, albeit briefly, to a peak of achievement. Like TR, Wilson discovered insoluble problems in his sincere attempts to improve the American political economy without undermining it. The Progressive Era was also the period when great industrial cities achieved their definitive spatial plan; giant industrial corporations finally achieved their definitive managerial and marketing revolutions; the motor car was mass produced; mankind learned to fly; and women gained the vote and began to change their appearance and sexual mores decisively.

The dramatic story of America's rise to global power was not enacted in a vacuum, but against the major disaster of World War I, the decline of the British Empire, the Russian Revolution, and the establishment of Communist government in the Soviet Union. Thus it was the political forces reshaping the world that were also titanic and were establishing the sort of modern, continuously industrializing world that mankind would subsequently inhabit.

The term of titans connotes something of prehistoric dinosaurs. The United States was not simply led by its presidents and inventors but also by the great industrialists and the teams of salaried managers who reorganized industrial enterprises on the most efficient and economic scales. The term titan and other similar terms are generally applied to the great inventors and industrial entrepreneurs of the period. We speak of Thomas Alva Edison as "the Napoleon of invention," of financier John Pierpont Morgan as "a titan of finance," and, using other classical allusions, also refer to Morgan as a Midas and a Jupiter. Morgan relished such nicknames as Jupiter. He was, after all, the preeminent financier who drew together the various threads of transportation and communication into his own banking empire and succeeded in unravelling the knots in each. When we talk of the great industrialists, such as John D. Rockefeller, Andrew Carnegie, and James Buchanan Duke, it is in the language of horror movies as "robber barons." Less pejoratively we refer to them as magnates, tycoons, and imperialists.

Auto manufacturer Henry Ford transformed the society into which he was born through an acute combination of mechanical genius, paternalist management, and pioneer spirit. It was the pioneer spirit of experiment and endurance that also characterized the determination of the brothers Wilbur and Orville Wright who first made powered airplanes and showed mankind how to fly. Progressive architects Louis Sullivan and Frank Lloyd Wright found new ways of accommodating more people more comfortably, whether in skyscrapers or town houses, and gave them a new perspective on urban life. The lost generation of American expatriate writers, led by Ernest Hemingway, F. Scott Fitzgerald, and T. S. Eliot, seized the initiative in the new realistic literature of profound psychological depth developed earlier by Henry James, Theodore Dreiser, and Edith Wharton and were primarily responsible for extending the horizons of modern literature in English.

The United States proved its ability to produce great political leaders in addition to the three great presidents. Senators Robert La Follette of Wisconsin and George W. Norris of Nebraska represented the progressive point of view in their states and in the national Capitol throughout long careers. Congress also fielded such formidable and highly-individual talents as Henry Cabot Lodge of Massachusetts and William E. Borah of Idaho. These men not only left their imprint on their times but also enduring testimony in terms of social legislation, foreign policy, and their ability to express the views of their constituents and to make administrations listen to them.

An important theme in the United States throughout the first half of the twentieth century is the extent to which government should (and must) intervene in the economy in the interests of the nation as a whole. In the Progressive Era the questions were how far the federal government should regulate business empires and monopolies, how far it should tax its wealthy citizens, how far it should extend democracy, and how far it should try and control its citizens' leisure and pastimes. For municipal government, it was a question of how far it should control such essential public utilities as gas and electric power, water, and sewage works, and such services as public transport, street cleaning, and refuse disposal. These questions were continuously posed in one form or another throughout the period. It took the national emergency of world war with its urgent need for absolute central control to unite armed forces and citizenry, agriculture and industry, in the common emergency.

CHAPTER ONE

Inventing America:
Expanding Industry

·꙳·

THE MOST spectacular building of the Pan American Exposition at Buffalo in the summer of 1901 was the central Electric Tower. It stood at the head of the Court of Fountains, rising 375 feet, "the high C of the entire architectural symphony." Julian Hawthorne wrote in *Cosmopolitan Magazine* how "the shaft of the Electric Tower . . . assumes a magical aspect, as if it had been summoned forth by the genius of our united people . . . and it makes a tender nuptial with the sky and seems to palpitate with beautiful life."

The exposition, known variously as the Rainbow City and the City of Light, was intended to look like a cityscape in oils lit by some splendid sunrise and, to a large extent, it succeeded. The whole exposition in general and its tower in particular were intended as a potent symbol of America's industrial prowess and its largely untapped potential as a first-class world power. Thus it embodied representation and reality of industrialism, imperialism, and republicanism, all at once. Moreover, the tragic climax of the exposition strengthened people's respect for these things.

The directors intended to draw visitors into the twentieth century that they projected as a utopian era of rising prosperity and continuous peace. In an attempt to woo Latin Americans, with whom the United States wanted greater trade, the buildings were designed in the style of the Spanish Renaissance, not in white as with past expositions but in a myriad of colors. In particular, the exposition celebrated the contribution of railroads to the recent settlement of the West, the achievement of the American Industrial Revolution, and the superiority of white peoples over blacks, Indians, Hispanics, and Asians. All colonial exhibits, including those of the Philippines (a Filipino village) and Hawaii (with acquiescent subjects), were intended to justify American acquisition of new territories, to show that the results were ample compensation for the sacrifice of the war with Spain of 1898 and the subsequent suppression of the Philippine Rebellion (1898–1901).

The Electric Tower was to be the climax, representing "the crowning achievement of man," and "dedicated to the great waterways and the power of Niagara (Falls)" whose water generated the current to illuminate and power the exposition. Mastery of the new technology of electricity made it possible to apply energy in precise quantities, wherever it was needed— something impossible in the old days of steam and waterpower. Electricity could light a house lamp, run a streetcar, work a sewing machine, and illuminate a skyscraper. Moreover, electric light could be transmitted for hundreds of miles, allowing manufacturing to choose the best sites for raw materials, labor, and transportation, rather than having to remain close to coal, water, or oil.

The expo directors intended the visit of President William McKinley on September 5 to be the supreme moment of self-congratulation but the plan miscarried. McKinley played his part beautifully. In his address on President's Day McKinley praised such expositions as "time-keepers of progress," praised industrial growth as the guarantor of progress, and proposed reciprocal commercial relations between the United States and the nations of Latin America. Expositions, he said, were important, because they set a record of material achievement, stimulated energy and enterprise, and gladdened people's daily lives.

The next day, September 6, McKinley returned to the exposition. In the Temple of Music he bent forward to offer his usual red carnation to a little girl. He was shot at close range by an unemployed artisan, Leon Czolgosz. McKinley had noticed the young man with a bandaged right hand and, thinking it injured, had reached to shake him by the left. At this point Leon Czolgosz blasted him in the stomach with two bullets from a revolver concealed in a handkerchief—not a bandage. "I didn't believe that one man should have so much service and another man should have none," the assassin told his captors afterwards.

However, McKinley did not die immediately of the gunshot wounds in his stomach but of gangrene that set in and killed him eight days later.

On September 12 Vice-President Theodore Roosevelt, his family, and some friends decided to ascend Mount Marcy in the Adirondacks. While the others were dismayed by impenetrable drizzle on Friday 13 and decided to return to base, TR went ahead with one guide. He could not resist the highest peak in any region. Just before noon the fog lifted and the clouds parted and he could see right across New York State with its splendid mountains, trees, and sparkling water. Here Roosevelt immediately recognized the metaphor and reality of his position. Would he ever rise further politically or would the blanket fog of anonymity roll over him again? Would the peak of political office be forever denied him? The mists descended and Roosevelt went down another 500 feet to a lake, Tear-of-the-Clouds, where he ate a sandwich lunch. As he sat he noticed a ranger below running toward him with a yellow slip in his hand. It was a telegram and could only contain one message. TR set out for Buffalo immediately and arrived after McKinley had died. On September 14, 1901, Roosevelt took the oath of office in the same house where McKinley lay dead.

McKinley's assassination exposed various divisions in American society along the lines of class, race, and ethnicity. Its very fact suggested something of the widening gulf between the huddled masses of immigrant workers and native artisans, dispossessed Indians and oppressed blacks, and the successful plutocrats of industry and finance, the politicos, and even the expanding

The spectacular Electric Tower dominated the Pan American Exposition at Buffalo in 1901 by day and night. Its monumental presence was taken as a symbol of America's industrial and imperial preeminence and a singular demonstration of electric power, the cheapest and most reliable form of energy yet known. (Photo by C. D. Arnold, Library of Congress).

middle class of professional men, progressive reformers, investigative journalists, and business executives. Czolgosz was a reputed anarchist. Although born in the United States, he was the son of Polish immigrants and this fact led to renewed calls for immigration restriction. Yet, paradoxically, the exposition with its trumpet fanfares of American industrial, democratic, and imperial supremacy, proved a means of maintaining cultural stability and confidence in the healing effects of progress at a time of acute political crisis.

Expanding Industry

The progressive generation of Americans who came to political maturity at the turn of the century, and among whom Theodore Roosevelt was preeminent, were sustained in their faith in political progress by the undoubted material progress of the American Industrial Revolution.

The extent of America's industrial development in the first half of the twentieth century is suggested in the accompanying table, indicating population, net national income, and net per capita income (both in dollars, according to 1929 prices). The table also reveals the sharp fall in the percentage of the population engaged in agriculture and its declining percentage share in the national income.

The overall growth of industrial production in the United States (and in western Europe) was accompanied by a marked shift in the relative importance of various sections of industry and agriculture. Thus in the early twentieth century food and textiles accounted for 47 percent of total manufacturing production, whereas by the end of World War II they accounted for only 19 percent. In the same period metal products rose from 10 to 41 percent, while chemicals rose from 5 to 13 percent.

That America led the world's agriculture and industry is suggested by export statistics that no other country could match. The value of American exports rose from $1.49 million in 1900 to $2.3 billion in 1914. Imports rose from $929 million (1900) to $2 billion (1914). During and immediately after World War I,

National Income of the United States, 1899–1948

	Population in Millions	Net Annual National Income in US $ Milliards	Net Annual National Income per Capita in US $	Net Capital Formation as Percentge of Net National Product	Percentage of Population Employed in Agriculture	Percentage Share of Agriculture in National Income
1899–1908	81.3	37.5	461	13.9	34	16
1909–1918	97.6	50.3	515	12.5	29	13
1919–1928	112.9	69.0	612	10.6	24	11
1929–1938	126.0	72.0	572	1.7	20	10
1939–1948	137.8	108.9	790	7.9	13	8

Source: Statistical table basd on material in Richard B. Morris, ed., Encyclopedia of American History (New York, 1982; first published, 1953) and Ben J. Wattenberg, ed., The Statistical History of the United States from Colonial Times to the Present (New York, 1976).

American exports rose sharply from $2.3 billion in 1914 to $8.1 billion in 1920. They fell sharply in the recession of 1921 and the level fluctuated throughout the 1920s between a low of $3.8 billion (1922) and a high of $5.2 billion (1929). We might also note that in 1914 the United States' principal trading partner was Britain, with Germany second, and Canada third.

There were five major keys to America's astonishing industrial success: a superabundant supply of land and precious natural resources; excellent natural and manmade systems of transportation; a growing supply of labor caused by natural growth of population and massive immigration; special facility in invention and technology; and superb industrial organization. Thus what brought the American Industrial Revolution to fruition was human initiative, ingenuity, and physical energy.

The Agricultural Revolution hastened the Industrial Revolution in various ways. The increase in production per farmer allowed a transfer of labor from agriculture to industry without reducing the country's food supply. Moreover, such expanding agriculture did not need the transfer of limited capital from industry to agriculture. Indeed, the profits derived from agriculture could be used for buying manufactured goods, thereby further stimulating industry and manufacturing. There were two manufacturing belts across the nation formed by the way cities were clustered. One stretched along the Atlantic coast from Maine in the North to Virginia in the South. The other was west of the Allegheny Mountains and north of the Ohio River, extending from Pittsburgh and Buffalo in the East to St. Louis and Milwaukee in the West.

By 1913 the United States was the world's leading producer of coal, mining 500 million tons. American coal was cheaper to mine than any other, largely because its mines were shallow and surface open cast mining was much increased at the turn of the century.

There were two types of coal, anthracite and bituminous. Pennsylvania was the principal coal-producing state, accounting for 60 percent of total U.S. production. Anthracite coal was mined in a number of small fields in eastern Pennsylvania and coal was transported along the Delaware Valley on the Delaware River

Tragedy struck the Buffalo Exposition when its principal visitor, President William McKinley, (center), was mortally wounded by an assassin on September 6, 1901, the day after he had made a successful speech extolling American supremacy in industry, empire, and politics. Unconventional photographer Frances Benjamin Johnston took this conventional posed photo of the president's party for the *Illustrated Express*. To the left of the president are Mrs. John Miller Horton (with parasol), and the Mexican ambassador; to his right are George Cortelyou and Col. John M. Brigham. (Library of Congress).

and its tributaries, and by canal and rail. Bituminous coal was mined in the west of the state in a region around Pittsburgh with its center at Connellsville that produced nearly all the coal used for coke in the United States. Illinois was second to Pennsylvania in coal production. West Virginia and Ohio also had coalfields that extended the Pennsylvania bituminous field and produced steam coal in the Pocahontas coalfield. Coal was also produced in the Appalachian states of Kentucky, Tennessee, and Alabama.

Whereas average annual coal production in the period 1896–1900 was 202.8 million tons, in the period 1906–10, it was 405.9 million tons. Moreover, this trend toward ever greater production continued during a period when world coal production was decreasing. Thus American production rose from 509 million tons in 1913 to 611 million in 1918, while world production fell from 1.32 billion tons in 1913 to 1.15 billion in 1919, partly, it must be admitted, because of economic dislocation in World War I. Only in 1919, when the United States' economy was disrupted by a series of strikes, including a coal strike, did American production fall briefly to 486 million. Furthermore, American coal resources seemed almost limitless and it was estimated at the Twelfth International Geological Congress of 1913 that U.S. coal reserves amounted to 1.94 billion tons altogether. At the turn of the century about 681,000 men worked at the mines, both above and below the surface, mining on average 596 tons each per year, in comparison with Britain, which had to employ a work force of 953,000 men who extracted, on average, 275 tons each per year. This was because American mines were easier to work and American equipment was superior to British. In the period 1906–10, the bulk of American coal was for domestic use. Average consumption per head of population was 4.43 tons. American coal exports were 12.85 million tons, compared with Britain, which exported 83.57 million tons.

The United States was also rich in iron ore that was abundant, well distributed, and of excellent quality. The only disadvantage was that most of the ore was some distance away from smelting fuel. About three-fifths of the iron ore produced in the United States in the early twentieth century was from the Lake Superior region. It came from the Marquette Range, Michigan, discovered in 1855; the Menominee, south of Marquette, discovered in 1877; the Gogebic, Wisconsin, discovered in 1865; the Vermillion in Minnesota, discovered in 1884; and the Mesabi, also in Minnesota, discovered in 1892 and considered the most important of all.

It was also easy to extract. The ore was buried beneath a mere skin of glacial drift that just needed to be stripped for the ore to be dug and extracted and then transported. The Mesabi iron range turned out to be the world's greatest field of iron ore. By 1900 it was yielding a third of all the ore mined in the United States, a sixth of the world's supply, and half of all the raw materials to make steel. The development of the Mesabi field led to the construction of new steel works by United States Steel at Duluth, Minnesota. In the 1880s the iron and coal fields of the Appalachians were also developed. Both Pittsburgh to the east and Birmingham to the south became centers of the iron, coal, and steel industries.

As is well known, the iron and steel industry was highly centralized and thirty-eight plants of U.S. Steel were sited along twenty-six miles of navigable waterways. The very center of the iron and steel industry was Pittsburgh, partly because it was a traditional center close to coal, and partly because haulage was relatively cheap. It was most accessible to other regions, being sited at the union of two rivers to form the Ohio River. Pittsburgh produced a quarter of all pig iron in the United States, although most of its ore came from Lake Superior since its local supply had ended. Ohio and Illinois were the next largest centers of the iron and steel industry and both used ore from Lake Superior, except that plants in southwest Illinois used ore from Missouri close by.

In the 1910s and 1920s northern Alabama was a growing area for iron production, with an industry centered on Birmingham close to deposits of iron ore and coal. However, its ore was used only for foundry iron, not steel. Alabama had the economic advantages of cheap black labor and deposits of limestone that were used in the iron-producing process. Besides Birmingham, the towns of Bessemer, Sheffield, and Anniston also produced iron and Anniston had the most extensive manufacture of cast-iron pipes. In the period 1901–9 the output of steel products rose from 10 million to almost 24 million tons, with open-hearth steel exceeding Bessemer production in 1908. In 1909 open-hearth production was 14.49 million tons, while Bessemer production accounted for 9.33 million tons. The abundance of steel led to elaborate engineering projects by way of massive bridges and high-speed rails, battleships, trains, and eventually automobiles and airplanes. World War I stimulated greater steel production. The total number of steel ingots and castings rose from 23.51 million long tons (1914) to 45.06 million long tons (1917).

In the 1900s coke became the principal fuel in the steel industry. Moreover, in World War I enlarged demands for munitions placed a premium on the construction of by-product coking ovens to provide coal tar for explosives. By 1919 by-product coke amounted to 56.9 percent of the total of 44.2 million tons.

In the West the Rockies and Sierras contained large deposits of metals, both precious (such as gold and silver) and industrial (such as copper, zinc, and lead). Of the precious minerals, gold was produced at Cripple Creek, Colorado, and silver from Colorado, Montana, and Nevada. Aluminum, used in the making of electrical equipment and aircraft, came from bauxite, obtained in Alabama, Arkansas, Georgia, and Tennessee, and was usually produced by electrical furnaces. Because World War I increased the demand for alloys, it stimulated the aluminum industry. To meet the needs for special alloys, electric furnace production was greatly expanded, rising from 27,000 long tons of aluminum in 1914 to 511,693 long tons in 1918. Since the production of aluminum required large supplies of cheap electricity in the period 1900–20, the aluminum industry was often sited near hydroelectric power stations, such as those at Niagara Falls, Massera, and Long Sault Rapids, New York.

Petroleum

Between 1900 and 1920 the petroleum industry grew rapidly in a region of oil fields, stretching across a 160 mile strip, running from southwest to northeast in western Pennsylvania and New York and only 40 miles wide at its broadest point. The strip included 20,000 wells, pipelines, and refineries, and the petroleum extracted was used in various industries, such as iron-smelting, and manufactures, such as glass-making, in the same region.

At this time any manufacture was usually sited near its raw materials and source of energy. Thus in 1885 this particular region produced 95 percent of petroleum. From 1900 its yield began to decline, although overall American production of petroleum continued to expand. Fuel oil production rose from 300 million gallons (1901) to 1.7 billion gallons (1909). Petroleum benefited from the creation of an enormous new market after the turn of the century, created by the automobile. The new demand for gasoline fuel occurred almost precisely when the dramatic increase in electricity for light was rapidly reducing the demand for kerosene. Moreover, just as new markets for oil were being created, great sources of additional supply were being discovered in such states as California, Oklahoma, Texas, the Lima field in northeast Indiana and northwest Ohio, Kansas, and Illinois.

The modern period of oil production opened on January 10, 1901, when the Lucas well at Spindletop, near Beaumont, Texas, yielded a huge gusher. For each of nine days before it was capped it yielded between 70,000 and 110,000 barrels. We can understand the hysterical enthusiasm with which the strike was greeted by recalling that the railroads provided special trains from New York and Philadelphia for oil prospectors and, within a year, 500 wells had been sunk in an area of no more than five acres. In its second year of production the Spindletop well produced 17.50 million barrels.

The strike at Spindletop was the first indication of a huge oil boom in the Southwest. Other strikes and wells followed in Texas at Powell (1901), Sour Lake (1902), Petrolia (1904), Beaver Switch (1909), and Bunkburnett (1912). Moreover, the new state of Oklahoma (admitted to the Union on November 16, 1907) yielded vast supplies at Red Fork (1901), Glenn (1905), Cushing (1912), and Healdton (1913). Soon the yield in Oklahoma surpassed that in Texas and in 1907 Oklahoma was the leading oil producer of all the states; by 1913 it produced a quarter of the nation's oil. Other pools were discovered in Louisiana at Jennings (1901), Ansela-Butte (1902), Caddo (1906), Vinton (1910), Pine Prairie (1912), and De Soto (1913).

These surprise boom pools were attended by a great herd of wild-cat prospectors, well drillers, and sharpers. Eyewitness Samuel W. Tait, Jr., observes in his *The Wildcatters* (1946), "Never before was a region assaulted by so numerous, desperate, determined, and plunging an army of wildcatters." Shantytowns appeared and disappeared overnight but some new towns prospered, including Tulsa and Port Arthur.

Because of its spectacular growth in oil production and the high proportion of oil exported, especially to Europe, by 1919 the United States was supplying two-thirds of estimated world production at 577 million barrels. Following World War I American oil production continued to grow, but in 1919 and 1920 explorers discovered various foreign oil fields of comparable, and sometimes greater, size, such as the Iranian oil fields being developed by the Anglo-Persian Oil Company. By the 1920s oil and gases refined from crude petroleum had over 200 commercial uses, not only as lubricant, illuminant, and gasoline but also as ink, paint, medicine, asphalt, and wax. Oil was sixth among the country's industries, worth $2 billion in 1925, and indispensable to the first manufacturing industry, automobiles. Primarily, it was the source of energy that allowed man to travel the surface of the earth at fifty miles an hour, to fly above the clouds and swim beneath the ocean, to drive 20 million automobiles, thousands of railroad engines, and hundreds of ships and submarines.

Labor and Income

Another factor stimulating America's economic growth was the ever greater reservoir of labor for industry. Natural population growth and the continuous flow of immigrants, chiefly from Europe, steadily increased the army of labor. In 1900 the population of the continental United States and its overseas possessions was 76,094,000. In 1910 it was 92,407,000. Of these numbers, in 1900 6.25 million people were employed in manufacturing; in 1910, 8.250 million. Another 1.64 million were employed in construction in 1900, rising to 2.31 million in 1910; in transportation, 2.02 million (1900), rising to 3.20 million (1910); in trade, 2.87 million (1900), rising to 3.62 million (1910). In the period 1900–10, when first-generation immigrants accounted for about 14 percent of the total population, they constituted about 25 percent of the labor force. Moreover, marginal farmers and agricultural workers who could not make agricultural work pay drifted from countryside to town. Of the total population of 76.09 million in 1900, 30.15 million lived in urban areas and 1.73 million lived in urban centers. Thus 39.7 percent lived in urban centers and 19 percent lived in cities of over 500,000 inhabitants. Industry was also supported by huge capital investment. Foreign capital flowed to invest in American industry, much of it British investment in railroad construction, rising from $3.4 billion in 1897, to $6.4 billion in 1908, and $7.2 billion in 1914.

The South, however, did not share in the great prosperity of the other regions. The earliest pure per capita income estimates available are for 1919. They disclose that southern per capita income was about 40 percent lower than the national average. The national average was $614, whereas the average of the thirteen southern states was $405. None of the southern states came near the national average. The state with the highest average per capita income was New York with $929. The poorest state was Alabama with $321.

In the Southeast the principal crops were cotton and tobacco, but maize was also grown as well as "southern fruits," groundnuts, pecans, and, in Florida, oranges and other citrus fruits. There was also a growth in arable farming in sandy pine barrens, occupying the plain from North Carolina to lower Mississippi, a growth made possible after reclamation of exhausted soil by use of phosphate fertilizers, mined locally. The southern economy was a colonial economy in which the North extracted farm produce, raw materials, and semifinished goods from the South and secured them at bargain rates. Southern historian C. Vann Woodward observes how "the penetration of the South by Northeastern capital continued at an accelerated pace" after the turn of the century. "The Morgans, Mellons, and Rockefellers sent their agents to take charge of the region's railroads, mines, furnaces, and financial corporations, and eventually of many of its distributive functions."

Although many southern industries prospered, it was a case of "branch plants, branch banks, captive mines, and chain stores." In the tobacco industry, factories were dismantled in the North, where wages were higher, and moved to the South, which was producing 40 percent of all tobacco in 1919. By far the greater part of products left the South's farms, forests, and mines as raw or semifinished materials to be further manufactured in northern factories. Thus 62 percent of employed southerners worked in extractive industries (agriculture, forestry, mining, and fishing), compared with only 10.7 percent in New England and 14.2 percent in the mid-Atlantic states.

Inventing America

Another key to America's astonishing industrial success was the aptitude of Americans for invention and their facility in adapting the inventions of others to their own purposes. Popular legend has it that the major technological achievements of the twentieth century were due to the pioneer creations of a relatively small number of classic inventors, notably Thomas Alva Edison, Alexander Graham Bell, Wilbur and Orville Wright, and Henry Ford. To Edison we ascribe the electric lamp, phonograph, motion picture, improved telegraphs and a thousand other inventions; to Bell, the telephone; to the Wrights, the first practicable airplane; and to Ford, the mass-produced motor car. Although Ford did not invent the motor car, as Edison invented the phonograph and incandescent lamp, he made it available to the masses, thereby extending democracy and earning himself a fortune. Popular lore has turned these inventors into mythic heroes, representing a cherished American ideal that ordinary man can produce the greatest leaps in technology by dint of supreme individual endeavor and perserverance. Thus their creations were taken as an affirmation of the greatness and vitality of the United States. The fact that the inventors often came from small towns and provincial backgrounds was something emphasized by themselves

The Midway, the section of the Buffalo Exposition that provided entertainment, refreshment, and relief played its part in the official cult of
white supremacy with an outsize white head inviting visitors to enter a
Dreamland of minstrel shows and fantastic voyages. "I've tol' ye wanst,"
observed Irish-American saloon keeper Mr. Dooley, "that f'r ev'ry wan
that goes to a wurrld fair to see how boots is made, there's twinty goes
f'r the hootchy-kootchy, an' that's where the wan ends finally." (Photo
by C. D. Arnold, Library of Congress).

and by others to support the myth of individuals rising from humble origins to great achievement.

One reason why American technology in general was so advanced was the relatively high cost of labor in America that encouraged industrialists to invest in mechanizing. Moreover, the large domestic market allowed for great economies of scale. In addition, Americans in general were far less bound than Europeans by tradition and thus far more willing to try out new methods. Contemporary editor Mark Sullivan traces this facility to a natural ingenuity and determination in the people: "Intellectual freedom and curiosity about the new, the instinct of the American mind to look into, examine, and experiment—this led to, among other things, a willingness to 'scrap' not only old machinery but old formulas, old ideas; and brought about, among other results, the condition expressed in the saying that 'American mechanical progress could be measured by the size of its scrap-heaps.' "

A principal purpose in improving technology was to make industry more efficient and cost-effective by speeding up production. In 1929 AT & T published a comparison of productiveness between the old order of industry and the new, shown in the accompanying table. It paid tribute to greater uses of power, whether steam, oil, or electricity, and improved technology. The streamlining of industry and manufacture excited very different reactions. Those who valued traditional craftsmanship professed themselves dismayed by the soullessness of modern industry and already were concerned by the possibility of built-in obsolescence. Mr. Dooley remarked, "Th' shoes that Corrigan th' cobbler wanst wurruked on fir a week hammerin' away like a woodpecker, is now tossed out be th' dozens fr'm th' mouth iv a masheen. A cow goes lowin' softly in to Armours an' comes out glue, beef, gelatine, fertylizer, celooloid, joolry, soft cushions, hair restorer, soap, lithrachoor an' bed springs so quick that while aft she's still cow, for'ard she may be anything fr'm buttons to Panny-ma hats."

American inventors Thomas Alva Edison and Alexander Graham Bell transformed the society into which they were born by an astute blend of inventive genius and technological knowledge.

In 1781 One Man Working One Day Produced:	*In 1925 One Man Working One Day Produces:*
500 lbs of iron	5,000 lbs of iron
or 100 ft of lumber	or 750 ft of lumber
or 5 lbs of nails	or 500 lbs of nails
or ¼ pair of shoes	or 10 pairs of shoes
or ½ ton of coal	or 4 tons of coal
or 20 square feet of paper	or 200,000 square feet of paper

Their fame was spread by the communications they devised. They seemed heroes because they combined technical expertise in the new field of communications with the sort of traditional pioneer spirit that had the tenacity to see a novel idea through from start to finish. In 1879, Edison, who rejoiced in ditties and word plays of all kinds, made up this cocky, self-assured rhyme in praise of his quintessential American skills. It might have been by W. S. Gilbert.

> I am the wizard of the electric light
> And a wide awake wizard, too,
> Quadruplex, telegraph or funny phonograph,
> It's all the same to me.
> With ideas I evolve and problems that I solve
> I'm never stumped, you see.

Yet his and Bell's inventions were not the happy result of accident and intuition but of backbreaking trial and error in painstaking experiments. In fact, Edison's most famous remark was "Genius is 1 percent inspiration and 99 percent perspiration." Edison, Bell, and the Wright brothers regarded science not as an absolute, but an infinitely expanding world, in which to seek was to find. Thus they were perfectly equipped for the competitive worlds of business and industry when business and industry were putting a special premium on increasing efficiency by improving communications.

Another common factor between Edison and Bell, and, also, the Wright brothers, was that their painstaking research was sustained by private incomes that allowed them the freedom and materials to work on their most cherished projects. Thus, in their early careers, Edison could rely on royalties from his telegraphs, Bell lived on fees from his successful schools for the deaf, while the Wrights made money from the sale of their bicycles. Moreover, lone inventors first achieved, and then sustained, their success by using conventional business methods. Thus Edison and Bell formed companies based on their research laboratories.

Were these inventors geniuses of true originality or, rather, bright, intelligent, and hardworking men who put fairly widely known scientific theories into practice? Edison was certainly the most prolific inventor in history with patents for 1,018 inventions. However, if we are to discover the man behind the formidable reputation, we need to pare away layers of anecdote and myth. Although he was a brilliant man whose unparalleled inventions transformed the world, his reputation as the inventor of almost everything in the modern world must be qualified. In fact, he was the titular, professional, and active head of a large research team, a factory, that produced pioneer inventions. He actively sought celebrity and had some inventions by other scientists attributed to him, such as the transformation of small kinetoscope slot machines into large-screen exposures, actually achieved by realtor Thomas Armat but accredited to Edison. By comparison, the Wright brothers freely admitted that their invention of the first practicable airplane depended largely on the preliminary research, construction, and testing of many other people. In short, they did not produce an airplane out of nowhere. Similarly, both Henry Ford's Model T car and his mass production assembly lines were derivative. It is significant that the men who actually discovered radio have been obscured by Guglielmo Marconi, the man who brought their ideas together and applied them into one practical package in 1896. Thus Marconi is famous; they are not. It was, apparently, Marconi, who created radio while, in the end, they only made a partial contribution to its creation.

The classic American inventors were distinct from many accomplished scientists of the past. They were far less interested in theory than in facts. They were essentially practical men who applied their practical knowledge and ability to find the means to meet the needs of industrial society for transportation, communication, and energy. They appreciated the need for team effort and were essentially organizers of men, planners of effort, and repositories of experience and knowledge.

Perhaps the greatest skill of these inventor titans lay in their ability to impose order and organization onto the whole field of invention in their specific area of interest and so to lay the foundations of modern corporate research. Thus it was the managerial, even more than the scientific, skill of Edison and Bell, the Wrights, and Ford that led to the transformation of society. In the Gilded Age and the Progressive Era it is impossible to separate inventors from businessmen in the crucial, early stages of new inventions. Inventors' successes led to spectacular profits and encouraged the institutionalization of invention in which their companies provided funds for the specific purpose of finding new processes, products, and means of power. All successful inventors had to have good business instincts and acumen. Otherwise, they would be exceeded by their avid competitors. This devotion to business is most clearly shown by the cautious, ordered methods in which they began to plan their route from the first inklings of a new idea or project to a finished invention with a minimum of waste, in particular by eliminating all impractical schemes in succession. Thus, for instance, the Wright brothers avoided all the usual pitfalls of previous aeronautic designs.

The next step after an invention was successfully proved was not to continue research but to safeguard sole rights to it by securing a patent, defending it legally when necessary, and then finding ways to manufacture and sell it. The early history of many inventions by Edison, Bell, and the Wrights was the history of court cases in which the inventor had to demonstrate and prove his title against all competitors. Such legal wrangles suggest something about the state of inventions in the late nineteenth and early twentieth centuries. Firstly, it reveals that more than one person was making progress and achieving results at roughly the same time. This was certainly true of the telephone and telegraph. Bell and his associates had to win the notorious Dowd case of 1879 to prove that he had conceived, made practical, and patented the telephone before anyone else. Similarly, the young Edison found himself caught between his employers, Atlantic and

Pacific, and his great rival, Western Union, who sought to detract from his achievement in the creation of the quadruplex telegraph in 1877. Indeed, it was this case, settled out of court, that made Edison's name widely known. The *Telegrapher* of March 25, 1876, had already dubbed him "the professor of duplicity and quadruplicity." Secondly, such cases show how imitation and piracy were very real threats to the financial success and future of inventors and their entire research teams. Thus the most successful were determined to retain firm control of their inventions. Indeed, the Wrights hid their planes behind a shroud of secrecy for a year or so in order to insure themselves against patent infringement.

Those inventions indelibly associated with modern societies in the twentieth century, such as the telephone, electric light and power, and the internal combustion engine were all invented in the nineteenth century. This is not to say that other, crucial inventions were not made in the twentieth century. Early twentieth-century inventions included the airplane, radio, and television. However, the twentieth-century history of science and technology was far more characterized by innovation, the introduction of new methods, than it was by invention, the creation of original products.

As nineteenth-century inventions were being manufactured in ever larger numbers, they became more conventional industrial property and, as such, products to be made and distributed by the new giant corporations that were evolving at the same time. In the changing world of industrial corporations, the lone inventor of myth was being replaced by the newly emerging teams of research scientists. Moreover, the thrust of innovation was to make new inventions and technologies available to the widest number of people in the fastest possible time. Thus it was essential for Henry Ford (and herein lies his significance) not only to design and make a popular car but also to operate a mass production process that was continuously expanding existing markets and creating new ones. A successful invention was one that created and held its own mass markets. Thus the development of such inventions as the telephone, automobile, and airplane depended more on the development of consumer society than on the development of technology. Accordingly, airplanes were made more comfortable for passengers by way of improved cabin design, seating, and facilities before they were made faster and fuel-efficient.

Inventors often failed to appreciate the significance and application of their own inventions. Thus Edison first considered the phonograph as a secretarial device for recording and then transcribing messages, a convenience for dictation. What happened was a revolution in popular entertainment, primarily the recording and playing of all kinds of music for listening at home. Yet the original intention remains in the noun for the new invention—phonograph—from phono (sound) and graphy (writing). Indeed, shorthand secretaries were then known as phonographers. Bell initially saw the telephone as a means of improved communication for deaf people. Edison never realised the full cultural potential of motion pictures, an invention to which he was, nevertheless, glad to lend his name. The Wrights recognized the distinct military potential of the airplane, especially for surveying enemy terrain, but they did not appreciate its potential for mass transportation. Long-distance air travel was then more associated with airships, at least until the 1930s.

Thomas Alva Edison: The Napoleon of Inventions

The history of electricity in the nineteenth century was almost indissoluble from the meteoric career of Thomas Alva Edison. In 1876 he also established the first ever industrial research laboratory at Menlo Park, twelve miles south of Newark, a prototype of company laboratories of the future. His creation of an invention factory showed how Edison, in the words of German analyst Werner Sombart, was the classic example of the man "who made a business of invention." Menlo Park was a precursor of the large-scale research centers established by the great industrial corporations. It enjoyed considerable financial support from a syndicate of financiers, including J. P. Morgan and William Henry Vanderbilt. The syndicate advanced Edison $50,000 for research into, and the development of, the electric light and the establishment of the Edison Electric Light Company. Their faith in Edison was such that in November 1878 they founded the Electric Light Company before the invention of the incandescent lamp was actually made.

Edison determined to find a way of retaining light. By the 1870s various types of electric arc lamps were available, but because of the enormous power and the gases they gave off they were suited only to large halls or open spaces. The crucial breakthroughs in the search for a practicable electric lamp were the invention of a special generator (the long-waisted Mary Ann) and the carbon-filament lamp. Edison discovered that carbon remained stable in a nearly perfect vacuum. But he was unable to bake carbon wire in spiral form. It was only when his associate, Charles Batchelor, shaped the wire into a horseshoe that the first viable incandescent lamp was realized. It burned for sixteen hours on November 17, 1879. A subsidiary but equally important discovery by Edison was of the flow of current between hot and cold electrodes, the emission of electrons, and the basis of the electron tube, thereby leading to the electronics industry.

In order to gain as much publicity and credibility as possible for the new invention, it had to be accepted in Europe. The first public electrical power station was opened in London in January 1882, the second in New York in September that year. At first, use of electrical power was limited because it was dependent on low voltage direct current that could only be distributed over short distances. The losses in transmission were too great to allow for a distribution of electricity between cities and each city required several different sources. Thus the next important stage was the replacement of direct current by a superior alternative. This was achieved by George Westinghouse of Pittsburgh who in 1885 bought patents for a system of alternating current and had one of his team of scientists, William Stanley, perfect it and then developed an alternating current constant-potential generator. In 1886 Westinghouse demonstrated the practicability of alternating current in Great Barrington, Massachusetts, by transmitting electricity over 4,000 feet, using one transformer to increase the voltage to 3,000 volts en route and then to reduce it to 500 volts at the receiving end. Westinghouse invested heavily in this system. He acquired a patent for Hungarian immigrant Nikola

Tesla's polyphase alternating current system that possessed an induction motor worked by a rotating magnetic field. The first major demonstration of the complete system was given at the World's Columbian Exposition in Chicago in 1893 with a two-phase generator supplying electrical power to lights and motors.

The use of electric motors in manufacturing made electricity the cleanest and most convenient form of industrial power yet known. Artificial light could continue the day through the night, allowing work beyond sundown and increasing the industrial potential of factories, the commercial potential of offices, and the social life of city and home. Electric power was being used widely in transportation by the 1890s. Frank J. Sprague introduced the first electric street railway in Richmond, Virginia, in 1888 and his invention, affording cheap, rapid, and clean transport, was soon adopted by other cities anxious to free themselves from the pollution and risk of fire of steam trains.

Edison, who always plowed his money back into new research, opened a new laboratory of grand design, ten times larger than Menlo Park, at West Orange, New Jersey, in 1887. He now employed 120 research assistants and eventually the laboratory was surrounded by an industrial estate of 5,000 people making goods from his inventions.

The competitive claims of the rival systems direct and alternating current, were hotly contested by Edison and Westinghouse. During the 1890s and in the 1900s the benefits of alternating current above direct current became increasingly evident. Gradually, the United States was converted to alternating current. One important victory for the proponents of alternating current was its adoption by the hydroelectrical power plant at Niagara Falls in 1893 for the International Niagara Commission to transmit electricity to Buffalo, New York, twenty-two miles away. (The first hydroelectric plant had been opened in Appleton, Wisconsin, in 1882.) By 1898 the use of alternating current had developed to the point that it was in use carrying 30,000 volts along a three-phase 75 mile line service between Santa Ana and Los Angeles, California. In 1899 a seventy-mile line from Colgate Hydro Station to Sacramento, California, carried 40,000 volts. The pattern was set for ever longer lines, carrying ever

Thomas Alva Edison, the most prolific inventor in history, whose numerous inventions, notably in electricity and sound recording, were transforming the world, photographed with one of his dictating machines in 1906. The impetuous, obsessive inventor of the Gilded Age had become a more reflective, sadder man in the Progressive Era who had lost his early lead in electricity but remained the titular and professional head of a large scientific laboratory of research scientists at Menlo Park, a sign that the earlier stage of inventions was being superseded by a later one of technological innovation. (Library of Congress).

higher voltages. In 1907 engineers Edward Hewlett and Harold Buck developed suspension insulators. By 1920 some lines were carrying up to 132,000 volts and a few up to 150,000 volts.

Electricity was a new form of physical energy, greater than the sum of all previous forms of energy. Journalist Mark Sullivan described how, at the turn of the century, "Electricity was streaking up and down the country, literally like lightning—wires to provide it with a pathway were everywhere being extended, like long nerves of new growth, from central power houses, from the city to the suburb, longer and longer capacity for transmission carrying it to distant villages, from the villages to the farm—everywhere ending in a switch, by the turning of which man could tap for himself a practically limitless reservoir of physical power." It was a case of many lights make hands work.

In the twentieth century the history of electricity and Edison's career diverged. Electricity, and its uses, were no longer the property of Edison alone. Because of a parallel public demand for ever more electrical power, engineers devised new propulsion systems to carry it. During the 1890s they used steam-reciprocity engines to drive electrical generators but these proved too large and heavy and tended to pulsate whilst rotating. In 1903 they began using 5,000 kilowatt steam-turbine driven generators that allowed for increased output. Yet they, too, had problems, primarily output capacity and high consumption of fuel.

Meanwhile, Edison was beset by financial problems. Partly because of mistakes in strategy, he lost control of his company to his business associates. In February 1892 Edison's company merged with its great rival, Thomson-Houston. The new corporation, capitalized at $50 million, was entitled, quite simply, General Electric.

Although Edison kept financially solvent, thanks to such inventions as the motion picture projector, he lost his initial lead in electrical research and practice. Edison's mistaken loyalty to, and preference for, direct current reflected his limits—that he was not strong in theoretical science. Yet he continued to produce successful inventions, such as the efficient cement kiln that made it possible to create structures of poured concrete and thereby build low cost housing. He undertook research into torpedoes and anti-submarine devices for the Naval Consulting Board in World War I. As a result of his arguments, in 1920 the federal government created a Naval Research Laboratory, the first institution for military research.

Edison relished his mythic reputation as a hero who had risen from rags to riches. His highly egotistical temperament and somewhat calculated eccentric persona were, nevertheless, at odds with the traditional character of the long-haired, absent-minded scientist. In professional terms, he was a transitional figure among inventors. He bridged a gap between untutored mechanically minded lone inventors of the nineteenth century and professional inventors of the twentieth century whose experimentation was systematic and who were likely to work as one among a team of specialized scientists. For all his contempt for scientists who turned theory into a god, Edison employed such men as Tesla and Kennelly, who were mathematical physicists. Thus Edison took his place in the procession of inventors who were leading mankind to a new age of the machinists. Nevertheless, within this research group with its commitment to, and financial dependence upon, corporate interests, Edison remained individually creative and extraordinarily so. In his later years in the 1920s and 1930s he sought celebrity and encouraged his reputation as a "wise man," a sort of Merlin figure, who had held the keys to the secrets of the modern world.

Advances in Electric Power

Like other pioneer inventions of the late nineteenth century, electric power became ever more widely used in the early twentieth century. By 1903 three electrical companies were operating over 1,000 central power stations that lit 1.25 million electrical lamps. It was electric power above all else that led to higher standards of living and more advanced levels of industrialization and urbanization, not only across the United States but also across the world. In the period 1909–14 electric power installed in manufacturing rose from 1.7 million horsepower (1909) to 3.8 million horsepower (1914). In 1914 energy produced by electric current accounted for 17.3 percent of all installed primary power in manufacturing. In the period 1914–19 installed primary electric power more than doubled, reaching 9.34 million horsepower and this accounted for 31.6 percent of the total horsepower of manufacturing industries.

In the period 1900–20 alternating current was widely adopted throughout America by public utility companies anxious to satisfy growing public demand for greater production. This required larger and more efficient generators driven by steam turbines or hydroelectric power and from the 1920s state and local authorities began to undertake large hydroelectric projects. By 1922 Pit River and Big Creek hydroelectric power was being transmitted at 220,000 volts in California. In 1934 the Hoover Dam (originally, the Boulder Dam) on the Colorado River transmitted electric power at 287,000 volts to Los Angeles, 270 miles away. During the 1930s a growing problem in electrical transmission was a loss of electricity from lines operating at high voltage. The remedy at that time was the corona discharge to increase the conductor diameter by over an inch.

During the 1920s and 1930s hydroelectric power was becoming established as the principal power source, with steam power being used as an auxiliary source. Electric power had to cope with growing public demand and needed to develop a grid linking power sources to the markets, the large cities, usually hundreds of miles away from the source and from one another.

Realizing just how critical was electrical power for the industrial and social transformation of the United States, government (federal, state, local, municipal) decided to act and ensure the greatest use by the greatest number. In the early days of electrical power the industry was dominated by private utility companies and some utility companies owned by municipalities. Moreover, the Newlands Reclamation Act of 1902, as amended in 1906, included a clause allowing for a lease of surplus power from dams for irrigation to be leased for up to ten years and gave preference to municipal authorities over private companies. From the early 1930s onwards federal agencies, public power districts, and rural cooperatives became part of the industry. However, the major piece of legislation governing hydroelectrical power was the earlier Federal Water Power Act of 1920 that limited licenses to hydroelectric power sites to fifty years and thus allowed for their repossession by the federal government. In an important subsidiary clause it gave preference to states and municipalities and other sectors of government over private organizations.

The Department of the Interior also played a crucial part in this development. The Bonneville Power Administration was created in 1937 to market electric power from the Bonneville Dam on the Columbia River, Oregon; the Southwestern Power Administration was created in 1943 to market power from Corps of Engineers' projects in Arkansas, Missouri, Oklahoma, and Texas. The reform administration of Franklin Delano Roosevelt created the Tennessee Valley Authority (TVA) in 1933 to enrich the entire Appalachian region of seven states, providing new dams, improvising existing ones, and to generate cheap hydroelectric power. The federal government also established the Rural Electrification Administration in 1935. As a result of these developments, the percentage of installed capacity produced privately began to decrease, at first slightly, but decisively, from 91 percent in 1936 to 80 percent in 1946. Meanwhile, the percentage production by federal-owned utilities grew from 2 percent in 1936 to 13 percent in 1961.

Alexander Graham Bell and the Telephone

Whereas Edison became the most prolific inventor in the history of the world, his equally great rival, Scottish immigrant Alexander ("Graham") Bell, held patents for only eighteen inventions. He had, however, just as fertile an imagination as Edison and preferred to concentrate on what he regarded as his true profession, teaching the deaf.

Bell was the first to realize that the electrical transmission of the human voice was physically possible and commercially practicable and conceived the idea of the telephone in July 1874. The caller would speak into vibrating plates or reeds, thus inducing a continuous fluctuating current that would carry the exact amplitude and frequency of his voice along a wire. At the receiver an electromagnet would transform the current into pulses or undulations of magnetic force that would then act on another array of tuned reeds to reproduce the original sound. On March 10, 1876, he and his assistant, Thomas Watson, had their first intelligible, if muffled, conversation by telephone from adjacent rooms. The new invention in an imperfect state was demonstrated to a large audience at MIT on June 23, and, on June 25, 1876, at the instigation of Bell's father-in-law, Gardiner Greene Hubbard, to three judges at the Philadelphia Centennial Exhibition. Bell obtained a second patent, no. 186,787, for an improved model on January 30, 1877.

In the meantime, Hubbard organized the Bell Telephone Company in 1878 and secured the outstanding services of Theodore N. Vail as its president who had it incorporated in July 1878. The first commercial telephone switchboard was established in New Haven, Connecticut, in 1878. By March 1880 there were 138 exchanges and some 30,000 subscribers. In 1880 the various companies were reorganized as the American Bell Telephone Company; then, in 1885, as the American Telephone and Telegraph Company (AT & T).

Heavy demand for telephone services at certain peak times quite early in the history of the telephone necessitated complex switchboards and technical developments had to be swiftly utilized in order to keep up with the demands. The first central office with a central battery opened in Lexington, Massachusetts, in 1893. This improvement led to another by which a caller could now signal the operator simply by lifting the receiver, instead of dialing the operator who then placed the call.

As ever more people wanted to use the telephone in the new century, instruments, connections, and exchanges all proliferated. The demand for service over long distances and better quality sound caused new technical problems. Early solutions included the replacement of steel wire with hard-drawn copper wire, a better and stronger conductor, the laying of underground cables, and the development of a dry-core cable (achieved by surrounding the wire with paper and air and a watertight binding).

Because electrical distortion was considerable over long distances, it was thought that telephone communication between Boston and Chicago, a distance of 1,200 miles, was the farthest practical maximum for long-distance transmission. Then British scientist Oliver Heaviside suggested how actual transmission could be improved by increasing the inductance of the circuit by placing loading coils at strategic points along the cable. American engineers applied and developed this idea by siting coils along cables at regular intervals. The technique of loading had the effect of doubling possible lengths of line and was in public use in May 1900. In 1906, in order to overcome distortion and get good voice quality, Lee De Forest devised the three-element vacuum repeater, a vacuum tube, consisting of a filament and plate with a wire mesh in between. Signals entering the repeater agitated the filament, producing electrons that passed through the grid and were received at the plate. The grid amplified the signal. The three-element vacuum repeater was in commercial use in 1915 and it required only three repeaters to get good voice quality from coast to coast.

However, the early vacuum repeater with its short life was impractical for telephone links across oceans. Yet the problems of distortion of sound would be even greater along transoceanic cables since the two conductors (wire and water) would dilute the signal. Nevertheless, public demand for transoceanic telephone links was such that the companies succumbed to pressure and established radio links across the Atlantic by 1926. Transoceanic cables would have to wait until after World War II for the development of a repeater with a life expectancy of twenty years.

AT & T naturally wanted to economize on equipment by sending a series of voice signals on a courier wire simultaneously by a system of superimposition. This was achieved by a coaxial cable, consisting of a tubular conductor and another conductor concentric to it, first used commercially between New York and Philadelphia in 1937. The automatic switching system, first patented in 1889, was a mechanism for making contact by sending out a series of pulses to raise, then rotate, a shaft through a corresponding series of steps. Its first large test installation was in Newark, New Jersey, in 1914, and in 1921 a fully automatic switching system was opened in Omaha, Nebraska.

Not all inventions were as spectacular as telephone and electric light yet were just as instrumental in expanding production— such as the sterile tin can and sanitary canned milk that stimulated whole new industries of canning and food processing. Similarly, the development of machine tools by Pratt and Whitney was a pivot in rapid mechanization. Mechanized refrigeration revolutionized meat packing and the preservation of perishable foods.

In 1874 I. Solomon of Baltimore introduced pressure-cooking for preserving food to be canned. Sealing of cans was improved by the invention of the drop press by Allen Taylor (also in 1874) and the flow machine (1876). By 1880 one machine could make 1,500 cans a day. From 1900 the open sanitary can, sealed by the crimping method, eliminated faulty canning and contamination and became widely used. In 1914 55 million cans of vegetables were sold around the world. Between 1890 and 1917 the chilling and transportation of frozen foods greatly expanded, despite public prejudice about frozen food being second rate, and after World War I frozen food came to be generally accepted. Also, the Kelvinator Corporation and the Frigidaire Corporation began production of small-scale refrigerators for family homes in the 1910s. Thus by 1927 over 2 million refrigerators were in use. In 1925 Birdseye and Hall extended deep-freezing to precooked foods and in the 1930s the Frosted Foods Corporation began commercial production.

Certain natural substances became important sources for chemicals. Once it was understood that nitrogen formed an important constituent of air, chemists tried to use nitrogen. Thus the Atmospheric Products Company of Niagara Falls in 1902 and Birkeland and Eyde in 1903 bound nitrogen to nitrates and nitric acid. Processes were invented to compound rubber, first vulcanized (or hardened) by Charles Goodyear in 1839, with mineral powders, oils, waxes, tars, and fibers. Advances in chemistry and bacteriology also promoted the supply of good potable water and led to the abandonment of public cesspools and privy-bucket systems.

Sometimes the smallest inventions were among the most significant, such as the razor blade. Among metal fabricators, one, the Gillette Safety Razor Company, produced for the consumer market. In 1903 King Camp Gillette, the inventor of the safety razor, produced 51 razors and 168 blades. The following year his factory manufactured 90,000 razors and 12.4 million blades. By the 1910s, in addition to a worldwide marketing organization, he had factories in Britain, France, Germany, and Canada. All this huge expansion was financed by retained earnings.

Edison, Bell, and their contemporary inventors did not establish a continuous tradition of American invention. Rather, their work led to the management of industry based on science that continuously assimilated the most recent advances of technology. Managers wanted to protect their investment, the inventions, and get the best profits out of them by keeping them as competitive, that is as up-to-date, as possible by incorporating improved technology. Thus AT & T began using radio for some long-distance telephone lines. Sometimes, it was the public who gained more than the companies. Thus AT & T's use of radio demonstrated its superiority for person to person communication in certain circumstances and, in time, AT & T's wire communication was, in effect, neutralized.

Industrial Organization

How such inventions as electric light, telephone, and synthetic fibers transformed society depended largely on superb industrial organization, another special characteristic of the American Industrial Revolution. Large industries achieved economies of scale in production, distribution, and marketing. Whereas in the 1870s a manufacturing firm was simply a company that made goods, in the 1900s many important industries were dominated by a few large corporations that often controlled their source of raw materials, certainly did their own purchasing, their own production, their own distribution, and possibly their own wholesaling. This was vertical integration.

Glen Porter in *The Rise of Big Business 1860–1910* (1973) finds several characteristics that separated big business from such earlier enterprises. First, it used far larger numbers of workers. Second, in order to rebuild, maintain, and operate large factories, it was necessary to attract larger investment from more people. Third, big business used complex technology and many factories now had far higher costs than before and were thus reliant on regular levels of operation to achieve low costs per unit of output.

Fourth, the nature of ownership changed from the time when individual businesses were owned by a few people to a period when there were many part owners. Before the American Civil War the owners of a business were also the managers. Thereafter, a cardinal feature of modern business enterprise was the separation of ownership from management. Because it was necessary to raise large sums of money to fund the company, ownership was dispersed among a large number of investors who usually had little part to play in the actual running of company affairs. Thus, instead, and fifth, firms came to be run by a new tier of salaried managers, professionals who, usually, had little or no ownership in the business. Sixth, the spatial, or geographical, scale of business moved from a single town or city or region to a fair number of widely scattered locations. Seventh, big business abandoned its traditional pattern of narrow specialization, expanding the range of functions to achieve vertical integration. Last, big business was also characterized by an elaborate managerial structure to coordinate the different but interrelated activities.

Many firms, first organized shortly after the American Civil War, had achieved nationwide success by the turn of the century. They included John D. Rockefeller's Standard Oil Company, James Buchanan Duke's American Tobacco Company, Andrew Carnegie's steel company, and the House of Morgan. Others remained desultory enterprises until the very end of the century. They included Coca-Cola, Levi Strauss, Kellogg, Eastman Kodak, Sears Roebuck, and R. J. Reynolds. Others organized in the

Gilded Age expired or were absorbed by their most successful competitors, notably certain oil and railroad companies.

Monopoly capitalism, represented by big business, entailed a great conglomeration of wealth and power, a veritable plutocracy. By 1904 the top 4 percent of American businesses produced 57 percent of America's total industrial production. The depression of 1893–97 had undermined many firms that were only marginally competitive, paving the way for several hundred mergers. In the period 1898–1902 there were 319 major consolidations. Between 1895 and 1904 an average of 300 firms disappeared every year. As a result of this wave of mergers and consolidations, a single firm came to account for 60 percent of production in 50 different industries. Thus Dupont and General Electric came to control 85 percent of their respective markets, chemicals and electric power.

The most prolific historian of industrial consolidation, Alfred Dupont Chandler, Jr., explains in his *Visible Hand* (1977):

The rise of modern business enterprise in American industry between the 1880s and World War I was little affected by public policy, capital markets, or entrepreneurial talents because it was part of a more fundamental economic development. Modern business enterprise . . . was the organizational response to fundamental changes in processes of production and distribution made possible by the availability of new sources of energy and by the increasing application of scientific knowledge to industrial technology. The coming of the railroad and telegraph and the perfection of new high-volume processes in the production of food, oil, rubber, glass, chemicals, machinery, and metals made possible a historically unprecedented volume of production. . . . Changes in transportation, communication, and demand brought a revolution in the processes of distribution. And . . . the manufacturers integrated mass production with new distribution. The result was the giant industrial enterprise which remains today the most powerful privately owned and managed economic institution in modern market economies.

Giant industrial enterprises were often controlled by so-called holding companies. Holding companies were formed by promoters who bought a majority of the stock, or enough to control voting in two or more corporations and then elected common directors who ran the several corporations as one business. Thus a corporation worth $1 million could be acquired for $500,001. By a system of tiers, a process of building the holding company atop another in a pyramid, such acquisitions became less expensive and more profitable. The most significant holding company movement came in the period 1898–1901. Many were based in New Jersey which was geographically close to Wall Street and where state laws tolerated and encouraged holding companies.

In the 1800s and 1890s the multiunit industrial corporation was a new phenomenon. However, soon after the turn of the century, it became the standard instrument in manufacturing for production and distribution. Of a sample of 278 companies among the largest 500 industrial firms, compiled by Thomas R. Navin in *Business History Review* for August 1970—those involved in agriculture, forestry, fishing, mining, construction, and manufacturing—236 manufactured or processed raw or semifinished materials into finished products. Thus they were in industries with similar characteristics to those in which integrated corporations first appeared in the 1880s and 1890s. Thus 171 (72.5 percent) were in primary metals, food, transportation equipment, machinery, petroleum, and chemicals, while 23 (9.7 percent) were in textiles, lumber, leather, printing, clothing, and instruments.

However, the most modern forms of industry failed to thrive in any manufacturing that was labor-intensive but required little heat, energy, or complex machinery, or where middlemen had no difficulty in selling the product. Thus there were few large firms in such traditional industries as wood, clothing, and leather, or in printing and the making of specialized instruments and machinery. Of the 23 firms listed by Thomas R. Navin whose processes were labor-intensive, most were at the lower end. Of 218 firms that were fully integrated, over 80 percent managed their properties through functional departments, such as production and sales, rather than through autonomous subsidiaries.

Modern enterprise had its beginning in machinery, food, and tobacco. By 1917 there were thirty-nine large-scale enterprises in machinery, thirty-five in food. The largest food enterprises included the first processors of perishable food, notably meat packers (Armour, Swift, Wilson, Morris, and Cudahay) and brewers (Anheuser Busch and Schlitz). By 1917 United Fruit (technically in agriculture, rather than food processing), American Ice, and Booth Fisheries (which failed), used refrigeration and were operating comparable networks for distribution. The early producers of cheap packaged goods used continuous-process machinery and were still leaders in their industries: Quaker Oats, Washburn-Crosby (flour), Heinz, Borden's, Libby, and Coca-Cola all flourished. The only new company of this type to be formed after 1900 was California Packing (Del Monte), a merger of local canning companies in 1916 that created a nationwide marketing organization. The first merged companies, such as American Cotton Oil and Southern Cotton Oil, often dominated their industries. Royal Baking Powder and United States Milling (later Standard Milling), which had merged at the turn of the century, accomplished the change from loose federations of single-function family firms to cohesive, centrally controlled and integrated businesses.

The makers of complex machines began to create extensive marketing organizations almost from the beginning and soon became huge global enterprises. If we add together the leading companies in electrical machinery with those in transportation equipment, and machinery, the total is fifty-eight, a quarter of all manufacturing firms in the United States with assets of more than $20 million in 1917. The leaders in machinery making were Singer Manufacturing, Remington Typewriter, Burroughs Adding Machine, Deere and Company, Moline Plow, J. I. Case, Babcock and Wilcox, Worthington Pump, Otis Elevator, Mergenthaler Linotype, Westinghouse Electric, and Western Electric.

Alfred Dupont Chandler concludes, firstly, that the nature of the market was more important than methods of production in determining the size and defining the scope of the modern industrial corporation. Secondly, while the strategy of vertical integration led to industrial concentration, it rarely resulted in monopoly. The various integrated firms competed with one another as oligopolies. Thirdly, the large firms came to dominate their industries overseas as well as at home. Finally, the twenty years between the great merger movement of 1898–1903 and American intervention in World War I in 1917 was the formative period in American industry in which most industries acquired their definitive structure. Because marketing was now the key to commercial success, any newcomers seeking to compete with the most successful firms could not hope to challenge their hold on the market unless they could first create an effective marketing organization. However, small integrated firms continued to prosper in those industries where technology did not lead to mass production and where distribution did not gain from specialized scheduling.

The concentrated industries were in the same industrial groups as the large industries. Thus in 1909 six oil companies accounted for 34 percent of petroleum; in 1919, they accounted for 44 percent. In 1909 one tobacco company accounted for 75 percent of tobacco; in 1919 two tobacco companies accounted for 80 percent. However, in some industries consolidation was not especially successful. It took seventeen textile companies to account for less than 1 percent of textiles in 1909 and twenty-three textile companies accounted for less than 1 percent in 1919.

The integrated companies were forced to compete with one another, rather than with the nonintegrated firms. The fuller their use of their facilities became, the more complete their integration, the more likely this was to be the case. Thus National Lead became a natural competitor of National Linseed in the production of linseed oil. And National (or, as it became, American) Linseed was drawn to compete in the fertilizer markets with the large cotton oil and fertilizer firms. When companies in cotton oil and meatpacking began to make soap as a by-product, they were thrown into competition with Proctor and Gamble.

The United States' fundamental industrial organization was achieved and made firm by World War I. As the century progressed, it was the same large industrial enterprises that continued and dominated the same large industries. In 1929 88 percent of the largest 81 manufacturing companies were in food and tobacco, oil, rubber, chemicals, primary metals, and machinery making. If we include integrated companies in paper, glass, cans, and photographic equipment, the total is over 90 percent. These were all industries with concentrated forms where the visible hand of management had greatest scope for increasing productivity and was crucial to the health of America's industrial economy.

Moreover, once a firm had created a hierarchy of managers, and once that organization had become efficient, it became self-perpetuating. Such centralized decision making and concentrated economic power were of crucial significance as they took place in industries central to the economic growth and well-being of the nation as a whole. However, it was markets and technology that determined whether it was manufacturers or their salaried managers in marketing who did the coordinating. Chandler concludes that the marketing managers "had a far greater influence in determining size and concentration in American industry than did the quality of entrepreneurship, the availability of capital, or public policy."

In the hands of their tiers of talented, salaried managers, the great industrial companies developed a momentum and logic of their own. They could overcome whatever problems stood in their way, whether of supply and demand, or of labor, production, or governmental regulation.

CHAPTER TWO

Bear Necessities:
Theodore Roosevelt and
the Square Deal

·ॐ·

THEODORE ROOSEVELT'S accession to the presidency, albeit in tragic circumstances, signaled the end of the Gilded Age of 1865–1901 and the opening of the Progressive Era of 1901–17. It seemed that progress, whether in inventions, industry, or democratic government, was the key to modern America. It was an insistence on progress that underlay the reform movement we call Progressivism and that was at its zenith in the early twentieth century. Reformers tried to bring rational order to politics, industry, and cities as the United States was being transformed from a rural to an urban and industrial economy. Progressives thought that they could correct such dislocations and evils as: excessive concentration of economic power in a few monopolies; wasteful consumption of the nation's resources; corrupt party machines; sweatshops, child labor, and overcrowded slums.

The first centers of the progressive movement in the 1890s were the large cities of the Northeast and Midwest and the mainly agrarian communities of the Midwest and parts of the South. After what novelist Theodore Dreiser called "the furnace stage" in the making of major cities, an optimistic and energetic middle class first moved to improve facilities, remodel government, and enhance its social status. The Progressive movement then moved to state government with the election of reform governors like Robert M. La Follette of Wisconsin (1901–6), and gained a national voice during Theodore Roosevelt's presidency (1901–9), scoring legislation in his second administration. It concentrated its reform ideas during the disappointing presidency of William Howard Taft (1909–13), formed a third political party in 1912, and achieved several fundamental federal reforms during the first administration of Woodrow Wilson (1913–17). It was divided by Wilson's policies during World War I and resurfaced briefly in the elections of 1924 when La Follette stood as a third party presidential candidate.

Its impact on the federal Constitution can be seen in the adoption, after a gap of over forty years from 1870, of no fewer than four new amendments sponsored by various Progressives: the Sixteenth, allowing for federal income tax (1913); the Seventeenth, providing for the direct election of U.S. senators (1913); the Eighteenth, imposing national prohibition of alcohol (1919); and the Nineteenth, introducing female suffrage (1920).

We might say there were two sorts of Progressives: those who promoted reforms in government and business on the grounds of efficiency—such as business modernizers and efficiency experts, and those who supported humanitarian policies in government and whom we would now call liberals. However, these two sections were not self-contained entities. The aims and political will of each frequently overlapped with the other. What they had in common was a commitment to a new identity—a generation that had reached political maturity at the turn of the century and saw itself as the new men and women of a new progressive age.

Several historians have shaded the motives of some Progressives, blurring their objectives, and softening the outlines of their priorities, while adding much detail on the great diversity of the movement as a whole. Richard Hofstadter in *The Age of Reform* (1955) and George E. Mowry in *The California Progressives* (1951) have emphasized what the Progressives owed to their anteced-

"The President's Dream."
When Theodore Roosevelt went on a bear hunt in Mississippi in November 1902, but refused to shoot a defenseless, small bear, Clifford Berryman provided the *Washington Post* with a cartoon showing TR "Drawing the Line in Mississippi." Thereafter, the teddy bear was indissolubly associated with Roosevelt. In this cartoon Berryman extends his symbol to show TR's own political distinction between good trusts, subservient to government, and bad trusts, rampaging all over it, until Roosevelt sets his foot upon them. (Library of Congress).

ents, notably in adopting earlier moral values. Samuel P. Hays in *The Response to Industrialism, 1885–1914* (1957) and an article, "The Policies of Reform in Municipal Government in the Progressive Era," for *Pacific Northwest Quarterly* (1964), has shown how interest groups reshaped the democratic principles involved in such matters as the reform of local government to elitist solutions. Gabriel Kolko in *The Triumph of Conservatism* (1963) has argued how the establishment of federal agencies to regulate business, such as the Federal Trade Commission and the Federal Reserve Board, served business and allowed the triumph of a political capitalism that was to characterize modern America.

In comparison with the Populists, Progressives were urbane and middle-class, including the most articulate, literate, and expert members of the new professional classes. Their leaders were usually white Anglo-Saxon Protestants from affluent backgrounds and with a college education, as well as occupying a professional or commercial position, allowing them a certain economic independence and social status. By virtue of their education and their Christian ideals, they were particularly sensitive to exposures of mismanagement, corruption, and accounts of economic and social distress. They were also equipped with the necessary eloquence and with leisure time to engage in serious and considered protest.

Moreover, the middle class was not a dwindling but an expanding group at the turn of the century. Robert Wiebe explains this phenomenon and analyzes its significance in his *The Search for Order, 1877–1920* (1967). The genesis of a new professional middle class was, in part, a progressive creation and helped shape progressive politics. According to Wiebe, the emerging and expanded middle class spanned two groups. The first comprised such professions as medicine, architecture, law, economics, administration, and social work. The second was composed of the special fields of business, labor, and agriculture. Both groups were proud of specialist skills, common aims, and a general desire to improve the quality of life of society as a whole. The special needs of cities and industry encouraged their self-confidence and raised standards of professional expertise.

Reform Administration in Cities and States

The first historian of the progressive phenomenon, Benjamin P. DeWitt, said in *The Progressive Movement* (1915) that "the social phase of the progressive movement in the state is by far the most important." The cities were, to borrow a phrase from Congregationalist minister and writer Josiah Strong, both the nerve center and the storm center of American civilization. It was in the city that the cultural, social, political, and economic dislocations of industrialization were most strongly felt and most openly displayed. Immigrants congregated in the slum housing of ethnic ghettos, and were exploited in poorly paid and often dangerous jobs, and used as political pawns by party bosses who were unrestrained by the law. The existing and rudimentary municipal services, such as public transport, gas heating, street paving, and refuse collection, could often not cope with the sheer growth in the number of residents. As late as 1900, cities such as Baltimore and New Orleans had no sewers while two-thirds of Chicago's streets were mud.

Progressives believed that one solution to the problems would be to replace the city's formal system of government and its large number of elected officials, who held little real authority, with a system of appointed commissioners who would wield strong municipal control against vested interests, such as those of utility tycoon Charles Tyson Yerkes who dominated the traction and gas monopolies of Chicago.

In 1900 in Galveston, Texas, a hurricane and tidal wave overwhelmed both the city and the city's council government, and leading local property owners appealed for emergency government by commission. The state legislature responded positively to this appeal and appointed five commissioners to take over the management of Galveston. So successful was this system that in 1903 the system of commissioners was made elective and by 1913 more than 400 other cities had followed suit. Another flood, this time in Dayton, Ohio, in 1913, led to a variation on municipal government by commission with the appointment of a professional city-manager to administer city government. By 1919 more than 130 cities had adopted the city-manager plan. Business interests, often in the form of the local chamber of commerce, were the most consistent supporters of both the commission and city-manager systems. These specific progressive reforms were confined mainly to small and medium-sized cities in New England, the Midwest, and the Pacific states, but even in the larger cities governmental reform was often instigated and shaped by business and professional groups who were motivated by a desire for greater efficiency.

It became ever clearer that the old patchwork system of government was quite inadequate to meet new demands for essential services. In city after city Progressives extended the scope of utility regulation and began to limit the profits and duration of franchises for street lighting, gas, electricity, intracity transport, and refuse disposal. The sort of one-sided contracts exacted by construction companies for laying pipes, that had once been excused when the demand for fresh water, piped gas, and sewage disposal was urgent, were now scrutinized anew by sober Progressives, intent on maximum efficiency, minimum profit, and optimum fairness.

In city after city genuine and progressive reform candidates found that they could get themselves elected as mayor, despite the opposition of previously entrenched political machines. Seth Low was elected in New York (1901–3) and James D. Phelan took San Francisco (1897–1902).

Let us look at the political career of one of these reform mayors to see how Progressivism worked in the cities. Former congressman Tom Johnson of Cleveland was a steel manufacturer who also had a majority interest in the franchise and property of street railways in Indianapolis, Cleveland, St. Louis, Detroit, Brooklyn, and other cities. Nevertheless, he waged an attack on the selfishness of business ownership of public utilities and was a strenuous advocate of municipal ownership. His campaign provoked vigorous opposition to business operation of public utility interests and led him to campaign for mayor of Cleveland. He served as mayor for the period 1899–1909, had a uniform 3 cent street carfare introduced in 1907, but was defeated for reelection.

What transformed Johnson's war in Cleveland was the expert advice of his young counselors Frederic Howe, Newton D. Baker, and Edward Bemis, who provided him with a continuous series of ideas on tax assessment, the treatment of offenders, and more rational government. In short, they provided the cooperative and unassuming Johnson with expert knowledge that was quite outside his own experience. Newton D. Baker, city solicitor of Cleveland in Tom Johnson's time, thought Johnson's mayoralty marked a decisive turning point against inefficient and corrupt municipal government. "Johnson became at once the outstanding municipal executive—was guide, counsellor, and friend to all other American cities; was visited almost daily by men from everywhere who were interested in rescuing city government. When Johnson ceased to be Mayor of Cleveland, he had set new standards of city government throughout the nation."

At first, only prominent businessmen had the sort of financial resources and prestige to command some immediate response from local government. Hence, they became prime targets for progressive recruitment. Similarly, reformers tried to win over local bosses who had the connections to make politics work. In return, political bosses gained insight into city problems and special skills about how to solve them from rank and file Progressives. Both businessmen and political bosses liked to parade as public benefactors and enjoyed their new reputations.

Following their successes in cities, Progressives turned their attention to state government, first fielding charismatic leaders, and then proposing major reforms. Once again, the same mix of factors yielded Progressives success and failures in state government. Apart from certain exceptions, such as Braxton Bragg Comer of Alabama (1907–11), the important progressive governors began their careers as leaders of intraparty factions, intent on power rather than a specific program that was sometimes forced on them by certain sections of their middle-class followers. This could lead them away from progressive reforms. Albert Cummins of Iowa (1902–8) created his first coalition from Republicans opposed to prohibition. Hoke Smith of Georgia (1907–10; 1911) was obliged by his adherents to include Jim Crow racism in his plans.

Once in office, progressive governors had the unenviable task of having to pilot legislative programs, direct administration, and hold somewhat diffuse coalitions together, all at once. The most skillful, like Robert La Follette of Wisconsin (1901–6), Albert Cummins of Iowa, and Hiram Johnson of California (1911–17), did so by getting their bands of progressive reformers to concentrate on lobbying, and otherwise persuading, state legislators to pass certain measures whilst they, themselves, attempted to unite their constituencies by traditional appeals to local spirit. The most successful and controversial of all progressive governors was Robert ("Battling Bob") La Follette of Wisconsin who first campaigned for a direct primary in Wisconsin, then wrested the governorship from the Republicans, and, ultimately, created his own progressive machine that continued to provide him with strong support throughout a long political career. Journalist and contemporary historian Mark Sullivan recorded how

As Governor, La Follette, after years of denunciation of the boss system, was himself the boss of Wisconsin. He was a boss of a new and utterly different type, who worked always in the interest of the common man as he saw it, who discarded the sordid methods of the older type—and yet a boss, autocratic, imperious, peremptory, practising toward his apostles a dictatorial insistence upon obedience such as no boss of the older type would ever have dared attempt.

La Follette's governorship was extremely controversial. He harried a reluctant legislature into imposing heavier taxes upon the railroads, an inheritance tax, and a graduated income tax, and introducing direct primary elections and a railroad commission with far-reaching powers.

Extending Democracy

Progressives moved, logically enough, from local social and economic reforms, to reforms of the political structure that would extend democracy. Progressives wanted to make governments truly responsive and responsible by a package of democratic measures, including the initiative, referendum, recall of judges and other public officials, accurate registration of voters, direct election of senators, proportional registration, direct primaries, secret and simpler ballots, corrupt practices acts, and lobbies in the public interest.

Furthermore, Progressives believed that good legislative reforms would bring good men into government who would pass good laws to reduce inequality and achieve true justice. The process would also benefit the huddled masses who would become educated and enlightened citizens. Thus they wanted to retain the advantages of the representative system, notably its compactness, experience, and legal knowledge, and eliminate its disadvantages, notably both haste and delay, complexity, corruption, errors, and legislative excesses and shortcomings.

The general principle of the referendum was to enable state acts and local ordinances to be scrutinised by the electors. If within thirty days of the passing of a city ordinance, or ninety days in the case of a state law, 5 or 10 percent of the voters signed a petition asking that the ordinance or law be submitted to the entire electorate at the next election (or at a special election if 15 or 20 percent of voters so petitioned), it was; then, if a majority of those voting favored the measure, it became law; if a majority were against it, it was vetoed by the people. The exceptions to this practice were measures governing immediate public health, peace, or safety. In the case of the initiative, the public took the initiative in requesting a certain law, again by use of a petition signed by 5 or 10 percent. If 15 or 20 percent so petitioned, then the measure had to be submitted to the electorate at the next election. The first state to adopt the initiative and referendum was South Dakota in 1898; by 1912 seventeen states had adopted either or both of these devices.

Primary elections were the means by which voters who were registered with either party directly chose that party's candidates for election. In 1899 Minnesota provided for a "direct primary" to select nominees for election to political office, in place of a system of party conventions or caucuses, and the first primary election was held in Minneapolis in September 1900. The previous month a state convention in Madison, Wisconsin, also declared for direct primaries. The recall was the means by which the people could oblige officials, whom a petition, signed by a certain proportion of the electors, had deemed to have failed them, to submit themselves to a special election before their term of office had expired. The recall was first applied in cities in 1903, adopted by Oregon in 1908, and used by ten other states by 1914.

Another bone of contention between Progressives and diehard conservatives was the system of having U.S. senators elected by state assemblies, a system that had led in the past to some senators being nominated by state bosses and representing certain economic interests rather than the people. During the 1890s the Senate had been known as the Millionaire's Club. Senator James McMillan (1889–1902) represented shipping and lumber rather than Michigan; Joseph Foraker (1897–1909) served Standard Oil rather than Ohio. The *Outlook* of April 7, 1906, spoke for many when it described the general distrust aroused by a few senators, that the Senate "includes altogether too many managers of political machines who control the entire political organization of their States; that a small group of Senators stand together too definitely for business in politics—that is to say, for that 'system' of interweaving business and political interests which more than any other single thing has corrupted and lowered the tone of our public life."

By 1912 twenty-nine states were experimenting with various ways of electing senators directly, having instituted primaries and putting the name of the winning candidates at the primary on the ballot paper at the election and pledging the candidates for the state legislature to elect the senatorial candidate with most votes. The widespread acceptance of this reform led to its formal adoption by the federal government. The Seventeenth Amendment, passed on May 13, 1912, and ratified on April 8, 1913, declared that "The Senate of the United States shall be composed of two Senators from each State, elected by the people thereof, for six years; and each Senator shall have one vote." Those qualified to vote would be those qualified to vote for "the most numerous branch of the State legislature." When vacancies occurred in Senate seats, the executive of the states had to issue writs of election to fill the vacancy. However, the state legislature could empower the executive to make temporary appointments to the Senate until the election. In the end, diehard conservatives in Congress

The San Francisco earthquake of 1906 fueled a devastating fire that laid waste to large sections of the city and, incidentally, drove Theodore Roosevelt's crusade for railroad regulation off the front pages of newspapers across the nation. Here the Grand Palace is engulfed by flames. (Library of Congress).

accepted the measure and supported it, knowing that they could not deny it for long, and that frank opposition to it would surely result in their own defeat at the next election.

The Progressives' tendency to elitist solutions also led them to urge proposals that would curtail, rather than extend, the part played in government by the people. Thus some advocated a "short ballot," to reduce the number of elected officials, on the grounds that the "long ballot" was democratically specious, because voters could not be expected to pass informed judgments on the merits of minor officeholders and, in practice, tended to endorse an entire party ticket. Instead, Progressives, assuming high professional expertise from chief administrators, would have simply turned over the authority to run a whole administration to a few senior executives.

Theodore Roosevelt

It was Theodore Roosevelt more than any other single person who united the diverse impulses of Progressivism and turned them into effective national politics when he became president in 1901.

Theodore Roosevelt was born in New York City in October 1858, son of a middle-class banker of Anglo-Dutch descent, who provided him with a comfortable youth that included extensive world travel capped by education at Harvard. In 1880 he took his B.A. degree and embarked on a remarkable early career that included brief spells as a law student, a historical writer, a mayoral candidate in New York City, a civil service commissioner, and president of the board of police commissioners of New York. In 1897 he was appointed assistant secretary of the navy in the first McKinley administration (1897–1901) where he helped prepare for war with Spain. When America went to war to free Cuba in 1898, he made a most audacious move and assured himself of lifelong fame and popularity. Together with Leonard Wood, a professional soldier, he organized the 1st U.S. Volunteer Cavalry—"the Rough Riders"—and, as Colonel Roosevelt, personally led a successful charge up San Juan Hill in Cuba. On his return, he was elected Republican governor of New York and alarmed the old guard of party bosses with reforms that threatened their oligarchy. However, such was Roosevelt's popular appeal that he proved to be a major asset to the Republican party. Thus, initially against his will, he was nominated as McKinley's running mate in 1900. Party chairman Mark Hanna wanted to exploit his popularity while silencing his political opinion. His presence on the ticket helped ensure the Republicans' victory over William Jennings Bryan and the Democrats. When Boss Thomas

Collier Platt of New York was asked if he would attend the McKinley-Roosevelt inauguration he replied, "Yes, I am going to see Theodore Roosevelt take the veil." Whatever the old guard would have preferred, the first of the political titans was now president and in command. "Do you know the two most wonderful things I have seen in your country?" asked English diplomat John Morley. "Niagara Falls and the President of the United States, both great wonders of nature." What these two natural phenomena had in common was a continuous flow of torrential energy, a sense of perpetual motion. Thus Theodore Roosevelt was a man of overwhelming physical presence.

He stood five foot eight inches and weighed 200 pounds but 200 pounds of thick muscle on thighs, arms, and chest carried on a small-boned frame. Since his early childhood had been marred by continuous illness, especially violent attacks of asthma, TR built up his body, spending thousands of assiduous hours in gyms, exercising his body into fighting shape. Even his speeches were punctuated by expressive physical jerks, intense concentration, and contorted expressions. His head was too large, his ears too large, and his jowls too heavy for him to be handsome. However, he had a high brow to set off his pugnacious features and a dazzling smile. His large pale blue eyes under the pince-nez, one of which was blind, betrayed what editor William Allen White called "the shadow of some inner femininity deeply suppressed," a sort of wistful perplexity. This expressed what Owen Wister called "the sign of frequent conflict between what he knew, and his wish not to know it, his determination to grasp his optimism tight, lest it escape him." His full mustache partly hid a large, somewhat pouting lower lip but never concealed his gleaming white and even teeth. When he spoke in his precise, enthusiastic way, people were reminded of engines starting, and light artillery firing away. If Roosevelt started to clean out some government department, the press responded with cartoons of the "Old Dutch Cleanser." Without exception, the cartoons showed Roosevelt in action and, nine times out of ten, in active combat.

He had a lively sense of humor with an irresistible chuckle, ready for absurd incidents, cowboy stories, children's games, and to laugh at himself. He indulged in eccentric exercises—wading naked into the icy Potomac and taking up jujitsu with a Japanese wrestler (and forcing the outsize William Howard Taft to do so on one occasion). "You must always remember," observed the Englishman Sir Cecil Spring-Rice, "that the president is about six." Yet he was courteous to both great and grotesque, until roused to anger by sudden familiarity or the use of the nickname "Teddy" that he regarded as vulgar and impertinent.

He had considerable charm, much of it derived from his amazing self-confidence, and this made him enchanting to women. Novelist Edith Wharton recalled, "I do delight in him," and found her every encounter with TR glowed "like a tiny morsel of radium." His friend, Henry Cabot Lodge, admitted, "Theodore is one of the most lovable, as well as one of the cleverest and most daring men I have ever known." Yet he weighed friendships according to the use he could put them to. When he met someone, "the camera of his mind is busy taking photographs," according to the *Philadelphia Independent*. If that person could be of future use, TR would ensure that his guest would never forget him. His memory was legendary, especially for the way he could quote passages from literature and place people last seen years before. Roosevelt's victories were those of St. George; his activity was that of St. Vitus. Yet his every gesture told; nothing was wasted.

Roosevelt was a major force behind Progressivism, yet his commitment was a direct consequence of the new mood. Until 1902 his political record was one of unrelieved, but upright, conservatism: reform in the interests of honesty and efficiency. Roosevelt's genius was not for crusades but for poses. He could show conclusively that he was a committed Progressive while doing no more than going down the middle of the road. As president, Roosevelt had three goals: to make himself the preeminent leader in his party; to transform the office of president into the most important in the federal government; and to make the federal government the most important and decisive influence in national affairs. His every step was scrutinized by a minority of corporation magnates who, sensing his intentions, showed him their power in a vain attempt to deter him.

Few presidents have been as learned. His grasp of history, great literature, biology, and military and naval strategy reflected his unique mind with its highly developed curiosity, analytical skills, and zest for knowledge. While neither profound nor systematic, he drew on these qualities in others, inviting novelists and poets, inventors, and explorers, men of business, labor, and war to the White House, all of whom he probed for information and insight.

Roosevelt's second wife, Edith Kermit Carow Roosevelt, had far greater insight into men, their motives, and character than he, and her judgment was much sounder. Those who worked in the White House during the Roosevelt years thought that, despite the code of conduct that kept her in the background, she was even greater among women than TR was among men. Mark Sullivan recorded how "For much that Roosevelt got approval for, Mrs. Roosevelt was not only inspiration and partner, but actually principal. Her education was broader than Roosevelt's, her reflection deeper." Through an astute combination of humor and graciousness, she put a brake on TR's recklessness. When Roosevelt had his wife's judgment, he never went wrong, Owen Wister, one of the White House visitors in these years, said, "She was the perfection of 'invisible government.' "

TR maintained that he would be president of the United States and not of any one section, thereby refusing to abide by precedents associated with the spoils system. "If I cannot find Republicans, I am going to appoint Democrats." Thus he gave the pivotal spoils position of the collectorship of the Port of New York to an independent Republican, ignored the Repbulican machines in certain states, and restored to civil service rules and protection 1,500 positions in the War Department removed by a McKinley executive order of 1899. Thus the Detroit *News* declared, "Every day or two he rattles the dry bones of precedent and causes sedate Senators and heads of departments to look over their spectacles in consternation." Roosevelt realized he had the singular advantage above the restraints imposed by Congress and the Supreme Court, and one unused for decades, and that was to use the platform of the office of president as an organ of propaganda. He called it a "bully pulpit." It provided a special opportunity for defining the great national problems and proposing a practicable solution to them. To Roosevelt, "the bulk of government is not legislation but administration." In all, Roosevelt sent 421 messages and 40 vetoes to Congress, a record until his time.

Roosevelt's exuberance was infectious. Across the country there spread the legend of a new, especially vital man in the White House with enormous capacity for work and an energizing, forthright approach. Harry Thurston Peck commented on how "he brought in a stream of fresh, pure, bracing air from the mountains, to clear the fetid atmosphere of the national capital." One author, Richard Washburn Child, described his own visit to the White House and concluded, "You go into Roosevelt's presence, you feel his eyes upon you, you listen to him, and you go home and wring the personality out of your clothes."

In his aims, Roosevelt was also much aided by his trusted advisers and most senior civil servants. Lord Bryce remarked how he had never seen a more high-minded, efficient, and keen set of public servants than those of Roosevelt's administration. Indeed, during these years, the federal government acquired the services and skills of a wide range of professionally trained experts in the fields of architecture, education, engineering, and public health. They included Dr. Harvey Wiley, chief chemist in the Department of Agriculture, whose specialised knowledge was most useful in the drafting of the Pure Food and Drug Act, and forester Gifford Pinchot and geologist W. J. McGee, who helped plan conservation projects based on fire control and sustained-yield forestry. Roosevelt also delegated responsibility to those cabinet members he trusted, notably Secretary of War Elihu Root (1899–1904), who continued the reform of the army he had begun under McKinley, and Root's successor William Howard Taft (1904–8), Secretary of the Interior James R. Garfield (1907–9), and Attorney General William H. Moody (1904–6).

Roosevelt spent most of his first three years consolidating his position of authority, not only within the nation but also within his own Republican party. Congress was under the control of conservative old-style politicians. Joseph G. ("Uncle Joe") Cannon was the authoritative speaker of the House of Representatives (1903–11), while in the Senate Nelson Wilmarth Aldrich of Rhode Island (1881–1911) led a powerful conservative oligarchy. Roosevelt had both to court the favor of these men and also remain true to his character as a moderate reformer. He himself was well aware of the conflict, as a letter written to Senator Chauncey Depew of New York in 1901 shows: *"How* I wish I *wasn't* a reformer, oh, Senator! But I suppose I must live up to my part, like the Negro minstrel who blacked himself all over!"* Indeed, in the fall of 1901 Roosevelt caused a sensation by inviting black leader Booker T. Washington to the White House, ostensibly to discuss the appointment of blacks to political office through the Republican party in the South. By his various actions, Roosevelt set a precedent, that the president can do whatever he is not forbidden to do by the Constitution or in law.

The style of Roosevelt's presidency was made clear to all by the way he intervened in a long coal strike of May–October, 1902, bringing together labor leaders and management. The strike of 147,000 anthracite miners led by Johnny Mitchell had threatened consumers with a serious coal shortage and Roosevelt's insistence that the rights of the public be respected forced operators, led by the truculent George F. Baer, and miners into an agreement to settle the dispute by arbitration. Roosevelt's disinterested intervention was in marked contrast to President Grover Cleveland's intervention in the Pullman strike of 1894 on the side of management, by ordering troops to move mail trains. Roosevelt later concluded that his unprecedented intervention for the settlement of the coal strike in October 1902 was the time he "struck his own note" about big business.

In November he went on a bear hunt in Mississippi but refused to shoot a small bear brought into camp for him to destroy. Thereupon Clifford K. Berryman of the *Washington Post* drew a cartoon showing TR "Drawing the Line in Mississippi." For reasons both symbolic and whimsical, public opinion interpreted the story as disclosing the bare necessities of Roosevelt's personality. Thus the Berryman cartoon of TR and the Teddy-bear was adapted and repeated thousands of times in different forms. Toy makers took advantage of the vogue and created new bear toys for children of all ages that superseded the traditional woolly lambs.

Roosevelt's fame was spread by the newspapers because everything he did was good copy. As one editor, who was highly critical of Roosevelt, reluctantly admitted, Roosevelt had a way of "slapping the public on the back with a bright idea." Roosevelt knew that everything emanating from the White House was potentially news and capitalized on the fact. His incessant activity was a godsend to cartoonists who never lacked a subject while this most temperamental, impetuous, and masterful of politicians with his facile gift for pointed phrases, was in office. He had only to say "Speak softly—but carry a big stick" (in an otherwise academic address on foreign policy) or "the spear that knows no brother" or "square deal" to invite a series of melodramatic cartoons of himself as fearless opponent of the dragon trusts. His protruding teeth and thick spectacles could be used to convey a wide range of facial expressions, notably joy and determination. In scores of drawings by W. H. Walker, an innocent child, "common people," was rescued by Roosevelt from the villain "Trusts."

The Problem of the Trusts

Indeed, during the Progressive Era the pivotal question was that of the "trusts," the giant corporations that seemed to be consolidating industrial production and distribution in the hands of a few finance capitalists. At the turn of the century a "merger boom" was reshaping corporate capitalism decisively. Whereas between 1887 and 1897 there were only 86 industrial combinations with a total capital of less than $1.5 billion, in the period 1897–1902, 2,653 independent companies in mining and manufacturing were swallowed by combinations with a total capital of $6.32 billion. The trusts challenged the assumption of American liberalism because their overwhelming economic weight allowed them to crush the separate interests of their suppliers, employees, competitors, and customers. The Progressives' concept of popular government could only be achieved and maintained by an independent citizenry. A capitalist economy in which only a few corporate executives managed a huge work force was far from this traditional republican ideal. The increasing use of money in politics by industrial entrepreneurs promoting their own interests was disrupting the traditional operation of the political system. "I do not expect to see monopoly restrain itself," observed Democratic presidential candidate Woodrow Wilson during the campaign of 1912. "If there are men in this country big enough to own the government of the United States, they are going to own it."

Progressive journalist Walter Lippmann summed up the situation thus in his *Drift and Mastery* (1914):

The trusts made enemies right and left; they squeezed the profits of the farmer, they made life difficult for the shopkeeper, . . . they closed down factories, they exercised an enormous control over credit through their size and through their eastern connections. Labor was no match for them, state legislatures were impotent before them. They came into the life of the simple American community as a tremendous revolutionary force, upsetting custom, changing men's states, demanding a readjustment for which people were unready. Of course, there was antitrust feeling; of course, there was a blind desire to smash them. Men had been ruined and they were too angry to think, too hard pressed to care much about the larger life which the trusts suggested.

By 1890 public opinion was so incensed against monopolies that it demanded federal regulation to supplement state laws. Investigations in 1888 by a committee of the House and by a committee of the Senate of the New York State Assembly provided little by way of constructive proposals but confirmed contemporary hostility to the abuses of monopolies. The New York investigation was significant because many great firms were run from the city. There followed two years of intense discussion and presidential recommendations before a bill was passed in Congress. The Sherman Antitrust Act of 1890 had eight sections of which the first boldly announced the principle and theory behind the new law: "Every contract, combination in the form of trust or otherwise, or conspiracy, in restraint of trade or commerce among the several States, or with foreign nations, is hereby declared to be illegal. . . ." The act provided fines or imprisonment for violations and stated how an injured person might recover three times the damages sustained. Jurisdiction rested with the various circuit courts, but it was the attorney general who was instructed to institute proceedings against violations.

The Sherman Act proved ineffective for three reasons. First, the economic depression of 1893–97 deferred much business consolidation and what little consolidation actually took place was seen as an attempt to revive flagging industrial fortunes. Second, the general terms of the act required closer definition (and hence interpretation) to be effective and this was unlikely, given the prevailing conservative temper of the judiciary. Third, the federal government, somewhat crippled by the depression, had no interest in incurring extra expenses by enforcing the measure.

By 1901 the government had instituted eighteen suits but with singular lack of success. Clear-cut judicial decisions were impossible, given the prevailing conventional wisdom of laissez-faire, general political conservatism, and the complexity of corporate forms.

Public resentment was tempered by ever wider understanding that in certain cases monopoly was justifiable. Everyone conceded that in the interests of general efficiency certain public services must be part of a consolidated unit. Thus telephones, street railways, gas and electric power were considered public utilities that could be run by monopolies, provided they were controlled by laws. Accordingly, the Interstate Commerce Commission (ICC), established in 1887, had authority over interstate railroads and local intrastate utilities were subject to state public utility commissions. Thus progressive writers did not like the past so much that they wanted to forgo modern technology. They prized inventions, industry, and technology for their potential social benefits. Walter E. Weyl wrote in *The New Democracy* (1912) how "It is the increasing wealth of America which makes democracy possible and solvent, for democracy, like civilization, costs money." Progressives objected to the uneven distribution of wealth, not its existence. Perhaps it was, as Richard Hofstadter remarks, "the broad diffusion of property and power" that made the "preponderantly rural society" of bygone days seem so attractive, rather than its candlelight, horses, and buggies. While the problem of the trusts was easy to see, a solution was more difficult to achieve, and differences and irresolution on this point divided the progressive movement.

Progressive resentment against the trusts was intensified a few short months before Theodore Roosevelt took office by the activities of financier John Pierpont Morgan. Morgan was the preeminent financier of the Gilded Age, less personally wealthy than such "robber barons" as steel magnate Andrew Carnegie or oil tycoon John D. Rockefeller but probably more influential. He it was who drew together the various threads of transportation and communication into his own banking empire in a dazzling career, capped by consolidation of two giant holding companies: United States Steel, capitalized at $1.40 billion in January 1901; and a railway consolidation, the Northern Securities Company, capitalized at $400 million in November 1901.

Roosevelt's Challenge to the Trusts

While the rise of the trusts constituted a grave crisis for American liberalism, Progressives were unsure what to do about them. Mark Sullivan suggests the way Roosevelt's mind was working. "The trusts, through the holding-company device, were above the law. They were more powerful than the people, more powerful than Congress, more powerful than the government. That condition presented to Roosevelt a challenge such as his nature would never ignore . . . here was a challenge not merely to him personally, but to the government and people of the United States, of whose power and dignity he was now the custodian."

In his first message to Congress on December 3, 1901, TR set out his basic policy toward the trusts in vigorous yet moderate tones, proposing supervision and control rather than outright prohibition of monopoly. This ambivalent stance was ripe for lampooning and humorist Finley Peter Dunne captured the comic side of Roosevelt's philosophy in the words of Mr. Dooley: "Th' trusts, says he, are heejous monsthers built up be th'enlightened intherprise iv th'men that have done so much to advance progress in our beloved country, he says. On wan hand I wud stamp thim undher fut; on th'other hand, not so fast." Not so fast indeed. The vested interests of leading Republicans and their dominance of the party partly explain Roosevelt's hesitancy.

Nevertheless, prompted by Roosevelt, Congress passed three acts in 1903 to control big business more closely: the Expediting

Meat packing in the Chicago stockyards was grueling, hazardous work in unsanitary conditions that demoralized and brutalized workers and provided consumers with meat products not always fit to eat. Upton Sinclair's exposure of abuses in the stockyards in his best-selling novel of 1906, *The Jungle,* brought a twenty-year campaign for purer food and better meat products to a triumphant climax in Congress. (Library of Congress).

Act gave preference to federal suits brought under the Interstate Commerce Act and Sherman Anti-Trust Act; the Elkins Anti-Rebate Act tried to clarify the law on the notorious railroad practices of rebates and drawbacks; and the third act established a

Department of Commerce and Labor with a subsidiary Bureau of Corporations, created to make "diligent investigations into the organization, conduct, and management of corporations."

In 1904, when Roosevelt's position within the Republican party was far more secure, he encouraged proceedings already instituted in 1901 against a trust, the Northern Securities Company. J. P. Morgan tried to forestall any attempt at regulation. He visited Roosevelt and declared with his customary arrogant assurance, "If we have done anything wrong, send your man to my man and they can fix it up." Roosevelt later remarked that Morgan "could not help regarding me as a big rival operator, who either intended to ruin all his interests or else could be induced to come to an agreement to ruin none." The news depressed prices on stock markets everywhere. The Detroit *Free Press* satirized the gloom of the financial establishment: "Wall Street is paralyzed at the thought that a president of the United States would sink so low as to try and enforce the law."

The political tool that Roosevelt used in the process against the Northern Securities Company was the discredited Sherman Act of 1890. In the case of *Northern Securities Company* v. *U.S.,* decided on March 14, 1904, by five votes to four, the Supreme Court dissolved the holding company. Roosevelt was triumphant, declaring that the case established the government's power to deal with all great corporations and this was also the general opinion. Alexander Dana Noyes found in his *Forty Years of American Finance* how "the overthrow of the Northern Securities combination was the most positive achievement of the Roosevelt administration in the field of corporate finance."

Stimulated and encouraged, Roosevelt embarked on forty-four antitrust prosecutions against such giant corporations as the E. I. du Pont Company, American Tobacco, and Standard Oil, partly because he thought they were politically vulnerable and partly because he thought they were an economic nuisance. Roosevelt's antitrust prosecutions exposed a raw nerve among corporate executives. Just as they were confused by their inability to make their corporations truly cohesive and efficient, an aggressive president rubbed salt in their wounds of public odium.

Without doubt, Roosevelt was a skillful political opportunist.

In 1904 when he feared that Wall Street was pumping some $5 million into the Democratic campaign to elect the ultraconservative Alton B. Parker to the presidency, he abandoned his principles and allowed his campaign manager to tap the trusts. The money came flowing in from all areas of business. Edward H. Harriman, president of the Southern Pacific Railroad, personally contributed $50,000 and J. P. Morgan another $150,000. In the election on November 9 Roosevelt took 7,628,461 votes (57.4 percent), Parker, 5,084,223 votes (37.6 percent), while Eugene V. Debs, the Socialist, took 402,283 votes (3.0 percent) and Silas C. Swallow, the prohibition candidate, took 258,536 votes (1.9 percent). Thus Roosevelt took 336 seats in the electoral college to Parker's 140. He had gained the highest percentage of the popular vote to that time.

Yet, following his victory, Roosevelt felt no obligation to the trusts and embarked on a series of reforms to provide stricter regulation of railroad rates that culminated in the Hepburn Act of 1906 and the Mann-Elkins Act of 1910 (passed after he was out of office). Roosevelt's supposed duplicity provoked angry comment from steel magnate Henry Clay Frick who complained that "we bought the (son of a bitch) and he didn't stay bought." Among Roosevelt's most crucial appointments was that of able lawyer Henry L. Stimson, who became district attorney for the Southern Judicial District of New York, centered on Manhattan, and with unequalled responsibility to monitor the giant corporations. Stimson's lazy predecessor had brought to trial only 27 of 610 active cases against giant corporations. It was Stimson who brought Felix Frankfurter onto his staff and, together, they persuaded TR to have an extra federal judge appointed. This was to be Charles M. Hough, who was so vigorous in his handling of corporations that, within three years of his taking his seat, he had exacted fines of over $500,000 from two corporations for violations of the Mann-Elkins Act. Almost $3 million was recovered from other corporations that had withheld it from the federal government, and eight officers of three corporations were either imprisoned or fined for infractions of the antitrust laws.

Although Roosevelt and his lawyers secured twenty-five indictments under the Sherman Act and his successor, William

Howard Taft, obtained another forty-three, the actual results of trust-busting were very disappointing to more radical Progressives. For example, in 1911, in the case of *Standard Oil v. U.S.,* decided by eight votes to one on May 15, 1911, the court broke the huge oil monopoly but introduced a new concept, the rule of reason. Chief Justice Edward Douglass White wrote the majority opinion that declared that only unreasonable combinations and undue restraints of trade were illegal under the Sherman Anti-Trust Act. Previously, the court had held that any combination which restrained trade, whether "reasonable" or "unreasonable," was a violation of the Sherman Act. Government prosecutor Frank Kellogg had amassed detailed evidence of the way Standard Oil had created and organized its monopoly and disclosed its exorbitant profits—said to be almost $1 billion over the comparatively brief period of twenty-five years. John D. Rockefeller himself was summoned to give evidence. At sixty-nine he looked older, a shrunken man with hollow cheeks wearing a white wig, but he remained impassive. Although he no longer ran the company, because he was still president he was accountable to the court. To his own lawyers he affected a benign manner, gently describing the way he had created his empire. But when cross-examined by Kellogg, he pretended to be forgetful, his mind a blank, or, as one reporter had it, "his mind was as opaque as an oyster-shell." Rockefeller's considerable skills as an actor did not distract the Supreme Court. Chief Justice Edward Douglass White read out his opinion, all 20,000 words, describing how the "very genius for commercial development and organization" that had created Standard Oil had also created a monopoly to "drive others from the field and exclude them from their right to trade." Accordingly, the Supreme Court ruled that Standard Oil must divest itself of all its subsidiaries within six months. The actual dissolution was achieved by apportioning shares in the various constituent concerns pro rata to the stockholders of the holding company. However, the introduction of the rule of reason created a loophole for trusts to justify their existence as a natural growth of a single business.

The enforced dissolution of Standard Oil resulted in a fair number of single-function companies because, apart from Standard Oil of California and Standard Oil of Louisiana, no Standard subsidiaries were truly integrated. However, by 1918 eight of the former Standard companies with assets of over $20 million had extensive refining and marketing facilities and four had moved into production of crude oil. A fifth Standard company, Standard Oil of Indiana, would do so in 1919. However, the three former Standard companies in crude oil and pipelines managed to find enough markets, especially through their Standard allies, and did not choose to become fully integrated companies until after World War I.

Although the Supreme Court returned each of Rockefeller's thirty-eight companies to the state where it operated, the companies were still owned by Rockefeller and his associates. By far the largest was the New Jersey company that had provided the holding company for the rest, Standard Oil of New Jersey, subsequently known, much later, in the 1960s, in the United States as Exxon, and elsewhere as Esso, and led by Rockefeller's favorite young lion, John D. Archbold. Standard Oil remained an object of intense distrust and the *Congressional Record* of 1914 referred to it as "the invisible government." Exxon had greatly profited from the 1911 dissolution because it came when Rockefeller and the other directors were well over sixty and inclined to be too complacent. After the dissolution, Exxon became far more aggressive. It had managers, money, and markets but very little oil. In its search for new reserves, it started to look outside the United States.

Moderate political Progressives, like Theodore Roosevelt, were more concerned with modifying and reshaping rather than completely restructuring the American economy. What they wanted, and to a large extent achieved, was regularity and efficiency. One historian of Progressivism and railroads, Otis Graham, expressed this phenomenon succinctly when he wrote, "No man can demonstrate with exactitude that justice was the end result of the progressive regulation of railroads, but regularity of procedure was accomplished, and this was close to the heart of progressivism." The bitterly debated Hepburn and Mann-Elkins Acts, of 1906 and 1910, respectively, brought regularity and efficiency to the administration of the railroads by breathing life into the powers awarded the Interstate Commerce Commission, powers that had, like the authority of the Sherman Act, been nullified by the courts during the 1890s. The two new acts combined to empower the Interstate Commerce Commission to effect "reasonable" rates, extended its jurisdiction to cover express and sleeping car services, separated railroad management from other enterprises such as mining, forbade unfair rebates and passes to favorite clients, and abolished the dubious distinction between "long" and "short" hauls.

It was touch and go whether the Hepburn bill would be passed at all and public interest in the way Roosevelt and his allies, including, surprisingly, the Democratic Senator Benjamin ("Pitchfork") Tillman of South Carolina, and his opponents, led by Nelson Aldrich, continuously regrouped was intense. Debate in the Senate lasted sixty frantic days. Any senator who wanted to study the subject adequately had to read 5,000 pages of evidence, study quite intricate tables of statistics, and master the complexities of long and short haul. The debates provided ample opportunity for obfuscation and delay. Opposition to the bill was of a quantity and quality that would have dismayed anyone less than Roosevelt. TR was even deserted by his trusty ally Henry Cabot Lodge, who turned words of the English poet Coleridge to advantage. "I have heard but two arguments of any weight adduced in favor of passing this reform bill, and they are in substance these: 1. 'We will blow your brains out if you don't pass it. 2. We will drag you through a horsepond if you don't pass it.' And there is a good deal of force in both." On his side, Roosevelt had the Democratic minority, only thirty-three senators out of the total of ninety, and it was by no means uniformly in favor of the bill. However, Roosevelt could count on support from progressive Republicans, including Jonathan P. Dolliver of Iowa and the as-yet untried Robert La Follette of Wisconsin whose lengthy impassioned plea throughout three daily sessions for rate regulation scandalized elderly senators, unaccustomed to such rigorous controversial assertions from a mere novice.

The crux of the matter was about the degree to which the

railroads should be allowed to appeal to the courts against rate-fixing decisions by the ICC. Regular Republicans and railroad senators wanted a court review to give the courts the right to overrule the ICC. Roosevelt's supporters accepted the idea of a court review, provided its powers were narrow. The Allison amendment required the ICC to issue an injunction within five days of a request to do so and provided that an appeal against its decisions must be lodged within thirty days and come to the Supreme Court. All recognized that, without Roosevelt's driving force, the bill would not have been passed. For Aldrich, it was a humiliating defeat. Public interest abated only once and TR was relegated to the inside pages of the morning's papers just as he was about to propose a new and stronger antitrust law by news of the San Francisco earthquake.

The San Francisco earthquake of 5:13 A.M. on April 18, 1906, killed hundreds as they slept and injured thousands. Immediately, the city was engulfed by fire. Scores of fires were started by gas from broken mains, by exposed electric wires, and overturned stores. Because the earthquake had damaged the water system, General Fred Funston, in charge of a division of infantry soldiers trying to stop the farther spread of the blaze, ordered his men to dynamite or raze buildings in the path of the blaze. Thus San Francisco lost, among others, half a mile of proud mansions in its most select residential district. Yet the fire raged for three days, wiping out at least half the city and making 200,000 people homeless. Roosevelt asked and received from Congress $2.5 million for relief and reconstruction and the nation as a whole also responded with gifts of extra supplies of food, medicine, and money, and special detachments of doctors and nurses. The people of San Francisco faced their terrible situation with characteristic grit. A dispatch to a New York paper declared, "She's crippled, thirsty, hungry, and broke; she has a few whole churches, only half her schoolhouses; not one French restaurant, not a theatre; she is full of people without homes, jobs or clothes; she is the worst bunged-up town that ever was. But the spirit of her is something to bring tears to an American's eyes."

The Muckrakers

What the public knew about the trusts in particular was their own experiences of public utility companies, railroad companies, and hearsay about the nearest giant corporation. What they knew about trusts in general was provided by the literature of exposure, beginning with Henry Demarest Lloyd's seminal work on Standard Oil, *Wealth Against Commonwealth* (1894). In 1899 and 1900 twenty-eight books were published critical of the trusts, as well as over 150 magazine articles, in addition to several of nineteen volumes of the official report of the United States Industrial Commission that had spent several months hearing evidence about monopolies.

Pioneer editor Samuel S. McClure created *McClure's,* a magazine retailing for fifteen cents, that employed scholars to make clear to ordinary readers the way their lives were being shaped by the intricate maneuvers of the great corporations. Thus, starting in 1902 with Ida M. Tarbell's "History of the Standard Oil Company," McClure went on to employ Lincoln Steffens, who contributed "Enemies of the Republic" and "Shame of the Cities," and Ray Stannard Baker, who provided "The Railroad on Trial." The impact of Steffens's various works owed much to his lively, colloquial style, with its dramatic contrasts and ironies, and his facility to get the reader to understand quite difficult points.

The commercial success of *McClure's* prompted other magazines to exploit public taste for ever more scandalous exposures, moving from the giant trusts to such subjects as municipal corruption, terrorism in labor unions, fake patent medicines, and the white slave trade. Charles Edward Russell exposed abuses of the so-called beef trust in a series of articles, entitled "The Greatest Trust in the World" for *Everybody's.* B. J. Hendrick disclosed illegal practices of insurance firms in "The Story of Life Insurance" for *McClure's* in 1907. Thus, in a short while, there existed, according to William Archer of the English *Fortnightly Review,* "a group of some half-dozen periodicals of extraordinary vital and stimulating quality, which must be reckoned among the most valuable literary assets of the American people; there is nothing quite like them in the literature of the world—no periodicals which combine such width of popular appeal with such seriousness of aim and thoroughness of workmanship."

More caustically, newspaper columnist Finley Peter Dunne's fictional Mr. Dooley complained to his favorite customer, Hennessy, about the new sordid element in literature:

Ivrything has gone wrong. Th' wurruld is little betther thin a convict's camp. . . . All th' pomes be th' lady authoresses that used to begin: 'Oh, moon, how fair!' now begin: 'Oh, Ogden Armour, how awful!'. . . . Read Wash'n'ton Bliffens's [Lincoln Steffens's] dhreadful assault on th' board iv education iv Baraboo. Read Idarem [Ida M. Tarbell] on John D. [Rockefeller]; she's a lady, but she's got th' punch. Graft ivry-where. 'Graft in th' Insurance Companies,' 'Graft in Congress.' 'Graft be an Old Grafter,' 'Grafter in its Relations to th' Higher Life,' be Dock Eliot [Charles W. Eliot, president of Harvard]; 'Th' Homeric Legend an' Graft; Its Cause an Effect; Are They th' Same? Yes and No,' be Norman Slapgood [Norman Hapgood].

Whatever their differences, investigative journalists and their most avid readers agreed on the need for the federal government to extend its powers and regulate economic activity and for municipal governments to set their house in order in the interests of clean, efficient, caring, and accountable government.

However, after five or six years, investigative journalism passed through a phase that not only impaired its value to Roosevelt politically but also disturbed him as to its general cast on American affairs. The more it was fed, the more the public appetite for exposure increased and certain journalists saw how to take purely commercial advantage by publishing sensational stories without the academic analysis and conscientious scholarship supplied by such as Ida Tarbell and Lincoln Steffens. For instance, stock market operator Thomas W. Lawson of Boston disclosed the shady secrets of his dealings with captains of industry as "Frenzied Finance" for *Everybody's*. Within a year the circulation of *Everybody's* rose from 150,000 to 750,000. Lawson's accounts contained hard facts of numerous dirty deeds by the "system." However, the facts that could be corroborated with certainty were

In 1908 the Democrats once again selected William Jennings Bryan, their somewhat shop-soiled but energetic, bible-thumping standard-bearer to run as presidential candidate, thereby inviting him to lose a presidential election for a third time. Comparing himself to a drunk bounced from an exclusive club, Bryan observed wryly, "They can't fool me; those fellows don't want me in there." (Library of Congress).

mingled with fantastic exaggeration. In the end, the public was sated and the rest of the press turned against him.

Roosevelt attributed such exaggerated literary attempts to a "lunatic fringe" but was not content to leave it there. He wanted to dissociate himself from extremists. At a Gridiron dinner on March 17, 1906, he took as a theme for his speech a passage from *Pilgrim's Progress* by Paul Bunyan concerning "the Man with the Muckrake, the man who could look no way but downward with the muckrake in his hand; who was offered a celestial crown for his muckrake but who would neither look up nor regard the crown he was offered but continued to take to himself the filth of the floor." Sensing the public was with him, Roosevelt expanded his remarks when he dedicated the cornerstone of the House of Representatives Office Building on April 14, 1906. "The effort to make financial or political profit out of the destruction of character can only result in public calamity. Gross and reckless assaults on character, whether on the stump or in newspaper, magazine, or book, create a morbid and vicious public sentiment." The conservative press chose to ignore TR's early reference to "swollen fortunes" and concentrated, instead, on the term "muckraker" that they applied uniformly to all investigative journalists.

By 1909 many of the muckraking magazines were in deep trouble, their staffs divided over editorial policy and their editors in conflict with management who wanted milder articles. Several magazines went out of print; others changed hands and policies. Thus by 1913 only two or three had survived as vehicles for protest. The decline in muckraking provided journalists Herbert Croly, Walter Weyl, and Walter Lippmann with the opportunity to try out a new kind of political journal with the *New Republic* in 1914. Within two years, the stature of the magazine soared.

Recognizing just how formidable was the charismatic president, the wisest corporation executives began to reconsider their strategy and moved toward a policy of accepting federal reform in order to strengthen their companies. Both Gabriel Kolko in *The Triumph of Conservatism* (1963) and James Weinstein in *The Corporate Ideal in the Liberal State, 1900–1918* (1968) see the most signficant reforms of the Progressive Era as representing a successful attempt by business to appropriate the authority of the federal government to regulate, that is to say, to stabilize and maintain, its dominant position.

Kolko argues how corporate executives wanted the creation of federal regulatory agencies, partly to establish order within their industries by limiting competition. He believes that many of the giant amalgamations were now overcapitalized, inefficient, and vulnerable to competition. Thus U.S. Steel, for instance, which produced 61.6 percent of the nation's steel in 1901, was manufacturing only 39.9 percent of the total in 1920. While Standard Oil was refining 90 percent of the nation's oil in 1899, in 1911, when it was being divided by order of the Supreme Court, the proportion was down to 80 percent. Other trusts, such as International Harvester, American Telephone and Telegraph, Amalgamated Copper, and the Big Four meat packers, were also losing their precious outsize share of the market. Another motive of corporate executives for welcoming federal regulation was to anticipate a plethora of state laws that were likely to be more varied and, therefore, harder and more inconvenient to meet. Moreover, they were more likely to be subject to public pressure and, therefore, more radical, as had been the experience of the railroads. Later, this thinking underlay the big meat packers' acceptance of the Meat Inspection Act.

James Weinstein extends these arguments to suggest that businessmen sought expansion, stabilization, and rationalization and realized that moderate federal regulation would undermine socialist appeals for an alternative, more dangerous form of social organization. Thus they accepted Progressivism, knowing they could bend it to their will. Accordingly, business would be regulated (but also licensed) by impartial federal agencies; labor would be represented (and held in check) by responsible unions; and social problems would be met by various, carefully calculated reforms. Such was the philosophy of the National Civic Federation that drew together the different talents of such as corporate executives Elbert Gary and George W. Perkins, labor leaders Samuel Gompers and John Mitchell, and civic official Seth Low.

Businessmen knew strength lay in numbers and during the progressive period they formed various business organizations to lobby Congress and the state legislatures.

Conservation

Perhaps Roosevelt's supreme domestic achievment was his sponsorship of effective conservation measures to save forests and minerals from exploitation and waste. In this respect, he showed himself many years ahead of his time. Previously, it was assumed that there were enough natural resources for all, and this assumption partly accounts for their exploitation by business with the connivance of the federal government in the late nineteenth century. Government policy of granting millions of acres to railroads and other enterprises that could freely use the oil, lumber, and metal lands was strengthened by the spirit of pioneer individualism, cherished by frontiersmen who expected to have complete freedom of action. Although there was, indeed, plenty for all, the best prizes went to the strongest and most unscrupulous. It was Roosevelt who was largely responsible for reversing this traditional, exploitive point of view.

The decisive influence on Roosevelt was pioneer conservationist Gifford Pinchot. Having graduated from Yale, Pinchot spent three years studying forestation in Switzerland and Germany. In 1896 he organized the National Forest Commission and subsequently became head of the Bureau of Forestry in the Department of Agriculture. On his accession, Roosevelt promoted Pinchot to his tennis cabinet, political allies with whom he shared leisure activities, and, under Pinchot's influence, made conservation a subject of his first message to Congress, declaring that "the forest and water problems are perhaps the most vital internal problems of the United States" and "the whole future of the nation is directly at stake." One of Pinchot's associates, P. P. Wells, defined conservation as "foresight and restraint in the exploitation of the physical sources of wealth as necessary for the perpetuity of civilization and the welfare of present and future generations." He said, furthermore, that conservation "was only a means to an end and the end was economic justice." Rebuking previous wastefulness, Pinchot predicted, quite accurately, the use of metal tables because forests would no longer be able to supply enough wood to make wooden ones. Even hardened industrial entrepreneurs, such as railroad magnate James J. Hill, saw the wisdom of Pinchot's point of view and realized that senseless exploitation would, in time, imperil America's supply of such essential minerals as iron and coal.

In 1902 Congress passed the Newlands Reclamation Act, sponsored by the appropriately named Francis G. Newlands, Democratic senator from Nevada. Roosevelt endorsed the act and managed to gain much of the credit for it. The act's purpose was twofold, including both reclamation and irrigation of farming land in the Great Plains. The Carey Irrigation Act of 1894 had tried to provide the means of irrigation for western states but had left ambitious projects to state governments, which simply did not have the resources to complete them. Under the Newlands Act, the federal government also accepted responsibility for the entire irrigation program. Money from the sale of western lands (sold in lots of 160 acres or less and paid for within ten years) went into a revolving fund and by 1915 the government had invested some $80 million in twenty-five separate projects, the largest being the Roosevelt Dam on the Salt River in Arizona.

While his name was being immortalized in concrete, Roosevelt was using the rhetoric of progressive conservation and rapidly extending the government reserves set up under the Forest Reserve Act of 1891. In 1907 western congressmen succeeded in getting some 68 million acres of coal lands (all known coal deposits in the nation), included in these reserves. In total, Roosevelt's administration added about 125 million acres to the National Forests and prepared the way for a new government policy on electric power by reserving some 2,565 water-power sites, including Muscle Shoals on the Tennessee River that would become the heart of the Tennessee Valley Authority a generation later, and a showpiece for the New Deal of Franklin Delano Roosevelt. In 1907 Theodore Roosevelt appointed an Inland Waterways Commission to prepare "a comprehensive plan for the improvement and control" of river systems. In 1908 it reported that future plans for navigation should take into account such things as water purification, power development, flood control, and land reclamation. In the following year the National Waterways Commission was created for such work. The rhetoric that accompanied these initial conservation measures was designed to attract wide public attention and was couched in terms of a struggle to protect national resources against vested interests.

Roosevelt used his authority to set aside forests from exploitation. When his opponents forced on him a rider to an Agricultural Appropriation bill, making future withdrawals the responsibility of Congress, rather than the president, Roosevelt had Pinchot and his team survey the public domain in six northwestern states to allow him to withdraw 16 million acres of forest lands before he signed the bill transferring the authority to Congress. Roosevelt commented how "the opponents of the forest service turned handsprings in their wrath; and dire were the threats against the executive; but the threats could not be carried out, and were really a tribute to the efficiency of our action."

Pure Food and Meat Inspection

The nation's health, too, had to be protected from vested interests. Dr. Harvey Washington Wiley, chief chemist of the Department of Agriculture (1883–1912), had long agitated for the protection of consumers from dangerous foods and adulterants.

Until the early twentieth century there were almost no rules on the processing and presentation of food, even though this was now becoming part of giant manufacturing. This led to grave and dangerous abuses of the trust between manufacturer and consumer. In fact, science was being turned against the consumer. Industrial chemists suggested the addition of some substances to prevent the decomposition of food, of coloring to mask decomposition, and of other things to simulate freshness in food that had already deteriorated. Thus, while stale, soiled, and rancid butter could not be sold, once it had been oxidized by a forced air process and rechurned with skim milk, it could be marketed as new. Stale eggs could be deodorized with formaldehyde and sold for making cakes.

Professor Edward F. Ladd, food commissioner (and later senator) for North Dakota, told the National Association of State Dairy and Food Departments, meeting in St. Louis in 1904, what he had discovered from analyzing food. "More than 90 percent of the local meat-markets in the State were using chemical preservatives, and in nearly every butcher shop could be found a bottle of 'Freezem,' 'Preservaline,' or 'Iceine.' . . . In the dried beef, in the smoked meats, in the canned bacon, in the canned chipped beef, boracic acid or borates is a common ingredient." Such adulteration extended to other food.

Of cocoas and chocolates examined, about 70 percent have been found adulterated. . . . Ninety percent of the so-called French peas we have taken up in North Dakota were found to contain copper salts. Of all the canned mushrooms, 85 percent were found bleached by sulphites. There was but one brand of catsup which was pure. Many catsups were made from the waste products from canners—pulp, skins, ripe tomatoes, green tomatoes, starch paste, coal-tar colors, chemical preservatives, usually benzoate of soda or salicylic acid.

Here the abuses of the trusts on unsuspecting consumers were plain for all to see.

Such practices were even more dangerous when applied to patent medicines, using undisclosed amounts of opium, morphine, cocaine, laudanum, and alcohol, and claiming preposterous curative powers for them. However, it was a lucrative business. In 1900 the total sums earned were $59.61 million. The secrets of the patent-medicine business were exposed in articles by Edward W. Bok in the *Ladies' Home Journal* of 1904–5 and by Samuel Hopkins Adams (entitled "The Great American Fraud") in *Collier's Weekly* in 1905. Bok knew that people who felt they could not afford a doctor would, nevertheless, obtain drugs from commercial companies through the mails. He showed how the confidence of his trusting woman readers was betrayed by companies intent only on a quick profit. He reproduced the American label of Mrs. Winslow's Soothing Syrup, for quietening teething babies, aside the English label for the same medicine, where British law required it to be clearly marked "Poison."

There was no federal law compelling manufacturers to use only wholesome foods or to describe their products accurately. Moreover, properly prepared and wholesome foods were at a disadvantage in the market because they were likely to look less vivid and to cost more. What Bok, Adams, and other crusaders wanted was an American law insisting on accurate, clear labeling of medicine, food, and liquor, including information on what drugs and chemicals had been used.

In states where they were a political force to be reckoned with, farmers had already supported the creation of official departments of food and drugs and this stimulated the wider analysis of food, the establishment of local and municipal boards of health, and the passing of city ordinances requiring certain standards of purity for milk and milk products. In 1898 official chemists of those states with departments of food and drugs formed the National Association of State Drug and Food Departments of which Robert McDowell Allen of Kentucky became secretary in 1902. (This was an instance of the drive toward professional recognition.) However, there was another side to otherwise welcome reforms. Among the states that had already adopted food and drug laws, standards varied greatly and it was clearly unfair to producers to have to meet greatly different requirements. Only the federal government had the power to control the interstate shipment of food and impose certain basic and uniform standards.

A leading pioneer in the crusade for a federal law, Dr. Harvey Washington Wiley of Indiana had a crusader's moral spirit, a physique strong enough to survive an arduous campaign, a great capacity for moral indignation, and skill at pitiless publicity. Let the public learn what the food manufacturers were doing, he believed, and their demand for reform would be irresistible. In 1903 he conducted "poison squad" experiments on volunteers whom he fed with foods containing preservatives to see if they were harmful. The New York *Sun* called him "diet janitor and policeman of the people's insides." He was more often known as "Old Borax," said affectionately by the public, and maliciously by those whose interests he threatened. One of Wiley's converts was Alice Lakey of Cranford, New Jersey, who was so moved by his revelations that she made it her task to rouse women through lecture tours arranged through the General Federation of Women's Clubs and the National Consumers' League. Although, for the most part, women did not have the vote, they were the most important consumers in the home. Middle-class, middle-aged women had lived through the transition from small-scale, local food production in towns and villages to the large-scale corporation food industry in cities and could recognize and explain the difference between natural and unnatural products. They were ideal recruits for the cause.

Thus the movement for pure food drew together associations of farmers, chemists, social reformers, women's groups, doctors, and consumers. (Here was a classic confluence of separate sections toward a progressive whole.) The various groups working for pure food laws staged a most effective piece of propaganda at the St. Louis Exposition of 1904. They produced samples of well-known foods that were artificially colored, extracted the various dyes and used them to dye pieces of silk and wool and exhibited the whole with very large notices explaining what they had done at a booth close to the displays of the food manufacturers. People knew what color their internal organs should be and knew that the vivid colors of red, blue, and green shown by the pure food display were wrong. R. M. Allen recalled years later how the exhibit was a public sensation, attracting politicians, journalists, and delegations from women's clubs. (Here was a superb instance of the Progressives' ability to dramatize an issue and thus rouse public opinion.) While the advocates of pure food were successful in working together, and in rousing public opinion, their efforts to secure appropriate legislation were doomed to failure, however, while organized capital could outbuy, outwit, and outmaneuver them.

The first attempt to secure federal legislation was a bill sponsored by Senators Porter J. McCumber of North Dakota and Weldon B. Heyburn of Idaho in 1902. Twice their proposal passed the House, only to be gunned down in the Senate by Republicans who did not want to jeopardize their party's finances, not to mention their own chances of reelection by offending the interests of big business.

In 1906 matters reached a head when western novelist and socialist Upton Sinclair published *The Jungle,* the powerful story of an immigrant worker in the Chicago stockyards. *The Jungle* described how a Lithuanian peasant, Jurgis, is enticed to America by steamship posters. He comes to the stockyards of Chicago, called "Packingtown," where he encounters every political, social, and industrial evil. He has to pay a bribe to get, and keep, his job and has to live in a lodging house where the keeper rents the same bed to alternate day and night shifts of workers. He and his family get infected by disease and acquire ulcers from anxiety. Sinclair's work was the product of close research. He lived for seven weeks among stockyard workers, financed by a grant of $500 from the socialist periodical *Appeal to Reason*. The way Sinclair told his bitter tragedy about an individual and a generation of immigrants who experienced the urban jungle owed much to Russian novels of despair and he used the hogs for slaughter as so many crude symbols of human suffering.

The Jungle was rejected by five publishers before Sinclair published it himself. However, it was subsequently published by Doubleday when it caused a sensation, became the best-selling book for a year, and was translated into seventeen languages. The book was intended to show how industrial workers were radicalized by their experiences to advocate industrial and social reforms, and to justify socialism. However, the main thrust of Sinclair's argument got lost in public revulsion for the processes of making meat products. Sausages would never taste the same again to customers who read about the true constituents of recycled meat and the rats that scavenged on it. "These rats were nuisances, and the packers would put poisoned bread out for them; they would die, and then rats, bread and meat would go into the hoppers together."

Sinclair recounted how a meat inspector appointed by the government was so engrossed in describing the dangers inherent in eating tubercular pork to a visitor that he let a dozen carcasses pass without testing them. Another inspector was horrified that the carcasses of tubercular steers were being sold in the city. He insisted that they be treated with kerosene to prevent anyone from eating them and was forced to resign. The packers were so indignant that they went further and had the mayor abolish the local bureau of meat inspection outright. Canned beef was made out

George William Norris of Nebraska, first as congressman (1903–13) and later as senator (1913–43), was the very embodiment of the progressive spirit among prairie Republicans. He led the House revolt of Insurgents against Speaker Joe Cannon in 1910, fought continuously for federal water power regulation and public ownership of hydroelectric plants, and saw his efforts come to fruition in the Tennessee Valley Authority, created in 1933. (Photo by G. V. Buck, 1908; Library of Congress).

of old or diseased cattle. It was this that had killed more soldiers in the War of 1898 than had died in battle. Potted chicken was made of tripe, pork fat, beef suet, hearts of beef, and waste-ends of veal.

Sinclair built his narrative to a climax, leading to a hard punch in the guts of his readers' consciences as he described the workmen and the dangers they encountered. Men in the pickle rooms who scraped their fingers on the trucks might have their finger joints eaten by the acid. Butchers and trimmers lost their thumbs, slashed away by knives. "Worst of any, however, were the fertilizer-men, and those who served in the cooking rooms. These people could not be shown to the visitor, for the odour of a fertilizer-man would scare any ordinary visitor at a hundred yards; and as for the other men, who worked in tank rooms full of steam, and in some of which there were open vats near the level of the floor, their peculiar trouble was that they fell into the vats; and when they were fished out, there was never enough of them left to be worth exhibiting—sometimes they would be overlooked for days, till all but the bones of them had gone out to the world as Durham's Pure Leaf Lard!"

Sinclar's principal intention was to fire public interest in the need for better protection and higher wages for stockyard workers in the interests of humanity. However, middle-class readers, revolted by his descriptions, were most interested in the consumer and developed a primary concern for safe and pure meat. Here was more proof of the weight that could be exercised by the new and expanded middle class in its role as consumer. Outraged by the poor quality of food products and the lobbying tactics of the manufacturers, a delegation of pure food crusaders, led by Robert M. Allen, secretary of the National Association of State Dairy and Food Departments, and A. B. Fallinger of the National Organization of Retail Grocers, had already called on Roosevelt in February 1905 and he was prompted by their arguments to investigate their claims informally.

Given public outrage and Roosevelt's commitment to pure food reform, a reform Pure Food bill could no longer be parried by the vested food interests. Nevertheless, they tried to do just that. However, opposition in the Senate collapsed in February 1906 when the American Medical Association told Republican leader Nelson W. Aldrich of Rhode Island how their 135,000 member physicians in 2,000 counties would get their patients to lobby the Senate if the bill were not passed. The Senate was in a jam and the Pure Food bill passed on February 21, 1906, by sixty-three votes to four. However, the House seemed about to bury the bill in committee. It was at this stage, in March 1906, that Roosevelt read *The Jungle,* published only the previous month.

Roosevelt was not only disgusted by *The Jungle* but he was also infuriated by it. He knew it reflected badly on government in general and on his administration in particular. There were government inspectors in the packing houses; if bad beef was being sold, then the government system of inspection was to blame. He ordered Secretary of Agriculture James Wilson to ascertain the facts. Roosevelt's investigating commission comprised two settlement house (or social) workers, James Bronson Reynolds and Charles P. Neill (who was also a United States labor commissioner). In their early report they showed how government labels were being misused as they carried the notice "Inspected and passed by the United States government," although the only federal inspection was on the killing floors where carcasses were examined and certified. Government inspectors were not required to, and did not, attend later stages of preparation and, clearly, the manufacturers were taking advantage of the fact.

The report emphasized the unhygienic conditions in which meat was prepared.

Usually the workers toil without relief in a humid atmosphere, heavy with the odors of rotten wood, decayed meats, stinking offal, and entrails. The tables on which meat was handled, the tubs, and other receptacles were generally of wood, most of which were water-soaked and only half cleaned. The privies, as a rule, were sections of workrooms, enclosed by thin wooden partitions, ventillating into the workrooms. In a word, we saw meat shovelled from filthy wooden floors, piled on tables rarely washed, pushed from room to room in rotten box carts, in all of which processes it was in the way of gathering dirt, splinters, floor filth, and the expectoration of tuberculous and other diseased workers.

Press coverage of the report supplanted *The Jungle* as the central indictment of the packing industry. Although one might think the nuances could not be best expressed in verse, the New York *Evening Post* was succinct.

> Mary had a little lamb,
> And when she saw it sicken,
> She shipped it off to Packingtown,
> And now it's labelled chicken.

Roosevelt used the report to persuade Congress to pass an amendment to the Agricultural Appropriation bill, and sponsored by Senator Albert J. Beveridge of Indiana, that would extend government inspection to all processes in preparing meat. It was passed by the Senate, after three days, on May 23, 1906.

It gradually dawned on the meat packers that it was to the advantage of the larger and better food manufacturers to have dangerous or dishonest practices eliminated among their competitors. Thus the packers came to realise how the Meat Inspection amendment might save their businesses, since it would provide a federal stamp on their products as a sort of certificate of character to restore public confidence and their lost trade. Thus they advocated limited reform. However, the large packers, often known collectively as the "beef trust," objected to the dating of meat and having to pay for inspection. Nevertheless, they could fulfill federal regulations more easily than could smaller meat packers who wisely decided to concentrate on intrastate sales, not touched upon by the bill. However, they used all their influence in Congress to prevent the dating of meat, make the government itself pay for inspection, and subject decisions of inspectors to judicial review. Their lobbying was successful with the House Committee on Agriculture headed by James Wadsworth of New York that could hold up passage of the entire bill. Roosevelt was willing to compromise and withdraw the clauses about dating. In order to bring the controversy to a conclusion, he published the second, more "sickening" part, of the report prepared by Neill and Reynolds. The report served to confirm Upton Sinclair's earlier account, cause further public uproar, and persuade the major packers that their entire reputation was being undermined by their own shortsightedness. Thus the Wadsworth substitute Meat Inspection amendment, providing for expanding federal inspection of meats for interstate commerce, was revised to meet Roosevelt's views and passed the House (without a roll call) and the Senate to be signed by Roosevelt on June 30 and take effect on July 1, 1906. During this same period, the House was also discussing the Pure Food bill that passed the House on June 23, 1906, by 240 votes to 17. The 17 negative votes were by Democrats whose opposition was on the traditional Democratic principle of states' rights. It went into effect on January 1, 1907.

One of the casualties in Congress was James W. Wadsworth of New York whose resistance to Roosevelt's meat inspection rider had alienated his constituents. At the next election he was defeated in a Republican district he had represented almost continuously since 1881. Wadsworth's defeat signaled that any congressman who resisted legislation Roosevelt wanted risked losing his seat and thereby marked an increase in the president's power that seemed most sinister to his opponents.

Modern Spelling and New Ideas

Progressive zeal for social improvement by the application of objective analysis also extended to the spelling of the English language. Here was another classic instance of progressive desire for reason, order, and efficiency.

The American Philological Association first proposed abrupt breaks with traditional English spelling in 1876. The changes included such amputations as "through" to "thru" and "axe" to "ax." The *American Anthropologist* printed a symposium on the subject in March 1893. It had noted considerable variations in the spelling of certain English words. Moreover, delegates to the symposium heard how, of 1,972 failures to pass the entrance examination for the civil service in Britain, 1,866 had failed because of poor spelling. The thrust of the symposium was that people spelled badly because English spelling was arbitrary and inconsistent. Francis A. March in the *History of Spelling Reform* (1893) noted how the word "could" was "a markt exampl of unpardonabl spelling; the 'l' is a sheer blunder, the 'ou' has a wrong sound."

It would be better to reform the spelling to "cud," "cood," "kud," or "kood." There were at least twenty different ways of spelling the sound "sh," as in *sh*ip, *s*ure, *p*shaw, o*c*ean, par*t*ial, man*s*ion, and so on.

A cardinal idea was that reformed spelling would be more efficient and more economical. According to Henry Holt, simplified spelling would cost less in printing, thereby saving $35 million per annum in printers' and compositors' fees. All newspapers would save one column in six. It would take between one-and-a-half and two years less to educate children, probably in third and fourth grades, thereby saving another $220 million a year. Convinced by such arguments and moved by the desire for greater efficiency, former steel tycoon Andrew Carnegie provided the Spelling Reform Association with first $10,000 and, later, $25,000 a year to promote the campaign.

On August 27, 1906, Theodore Roosevelt, roused by these considerations, ordered the public printer to modify and simplify the spelling of 300 words on all government publications. He defended his action as "not an attack on the language of Shakespeare and Milton" by the government but simply an attempt to exercise its weight toward bringing public sentiment up-to-date with the latest recommendations of scholars. Accordingly, unnecessary "u"s were to be omitted from such words as "honor," "labor," "color," and "rumor," and, with their final letters eliminated, "programme" would become "program," "omelette," "omelet," and "catalogue," "catalog." The French influence was to be expunged from words ending in "re," in which final letters were to be reversed, thereby creating "center," "theater," and "saber." Similarly, "cheques" would become "checks," "comptrollers" would become "controllers," and "judgement" would lose its silent middle "e." Some diphthong "ph"s were to be supplanted by "f"s in words like "sulfurous," while vowels in "mediaeval," "subpoena," and "phoenix" were to be eliminated, making "medieval," "subpena," and "phenix." In some words, "s" was to be superseded by "z," making "idolize," "legalize," and, though not permanently, "surprize" and "compromize." The soft "c" became "s" in "license" and "defense." The double "l" was condemned in "fulness" and "woolen."

The American press had a field day of pretended outrage. They were in the saddle, since press reporting of the news, and whether it decided to adopt the new spelling, would forcibly determine public acceptance or rejection of it. Andrew Carnegie, a proponent of more rational spelling, became "Andru Karnegi," while no one knew if the president would become "Rusevelt" or "Rucevelt." Henry Watterson in the Louisville *Courier-Journal* wanted the first syllable to rhyme with goose. "Nuthing escapes Mr Rucevelt," he averred. "No subject is to hi fr him to takl, nor tu lo for him to notis. He makes tretis without the consent of the Senit. He inforces such laws as meet his approval, and fales to se those that du not soot him. He now assalts the English langgwidg, constitutes himself a sort of French Academy, and will reform the spelling in a way to soot himself."

However, the Supreme Court continued to hand down its decisions in traditional spelling, while Congress also resisted the move, partly because the new spelling would, initially, cost more for government printers to compose but, principally, because it disliked Roosevelt's high-handed actions. However, a mere glance at any contemporary American book, newspaper, or magazine, highway sign or billboard will reveal who it was who triumphed in the end.

The ebb and flow of political tide is continuous and, despite his successes hitherto, Roosevelt's fortunes began to change with it. In November 1906 he had already lost his leverage with Congress when the Democrats gained enough seats in the midterm elections to increase his difficulty in holding a majority and his problems were compounded by the panic of 1907.

The Panic of 1907

The panic of 1907 was precipitated by wild speculations on the New York Stock Exchange engineered by the great financiers. In the fall of 1907 banks outside New York (interior banks) wanted to withdraw the funds they had deposited in New York banks in order to have the resources to finance farmers who wanted to harvest more crops. The total amount due to national banks and other banks was considerable—$410 million. Because they had been investing the money for their own purposes, the New York banks could not meet their obligations to the interior banks. Accordingly, on October 31, 1907, New York banks suspended payments and telegraphed their correspondents across the country that they could no longer honor drafts for money, although, in fact, they still had $224 million in their vaults. The New York banks were so selfish that they not only refused to repay the interior banks the money they owed them but actually increased their loans to their own clients by $110 million.

The crisis was exacerbated by gross individual acts of exploitation. Trust company executives and speculators Charles W. Morse and Augustus Heine were trying to corner the copper market and their failure led to a run on the companies with which they had been associated, including the Knickerbocker Trust Company, which was forced to close on October 23, 1907. When the crisis broke J. P. Morgan was at an Episcopal convention in Virginia. He stayed for most of the sessions but returned a day earlier, observing to Bishop William Lawrence how "They are in trouble in New York. They do not know what to do and I do not know what to do, but I am going back."

In a speech at Provincetown, Massachusetts, on August 20, 1907, Roosevelt declared that the depression was partly caused by "ruthless and determined men," hiding "behind the breastworks of corporate organization," who were retaliating at the "determination of the government to punish certain malefactors of great wealth," by ringing about "as much financial stress as they can" to discredit the government and try and get it to change its policies. Nevertheless, the way government and Wall Street responded to a desperate situation exposed the rather close and somewhat trusting relationship between them. At the height of the panic, leading financier J. P. Morgan conferred with entrepreneurs and industrialists, such as Henry Clay Frick, E. H. Harriman, James Stillman, and others, to save the situation by importing almost $100 million in gold from Europe. In addition, John D. Rockefeller provided $10 million in government bonds while Secretary of the Treasury George B. Cortelyou announced the government's willingness to deposit $150 million of federal money—all to support the banks and restore public confidence that they could redeem notes in gold or securities.

It seemed likely that an independent steel company, the Tennessee Coal and Iron, might fail and thereby disturb some of the Wall Street firms investing in it. Accordingly, J. P. Morgan agreed to a rescue attempt by which U.S. Steel would buy Tennessee Coal and Iron and thus put its immense financial power behind the company. He did this only after securing a tacit promise from Roosevelt, through his intermediaries Elbert Gary, president of U.S. Steel, and Henry Clay Frick, that the federal government would not object and use antitrust legislation against the merger. Once the crisis was averted, it was only too easy for critics to charge that U.S. Steel had exploited a general panic for its own advantage and used the occasion to acquire a most valuable company at a knockdown price.

Widespread unemployment accompanied the panic of 1907 and continued into 1908, with the effect of depressing wages for those in work. In New York the daily breadline of indigent poor seeking free coffee and rolls from the Bowery Mission was 2,000 more than usual. The panic aggravated existing pressures for financial reform and stimulated many citizens to reconsider their ideas on finance. What if the catastrophe should continue into 1908, or disappear simply to recur? Sensitive to public opinion, Congress established a commission to devise proposals to revise banking practices.

Roosevelt left the presidency in the hands of his close friend and political ally William Howard Taft, when, using patronage, he ensured Taft's nomination as Republican candidate at the Republican National Convention in Chicago of 1908. Taft was assured of victory in the election of 1908. No doubt heartened by Roosevelt's refusal to run, the Democrats returned to their old, if somewhat shopworn, former standard-bearer, William Jennings Bryan, thereby inviting him to lose a presidential election for the third time.

In the presidential election Taft took 7,675,320 votes (51.6 percent) and 321 votes in the electoral college, whereas Bryan took 6,412,294 votes (43.1 percent) and 162 electoral votes. Socialist candidate Eugene Debs took 420,793 votes (2.8 percent), while the prohibition candidate, Eugen W. Chafin, took 253,840 votes (1.7 percent). After his election, Taft wrote to Roosevelt in unstinted praise: "The first letter I wish to write to you, because you have always been the chief agent in working out the present status of affairs, and my selection and election are chiefly your work." After his third defeat, Bryan, a teetotaler, used to tell the story of a drunk who tried to get into a private club three times and was thrown out each time. After his third attempt, he picked himself up, and concluded, "They can't fool me. Those fellows don't want me in there."

On March 4, 1909, for the last time, the journey of president and president-elect from White House to Capitol was made in a horsedrawn carriage. Breaking with custom, Roosevelt did not ride back to the White House with Taft after the ceremony. In Roosevelt's place to the left of the new president rode Mrs. Helen Herron Taft who cared not a whit for various protests at her usurpation. This was the most glorious day of her life. Thus she established a new custom of presidents' wives returning with their husbands from the ceremony.

Shortly afterwards Roosevelt embarked on a world tour that included big game hunting in Africa and catching big fish in the little pools of European courts where he was feted beyond any precedent. Although Roosevelt's seven-and-a-half years of supreme power had ended, he remained the most interesting and mesmeric figure in American political life for the next seven-and-a-half. He and the public soon learned how tragic had been his mistake in not seeking and winning the presidency again in 1908. To H. G. Wells, Theodore Roosevelt was "a very symbol of the creative will in man, in its limitations, its doubtful adequacy, its valiant persistence amid perplexities and confusions. In his undisciplined hastiness, his limitations, his prejudices, his unfairness, his frequent errors, just as much as in his force, his sustained courage, his open intelligence, he stands for his people and his kind."

After he gave up being president, it was impossible for Theodore Roosevelt to enter private life. Everywhere he went he generated magnetism. America followed all his pursuits from the time he sailed out of New York on March 23, 1909, to the day he returned on June 16, 1910. Daily bulletins of his progress on African safari were received like the legend of Marco Polo. In Africa he and his son Kermit slew 512 animals, including 17 lions, 20 rhinoceroses, 11 elephants, 88 hippopotamuses, 9 giraffes, and 47 gazelles. Press reports informed the American people about his exploits among the bongo, the kudu, the dik-dik, the wildebeest, and the aardwolf.

In Khartoum he advised the English to continue their rule of Sudan and Egypt and told the Sudanese and Egyptians that they must remain loyal to the English. In Europe he met members of many royal families, including the aged emperor of Austria-Hungary. He called Franz Josef "the last representative of the old system" and spoke to him in French, which "I speak with daring fluency." Kaiser Wilhelm II of Germany allowed him to review his troops for five hours, prompting TR to observe later, "A king is a kind of cross between a vice-president and a leader of the four hundred." He also said Europe's kings and queens were "anxious to justify their own positions by the way they did their duty. The average among them was not very high as regards intellect and force." He received the Nobel prize for peace at Christiania, Norway, and various honorary degrees at Berlin, Oxford, and Cambridge.

On his return from Europe, Roosevelt had 2,000 invitations to speak in America. Some appeals were plangent.

> Teddy, come home and blow your horn,
> The sheep's in the meadow, the cow's in the corn,
> The boy you left to 'tend the sheep,
> Is under the haystack fast asleep.

Thus *Life* magazine of May 26, 1910, expressed the country's weariness with William Howard Taft.

Taft and the Insurgents

History has not been kind to William Howard Taft. The more responsible of Taft's critics praised his kindliness, candor, and

The outsize President William Howard Taft (1909–13) mounted on horseback in 1909, a ludicrous sight for public eyes that, as Theodore Roosevelt warned Taft, was not only absurd in itself but also "cruelty to the horse." Taft was an able judge but his standpat presidency was marred by continuous criticism that he was not Roosevelt and his deepening realization what a misfortune it was to have to follow the charismatic Roosevelt as president. (Library of Congress).

integrity, but attacked him for his obsession with the Constitution. They thought that he should have been a judge, rather than a president. This was true.

Taft was born in Cincinnati, Ohio, in September 1857 into a family of moderate wealth and some distinction within the legal profession. He graduated from Yale in 1879 and completed his formal education at the Cincinnati Law School, eventually gaining admission to the Ohio bar. Except for 1880, when he was a newspaper reporter, and the years 1883–1885, when he practiced law, all of the positions he held until elected as president—federal judge, Philippine commissioner, and Roosevelt's secretary of war—were appointive offices. This lack of experience in political elections contributed to Taft's clumsy handling of Congress that led to his downfall. He was habitually hesitant and cautious, even when he worked as an administrator under McKinley and Roosevelt—perhaps a result of his judicial turn of mind. Nevertheless, under McKinley and Roosevelt, Taft was a great success as one of the first shuttle diplomats, traveling over 100,000 miles between 1900 and 1908 on various assignments to Manila, Rome, Panama, and Cuba.

Although he was obese, weighing around 354 pounds, Taft carried his flesh majestically on a huge, wide frame. "He looks," said Arthur Brisbane, "like an American bison, a gentle, kind one." Frederick Palmer spoke for many when he wrote in *Current Literature* of June 1907 how "It is good to see Big Bill Taft enter a room after a number of other men. He reminds you of a great battleship following the smaller vessels, coming into port with her brass bright, and plowing deep. You feel that when a giant is so amiable it would be impolite not to agree with him; and, moreover, it would be unwise, considering that the power of the United States is behind him."

Taft's achievements were far from negligible. He exercised his executive powers more than Roosevelt in conservation, antitrust suits, and application of railroad laws. His most singular achievement was in persuading Congress to pass the Sixteenth Amendment, on July 12, 1909, empowering Congress to levy a general income tax, which was duly ratified and came into effect on February 3, 1913, just before Taft left office. He also recommended, and Congress enacted, a 2 percent tax on the net income of corporations. Taft also signed a bill creating a Bureau of Mines with authority to recommend safety improvements in mining. By executive order, Taft placed 8,000 assistant postmasters under the Civil Service, thereby considerably weakening the discredited system of patronage in the postal system. Also on Taft's recommendation, Congress established a postal savings system, allowing depositors up to $500 at 2 percent interest. Moreover, the parcel post was instituted on January 1, 1913, to carry up to eleven pounds weight by fourth class post at, initially, five cents for the first pound and one cent for each additional pound. In addition, Taft had more suits brought against the trusts than had Roosevelt.

The fact that he received less credit than TR perhaps suggests more about the way he and his policies were perceived than it does about the policies themselves. For one thing, Progressivism had now developed beyond the ability of the federal government to control it. Moreover, Taft lacked Roosevelt's true geniality, his irrepressible vitality, and his easy capacity to dominate others. "When I hear some one say 'Mr. President,' " Taft confided to White House aide Archie Butt, "I look around expecting to see Roosevelt." Thus Taft's chief fault was that he differed from Roosevelt; his chief misfortune was that he succeeded Roosevelt as president. At first, jokes about Taft's obesity were genial, such as the famous one of 1907 about Taft being "the politest man I know because he gave up his seat in a street-car to three women." Later, they took on a caustic ring, such as one of 1910 in which the stout Taft was trying to alight from a streetcar. Because he was so fat, he had to descend the steps backwards but at each stop the well-meaning conductor and passengers, seeing him face forward, assumed he was trying to get on the car, and by pushing and pulling, helped him back onto the car so that he was carried four stops beyond his destination. The cruel joke was intended as a parody of Taft's ambivalence toward progressive reforms.

The initial warmth between Roosevelt and Taft was dispelled by chills of lasting coldness, such as that when, having agreed to retain four members of Roosevelt's cabinet, including Secretary of the Interior James R. Garfield, Taft went back on his word and appointed an entirely new team. Roosevelt was the only person who did not foresee what would happen, especially as Taft's wife Helen and his half brother and financial sponsor Charles, were deeply jealous of Roosevelt for his role as architect of the Taft family's political fortunes.

However, in no time at all, Taft sank up to his neck in the treacherous quicksands of American politics. The first threat to his authority came from a group of committed midwestern Progressives in Congress, the Insurgents. At this time the terms "Progressives" and "Insurgents" were almost synonymous but "Insurgents," made popular by Mark Sullivan, was preferred. There were thirty insurgents in the House and fourteen in the Senate. Robert Wiebe considers them as representatives of state and local Progressivism who began arriving in Washington during Roosevelt's second term, determined to see their ideas put into effect and to unite middle-class Americans in a crusade against the injustices of monopoly capital. Senators Jonathan Dolliver of Iowa (1900–10) and Albert Beveridge of Indiana (1899–1911) joined newcomers Senators Robert La Follette of Wisconsin (1906–25), Joseph G. Bristow of Kansas (1909–15), and Albert Cummins of Iowa (1908–26) in identifying themselves with reform, even to the extent of defying party whips. They also favored better co-ordinated policies on such subjects as conservation, child labor, and labor legislation. In the House, they included Victor Murdock of Kansas (1903–15), George W. Norris of Nebraska (1903–13), and Charles A. Lindbergh of Minnesota (father of the aviator, 1907–17).

Moreover, they enjoyed complaining about their self-imposed exile from power and in the Senate the prime object of their criticisms was Republican majority leader Senator Nelson W. Aldrich of Rhode Island (1881–1911), whom they accused of being a despot and a tyrant, exercising more power than any other individual in any legislature anywhere in the world. This was probably true, for the rules of the Senate allowed the leader of the majority party to determine the composition of committees and thus he could use this power to extract and distribute campaign contributions.

Aldrich was a tall, imposing man with luminous eyes, an authoritative manner, and an easy temperament. He was also an acute judge of character. However, Aldrich had to endure a series of challenges to his authority. The first came when he had William E. Borah of Idaho (1907–40), then a newcomer to the Senate, appointed to the Committee on the Judiciary because he knew Borah was an outstanding lawyer in his state who had represented great corporations. However, Aldrich had miscalculated Borah's political allegiance. The Judiciary Committee was faced with a proposal for a constitutional amendment for the direct election of senators. Aldrich and other conservatives were strongly opposed to the reform. Borah cast the deciding vote, approving the proposal that was reported out of committee to the Senate and sent on its way to passage through both Houses (by May 13, 1912), and ratification by the states (on April 8, 1913) as the Seventeenth Amendment.

Aldrich also suffered a personal affront in the controversy surrounding the tariff. Taft had called Congress into special session for March 15, 1909, with the avowed intention of enacting a lower tariff, a subject TR had deliberately avoided. A lower tariff was exactly what the Republican insurgents wanted, because they thought the trusts could be thwarted by regulated exposure to foreign competition.

Buttressed by Taft's support, the Insurgents began a spectacular fight for reduction throughout the long hot Washington summer, dividing the various schedules among them, assigning cotton to Jonathan Dolliver of Iowa, wool to Robert La Follette of Wisconsin, sugar to Joseph Bristow of Kansas, and metals to Albert B. Cummins of Iowa, and so on, until each had mastered all the requisite information. Aldrich and the majority, who favored a protectionist tariff, were quite unprepared for this tactic. They had devised the schedules according to figures supplied by the respective industries. Aldrich and his allies were made to look ridiculous as their own bill was explained to them by the Insurgents. Dolliver's masterly oratory rubbed salt in the wounds. Aldrich was frequently so embarrassed by Dolliver's assaults that he simply left the Senate chamber, silenced and red in the face, having been successfully defied. Nevertheless, the Insurgents were in a minority and thus the Payne-Aldrich tariff passed Congress quite comfortably.

The strain of having to stand on his own two feet had already made Taft irascible. He was warned by Medill McCormick that, unless he vetoed the tariff, he would antagonize the West who would then saddle him with a Democratic Congress in the midterm elections and then defeat him in 1912. Nevertheless, he signed the bill on August 5, 1909, thereby sealing his fate and leaving Dolliver to crystallize public opinion against him in a damning indictment, "President Taft is an amiable man, completely surrounded by men who know exactly what they want." For his part, Taft admitted that the tariff was not perfect, but optimistically suggesting that it represented "a sincere effort on the part of the Republican party to make a downward revision." Indeed, the act did provide for a Tariff Commission that would bring tariff control under systematic, rather than purely political, control and this found support from many Progressives. Nevertheless, the Insurgents were angry at Taft's betrayal. By his approach to this delicate political problem, Taft added insult to injury when he went on a speaking tour of the nation. When he spoke in Winona, Minnesota, a hotbed of Republican insurgency, the bill that had been "not perfect" suddenly became "on the whole . . . the best bill that the Republican party ever passed." The speech caused uproar when it was reported in the West. "Shades of Theodore Roosevelt," exclaimed the Des Moines *News,* "may ghosts of the animals he has killed in Africa ever haunt him for having foisted on the country this man Taft." Journalist Charles Willis Thompson described western anger as "a reverberating roar; the Rocky Mountains stood on their heads, the Great Lakes turned inside out, and the Sierra danced like the hills of Scripture." So great was the resentment that the remainder of the midwest trip was "a polar dash through a world of ice."

In the House the Insurgents' grievances were directed at the Speaker, Joseph Gurney ("Uncle Joe") Cannon (1873–91; 1893–1913; 1915–23), of mixed Quaker and Huguenot ancestry and perhaps the most politically sophisticated, deceitful, and subterranean man in American public life at that time. He knew that the public thinks and acts according to its response to symbols and his pose of common simplicity was intended to inspire public faith in his political probity. It was nothing for Cannon to appear at three or four dinners in the evening, tell a funny story at each, and then at midnight sit down to a game of poker. These pastimes were for observation of the men, and their methods, with whom he would be dealing during the day. He was slim, erect, and poised, easily able to control 391 men in the lower house, half of whom heartily detested him. He considered that, of all proposals for change, half were harmful and the other half useless.

Cannon's great power was based on the existing rules of the House that allowed him to appoint a majority (all Republican members) of the all-important Committee on Rules and of various other committees. The recipients of his favors constituted a political bloc committed to reelect him as speaker every two years and to retard or advance bills at committee stage, according to Cannon's wishes. When Cannon tried, and failed, to dispose of "Calendar Wednesday" (a day giving congressmen extra prerogatives), Congressman George W. Norris of Nebraska presented a previously prepared motion to have the Committee on Rules elected by the House, instead of being appointed by Cannon. After twenty-nine hours of continuous debate it was passed on March 17, 1910, by 191 votes to 156. Taft greatly disliked Cannon ("Simply hates him," said Archie Butt) but, out of mistaken loyalty to his party, allowed himself to be photographed embracing the impotent speaker. As a result, Cannon carried Taft down with him as he sank. Norris, who had led the assault on Cannon, emerged as a congressional hero.

Taft had already found himself embroiled in another controversy that touched very sensitive nerves amongst all Republican Progressives. The root of the trouble was that Taft had replaced Roosevelt's secretary of the interior, James R. Garfield, with Richard Ballinger, a man who wished to distribute public natural resources to private interests for development. Yet Taft had retained Gifford Pinchot, a Roosevelt man, as chief of the forestry services in the Department of Agriculture. A clash between the two men was almost inevitable and it was certainly inevitable that public interest in such an issue would be very intense. With Roosevelt to inspire him, Pinchot was idealistic, exuberant, and charming in his championship of conservation. Once Roosevelt's leadership and restraint were gone, Pinchot became harsh, pugnacious, and intolerant. When the clash with Taft came, it was spectacular, with Pinchot charging that Ballinger was conniving to turn over valuable coal lands in Alaska to a Morgan-Guggenheim syndicate.

Taft accepted Ballinger's rebuttal and publicly exonerated him, but was, justifiably, forced to dismiss Pinchot for insubordination. A congressional investigative committee decided in favor of Ballinger by a Republican majority. Despite this decision, Pinchot was seen by Progressives throughout the nation as a defender of national interests against vested interests, after the fashion of Theodore Roosevelt. Taft was discredited because it appeared that he wanted to allow vested interests to tap the nation's resources. Six months later, on March 7, 1911, Ballinger resigned, his usefulness impaired by the evaporation of his credit. To the end, Taft staunchly maintained that Ballinger was the victim of a conspiracy of defamation, prompting the New York *Evening Post* to comment, "Mr. Taft consents to Mr. Ballinger's departure in a blaze of indignant relief."

In the spring of 1910 Taft showed his true colors irrevocably when he joined the Old Guard of the Republican party in a well-planned and generously financed campaign to eradicate insurgency. They wanted to secure the defeat of progressive Republicans in the forthcoming primary elections in the Midwest. Despite the use of federal patronage, large sums of money, and the best standpat orators of the region, Taft's campaign failed. State after state—Indiana, Wisconsin, Minnesota, the Dakotas, Kansas—renominated progressive candidates. By the summer of 1910 it was obvious that the insurgents would only leave the Republican party if, and when, they were ready. Indeed, many of them were prepared there and then to divide the party on the issue of political reform and some of them were looking to Theodore Roosevelt for leadership. Roosevelt blamed himself. It was he who had made Taft president. Now he saw him doing badly in a job that he knew he, himself, could do well.

Midterm Crises

Roosevelt returned to America on June 16, 1910, to a lavish reception bordering on hysteria. He knew this moment was the zenith of his love affair with the American public. He set about trying to heal the party's wounds. He tried to take a hand in organizing the state convention in New York but it was there that Taft declared himself firmly against him. Thus rebuffed, the ex-president set out upon a great tour of the West where first at Ossawatomie, Kansas, on August 31, 1910, he enunciated the advanced political and economic philosophy that came to be known as the New Nationalism and was seen as dangerously revolutionary by the Old Guard of conservative Republicans.

The election results of 1910 were a debacle for the Republicans. The Democrats took the House by 228 seats to 162, a majority of 66, and carried the governorships in 26 states, including Ohio (Taft's state) and New York (Roosevelt's state). They also succeeded in electing Woodrow Wilson, president of Princeton, as governor of New Jersey, the man widely recognized as the greatest threat to the Republicans' hold on the presidency since Grover Cleveland.

Roosevelt, who at heart was a Republican partisan, took the Republicans' election debacle as a personal rejection. The very western states and New York, in which he had campaigned, had gone Democratic. The defeated Republican candidate for governor in New York, Henry L. Stimson, was Roosevelt's protégé. His defeat led the New York *World,* which had previously declared that a vote for Stimson for governor in 1910 was a vote for Roosevelt for president in 1912, to say that Roosevelt was extinguished. Despite his brave face in public, TR recognized that this was true. For a year he suffered an eclipse. The only visitors to his homes were extremists whom he eventually repudiated as a "lunatic fringe."

Having captured the House in the midterm elections of November 1910, the Democrats were in the advantageous position of having a majority in one chamber without being responsible for the government as a whole. They exploited their position to embarrass Taft. Taft tried to counter this adverse publicity by starting a series of antitrust suits, twenty-two bills in equity and forty-five indictments in all, against corporations for having violated the Sherman Act, compared with Roosevelt's eighteen bills in equity and twenty-five indictments. The most notable of these was a suit for dissolution against U.S. Steel, filed by Attorney General George W. Wickersham on October 26, 1911.

Taft also tried to correct his mistakes over the Payne-Aldrich tariff by supporting what was intended as a progressive bilateral tariff arrangement with Canada. His attempt ended in a rout. The treaty, signed on January 7, 1911, proposed to place over 100 articles on the free list and to reduce the tariff on over 400 others. Both houses passed the treaty. Taft openly acknowledged the support of the press, notably magnate William Randolph Hearst. His statement enflamed hostile opinion both within and without the United States. Not only was it widely known that Hearst favored tariff reciprocity but also that he favored the outright annexation of Canada.

Taft's well-intentioned statement swelled fears in Canada and in Britain that reciprocity might be the first stage toward absorption. The Canadian prime minister, Sir Wilfred Laurier, had parliament dissolved and went to the country in an election that was widely interpreted as a referendum on reciprocity. So great was the fear of annexation in Canada that reciprocity was overwhelmingly repudiated, much to Taft's deep embarrassment.

Although the public was dissatisfied with Taft, the Republican reverses were not simply a consequence of the incipient feud between Roosevelt and Taft. They were an expression of the changing fortunes of the progressive movement in the country as a whole. Just as Progressivism was exciting ever more interest in Washington, it was declining in certain localities, partly because reformers had achieved their aims or reached a practical compromise with business and local government, partly because that achievement had dulled the urge to reform. They had also roused suspicion bordering on resentment among the people whose lives they were trying to improve. Millions of city folk did not care about city budgets or actually wanted their children to work instead of going to school, and the arrogance of some urban Progressives simply exasperated them.

In short, the Progressives, sometimes unintentionally, deepened the division between middle- and working-class people. As a result, certain local bosses survived the progressive onslaught and emerged strengthened by the knowledge and insight of progressive campaigns. Now it was Progressives who were on the defensive, as bosses appropriated, modified, and implemented their ideas. In certain states the old guard rallied and helped defeat progressive leaders who had become unpopular. This was the fate of Albert Beveridge of Indiana who lost his Senate seat in 1910, failed to get elected as governor in 1912, and in 1914 failed to get reelected to the Senate. Thus, as the federal government gained extra powers at the expense of the states, the tide of Progressivism began to ebb in local communities. However, some Progressives drew extra support from working-class constituencies to compensate for loss of middle-class support and thus survived the ebbing fortunes of the movement as a whole. This was what happened to Governor Hiram Johnson in California (1911–17), as interpreted by Michael P. Rogin in "Progressivism and the California Electorate" for the *Journal of American History* (1968). As governor, Johnson supported such measures as workmen's compensation, an eight-hour day for women, regulation of child labor, and factory inspection, which were anathema to his previously ardent supporters. Nevertheless, such regulation appealed to the very classes they most detested. Thus in 1916, when Johnson contested a primary election for the U.S. Senate, his strongest support came from Catholic and working-class constituents in the San Francisco Bay area.

CHAPTER THREE

The New Nationalism and the New Freedom: The Triumph of Woodrow Wilson

·❦·

THE FRIENDSHIP of Roosevelt and Taft had determined the presidency for one term; their estrangement determined it for two. For some time the growing rift between Roosevelt and Taft had been deepening inexorably. Suddenly, a chasm opened. On the morning of October 27, 1911, Roosevelt read how Attorney General George W. Wickersham had, the day before, begun a suit to have U.S. Steel dissolved, charging that the corporation was a monopoly. Furthermore, he read how Wickersham was supposed to have said that U.S. Steel had achieved its monopoly by acquiring the Tennessee Coal and Iron Company four years earlier and, to do so, had "misled" President Roosevelt. No other charges made against Roosevelt enraged him more than these and he denounced them indignantly before Congress, in the press, and on the stump.

Roosevelt's fury reached all parts of the country and roused his followers. His return had inspired a wide range of Progressives, from former Rough Riders, such as Frank Knox of Michigan, social workers, such as Jane Addams of Chicago, conservationists, such as Gifford Pinchot of Pennsylvania, and impetuous reformers, such as Everett Colby of New Jersey, to such unlikely businessmen converts as George W. Perkins, hard-line Republican regulars, such as Bill Flinn of Pittsburgh, and Insurgents, such as Albert J. Beveridge of Indiana. William Allen White compressed informed press comment right across the country into the slogan, "Roosevelt or bust." The majority wanted him as soon as possible, no later than 1912.

Robert La Follette had already organized a National Progressive Republican League that he expected would provide him with a clear path to the Republican nomination for president. However, La Follette was incapable of providing the sort of decisive leadership to unite his disparate band of followers. Roosevelt's reentry into national politics completely undermined La Follette's faltering authority as his members called, instead, for Teddy. La Follette finally ruined his chances by an overlong and wild harangue against businessmen and journalists at a newspaper publishers' dinner in Philadelphia. Almost the whole progressive movement shifted to Roosevelt overnight.

Seven Republican governors urged Roosevelt to enter the race against Taft. Roosevelt used their various letters as the basis for a joint request, purporting to come from the governors but actually drafted by himself and calling on him to stand for the nomination. At Columbus, Ohio, on February 22 he spoke of his proposed personal platform, a "Charter of Democracy." One phrase, "recall of judicial decisions," was erroneously interpreted to mean a popular vote on all court decisions and alienated outright conservatives even more. The *Wall Street Journal* subsequently suggested how "Those most enthusiastic about the recall of judicial decisions are prevented by prison rules from working for the Colonel." Roosevelt's official announcement on February 22 that he would seek the nomination aggravated Taft's poor health. "His flesh looks like wax, his lips are thin, he is getting unhealthy bags under his eyes," noted White House aide Archie Butt. Mrs. Taft reminded her husband how she had predicted what Roosevelt would do. "I told you so." "I know you did, my dear," observed Taft, "and I think you are perfectly happy now; you would have preferred him to come out against me rather than be wrong yourself."

"Goodness gracious, I must have been dozing." In this cartoon of 1912 mischievous kittens of Senate and House, cabinet and courts unravel woolen balls of Taft's policies of railroad regulation, income tax, postal savings bank, and corporation tax that have spilled out of the Capitol mending basket to the evident dismay of Taft who also dreads the reappearance of Teddy at the window. (Library of Congress).

1912—A Crash of Rhinoceroses

The two wings of the Republican party now joined battle. Already at the Lincoln Day dinner of the New York Republican Club on February 12, 1912, Taft had discussed the progressive movement and denounced its leaders. "Such extremists would hurry us into a condition which would find no parallel except in the French Revolution. . . . Such extremists are not Progressives, they are politically emotionalists or neurotics." This last word was used by Roosevelt's allies to imply that Taft thought Roosevelt was crazy. Then in Boston on April 25 Taft made a vehement personal denunciation of Roosevelt, whom he accused of trying to discredit him by "adroit appeals to discontent and class hatred," in a speech that filled ten columns of newspaper copy the next day. Roosevelt retaliated at Worcester, Massachusetts, on April 26.

President Taft has not only been disloyal to our past friendship, but he has been disloyal to every canon of decency and fair play. . . . President Taft served under me for over seven years without finding fault with me. He only discovered I was dangerous when I discovered that he was useless to the American people. I wanted from President Taft a square deal for the people of the United States. . . . I do not believe he has given the people a square deal. I believe that he has yielded to the bosses and to the great privileged interests.

Mark Sullivan spoke for many when he said of these extreme charges and countercharges, "It was appalling, terrible, yet also Titanic . . ."

By his actions, Roosevelt widened the circle of his critics, especially among those Republicans whose affection for the Republican party was such that they could not bear to see an incumbent president denied renomination, or to see the unwritten rule against a third term broken, or were simply outraged at the very idea of the recall of judicial decisions or at Roosevelt's violent personal assault on Taft. They included prominent old-time bosses such as Boise Penrose of Pennsylvania, William Barnes, Jr., of New York, and Murray Crane of Massachusetts who would rather see the Republican party torn apart than let Roosevelt have the 1912 nomination. Underlying the assumed outrage of some sections of the press at Roosevelt's audacity in wanting a third term was widespread humor, expressed in the Brooklyn *Eagle,* that "No place feels like home after you have once lived in the White House." *Life* was sarcastic in the extreme, claiming "The popular demand for Colonel Roosevelt is steadily increasing; but however great the demand may become, it can never be as great as the supply."

The Insurgents, led by the interested La Follette, had been advocating the use of direct presidential primaries to supersede conventions as the means of selecting and instructing delegates to national party conventions. Oregon had adopted presidential primaries in 1910; in 1911 the states of California, Nebraska, New Jersey, North Dakota, and Wyoming did so. However, campaigns for primaries elsewhere met with little interest until Roosevelt announced his candidacy, whereupon his ardent supporters realized that only by this reform could they achieve the requisite number of delegates to offset boss control of the Republican National Convention. As a result of the campaign, the states of Massachusetts, Pennsylvania, Illinois, Maryland, Ohio, and South Dakota held regular or special meetings of the state legislatures and adopted presidential primary elections in 1912.

Roosevelt won and took delegates in most of the states that had adopted the primary law to assist him. It was clear that he was, in fact, the overwhelming first choice of Republican voters across the country. It seemed that the ex-president stood more than a good chance of winning the Republican nomination. In fact, he stood no chance at all. When the Republican National Convention opened in Chicago in June, Taft used patronage to shut his erstwhile patron out of the contest. The Republican National Committee gave Taft 235 out of 254 contested seats at the convention, leaving only a humiliating 19 seats for Roosevelt. Taft was nominated on the first ballot as Roosevelt's followers walked out of the convention.

Roosevelt's arrival in Chicago on June 14 was a sensation and sparked off mob demonstrations of unknown frenzy. To a reporter who asked after his health, Roosevelt replied, "I'm feeling like a bull moose," an imaginative answer that was carried on the front pages of 10,000 newspapers the next day and gave the name "Bull Moose party" to his personal following. Roosevelt felt the humiliation of his rejection by the Republican convention most keenly and was more than ever determined to run for president. While the Republican National Convention continued, he agreed in principle to the formation of a Progressive party when Frank Munsey, a newspaper magnate, and George W. Perkins of United States Steel and International Harvester promised to help finance the venture—further evidence of the ambiguous attitude of Progressives toward big business. In Chicago on August 6, 1912, the Progressive, or Bull Moose, party came into being with distinguished social, political, and economic Progressives on the platform. Never before had all the various and disparate progressive groups gathered together to participate in national politics and they never would again. It is difficult to say with exactitude that the Progressive party was purely and simply Theodore Roosevelt's personal vehicle for the presidency, but it is certainly true that without him the party could not exist. In 1916, when he refused the Progressive nomination, it simply disintegrated.

The leaders of the new Progressive party were all united by one common characteristic. They were all business or professional men and women. Out of 260 leaders present at the inaugural convention in 1912, there were 95 businessmen, 75 lawyers, 36 editors, 19 college professors, 7 authors, 6 professional social workers, and a scattering of others in various professions. The vast majority of them were self-employed and none of them was dependent on waged work for their living. Progressive party leaders were people who were deeply aware of the social problems of American society, yet were somewhat divorced from them by virtue of their privileged status. The Progressive party was new and Theodore Roosevelt was its only trump card.

Roosevelt was taken aback when the delegates at the Progressive convention sang "Onward Christian Soldiers" and seemed ready for a crusade; crusades were not in his style of calculated and thoroughly prepared political maneuvering. In reply, he gave them his "Confession of Faith," a speech that was a classic synthesis of the most advanced political thought of the time. Not since the Populist platform of 1892 had such a significant political program been expounded. Roosevelt called for many reforms of social justice, including: a minimum wage, the prohibition of child labor, legislation to prevent industrial accidents, a system of workmen's compensation, and social insurance. In politics, he wanted the establishment of machinery for the direct election of senators; the referendum and recall of both legislative and judicial decisions; a nationwide presidential primary; full public declaration of campaign expenditure; woman suffrage; and the direct initiative that would have allowed citizens themselves to propose legislation. Proposed economic reforms included a federal trade commission to regulate business and industry and a tariff commission that would ensure the benefits of protection for consumers, as well as producers.

Roosevelt claimed that the "old" nationalism had been used since the Civil War, "by the sinister . . . special interests," toward their own ends, whereas he was promoting a New Nationalism that would bring those special interests under government control and help make them work toward his vision of progress that Europeans now call the modern welfare state. Despite the reaction of the conservative press, the New Nationalism was neither new nor revolutionary. In three messages to Congress between 1907 and 1908 Roosevelt had spelled out almost the entire program of the New Nationalism. It was not until 1910, with an obviously irreparable split in the Republican party, that Roosevelt was willing and able to present his platform in its concentrated form. By that time the debacle of the Taft administration had destroyed the middle ground on which Roosevelt had once thrived. Roosevelt had read a book in which he, himself, was the hero and in which his policies had been presented together in a group. The lack of middle ground in the Republican party led Roosevelt to be identified unequivocally as a Progressive, while the book's skillful synthesis enabled him to expound his philosophy and program fully.

The book was *The Promise of American Life* (1909) by Herbert Croly, then an obscure progressive journalist from New York. It was drawn to Roosevelt's attention by Henry Cabot Lodge early in 1910 in Europe and he read it in late spring or early summer of the same year. In late July, while preparing for his western tour, Roosevelt wrote to Croly saying, "I shall use your ideas freely in speeches I intend to make." In fact, the ideas in Croly's book were Roosevelt's own earlier ideas that he had never had the time to collate and express in considered written form. *The Promise of American Life* captured the sweeping impulse of Progressivism at its peak. As historian David Seideman observes, "Croly virtually redefined the American national interest, and thereby laid the theoretical cornerstone for modern liberalism and the welfare state." Croly was advocating a unified, central state to promote economic and political freedom. Under a strong, heroic leader the government would enact a broad social program to ensure the peaceful transfer of power from the privileged few to the community as a whole.

Since conservatives would not be voting Progressive in any case, no attempt was made to propitiate them in the Progressive platform as a whole. Quite simply, it was the most radical platform of any major party hitherto. Indeed, Socialist leader Eugene V. Debs surveyed the scene and observed that the Progressives' bandanas had replaced the red flag of socialism. In its final form, the Progressive platform recommended efective legislation to prevent industrial accidents, occupational diseases, overwork, and unemployment; to fix minimum standards of health and safety in industry; to institute federal control of interstate commerce and use taxation to maintain its standards; to prohibit child labor; to provide a "living wage" throughout industry; to safeguard the rights of women by establishing an eight-hour day for women and children and fix minimum wages for women and prohibit night work for women; to institute one day's rest in seven for wage earners and limit shifts in plants operating twenty-four hours continuously to eight hours.

In 1912 the whole concept and extent of governmental intervention into virtually every area of life as proposed by TR would have been anathema to Democratic presidential candidate Woodrow Wilson who challenged the New Nationalism with the New Freedom. Indeed, judging by the titles alone, it would seem that the two programs were entirely antithetical. In fact, there were more similarities than differences between Roosevelt and Wilson. While editor William Allen White's comment that the two were like Tweedledum and Tweedledee was a gross simplification, the two philosophies and programs were distinct only in the sense that they represented two different progressive approaches to the problem of government. If the United States Mint were ever to issue a series commemorating Progressivism, then Wilson and Roosevelt would find themselves side by side on the same coin.

In the same way that Roosevelt's brand of Progressivism tended to blur his political position somewhat, Wilson was equally par-

Rejected by the Republican old guard, Theodore Roosevelt campaigned vigorously for the presidency in 1912 on a Progressive ticket, promising American life a New Nationalism of effective government regulation. (Library of Congress).

adoxical. Richard Hofstadter encapsulated the contradiction when he remarked, "Woodrow Wilson: the Conservative as Liberal." Prior to 1911, Wilson was definitely a conservative. In 1896 he bolted his party to support the Gold Democrat ticket and held nothing but contempt for his party's presidential candidate, William Jennings Bryan. However, by 1912, he was enlisting the support of the radical Nebraskan and wrote to him with remarkable self-critical honesty, bemoaning Roosevelt's strong appeal to the voters' imaginations: "He is a real, vivid person, whom they have seen and shouted themselves hoarse over and voted for, millions strong; I am a vague, conjectural personality, more made up of opinions and academic prepossessions than of human traits and red corpuscles." However, what Wilson lacked in charisma, he more than made up for in intellect and moral leadership.

Wilson was born in December 1856 in the Valley of Virginia, the son of a Presbyterian preacher. He was brought up, first, in Confederate Georgia and, then, during Reconstruction, in South Carolina, and matured in an atmosphere of romantic nostalgia for the lost cause and of Calvinistic fervor for what was right and moral. As a professor of political economy and later as president at Princeton University, he inspired students with his respect for an idyllic American past and revitalized both curriculum and teaching methods. In October 1910 he was elected governor of New Jersey, having been nominated to the Democratic ticket by the party's leading conservative bosses. However, the campaign that brought him the governorship was far from conservative. Such was the strength of his political ambition and his political sense that he cut himself loose from the conservative machine and went over to the reform program that Progressives of both parties had been pressing for over a decade. One of his first actions as governor was to prevent the election of the conservative boss, James Smith, Jr., to the Senate. Then, during the winter and spring of 1911 he subdued the bosses once again and pushed through a reluctant legislature practically his entire reform program: a direct primary system; legislation against corrupt practices; workmen's compensation; and, belatedly, strict state control of railroads and public utilities. Coming from someone who drew his political inspiration from Jefferson and the English classical conservatives, Edmund Burke and Walter Bagehot, this progressive program constituted a surprising turn around.

Progressive Democrats throughout the nation began to look toward Wilson as a potential presidential candidate. In the spring of 1911 they began an organized campaign for his nomination.

Wilson himself campaigned strenuously throughout the nation and, although he had difficulty in attracting conservative Democrats, it seemed certain that he would win the nomination with ease. However, when the convention opened in June in Baltimore, it was obvious that Wilson had serious competition from another progressive politician, Beauchamp ("Champ") Clark of Missouri, speaker of the House of Representatives. Not until the forty-sixth ballot—after William Jennings Bryan had shifted his support to Wilson's camp—was Wilson nominated.

As for a Democratic platform, the New Nationalism of Roosevelt and Croly was far too sweeping for Wilson. He was committed to the ideas and ideals of social justice, while maintaining an essentially Jeffersonian philosophy. Federal power should be used only to sweep away special privileges and artificial barriers to the development of individual energies and to preserve and restore competition in business.

At first, Wilson's campaign seemed to flounder somewhat as he tried concentrating on the single, unpopular issue of the tariff. He seemed to be searching for something more appealing when he met progressive lawyer Louis D. Brandeis at Sea Girt, New Jersey, on August 28. Brandeis had achieved national fame in 1908 when he went before the Supreme Court in the case of *Muller v. Oregon* as counsel for the state. The "Brandeis Brief" was an unorthodox and innovative means of argument for a lawyer to use. Rather than simply relying on the traditional legal argument of precedent, Brandeis amassed statistical, historical, sociological, and economic data to support his case. Brandeis was successful in arguing that Oregon's law of 1903, setting a maximum of ten hours for women working in laundries, was valid. The court unanimously accepted on February 24, 1908, that longer hours might impair the childbearing of women workers. Thus state limitation of ten hours was justified as a health measure, properly within the state police power. Thereafter, Brandeis became one of the chief spokesmen of the philosophy of regulated competition, and of unhampered enterprise and economic freedom for the small businessman. It was Brandeis who helped clarify Wilson's thought and led him to the program of the New Freedom.

While Roosevelt preached regulation of monopoly, Wilson

preached regulation of competition with the avowed intention of destroying monopoly. Roosevelt promulgated a program of social welfare that Wilson dismissed as paternalism that would reduce workingmen to nothing more than wards of the federal government. In Wilson's view, freedom to compete had to be maintained at all costs because he feared that the middle class, the mainstay of Progressivism, was in danger of "being crushed between the upper and nether millstones." The middle classes were to be protected from the hegemony of labor on the one hand and the hegemony of capitalist monopoly on the other.

Thus the campaign of 1912 presented the electorate with an interesting choice of solutions to the problems caused by the trusts. Theodore Roosevelt argued that any attempt to restore competition was futile. Instead, he advocated regulation of giant corporations by a federal commission. Using phrases coined by former Secretary of the Interior James R. Garfield, TR distinguished between "destructive litigation" and "constructive legislation." By contrast, Woodrow Wilson emerged as the champion of antitrust legislation in order to restore and maintain competition throughout private industry. He told an audience in Indiana, "I stand, as the party behind me stands, for regulated competition of a sort that will put the weak upon an equality with the strong." In his *The New Freedom* (1913), a collection of his campaign speeches, he explained what he considered to be the inefficiency and economic wastefulness of giant trusts. Wilson based his opposition to Roosevelt's proposed reform of the trusts on his interpretation that, in Roosevelt's scheme, there would be a partnership between the government and the trusts, in which the junior member—the trusts—would be running business at the expense of the government.

Although the underlying issues were momentous for the whole future of American industrial society, at the time the election was generally interpreted as a duel between great personalities, rather than a conflict of principles. Most of the arguments centered around Roosevelt and Taft's role was to provide an alternative for Republicans who had come to hate Roosevelt. Thus many voters did not so much think about the various political philosophies on offer as feel the emotions roused by the slogans. Roosevelt and

Wilson acted like capricious rival prima donnas, each with a claque and determined to cause mutual friction. Their behavior was, perhaps, justified. By striking sparks off one another, they ignited the fuel that turned the election of 1912 into a blaze. Roosevelt's most widely publicized description of Wilson was a "Byzantine logothete," emphasizing Wilson's apparent predilection for abstruse thought. In public, Wilson deliberately ignored Roosevelt, in part lest he arouse the sort of controversy in which Roosevelt was bound to come off best and in part to exasperate Roosevelt who could not bear such treatment.

Roosevelt campaigned tirelessly in New England, the Midwest, the Pacific Coast, the South, and the Northwest. He was shot in Milwaukee on October 14 by an insane man, John Shrank. Even his opponents admired his mettle when he insisted on continuing his speech, despite being dangerously wounded with a bullet in his lower chest. The bullet lodged in his massive muscles, instead of penetrating the lung. He protected the would-be assassin from the fury of the crowd, holding up a bloody handkerchief for all to see and in general making the most of the drama. Not only was he deeply resented for having divided the Republicans but Roosevelt was also weakened by the fact that his most enthusiastic constituency was the Midwest and agricultural areas of the country whose Progressive leaders distrusted him or contented themselves with giving him meager support from the sidelines. Furthermore, Roosevelt's paternalism was essentially urban.

The results of the election of 1912 show that Roosevelt failed to attract progressive Democrats to his Progressive party and this fact alone ensured his defeat. Wilson polled 6,296,547 votes (41.9 percent), Roosevelt 4,118,571 (27.4 percent), Taft 3,486,720 (23.2 percent), and the Socialist candidate, Eugene V. Debs, 900,672 (6.0 percent). The prohibition candidate, Eugene W. Chafin, took 206,275 votes (1.4 percent). This multiple division of the popular votes meant that, although he took fewer popular votes than Bryan in each of his three attempts, Wilson's victory in the electoral college was of landslide proportions. He gained 435 electoral votes against Roosevelt's 88 and Taft's derisory 8. The split in the Republican party also gave control of Congress to the Democrats and for his first two years in office at least Wilson was assured of workable majorities of seventy-three in the House and six in the Senate. The two-party system was too resilient to be overthrown even by as charismatic a leader as Roosevelt. It was rooted in deep political habits and extensive organization at the local, state, and national levels. People responded to Roosevelt's character but he could not generate a new political mechanism. In the congressional elections the Progressives captured 9 seats in the House and 1 in the Senate. They won only about 250 local offices and 1 governorship.

A few months after the election both Roosevelt and Taft attended the funeral of editor Whitelaw Reid at Grace Church, New York. At the end of the service Taft was unsure if, as president, he should go first or follow the casket. Roosevelt remarked, "This is the first time I ever saw a competition for precedence between corpses." Even in defeat, the Republicans were financially secure and could afford to allow the Democrats temporary control of the federal government, knowing that when they did return to power, the Republican machine would be intact. Had Roosevelt won, it would not have been.

Wilson and Presidential Leadership

Wilson's various publications not only disclosed his admiration for such statesmen as Washington, Gladstone, and Lincoln and his belief in the orderly, organic growth of political institutions, but also his concern about the concentrated economic power of the great corporations and the inefficiency of Congress. He intended to become a leader who could master multitudes, teach them to keep faith with the past, and implement progressive policies that would conserve as well as reform.

Wilson admired Gladstone and the British parliamentary system that he compared favorably to the weak presidents and assertive congressional machines of America in the Gilded Age. In his *Congressional Government* (1885) he dismissed the president as a useless fifth wheel in the American system and called for the introduction of a more assertive and central cabinet system (like the British) to concentrate responsibility and leadership in an executive body accountable to Congress. Wilson never gave up such ideas, especially of making the president answerable to public opinion. In 1916 he planned to resign immediately should his Republican opponent win the presidential election. In 1918 and 1920 he tried to turn the elections into a "solemn referendum" on his foreign policy. Wilson's views on the possibility of effective leadership had been radicalized, firstly, by the emergence of the United States as a first-class power and, secondly, by the way Theodore Roosevelt had revived the presidency by asserting a national leadership responsive to public opinion.

Calvinists such as Woodrow Wilson may have tidings of great joy to bring but they are not often very cheerful. Wilson gave most people the impression that he was, at best, reserved, distant, and cold, and, at worst, self-righteous and vain. Many people disliked his habit of polishing his spectacles whilst they were talking to him. William Allen White said his handshake was like feeling a "ten cent pickled mackerel in brown paper." It was widely known that once Wilson had made up his mind, he was inflexible and intolerant of others' opinions. At Princeton he got into a quarrel with one of the deans and a faculty member tried to reason with him, saying, "There are two sides to every question." "Yes, the right and the wrong," replied Wilson frostily. There were times when his arrogance was boundless. After the election, Wilson told William F. McCombs, chairman of the Democratic National Committee, "Before we proceed, I wish it clearly understood that I owe you nothing." McCombs reminded him of his services during the campaign. Wilson resisted, "God ordained that I should be the next President of the United States. Neither you nor any other mortal could have prevented that!"

Behind the scenes Wilson was far from a prude. He enjoyed vaudeville and courted his second wife, Edith, with the song, "Oh, you beautiful doll." While hardly lascivious, his need and love of female company beyond his first wife, Ellen Axson Wilson, and their three daughters, had led him during his period in New Jersey into a few love affairs. The most persistent of such liaisons with Mrs. Peck cost him dear later. When he was president Mrs. Peck exercised a subtle form of blackmail upon him with periodic requests for financial aid. Some malicious gossips suggested that it was this most unwelcome pressure that contributed to the early death of Ellen Axson Wilson in late summer 1914. Wilson had other problems besides—a long history of illnesses, including a first stroke at age 39 and chronic bowel complaints. None of these experiences taught him much about human charity. The most cynical interpretation of Wilson the politician would be that he was an ambitious trimmer, far less progressive than many he led. He was successful in getting enabling or codifying legislation enacted where his general strategy and understanding of just when to compromise and when not to where seen at their best. But he was least successful when his passion for morality were roused and he became intemperate, as was the case in his relations with Mexico and with his allies and enemies over American membership of the League.

Yet in his domestic program Wilson showed that he was a practical idealist, a man with immense confidence in ideals, with enough vision to use broad conceptions of statesmanship, and with the capacity to plan for long-term objectives. The greater part of opinion in both parties wanted reform of tariff, tax, and currency; a program to regulate banks, railroads, public utilities, and manufacturing industry; various forms of protection for artisans, farmers, women, and children. Thus Wilson's task was straight-forward—to synthesize reform ideas, arrive at a consensus, and lead public opinion and Congress in getting the reforms enacted.

Moreover, Wilson decided to govern through his party, instead of relying on a coalition of reform-minded congressmen as Roosevelt had done. He chose to do so, partly because this was his theory of government and partly because he gauged, quite accurately, what was feasible politically. Moreover, he wanted to broaden the base of the Democratic party and to strengthen it for the future. He thought that the sort of party discipline upon which a British prime minister relied in Parliament could be applied to Congress by a strong president. In order to counterbalance the weight of southern Democrats who chaired important committees in Congress and who had considerable reservations about his policies, Wilson decided to deploy presidential patronage as effectively as possible through his postmaster general, Albert S.

Sir William Orpen's study of President Woodrow Wilson did full justice to Wilson's penetrating gaze, tight lipped tension, and general hauteur. (Library of Congress).

Burleson, and thus keep his critics in the party within manageable bounds. He also believed that his spirited leadership and natural eloquence could convince the party to accept his program.

The disruption of the Republicans in the period 1910–16 allowed the Democrats large majorities in the House and workable majorities in the Senate where they were strengthened by support from insurgent Republicans. The 114 novices among the 294 Democratic congressmen in 1913 were eager to pass reforms and eager to please Wilson because much of their future careers depended upon the success of the administration and the continuation of party patronage. Even conservative southerners reckoned it was better to support reforms rather than risk national opprobrium. Few congressmen dared challenge Wilson. They had no congressional machine to resist him and, if they opposed his proposals, they had to do so alone.

Wilson's most considerable advantage was that he was an untarnished newcomer in national politics at a time when the Democratic party was consciously shifting emphasis from a somewhat sectional party based largely on southern, agrarian, and innercity support into an effective nationwide organization, representative of all sections and classes. Unlike Bryan, Wilson was free from embarrassing political obligations that had accured over a long political career.

Furthermore, at a time when Americans rejoiced in oratory, Wilson was a spellbinding public speaker, being especially gifted in communicating high ideals and touching men's spirits. He was, argues prolific Wilson scholar Arthur Link, "a romantic moralist, who, using the poet's hyperbole to express political and moral truth, raised every issue and conflict to a high stage upon which the human drama was being played out." Wilson knew that language is the backbone of political style. Nevertheless, Wilson sometimes said things he did not really mean and his meaning was sometimes abstruse. During extemperaneous speeches his oratory took flight and became a virtuoso solo, meant to be felt rather than understood. Moreover, "there was always the temptation to idealize unpleasant situations and necessities, and this in turn sometimes led Wilson to romanticize objectives and to refuse to confront hard realities." A percipient critic, Herbert Croly, wrote of "The Other-Worldliness of Wilson" for the New Republic of March 27, 1915: "Mr. Wilson seems to be one of those people who shuffle off their mortal coil as soon as they take pen in hand. They become tremendously noble. They write as the monuments of great men might write. They write only upon brass, and for nothing shorter than a millennium. They utter nothing which might sound trivial in the Last Judgment, or embarrass them in the most august company . . ."

The closest of all Wilson's advisers was the shrewd and ubiquitous Colonel Edward M. House, who, through his constant attentiveness and his refusal to accept a cabinet position, came close to sharing presidential influence. Indeed, while Wilson went on vacation in Bermuda before his inauguration, it was House who drew up plans for the new cabinet that necessarily reflected the factional divisions within the Democratic party. Two of the more significant appointments were made when William Jennings Bryan was given the prestigious position of secretary of state, despite Wilson's distrust of him, and when William B. Wilson was appointed the very first secretary of labor. The inclusion of the Bureau of Labor in the cabinet in its own right marked the completion of a struggle that had begun when Roosevelt created the Department of Commerce and Labor. William Wilson, a former secretary-treasurer of the United Mineworkers and congressman, was appointed in recognition of his efforts to establish the Bureau. His appointment set a precedent, which lasted twenty-five years, that the position should go to a labor leader. Woodrow Wilson's Bureau of Labor was committed to "foster, promote, and develop the welfare of the wage earners of the United States," and constituted his first progressive action as president.

The New Freedom

The New Freedom was the first phase of Wilson's program from March 1913 to December 1914. Ironically, progressive supporters of Roosevelt discerned more of the New Nationalism in Wilson's subsequent domestic policies than of the New Freedom. The reforms of Wilson's first administration did not originate with Wilson but with others in both parties. Wilson's contribution was his leadership.

Wilson's first action in office was spectacular and dramatically successful. On the day of his inauguration he called a special session of Congress and on April 8, breaking a tradition in effect since Jefferson's administration, appeared in person to deliver a short message before a joint meeting of the House and the Senate. In the message he expressed his determination to achieve what Cleveland and Taft before him had resoundingly failed to do—substantially reduce the protectionist tariff that had kept foreign competition away from American industry since the American Civil War.

On April 22, 1913, Oscar W. Underwood of Alabama, chairman of the House Ways and Means Committee, presented the tariff that had been largely drafted two years earlier when Congress had passed three Democratic tariff bills vetoed by Taft. The Underwood-Simmons bill was not a free-trade tariff, but it did propose a reduction in the average ad valorem rate from the (approximately) 40 percent of the Payne-Aldrich tariff of 1909 to an average of about 29 percent. In addition, several important products were put on the free list, including wool and sugar. Moreover, where it could be shown that American products dominated the world market, then it was proposed that rates should be either abolished or drastically reduced. Agricultural machinery and most consumer goods went on the free lists, as did products such as iron and steel that were manufactured by the trusts.

To recover loss of revenue that would result under the new tariff, Congressman Cordell Hull of Tennessee drafted a section for the bill that provided for a graduated income tax under the Sixteenth Amendment (passed on July 12, 1909, and ratified on February 3, 1913), which authorized Congress to impose taxes on incomes from whatever source and without apportionment to the states. The income tax provided by the Underwood-Simmons tariff was modest. It levied a tax of 1 percent on incomes over $3,000, or $4,000 for married couples, and a surtax of 1 percent on incomes of $20,000 a year, increasing gradually to 6 percent on incomes over $500,000. The Supreme Court subsequently affirmed the constitutionality of the income tax law in its decision by seven votes to two in the case of *Brushaber* v. *Union Pacific Railroad Co.*, on January 24, 1916.

The Underwood-Simmons bill had a very stormy passage through Congress with lobbyists for manufacturers doing their utmost to have it rescinded. Surprisingly, the finished bill provided even greater reductions in the tariff than had originally been proposed. During debates and negotiations food and other farm products had been put onto the free lists, bringing the general level of rates down to between 24 and 26 percent. Similarly, the maximum surtax on incomes was increased from 3 to 6 percent. Wilson's impatience with vested interests in Congress shamed senators into a vigorous endorsement of a low tariff. However, the reductions of the Underwood-Simmons tariff were not especially effective, since the outbreak of World War I and the consequent disruption of trade was the equivalent of a prohibitive tariff.

Federal Reserve Act

Banking and currency reform was high on the list of potential legislation in 1912. The national system of banking was something of an anachronism, hopelessly inefficient in catering to the needs of a large industrial nation. At this time many banks were not under national control at all. So-called national banks—those interstate banks with substantial assets—operated as independent units under federal supervision. Their ability to issue notes was related to their holding of government bonds and bore no relation to the country's needs as a whole. The system did not allow for the expansion of credit when this was required, nor did it meet the seasonal needs of farmers. In 1907 a short-lived, but intense, bankers' panic had underlined the need for reform and the Aldrich-Vreeland Act of 1908 had led to the establishment of an interim system, providing for more mobile reserves and a more elastic money supply. The Aldrich-Vreeland Act also established the National Monetary Commission, headed by Nelson W. Aldrich, that investigated possible options and advised Congress of its recommendations in 1911 and 1912. The separate Pujo investigations of 1912 for the House disclosed how a small group of financiers controlled banks and trust companies, insurance companies, express companies, railroads, and industrial and public utility companies worth, collectively, $23 billion. This group of financiers constituted a "Money Trust," able to construct rail-road lines, foster manufacturing, or stimulate national prosperity or recession.

The Aldrich plan of reform was a banker's dream that would have meant the perpetuation of banking control by Wall Street. Together with his advisors, Wilson secretly formulated what was essentially a decentralized version of the Aldrich plan with control still in private, rather than governmental, hands. News of the plan was leaked to the press and a furor ensued because radical progressives would settle for nothing less than full governmental control of the banking system. For once, Wilson felt himself unqualified to take a strong line of leadership on this issue and, somewhat concerned by the factional dissent it was causing within his own party, looked beyond his cabinet for advice. On June 11, 1913, Louis Brandeis told Wilson that what Bryan and the Progressives were saying was right: that the government alone should issue currency and control the banking system. This forceful piece of advice convinced Wilson that he would have to make concessions to the Progressives.

The outcome of such discussions was the most important act of Wilson's administration, the Federal Reserve Act. It was the climax to a century of arguments about politico-economic reform and drew from the varied protests of a wider spectrum of opinion than any other single piece of legislation. Nevertheless, the act still put into effect the bankers own wish for a bankers' controlled central bank. Wilson used party discipline to ensure passage of the act. After it passed the House on September 18, 1913, by 287 votes to 85, following explosive debates, the same sort of struggle took place over it in the Senate. When Senator Elihu Root of New York denounced it as a sure cause of inflation and national disaster, proponents of the bill reviewed it and tightened its reserve requirement. The Senate passed the bill on December 19 by 54 votes to 34 and it was signed by Wilson on December 22, 1913. Wilson won by leading rather than by driving.

The Federal Reserve Act—also known as the Glass-Owen Act—established the Federal Reserve System with twelve private regional Federal Reserve Banks that were controlled and supervised by the Federal Reserve Board in Washington. The Federal Reserve Board comprised six men (of whom two must have banking experience) appointed by the president, and the secretary of the treasury and the controller of the currency. Each reserve bank was to be controlled by a board of nine directors, six to be elected by the banks and three to be elected by the Federal Reserve Board. Of the six directors selected by the banks, three had to be selected to represent the general public interest of the reserve district by the stockholding banks. The Federal Reserve Board had power to remove these three directors if they did not fairly represent the general public interest.

The act provided for the creation of a flexible currency, allowing the Federal Reserve Board to issue, through its member banks, currency equal in amount to collateral (such as notes, drafts, or bills of exchange arising out of commercial transactions) deposited in the banks with a permanent reserve fund of 35 percent to provide for prompt redemption. The regional banks would have, initially, $105 million in capital and $531 in deposits. All national banks were obliged to join the system while state banks and trust companies were encouraged to do so. The system was essentially a successful compromise between governmental and private control and within its first year in operation represented nearly half the nation's banking resources, increasing to four-fifths by the 1920s. Here again, we see a reform that partially expressed the philosophy of Progressivism. It was a reform of efficiency rather than a reform of justice or social restructuring. The Federal Reserve Act improved the capitalist economy of the industrialized United States, making it run more smoothly by providing an absolutely sound, yet elastic, currency that would be flexible.

The FRB had much control but the regional banks, notably the richest of them, the Federal Reserve Bank of New York, exercised great independence and had far more influence over interest rates. Moreover, officers of regional banks were to be elected by member banks in those regions. Thus Wall Street came to dominate the New York bank.

Although the act empowered the president, with the consent of the Senate, to appoint members of the FRB, the candidates were, necessarily, going to be professional bankers, or men of affairs sympathetic to them, who would also be acceptable to the conservative Democrats on the Senate Banking and Currency Committee. Public interest depended on the appointment of disinterested and informed experts to the FRB and those who were truly experienced, professional, and impartial were likely to be in short supply.

Progressive Pressure on Wilson

Despite the singular achievement of the Federal Reserve Act, Woodrow Wilson's administration still faced a serious challenge from diverse progressive groups. By 1913 calls for economic and social justice were as strong as they had ever been with campaigns for regulation of industry, federal child labor legislation, and governmental aid to labor, farmers, tenant farmers, and the unemployed. Organized groups dedicated to these causes included: the American Association of Labor Legislation, the National Consumers' League, the National Child Labor Committee, and National Association for the Advancement of Colored People (NAACP), and organized social workers. Organized labor, too, should be included in this list, despite the reluctance of unions to be associated with either middle-class or professional students of labor problems. Farm organizations, such as the National Farmers' Union and the Non-Partisan League, were demanding a program of government intervention on behalf of farmers, especially the establishment of a governmental system of long-term rural credit. The question of the day was whether or not Woodrow Wilson and his New Freedom were sufficiently flexible to satisfy these various progressive groups.

All things considered, the answer to the question must be a qualified no. In the summer of 1914, Wilson rebuffed farmers who wanted government-backed, long-term credit. Not until 1916, when political circumstances left him no choice, did he lend his support to a policy of farm credit, resulting in the Federal Farm Loan Act and the Federal Farm Loan Board.

The Federal Farm Loan Act of 1916 provided farmers with long-term credit facilities, similar to those made available to industry and commerce by the Federal Reserve Act. The country was divided into twelve farm districts under the general administration of a Federal Farm Loan Board, consisting of the secretary of the treasury and four other members. Each district was given a Farm Loan Bank, capitalized at $750,000, in which cooperative farm loan associations held membership. Farmers belonging to these associations could secure long-term loans (of between five and forty years) on farm-mortgage security at interest rates between 5 and 6 percent, rather lower than those of commercial banks. The Bonded Warehouse Act of 1916 authorized licensed and bonded warehouses to issue against specified agricultural commodities (including grain, cotton, tobacco, and wool) warehouse receipts negotiable as delivery orders or as collateral for loans. The measure assisted farmers in financing their crops.

Early in 1914 Wilson had refused to give his crucial support to a child labor bill drafted by the National Child Labor Committee, on the grounds that it was unconstitutional. Throughout his presidency he refused to support woman suffrage. On this issue he was utterly conservative but consistent. Years earlier the mother of a Princeton student suggested Wilson make the college coeducational "to remove the false glamor with which the two sexes see each other." "My dear Madam," said Wilson, "that is the very thing we want to preserve at all costs!"

The legislation achieved by Wilson's administration baffled many Progressives because of its inconsistency. It was, nevertheless, difficult for them to decide what sort of Progressive Wilson was. Wilson did not make that judgment any easier when he supported the Furuseth Seaman's Bill, to improve safety and conditions of work for merchant sailors that was enacted and signed on March 4, 1915. This act, often known as La Follette's Seamen's Act because of La Follette's sponsorship, was one of the great measures of social justice to come out of the Progressive Era. The proposal gained additional support in 1912 when the British ocean liner *Titanic* hit an iceberg on its maiden voyage on April 15 and sank with the loss of many lives. Of over 2,000 on board, only 705 passengers and crew were saved. The crisis dramatized in spectacular and tragic fashion the dangers at sea for sailors as well as passengers. The Furuseth or La Follette measure pertained exclusively to seamen, a fact that may account for Wilson's willingness to support it. Andrew Furuseth, president of the Seamen's Union, had campaigned for this bill for twenty years. The act was designed to improve the living and working conditions for seamen and to attract more people to the sea. It applied to crews of vessels registered in the United States and to foreign ships while they were in American ports. It regulated hours of work at sea and in port, and the payment of wages; fixed minimum amounts of food; and set certain standards of quality. It increased the required number of able seamen to 65 percent of the total crew, excluding officers, and required employment of at least 75 percent of members in each ship's department who could understand the language spoken by the officers.

Wilson's lack of concern over issues of social justice was nowhere more clearly expressed than in his administration's policy toward blacks. Oswald Garrison Villard, one of the founders of the National Association for the Advancement of Colored People (NAACP), called at the White House soon after Wilson's inauguration and presented a plan for the appointment of a National Race Commission to study the problem of race relations throughout the nation. Wilson appeared to be "wholly sympathetic" to the suggestion and Villard left for a visit to Europe, confident that the Commission would soon be appointed. However, on his return, Wilson refused to grant him an interview and wrote explaining that the political situation was far too delicate for any such action. He explained that the National Race Commission would incite the resentment of southerners in Congress whose votes he needed for the success of his legislative program. Indeed, throughout his presidency, Wilson did nothing to prevent the Jim Crow racism of Democratic white supremacists. In the spring of 1913 the Bureau of the Census, the Post Office Department, and the Bureau of Printing and Engraving quietly began to segregate workers in offices, shops, restrooms, and restaurants. Employees who objected were discharged. In the South, post office and treasury officials were given free rein to discharge and downgrade black employees. In Georgia, the collector of Inland Revenue announced, "There are no government positions for Negroes in the South. A Negro's place is in the cornfield."

For the first time since the Civil War, it seemed the federal government was endorsing and encouraging segregation. Black leaders strongly protested this perfidy from the man whom they had supported only a year before. Much of the progressive leadership of the Midwest and North also protested. Wilson was surprised and disturbed by the furor caused by the moves toward segregation. He himself approved of segregation and it was only the protest from other progressive quarters that put a check on the spread of Jim Crow segregation throughout the entire federal government. Progressives were perplexed by Wilson's lack of commitment to the egalitarian ideals of the New Freedom and their confusion was further compounded when Wilson began his moves toward regulation of the trusts.

In his address to Congress on January 20, 1914, Wilson spoke of breaking up interlocking directorates, of defining, forbidding, and punishing "hurtful restraints of trade," and of creating a commission to inform and advise business. The emphasis was to be on legal prohibition rather than on federal supervision. However, once the legislative debate was under way, Wilson began to shift emphasis. His insistence on prohibition waned and his interest in a strong commission to administer antitrust rules and prevent unfair competition waxed. Congress responded with two acts, the Clayton Act and the Federal Trade Commission Act.

The Clayton bill was discussed by Congress in 1914 and was designed both to modify and intensify the terms of the Sherman Antitrust Act of 1890. It concurred with the somewhat vague principles of the New Freedom campaign of 1912 in that it sought to establish fair competition by providing precise definitions of restraint of trade and clarification of the rule of reason. It was a long way from the desires of labor leaders, such as Samuel Gompers of the AFL, who had supported Wilson in 1912 on the understanding that his antitrust laws would exempt both labor and farm organizations from the penalties of the Sherman Act. When Gompers saw the text of the Clayton bill, he was deeply disappointed. However, Wilson and his congressional leaders stood firm and only offered labor a compromise amendment that provided for jury trials in cases of criminal contempt; limited the issue of injunctions in labor disputes; and declared that neither labor unions nor farm organizations should be declared in restraint of trade when they sought legitimate objectives by lawful means. The House passed the bill on June 5, 1914, but when it came through the Senate on August 5 it was in many ways unrecognizable from the original.

In the interim, Wilson had rethought the question of business regulation and, under the influence of Louis Brandeis, had moved toward Roosevelt's idea of a strong, independent trade commission. Thus the Clayton bill was left adrift in the Senate and virtually every one of its strong provisions was seriously weakened. The prohibition against mergers was modified by conservatives who wanted it to apply only to those cases where mergers would tend to decrease competition. The upshot of these revisions was that over the next twenty years the Supreme Court, by its decisions, weakened the act.

The Federal Trade Commission Act outlawed unfair trade practices in general terms and gave the commission plenary authority to oversee business activity and issue cease and desist notices. However, like all commissions, the Federal Trade Commission was entirely dependent on its members for its character, and Wilson deeply disappointed Brandeis and other Progressives by appointing a board that was sympathetic to the needs and wishes of big business.

In 1914, Wilson began to welcome men such as financier J. P. Morgan and automobile manufacturer Henry Ford to the White House where he listened to their advice. Also in 1914, Wilson's attorney general, Thomas Gregory, began to use a new method in dealing with alleged combinations in restraint of trade. He invited any large corporation with doubts over the legality of its structure to come and talk it over amicably with the Justice Department. Many corporations did so, including American Telephone and Telegraph and the New Haven Railroad. In effect, the president of the United States was saying to business leaders, "Send your man to my man and they can fix it up."

Wilson's declining interest in domestic reform, his increasing absorption in foreign policy, and part in the tragedy of World War I have somewhat obscured his significance in American domestic policies. Yet he had come to dominate American politics in the

1910s as Roosevelt had done in the 1900s. Moreover, the Underwood tariff, Federal Reserve, Clayton Antitrust, and Federal Trade Commission Acts were all Wilsonian measures in the sense that it was Wilson, above all others, who provided a synthesis of demands, achieved political consensus, and, by sheer force of will, ensured that Congress enacted the legislation. In the second phase of his domestic program in 1915 and 1916, Wilson had drawn the fire from advanced Progressives in both main parites who wanted a stronger program of federal support for farmers, industrial workers, women, children, and the huddled masses in general.

Wilson's outsize contribution has prompted Arthur S. Link to conclude in his essay of 1957, "Largely through Wilson's leadership, . . . the United States for the first time attempted squarely to confront the enormous domestic problems of the twentieth century. The program begun by Theodore Roosevelt and aimed at building public administrative power to offset the aggregations of private power came to its first culmination under Wilsonian auspices and to an even fuller fruition after 1932." Underlying this was a major achievement of American politics in general for "historians a century hence will probably describe the Wilson era as the time when the American people through their leaders found the first, though incomplete and imperfect, answers to the question of how to bring a dynamic, growing, and competitive economy under effective social control."

Finally, we should consider a phenomenon that achieved a signal victory for Progressivism—the prohibition movement of the late nineteenth and twentieth centuries.

The Prohibition Movement

The introduction of the national prohibition of alcohol by the Eighteenth Amendment, passed in 1917, ratified in 1919, and put into effect in 1920, was also a direct consequence of a concerted progressive campaign. To its admirers, it was a fulfillment of the best traditions of urban reforms, a means of cleansing cities and their inhabitants of social and political ills. To its numerous critics, it was a gross and crude mistake, a parody of reform, a joker in the mixed pack of Progressivism. As with the campaigns for major reforms of food and drugs, the campaign for the prohibition of alcohol served to unite middle-class Progressives from various professions, notably medicine and sociology, and to link them to the Populist tradition of agrarian dissent and rejection of the new values of the cities. James H. Timberlake in *Prohibition and the Progressive Movement 1900–1920* (1963) has remarked on the associations of personnel and aims of Progressives and prohibitionists; Andrew Sinclair in *Prohibition—the Era of Excess* (1962) has traced the roots of the prohibition movement in the agrarian revolt; and K. Austin Kerr in *Organized for Prohibition* (1985) has explained the way the Anti-Saloon League mobilized its forces.

After the American Civil War a prohibition wave began with the rapid spread of scientific information on the physiological effects of alcohol. It convinced many thousands of middle-class people that even moderate drinking damaged the body and that total abstinence provided the only assurance of long life. Whereas alcohol had once been thought a source of energy, it was now considered a cause of disease. Scientists showed how alcohol depressed the heart and made alcoholics prone to illnesses such as arteriosclerosis, gastritis, fibrous liver, and tuberculosis. As a result of investigations into alcohol and health, life insurance companies turned their attention to the relationship between alcohol and mortality.

A joint committee of the Medical Directors' Association and the Actuarial Society of America published a report in 1915 based on the statistics of forty-three life insurance companies in America and Canada between 1885 and 1908. The nub of the report was that alcohol shortened life: even two or three glasses of beer a day were dangerous. Thus life insurance companies favored total abstainers with lower premiums and bonuses. Such conclusions, important in themselves, would have had less political significance were it not for the wider social issues they raised. Alcohol was to assume greater importance in a society that was, through industrialization and urbanization, becoming more tightly knit than ever before.

It was not coincidence that the prohibition movement and the industrial revolution originated, developed, and culminated in the

Organized for the national prohibition of alcohol, the Anti-Saloon League, through its giant press in Westerville, Ohio, distributed thousands of pamphlets and posters warning people of the evils of demon drink, such as this cartoon of little children orphaned of parental care by the saloon. (Library of Congress).

same periods. In the late nineteenth and early twentieth centuries accidents arising from drunkenness at work were more dangerous than before. Mistakes with mechanical drill, loader, and conveyor belt had more damaging consequences than those with pickax, shovel, and wheelbarrow operated by hand. Abstinence was an absolute prerequisite of employment for many an industrial boss obliged to protect his workers and his machines as well as production. Henry Clay Frick, du Pont Powder, and American Sheet and Tin Plate were among these manufacturers. The most famous automobile manufacturer, Henry Ford, was an ardent prohibitionist.

Agrarian discontent in the 1890s provided fertile soil for the seeds of prohibition sown by the Protestant churches who sought to make temperance a major issue. Evangelical emphasis on personal conversion as the crux of religious experience made the converted intolerant of anything that interfered with that experience. However, Protestant churches did not simply criticize drinkers. They blamed the liquor interests for aggravating a social problem by inducing those who drank to drink more and by working to create new drinkers.

The liquor industry comprised the manufacture of beer, wine, and spirits by brewers, vintners, and distillers. Not only did it have huge financial resources but it was also associated with machine politics and commercial vice and used its influence to block reforms that did not suit its interests. In particular, it sought through its principal lobby, the United States Brewers Association, formed in 1862, to get federal tax on beer reduced. Naturally, it was also in the interests of the liquor trade to encourage more Americans to drink and to drink more alcohol. Thus it became a prime target of progressive reform.

Although the liquor trade was the target of prohibition, it was the saloon that became its first goal. In 1909 there was one saloon for every 300 people. There were more saloons in the United States than there were schools, libraries, hospitals, theaters, or parks, more certainly than churches. By the turn of the century many saloons were controlled by the brewers. Intense competition among the brewers drove them to control the retail sale of their beer. Moreover, high license fees imposed on the saloons by Progressives who wanted to drive disreputable places out of business resulted in alliances between saloon keepers and brewers. Individual owners could not always raise the $500 or $1,500 for a license and borrowed from the brewers directly or by mortgaging the bar. In return for the loan, they undertook to sell only the brewer's particular brand of beer. One prohibitionist, D. Leigh Colvin, estimated that by 1900 the percentage of bars controlled by brewers in midwestern cities was as high as 65 percent in St. Louis, 70 percent in Kansas City, 75 percent in Toldeo, and 90 percent in Indianapolis, Minneapolis, and St. Paul.

As far as Progressives and prohibitionists were concerned, the supposed "liquor trust" was accused of corrupting government and holding the huddled masses in a slavery of alcoholic dependence. Progressives believed that liquor impeded the integration of immigrants and their assimilation into American society. One social worker, Paul H. Benjamin, had the obvious answer: abolish the saloon "and the task of Americanizing the conglomerate foreign population would be lightened 50 per cent," he declared in 1915. Thus, for some Progressives, prohibition was as crucial as other social reforms. Moreover, to the middle classes the saloon was politically subversive as well as socially undesirable. The low saloon could always provide politicians with fraudulent votes to keep the party machine in power. Sometimes, these were the paid votes of pimps, pickpockets, and tramps. Sometimes, they were the misappropriated votes of local residents rounded up by gangs of thugs.

The two most effective prohibition organizations were the Women's Christian Temperance Union (WCTU), founded in 1874, and the American Anti-Saloon League (ASL), given definitive form in 1895. The League declared for one object only, closing the saloon, and thus appealed to a wide catchment area, including those who detested the saloon and the social evils it maintained but were, themselves, advocates of temperance rather than of prohibition.

The ASL was one of the most persuasive pressure groups, working within the traditions of agrarian dissent, urban Progressivism, and the managerial revolution in big business. It created an elite of highly skilled leaders whose task was to mobilize a mass constituency. Thus the ASL was a complement both to the various professional associations emerging at the turn of the century and to the specialized groups being established to transform local government. The ASL had developed a major organ for publicity in its American Issue Publishing Company at Westerville, Ohio, which by 1912 had produced a total of forty-one tons of literature. This included a paper, *The American Issue,* which, by 1919, had a total circulation of 16 million.

The ASL focused the prohibition movement on a succession of concrete political objectives: legislation by local option to bar the saloon from individual districts; state prohibition laws; and, from 1913 onward, a constitutional amendment to bar the manufacture, distribution, and sale of alcoholic beverages. Moreover, the ASL was securing the support of other reputable associations. At its quadrennial meeting in December 1916, the Federal Council of Churches of Christ in America declared for total abstinence and supported the idea of a constitutional amendment. Charles H. Mayo, president of the American Medical Association, came out in favor of prohibition on June 6, 1917.

States began to accept the anti-alcohol arguments of prohibitionists. Some went dry, prohibiting the manufacture and sale of intoxicating beverages, led by Kansas (1880), Maine (1884), North Dakota (1889), Georgia (1907), the new state of Oklahoma (1907) with prohibition written into its constitution, and Tennessee (1909). Other states experimented with different ways of controlling the liquor trade, notably Illinois, Massachusetts, Missouri, Pennsylvania, and South Carolina. At the outbreak of World War I, the situation was most promising from the prohibitionists' point of view. West Virginia went dry in 1912 and, by the end of 1914, Arizona, Colorado, Oregon, Virginia, and Washington State had adopted prohibition, bringing the total number of states to do so to twelve. Many pockets within other states had gone dry by local option. Thus 74 percent of the total territory of the United States in which 47 percent of the population lived was dry. The exception to this general trend was provided by industrial centers, mill towns, and large cities. There were, for instance, more bars in Chicago than in all the South. In the period before American intervention in the war, the number of states with total prohibition almost doubled. In their attempt to purge them of vice and poverty, crime and corruption, prohibitionists were determined to impose temperance on cities against the will of the huddled masses.

According to statistics disclosed by Jeremiah W. Jenks and Walter E. Clark in *The Trust Problem* (1919), prohibitionists exaggerated the evils of alcohol and made excessive claims about per capita consumption. Whereas annual per capita consumption of beer was increasing from 3.5 gallons in 1865 to 20.2 gallons in 1915, per capita consumption of distilled spirits was decreasing over the same period from 2.1 gallons in 1865 to 1.2 gallons in 1915. Nevertheless, consumption of beer by adults rose fourfold between 1880 and 1915, rising from about six-tenths of a gallon to 2.4 gallons.

The Anti-Saloon League now openly changed its emphasis. Instead of calling for prohibition within the states, it projected national prohibition by constitutional amendment. When Congressman Richmond P. Hobson of Alabama first proposed a prohibition amendment to the House on December 22, 1914, he and his allies presented a petition signed by 6 million people and extending 150 feet across the visitors' gallery and onto the floor of the House. Although the measure was passed by 197 votes to 190, it did not receive the necessary two-thirds majority. Nevertheless, it helped dramatize the significance of the prohibition movement. Moreover, that month Congress passed the Harrison Act, outlawing the use of narcotics. Both proposals served to educate the public and to warn congressmen that their stands would be noted.

Congress was well aware that the liquor trade was a central part of national commerce and that it yielded the largest single source of tax revenue. Therefore, congressmen were, initially, reluctant to do anything to damage it. When the sixty-fourth Congress assembled for its last session in December 1916, nineteen states were dry and four of them had gone dry that year.

The most significant victory was in Michigan where a majority of the electorate had decided to eliminate the liquor traffic, the first breach in the hitherto impregnable wet defenses of the industrial North and East. Politicians inferred from these last victories that the electorate wanted prohibition and that a politician who was on record for having voted against prohibition risked wrecking his future career. All commentators agreed that the ASL had won the propaganda battle and profited from the great weight of medical and scientific, business, and social science opinion ranged against drinking.

Unlike other ASL executives, Ernest Cherrington thought that the legislative battle would take only five years and chose the elections of 1918 as the optimum time to press the case. For one thing, there would not be a presidential election that year to distract the electorate; for another, the future sixty-sixth Congress would be the first with all senators elected by popular ballot and thus free of the wet funds that had traditionally influenced the decisions of party caucuses in the state legislatures. The most formidable obstacle was the House where there were always enough urban representatives to make it nigh impossible to secure the necessary two-thirds majority. Moreover, such reapportionment of seats in the House that must follow the 1920 census would reflect the growth in city population and produce an even greater proportion of wet congressmen.

Controversial constitutional amendments get passed and ratified only when two conditions are fulfilled. The first is that their proponents must demonstrate that only a constitutional amendment can rectify a profound social problem. The second is that there must be a wide and regionally diverse consensus across the states that the particular amendment is necessary and desirable. This was the case with the Eighteenth Amendment and the various strands of the argument were drawn conclusively together by World War I. The war brought to the political fore a special mix of factors that encouraged Congress to pass the Eighteenth Amendment in December 1917: the need to conserve grain; excessive patriotism and hatred of all things German, including beer gardens; and the countryside's last great defiance of the new values of the cities. Moreover, while some men were sacrificing their lives for their country, the least those at home could do was to give up drink during the war. Despite the tragicomedy of prohibition enforcement in the 1920s, the aim of prohibitionists and Progressives was the improvement of society and the elimination of corrupt politics.

CHAPTER FOUR

A Future out of the Past: The New Immigration

·꣟·

O N DECEMBER 10, 1910, the Metropolitan Opera gave the world premier of an opera by the most famous living Italian composer, Giacomo Puccini. *The Girl of the Golden West* was a romantic melodrama set in a gold-mining camp in California at the time of the gold rush. It was performed by a brilliant cast led by the world's leading tenor, Enrico Caruso, and Emmy Destinn and Pasquale Amato, under the baton of Arturo Toscanini. It met with a rapturous response and the composer himself took fifty-two curtain calls.

The heroine, Minnie, is the miners' schoolteacher on Sundays and the hostess of a mining camp saloon at night. It is she who provides the driven but homesick miners with emotional support during crises. When she falls for the handsome but notorious bandit Ramerrez, alias Dick Johnson, she protects him, first, from the sheriff, lascivious gambler Jack Rance, waging his life in a crooked card game and, then, from the miners who are ready to lynch him. In the end the miners agree to free Ramerrez. Not least of his crimes is the theft of Minnie's affection. Yet when she reminds them of her many kindnesses to them, they are moved and let him go away with her.

Children of the Wind.
New immigrants about to arrive in New York, huddled together on board ship in 1906, exhibit a mix of curiosity and bewilderment. The central trio of apprehensive women offers a photographer's variation on a traditional artistic theme of the Three Graces. (Library of Congress).

Whatever its limitations as music drama, *The Girl of the Golden West* can be seen as a metaphor for the experience of new immigrants with the United States in which Minnie represents the American dream. She is an object of desire who shares the min-

ers' wants and worries. "There is no sinner/for whom there is
no possibility of redemption." This is the promise that drives
immigrants to America. Yet she is an idealized figure set against
a dark background; the obsessive search of a community for material riches, represented by the gold that "poisons the blood of
those who look at it." Moreover, the little mining community is
torn by ethnic rivalries and the last act focuses on a lynch mob,
another fact of American life. It seems that Puccini and his li-
brettists are aware that each immigrant group fears competition
from the next arrivals. It is only when the mining immigrants
realize that the essence of the American dream is a universal welcome, that they can overcome their fear and suspicion of the most
recent newcomer, Dick Johnson. One of the reasons that *La Fan-
ciulla del West* remains on the fringe of the operatic repertoire is
because it enshrines these truths that enfold the story of American immigration.

The part played by the United States in the mass migrations
of the nineteenth and twentieth centuries is most distinctive—and
not for quantity alone. Americans looked to the future, not the
past. Where people had come from was less important than where
they were going. The very word "immigrant" was invented by
Jedidah Morse in 1789 (the same year as the federal Constitution)
to describe foreign settlers in New York. Distinct from "emigrant," the American language henceforth identified newcomers
with the country they entered rather than the one they had left.
The term presupposed an established society founded by the
original colonists who determined the terms of admission of others.

American immigration was continuous throughout the nineteenth century. Nevertheless, there were three distinct waves, each
greater than the one before. According to historian Marcus Lee
Hansen, they were dominated successively by the Celts, the Germans, and the Slavs and Mediterranean peoples. The first to arrive, the British, Irish, Germans, Scandinavians and northwest
Europeans were the old immigration. The Slavs and Mediterranean peoples were the new.

The period 1905–14 saw American immigration reach its zenith. Over a million immigrants entered the United States in each

Immigration to the United States, 1890–1917

Origins	Number	Percentage
Central Europe	4,879,000	27.1
Southern Europe	4,369,000	24.3
Northwest Europe	3,637,000	20.2
Eastern Europe	3,328,000	18.5
Canada and Newfoundland	744,000	4.14
Central and South America	473,000	2.63
Asia	468,000	2.6
Australia and New Zealand	23,500	0.13
Africa	15,000	0.08
Pacific Islands	3,500	0.02

of six separate years: 1905, 1906, 1907, 1910, 1913, and 1914. The year 1907 marked the absolute peak of immigration in any one year with 1,285,349 immigrants. If we take the period 1890–1917 in which this momentous shift occurred as a whole, we find that altogether 17,991,486 immigrants entered the United States. The numbers and percentages are shown in the accompanying table.

The essential forces underlying expanding immigration in the period 1890–1917 were political and religious discontent, increasing awareness of economic opportunities in the United States, the collapse of the agrarian order in the wake of European industrialization, and the pressures of rapidly increasing population. These were much the same reasons as had fueled immigration in the early nineteenth century. Thus, as these causes of discontent moved eastward across Europe successively from Britain and Ireland, to Germany and central Europe, and thence to eastern and southern Europe, so the sources of immigration moved eastward with them. In the period 1901–5 America received 959,763 immigrants from Italy; 658,735 from Russia; 944,239 from Austria-Hungary; but only 176,995 from Germany and 385, 469 from Britain and Ireland. By 1914 73.4 percent of the total number of immigrants came from southern and eastern Europe, compared with 13.4 percent from northern and western Europe. Thus the new immigration now exceeded the old.

This shift had profound consequences. Alan M. Kraut explains in *The Huddled Masses* (1982):

The immigrants who came to the United States in such numbers between 1880 and 1921 dramatically affected the shaping of the American population. By their very presence, these newcomers altered the economy, politics, and culture of the country. In turn, the immigrants were changed, in varying degrees, by the society they entered.

Immigrants widened the market for manufactured goods, increased city populations, and, in time, swelled the electorate. Their very presence required additional and larger churches, schools, and hospitals, and, ultimately, more and more accountable government.

The Transatlantic Exodus

Of all the factors stimulating the new immigration the most obvious was an increase in population. At the close of the century the annual rates of increase in eastern Europe were more than ten in every previous thousand. Increased population threatened traditional standards of living. There was not enough food to go round. Developments in the three states whence Slavic and Mediterranean emigration flowed (Austria-Hungary, Russia, and Italy) illustrate this. The catchment area of Slavs was especially wide. The term Slav covers a western division of Poles, Bohemians (Czechs), and Slovaks, and an eastern division of Russians, Ruthenians (Ukrainians), Bulgarians, Serbs, Croatians, and Slovenians.

Peasants in Italy, Austria-Hungary, and eastern Europe were being displaced in an agricultural system that no longer worked. The mania for subdivision of accessible arable land reached epidemic proportions. Sometimes, the tiny farms were too small to support a family. Thus in Bulgaria less than 4 percent of all holdings exceeded 50 acres while over 100,000 farms were smaller than 2.5 acres. Such precarious agrarian economies could not withstand the additional pressure of increased competition on the world market from agriculture in America or elsewhere in Europe. Furthermore, national revivals of minority cultures in Austria-Hungary incurred hostility and political repression from the ruling elite. Immigration from Austria-Hungary rose from 1.02 million in the period 1820–1900 to 2.14 million in the decade 1901–10.

In Italy, successive governments dominated by northerners failed to address the chronic problems of the impoverished south, *Il Mezzogiorno,* considering southerners irresponsible primitives. Cruel policies of taxation, internal tariffs, and landlords' harsh practices toward their tenants, the *contadini,* exacerbated the gulf between government and region, farmer and artisan, absentee landlords and stricken tenants. The agony of the Mezzogiorno was intensified by a series of terrible natural disasters. Vineyards were blighted by phylloxera; heavy French duties on Italian wines and competition by American citrus fruits from Florida and California decimated the fruit and vinegrowing economy of Calabria, Apulia, and Sicily. Then earthquakes jolted Basilicata and Calabria (1905), Campania (1906), Messina (1908), and Catania (1910). The worst earthquake was that in Messina, Sicily, followed by a tidal wave in the Straits, that leveled the city and killed 100,000 inhabitants, as well as destroying 300 small towns. Of 3 million Italians who crossed the Atlantic between 1876 and 1901 about 2 million went to Argentina and Brazil, both Catholic countries with Mediterranean-type climates and Latin cultures. However, Italian immigration to America rose from 1.04 million in the period 1820–1900 to 2.04 million in the decade 1901–10.

The impulse for migration from Russia was somewhat different. It was as much political and religious as it was economic. The greatest exodus was of Russian Jews, fleeing persecution. The assassination of Alexander II in 1881 set off antisemitic riots in the south and west. By 1897, 4.5 million Jews, 94 percent of the total Jewish population, were confined to the Pale of Settlement, an area of about 386,000 square miles from the Baltic Sea to the Black Sea. It comprised Poland, Lithuania, Byelorussia, and the Ukraine—except for Kiev. Only six categories of Jews could live beyond the Pale. The oppressive May Laws of 1882 also drove all Jews who could not prove a prior right to live in the country into the towns. Furthermore, it was becoming harder for Jews to earn a living. They were excluded from agriculture, industry, the professions, and public office. "The vast majority of them are in poverty," observed the American minister to St. Petersburg in 1893, "and a very considerable part in misery—just on the border of starvation." In one of Russian emigrant Sholom Aleichem's short stories a poor Jew promises a wealthy Rothschild the secret of eternal life. "Move to my shtetl," he advises the banker, "for in the history of our town, no millionaire has ever died there." Outright persecution followed economic restrictions. The brush fire of violence and intimidation inaugurated the first of three terrible pogroms, each more terrifying than the last: 1881–84, 1903–6, 1917–21. Forty-nine people were killed and over 500 injured in the massacre of Kishinev in 1903. Sculptor Chaim Gross, who emigrated from the Russian section of Poland in 1919, recalled a horrifying experience during World War I when the Cossacks went on the rampage.

They broke up the door, they broke the window—three large Cossacks came in with their sabres and guns and so on. My mother jumped out of bed, and my father and brother, and I, and the first thing, one of the Cossacks grabbed my mother—the idea was to rape her. My father tried to stop them, and they took a sabre, and as they were pulling my mother, one of the Cossacks, I don't know if it was the same one, started chopping at my father's head. And my mother put her hands over my head, and he chopped her fingers and then he started chopping my mother's head and my father put his hands out to her and they chopped his fingers again. . . . After the Cossacks had gone both my father and mother were unconscious for a long time . . . my mother for many, many weeks.

Displaced from their original homes but unable to own new land, the Jews had no loyalty to the land itself or the country of their birth whose government was oppressing them with such relentless cruelty. Nevertheless, their heritage was a disciplined religion that defined an appropriate code of morality and sustained them in adversity. Irving Howe explains in *World of Our Fathers* (1976) how "the world of the east European Jews was a world in which God was a living force, a Presence more than a name or a desire." These forms of strict religious observance were demanding but protecting, and they came under scrutiny from liberal Jews of western Europe. The challenge of this Western

European enlightenment, or *Haskala,* appealed to many younger Russian Jews whom they stirred with ideas of individual freedom, of socialism, and of Zionism. Moreover, there was the possibility of escape to the United States. "We do what all Jews do," remarks one of Sholom Aleichem's characters, "we emigrate to America." Consequently, we should note that Jewish emigration was as great from areas in eastern Europe where there was little overt persecution, such as Austrian Galicia. In Russia terrible pogroms, such as that of 1903–6, coincided with an economic depression following the Russo-Japanese War and the abortive revolution of 1905. It was this depression that led to an increase in Christian emigration from Russia among Finns, Poles, Lithuanians, and Ukrainians. For Jews, it was not outright persecution of Jews that encouraged them to move so much as the harsh economic restrictions within the Pale. The statistics are dramatic. The number of Russian immigrants to America rose from 761,742 in the period 1820–1900 to 1.59 million in the single decade 1901–10. Even when Poles made up a quarter of the Russian exodus, and Finns, Germans, and Lithuanians accounted for almost another quarter, Jews comprised the largest single group, 43.8 percent of the whole. Less than 5 percent of immigrants from Russia were Russian in anything but birth.

There were two phases of Jewish immigration. Between 1880 and 1900 Jewish immigrants comprised displaced merchants and improverished artisans from the Pale. Their motive was greater economic opportunity. Then in the period 1900–21 the second phase comprised rabbis, intellectuals, socialists, and affluent businessmen.

Not all immigrants came across the Atlantic. Between 1860 and 1900 about 1.05 million Canadians, mainly French-Canadians, left Canada. These French-Canadians came from the province of Quebec were neither agriculture nor industry could support the population. By the end of the nineteenth century French-Canadians constituted one of the major minority groups in New England and rather smaller ones in northern New York, Michigan, Wisconsin, and Illinois. They became itinerant workers, planning to save money earned in America and then return home and rebuild their family farms. Only when the Canadian frontier reached the prairies at the turn of the century did immigration from Canada begin to decline. Thus, in the decade 1901–10, immigration from Canada fell to 179,226.

A small number of Mexicans immigrated—according to official statistics, 28,003 between 1820 and 1900. Some historians believe the actual numbers were twice that. In the decade 1901–10 Mexican immigration increased to 49,642 and went on rising in successive decades until the 1930s: 219,004 in 1911–20; 459,287 in 1921–30. Mexican immigrants assisted the growing agrarian economy of the Southwest. As Alan M. Kraut puts it, "Whether they came legally or illegally, permanently or temporarily, for the day or until the planting and harvesting cycle was completed, Mexican laborers were plentiful and worked cheaply. They helped complete southwestern railroad lines; made southern California, Texas, and Arizona into cotton country; and dug irrigation ditches that turned California's Imperial and San Joaquin valleys into a fertile cornucopia. Mexicans mined in Arizona, harvested fruit in Texas and California, and staffed packing plants all over the Pacific coast."

A comparatively small but significant number of Orientals crossed the Pacific. Between 1849, when gold was discovered in California, and 1882, when the Chinese Exclusion Act was passed, 305,455 Chinese settled in California. Like many Europeans, their primary motive was economic. There was no significant immigration from Japan until 1891. From then until 1900, 25,942 Japanese, encouraged to immigrate by various domestic factors, entered the United States. However, the number rose to 129,797 in the period 1901–1910.

We should recollect that neither the United States nor such other countries receptive to emigrants as Australia, New Zealand, Argentina, Brazil, and Canada were impartial to the moving millions. These countries were at one or another stage of industrialization. They needed additional workers and industrialization made them competitive to attract as many cheap workers as was necessary to stoke their industrial furnaces. By 1900 Canada was spending over $1 million annually, much of it in offices in sixteen American cities, to entice foreign labor recently arrived in the United States. Agents were awarded a commission of $300 for every immigrant they persuaded to cross over the border into Canada. Ironically, just when Canada was advertising for European workers, French Canadians were crossing into the United States, seeking higher wages.

Europeans heard about the United States through newspaper articles, advertisements, and letters from former residents who had become immigrants and settled in America. Whatever their problems in the New World, the first immigrants in any ethnic group to arrive usually put a brave face on the situation. They emphasized what was good. Advertising copy was intended to sell ocean passages, railway seats, or land and also emphasized opportunity. A good deal of the information was out-of-date. By the turn of the century, there was precious little land to be had from railroads, who had previously compaigned to attract settlers and sold them land, at prices immigrants could afford. Yet the agent for Thomas Cook in Antwerp continued to distribute the company's pamphlet, *Homesteads For All,* with its assurance of plentiful supplies of cheap land. Despite the shift in sources of immigration, American agents continued to address northern Europeans, because they were considered more desirable than southern and central Europeans.

States and railroads were even more responsible than steamship companies for stimulating immigration. After 1865 almost all the northwestern states and territories formed separate agencies. They wanted to dispose of unsold land and they realized that increased population was essential for material growth. In 1870 midwestern governors called a national convention on immigration to Indianapolis. It was attended by delegates from twenty-two states who petitioned Congress to establish a national bureau of immigration in place of one closed down in 1868.

The impact that advertisements, letters, and rumors had as they circulated in Europe was considerable. Thus Mary Antin in her memoir, *From Plotzk to Boston* (1899), recalls how in Russia,

America was in everybody's mouth. Businessmen talked of it over their accounts; the market women made up their quarrels that they might discuss it from stall to stall; people who had relatives in the famous land went around reading their letters for the enlightenment of less fortunate

A young immigrant girl faces the routine medical examination at Ellis Island, including, here, a sight test as well as a test checking her heartbeat. (Library of Congress).

folk. . . . children played at emigrating; old folks shook their sage heads over the evening fire and prophesied no good for those who braved the terrors of the sea and the foreign goal beyond it; all talked of it, but scarcely anyone knew one true fact about this magic land.

The Journey

Prospective immigrants were shown why, where, and how to go. The advent of steamships revolutionized the transatlantic traffic. By 1867 92.86 percent of passengers were arriving in New York by steamship. The crossing by steam lasted, on average, fourteen days in 1867 and only five-and-a-half forty years later. The journey was much safer in the 1900s than forty years earlier for ships were getting bigger and better. The introduction of steel hulls, improved boilers, and the triple expansion engine made possible ships of 5,000 tons. Each could accommodate about 300 passengers first class and more than 1,000 in the steerage. Ships' lengths extended almost as far as many building ashore rose in height. The Inman Line's *City of Paris* was, at 10,650 tons, the largest ship in the world when she was launched in 1889. In 1907 the Cunard liner *Mauretania* was 31,950 tons.

During the American Civil War British and German steamship lines had seized the bulk of the transatlantic traffic from American companies. Lines such as the Inman and Cunard from Liverpool, the Hamburg-Amerika from Hamburg, and the North German Lloyd from Bremen built new fleets of passenger ships and expanded their trade. They were joined by new lines: by 1882 there were forty-eight steamship companies competing with one another in the Atlantic. Shipping companies began to improve their standards after the turn of the century, firstly by building third-class accommodation in new ships to supersede steerage. Emigrants traveling third class were boarded in two-, four-, or six-berth cabins, had far more washrooms and lavatories than in the old days of steerage, and had meals served in dining rooms. Bars sold beer, tobacco, and soft drinks, and kosher food was served in dining rooms.

At the turn of the century German shipping lines were better placed to carry immigrants from central and eastern Europe than were British lines. Moreover, between 40 and 65 percent of immigrants came on tickets prepaid by immigrant relatives already in America. Over the years the sums raised and distributed were considerable. Thus immigrants from Austria-Hungary received $95 million from relatives between 1893 and 1903.

Having made it difficult for prospective emigrants for many years, the governments of Austria-Hungary now accepted the inevitable and decided to try and make some money from mass migration. In 1904 Hungary reached an agreement with the Cunard Line, based in Liverpool, to sail direct from Fiume on the Adriatic Coast to New York as the Cunard-Hungarian American Line. In exchange for abiding by Hungary's laws on emigration, including accepting only passengers with proper documents, the line would have a monopoly of transporting immigrants to America. However, the alliance did not prove especially profitable for Cunard. Rival shipping lines lowered their charges to eight dollars and this induced Hungarians to cross Hungary's borders and sail from other ports. Thus no more than a third of Hungarian emigrants left from Fiume on Cunard's overcrowded vessels.

As a result of more strenuous American standards of health for immigrants, introduced in 1903, all emigrants had to undergo a medical inspection in Europe. Thus American doctors, chosen by American consuls, worked at the ports of Liverpool, Le Havre, Trieste (Fiume), and Palermo, inspecting prospective immigrants. An American inspector in Liverpool in 1909 reported on the high standard of the Cunard hotel system, "a village by itself in the center of Liverpool," comprising several buildings that could accommodate 2,000 guests. He stayed in a room with clean bed, steam heat, and electric light and supplied with soap and towels. At Naples, shipping companies provided passengers with ration-tickets, sent them to a hotel and restaurant for a dinner of soup or stew, melon, and wine, and then they were inspected by a doctor who also vaccinated them, and their papers were checked again. The Hamburg-Amerika Line provided the most extensive facilities, constructing a special village with station, churches, and synagogue for passengers. It could house 4,000 emigrants. Travelers, already weary from their journey across Europe, could bathe while their clothes and luggage were disinfected. It was, of course, in the shipping companies' interest to allow and assist at proper medical inspection, rather than endure an epidemic on board ship or have to return emigrants from America to Europe because they had been refused entrance to the United States by American officials.

The arduous voyage had its productive side, being an education for passengers in the art of living in close proximity to others of different countries with different customs. It allowed immigrants to adjust and vary their expectations according to the environment. Thus the voyage taught survival in unfamilar surroundings. French and Italian ships were poorer than British and German vessels, being notorious for poor ventilation, rotten food, and overcrowded quarters. "How can a steerage passenger," asked a journalist aboard a White Star liner traveling from Naples, "remember that he is a human being when he must first pick the worms from his food . . . and eat in his stuffy, stinking bunk, or in the hot and fetid atmosphere of a compartment where 150 men sleep, or in juxtaposition to a seasick man?"

Guardians of the Gate

The first stage in the integration of immigrants into American society was their reception. In 1892 the federal government opened a special immigration depot on Ellis Island in New York harbor. Ships docked in the harbor and immigrants were ferried to the island where all stages—quarantine, customs, and registration—were completed. The first floor of the main building contained facilities for handling luggage, railroad ticket offices, counters selling food, and a waiting room for travelers going farther. The registry room on the second floor, and usually called the Great Hall, was the largest room of all, being 200 feet long, 100 feet wide, and 56 feet high. It was, however, divided by iron railings into a sequence of narrow passageways. It was these iron railings, above all else, that intimidated newcomers since they reminded everyone of prison bars. Moreover, special detention areas were surrounded by wire fencing and thus looked like cages.

Registration covered, in turn: name; nationality; last residence; destination; occupation; age; sex; marital state; number in family; literacy; amount of money; whether a former prisoner or pauper; health; vessel; date. The clerks' methods were rough and ready, their knowledge of other languages rudimentary. If immigration statistics are misleading, it is largely due to them. They were quite likely to call Czechs Germans, and Serbs Hungarians. The Jewish Cooperstein became Cooper, the Dutch Kok became Cook, and the Greek Kiriacopoulis became Campbell. One German Jew was so confused by the barrage of questions that he forgot his own name. "Ich vergesse," he admitted when asked. The clerk accordingly registered him as Ferguson.

Ellis Island existed to examine all immigrants and to exclude some. By an act of 1891 the federal government denied entry to paupers, polygamists, and persons suffering from loathsome and contagious diseases. Medical inspectors double checked immigrants (already tested in Europe) and marked suspects with chalk letters on their coats: E for trachoma, G for goiter, K for hernia, and X for mental illness. Everything in the registration process was calculated. Even the first ascent of a staircase while carrying luggage was a test of physical stress and provided immediate clues above the immigrant's stamina, posture, and heart condition. Immigrants usually had their future address written on a scrap of paper, sometimes illegible, sometimes garbled. Thus "Neihouk, Nugers" was Newark, New Jersey, and "Pringvilliamas" was Springfield, Massachusetts. Someone traveling farther west would be expected to show he could pay the fare, as would an unaccompanied child. Old people would be expected to prove they were meeting friends or relations. In all, 92 percent of people arriving in New York in the years from 1908 to 1910 declared they were joining family or friends who had sent for them.

Although as many as 20 percent of immigrants were detained each year, about half were released as soon as funds arrived or minor ailments were treated. In 1907 1,004,756 immigrants were admitted through Ellis Island and another 195,540 people were detained. Of those detained, 121,737 were held only temporarily, 64,510 were held for some specific inquiry, and 9,203 were sent to a hospital. In the end, the Board of Inquiry excluded about 15 percent of the people whose cases it heard. However, many other ports conducted only the most casual inspection of immigrants. Thus passengers who arrived by first or second class escaped close inspection. In Boston, Philadelphia, and Baltimore, inspectors and doctors simply raced through the processes aboard ship or in a small building on shore.

In the act of March 3, 1903, that provided for a more comprehensive inspection of immigrants at European poets, Congress also gave the American government the right to deport any immigrant entering illegally and it added epileptics, prostitutes, and professional beggars to the list of excluded persons. The proscribed list also included anarchists and persons believing in the overthrow by force or violence of government. This was a direct result of William McKinley's assassination by Leon Czolgosz in 1901.

Ellis Island's poor reputation as the "Isle of Tears" developed largely because of the state of exhaustion in which most immigrants landed. Wearied by the journey, confused by the unfamiliar immigration procedures, and the impersonal attitude of many officials, many newcomers associated their treatment with all the severe trappings of law enforcement in repressive European countries. In 1901 a scandal broke about exploitation of immigrants. Corrupt officials had issued fraudulent naturalization papers allowing those who could pay a fee of five dollars to land to bypass Ellis Island. President Theodore Roosevelt intervened and appointed William Williams, a young Wall Street lawyer, as commissioner of immigration at Ellis Island. In order to expose the corrupt officials, Williams had his friends disguise themselves as immigrants, and go through the full process of inspection until they discovered which inspectors were breaking the law, exploiting immigrants, and taking bribes. A consortium of swindlers who ran a lucrative racket in exchanging foreign currency was also exposed and the contract to exchange foreign currency was subsequently awarded to the American Express Company. As part of the federal government's desire to supervise immigration, the Bureau of Immigration was established in 1906 to keep records and statistical information.

Patterns of Settlement

While the proportion of immigrants in 1910 was only 14.5 percent of the total population (much as it had been in 1860 when it stood at 13.2 percent), the immigrants were increasingly concentrated in the industrial Northeast. Indeed, four states contained almost half the foreign-born population: New York, Massachusetts, Pennsylvania, and Illinois.

Although the new immigration had now exceeded the old, we should note that even in 1910 Germany still accounted for the largest number of first-generation immigrants, over 2.5 million. However, Russia and Austria-Hungary came next, each with over 1.5 million. Then came Ireland and Italy with over 1.3 million while Scandinavia, Britain, and Canada had about 1.25 million. The largest German contingents had settled in the Midwest, notably Illinois, Wisconsin, Ohio, and Minnesota, with lesser (but still large) numbers in New York, Pennsylvania, and New Jersey. Scandinavians were concentrated in Minnesota, Illinois, Wisconsin, North and South Dakota, and Washington State. Finns settled in Massachusetts, Michigan, and Minnesota. Almost half the Canadians settled in New England, and most of the rest in New York, Michigan, and the states round the Great Lakes. The Irish settled in New England and the mid-Atlantic states as well as California and Illinois, states that received the greatest numbers of Italians. Immigrants from Russia and Austria-Hungary settled in New York, Pennsylvania, New Jersey, Massachusetts, and Illinois.

Polish immigrants settled in thousands of communities in at least thirty-six states, but primarily in the industrial cities of the Northeast from Illinois to New York. They became miners in Scranton, Pennsylvania, meat packers in Chicago, and steelworkers in Buffalo. Although most Greeks settled in the industrial cities of the Northeast and worked as artisans or in menial service jobs, others ventured west. By 1907 between 30,000 and 40,000 Greeks had settled west of the Mississippi. In Colorado and Utah they worked as miners and smelters; in California as construction workers for railroads. Few moved to the South, although John Cocoris and his family established a sponge business in Tarpon Springs, Florida, in which they employed 500 Greek immigrants to dive for, clean, and pack sponges.

Observers of early twentieth-century America remarked how immigrants seemed far more in evidence in the largest cities than ever before. It seemed there were masses of newcomers in unusual costumes speaking foreign languages and following strange customs. When novelist Henry James returned to the United States in 1907 after being away for twenty-five years, he experienced a profound "sense of dispossession." Whatever their numbers, immigrants never threatened to overwhelm the native-born population. Although there were times when the foreign-born comprised a fifth of the population of Canada and a third of the population of Argentina, they never exceeded more than a seventh of the population of the United States, although sometimes in such midwestern states as Wisconsin the fraction rose to a quarter.

In 1910 78.6 percent of new immigrants lived in towns or cities but the percentage of old immigrants in cities was only slightly lower—68.3 percent. The two immigrant groups most likely to cluster in cities, the Irish and Russians, represented both old and new with over five-sixths in urban communities. Among Italians and Hungarians the proportion was three-quarters; among the English, Scots, Austrian, Greek, and Chinese, it was over seventenths; among Germans, two-thirds, and among Swedes, threefifths.

The South tried to attract immigrants, especially to man its expanding railroad systems or work the land. In 1903 the Southern Railway settled 2,000 families on 2.27 million acres. The Southern Pacific sold 3 million acres in the ten years from 1894; the Mobile and Ohio sold off 600,000 acres and the Illinois Central sold off almost as much in Alabama, Kentucky, Louisiana, and Mississippi. The Louisville and Nashville sold 105, 143 acres of farm land and 255,540 acres of timber and mineral lands along its lines in 1903. Twice a month the main southern railroads ran special homesellers' trains charging prospective settlers half fare. Yet these efforts resulted in only small colonies of Danes, Germans, Hungarians, Italians, and Swedes settled along the southern railroads, as were some migrants from the Midwest. Dunkers and other religious sects settled in Alabama and Georgia. Nevertheless, as southern historian C. Vann Woodward concludes, "The flood tide of European immigration, in 1899–1910, swept past the South leaving it almost untouched and further isolating it in its peculiarities from the rest of the country." Thus the small northern state of Connecticut received more immigrants than the entire South and New Jersey received twice as many.

It is, however, true that most immigrants preferred cities to the countryside. Attempts to induce old immigrants with neither aptitude nor experience to take up farming fell by the wayside. Thus organizations like the Irish Catholic Benevolent Union could not turn Irish laborers into independent farmers in Virginia, Kansas, and Minnesota. Potato farming back home was simple. It involved planting, trenching, and digging potatoes. This was no preparation for running a farm of 160 acres in the Golden West. Among the new immigrants only Czechs and Germans from Russia took readily to agriculture. They had the advantage of arriving early enough to find land still available on the prairies. Moreover, it was similar terrain to that of their native steppes. Pioneer farmers cleared the trees or prairie grasses and exploited the land. They grew the same crop again and again until the soil was too impoverished for them to continue. In Marcus Lee Hansen's striking phrase, "The land was mined, not farmed."

Most new immigrants lacked the capital necessary to start a farm. Difficulty in understanding English was a greater handicap on a farm than in a factory. In comparison with the convivial atmosphere of European farming communities, rural life in America was solitary. Understandably, prospective immigrant farmers preferred densely settled areas where they could use specialized, intensive methods without much capital outlay. Thus Poles in Connecticut and Massachusetts grew tobacco and onions. Italians cultivated vegetables in New York and New Jersey, vines in California, and fruit and cotton in Texas and Louisiana. Here they could make a novel contribution to America. For example, Portuguese immigrant J. B. Avida introduced the sweet potato. When new immigrants did become involved in traditional farming, it was as hired hands during harvesttime.

Many new immigrants concluded from their harsh experience in the Old World that farming was physically and psychically draining. Thus Joseph Lopreato studies Italian patterns of settlement in his *Italian Americans* (1970) and concludes how Italian immigrants considered farming a punishment for both stomach and soul. The contadini's reliance on agriculture had "reduced him nearly to the status of the donkey and goat." Hence, for such people immigration was a liberation from the arduous work and penury of agricultural labor and they did not want to return to it.

Moreover, it was primarily the industrial revolution with its splendid promise of opportunity that had attracted immigrants, old and new. Indeed, without massive immigration the United States could not have developed industrially at anything like the rate it did. More significantly, the new immigrants' willingness to take on menial work enabled earlier groups to assume more skilled work or to enter the professions. The Dillingham Commission of 1907–10 disclosed that immigrants accounted for 57.9 percent of employees in twenty-one industries and, on average, some two-thirds of them came from southern and eastern Europe. The fraction was higher in certain industries: clothing, textiles, coal mining, and meat packing.

In any ethnic group the first group of immigrants were young men in their late teens or twenties. Thus up to the turn of the century 78 percent of Italian and 95 percent of Greek immigrants were men. Twenty years later the emphasis had shifted in some ethnic groups. In 1920 the proportion of men and women among Polish immigrants was about even, whereas among Slovaks 65 percent were female and among Italians 48 percent were female. However, almost 80 percent of Greek immigrants were male. Some male migrants were known as "birds of passage" because they moved across the Atlantic in either direction. According to seasonal employment prospects. Thus in the period 1908–14, 6,709,357 immigrants arrived in, and 2,063,767 people departed from the United States, either temporarily or permanently. In this same period over half the Hungarians, Italians, Croatians, and Slovacs went home. After all their original intention was to earn money for their families at home and return with it. Between 1908 and 1916 1,215,598 Italians left America. In the end, only 67 percent of all immigrants settled permanently in the United States. However, many immigrants who had originally planned to return home once they had made some money kept postponing the journey and, in the end, settled as naturalized citizens of their new country.

As the nature of immigration was changing, so, too, was industry itself. Historian Philip Taylor finds that: "Rapid economic growth in the United States did not merely draw in more immigrants: it provided an especially large number of opportunities for the lower grades of worker." As we have already observed, technological developments had altered not only industry but also its needs. New processes and mechanical inventions eliminated traditional methods. Specialized skill was no longer at a premium among the work force. Brawn replaced brain. What manufacturers and mine owners sought was unskilled, cheap labor. After a brief training, inexperienced novices could operate automatic looms and frames as successfully as had skilled weavers in the old days. Mechanical cutters ate through coal faces with a speed that the most experienced miner could not match. Before 1890 most miners in the bituminous coalfields of Pennsylvania had been native Americans or immigrants from Britain, Ireland, and Germany. Thereafter, they were usually new immigrants—Poles and Italians, Magyars and Slovaks. In the same way the textile factories of New England at Fall River, New Bedford, Lowell, and elsewhere underwent a change in personnel. From being exclusively British, Irish, and French-Canadian, they became heterogeneous, employing Poles and Portuguese, Syrians and Greeks.

For a long time it was said that immigrants found employment according to their physical and mental abilities. Thus Poles and Slavs worked in heavy industry because they were supposed to be strong, stupid, and submissive. But Victor Greene in *For God and Country* (1975) dismisses any notion that Slavs were submissive and stupid. While it is true that Slavs were the most physically robust of immigrants and tolerated degrading conditions in mines, their original aim in coming to America was to earn enough money to be able to return home and buy land there. Thus they accepted a harsh lot. In the mines they could earn more than in mills. English workers were noted for their skill and versatility. For example, cutlers from Sheffield, who had had a long and careful training, were in special demand because they could turn their hand to anything in the iron industry. In New York and

At the turn of the century, street and market were one in such thoroughfares as Hester Street, a social center of the Jewish immigrant community from eastern and central Europe, on New York's Lower East Side. (Detroit Publishing Company; Library of Congress).

Chicago Russian Jews, widely known for their dexterity, made women's clothes their particular specialty.

However, who worked where and when depended on all sorts of social and economic factors. Italians preferred to work outdoors, rather than in factories. It was largely Italian labor that built the New York subways and some major bridges. In Florida they rolled cigars; in California they cultivated vines; on the prairies they helped lay tracks for the transcontinental railroads. French-Canadians worked in the textile factories of New England because their immigration coincided with increased demand for labor in the cotton mills of states close to Quebec. Moreover, the mills of Maine, Massachusetts, and Rhode Island took on women and children as well as men. Thus whole families could be employed together.

Only 11 percent of Jewish immigrants had worked as tailors in Europe but they now turned to the rag trade, despite its exploitation, for a mix of cultural, social, and career reasons. In New York the rag trade employed about 50 percent of Jewish men and boys living in the city and two-thirds of the city's Jewish wage earners. Journalist Hutchins Hapgood described in his *Spirit of the Ghetto* (1902) how homes became work rooms. "During the day the front room, bedroom, and kitchen became a whirling, churning factory, where men, women and children worked at the sewing and pressing machines." The clothing industry was not attractive to Russian Jews because it offered work to women and children. Their women usually stayed at home after marriage. Their children stayed at school until they were in their teens. The principal attraction of the rag trade was as an avenue to commerce. Pay was by piecework. Thus earnings were related to individual effort. Workers could therefore amass capital and invest in their own businesses. Jewish workers also found employment in cigar factories, printing works, and book binderies. It has been thought the sweatshops offered the opportunity to discuss Zionism. Yet the World Zionist Organization, founded in Basle in 1897, was slow to attract Jewish Americans and had no more than 20,000 active supporters in the United States by 1914. It ran counter to the philosophy of the Reform tradition that had no interest in the idea of a restored Jewish state. Socialists such as Morris Hillquit considered the Jewish state an irrelevance.

Moreover, the major cities were centers of commerce and provided extra opportunities for skilled work in handicrafts and such household manufacture as shoes, clothes, tableware, and toys. In his study of Italians, Rumanians, and Slovaks in Cleveland, *Peasants and Strangers* (1975), Josef Barton finds that it was those immigrants who had developed skills as merchants or artisans in Europe who adapted themselves most easily to American towns. About half the subjects he studied entered skilled work in the United States and another 40 percent immediately took white-collar jobs. Within twenty years such immigrants had settled comfortably in the middle class. Sixty-six percent of all Jewish men and boys who immigrated to the United States in the period 1899–1914 were classified as skilled, compared with an average of only 20 percent for all male immigrants in the same period. Their adjustment to life in American towns was made easier because they had valuable skills. Sicilian fishermen also adjusted quite easily. They immigrated with their families and were thus better able to cope with social dislocation. Moreover, they were used to business, originally fishing and selling their catch. In comparison, peasants, laborers, and their sons found it far more difficult to rise socially in the United States. Yet Andrew F. Rolle observes in *The Immigrant Upraised* (1968) how some Italians went west and prospered. In fact, the few who moved to the country succeeded better and became more quickly assimilated than those who remained in urban ghettos. However, for the majority, such a move was out of the question, especially if they ever intended to return to Europe.

Many immigrants became entrepreneurs, first on a small scale, as peddlers. According to contemporary observer Charles Bernheimer, in 1905 New York had almost 1,000 Jewish "peddlers and keepers of stands, the number varying according to the season of the year." In Sholom Aleichem's stories, the young men are willing to try any jobs. Eli works as a tailor, as a waiter in a delicatessen, and is ready to shovel snow—but not on the street. "Do you want your portion of snow brought to you in the house?" asks Pinney. When the family of seven decide to sell candy and cigarettes, they scare away prospective customers because there are so many of them behind the counter.

Greek entrepreneurs moved into confectionery as described by Theodore Saloutos in his *The Greeks in the United States* (1963).

It has been estimated that 70 percent of Greek makers of candy in the United States were in Chicago, "the Acropolis of the Greek-American candy business," according to Saloutos. The Greek newspaper, *Hellinikos Astir* reported in 1904 how "practically every busy corner in Chicago is occupied by a Greek candy store." It was their strict dietary laws that led many Jews into the meat and poultry trade. In 1900 80 percent of the wholesale meat trade in New York and 50 percent of the retail trade was run by Jews. There were about 500 Jewish bakers in New York at this time. As immigrants prospered, ethnic restaurants opened to cater to their special tastes and some, such as *Mama Leone's* (1906) which specialized in Italian dishes, quickly gained a reputation nationwide.

Acculturation

"We call England the mother country," observed humorist Robert Benchley, "because most of us come from Poland or Italy." Indeed, it was only the British, with conspicuous advantages of language and literacy, who remained indifferent to American citizenship. John Spargo, Cornish-born writer and leading Socialist, recalled his naturalization process in 1908 with some distaste. He thought himself insolently treated by the clerk, a "young man of a class closely related to the yahoo and the hoodlum," who was about to be indicted for election fraud. He found himself having to wait in line behind other candidates advanced by crooked politicians cultivating votes and was affronted by questions about anarchism and polygamy. Yet to many new immigrants American citizenship was a precious prize. In his *Destination America* (1976), Maldwyn Jones relates how Moses Kirshblum, a Polish Jew who emigrated from Bialystok in 1923, came to be naturalized. The story was first told by his son, a New York rabbi.

He knew well enough that a man who cannot speak English—how is he going to become a citizen? But he persevered and the day came when he went before a judge, who questioned him. I remember he was asked: "Are you a bigamist?" He had never heard of the word, and he said "yes" with great pride. "Do you have any prison record?" and again he said "yes." He figured he can't go wrong by saying "yes."

Then the judge began to ask him about certain American holidays. He said: "Do you remember what the Fourth of July is?" And he said "Labor Day." But toward the end he turned pleadingly to the judge and says, "Mr. Judge, please do me a taver (favor). I want to be an American citizen." And the judge—because he was deeply moved by this old man pleading for American citizenship—said tearfully, "A citizen you shall be," and granted him papers.

The immigrant's key to acculturation in America was his new citizenship. It confirmed a new identity. However, for a long time immigrants were American only in name. Their language, customs, and religions were quite different from those of many natives. Their lives revolved around their own ethnic group.

Cities became clusters of ghettos. Older cities in particular became centers for immigrants. The census of 1910 disclosed how roughly 75 percent of the population of New York, Boston, Chicago, Detroit, and Cleveland was composed of first- and second-generation immigrants, mainly new immigrants. There were also large numbers of immigrants in Philadelphia and Providence, cities closely linked to industrial sites by rail. San Francisco was noted for its immigrant communities, especially Chinese and Japanese. In 1916 the mother tongue of 72 percent of its population was a language other than English.

At the outset of World War I 1.4 million Jews lived in New York—more than the city's entire population in 1870. In time the Lower East Side had the largest Jewish community in the world, crammed into an area a little more than a square mile eastward from the Bowery almost to the East River and southward from 14th Street to Brooklyn Bridge. The east European Jews who lived there include Galicians, Lithuanians, Poles, Rumanians, Ukrainians, and Levantines, each at first living in distinct neighborhoods. Sholom Aleichem's fictional shtetl of Kasvilevka, "a town no bigger than a yawn," was transported entire to New York. "All Kasvilevka is here!" cries the boy Mottel. "Velvel" has become "Willy," "Mendel" has become "Mike." The butcher has become a rabbi while the doctor pushes a peddler's pushcart. Nevertheless, the sounds and smells are those of the old shtetl. "He who has not seen a New York street has never seen anything beautiful," says Mottel. However, in a private letter Sholom Aleichem confesses, "You know well the ghetto of this hell they call New York."

Chicago was divided among Germans (north of the Loop), Poles (northwest), Italians and Jews (west), Bohemians and Lithuanians (southwest), and Irish (south). These distinctive ethnic communities survived until after World War II. Immigrant groups that took over particular districts were as much regional as national in character. New York's Italian districts comprised Neapolitans and Calabrians (Mulberry Bend); Genoese (Baxter Street); Sicilians (Elizabeth Street); and Tyrolese (West Sixty-ninth Street).

The culture of ethnic ghettos owed little to English tradition. The facades of city houses and apartment blocks would not have been out of place in continental Europe. Thus Orchard Street was reminiscent of old Vienna, Hester Street of Warsaw. Taste and smell were as much affected as sight and sound. The new American cuisine included Irish stew, Hungarian goulash, German liverwurst, Russian borscht, Rumanian pastrami, Italian lasagne, Greek moussaka, and Jewish bagels and lox.

The process of immigrants' acculturation in American cities was made more complicated by the fact that the cities themselves were in transition. Although the cities offered special opportunities for work and leisure, they had numerous problems. The worst consequences of precipitate urban growth included low wages, bad housing and sanitation, general squalor, and high levels of mortality. Moreover, although economic life was more structured in cities, everyday social life became somewhat impersonal, and social divisions between classes widened. Immigrants, especially those from far less developed nations, endured hardship and, sometimes, degradation and morbid disillusionment.

A particular problem was finding enough room to live in, even to breathe in. In 1912 English novelist Arnold Bennett noted of tenements in Rivington Street how "the architecture seemed to sweat humanity at every window and door." Moses Rischin in *The Promised City: New York's Jews 1870–1914* (1962) comments how "New York's division of city lots into standard rectangular plots, 25 feet by 100 feet deep made decent human accommodation impossible" and his observation is shared by other authors. Builders found it impossible to construct profitable blocks that allowed for proper light and ventilation to inner rooms. Such was the value of land and the pressure for accommodation that space was at a premium. Architects had a solution for compressing the maximum number of people into the minimum amount of space, the double-decker dumbbell tenement, so called because the middle part of the ground plan tapered in. The idea was to allow light and air to the central portions of the building without reducing the width of front and back. The dumbbell tenement usually had four apartments to each of its six or seven floors, two on either side of the separating corridor. Only one of the three or four rooms received light and air from the street at the front or the yard at the back. The air shaft separating the tenements at the sides was no more than five feet wide along its fifty or sixty feet length. Lavatories were communal with four per floor situated off the airshafts.

In a fire, tenement blocks were deathtraps. Of 250 reported deaths by fire in Manhattan in the period 1902–9, a third were victims of fires in the Lower East Side. Sometimes overcrowded families increased danger to themselves by piling extra furniture and belongings on fire escapes and thus impeding their only escape route.

The problem of overcrowding was not confined to New York. Some parts of Chicago had three times as many people as the most crowded parts of Tokyo and Calcutta. In one Polish ghetto there was an average of 340 people to every acre in 1901. In one sector of only three blocks there lived 7,300 children. This Polish district was described as "nothing more than an infested wall-to-wall carpet of rooted wood and crumbling concrete." Whole neighborhoods were congested, filthy, and foul. Offal and manure littered the street along with trash and garbage. Thus it was hardly surprising that, in the large cities, consumption and pneumonia, bronchitis and diarrhea were endemic. Immigrant communities were prone to outbreaks of cholera, typhus, and typhoid. Indeed, at the turn of the century Pittsburgh had the highest mortality rate for typhoid in the world, 1.30 per 1,000. Because immigrants found food expensive, they restricted their diet to the cheapest food, heavy in fats and starches and low on protein. Reformer John Spargo in *The Bitter Cry of the Children* (1906) commented that some immigrants' children had to go for long periods without sufficient nutrition and then their stomachs became "too weak by reason of chronic hunger and malnutrition to stand good and nutritious food."

A principal cause of tuberculosis was the abrupt move from a life in the open air to the confinement of a dense urban ghetto. New York physician Dr. Antonio Stella remarked in 1904 how "Six months of life in the tenements are sufficient to turn the sturdy youth from Calabria, the brawny fisherman of Sicily, the robust women from Abruzzi and Basilicata into the pale, flabby, undersized creatures we see dragging along the streets of New York and Chicago, such a painful contrast to the native population. Six months more of the gradual deterioration, and the soil for the bacillus tuberculosis is amply prepared." Dr. Stella knew that conditions in sweatshops aggravated the danger of contracting tuberculosis. Italian women, already exhausted by much childbearing, now spent their precious little energy working excessive hours in factories. Thus there was a higher death rate from tuberculosis among Italian women than Italian men. Although the tenth ward had the highest rate of occupancy in New York, it had one of the lowest death rates, a fact ascribed to high standards of cleanliness and strict dietary laws among the Jewish population.

In their new and alien environment immigrants required special services: mutual aid societies; foreign language businesses and newspapers; churches and synagogues for culture, ceremony, and consolation. Various mutual aid societies were first organized on a local basis but, in time, joined federations organized according to ethnic groups. Thus such societies as the Polish National Alliance (1880), L'Association Canada-Américiane (1896), the Order of Sons of Italy (1905), and the Pan Hellenic Union (1907) developed. Those immigrants who were ambitious sought assistance from others thus motivated and together they might found a mutual benevolent society to provide loans or grants. Thus the Japanese *ken* and the Chinese *hui* associations provided the advice and means whereby immigrants secured loans and started business enterprises.

Italians also had fraternal associations but their funds were used to support individuals in need, rather than businesses. Thus the *Societa Calabria,* founded in Utica, New York, in 1903, was an exclusive lodge to encourage "concord, brotherhood, education, instruction, work, honesty." Edward Banfield in *The Moral Basis of a Backward Society* (1958) traces the Italians' emphasis on family needs and loyalty above all to the isolation, poverty, and feudalism of the Mezzogiorno, which sometimes perpetuated rivalries from the Old World.

Since bankers were unsympathetic to the needs of immigrants and reluctant to finance their business ventures, various immigrants created their own ethnic banks. One, Amadeo Pietro Giannini's Bank of Italy in San Francisco, evolved into a major financial institution. Giannini was a successful merchant who founded his bank to protect other Italian immigrants from loan sharks and to encourage Italian businesses. After he lost his building in the San Francisco earthquake and fire of 1906, he did business on the wharves, rather than wait until his new building was ready. When he died in 1949, the bank, retitled Bank of America, was the largest bank in the world.

Of all the different ethnic groups the Jews were most prepared to unite for the sake of their people as a whole. Successive Russian pogroms provided a continuous reminder of cultural obligations to others in distress. Moreover, Jewish religious observance preserved cultural identity and solidarity. However, with the passing years many German Jews became Americanized in their entire attitude. The economic status of German Jews was especially high—higher than that of any other group of immigrants. A federal survey of 1890 disclosed that about half the German Jews were in business, a fifth were clerks or accountants, an eight were artisans, a tenth were salesmen, and one in twenty was a doctor, lawyer, or other professional. Only one in two hundred was a peddler. In Germany they had mixed freely with other Germans and in the United States the Ashkenazim (mainly German Jews, from the German word for Hebrew) were closely identified with Germany. Indeed, many seemed more German than Jewish since they spoke German, lived alongside other German-Americans, and were generally devoted to German culture. Reform synagogues abandoned ancient rituals and introduced

"Knee pants at 45 cents a dozen," a study of a Ludlow Street sweatshop in the rag trade by Danish immigrant, police journalist, and amateur photographer Jacob Riis. Riis first revealed the hazards and poverty of tenement life on the Lower East Side in his *How the Other Half Lives* of 1890 but it was only later, when printing techniques could render half-tone photos accurately, that Riis's stark photos were published in successive editions of his book, thereby motivating social reformers. (Library of Congress).

sermons, mixed choirs, and family pews. The Reform movement was given theological respectability by the arrival of learned rabbis from Europe. The most influential was Isaac Wise who published the *Israelite* and made Cincinnati the center of Reform Judaism. By 1890 there were more members of Reform than Orthodox synagogues. Yet without the whip of persecution religion flagged. Many Russian Jews preferred socialism to religion. They could discuss it freely in the garment factories of New York.

The influx of Russian and other east Europeans Jews prompted the established community to offer help by way of the Hebrew Immigrant Aid Society, the Educational Alliance, and other organizations. The newcomers disliked charity from Americanized Jews and were quite capable of founding their own Hebrew Sheltering Society in 1890. They also established 300 schools to teach Hebrew. The newcomers brought an intense piety, sustained by strict religious observance, and deep commitment to secular causes—socialism, anarchism, and Zionism.

On the Lower East Side east European Jews created and preserved special religious practices. Thus they established religious functionaries: the *shohet* (ritual slaughterer); the *mohel* (circumcizer); and the *masgiach* (inspector of dietary laws). They also founded a special religious school, the *cheder,* a school with one teacher meeting after public school was finished for the day. These attempts slowed down but could not prevent the ultimate erosion of Mosaic law and Jewish religious practices. A survey of 1908 disclosed that only 28 percent of Jewish children in New York received even the most rudimentary religious education. Second-generation Jewish-Americans discovered they had to make a living in a business world that worked according to the Christian calendar.

Established Jewish-Americans were much disturbed by the appearance of Jews from eastern Europe and also disliked their religious orthodoxy and political radicalism. They were concerned that the advent of such unwelcome strangers might stimulate antisemitism and upset their own cherished status. In the early 1900s the American Jewish community was dismissed by learned European Jews as a community of peddlers. Sholom Aleichem parodied this point of view and its underlying arrogance. "Those who have changed the verse of 'From Zion will come forth the Law and the word of the Lord from Jersusalem' to read 'From Kiev will come forth the Law and the word of the Lord from Amsterdam,' will now have to change it once again to read: 'From America will come forth the Law and the word of the Lord from New York.' . . . I, who often indulge in jest, mean this very seriously."

The Roman Catholic church was the principal church of immigrants. In 1900 there were 70 dioceses and 10,000 churches. For, as historian John Higham explains, "immigration transformed the church into an ethnic fortress." Yet the Roman Catholic church became a source of controversy among immigrants rather than a means of assimilation. Catholicism divided, as well as united, new immigrants from old. The newer groups wanted to create autonomous religious groups but found this desire in conflict with the need to conform to a centralized authority. Moreover, the Catholic hierarchy, many of whom where Irish-Americans, staunchly opposed attempts to create national or ethnic parishes because they considered them a potential threat to church unity.

However, German-Americans who were Catholic resented Irish-American dominance of the church and now found that Italian, Polish, and French-Canadian immigrants did so, too. Thus controversies arose over the ethnicity of the priest, the nature of festivals, and the language of worship. In New England parishes Irish-American priests gave their sermons in English and this alienated French-Canadians. They regarded sermons in English as yet another attempt to undermine their ethnic culture.

Polish-Americans were equally disturbed by Irish-American domination in the Roman Catholic church. Here, it was also a matter of beliefs, as well as language. Helen Znaniecka Lopata in *Polish Americans* (1976) explains how "Polish peasants . . . combined a Polish version of Catholicism with pagan and magical beliefs in animated natural objects and spirits." Alan M. Kraut provides general examples. "A Polish immigrant . . . might sprinkle the floors of a newly acquired apartment with salt or coins before moving in to ensure his family's prosperity in their abode. Charms to ward off illness, assure fertility, or attract a particular member of the opposite sex were sometimes used in tandem with lighting candles in church or praying, rosary beads in hand." Catholicism in Italy, according to Rudolph Vecoli in "Contadini in Chicago," for the *Journal of American History* of December 1964, was much influenced by a system of *clientelismo,* in which local saints were invoked to act as intermediary between simple man and God, a "lofty, distant figure." Thus Italians prayed to individual saints, who had a right to oversee particular areas of human activity. The high point in the year of many a small Italian town was the saint's festival, in which a statue of the patron saint of the town was carried aloft through the streets as part of a long procession. Thus in Naples they honored San Gennaro, in Palermo Santa Rossilia, and in Catania, Sant' Agata. American Catholics were somewhat disturbed when the new immigrants continued such practices in the United States. Protestants regarded them as pagan rites.

There were schisms in the church. After confrontations with Irish-American bishops in Buffalo, Scranton, and Chicago, several Polish parishes created their own separate Polish National Catholic church and used the Polish language, partly to emphasize their differences from other ethnic groups that had, in Europe, oppressed them—Russians, Prussians, and Austrians. To prevent further schisms, the Vatican tacitly conceded to demands for national or ethnic parishs. In 1908 Bishop Paul Rhode, the first American bishop of Polish origin, was appointed auxiliary bishop of Chicago.

Second-generation immigrants began to dispense with any religious customs that conflicted with the new social or economic expectation of American life. However, whether Catholic or Jewish, they did not seek conversion to Protestantism, despite periodic attempts by some Protestants to claim them. For Orthodox Jews changes in dress conflicted with religious observance. As a sign of modesty married women were expected to wear a *sheitel,* or wig, in public. However, many young immigrant wives abandoned the sheitel to conform to American styles that their husbands found more attractive. After all, their husbands had shaved off their beards. The elimination of the wig was women's compromise with American customs. As young immigrants became more acclimatized, women from societies that had prearranged marriages expected to be able to choose their own husbands on the basis of romantic love, and immigrant men also wanted to make such a choice of wives.

The foreign language newspaper was a crucial immigrant institution. It nourished group solidarity. Between 1884 and 1920 3,500 new foreign language papers appeared. Only a fraction survived and the total number of foreign language papers increased only a little, from 794 to 1,052 in this same period. In 1920 there were 276 German language newspapers. Some of these were city dailies such as the *New Yorker Staatszeitung,* the *Anzeiger des Westens* of St. Louis, the *Cincinnati Volkesblatt,* and the *Wisconsin Banner.* In 1920 there were also 118 newspapers in Spanish and Portuguese, 111 in the various Scandinavian languages, 98 in Italian, 70 in Polish, 51 in Czech, 46 in French, 42 in Slovenian, 39 in Yiddish, as well as others in Dutch, Finnish, Greek, Japanese, Lithuanian, Magyar, Russian, and Ukrainian.

These papers were not simply national or religious journals based on European models. To appeal to uneducated immigrants they had to be written in a popular, even vernacular, style. For example, from 1897 immigrant novelist Abraham Cahan began to transform the *Jewish Daily Forward* from a sectarian journal into a popular newspaper with a circulation of 250,000 copies. He simplified its style, substituting American Yiddish for its previous highbrow language. Its agony column, *Bintel Brief* (Bundle of Letters), advertized the plights of immigrants and answered their problems. It was just as important for other language papers to sell copies. Thus conventional commercial values superseded nationalist or radical ethics. In time sensational stories and special features replaced prolix editorials. It was, after all, a Hungarian immigrant, Joseph Pulitzer, who had led the way with a tabloid written in English, the *New York World.*

Unlike native Americans, first-generation immigrants had not been inculcated with faith in progress. Their experiences in Europe had made them fatalistic. As far as they were concerned, government was not a tool to be used but an obstacle to be evaded. Proposals to regulate trusts, reform municipal government, and give women the vote were important moral and political issues to native Americans. However, to first-generation immigrants they were meaningless abstractions. What immigrants preferred was immediate practical solutions to the problems of acculturation in a strange land. Reformers could not hope to retain immigrant loyalty when they offered devices such as the referendum and the recall. Help was at hand. It was the local political boss who gave immigrants employment, protection, and accommodation. It was he they repaid. As Oscar Handlin puts it, "the machine was the means through which the immigrants sought services no one else performed."

Urban bosses gained money and patronage by supplying cities with public utilities—water, gas, public transport, and electricity—and the construction of civic buildings, sewage systems, street pavements, and docks. They also ensured that enough hospitals, schools, museums, and concert halls were built. Bosses owed their power to their ability to deliver votes at elections. They found immigrants accommodation and work, and helped them solve certain problems, in exchange for political support. Although they were opportunists, bosses provided genuine (and badly needed) services.

George Washington Plunkitt, a Tammany boss, recorded his impression of ethnic politics in New York at the turn of the century. He admired the skill of his man Johnnie Ahearn who had to build a coalition in the fourth district that was half Irish and half Jewish. Johnnie Ahearn was liked by both groups. "He eats corned beef and kosher meat with equal nonchalance, and it's all the same to him whether he takes off his hat in the church or pulls it down over his ears in the synagogue." Unlike well-intentioned but insensitive reformers, both men realized that immigrants were most supportive of those politicians who respected their need to retain their cultural identity, even as they were becoming acculturated to life in America. Social worker Jane Addams of Chicago knew only too well why bosses succeeded where middle-class reformers failed. "Primitive people such as the southern Italian peasants who live in the 9th ward, deep down in their hearts admire nothing so much as a good man. The successful candidate must be a good man according to the standards of his constituents. He must not attempt to hold up a morality beyond them, nor must he attempt to reform or change the standard."

First in the political field were Irish machines. The criminologist Mark Haller explains, "A complex system of Irish politicians, gamblers and police shared in the profits of gambling, protected gambling interests and built careers in the police department or city politics." The heyday of Irish bosses was from 1870 to 1920. The Irish had arrived earlier and, unlike many who followed, spoke English. They also knew how democratic government was supposed to work. As Leonard Dinnerstein and David Reimers acutely observe, "For two centuries they had been oppressed by the English in Ireland and during that period they had learned how Anglo-Saxon law could be manipulated to satisfy the ends of those who governed and work against those who did not." From the Catholic church they learned organization and discipline. Thus among ethnic groups they alone had the understanding and techniques to dominate politics after the Civil War. "Honest John" Kelly, Richard Croker, and Charles F. Murphy in succession ruled Tammany Hall. Mike McDonald, Johnny Rogers, Michael ("Hinky Dink") Denna, and ("Bathhouse John") Joseph Coughlin dominated Chicago. Colonel Ed Butler was the Democratic boss who ruled the Republican city of St. Louis. Hugh O'Brien and Patrick A. Collins were first and second in a long line of Irish mayors of Boston. In 1913 Massachusetts elected its first Irish senator, David Ignatius Walsh. These men led the first and most enduring ethnic bloc in American politics. On the whole the Irish remained loyal to the Democrats and resisted Republican attempts to entice them away.

Middle-class reformers based on settlement houses that were usually secular were far more successful in helping immigrants than interfering Protestant reformers who wanted immigrants to renounce their old life-styles and religions. Settlement houses were part residence, part club, part school. The most famous settlement houses were the Hull House of Jane Addams in Chicago (1889), the New York City University Settlement of James B. Reynolds (1886), and the Henry Street Settlement of Lillian Wald (1893). The Henry Street Settlement was opened in 1893 when philanthropists invited Lillian Wald, a nurse who had recently qualified, to look after the poorest immigrants on the Lower East Side. She was inspired to devise a course on home nursing, taught in an old building on Henry Street. Its success led to her extending the services offered there. Settlement house workers were ahead of their time in creating responsible day-care centers for working mothers. They provided children with meals, schooling, and health care. They offered classes in cooking to teach immigrants about American preparation of food. Sometimes the educational process worked both ways. In Milwaukee settlement workers and immigrants compiled German, Polish, and Russian recipes into *The Settlement Cook Book,* which provided the house with a welcome source of extra income.

Immigrant Perspectives and Creative Achievement

Although the political contribution of new immigrants was, at first, hesitant, their cultural contribution was distinctive from the outset. Through the simultaneous experiences of displacement and assimilation many second-generation immigrants showed a special feeling for the theater. Playing a part and projecting a personality were second nature.

It was in the theater that Jewish artistry in particular first achieved its fullest expression. Three Yiddish theaters on the Bowery specialized in problem plays. The plots were drawn from comic operas and melodramas, the dialogue from vaudeville patter. They were immensely popular among audiences of all classes. It is estimated that 2 million people attended 1,100 performances each year at the turn of the century. The opening of the theatrical season was as important an annual event in the life of New York Jews as the Feast of Passover. The extraordinary popularity of the Yiddish theater was due to its realism. In the plays of Jacob Gordin audiences could recognize and identify with situations from everyday life. The most influential statement about assimilation was *The Melting Pot* (1908), a play by Israel Zangwill, an English Jew. The subsequent contribution of American Jews to vaudeville, radio, and cinema became a legend of show business.

The Melting Pot received mixed reviews when it opened at the Columbia Theater, Washington, D.C., in 1908. It told of Jewish immigrant David Quixano who had fled from Russia after his family were slaughtered in a pogrom. He writes a symphony, falls in love with a Christian aristocrat, who is also an immigrant, and, defying Jewish law against intermarriage, decides to marry her. The play was most welcome to those who argued for an American melting pot, such as President Theodore Roosevelt who sat beside the author's wife at the premiere. TR thought so many different immigrant languages and cultural traditions were an impediment to true American nationalism. He declared:

The man who becomes completely Americanized—who celebrates our constitutional Centennial instead of the Queen's Jubilee, or the Fourth of July rather than St. Patrick's Day and who talks 'United States' instead of the dialect of the country which he has of his own free will abandoned—is not only doing his plain duty by his adopted land, but is also rendering himself a service of immeasurable value.

The idea of the melting pot was not, in itself, new. Hector St. John de Crèvecoeur wrote in *Letters from an American Farmer* (1782):

He is an American, who, leaving behind all his ancient prejudices and manners, receives new ones from the mode of life he has embraced, the new government he obeys, and the new rank he holds. He becomes an American by being received in the broad lap of our great *Alma Mater*. Here individuals of all nations are melted into a new race of man, whose labours and posterity will one day cause great changes in the world.

The concept of the melting pot was flattering to Americans in a number of ways. It suggested the United States was a haven for refugees and that once these refugees had been exposed to American culture and democracy, they would undergo a special metamorphosis. They would become Americans, culturally and biologically better than any European.

In the first act of *The Melting Pot* David Quixano remarks, "America is God's Crucible, the great Melting Pot where all the races of Europe are melting and reforming!" However, immigrant papers criticized *The Melting Pot* as a sentimental and idealized view of assimilation. In particular, Jewish papers were offended by the idea of intermarriage as an avenue to assimilation. They also disliked the idea of different ethnic groups arriving in America, each with its distinct cultural identity, soon to be submerged in a melting pot. In the last act David declares, "A fig for your feuds and vendettas! Germans and Frenchmen, Irishmen and Englishmen, Jews and Russians—into the crucible with you all! God is making the American!" However, the play offended those who were trying to find a way of preserving their ethnic culture and identity whilst becoming acculturated to American society, because it implied that losing the first was the price to be paid for gaining the second.

Immigrant literature, sometimes written by first-generation immigrants, sometimes by their descendants, took different stands according to the interest of the particular ethnic group. The Britons emphasized the problems of settlement and colonization; the French explored a romantic dream of freedom. In the nineteenth century two distinctive traditions emerged in which writers focused their attention on either the land or the city. Thus, for example, Scandinavian writers were primarily responsible for literature about pioneer settlement on land in the West, a crucial experience of their ethnic group, while Jewish writers concentrated on American cities with their numerous promises of freedom and individual freedom but also Americanization.

The Jewish contribution to American literature was outstanding. It began with *Yekl: A Tale of the New York Ghetto* (1896) by Abraham Cahan, the first novel of American immigrants written by a naturalized citizen in English. While Cahan's numerous short stories show just how painful was assimilation for Jewish immigrants, his masterpiece, *The Rise of David Levinsky* (1917), is a classic distillation of the Jewish immigrant experience, the search for individual economic success within the social context of assimilation. David Levinsky, a Russian immigrant, compromises his religious values and his enthusiasm for scholarship in exchange for material success. He becomes a clothing manufacturer, employs cheap labor to maximize profits, evades union regulations about work, and becomes virulently opposed to socialism. Early on, young David laments how the process of becoming Americanized undermined his religious practices. "The very clothes I wore and the very food I ate had a fatal effect on my religious habits." Later, after success has changed him, he mourns his lost self, how "David, the poor lad swinging over a

Talmud volume at the preacher's Synagogue, seems to have more in common with my inner identity than David Levinsky, the well-known cloak manufacturer." Thus the novel expresses the intense love for America of those immigrants who have succeeded but also a sense of loss of part of themselves. Cahan thought American capitalism had created an unjust society but believed the best way to further the cause of socialism was to describe society with all its corruption.

Assimilation

In *The Uprooted* Oscar Handlin described the immigrant as a man at the crossroads who moved alone. For although his neighbors were equally affected by adverse circumstances, many would never leave. He stood alone, sometimes with his family, sometimes not. Stoyan Christowe, a Bulgarian immigrant, reviewed his feelings in "Half an American," an article of 1929 and asked himself, "Has the storm in my being lulled now that I have spent two-thirds of my life in a struggle for readjustment and adaptation?" He answered "Yes" but could still not feel completely American. "I shall always be the adopted child, not the real son, of a mother that I love more than the one that gave me birth."

At first immigrants felt isolated, not only because they were unfamiliar with America itself but also because other members of their ethnic group treated them as misfits and put pressure on them to conform and become American as quickly as possible. English historian P.A.M. Taylor in *The Distant Magnet* (1971) challenges an old assumption that assimilation was a smooth transition. He believes that the whole process of assimilation "was a series of conflicts between competing influences from the wider American society battling with the entrenched leadership of families or of ethnic institutions." Immigrants were also influenced by advice from benevolent societies, public schools, and urban politicians.

Stephan Thornstrom described America's "ideology of mobility" in *Poverty and Progressive* (1964). In theory, the United States ran a fluid society based on competitiveness in which individuals succeeded according to their enterprise and merit. Failure must be ascribed to individual inadequacy, and not, as was the case in the Old World, injustice. For immigrants, the first sign of success was rising above manual labor, whether as foreman, clerk, or manager. A second sign was owning property. James Henretta in his article, "The Study of Social Mobility," for *Labor History* in Spring 1977, observes how each ethnic group defined success differently and its evaluation was never exclusively based on economic factors. While immigrants wanted to achieve a satisfactory position in the American economy, they did not simply want to abandon certain cultural values and habits. Family ties were more important to Greeks and Italians than education and success at work. Indeed, for Greeks and Italians, any aspirations beyond an income to meet basic necessities was sometimes regarded as social deviance, an attempt to surpass, and thereby insult, earlier generations.

Public school education opened a door to success but also led children down a corridor of assimilation away from their parents. The public school was a warehouse of American culture from which each immigrant group decided for itself what it wanted and what price it was willing to pay in terms of assimilation and compromise with hold values. The school day opened with a communal salute to the American flag, a patriotic exercise intended to stimulate common loyalty. So, too, did lessons on such national heroes as Washington, Jefferson, and Lincoln.

By the end of the nineteenth century most states had made attendance at school compulsory. Schooling was a prime center of assimilation. By learning to read and write in English and to do arithmetic, children were being taught to strive for material rewards. Adults who attended night schools learned not only English but also about civic government so that they could qualify for citizenship. Both children and adults received a large amount of socialization, notably the importance of hard work, cleanliness, thrift, perseverance, individualism, and patriotism.

Nativism

Immigration was now beginning to divide American society. Thus Americans began to lose confidence in the process of assimilation. The outcome was nativism, what John Higham calls "a defensive type of nationalism." Nativist agitation was the work of three groups: unions who regarded unskilled immigrants as a threat to organized labor; social reformers who believed the influx of immigrants exacerbated the problems of the cities; Protestant conservatives who dreaded the supposed threat to Nordic supremacy.

New immigrants were open to criticism for what they were not. They were Catholic, Jewish, or Greek Orthodox, rather than Protestant; they were supposed to be radical, rather than conservative; they were Latin, Jewish, or Slav, rather than Anglo-Saxon. Religious and racial minorities had played only insignificant parts in winning, or shaping, American political liberties.

The most persistent charge made against immigrants was that they were political radicals and some were terrorists. Nativists pointed to the indisputable fact that every radical movement of the period had a large immigrant following. The Socialist party of America was dependent on first-generation immigrants, especially Jews, Finns, and Slavs. In 1919 over half the SPA's members belonged to the various foreign federations and two prominent leaders, Morris Hillquit and Victor Berger, had been born abroad. Moreover, it was Russian immigrant and anarchist Alexander Berkmann who had tried and failed to assassinate coke and steel baron Henry Clay Frick in 1892 and Leon Czolgosz, a native-born anarchist with a Slav name, who had succeeded in assassinating President William McKinley in 1901. However, the great majority of immigrants were far from being anarchists, socialists, or even radicals: they were true conservatives. Not only did they resent European ideas on revolution but they were also opposed to domestic programs for social reform. Thus the Progressives attracted little support from first-generation immigrants. The most widespread hostility was directed at Roman Catholics, or, more precisely, their church and its increasing strength. In 1890 Catholics claimed 600,000 children were enrolled in their schools. They renewed demands for a share of public school funds. This enraged staunch Protestants.

The distinction between old and new immigrants was first put forward by New England academics who resented the intrusion of outsiders in politics. They provided the nativist movement with plenty of social cachet but very little intellectual respectability. In 1894 a group of Bostonians, Charles Warren, Robert DeCourcy Ward, and Prescott F. Hall, founded the Immigration Restriction League (IRL). A developing science of eugenics transformed the previously wooly thinking of the scatterbrained but biased New England intellectuals into hard-and-fast rules of racial superiority and inferiority. They were applied with indiscriminate enthusiasm to race relations, imperialism, and immigration. The rigorous application of these rules awarded the IRL scientific evidence that immigration restriction was essential if the United States were to preserve its racial purity.

In his *The Races of Europe* (1899), economist William Z. Ripley classified Europeans into a northern race of Teutons, a central race of Alpines, and a southern race of Mediterraneans, each with distinct, immutable physiological traits. In 1908 he suggested that racial intermarriage, such as America was experiencing among its various ethnic groups, was a form of reversion that would lead to a weakening of the dominant stock.

The nativist movement ebbed in the Progressive Era on account of domestic prosperity and patriotic fervor for imperialism. Domestic prosperity restored national confidence; imperialism provided a new outlet for dislike of foreigners. The financial panic of 1907 momentarily depressed national confidence and nativism was again more evident. Yet by now nativists met with organized opposition against literacy tests from the National Association of Manufacturers and from all the immigrants' associations, including those representing the old immigration. In 1907 the German-American Alliance and the Ancient Order of Hibernians agreed to oppose all forms of immigration restriction. Furthermore, new immigrants, especially Russian Jews, were effective critics of restriction. For, by now, an increasing number of first-generation immigrants were naturalized, had the vote, and began to influence the policies of both major parties who were obliged to take notice of their opinions. Thus in 1906 Joe Cannon, Republican speaker of the House, made a vigorous attempt to defeat a proposal to include a literacy test in an immigration bill. Moreover, in the elections of 1904 and 1912 the Republicans dropped their earlier restriction plank from the party platform.

Nevertheless, the restrictionist movement achieved some congressional successes. A consolidating act of 1907 extended the excluded list to include imbeciles, people suffering tuberculosis, and those who had committed a crime of moral turpitude. It raised the head tax levied on immigrants at entry to $4. The funds voted for enforcement were inadequate and those who needed to evade the act to gain entry could do so, either because there were not enough inspectors at ports to process the mass of immigrants, or by entering the United States across the land border with Canada.

Senator William Paul Dillingham of Vermont (1900–23) led a joint committee of both houses on immigration (1907–10) that in 1911 published a lengthy report in forty-one volumes on every aspect of immigration. Its general tenor was that new immigrants were less fit than earlier settlers in all aspects—physical, intellectual, economic, and cultural. It endorsed the ideas of a literacy test and some measure of restriction according to nationality. Nativists also urged the myth of immigrant criminality. The Dillingham Commisssion charged that "certain kinds of criminality are inherent in the Italian race." This was a covert reference to syndicate gangs involved in extortion, notably La Mano Nero (Black Hand), and others in labor racketeering. The whole accusation was based on inaccurate reading of criminal activities. An investigation in Massachusetts disclosed that while Italian-Americans accounted for 8 percent of the population, they comprised only 4.2 percent of prisoners.

It was now the turn of the Japanese to be characterized as subversive and servile. As had been the case with the Chinese, so with the Japanese, it was California that led the wave of hostility. Moreover, the Russo-Japanese War of 1904–5 provoked renewed fears of a "Yellow Peril" on the West Coast and led to demands for Japanese exclusion. In the first so-called "Gentlemen's Agreement" of August 1900, Japan agreed to impose limits on the number of its emigrants by refusing to issue passports to laborers. This did not satisfy Californian nativists and proponents of exclusion organized the Japanese and Korean Exclusion League on May 7, 1905.

However, the central crisis was over the crucial subject of education. On October 11, 1906, the San Francisco School Board ordered Chinese, Japanese, and Korean children to attend a separate public school. Ostensibly a measure to prevent overcrowding in white schools, where buildings had been destroyed in the recent earthquake and fire, it was really an attempt by municipal leaders about to face an accusation of graft to use the racial issue to distract public opinion from their own crimes. However, as a result of a conference with President Theodore Roosevelt, the San Francisco School Board later rescinded its action on March 13, 1907.

This, of course, did nothing to propitiate racist opinion and the federal government now moved toward a definitive Gentlemen's Agreement in a series of notes of 1907–8. In these Japan repeated its earlier undertaking to stop laborers emigrating. However, the agreement allowed Japanese residents in the United States to send for their wives and thousands did so, including wives married by proxy in Japan. Moreover, a series of state laws, primarily in California, limited the right of the Japanese to own (1913) and then lease (1920) farm lands. The law was upheld by the Supreme Court in 1923. To a certain extent Japanese-Americans evaded the laws by registering property in the names of their children born in the United States.

The anti-Japanese hysteria subsequently developed into an attack on the entire new immigration. Now imperialism served to enforce Anglo-Saxon notions of racial superiority. Thus Homer Lea, prominent California critic of the Yellow Peril, warned in 1909 how the racial purity of the United States was as much threatened by entry of the wrong sort of Europeans as it was by Asian immigrants.

The case of Leo Frank demonstrated how economic tensions fueled nativism. Leo Frank, son of Russian Jews engaged in manufacturing, had been educated at Cornell. He came South to run an Atlanta pencil-making factory owned by his father. In 1914 he was found guilty on flimsy evidence of murdering Mary Phagan, a factory employee. He was attacked by politicians, residents, and the press for exploiting southern workers and degrading the flower of southern womanhood. When the governor of Georgia commuted his sentence to life imprisonment, some people organized a boycott of stores owned by Jews. Worse, a virulent mob stormed the jail and lynched the hapless prisoner.

The concentration of xenophobia upon German-Americans during World War I gave other first-generation immigrants a welcome respite and allowed them to immerse something of their ethnic loyalties in general cooperation with the war effort. This was insufficient to prevent the adoption of a literacy test as a bar to further immigration. The justification was the need to achieve a new kind of absolute loyalty to be controlled by command of language. On January 28, 1915, Woodrow Wilson vetoed another literacy test bill on the grounds that it would reverse a fundamental historical policy without the support of any popular mandate. Then Wilson vetoed a similar bill on January 2, 1917, on the grounds that a literacy test was "not a test of character, of quality, or of personal fitness" but, in fact, of prior opportunity. Nevertheless, Congress overrode Wilson's veto. The act required all immigrants over sixteen to read "not less than 30 nor more than 80 words in ordinary use" in English or another language or dialect. However, the literacy test was waived for immigrants fleeing religious persecution and it could not be used to bar otherwise eligible aliens from joining members of their immediate family already settled in the United States. The Immigration Act also codified previous legislation, doubled the head tax to $8, and added to the list of excluded persons: chronic alcoholics, vagrants, and persons of psychopathic inferiority. It also set up a barred zone for the southwest Pacific, thereby excluding almost all Asian immigrants not covered by the Chinese Exclusion Act (1882) and the Gentlemen's Agreement with Japan (1907–8).

The Return of the Vanishing American

The heinous massacre of Indians at Wounded Knee, South Dakota, in 1890 was an event of profound symbolic significance, signifying a final white absorption of Indian land. Nevertheless,

Chief Red Cloud Cayuga's nobility and stoicism were caught in this impressive portrait by photographer C. D. Arnold at the Pan American Exposition in Buffalo in 1901. (Library of Congress).

it did not signal the eclipse of Indians as a resilient American people. Although no census figures are truly accurate, there were about 248,253 American Indians living in the United States in 1890. The number remained fairly stable until the 1920s when it began to rise again. The Bureau of Indian Affairs (BIA), operating within the War Department, recognized several hundred separate tribal units of which 300 enjoyed some degree of sovereignty protected by treaty. In fact, Indians are the only group specifically identified in the Constitution as a distinct political group. Each tribe has had a specific, but not precise, relationship with the federal government. Together, Indians and whites have resisted all attempts by interested parties to eliminate that relationship, whether by alienation, allotment, reorganization, or termination (after 1946). Yet the tribes remained the most dispossessed of all ethnic groups and the most disadvantaged in terms of poverty, health, and education. One of the most succinct and penetrating scholarly analyses of the problems facing modern Indians has been provided by English critic David Murray in his pamphlet *Modern Indians* (1982), from which much of the following material has been drawn.

The Dawes Severalty Act of 1887, also known as the General Allotment Act, was intended by its sponsor, Senator Henry Dawes of Massachusetts, and his supporters to provide Indians with a preferable alternative to their demoralized life upon reservations. Hitherto, many tribes had been transplanted from their original homelands where they had been nomadic hunters to reservations where they were expected to become farmers. The earlier policy had failed, partly on account of poor soil, partly because of Indian inexperience of, and resentment toward, farming, and partly because of inconsistencies in governmental policy. Most notorious was the periodic reversal of land cessations on account of pressure from white settlers and railroads greedy for ever more territory. Americans, much influenced by Social Darwinism, assumed that weaker Indians would be disease-ridden, demoralized, or drunk and thus eventually die off. Stronger Indians—the most fit and talented—would then become integrated, indeed, absorbed, into white society. Thus many federal administrators considered the policy of reservations as a temporary expedient, almost a strategy, toward eventual assimilation. This policy completely ignored the Indians' creative adaptation to, and use of, the dominant white culture around them.

In contrast to the policy of herding Indians onto reservations,

Henry Dawes proposed to transform Indians from wards of the federal government into American citizens. Each head of a family or household was allotted 160 acres of land and all single people over age eighteen and orphans were awarded 80 acres. The land was to be held in trust by the secretary of the interior for twenty-five years and it could not be sold. After twenty-five years it became the Indian owners' full property, subject to federal and state laws. The intention was not only to redefine Indians' legal and economic status but also to persuade them to see themselves as individuals within families rather than as members of a tribe holding land in common.

The Dawes Act failed because it attempted too much too quickly and with too few resources. The reservations were already proving quite inadequate for tribes. Subdivided, they were hopelessly inadequate for individual families to farm, providing plots too small and inhospitable to grow enough food. Many Indians got into debt, mortgaged land for seed or equipment, and, as soon as it was legally possible for them to do so, were obliged to sell or lease it to whites. Moreover, under the terms of the Dawes Act, the federal government was to acquire the residue of land after the wholesale allotment to families and keep the money in trust for the tribe. In 1901 President Theodore Roosevelt proposed to divide up and allot the tribes' funds as well as their lands. He declared that the Dawes Act was a "mighty pulverizing engine to break up the tribal mass. It acts directly upon the family and the individual."

In short, whatever the original intentions of the Dawes Act, the cumulative consequence was to release ever more land to whites. Indian land holdings fell from 138 million acres in 1887 to 47 million acres in 1934, a loss of two-thirds. Since white speculators wanted the best land, most of the land still owned by Indians was poor.

Furthermore, the federal government made an additional attack upon tribal culture in schools. Indian children at boarding schools were forbidden to wear traditional clothes, speak their Indian languages, and observe their religions. Thus education was another way of eradicating Indianness and it was practiced on the Indians' most important and most vulnerable asset—their children. White education was synonymous with competence in civilized society.

However, none of these policies, whether benevolent or malevolent, succeeded in extinguishing tribal communities. The Indians were supposed to have disappeared as an identifiable group yet they had not. Moreover, Indian communities were astonishingly diverse, ranging from the advanced agricultural communities of Pueblos in the Southwest, the confederacies of the Northeast woodlands, and various fishing societies in the Northwest. Some communities amounted to no more than twenty individuals, while the Navaho had 132,000 people on one huge reservation of 16 million acres in Arizona. Moreover, their responses to centuries of white contact were also very different. For example, whereas geography shielded the Hopi of New Mexico from early Spanish and American culture and allowed them to preserve much of their original culture, sometimes in settlements occupied for over 6,000 years, several other Pueblo tribes forged a mix of Christian and Indian religions and ceremonies.

The Peyote cult that developed into the Native American church mixed the Plains Indians' traditional emphasis on individual vision and the Indians' political realization that they must share spiritual experiences in order to keep the spirit of community alive. Peyote buttons are the tips of Lophophora Williamsii, a cactus growing in southern Texas and northern Mexico. The drug produces sensations variously described as exhilaration and nausea. Believers met together at night before an earthen mound in the shape of a crescent, ate a few Peyote buttons, sang, and passed around a ceremonial drum, rattle, and staff. The Peyote cult spread across the Kiowa, Comanche, and Wichita reservations and helped these Indians maintain a sense of being Indian. Bryan Wilson suggests in *Magic and the Millennium* (1973) that this form of Indian solidarity was only spiritual: "Dreaming both symbolized withdrawal from the world of white men, and was its realization. Peyote was the agency through which such introversion could be manifested." The Peyote cult was not uniform among all Indians. For example, amongst the Ute and Shoshone a new version of the Sun Dance held more believers as a redemptive religion.

Whites disapproved of Indian use of the Peyote cult and tried to ban both drug and ceremony. However, in 1918 believers formed the Native American church (NAC), an intertribal association based in Oklahoma. Believers claimed that use of the peyote was a sacrament to a "Heavenly Father," akin to the Plains Indians' "Supreme Being," and that the peyote contained part of the Holy Spirit and was thus equivalent to the transubstantiation of Jesus in the Catholic mass. Nevertheless, conservative Christians were outraged and condemned the ceremony as a pagan rite. Indian believers were eventually protected from persecution by Commissioner of Indian Affairs John Collier. The upshot of the controversy was another irony—the peyote was generally prohibited as a narcotic (although it is not habit forming) but members of the Native American church were allowed to use it.

In the early twentieth century, anthropologists, supposedly sympathetic to Indian cultures, were fascinated by those cultures endangered by white culture but far less aware of those Indian cultures that were surviving by adapting. In other words, anthropologists wanted to reconstruct, at least in their papers, the original culture (before white contact) from whatever material or sources they could salvage, rather than to chart the continuous evolution of Indian cultures. Thus American Indians were living in two vacuums at once—the empty geographical spaces unwanted by whites and a void of knowledge and understanding even among interested parties too intent on the polarity between an idealized Indian culture before white contact and a degraded Indian culture thereafter to appreciate any Indian culture that was still alive. Popular attitudes among the public at large toward Indians were largely formed by the presentation of Indians in western novels and films. Among novelists Ernest Hemingway and Hart Crane used Indians to embody quintessential American values. Yet, from the late 1930s onward, the presentation of Indians in feature films and serials was almost entirely as savages, based on the stereotype of the warrior Indians of the plains who wore feathers, rode fearlessly, and killed and scalped their enemies without mercy. The actors who played Indians were usually white or Hispanic and never spoke dialogue in any Indian language. The stereotyping of Indians was artistically no worse in its way than the stereotyping of their white enemies as vagabond cowboys and gunslingers but its sociological consequences were far more damaging. No one expected modern whites in the Southwest to tote guns or ride in posses. However, as analyst David Murray puts it, "modern Indians are made invisible by the presence of their mythic predecessors."

By the 1920s and 1930s the conventional wisdom on Indian policy was itself changing. In 1924 the federal government conferred American citizenship upon all Indians. Then, in the mid-1920s, Secretary of the Interior Hubert Work commissioned an independent report on Indians, *The Problem of Indian Administration,* usually known as the Meriam Report. It disclosed the calamitous failure of the Dawes Act and the desperate plight of Indians as regards poverty, health, and education. Sensitive to shifts in anthropology, the report suggested that (but not how) Indian culture should be allowed to follow its own path. Nevertheless, it assumed that the proper course for the federal government to follow must be to encourage Indians to adjust to white society, using newly expanded knowledge in social sciences to this end. As to the growing number of Indians living in cities, the BIA followed the ideas of the Meriam Report of 1928. It indicated how Indians who moved to cities were soon assimilated and quickly attained standards of living close to those of whites. Research many years later showed otherwise but the facts were scarcely known at the time.

CHAPTER FIVE

Labor in the Progressive Era

·ꙮ·

I N THE opening scene of his film *The Bank,* Charlie Chaplin demonstrated the gulf between capital and labor. He strode purposefully into a bank and across to the safe. Having carefully dialed the correct combination, he opened the door, entered, and reemerged carrying a mop and pail. In *Why is there no Socialism in the United States?* (1906), by German political scientist Werner Sombart, Sombart believed that American workers were so well provided for that socialism was not needed in the United States. This would not have been the opinion of Russian playwright, novelist, and revolutionary Maxim Gorky. Gorky prophesied in *In America* the revolution and horror he foresaw for the United States from the unemployed who would one day spring upon New York, their hands "unfettered and unrestrained," and who, "like rapacious marauders," would reduce the city to "dust and ashes—bricks and pearls, gold and serf-flesh, the unwashed and the idiots, the churches, the dirt-poisoned hotels, and the subtle 20-storey skyscrapers . . . yes, reduce the whole city to a muck-heap, a pool of stench and human blood, into the original chaos whence it came." Gorky's prophesy did not come true although there were times when the federal government feared a workers' revolution, notably in the Great Red Scare of 1917–21.

From the great railroad strikes of the 1870s through to the great sit-down strikes of the 1930s, American labor history was violent and turbulent. American labor was by no means passive to the rise of industrial capitalism, but when its vigorous struggles were turned into sensational stories on the front pages of the nation's newspapers, public opinion was antagonized against it. This partly explains why a coherent, working-class movement failed to develop and sustain itself for any length of time.

Working in the Progressive Era

The center of labor conflict was the workplace. Whether that place was located in a steel mill, down a coal mine, or on the waterfront, the world of the worker was continuously changing.

During the Progressive Era industrialists were trying to reduce the sudden fluctuations of economic fortunes attending the capitalist cycle of booms and slumps and, also, to reorganize the work process in order to improve efficiency, stability, and management power. At the same time factories were growing rapidly in size, while the form of their operations was lengthening the distance between worker and boss. In 1870, only a few factories employed more than 500 people. However, by 1900, over a thousand had work forces in excess of 500. For example, the packing firm Swift & Co. expanded from its single plant with 1,600 workers in 1886 to seven packing houses, employing an aggregate of 23,000 people, in 1903. Everywhere the place and pace of work was changing. In the mines such tasks as timbering, track laying, drilling, and shot firing became subdivided and more tightly supervised. In his *Workers in Industrial America* (1980), labor historian David Brody concludes that "Once loading became mechanized, the miner lost control over the pace of his work. The deadly speed-up began. The climax of this relentless drive for efficiency was to eliminate the underground work by stripping off the overburden and digging out the coal seams with power shovels." Workers in industries such as glass, chemicals, steel, and cement were affected by new technologies and auto-

The Boss

An outsize political boss manipulates rival processions of workers moving in different directions like so many diminutive marionettes in this cartoon by Walter Appleton Clark for *Collier's Weekly* of November 10, 1906. (Library of Congress).

mation even more profoundly than were coal miners. Skilled workers represented 17 percent of the industrial workforce at the turn of the century, and, although the introduction of overhead conveyors and power-driven machine tools boosted the numbers of semi-skilled laborers, the distinct traditions, identities, and powers of craftsmen were being increasingly eroded. With machinery requiring lower levels of skill and training to operate, management found it easier to discharge troublesome workers and replace them from the ever willing supply of surplus immigrant labor.

Dramatic though these changes were, the ability of workers to regulate production themselves and to hamper attempts by management to systematize the work process, nevertheless, remained very significant. In particular, foremen on the shopfloor still held enormous powers as to the hiring and firing of workers, and even over the setting of production levels and individual rates of pay. Workers frequently ignored management schemes to create artificial sections of workers, and, instead, continued to operate within informal work groups of friends who established their own production quotas. Individuals who exceeded quotas were known as "rate busters" and were disciplined by fellow workers. David Montgomery makes such points in his article, "The 'New Unionism' and the Transformation of Workers' Consciousness in America, 1909–22," for the *Journal of Social History* of summer 1974.

The survival of distinct social orders on the shopfloor and of workers' control in the face of advancing technology suggests that managerial techniques had, somehow, fallen well behind the physical changes in the workplace. Philadelphia engineer Frederick W. Taylor was among the first to use a rational, scientific, and methodical analysis to aid management in its review of the process of work. Taylor himself was one of the turn-of-the-century workaholics who showed no interest in alcohol, sex, or recreation. Instead, says novelist John Dos Passos in *USA,* "Production went to his head and thrilled his sleepless nerves like liquor or women on a Saturday night. He never loafed and he'd be damned if anybody else would. Production was an itch under his skin."

Taylor devised a scheme to eliminate the possibility of workers producing less than their maximum possible rate (a practice known as "soldiering"). Wages and bonuses would be set according to rates determined by the management once it had penetrated the craftsmen's domain and familiarized itself with the production process. According to its originator, scientific management, in its purest form, constituted "the deliberate gathering in on the part of those on management's side of all of the great mass of traditional knowledge, which in the past has been in the heads of the workmen." Taylor's system was based on four principles—research, standardization, control, and cooperation. The first two involved changes in machinery and, especially, wider use and standardization of machine tools. It was Taylor's advanced designs in cutting blades that had first made him well known among engineers and industrialists. The third principle suggested that management would have an increased control of such matters as routing of materials, scheduling of machines, temporary availability of tools and materials, and so on. The fourth principle necessitated the cooperation of workers with management.

Few large corporations adopted Taylor's proposals in the comprehensive schemes he regarded as essential for effective control. In industries where management tried to increase efficiency by excessive supervision and began to have foremen stand over employees with stopwatches, workers frequently responded either by walking out or by deliberately slowing down production. Highly publicized strikes at government munitions factories and American Locomotive alerted organized labor to the threat of Taylorism. In order to entice workers, management restricted the scope of Taylorism and rewarded work forces that complied with a system of bonus payments.

Legislation placing controls on industry, and the notion of corporate responsibility, had been long in coming and remained only partially effective throughout the early twentieth century. As was the case in many European industries, working in America's industries was grueling, dangerous, and low-paid. In 1910, only 8 percent of workers had regular schedules of 48 hours a week or less, while almost 70 percent labored for more than 54 hours a week. In 1914 the average number of hours of all workers was 55.2 hours a week.

Long hours and intensive labor practices in the United States combined to produce, then, one of the highest industrial accident rates in the world. In one Pittsburgh steel mill, nearly 25 percent of recent immigrant employees were injured or killed each year between 1907 and 1910 (3,723 in all). A national survey of industrial accidents in 1913 found that 25,000 persons had been killed and 700,000 seriously injured at work. The relentless drive for efficiency, increased production, and profits, almost always took precedence over considerations of health and safety. In New York's notorious garment industry, row upon row of women sat operating sewing machines at an ever quickening pace. One young clothing worker wrote of her job:

> The machines go like mad all day, because the faster you work the more money you get. Sometimes in my haste I get my finger caught and the needle goes right through it. It goes so quick, tho', that it does not hurt much. I bind the finger up with a piece of cotton and go on working.
>
> All the time we are working the boss walks about examining the finished garments and making us do them over again if they are not just right. So we have to be careful as well as swift.

The dreadful environment in which thousands of women worked in the garment industry was made tragically obvious when a fire swept through the Triangle Shirtwaist Company's building on New York's East Side on March, 25, 1911. Several doors from the building remained locked and 146 women were burnt to death or died jumping from windows on the upper stories. A reporter who witnessed the fire was frank and heartfelt in his conclusions:

> The floods of water from the firemen's hose that ran into the gutter were actually stained red with blood. I looked upon the heap of dead bodies and I remembered these girls were the shirtwaist makers. I remembered their great strike of last year in which these same girls demanded more sanitary conditions and more safety precautions in the shops. These dead bodies were the answer.

Moreover, most businessmen opposed progressive social legislation. The few who did support it had ulterior motives. When northern textile manufacturers discovered their labor costs were driven up by state legislation, they supported federal child labor legislation, knowing that their southern competitors in the textile industry would then be at a disadvantage.

The final report by the Commission on Industrial Relations of

1916 listed four principal causes of industrial unrest: the unjust distribution of wealth and income; unemployment and denial of an opportunity to earn a living; denial of justice in the creation, adjudication, and administration of law; denial of the right to form effective (labor) organizations.

Drawing on the research of Professor Willard I. King, the commission divided the distribution of wealth in the United States between a rich 2 percent of the population who owned 60 percent of the wealth; a middle class of 33 percent of the people, who owned 35 percent of the wealth; and a poor of 65 percent of the population, who owned 5 percent of the wealth. In short, 2 million people owned 20 percent more of the national wealth than the remaining 90 million.

The highest paid occupations among wage earners were those of railroad engineers and conductors, glass blowers, and certain steel and construction workers who could usually expect to earn between $1,500 and $2,000 per annum. This would provide a modest standard of living for a family of moderate size, including high school education for the children and an insurance policy. However, it was not enough to tide the family through some misfortune. Moreover, a worker who attained such wages would have to be well above average in terms of physical strength and endurance, as well as having served a long apprenticeship. In addition, either he or his predecessors in the trade would have had to fight a long, aggressive battle for better wages, a battle that would entail the victory of some trades at the expense of others. Such occupations were but a handful compared with the mass of workers. The commission disclosed that between a quarter and a third of men above eighteen working in factories and mines earned less than $10 a week; between two-thirds and three-quarters earned less than $15 a week; only a tenth earned more than $20 a week. These figures did not take into account time lost for any reason.

In the 1910s the number of working women was growing both absolutely and in proportion to the work force as a whole. Their participation had momentous significance, partly because they were supplementing the meager earnings of their men, and partly because, by the way they were exploited, their presence threatened the existing basis of the wage scale. Between two-thirds and three-quarters of women workers in factories, stores, and laundries earned wages of less than $8 a week. About a fifth earned less than $4 and almost half earned less than $6 a week. The commission's report was moving and eloquent as to what $6 would buy: $6 was, then, the price of three tickets to the theater, or a week's supply of gasoline for an automobile, or the cost of a dinner for two, or a pair of shoes or three pairs of gloves. "To the girl it means that every penny must be counted, every normal desire stifled, and each basic necessity of life barely satisfied by the sacrifice of some other necessity. If more food must be had than is given with 15-cent dinners, it must be bought with what should go for clothes. . . . If the breaking point has come, and she must have some amusement, where can it come from? Surely not out of $6 a week."

More even than the exploitation of women, the commission was concerned about the exploitation of children. "Last of all are the children, for whose petty addition to the stream of production the Nation is paying a heavy toll in ignorance, deformity of body or mind, and premature old age." The commission also discovered that as many as 20 percent of children in the largest cities were underfed and undernourished, and that poor children were dying at three times the rate of middle-class children. "It is certain," concluded the commission, "that at least one third and possibly one half of the families of wage earners employed in manufacturing and mining earn in the course of the year less than enough to support them in anything like a comfortable and decent condition."

The report emphasized the gross injustice of the unequal distribution of wealth.

Massed in millions, at the other end of the social scale, are fortunes of a size never before dreamed of, whose very owners do not know the extent nor, without the aid of an intelligent clerk, even the sources of their incomes. Incapable of being spent in any legitimate manner, these fortunes are burdens, which can only be squandered, hoarded, put into so-called 'benefactions' which, for the most part, constitute a menace to the State, or put back into the industrial machine to pile up ever increasing mountains of gold.

The commission discovered that, according to tax returns for 1914, there were 1,598 fortunes yielding an income of $100,000 or more each year. Of the fifty largest American fortunes, almost half had already been passed to heirs of the founders and the remainder would pass to future heirs within the next twenty years. Forty-four families had annual incomes of $1 million or more "whose members perform little or no useful service, but whose aggregate incomes, totaling at the very least" $50 million per year, are "equivalent to the earnings of 100,000 wage earners at the average rate of $500."

The commission concluded that "with a reasonably equitable division of wealth, the entire population should occupy the position of comfort and security which we characterize as middle class." Accordingly, the commission proposed that Congress should redress inequalities by introducing a federal inheritance tax. The revenue raised should be used to extend education, develop social services, and undertake construction of roads and irrigation, and provide reforestation. During the Progressive Era the number of states with inheritance taxes rose from twenty-six to forty-two.

Labor Unions and Working-Class Radicalism— The AFL, IWW, and SPA

Trade unionism, industrial unionism, and socialism were the main forms of organized labor, yet rarely did these shifting currents flow in complementary ways that might appeal to the vast majority of struggling workers. The three most important formal organizations were the American Federation of Labor; the Industrial Workers of the World; and the Socialist party of America. Their turbulent histories reveal many of the factors behind the weakness and division that have, historically, retarded left-wing radicalism in the United States.

Skilled workers combined in organizations that sought to maintain the traditions and "rules" of work in their particular occupations. In industries where this proved impossible, workers attempted to organize, regardless of craft or skill. However, for the impoverished mass of immigrant and unskilled native-born workers, protest could rarely take forms other than spontaneous and ephemeral strikes. Radicals found it extraordinarily difficult to raise working-class consciousness among a labor force fractured by conflicting cultures and aspirations.

The American Federation of Labor (AFL) was founded with the intention of building the class consciousness and economic power of workers by organizing them on occupational lines. The AFL was first established as the Federation of Organized Trades and Labor Unions of the United States and Canada from several independent national trade unions in 1881 and it took its definitive form and new name in 1886. However, the AFL retreated from its Marxian origins to become a profoundly conservative organization restricted to the ranks of skilled, white males. Under the long leadership of Samuel Gompers (1886–1924), the AFL pursued policies designed to win short-term, concrete, economic gains for a membership that, at the turn of the century, represented fewer than 5 percent of wage workers.

Gompers believed that labor should accept the existing capitalist economy but try and get a larger share for labor by way of higher wages, shorter hours, and better conditions of work. He thought that the idealistic goal of a fundamental economic reform was an illusion. It was, therefore, better to take all that could be attained now. Thus Gompers believed in negotiation and conciliation in labor disputes and in resort to strikes only after other methods had failed. He consistently opposed alliances between labor and political parties and the formation of a political labor party. His prime concern was the status of skilled labor. Under his leadership, it attained greater stability than ever before. The cost was borne not by the middle class but the unskilled. In concentrating almost exclusively on the needs of craftsmen, trade unions were increasingly supporting practices that severely undermined the solidarity of the working class as a whole.

The policy of restricting membership to skilled labor was often justified on the pragmatic grounds that these workers had more power in a society that barely acknowledged the right of workers to organize at all. In an industry with a simple production pro-

The debonair but determined John Mitchell, leader of the United Mine Workers, in 1903. Mitchell conducted various strikes to bind miners together, culminating in the successful, long strike of 1902 in which he received unexpected but most welcome support against the mine operators from President Roosevelt. (Photo by William Clarke; Library of Congress).

cess, such as cigar making, a craft union might well represent almost all employees. However, the system of craft organization broke down for those complex industries, such as automobile production, that employed a mix of skilled, semiskilled, and unskilled workers. In the AFL the only important industrial unions—those that included all employees of a particular industry—were the United Mine Workers (UMW) of 1890 and the International Ladies' Garment Workers' Union (ILGWU) of 1910.

There is no doubting the elitest and often racist slant of many union policies. Unskilled immigrant labor was regarded by most union leaders as either "unorganizable," or undesirable, or both. Indeed, the AFL was a leading advocate of immigration restriction on both economic and nativist grounds. Writing in his autobiography, Samuel Gompers said that it was about time that people understood "the principle that the maintenance of the nation depended upon the maintenance of racial purity and strength." In 1902, blacks constituted just 3 percent of total union membership and were largely segregated into ineffectual locals. The AFL's record with women was almost as poor. High union dues, apprenticeship requirements, and the autonomous structures of individual unions meant that few women entered craft unions. This was in spite of the important role played by women in the revival of unionism at the turn of the century. Between 1895 and 1905, they were involved in 1,262 strikes, including 83 in which they struck alone. Increasingly disillusioned with the AFL, women's groups turned their attention toward securing minimum wage laws and protective legislation.

The AFL was decentralized and organized something like the Trades Union Congress (TUC) in Britain, as a loose coalition of almost autonomous national unions (and international unions if there were Canadian locals). The advantage of this was that decisions were made in each union where the leaders understood the situation. The disadvantage was that the central body was almost powerless to settle disputes between unions, such as jurisdictional disputes over whether workers at a given task should be members of one union or another, and to discipline organizations whose policies were damaging to labor in general. The AFL wanted legislation that aided trade unions whilst being, at best, indifferent to general welfare legislation. Indeed, the AFL convention condemned legislation providing for an eight-hour day.

By 1917 total AFL membership stood at 2.37 million workers. Remaining outside the AFL, but with a similar philosophy and tactics, were the four railroad unions—the Brotherhoods of Locomotive Engineers, of Trainmen, and of Firemen, and the Order of Railway Conductors. By 1916 they had, altogether, about 400,000 members. During this period trade unions represented only a small part of the total labor force, never more than between 8 and 12 percent of those in work. In such industries as steel, textiles, and automobiles, union membership was almost nonexistent. This was one consequence of the bitter, divisive, and unproductive labor strikes of the late nineteenth century, often fought for union recognition. The failure of steel workers to secure union recognition in the Homestead Strike of 1892 ensured there would be no effective steel union for over forty years.

A small number of businessmen were ready to tolerate and work with labor. In 1901 a group of employers met with labor leaders and founded the National Civic Federation (NCF) with Marcus Hanna as president and Gompers as one of the vice-presidents. To socialist leader Eugene Debs, Gompers's role in the NCF was a sell-out for which he had nothing but contempt. For their part, most industrialists regarded the NCF much as Debs regarded Gompers. Most employers regarded the running of a business as the exclusive prerogative of the owners and this included all decisions about hours, wages, and conditions of work.

Skilled workers at General Electric, International Harvester, the Big Four meat packing firms in Chicago, and several smaller textile and building companies, forced management to make concessions regarding work rules and practices. However, the newly formed U.S. Steel Corporation chose to force a confrontation with the Amalgamated Association of Iron, Steel and Tin Workers—a union that had fallen apart and almost disintegrated after the Homestead strike of 1892. In 1901, this giant corporation mobilized private police forces as well as state and local authorities to establish open shops in all its plants.

Not all of America's unions were led by conservative leaders or operated exclusionary membership requirements. In the coal mines, where skilled miners could not control the flow of coal cars or the weighing of coal, the United Mine Workers (UMW) could not rely solely on the strategy of organizing craft unions. By the late 1890s, the UMW was operating as a genuinely multilanguage, multiracial organization, and in 1897 had won union recognition in the bituminous fields of the Midwest. Most accepted the institution of private ownership in mining and their grievances were about pay, hours, and conditions of work. In his *Autobiography* Samuel Gompers described the domination of the mine operators in the anthracite region thus:

The miners' families had not only to pay rent to the corporations which owned the shacks but they had to make their purchases of all the necessaries of life, meager as they were, from the company stores at double the prices for which they could be had elsewhere. If the full amount earned had not been purchased, they were hauled before some overseer and threatened with eviction and discharge. The tools, gunpowder and clothes, such as they were, all had to be purchased from the company. There was the company doctor for which men had to pay, the company graveyard, the company parson or preacher, so that it was a common saying that children were brought into the world by the company doctor, lived in a company house or hut, were nurtured by the company store, baptized by the company parson, buried in a company coffin, and laid away in the company graveyard.

After a successful strike in 1900, the miners, led by the charismatic John Mitchell, sought additional demands in 1901 not only for a wage rise but also for shorter hours, payment in cash by weight (rather than by cars) and every two weeks, and for the abolition of company stores and company doctors. They also wanted union recognition. This demand was most unwelcome to the operators because it would give miners the right of collective bargaining. George F. Baer, president of the Philadelphia and Reading Railroad, who became the spokesman for the operators, refused point blank to negotiate on this subject. The entire body of anthracite miners, about 147,000 in all, abandoned work on May 12, 1902. No work was done throughout the summer and by early fall coal stocks were almost exhausted. Not surprisingly, by September 1 the price of anthracite coal, usually $5 a ton, had risen to $14.

Concerned by the disruption, President Theodore Roosevelt invited both sides to meet him in Washington on October 3. John Mitchell made constructive suggestions, including the establishment of an independent tribunal to determine the issues and to be appointed by Roosevelt himself. Baer did not know how to parry this disingenuous offer and went red in the face. At this point, the strike became a political battleground for the titans with Roosevelt, his cabinet, and Mitchell on one side, and the mine owners and J. P. Morgan on the other. Secretary of War Elihu Root and banker J. P. Morgan met secretly and together hammered out a compromise, agreed by the six main mine operators. It also proposed a commission to be appointed by the president but without a representative from organized labor. In order to satisfy the miners, Roosevelt chose E. E. Clark, grand chief of the Order of Railway Conductors; in order to outwit the operators, he chose this union man not as a formal representative of labor but as an "eminent sociologist." Newspaper comment on Roosevelt's decisive action and masterly tactics was carried in superlatives. Walter Wellman opined for the *Review of Reviews* of November 1902 that the settlement was "the greatest event affecting the relations of capital and labor in the history of America." The miners returned to work on October 23, 1902.

At the arbitration proceedings the UMW had the advantage of the most able labor counsel, Clarence Darrow, "attorney for the damned," who had defended socialist leader Eugene Debs after the Pullman strike of 1894. Darrow narrowed the discussions to what was a fair wage. He calculated that a fair average of miners' wages would be $528 per year, less $40, because miners used their own tools, making net wages of $488. However, coal loaders below ground earned only $333. Moreover, the owners used child labor extensively throughout Pennsylvania. Darrow emphasized the plight of children in a moving speech. "Every mill in that region is a testimony to the fact that the wages that you pay are so low that you sell your boys to be the slaves of the breaker and your girls to be slaves in the mills."

The Anthracite Coal Commission made the following awards in its final report of March 21, 1903: a retroactive wage increase of 10 percent for contract miners but no increase for the remaining two-thirds who were, instead, to be paid the same rate for nine hours that they had previously received for ten; a reduction in the workday from ten hours to nine. The old system of payment was to be retained. Instead of union recognition, a six-member conciliation board was to be created to adjudicate all disputes. Mitchell and Progressives in the Civic Federation hailed the settlement, but more militant miners accused the union leadership of selling out. There was one further consequence of Roosevelt's baptism by fire into labor politics. The significance of labor to American industry was officially recognized by the government when Roosevelt signed the bill creating a new Department of Commerce and Labor on February 14, 1903, subsequently divided into two departments in 1913.

When the economy dipped into an, albeit brief, recession in 1903–4, employers began a determined counterattack that put labor on the defensive throughout the second half of the decade. Smaller employers in competitive markets had been hit hardest by the gains craft unions had made over job control and customary rights. Already in 1900 employers in Dayton, Ohio, formed a citywide association against what they called "restrictive" trade union practices and by opposition to the closed shop through a blacklist of union members they had routed organized labor from Dayton. The Dayton plan was imitated in Chicago, Indianapolis, Louisville, and elsewhere in the Midwest. By 1903 these anti-union employers had assumed control of the National Association of Manufacturers (NAM), first formed in 1895 to encourage exports. Now it spent money on campaigns at elections to defeat candidates it considered too friendly to labor. They established agencies that recruited strikebreakers on a nationwide scale; detective firms and company spies infiltrated union locals; work was transferred between striking and operating plants; and a central blacklist of so-called known agitators was maintained.

Employer associations also used their influence with state legislatures to create anti-union state police or convert existing police forces into a weapon. The best known of the new state police

A dreary routine of manufacturing for women workers slotting fuses in the Gray and Davis ordinance plant at Cambridge, Massachusetts, in World War I. (Library of Congress).

forces was the Pennsylvania State Constabulary of 1905, a mounted police known as the "Cossacks" or the "coal and iron police." International Harvester and the meat packing companies drove unions from their factories in 1904; metal working shops increasingly ignored the rules of the machinists' union by substituting handymen and specialists for journeymen. Roosevelt even threatened to use federal troops to break a strike by the Chicago Teamsters in 1905. Fourteen people died in the bitter dispute that finally saw the Teamsters defeated by a solid front of open shop employers. Elsewhere in the country, private police forces, vigilante groups, and Citizens' Alliances of the local middle class terrorized union members and communities of strikers.

Business could also count on the support of the state's legal institutions in handcuffing working-class militancy. Injunctions were issued against strikes, picketing, and sympathy boycotts. In *Loewe* v. *Lawler,* the so-called Danbury Hatters' case, the Supreme Court ruled unanimously on February 3, 1908, that a union attempting to organize workers in a factory in one state by secondary boycotts of stores in other states selling the factory's products was in violation of the Sherman Antitrust Act of 1890 because it was combining in restraint of trade. This decision opened the door to other suits against unions for actions "in restraint of trade," which was partially closed by an enabling clause in the Clayton Antitrust Act of 1914. Faced with the twin assault of the employers and judiciary, the cautious Samuel Gompers now became more militant in his defense of union rights. Referring drily to the rush of anti-union injunctions, he said, "Yes, there is no hesitancy on the part of our courts to grant us certain rights—for instance, the rights to be maimed or killed without any responsibility to the employer; the right to be discharged for belonging to a union; the right to work as long hours for as low pay as the employer can impose. . . ."

In the western states, industrial conflicts were invariably intractable and violent. In the gold, silver, and copper mines of the Rockies, the Western Federation of Miners (WFM) became the country's foremost radical industrial union. But violent conflicts at Leadville in 1896, Coeur d'Alene in 1899, and Cripple Creek in 1903–4 led WFM leaders to the conclusion that even an industrial union fighting with all its might for secure jobs and higher wages was inadequate in the prevailing economic system. Some felt the only way to counter the martial law and mob rule of the mining districts was to use industrial unionism as a revolutionary weapon. In January 1905, WFM leader William D. ("Big Bill") Haywood, together with a small band of labor radicals, and various left-wing socialists, including Eugene Debs, converged on

Brand's Hall, Chicagò, to form the most adventurous radical organization in American labor history, the Industrial Workers of the World (IWW). Not only did it draw support from the WFM but also from antecedents—the Western Labor Union (WLU) and American Labor Union (ALU).

Bill Haywood had begun work in the Nevada mines at the age of fifteen, and became radicalized in the brutal conflicts between the WFM and the mine owners. Haywood was a big, sturdy man with a square head and a jaw like a prizefighter. He had lost one eye in a boyhood accident and overworked the other in reading socialist literature. Bringing the 1905 IWW convention to order in his booming voice, Haywood declared, "What we want to establish at this time is a labor organization that will open wide its doors to every man that earns his living by his brain or his muscle."

The IWW manifesto, adopted in June 1905, declared:

The worker, wholly separated from the land and the tools, with his skill of craftsmanship rendered useless, is sunk in the uniform mass of wage slaves. He sees his power of resistance broken by craft divisions, perpetuated from out-grown industrial stages. His wages constantly grow less as his hours grow longer and monopolized prices grow higher. Shifted hither and thither by the demands of profit-takers, the laborer's home no longer exists. In this hapless condition he is forced to accept whatever humiliating conditions his master may impose.

The remedy was obvious. "Universal economic evils afflicting the working class could be eradicated only by a universal working class movement. Such a movement of the working class is impossible while separate craft and wage agreements are made favoring the employer against other crafts in the same industry, and while energies are wasted in fruitless jurisdiction struggles which serve only to further the personal aggrandizement of union officials." The manifesto proposed that the new union must be founded on the class struggle, "with the recognition of the irrepressible conflict between the capitalist class and the working class," but "without affiliation with any political party."

Better known as the "Wobblies," the IWW were singularly free of prejudice in an intolerant age. In the IWW's drive to organize all workers as a class against the capitalists, they employed foreign language organizers and published multilingual materials. The creation of dual unions, in direct competition to the AFL, reflected the enormous gulf that existed between the outlook of business unionists such as Gompers, and radical industrial unionists of the IWW who stated, "The working-class and the employing class have nothing in common. There can be no peace so long as hunger and want are found among millions of working people and the few, who make up the employing class, have all the good things of life."

By organizing the mass of workers who were excluded from the AFL, the Wobblies aimed to engage the employers in an unrelenting class war, culminating in a general strike to redistribute power and wealth. Indeed, leaders of the IWW were openly antagonistic to the AFL. However, for the first five years, the IWW's revolutionary plans remained no more than utopian rhetoric. Internal disputes over organizing tactics and political ideology splintered the Wobblies: even the WFM left the IWW in 1907. Unfortunately, signs were already developing to suggest that IWW activities would generate fear and notoriety across America's treacherous industrial terrain over the next decade.

One of the first came when shepherd Frank Steunenberg was murdered in his front garden at Caldwell, Idaho, on December 30, 1905, by a bomb attached to the garden gate. Subsequently, Harry Orchard, a miner of Baker County, was arrested and confessed that he had, indeed, murdered Steunenberg and various other people over the previous ten years. Orchard said he had done these things on the instructions of an inner circle of the WFM including Haywood. The murder was in revenge for Steunenberg's action six years earlier when, as governor of Idaho, he had intervened against the workers in a labor dispute. There were, altogether, five trials in Boise, Idaho, of various persons indicted for the murder of Frank Steunenberg. The second trial, that of Haywood, in the summer of 1907, was the most discussed. Across the country Haywood was supported by organized and unorganized labor and by radicals of all persuasions who raised the sum of $250,000 for his defense.

The defense team was led by Clarence Darrow and the prosecution team included William E. Borah, recently elected senator for Idaho. Haywood, with his lopsided face and one eye, looked like a desperado. Orchard, with his steady gaze, bluff manner, and generally affluent appearance, looked the picture of sobriety and respectability. Orchard claimed to have killed a total of 1,900 people in various bomb attacks in Idaho and Colorado, all at the direction of Haywood and other defendants. Orchard's evidence sent a thrill of outrage and horror across America. Darrow tried to show how the trial was part of the class struggle, in which "the spiders and vultures of Wall Street" and those "who hate Haywood because he works for the poor" wanted Haywood convicted at all costs. Darrow threw caution to the wind in one of his most eloquent political speeches:

"I don't care how many wrongs they committed. I don't care how many crimes these weak, rough, rugged, unlettered men who often knew no other power but the brute force of their strong right arm, who find themselves bound and confined and impaired whichever way they turn, who look up and worship the god of might as the only god they know—I don't care how often they fail, how many brutalities they are guilty of. I know their cause is just. I hope that the trouble and the strife and the contention has been endured. Through brutality and bloodshed and crime has come the progress of the human race.

Borah's response was logical and dismissive. "This is merely a murder trial; we are not fighting organized labor."

Indeed, the middle-aged jury of farmers found Haywood not guilty on July 28, 1907, because no one could be convicted in Idaho on the unsupported evidence of an accomplice.

The public impression that the IWW and all union leaders were anarchists hardened into deep conviction as a result of the McNamara case of 1910–11. Union organizers and brothers John J., and James B., McNamara were found guilty of having caused an explosion that wrecked the plant of the Los Angeles *Times* on October 1, 1910. Nineteen people died and another thirty were injured. The affair was deeply embarrassing to labor.

During the Progressive Era organized labor continued to debate the merits of forming a working-class political party. At local levels, labor showed some enthusiasm for politics and occasionally had notable successes. In San Francisco, a Union Labor Party saw its candidate for mayor elected in 1901 and win three out of four of the following elections. Hitherto, organized socialism in the United States had essentially revolved around Daniel De-Leon's dogmatic Socialist Labor party (SLP). According to labor historian Melvyn Dubofsky in *Industrialism and the American Worker* (1975), "DeLeon and his few followers were purists and perfectionists, who scorned reform, and ridiculed trade unions and their leaders as the labor lieutenants of capitalism, and [instead] preached true revolution." Yet the fragmented American working class, however exploited or poverty-stricken, would never be swayed by "a narrow set of true believers" who refused to confront the actual issues of day-to-day work. As progressive journalist Walter Lippmann later put it, "A man standing on a soapbox has to be cocksure. But about the tactics of a revolutionary movement only a fool is convinced that his is the last word."

In 1901 the Socialist party of America (SPA) was formed. Eugene V. Debs, veteran hero of the Pullman strike, moved forward to lead the SPA's campaigns for the next two decades. Growing up in the small town of Terre Haute, Indiana, and then going to work on the railroads, Debs's life and career reflected the turbulence and trials experienced by many workers as industrial capitalism remolded the nation. Perhaps Debs's most quoted remark was "While there is a lower class I am of it, while there is a criminal class I am of it, while there is a soul in prison I am not free."

Socialism flourished in the period 1901–12 and came to have an important impact on the lives of significant numbers of Americans, only to fall away sharply in the various domestic conflicts that accompanied World War I. Starting with 10,000 members in 1901, the party grew steadily, achieving 120,000 members by 1912. In 1912 it also held 1,200 public offices in 340 municipalities, among them seventy-nine mayors in twenty-four states. In 1912 socialists published 300 periodicals of all kinds and the *Appeal to Reason* had a circulation of 760,000. That year Eugene Debs took 900,672 popular votes (6.0 percent) in the presidential election. Two years later radical immigrants in New York's Lower East

Side elected SPA labor lawyer Meyer London to Congress. The party's principal strength was limited to a few groups—the tenant farmers of the southern plains, particularly Oklahoma, the German trade unionists of Milwaukee, the eastern European Jews in New York's rag trade, lumbermen in the West, and metal miners and migrant laborers in the IWW. James Weinstein concludes in *The Decline of Socialism in America, 1912–1925* (1967) how in 1911 socialist strength was strongest in small cities and towns; by 1917 it had increased its hold in larger cities of the industrialized East and Midwest. However, it was after 1912 that the organization began to crumble. In the Southwest, Socialism had a strong appeal to thousands of workers and farmers who were still influenced by the legacy of Populist agrarianism. Historian James Green argues in *Grass Roots Socialism: Radical Movements in the Southwest, 1895–1943* (1978) that what distinguished the Debsian from earlier Socialists was that they wished to reform the system, and not overthrow it. Despite their recognition of this fact, the party still quarreled over the means by which a new society could be achieved.

The first city to elect a socialist mayor, and the most influential in municipal socialism, was Milwaukee. When socialists gained office elsewhere, it was to Milwaukee that they looked for guidance. Thus Mayor George R. Lunn of Schenectady imported his commissioner of public works from Milwaukee. Like some other analysts, Sally Miller believes that socialism in Milwaukee "epitomized progressive municipal reform more boldly than those who bore the name."

In his introduction to *Socialism and the Cities* (1975), Bruce Stave concludes that socialists often came to power in the cities as a result of voters' dissatisfaction with corruption within the two major parties. Thus in office socialists proved cautious, fearing to alienate business and the public by introducing reforms that would necessitate higher taxation, sometimes finding themselves limited by city charters, or at odds with hostile state legislatures. Thus they concentrated on trying to win elections, stay in power, and work for reform within the existing political framework. As a result, their policies favored economical, efficient government, especially as regards sound city credit rating for the extension of

"Workers of the World Unite" was the campaign slogan of Eugene Debs when he ran as Socialist party candidate for the second time in 1904. One of the most charismatic men in American labor history, Debs inspired great affection among the radicals who followed him and great fear among conservatives. (Library of Congress).

municipal services and establishing public ownership of utilities and transportation. Bruce Stave concludes:

It appears that American Socialism was most successful in winning power when it was most progressive; as 'gas and water socialism,' it espoused democracy rather than revolution. . . . Preoccupation with immediate demands left the ultimate demands of socialism unsatisfied; nationalization of the means of production and distribution, democratic planning, and production for use rather than profit have not been accepted in this nation. Municipal socialism in the United States did little to further these goals.

While there was a considerable overlapping between socialist and progressive intentions, James Green reminds us in an article for *Socialism in the Cities* that the working-class membership of the SPA clearly distinguished it from the Progressives. The proximity and social structure of city and small town allowed SPA members, drawn from the working class, to join closely with middle-class professional workers in reform campaigns. Moreover, socialists generally opposed progressive plans to institute city manager or commission forms of government because these forms weakened local socialist strength and neighborhood control of municipal politics.

After election victories in 1904, socialists lost votes in 1905 and 1906 as the major parties, realizing the danger to their duopoly, began to nominate reform candidates. Socialists in the center were concerned by these losses and moved to the right, openly promoting reform (or compromise) platforms as advocated by the right-wing leader Victor Berger. Berger and the right and center wings began to call for a program of progressive (or piecemeal) nationalization and ended up with the more conservative solution of municipal ownership of public utilities. This was different from the more fundamental reforms sought by Eugene Debs and the left wing. In time, more professional people and Protestant ministers were attracted to the party and began to have a larger voice in its affairs. These new members were motivated by humanism and the Social Gospel and were much less interested in the class struggle than were blue collar members. For the new industrial working class, socialism was a way of attaining concrete material, political, and social gains. For the new intellectual class, socialism served as a metaphor for their own alienation and a blueprint for the reform of society in the interests of social justice and a more equable distribution of wealth.

Superficially, President Woodrow Wilson's reforms in his first administration did not seem very different from the promised reforms of the socialists, and, consequently, won such unions as the UMW over to the Democrats. The Furuseth or La Follette Seaman's Act, the Adamson Act (providing an eight-hour day for railway employees), the Federal Farm Loan Act, and the Clayton Antitrust Act won over workers and farmers. Moreover, Wilson's administration also established a new cabinet post of secretary of labor and appointed a former miner (William B. Wilson) to it, the UMW endorsing Wilson in his reelection campaign. Moreover, after 1912 the SPA began to emphasize reforms somewhat devoid of overt class conflict—national prohibition of alcohol, woman suffrage, and pacifism.

One of the most enduring testaments to the vigor of socialist thought in America during these years was the journal, the *Masses,* as transformed by pioneer editor Max Eastman.

The first issue of the *Masses* edited by Max Eastman appeared in December 1912 and, from the start, Eastman changed its character from a somewhat staid socialist magazine to a cooperative magazine promoting various experiments in economic, social, and artistic matters. The *Masses* looked toward "a radical democratization of industry and society." Perhaps the single most distinguished feature of the *Masses* was its art work. The cartoons of Art Young and Robert Minor were angry and irreverent as well as humorous and, more than anything else, determined the iconoclastic temper of the magazine. The illustrations of blue collar life were contributed by artists of the Ash Can School, such as John Sloan and Robert Henri. A younger generation of realists, including Glen O. Coleman, Stuart Davis, and Abraham Walkowitz, drew on European styles of socialist art to produce exciting original work.

It is, perhaps, not surprising that the IWW shunned conventional party politics. The character of its constituency had nothing in common with socialist groups. The workers to whom the Wobblies were increasingly directing their appeals were women, the newest immigrants, hobos, and native-born migrant workers, who either moved too often to establish voting residences, or were disfranchised. After the SPA convention of 1912 passed an amendment opposing the use of sabotage, Haywood was expelled from the party's national executive committee. When the working class behaved at its most militant, it tended to do so in a spontaneous, ephemeral manner. Strikes erupted most often when either the level of unemployment fell off sufficiently to encourage the rank and file to believe that they had a chance of success, or when their standard of living fell so sharply that they could tolerate poverty no longer. In the 1910s the labor movement would surge forward again to protest the arbitrary and vindictive policies of management, but, typically, it did so in erratic currents that usually flowed beyond the control of both union leaders and radical groups.

In 1909, the management at the Pressed Steel Car Company in McKees Rocks, Pennsylvania, introduced a new pay system by piece rate, designed to increase output by ending the practice of paying workers by the hour. Under the new system wages were to be pooled so that a slowup by one worker would also affect the pay of the others in his group. Unskilled immigrant workers at the plant responded with a spontaneous walkout that spread to the skilled English-speaking workers. IWW organizers helped to mobilize the strikers and distributed multilingual newspapers during the violent forty-five–day dispute. In all, 500 people were injured and 13 killed, but the strikers succeeded, nevertheless, in defeating the new proposals of the steel trust. Mass strikes began to occur in other industries, heralding a new period of labor unrest in which unskilled workers began demanding higher wages and the right to organize, and skilled workers revived the battle against scientific management and mechanization.

In New York, a militant group of women clothing workers initiated the 1909 "uprising of the 20,000." Enlisting the support of the International Ladies' Garment Workers' Union, the women shirtwaist makers battled police on picket lines, and forced the clothing companies into accepting collective bargaining under the famous Protocol of Peace. A similar revolt by the city's 50,000 cloak makers (75 percent of whom were men) gained advantages for union members in the hiring process, but the old guard United Garment Workers were increasingly faint-hearted in supporting militant actions. The inevitable split came in 1914 when a dynamic young Jewish cutter, Sidney Hillman, led rebel workers in founding the Amalgamated Clothing Workers of America. The new industrial union maintained socialist principles in recruiting urban immigrants, but remained unrecognized by the AFL for a number of years.

Although progressive reforms weakened the power of the left in elections, in some instances they provided the context for important revolts. In Massachusetts, a law passed by the state legislature, reducing the maximum workweek for women and children from fifty-six hours to fifty-four hours, resulted in possibly the most important industrial conflict of the Progressive Era. Employers in Lawrence's textile industry complied with the new law, but they also cut wages accordingly. When a group of, first, young Polish women received their lower wages on January 11, 1912, they protested and their action, and that of women from other ethnic groups, sparked off a walkout that polarized opinion across the whole town. At this time the town of Lawrence was effectively ruled by the giant American Woolen Company. Nearly 35,000 people worked in various textile mills, all infamous for their poor wages and wretched conditions of work. The employers had been able to maintain their power by manipulating the work force, most of whom were foreign-born, and deeply divided on ethnic lines, and by tapping the supply of surplus immigrant labor to replace any recalcitrant employees. However, when 23,000 workers walked out in 1912, a new feeling of militancy and solidarity swept the community.

During the bitter three-month conflict, Italian anarchists and IWW organizers established a multilingual strike committee that resolutely kept decision making in the hands of the rank and file. Many leading figures of the IWW, including Bill Haywood, Joseph Ettor, and Elizabeth Gurley Flynn, went to Lawrence to inspire and lead the strike. A Lawrence businessman placed dynamite around the city and blamed it on IWW leaders Joseph Ettor and Arturo Giovanitti, who were arrested until news spread that they had been framed. The IWW exploited newfound public sympathy by arranging to send the children of the strikers out of the city on the grounds that their parents could not feed them and that they were not safe from the police. Fighting police and state militia, the strikers held their lines to win a famous victory that included significant wage increases.

In 1913 the IWW organized a strike of silk workers in Pater-

COPYRIGHT APL'D FOR
BY MYERS BOISE
IDAHO 1907.

William D. ("Big Bill") Haywood, an assertive leader in the Industrial Workers of the World, or Wobblies, the most radical and controversial of all American labor movements. Haywood's unconventional methods and uncompromising stands frequently set him at odds with allies and opponents alike. (Library of Congress).

son, New Jersey, for an eight-hour day. The nearness of Paterson to New York City brought this industrial conflict within commuting distance for radicals, intellectuals, and artists in Greenwich Village. In a report for the *Masses* of June 1913, radical poet John Reed described the brutal way the strike was repressed—a fact ignored by the established press. He also described the refusal of the AFL and SPA to back the strike, the hardship endured by the workers, and his own arrest and imprisonment for four days. For John Reed the Paterson strike was a crucial experience and his report was instrumental in turning young intellectuals toward the IWW. For Reed, Paterson illustrated the poverty of thought and action among native English-speaking socialists. "It is the English-speaking contingent that remains passive at Paterson, while the 'wops,' the 'kikes,' the 'hunkies'— the 'degraded and ignorant races from Southern Europe—go out and get clubbed on the picket-line and gaily take their medicine in Paterson jail." However, that summer the strike collapsed.

Moreover, the IWW found it extremely difficult to build strong organizations, particularly in the South and West, where they recruited lumber and agricultural workers in the face of stiff opposition from employers, trade unions, and vigilante groups. Such fears were raised by the IWW's message that the California Commission of Immigration and Housing sent agents into the field to investigate the reaction of farm workers, hobo harvesters, and itinerant construction workers. One of the commission's agents, Frederick C. Mills, was stunned by the apparent notoriety of the Wobblies among California's migrant groups. IWW activists encouraged intermittent strikes, slowdowns, sabotage, and often refused to sign contracts with employers. Such militant tactics were suited to the spontaneous revolts of unskilled workers, but the ultimate syndicalist aim of a general strike to displace the capitalists from power and place the means of production in working-class hands remained a utopian vision in the heads of the IWW's ideologues.

The transient nature of the IWW's main constituency hampered its attempts to establish a stable grassroots infrastructure prior to strikes, and prevented consolidation of achievements after strike victories. For example, at Lawrence, the American Woolen

Company, by adroit use of espionage, blacklists, and mass lay-offs, was able, within two years, to reverse most of the gains made in 1912. Many workers also opted for accepting the concrete, so-called bread-and-butter, improvements offered by employers, instead of maintaining perpetual class war as urged by the IWW's vanguard. The Wobblies' most practical contribution to American labor history was their role as a shock force in leading unskilled workers when they rose in spontaneous strikes, and their ready ability to mobilize migrant, displaced workers at the bottom of society. Although at any one time the dues-paying membership probably never exceeded 100,000, it is estimated that 2 or 3 million workers passed through the ranks of the IWW between 1909 and 1918, thereby creating a radical subculture whose influence must have been felt by millions more. Frederick C. Mills, contemplating his experiences at IWW meetings and locals, wrote on July 20, 1914:

I am living, eating and breathing agitation, agitation that is really anarchy. . . . It is easy to say that the conception of any such dangerous discontent is imagination, it is so vague and strange to us. I felt it vaguely at first, then strongly when I came into personal contact with members of a great floating army, homeless, unmarried, denied any of the joys of life, over half of the millions of this army of casuals dying before they are forty years old. And I feel it vividly and keenly now. I have seen, to a very limited degree, some of the workings of the inner circle, the brains of this great army, the organizing force that is trying to teach them how to get their share of the goods of this world.

Violence was not limited to disputes involving the IWW. A strike launched by the UMW in the Rockefeller-owned Colorado Fuel and Iron Company in the Colorado fields in September 1913 over the refusal of the operators to allow unionization of the mines flared into a pitched battle at the tented encampment of Ludlow, Colorado, on April 20, 1914. Twenty-five people, including eleven children and two women, were either shot and killed by machine guns or burned to death as the camp was set afire. The strikers retaliated on April 23 by bombing and setting fire to mines and mine property, and, early on April 28, by killing seven mine guards. Federal troops were sent to the district to maintain order and remained there until the strike ended in September 1914 after the intercession of Woodrow Wilson.

As the American economy gained momentum on the tide of the Allies' war orders, so did the agitation of both skilled and unskilled sections of the working class. In the summer of 1915, a series of munitions strikes swept across the northeastern states, in defiance of directives from many AFL unions who disowned the stoppages. In the following year unemployment dropped, from 15 percent to, possibly, 9 percent of the labor force (statistics are really estimates in this period) and the number of strikes reached 3,789, a record for the twentieth century.

The Socialist party began a strong antiwar campaign that attracted thousands of dissenters, and was translated into several important successes in the 1917 municipal elections. Eugene Debs, the embodiment of the socialist spirit, opposed the war for broad ideological reasons and he thought that individual liberty would fall victim to jingoism and patriotic hysteria. SPA opposition to American intervention drew support from others opposed to intervention and thus membership climbed to over 109,000 in 1919. However, the party was already weaker within the working class. Gains due to SPA opposition to the war were offset by the departures of members from the giant UMW and IAM, whose members worked in war industries and supported Wilson's policy of intervention.

However, if the new demand for goods and labor stimulated working-class militancy, America's formal and irrevocable entry into World War I on April 6, 1917, also facilitated a savage reaction from both government and employers. By disrupting the important lumber and copper-mining industries, the IWW made itself a prime target among labor groups for the counterattack. In Bisbee, Arizona, 1,200 striking miners were rounded up and shipped out in boxcars to the New Mexico desert. Vigilantes lynched Wobbly organizer Frank Little in Butte, Montana. Individual Wobblies were attacked and beaten in the woods of Washington and Oregon and the oil fields of Kansas and Oklahoma. On September 5, 1917, Justice Department officers raided IWW offices in twenty-four cities across the country, seizing various documents, and, within a few weeks, began to arrest key leaders for conspiring to violate federal sedition laws. Deprived of its most experienced and dedicated cadres of organizers, and financially crippled by legal costs, the IWW would never recover.

To anticipate possible labor disputes a special labor commission, of which the secretary was Felix Frankfurter, recommended the creation, first, of the War Labor Board (WLB) and, then, in April 1918 of the National Labor Board with five members from industry, five from labor, and two joint chairmen, William Howard Taft and Frank P. Walsh, a labor attorney. Woodrow Wilson also established the United States Employment Service as a subsidiary agency of the WLB to place almost 4 million workers in essential war jobs. Taft recognized the need for, and place of, labor unions in the economy and, under his leadership, the board established a set of principles: union shops were not to be broken; employers could not fire workers because they belonged to labor unions; the eight-hour day was to be maintained; it was essential to pay workers a reasonable living wage. By such principles, the board averted 138 strikes, and made awards affecting 700,000 employees in 1,100 businesses. In short, the board ensured labor peace during the crisis. From their new leverage as crucial components in the war effort, many unions were able to win new contracts with employers, a system of arbitration, and a forty-eight–hour week for 49 percent of all workers.

When the Western Union Telegraph Company locked out some of its employees in spring 1918 because they were trying to organize a union, the War Labor Board insisted that they be allowed back to work. When the company refused, Congress authorized Wilson to take over the telegraph lines. Under this threat, Western Union gave in. Sometimes the WLB persuaded Wilson to intervene on the side of management. In August 1918 munitions workers in Bridgeport, Connecticut, went on strike. Wilson, concerned about disruption to a special industry, vital to the war effort retaliated with a blistering proclamation, warning them that if they did not return to work, they would be barred from working in any war industry and would lose their exemption from the draft.

The advances made by organized labor in the context of a comparatively amicable dialogue between politicians, employers, and patriotic AFL conservatives had a disastrous effect on the Socialist party. David Brody states in *Workers in Industrial America* (1980) how socialism had always claimed it would not detract from traditional trade union operations. However, the war undercut this crucial condition. For, as we have observed, in the military emergency, the federal government was prepared to concede a great deal to organized labor, in exchange for labor's enthusiastic cooperation in the war effort. "The choice that unions would make could never be doubted, even, as in the needle trades, by those deeply committed to the Socialist cause: they would take the concrete benefits and let the ideological loyalties go. That choice, deeply damaging as it was to the fabric of shared agreement, began a fundamental erosion of the Socialist hold with the labor movement."

Moreover, the industrial work force began to change in World War I and the 1920s. America's traditional source of new labor, Europe, was, first, isolated by the war and, then, the restrictive immigration acts of the 1920s reduced the flow of immigrant labor to a trickle. Employers now recruited women, southern blacks, and Chicanos into industry. For example, the number of women employed in railroad work almost doubled in 1918 to over 100,000. Moreover, the Great Migration of half a million blacks to the North from 1915 onward exacerbated divisions among the working class.

CHAPTER SIX

The New Woman

·ॐ·

WHEN NORA slams the door of a doll's house shut at the end of Henrik Ibsen's play, the bang signals the advent of a new woman. The new, assertive woman of the rising middle class was not content to be toy or drudge to her husband, but willing to fight to make her opinions known and secure her rightful place in society. The idea of the woman as business organizer and as sexual predator was further developed by Norwegian playwright Ibsen in such plays as *Rosmersholm* and *Hedda Gabler*. It was taken further by Swedish dramatist August Strindberg who presented bourgeois marriage as a vicious tissue of deceit and revenge in such plays as *The Dance of Death* and by Irish playwright George Bernard Shaw in his *Plays Pleasant and Unpleasant*. And when Shaw wrote *Man and Superman* (1901–3), he showed his manipulative and assertive heroine, Ann Whitefield, as superman, a Donna Anna who is more than a match for her Don Juan, Jack Tanner.

During the Progressive Era American women were becoming sufficiently active and independent socially to anticipate the emancipation of the 1920s. At first glance this may seem surprising, especially if we take fashion, an obvious index of cultural attitudes, as one instance.

Dressed to Kill

The decade 1900–10 was famous for elaborate fashions, with affluent women forcing their figures into tight steel corsets to give them tiny waists and ample figures above and below, aided by frills, padding, and trailing skirts, and crowned by long, luxurious hairstyles. The ideal of feminine beauty was still the Gibson girl, as idealized in the drawings of his wife by artist Charles Dana Gibson, mainly executed in the 1890s. Thus in June 1907 *Puck* jibbed:

"And her hair," cried Claude, "is something to dream over!"
"It would make a good mattress, for a fact," answered Meltravers, ever anxious to display fine sensibilities.

Out of doors the whole effect could be crowned by a wide, outsize, and lavishly decorated hat. The perils of the theater lobby in 1908 included being jabbed by protruding and ostentatious hat pins. (Twenty years later, they included being burned by cigarettes from extended cigarette holders.) Thus a jest of the early century is based on a conversation between two men. "What did you see at the theater?" "A black velvet bow, some tortoise-shell combs, a couple of plumes, a chiffon knot and a stuffed bird the size of a hen." This was also a period of chenille dotted veils and of boned collars, sometimes as high as five inches from the shoulder and with an extra inch of lace ruffles.

However, in keeping with other social and technological changes, women's fashions began to change quite sharply even before the 1910s. The hobble skirt had a brief vogue. Bloomers lasted longer and were promoted in city playgrounds by women gymnasium teachers, despite the professed outrage of Dr. Edward E. Bruce, who headed a committee of inspection of the Board of Education that visited city playgrounds and described bloomers as "unnecessary and unladylike, giving the children a false notion." Then, in November 1908 the sheath gown arrived in New York from Paris and "rang the knell of the rustling pet-

In this tobacco advertisement of 1900 American woman is transformed into a beguiling serpent of Old Nile by a paraphernalia of baubles, bangles, and beads, a succulent, exotic object at the service of Egyptian Deities Cigarettes. (Library of Congress).

ticoat." When a woman first wore one in Chicago, the police had to rescue her from jeering crowds. *Life* of November 19, 1908, contrasted the svelte effect of the sheath gown, hugging the figure, compared with the cultivated amplitude of hips previously in fashion by means of bustle and petticoats.

> We don't wish to insinuate
> That they were not real before:
> But where, oh, where are the hips that we
> Don't notice any more?

The satiric magazine *Punch,* of London, ridiculed the new fashion:

> A skirt whose meagre gores necessitate
> The waddle of a Chinese lady's gait . . .
> A waist promoted half way up the back
> And not a shred that's comfortably slack.
> A figure like a seal reared up on end,
> And poking forward with a studied bend.

The change from full to svelte lines arose largely from what was practicable and what was convenient. Whether in street, bus, automobile, or elevator, elaborate clothes impeded movement and made it difficult for women to work in the world of commerce. Moreover, new artificial fibers made possible a whole range of clothes that were easier to wear and maintain, provided the styles were simpler. Arthur D. Little, together with William H. Walker and Harry S. York, created rayon (cellulose esten) and artificial silk, both in 1902. Between 1905 and 1907 Leon Baekeland succeeded in condensing phenol (from coal tar) and formaldehyde into a plastic, Bakelite. It was entirely synthetic, since both primary substances could be produced from coal, lime, water and air. It was the first of a series of resins to revolutionize modern economic and technological life. Such creations led to entirely new forms of clothes and this was but a beginning in changes in chemical technology. Years later Wallace H. Carothers synthesized a superpolymer material, marketed by Du Pont as nylon, beginning with toothbrush bristles, on May 23, 1938. All fibers before nylon were dependent on nature for their molecular structure. Nylon and, later, synthetic fibers could be constructed artificially to yield certain desired qualities. Such synthetic fibers are often first made in the form of yarn (as Du Pont first produced nylon yarn in 1939), cut into small lengths to be spun and woven like wool, or to be admixed to cotton and wool and then spun.

Like much new art, new fashion seemed ugly at first, almost unfeminine. The effect of a pencil-line figure for women was stark for a society used to a fuller figure. The Haute Ton Whist and Literary Club of South Norwalk, Connecticut, proclaimed "that the sheath gown was but one big step backward toward the fig-leaf" and decided that "the sheath gown is both immodest and homely and this club will do everything in its power to put it down."

Mourning the changes entailed in new, simpler fashions, *Life* of November 26, 1914, said that "of all the details of underraiment that belonged in a woman's wardrobe ten years ago, the only one that survives is the stocking." There were, indeed, momentous economic repercussions to the changes in women's fashions. The New York *Tribune* of April 4, 1912, reported how George W. Neville, president of the New York Cotton Exchange, deplored the scantiness of women's underclothes and how it "has reduced consumption of cotton fabrics by at least twelve yards of finished goods for each adult female inhabitant." In 1900 the average expenditure for a year's supply of stockings was less than $5. They were made of cotton or wool in either black or white. Fewer than one woman in 10,000 wore silk stockings. As skirts began to rise and show more of a woman's legs, stockings became an important decorative feature and had to be of better quality textiles (including even silk), and were made in a wide range of colors. *Judge* of February 10, 1912, estimated how women spent, on average, $25 a year on stockings. Shoes were also more expensive than in 1900 and so were dresses and hats. "The silk stocking," observed *Judge,* "is the foundation of needless extravagance." Moreover, the magazine, with due decorum, referred not to leg but to limb. Changes in dress were both a symptom and emblem of more dramatic changes in lifestyle made possible by the growth of cities and their ambience so different from the country.

A special development was the blurring of appearance and behavior between younger and middle-aged women by means of cosmetics, dress, and corsets. Eleanor Chalmers in "Facts and Figures" for *Delineator* of April 1914 warned matrons, "This is the day of the figure. . . . The face alone, no matter how pretty, counts for nothing unless the body is as straight and yielding as every young girl's." The preferred style for women's dress between 1910 and 1918 was the close fitting sheath. The fashion for bobbed hair began in 1912 when young women began to tuck under their hair with a ribbon and by 1913 actress Pauline Frederick and dancer Irene Castle began to wear their hair short. In July and September of 1915, *Ladies Home Journal* showed women with short hair on its covers.

As technological advances and economic progress began, superficially, to narrow the gulf between the classes, middle-class and lower-class women were becoming free to do the same things as those in the upper classes. Traditional morality was already dissolving in the Progressive Era as families became smaller and as communities became larger. The developing cities allowed freedom from the constant supervision of the church, home, and small communities, allowing individuals more opportunities to determine their social behavior. By the early 1900s, social commentators saw how the automobile, in particular, was changing dating and allowing more sex outside marriage, while the telephone allowed a new and regular intimacy between people separated by distance, and factories and offices offered a much wider assortment of partners for friendship and love. Thus Louise Collier Willcox found in "Our Supervised Morals" for the *North American Review* (1913) that "The time is past when parents supervised the morals of their children. . . ."

Greater freedom and opportunities tended to dissolve confidence between generations and establish a prefigurative bourgeois culture in which it was the young people who led their elders. Thus Dorothy Dix observed for the Boston *American* of August 21, 1913, how there had been "so many changes in the conditions of life and point of view in the last twenty years that the parent of today is absolutely unfitted to decide the problems of life for the young man and woman of today. This is particu-

larly the case with women because the whole economic and social position of women has been revolutionized since mother was
a girl." Marion Harland lamented "The Passing of the Home
Daughter" for the *Independent* of July 13, 1911, and noted the rise
of the independent young woman who preferred the welcome
anonymity of city life to "dying of asphyxiation at home."

Advertising also shows how the popular stereotype of fulfilled
women changed in these years. At the turn of the century illustrations in advertisements in *Cosmopolitan* and *Ladies Home Journal* show curvaceous women with billowy hair, delicate hands,
and gentle motherly expressions who stand motionless. By 1910
advertisements show women active with a vacuum cleaner, talking on the telephone, and moving outside the home. *Ladies Home
Journal* of May 1917 shows a woman entertaining elegant friends
and driving an automobile. *Cosmopolitan* of June 1915 has a manufacturer of vacuum cleaners, promising "Push the Button—and
Enjoy the Springtime!" *Collier's Weekly* of September 25, 1915,
has Van Camp's Pork and Beans offering to save the housewife
"100 hours yearly," while Campbell's Soups wanted her to "get
some fun out of life," now that it was not necessary for her to
let the "three-meals-a-day problem tie you down to constant
drudgery." In short, the shifting emphasis of advertisements was
that, by buying such products as Wizard Polish and Minute Tap-
ioca, women would have greater time to enjoy themselves at leisure outside the family home. A woman in *Ladies Home Journal*
for April 1918 can tell her friend, "I don't have to hurry nowadays. I have a Florence Automatic Oil Stove in my kitchen." As
the same magazine showed in several issues from 1915 onward,
she could make the most of driving the car to her social engage-
ments. Novelists David Graham Phillips, in *The Hungry Heart*
(1909) and *Old Wives for New* (1908), and Robert Herrick, in *Together* (1908), noted the newfound leisure of middle-class women.

The Flapper

This was the social context in which the flapper, the nymphet
with the Ponjola, bobbed hair, boyish figure, and mass-produced
clothes first made her appearance. The term "flapper" was first

used in England and introduced by journalist H. L. Mencken to the United States in 1915. A girl who flapped had not yet attained full maturity and her flapper dresses were intended to transform juvenile, angular figures into an aesthetic ideal. She was a creation of the towns and really belonged to the middle and upper classes. "Young—whether in fact or fancy—assertive, and independent, she experimented with intimate dancing, permissive favors, and casual courtships or affairs," comments James R. McGovern in "The American Woman's Pre-World War I Freedom in Manners and Morals," an article for the *Journal of American History* reproduced in *Women's Experience in America,* a historical anthology edited by Esther Katz and Anita Rapore, (1980). It now seemed that women, freer in morals and less feminine in the traditional sense, could now take on the role of hunter in pursuit of their sexual quarry (as all women with leisure had had the opportunity to do in the past) and be seen to enjoy their active role. In *Independence* Nell Brinkley described this period as the "Day of the Girl" (November 14, 1916) and Dorothy Dix described the new type that men fell for as a "husky young woman who can play golf all day and dance all night, and drive a motor car, and give first aid to the injured if anybody gets hurt, and who is no more in danger of swooning than he is" (May 14, 1915). She was celebrated in lyrics like *A Dangerous Girl.* Indeed, young girls dispensed with maidenly reserve, kept their own keys to the front door and their parents in ignorance of the identities of their escorts to nightly entertainment. Ethel Watts Mumford asked anxious parents, "Where is Your Daughter This Afternoon?" for *Harper's Weekly* of January 17, 1914. In the Boston *American* Cliff Sterrett's cartoon series about a modern young miss had Polly washing dishes in the shower and drying them with an electric fan.

Since young women could move more freely with men at work and play, it was inevitable that they would begin to share their expectations of both. This led older people to lament the death of romance, such as Allen Duer Miller in "The New Dances and the Younger Generation" in *Harper's Bazaar* of May 1912. Margaret Deland wrote in "The Change in the Feminine Ideal" for *Atlantic Monthly* in 1910 how "This young person . . . with sur-

prising bad manners—has gone to college, and when she gradu-
ates she is going to earn her own living . . . she won't go to
church; she has views upon marriage and the birth-rate, and she
utters them calmly, while her mother blushes with embarrassment; she occupies herself, passionately, with everything except
the things that used to occupy the minds of girls."

Novelist Owen Johnson described unmarried flappers as determined pleasure seekers, "determined to liberate their lives and
claim the same rights of judgment as their brothers." They were
the products of an abrupt feminine revolution, living in cities
independent of their families. "She is sure of one life only and
that one she passionately desires. She wants to live that life to its
fullest. . . . She wants adventure. She wants excitement and
mystery. She wants to see, to know, to experience. . . ." Dure
Baxter, heroine of his novel *The Salamander* (1914), embodied his
interpretation as she said, "How do I know what I'll do tomorrow?" and uttered a nightly prayer, "O Lord! give me everything I want!" Like Bizet's Carmen, her "supreme law of conduct" was love and she dreaded "thirty as a sort of sepulcher, an
end of all things!" Stephanie Cleland in *The Restless Sex* had a
trial marriage in order to learn what it was like. Gertrude Ath-
erton observed in *Current Opinion* of November 1914 how girls
were as determined as men to have a fling. They kissed and pet-
ted and enjoyed sex though they did not intend to marry.

Kenneth A. Yellis argues in "Prosperity's Child" in *Women's
Experience in America* (1980) of these two feminine ideals how

The Gibson girl was maternal and wifely, while the flapper was boyish
and single. The Gibson girl was the embodiment of stability. The flapper's aesthetic ideal was motion, her characteristics were intensity, energy, volatility. While the Gibson girl seems incapable of an immodest
thought or deed, the flapper strikes us as brazen and at least capable of
sin, if not actually guilty of it. She refused to recognize the traditional
moral code of American civilization, while the Gibson girl had been its
guardian.

Thus the American woman, circa 1910, was showing changing
tastes in beauty of face and figure and in the 1910s the modern
appearance of women was created to last—with various and suc-

cessive modifications—until the end of the century. Beauty included more expressive use of powder and rouge, lipstick, and
eyelash and eyebrow liners. *Cosmopolitan* of July 1915 showed
"How to Become Beautiful, Fascinating, Attractive." From 1910
onward women also disclosed more of their bodies, as what had
once been referred to as limbs became legs as skirts were raised.
The style of rolled down hose, that is partly rolled down the leg,
first appeared in 1917. Dresses for the opera and restaurants
plunged in front and back. The *Delineator* of January 1910 remarked how "The conventions of evening dress have changed
radically in the last four or five years. Not so very long ago a
high-necked gown was considered *au fait* for all evening functions except formal dinners and the opera. Nowadays, well-dressed
women wear décolleté dresses even for home dinners, and semi-
décolleté gowns for restaurants and theaters."

Cosmopolitan of July 1915 opined how "Fashion says—evening
gowns must be sleeveless . . . afternoon gowns are made with
semi-transparent yokes and sleeves." The *Unpopular Review* of
spring 1915 complained of the vogue for transparent dresses and
blouses that "At no time and place under Christianity, except the
most corrupt periods in France . . . certainly never before in
America, has woman's form been so freely displayed in society
and on the street." Not only were middle- and upper-class women
following their youngers in dress and makeup but also in smoking, drinking, and permissive manners. Their new modes of behavior extended to other classes. It was now considered smart
for a woman to smoke cigarettes and drink cocktails. This was a
radical change.

Among other cities, New York City had previously passed a
municipal ordinance, the Sullivan ordinance on January 21, 1908,
making it illegal for women to smoke and for a manager of a
public place to allow women to smoke therein. A press report of
July 22, 1910, that Alice Roosevelt Longworth smoked cigarettes
provoked a lively discussion among members of a women's club
in Pittsburgh which reached a conclusion when a prominent
member of the DAR said, "We needn't all get up our feathers
simply because Mrs. Longworth smokes cigarettes. Why, a

hundred years ago our great-grandmothers sat with their husbands and smoked corn-cob pipes." Gradually, the license to smoke, first granted to the wives of foreign diplomats, was extended to all women as to all men.

The Women's Movement

If all men citizens were to have the vote, and to be able to vote for more than their representatives, we might expect the Progressives to support woman suffrage, also. However, the campaign for woman suffrage both united and divided Progressives. The proponents of woman suffrage not only argued for this extension of democratic rights on the grounds of civil rights but also claimed it would introduce both the superior ethics of women into politics and their skills as housekeepers into government. Eventually, woman suffrage was adopted by the federal government and the Nineteenth Amendment, ratified in 1920, represented what Robert H. Walker calls "more quantitative progress in extending democracy than any other single act in the nation's history."

The franchise was extended to women first in western states, led by Wyoming (1893), Colorado (1893), Utah (1896), and Idaho (1896). These were all sparsely populated states that were trying to attract settlers. Moreover, historian Alan Grimes has argued that in such areas women proposed, and men supported, woman suffrage as a conservative device to ensure the dominance of white Anglo-Saxon Protestants in politics. By 1912 five more states had adopted woman suffrage—California, Arizona, Washington, Oregon, and Kansas. Another twenty-two had woman suffrage on certain subjects.

In the 1870s and 1880s such agrarian organizations of the West as the Grange and its successsors, the Alliances, had encouraged women to work alongside men, albeit in supportive, secretarial roles, rather than as equal officeholders, and perhaps as many as a quarter of Southern Alliance members were women. Nevertheless, the agrarian revolt stimulated the activity of women in politics. The Populists included certain prominent women speakers,

Ida Minerva Tarbell, one of the most articulate of progressive investigative journalists, most noted for her well argued criticisms of the way John D. Rockefeller had achieved the Standard Oil monopoly. A champion of several feminist causes, she nevertheless opposed woman suffrage because she believed the achievement of a fictional social equality between the sexes would enable unscrupulous industrialists to evade legislation protecting women and children in factories. (Library of Congress).

notably Mary Elizabeth Lease and Annie L. Diggs, both of Kansas, Eva McDonald of Minnesota, Marion Todd of Chicago, and Sarah Emery of Michigan.

The pivotal figure in the movement for woman suffrage was

Susan Brownell Anthony, originally of Massachusetts, whose first crusade was for the abolition of slavery. During the American Civil War she was already the country's leading suffragist and by her campaign in 1860 won the right of women in New York State to control their own wages and to be guardians of their own children. As publisher of the *Resolution,* a short-lived weekly journal in New York City, she propounded the slogan "the true republic—men, their rights and nothing more; women, their rights and nothing less." She formed the National American Woman Suffrage Association (NAWSA) in 1889, which she served as president (1892–1900), with the aim of a constitutional amendment to grant women the vote. Although she died in 1906, fourteen years before the Nineteenth Amendment was adopted, she also helped create the International Council of Women (1888) and, with Carrie Chapman Catt, the International Woman Suffrage Alliance in Berlin (1904). An indefatigable speaker to audiences, both welcoming and hostile, she endured the hardships of frontier travel and the rigors of resentful audiences to survive and become almost a national institution, widely respected as a superb organizer and executive.

Another activist feminist whose campaign began with the movement to abolish slavery was Elizabeth Cady Stanton of New York, one of the most influential women's rights leaders and renowned as a journalist and superb orator. When she married the abolitionist lawyer and journalist Henry Brewster Stanton in 1840, she insisted upon the word "obey" being struck from the ceremony, a decision that seemed, then, a most radical act of defiance. She and her husband had seven children. Together with Lucretia Mott she organized the first convention on women's rights in the United States at Seneca Falls, New York, in 1848. Overriding Lucretia Mott's objections, she insisted on the bill of rights for women containing a suffrage clause. After meeting Susan B. Anthony in 1851, she decided to join her and they became a remarkable team. Elizabeth Cady Stanton became the first president of the National Women Suffrage Association (1869), the precursor of NAWSA, which she also served as president. Together with Susan B. Anthony and Matilda Joslyn Gage, she compiled the first three volumes of the *History of Woman Suffrage.*

Whereas it was possible for certain critics to dismiss Susan B. Anthony as a bottled-up old spinster, the same could not be said of the engaging wife and mother Elizabeth Cady Stanton. Indeed, her very association with the women's movement was a reason for widening discussion about the proper roles for women in modern society.

The suffrage movement was part of a broader trend of feminism, the freeing of women from all sorts of outdated taboos. In society as a whole, women suffered various legal disadvantages, as litigants, as property owners, and as heirs to it. In marriage, the law gave husbands many rights that made their wives less equal and custom gave the husbands other privileges, notably absolute sexual rights. This was still the period when convention assumed that marriage was the price men paid for sex, and that sex was the price women paid for marriage.

Women working for an improved quality of life for women, whether by an extension of the franchise or the introduction of social reforms, recognized that they could only achieve their aims by creating organizations to rally support, educate the public, and lobby politicians. Thus active suffragist Carrie Chapman Catt estimated that the campaign for the Nineteenth Amendment took 52 years of active campaigning, 56 referenda of men voters, 480 campaigns on legislatures to submit suffrage amendments to voters, and 47 campaigns to induce state constitutional conventions to write woman suffrage into state conventions. While half of the important women's organizations were established in the 1890s, many professional women's groups were founded during the first twenty years of the new century, including the National Organization of Public Health Services (1912), the International Association of Policewomen (1915), the Medical Women's National Association (1915), the Federation of Teachers (1916), the National Association of Deans of Women (1916), and the National Federation of Business and Professional Women's Clubs (1919).

This new development of women's groups was encouraged by urbanization, industrialization, and increased opportunities in higher education. However, perhaps the most important single factor was the increased leisure time of middle-class wives, introducing them, through lectures, to such subjects as prohibition, political corruption, and international affairs. Many clubs were active forces for change and helped establish such community services as kindergartens, playgrounds, public laundries, public baths, parks, and libraries. In New York it was the Women's Municipal League that decided in 1906 to investigate the reception procedures for immigrants at Ellis Island in an attempt to protect newcomers from harassment and fraud. It was women's groups that were chiefly responsible for getting streets cleaned and for improving the quality of milk and processed foods.

By 1890 some 100,000 women belonged to various clubs and in 1898 800 delegates representing 160,000 members attended the National Convention of Women's Clubs. Jane Addams, the settlement house organizer, and Beatrice Webb, the British Fabian socialist, addressed them on "The Industrial Problem as it Affects Women and Children." The meeting then turned to discussion about ensuring certain standards of work for women and children in industry. Each constituent association agreed to establish local committees to check on how far these standards were maintained in nearby industries. The national organization became increasingly immersed in social and economic reform. In 1910, the year Congress granted a national charter to the General Federation of Women's Clubs, national membership was 800,000; in 1914 it was over a million.

Despite the growth of activities open to women, almost all of them fell within the traditional pattern of women's activities, such as domestic work and child rearing. Thus they reflected the old idea of separate spheres for men and women. In *Everyone was Brave* (1969), historian William O'Neill describes women whose primary concern was to serve others and society and calls them "social feminists," in comparison with those (political and economic) feminists whose main aim was to widen opportunities for individual women workers, irrespective of the ends to which new opportunities might be put. This second class of feminists rejected "the social feminist compromise that enlarged women's sphere of action while channelling their energies" in directions acceptable to a society run by men. Thus "Social feminists wanted the vote on the perfectly reasonable ground that it would advance their reforms. Ardent suffragists wanted it for its own sake."

Thus William O'Neill sees in the growth of social feminism a primary shortcoming of the women's movement in America. "The chief feature of social feminism was that it created roles for women that militated against their full emancipation. Their benevolent enterprises met women's desire for useful and satisfying work without touching the sources of their inequality."

We should ask why it took fifty years to achieve woman suffrage after the development of a professional middle class. Some of the opposition was antiquated, sexist, and alarmist, and made its points in labored jests. Thus, the satirical *Puck* resorted to a caricature of feminist stereotypes in its jibe: "Imagine a long line of skimpy skirts tackling an electionbooth—each one having to stop and powder her nose, and fix her hair, and adjust her belt, and look through her handbag, and wonder who the occupant of the next booth is voting for; the elections would have to be held 'the first two weeks in November,' or perhaps longer."

In one respect, the opposition was surprising, given the gradual social improvement in the position of women that might suggest that there would not have been any serious objection by men to women voting. Following the example of Mississippi in 1839, many states granted married women control of their own property. Between 1869 and 1887 thirty-three states and the District of Columbia allowed married women control of their wages, while thirty states provided for a separate estate for women. Moreover, California, Louisiana, Texas, New Mexico, and Arizona, and, later, Idaho and Washington, had laws of common property, whereby the property of a family was declared to be held in equal shares by husband and wife. Thus Susan B. Anthony and Ida H. Harper in their *History of Woman Suffrage* assessed the progress in married women's rights by 1900: "The wife now may own and control her separate property in three-fourths of the states and in the other fourth only one Northern State is included. In every State a married women may make a will, but can dispose only of her separate property. In about two-thirds of the States she possesses her earnings. In the great majority she may make contracts and bring suit. The property rights of unmarried women always have been nearly the same as those of married women." Moreover, the husband's right to use his wife's real estate "has now been abolished in over one-half of the States . . . and the wife's separate estate has been made so liberal that in comparatively few States is she left in the helpless condition of olden times."

Nevertheless, in the early twentieth century women were being admitted to all levels of education, including higher, professional, and technical education, and they were organizing themselves into groups for all sorts of careers. By comparison with the suffragists, who still had little to show for all their hard work, social feminists could point to their achievements in the fields of education, careers, and social work. Unlike suffragists, they could also show how they had brought women's influence to bear in the spheres of state and local government. Yet none of these admittedly significant advances was a serious challenge to the traditional roles of men and women. Thus, according to William O'Neill, social feminists, by their very activities outside the family, actually undermined the movement for political and social equality by simply increasing a range of opportunities for women that were usually extensions of women's activities in the home. "Their benevolent enterprise met women's desire for useful and satisfying work without touching the sources of their inequality."

The movement for woman suffrage attracted support from men and women we might think of as conservative and opposition from those we prefer to think of as liberals. For instance, it received support from certain nativist and racist sections. "I have rarely heard a ringing suffrage speech," declared social worker Florence Kelley in 1906, "which did not refer to the 'ignorant and degraded man,' or the 'ignorant immigrants' as our masters. This is habitually spoken with more or less bitterness. But this is what the workingmen are used to hearing applied to themselves by their enemies in times of strike."

The most concentrated opposition to woman suffrage came from the South in states favorable to prohibition and most intent on denying their citizens access to liquor. In the end, only ten states refused to ratify the Nineteenth Amendment, nine in the South, and Delaware on the border between North and South. However, all of these states ratified the Eighteenth (or National Prohibition) Amendment. David Morgan explains how the Democratic party, dominated by its southern section, refused to support woman suffrage by constitutional amendment as late as 1916. What the South feared was that the entire issue of suffrage would be reopened. The South had recently disfranchised black men by a series of subterfuges such as grandfather clauses, poll taxes, and literacy tests. Such devices were subversive of the Constitution but technically unassailable while the North accepted the racist arguments of the South. If woman suffrage were adopted, reasoned bigoted racists, then black women, as well as white, would be legally entitled to vote. The sort of systematic violence and coercion that had been used to intimidate black men as a matter of terrible routine could not so easily be applied to black women without attracting unfavorable publicity and leading to adverse political repercussions. Moreover, southern politicians from states producing textiles feared that if women gained the vote, then middle-class women would work to reduce, and possibly eliminate, the very child labor upon which southern industry relied.

Another crucial factor in the delay was growing awareness of just how radical a proposal was woman suffrage. On the surface, it seemed that little would change socially. However, more was expected of woman suffrage by those in favor and those opposed. Radicals such as Charlotte Perkins Gilman thought the upshot would be that middle-class women would have a chance to influence those politics directly affecting women. They were proved correct. However, as Carl Degler explains, woman suffrage appeared radical because it could not be accommodated in the traditional idea of separate spheres. "In fact, the aim of woman suffrage . . . was to break down the barriers or separation between the two spheres." Some of the early feminists, such as Frances Willard, had recognized this, and saw that wider public understanding of it would work against other causes supported by women, such as temperance. Thus, in the early days of the Women's Christian Temperance Union (WCTU) she was careful to dissociate her lobby from outspoken suffragists Elizabeth Cady Stanton and Susan B. Anthony. In 1874 she joined with others to form the Association for the Advancement of Women (AAW) and it deliberately and pointedly excluded leading suffragists.

Another factor was that many married women were reluctant to consider suffrage, partly because the doctrine of separate spheres was enough for them, providing them with considerable influence over their husbands, control of the home, and enough autonomy to work for social causes, and partly because they thought that women suffrage would disrupt the family as an institution. Woman suffrage implied the full rights of women as individuals and asserted their particular interests.

However, if women were never to free themselves from hearth and home by some sharing of responsibility they would remain cut off from all sorts of professions. Charlotte Perkins Gilman first raised the problem in *Women and Economics* and continued to discuss it. She proposed cooperative kitchens, professional house maintenance, and professional baby care as ways of allowing women to have careers without having to sacrifice marriage and family life. Another related obstacle was what Susan B. Anthony and Ida H. Harper described as "the indifference, the inertia, the apathy of women." It was, they said, women, rather than men, who put a brake on the movement. Where women did have the vote, they did not always use it. Thus in Massachusetts, after forty years of school suffrage for women, only 5 percent of women eligible actually cast their votes. In a special referendum on woman suffrage in Massachusetts in 1895 the vote was 187,000 against, compared with 110,000 in favor. What was worse from the suffragists' point of view was that while 87,000 men voted for woman suffrage, only 23,000 women did so.

Not only men but also women worked against the suffrage in various groups of "Antis," especially in those states where the suffrage movement was strongest (Illinois, Indiana, Iowa, Massachusetts, New Jersey, New York, Ohio, and Pennsylvania). Moreover, women prominent in public life took part in the campaign against woman suffrage, notably investigative journalist Ida Minerva Tarbell, economist Annie Nathan Meyer, writer and art critic Mariana van Rensselaer, prison reformer Kate Barnard, and a special agent of the Labor Department, Minnie Bronson.

The reason for organized opposition by women was the fear that woman suffrage would disrupt the family. Underlying their arguments lay the traditional assumption that the differences between men and women extended beyond biology into the suitability of one sex for a social and political role and the suitability of the other for a social role only. Ann Watkins declared in 1912, "You cannot dodge the fact women have work in the world that men cannot do, and it is equally true that men have work that women cannot do. Neither man nor woman is superior or inferior to the other; the two are just different, positive and negative, two great manifestations of a still greater force." The *Anti-Suffragist* asked in 1909 "What sort of a 'next generation' would evolve if all women considered their 'first duty' to be themselves, and overlooked the fact that their strongest power and highest possibility is that of unselfish—and often unnoticed—service." Antis also opposed reform in divorce laws because they thought the possibility of easier divorce would undermine family stability.

About 1910 suffragist leaders decided to forego the piecemeal campaign to win suffrage state by state and to concentrate upon a constitutional amendment. This was adventurous, especially when we recall that, hitherto, only four western states, all with small populations, had provided women with full suffrage. However, Congress and the president proved much easier targets than forty state legislatures because they could be embarrassed by the sort of publicity associated with the strategy of nonviolent resistance. Led by radical Alice Paul, suffragists borrowed the sort of tactics also being used by English suffragettes—picketing government buildings (notably the White House) and chaining themselves to railings, and, once in jail, going on hunger strikes. The aim was to bring shame on the authorities. Referring to the wave of militant tactics, *Judge* reported a jingle in its issue of February 10, 1912:

> Peter, Peter, pumpkin eater,
> Had a wife and tried to beat her;
> But his wife was a suffragette,
> And Peter's in the hospital yet.

The publicity associated with middle-class women who defied the law, got arrested, endured prison, and resisted force feeding and then, when freed, did everything all over again began to convince thousands of hitherto apathetic women that here was a

During the Progressive Era women's fashions moved dresses away from the hourglass figure of frills and bustle toward a more svelte look with straight outlines and shorter skirts. Here the fashions were designed with more consideration given to how they would look as illustrations reproduced on the flat printed page than as clothes to be worn by fully rounded women, breaking resolutely with past tradition. (From *The Home Book of Fashions* for Winter 1914).

cause worth fighting for. In 1915 four eastern states held referenda on woman suffrage and, although the motions were defeated, they came close to being carried, taking 46 percent in Pennsylvania, 42 percent in New York and New Jersey, and 35 percent in Massachusetts. Membership in NAWSA climbed close to 2 million, with a gross annual income of $750,000.

Thus the second generation of suffragists argued that it was not women's individual interests that should be represented but women's character as a sex. Thus politics were now interpreted as an extension of the home and needed a woman's touch to improve them. Jane Addams now emphasized that the central problems of modern cities were those with which women were most familiar—child labor, slum housing, and adulterated food. "May we not say," she opined, "that city housekeeping has failed partly because women, the traditional housekeepers, have not been consulted as to its multiform activities?"

Among the leaders of the second generation of suffragists was Carrie Chapman Catt, originally of Wisconsin, who succeeded Susan B. Anthony as president of the NAWSA, serving two terms (1900–4 and 1915–20). It was Carrie Chapman Catt who led NAWSA to the climax of its crusades to get the Nineteenth Amendment passed and ratified. She then helped form the nucleus of the suffrage association for what became the League of Women Voters of the United States (LWVUS), with the object of teaching American women to exercise their right to vote. She also served as president of the International Woman Suffrage Alliance (1904–23), and, as a committed pacifist, as chairman of the Conference on the Cause and Cure of War (1925–32).

The Nineteenth Amendment eventually passed Congress on June 4, 1919, and was ratified on August 18, 1920. It simply announced how "The right of citizens of the United States to vote shall not be denied or abridged by the United States or by any State on account of sex."

The initial results of woman franchise were most disappointing for the feminists. In the elections of 1920 and 1924, for the only times in American history, less than half the electorate turned out to vote. Women were enfranchised only a few weeks before the election of 1920 and, perhaps, needed time to get used to exer-

cising their rights. However, according to Gallup polls, the proportion of women who voted did not equal that of men until
1956—thirty-six years after they gained the vote.

More disturbing from the feminists' point of view was that,
although the suffrage movement had become central to the whole
feminist cause, woman suffrage had almost no discernible effect
upon the position of women. This was ironic because advocates
of woman suffrage had predicted how it would lead to social
reform, even to a reduction in vice and crime and the possible
elimination of imperialism and war. Thus, within three years after
the Nineteenth Amendment had been ratified, radical feminist
Alice Paul proposed a new amendment, which she called the Equal
Rights Amendment (ERA). It would forbid the federal government or any individual state from discriminating between male
and female in any way, thereby requiring the law to recognize
the treat women as individuals rather than as members of a particular sex.

Many women who had campaigned for the Nineteenth
Amendment regarded the ERA as a betrayal of all they had worked
for. For one thing, it would nullify special protective legislation
for women workers. Thus Jane Addams, Florence Kelley, and
Carrie Chapman Catt rejected ERA. For another fifty years leaders of women's organizations opposed ERA because they thought
it would actually damage women's place in society.

Divorce in the Progressive Era

During the Progressive Era the divorce rate rose dramatically. In
1880 there was 1 divorce in every 21 marriages; in 1900 there
was 1 divorce in every 12 marriages; in 1909 the ration was 1 to
10; in 1916, 1 to 9. In his article "Divorce in the Progressive Era"
for the *American Quarterly* of Summer 1965, later the subject of a
book, historian William L. O'Neill explains the impact this change
had on the defenders of marriage and the defenders of women's
rights.

The rising tide of divorce alarmed many conservatives. In 1881
the New England Divorce Reform League was founded to study
family problems, educate the public, and lobby for stricter di-

vorce laws. Yet its leader, Samuel Dike, a Congregational minister, was reluctant to face the underlying problems of divorce and to propose effective legislative solutions. Others pursued state campaigns to revise local divorce laws, while some reformers concentrated on achieving uniform federal laws on marriage and divorce. A particular target was the trade in migratory divorces, whereby prospective divorcees would take up somewhat fictitious, impermanent residences in such cities as Sioux City, South Dakota, simply to fulfill a vestigial residence requirement of ninety days and get divorced. In 1893 Bishop William Hobart Hare of the Episcopal church led a mixed campaign of Catholics, Protestants, and Populists against the ninety-day residence requirement that ended when the state legislature extended the requirement to six months.

In response to various lobbying campaigns, President Theodore Roosevelt requested a new census study of marriage in 1906 and, at the suggestion of Governor Pennypacker of Pennsylvania, a National Divorce Congress attended by delegates from forty-two states met in Washington to draft model legislation.

The Episcopal church was generally opposed to divorce and William Croswell Doone, bishop of Albany, was its most outspoken moral advocate. He would have preferred prohibiting divorce altogether and was absolutely opposed to the Church allowing even the innocent party in an adultery suit to remarry after divorce. After a series of attempts, his amendment to canon law to this effect was passed by the House of Bishops in the 1904 Triennial Episcopal Convention but failed in the House of Deputies where laymen regarded it as too far removed from the ideas of most Americans.

The social critics of easy divorce attacked it on two grounds—as immoral and antisocial. However, having declared that divorce was immoral, critics could not elaborate much further on that point and, therefore, moved on to its antisocial character. According to Theodore Schmauk, president of the Lutheran General Council, divorce destroyed the family, a prime source of civilization. This was also the view of TR. Marriage and the family are not exactly the same but critics of divorce did not usually bother to distinguish between them. By 1915 Felix Adler, founder of Ethical Culture and an advocate of liberal religion, had modified his earlier tolerance of divorce and had come to believe that divorce must be suppressed if society were to survive in its present form.

Two-thirds of all divorces were granted to women. Critics of easier divorce began to question women's traditional role as guardians of family stability and morality. They feared that the swelling tide of divorce would undermine this role and, then, society. In a symposium on divorce, "Are Women to Blame?", the *North American Review*'s women panelists accused American women of responsibility for the soaring divorce rate, charging them with being spoiled, impatient, and jealous of men. Margaret Deland, an enthusiastic supporter of Progressive causes and the champion of unmarried mothers in Boston, believed that civilization "rests upon the permanence of marriage." Easier divorce would undo civilization. She said, "If we let the flame of idealism be quenched in the darkness of the senses, our civilization must go upon the rocks." She argued that adultery did not constitute true grounds for divorce because men were promiscuous by nature and their adulteries had to be tolerated for the sake of social harmony. In this instance, the rights of the individual woman were less important than society as a whole.

Those who favored easier divorce laws were mainly sociologists, liberal clergymen, and feminists. Like critics of divorce, they argued their very different case on the grounds of morality and social need. Once Ibsen's plays, notably *A Doll's House* (1879) and *Ghosts* (1880), had been produced in the United States, they did much to expose the sham of many Victorian marriages. English feminist Mona Caird argued that marriage and divorce should be superseded by short-term marriage contracts, leaving both partners free to separate or to renegotiate a new contract upon expiry of the first. Grant Allen advocated free love and an end to marriage in a sensational novel, *The Woman Who Did*.

Many American liberals felt that conventional marriage was repressive, that it discriminated against women, and that easier divorce offered opportunities for reform of marriage. A widely known argument was that women needed to be protected from their husbands' excessive sexual demands. Feminist playwright

Jesse Lynch Williams asked in 1914 if a woman "allowing herself to be owned body and soul by a man she loathes [is] doing right?" Not only did their husbands' sexual rights make victims of many wives but they also exaggerated the significance of sex and denied women the right to develop fully because they placed too high a premium on nubility, pulchritude, and desirability. In *A History of Matrimonial Institutions* (1904), social scientist George E. Howard explained the rising tide of divorce in the context of the forces reshaping and improving society, such as industrialization and urbanization. Not only was the old patriarchal family being dissolved but new forms of marriages with higher spirituality were coming into being as the single individual, rather than the family, became the functional unity of society.

In 1908 the American Sociological Society devoted its third annual meeting to the subject of the family. Its president, William G. Sumner, commented pessimistically how "the family has to a great extent lost its position as a conservative institution and has become a field for social change." George E. Howard repeated his familiar argument in a controversial address, "Is the Freer Granting of Divorce an Evil?" Catholic lawyer Walter George Smith accused Howard of approving a social revolution that conspired to undermine the divine order of society. Nothing could change the immutable fact of female inferiority, he argued. He wanted stricter and more uniform divorce laws. Howard replied that marriage was not a divine but a social institution "to be freely dealt with by men, according to human needs." Smith's ostentatious and plangent moralism suggested how isolated was his position. By now the profession of social science was almost entirely committed to a progressive view of divorce at a time when almost all other professional groups were against it.

Sociologists could speak from knowledge and their expertise was widely admired by a society that placed trust in professional knowledge. It was the task of sociologists to allay public fears about the effects of easier divorce and, in particular, a general conviction that divorce was explicitly forbidden in the Bible. In this aim, they were aided by liberal ministers who showed that divorce was morally acceptable and legitimate provided it was not abused. Classicist and biblical scholar William G. Ballentine explained contradictions within the Bible on such matters and showed how Jesus had had to struggle continuously against Talmudic literalism in his own day. "He fought against the tyranny of mere words. . . . He suggested great truths by parables, by questions, by metaphors, by paradoxes, by hyperboles, by every device that could elude the semblance of fixed judicial formulas. It is the irony of history that such language should be seized upon for statute law." The impact of Ballentine's argument and the arguments of others was to undermine a widespread conviction that the Bible forbade divorce absolutely. The Reverend Minot J. Savage said that, as love was the essence of marriage, a couple who no longer loved one another should have the right to get divorced.

Gradually, public opinion began to change and organizations opposed to divorce, such as the New England Divorce Reform League (1881–1913) and the Committee on the Family of the Federal Council of Churches (1911–19), failed. The press, once staunchly opposed to divorce, began to shift emphasis and adopted the critical stance of such progressive journals as the *North American Review,* the *Outlook,* and the *World's Work.* The *World's Work* published "The true view of Increasing Divorce" in 1910. The rate of divorce had not reached epidemic proportions and divorces should not be excessively restricted. This is not to say that the press went to another extreme of advocating divorce as social therapy; it simply explained that there were several different ways of looking at a complex issue. William L. O'Neill concludes his article, "Divorce in the Progressive Era," with an assessment of the changed situation:

Divorce was a part of the complex transformation of moral values and sexual customs which was to help give the 1920s their bizarre flavor. It was not only the most visible result of this vast social upheaval, but in many ways it was the most compatible with traditional modes of thought. It was, on the whole, an orderly public and institutionalized process which took due account of the formal difference between right and wrong, guilt and innocence. It had the blessings of the highest sociological authorities and it was recommended by many feminists as a cure for the brutalizing sexual indignities known to occur in some marriages. Conservatives could, therefore, more easily resign themselves to

A flapper alights from her motor car. Suzette Dewey, daughter of Assistant Secretary of the Treasury Charles Dewey, photographed in full flight in December 1927. The photograph records examples of two icons of the postwar period: the adolescent girl with bobbed hair and short skirt and the automobile. (French Collection, Library of Congress).

divorce than to other, more extravagant, demonstrations of the changing moral order.

New Moral Values

In *Years of Discretion: A Play of Cupid at Fifty* by Frederic Hatton and Fanny Locke Hatton, staged by David Belasco in New York and Chicago in 1912, the widowed heroine of forty-eight declares, "I intended to look under forty—lots under. I have never attracted men, but I know I can." Also, "I mean to have a wonderful time. To have all sorts and kinds of experience. I intend to love and be loved, to lie and cheat." Deploring the newfound interest in sexual sensation, Dorothy Dix wrote in the Boston *American* of April 10, 1908, "I'll bet there are not ten thousand women in the whole United States who couldn't get one hundred in an examination of the life and habits of Evelyn Nesbitt and Harry Thaw." Evelyn Nesbitt was the wife of Harry Thaw who had an affair with architect Stanford White, whom Thaw shot and killed. Possibly in keeping with the implied sexuality of Elinor Glyn's novels, William M. Reedy, editor of the St. Louis *Mirror* coined the phrase "sex o'clock" in 1913. Already, in the 1910s, such writers as H. W. Boynton in "Ideas, Sex and the Novel" for the *Dial* (1916), Robert W. Chambers in *The Restless Sea* (1918), and Arthur Pollock in "Are We Immoral" for *Forum* (1914) thought that society and literature were liberating themselves from Victorian values and enjoying a new freedom in morals.

Married women in fashionable society in the 1910s threw lavish parties, hiring black orchestras at Newport, and performing such daring dances as the turkey trot, bunny hug, and grizzly bear. One of them, the chicken flip, was invented by a Boston society woman. In retrospect, their parties were scandalous and the more famous ones of the 1920s were quite staid by comparison.

These hostesses practiced birth control on lines discussed by Louis J. I. Dublin in *Social Hygiene* of January 1920. Novelist Robert Herrick described the pleasure seeking, aimless lives of upper-class and professional women in which childbearing was repudiated as a waste of a year while infidelity was accepted as providing a welcome relief from social routine. In *Together* Herrick describes the temperament of the modern woman as one of the "mistress rather than the wife . . . . 'I shall be a person with a soul of my own. To have me, man must win me not once, but daily.' " In F. Scott Fitzgerald's *This Side of Paradise* (1920), Rosalind tells her lover, "I have to be won all over again every time you see me."

It could be the same for lower classes in the towns. The Chicago *Herald and Examiner* of March 10–17, 1920, ran a series of extracts from the diary of Ruth Vail Randall, a woman dissatisfied with her husband and routine work in a department store because there was no romance in either of them. She took a series of lovers, and, fearing that the last would eventually leave her, she killed him and herself on March 6, 1920. The diary discloses the sort of conditions and events that show how the revolution in morals could flourish. Because Mrs. Randall and her husband, Norman, lived in a neighborhood with a continuously shifting population, they could live somewhat anonymously and choose their own moral values. Ruth Vail Randall did not want children and had an abortion. She also chafed at the traditional womanly role of submission expected by her husband. "Why cannot a woman do all a man does?" she complained and set out to make her social life as independent as any man's, and, consequently, drank, flirted, and had sex freely with other men. Her promiscuity was facilitated by telephones and automobiles. Her diary disclosed her excessive hopes of love but her various lovers disappointed her as much as her husband by their lack of companionship and tenderness. She often thought of suicide and, once in her disillusionment, noted, "I am miserable. I have the utmost contempt for myself. But the lake is near and soon it will be warm. Oh, God, to rest in your arms. To rest—and to have peace."

The shifting sands of new moral values disturbed various civic officials. They found that, despite their censure of divorce, liquor, and prostitution as evils and of dancing, loosened dress, birth control, and ever-increasing forms of entertainments as the way to hell, women were racing down the primrose path. *Mrs.*

Warren's Profession, George Bernard Shaw's play unpleasant of syndicated prostitution and its causes, was withdrawn from the New York stage after only one performance in 1905. The *New York Times* of May 28, 1913, reported how a grand jury had condemned the turkey trot and other dances as indecent, leading to the bench insisting on licensing public dancing. The issue of June 29, 1913, reported that the police chief of Louisville, Kentucky, had all women arrested who appeared on the streets with slit skirts.

Fearing that spreading information on contraception would encourage greater sexual license, both the federal and various state governments enacted sumptuary legislation. The two most widely publicized cases involved Van K. Allison in Boston in July 1916 and Margaret Sanger in New York in February 1917 who were both prosecuted, convicted, and imprisoned. When Mrs. Sanger was arrested for publicizing information on birth control, she said, "I have nothing to fear. . . . Regardless of the outcome, I shall continue my work, supported by thousands of men and women throughout the country."

Margaret Sanger and the Campaign for Birth Control

Margaret Sanger's great will to create a widely based movement of birth control and the skill with which she conceived it probably affected a wider social and ethnic spectrum of women than any other movement of social reform in the twentieth century.

Born into circumstances of abject poverty in Corning, New York, in 1879, Margaret Sanger tried to transcend her personal situation whilst freeing other women from any exploitation of the fact that biology must be destiny. From her Irish-American stonecutter father, Michael Higgins, she learned socialist ideas and her understanding of the relationship between capital and labor was reinforced by poverty. Cheated by domestic circumstances of her preferred careers as teacher, actress, and doctor, she, nevertheless, completed her training as nurse at the Manhattan Eye and Ear Hospital. Her marriage to William Sanger proved unhappy and deepened her understanding of the way men who were domestic bullies damaged women's potential for self-fulfillment. She became a campaigner for birth control to free women in the home rather than the workplace. Her experience of life in the Lower East Side was pivotal. She learned how working-class women were chained to enforced motherhood and poverty. Their only alternative recourse was from a "five-dollar abortionist." One victim, Sadie Sachs, a mother of twelve, died from infection following a second self-induced abortion after a doctor withheld advice on how to anticipate and prevent another pregnancy. Roused by such tragedies, in March 1914 Margaret Sanger published the first issue of the *Woman Rebel,* trying to make working-class women think for themselves and not simply accept the general dictates of their husbands. Its slogan was "No Gods, No Masters." Margaret Sanger's demand for public information on birth control was an initial step in the revolt against paternalism. She declared how "Suffragists, feminists and all women's organizations will never make progress until they recognize the fact that women cannot be on an equal footing with men until they have full and complete control of their reproductive functions."

The paper was an immediate success and Margaret Sanger decided to use some of the money from subscriptions to publishing a pamphlet, *Family Limitation,* that would provide information on contraception. It was before *Family Limitation* was in print that she was indicted by the federal government for violation of the mails by having used them to distribute an "obscene" article in the *Women Rebel.* Rather than face trial and a possible jail sentence of forty-five years, she left for Europe in fall 1914 but not before *Family Limitation* had been published. In the end, the federal government chose not to prosecute her and raise a controversy.

By the time she returned to New York in 1916, a group of liberal women had created the National Birth Control League with the aim of getting laws on birth control revised. Their leader, Mary Ware Dennett, tried to recruit members from the subscription lists at the *Women Rebel* but failed to gain enough members. She rejected Margaret Sanger's overtures and the two were at loggerheads for the next ten years. Arrested for publication and distribution of the *Family Limitation,* Margaret Sanger, nevertheless, set off on a nationwide tour to elicit support and funds for her plan to establish birth control clinics. In Portland, Oregon, she was again arrested for distributing *Family Limitation*. The publicity was such that her name and the idea of professional birth control were spread by newspapers right across the country.

Margaret Sanger opened her first birth control clinic in the United States in the Brownsville section of Brooklyn on October 16, 1916. For a fee of only 10 cents, she explained to Italian and Jewish immigrant women how to use various birth control devices and helped about 500 women to get a diaphragm fitted. After ten days she was arrested. She challenged police interpretation of the law, claiming the specific code, Section 1142, was unconstitutional because it compelled women to run risks of death in childbirth: thus it did not promote the health and welfare of the community. After she spent thirty days in jail, the judge who reviewed her case ruled that doctors could prescribe contraception but, also, that birth control was a matter for the legislatures, not the courts. It was another five years before Margaret Sanger had the court decision widened so that she could open a birth control clinic that employed a physician.

In this period she founded the American Birth Control League and a new periodical, *Birth Control Review,* wrote two popular books, and remarried. She was now convinced that her best stragegy was an alliance with affluent society people. This move from her working class, radical origins was symbolized by her marriage to J. Noah Slee, the manufacturer of Two-in-One Oil whom she did not love but whose wealth could supply her campaigns. They lived separately. Because the American Birth Control League was a membership organization, it could not legally distribute contraceptives. Thus Margaret Sanger persuaded a young doctor, Dorothy Bocker, to open, on January 2, 1923, a separate, private clinic, the Birth Control Resources Center, across the hall from her office. Dr. Bocker's inability to collect precise information from patients on the success of her measures was much criticized and, in 1924, Sanger replaced her with Dr. Hannah Stone whose aftercare research findings supported her own ideas on birth control.

After World War I laws spreading contraceptive information

remained on the statute books but were more honored in the breach than the observance. As Margaret Sanger's organization, the American Birth Control League, developed into a middle-class reform movement and gained support from doctors, the number of birth control clinics multiplied. Margaret Sanger maintained that effective birth control would produce "more children from the fit, less from the unfit." It would eradicate the degenerate and the diseased, rid society of "poverty, mental defects, feeble-mindedness, and other transmissable traits." (Thus many of the earlier progressive arguments for birth control were like those for prohibition of alcohol.) In time, the movement for birth control capitalized on its scientific and eugenic intentions, rather than on its radical origins. Thus, it won over many from the middle class and the medical profession and became a pivot of the new morality.

Prostitution was known as "white slavery" and was investigated by Congress and certain state legislatures, including Wisconsin and Massachusetts. General Theodore A. Bingham, a former head of the New York police, wrote an account, *The Girl That Disappears,* and such varied cities as Chicago and Minneapolis established commissions to study the problem. Show business exploited the more sensational aspects in a series of white slave films and plays. Censorship served to increase the appetite for so-called vice films, such as *Traffic in Souls,* which earned $450,000 gross at the box office. If anything, prostitution was declining but the public enjoyed the titillation of a white slave panic in 1912–13. Public officers also deplored what they interpreted as the corrosive effect of movies. Four states established boards to review and censor movies—Pennsylvania (1911), Ohio (1913), Maryland (1916), and Kansas (1917)—as did various cities beginning with Chicago (1907).

A legend developed that white slavers procured victims by stupefying young women on streetcars by injecting them with poisoned needles and carrying them off to brothels to be broken in by professional rapists. "How far," complained the New York *World,* "is this ridiculous delusion to go? If the popular imagination is to become heated to a point where it discerns an attempt at abduction in every dizzy feeling of momentary illness suffered by a young woman in a public place, it will be unsafe for a man to offer the slightest civility to a person of the opposite sex whom he does not happen to know." Having roused public disquiet, the press then quoted testimony from doctors about how impossible it would be to drug an unwilling person by a hyperdermic needle on a crowded streetcar. In *My Little Sister* Elizabeth Robins wrote a best-selling fictional account of two young girls lured into prostitution in London whence one survives to tell a cautionary tale. The Mann Act, passed on June 25, 1910, and named after its sponsor, Congressman James R. Mann of Chicago, but also called the white slave traffic act, proscribed interstate traffic of women for commercial sex "or for any other immoral purpose."

The 1920s quickened rather than started a revolution that had already begun by encouraging women from small towns to adopt attitudes and dress that were becoming increasingly accepted in the great cities.

CHAPTER SEVEN

History Written in Lightning:
The Transportation Revolution of
Henry Ford and the Wright Brothers

·ॐ·

"HISTORY WRITTEN in lightning" was Woodrow Wilson's comment on D. W. Griffith's film, *The Birth of a Nation* (1915). His remark also rings true for the way science and technology were extending American industry and manufacturing, notably in the creation and mass production of automobiles and airplanes. When we speak of the world in the twentieth century as a global community, we are not only acknowledging the controversial contributions of imperialism, mass migration, and economic ties between nations geographically far apart, but also advances in communication and transportation. Telephone, radio, television, and satellite links have made communication truly instantaneous. In the field of transportation, automobiles and airplanes have reduced distance and all but eliminated it as an impediment for politics, trade, and socializing, and, it must be admitted, for war. The United States led the way in motor cars and airplanes and changed the world irrevocably.

After the turn of the century the primary leaders in American industrial growth were the automobile, electric-power, and chemical industries. These industries affected production in re-

GENTLEMEM
OUR
COUNTRY

HENRY FORD, AND HIS FIRST CAR.

Henry Ford and his first car. Automobile manufacturer Henry Ford transformed society by an acute combination of technical prowess in a new field, self-interested paternalist management, and rugged pioneer determination. (Library of Congress).

lated industries and the structural nature of industry in general, just as they reshaped social patterns and life-styles. Early statistics on automobile production and sales indicate something of the extent of the changes set in motion by public appreciation of the possibilities of motor cars. In 1900 4,192 passenger cars were sold for a total of $4.89 million; in 1910 181,000 were sold for $215.34 million; in 1920 1.90 million cars were sold for $1.80 billion. The value of the automobile industry rose from 150th in 1900 to first in 1925, when it also accounted for 6 percent of the total value of American manufacturing. However, the story of car production was not one of consistent growth. After a peak of 3.73 million cars were sold in 1925 for $2.45 billion, sales slumped slightly. In 1930 2.78 million cars were sold for $1.64 billion. Thereafter, sales increased and in 1940 3.71 million cars were sold for $2.37 billion. Nevertheless, it was the automobile that made possible the development of the modern city and its suburbs and provided the stimulus for further industrial revolution. The automobile stimulated construction of roads and suburban houses, and aided the development of advertising, insurance, and banking. In short, the automobile revolution was the cutting edge in a social revolution that made Americans more independent because more mobile than ever before. In addition to the more obvious innovation in transportation and the extra expansion of industry and manufacturing, automobile production also stimulated three profound changes in manufacturing: the further introduction of mass assembly production; greater emphasis on marketing, as distinct from sales; and yet another version of executive management with a more flexible form of centralized control.

The Early Years of Automobiles

The invention of automobiles was the product of many minds, but Nicholas Joseph Cugnot is usually credited with having first perfected a primitive car in 1769 and Richard Trevithick with another in the 1830s. Charles Brady King manufactured the first American car in Detroit in 1869. Charles E., and J. Frank Duryea were credited with building the first gasoline-powered car, the Duryea, that ran a secondhand carriage chassis from a one cylinder electrical ignition. It was first run by Frank at Springfield, Massachusetts, on September 21, 1893. However, the Duryeas' title was contested by John William Lambert of Ohio City, Ohio. George B. Selden of Rochester, New York, applied for the first gasoline auto patent in 1879, before he had actually built a car, and it was granted as patent 549, 160 in 1895, after he had built one.

However, it was Ransom Eli Olds who was the first automaker who tried to produce motor cars en masse. Having obtained credit from local banks in 1897, he set up a business in Lansing, Michigan, that failed, partly because he did not have enough capital and partly because he could not find enough local customers. In the end, he survived by obtaining a capital-stock subscription of $200,000 from S. L. Smith that left him with only a 5 percent interest in the business. In 1899 he began to make a complex, quality, and expensive automobile in Detroit but soon returned to Lansing where he began to make the Oldsmobile in 1901. Instead of making each part himself, he bought parts in quantity from various suppliers, and concentrated on the assembly of vehicles. By dividing his labor force into sections and assigning a special task to each, he introduced a rudimentary assembly line into automobile manufacture. Olds demonstrated the commercial potential of motor cars by selling 425 cars in 1901. His mass-produced Oldsmobile sold for $650, a competitive price, and in the first three years of 1901–4, Olds paid investors 105 percent on their securities. In 1904 he sold 5,000 vehicles but parted with Smith when Smith would not agree to concentrate on mass-produced motor cars for the general market. Olds's success encouraged other automobile manufacturers who wanted to enter and exploit the new market. Thus 241 new automobile companies were created in the period 1904–8.

The expansion of the automotive industry occurred in three distinct phases: a pioneering stage in the period 1893–1903; a stage of mass production between 1903 and 1927 in which the central problems of production and capital accumulation were first discovered; and a mature phase of prosperity since 1927. It was somewhat interrupted by the Great Depression and World War II but it was characterized by underlying continuous expansion in which the problems to be solved included marketing, labor relations, and then safety standards and environmental impact.

The earlier years of the automobile industry were characterized by technological innovations and commercial uncertainties.

The steering knuckle was invented in 1902 by Sterling Elliott. It allowed both front wheels to turn while the axle remained stationary and thus introduced the principle of a steering wheel to replace the old tiller. Car tires went through a series of improvements. The pneumatic tire of 1892 was succeeded by clincher-type tire (1899), standard quick demountable tire rims (1904), the nonskid tire (1908), the cord tire (1910), and the balloon tire (1914). Other improvements included automatic lubrication (1904); front bumpers (1906); the first v-8 engine (1907 Hewitt, made by Hewitt Motor Co., New York); left-hand steering (1908); all-steel automobile body (1912) by Edward G. Budd; 4-wheel hydraulic brakes (1918) by Malcolm Loughead (later, Lockheed); ethyl gasoline (1923), developed by Thomas Midgley, Jr., and Charles F. Kettering.

Charles Franklin Kettering of Ohio was a most significant pioneer. After inventing an electric motor for cash registers, he organized the Dayton Engineering Laboratories Co. (Delco) in 1909 and, in the next two years, achieved significant improvements in automobile ignition and lighting systems. His perfection of the self-starter in 1911, thereby dispensing with manual starting with an axle and first installed in the 1912 Cadillac, greatly enlarged the market for cars.

It was by no means a foregone conclusion that automobiles would be powered by gasoline. At the turn of the century about 40 percent of American cars were driven by steam, about 38 percent by electricity, and about 22 percent on gasoline. Makers and consumers alike tended to agree that gasoline was unreliable, causing excess noise and making the cars vibrate too much. Steam was also problematic, making the car thirsty. It seemed that electricity provided the optimum form of energy for cars. Electric power was clean and quiet, instantly self-starting and easy to maintain. Moreover, the first automobile to exceed 100 kph (60 mph) was electric, Camille Jenatzky's La Jamais Contente (1899). As the market widened, the major limitation of electric-powered cars became ever more apparent: electric batteries needed recharging every few miles and this could only be done easily in towns. The gasoline-powered engine proved its superiority over electric- and steam-powered engines largely because it was lighter, could reach higher speeds, and was simpler to run. Charles Kettering's invention of the electric self-starter for gasoline cars made the gas-driven car seem far more convenient. Moreover, it could serve a wider market, beyond the confines of cities and towns where it was easier to recharge the battery.

Among the first entrepreneurs to appreciate the social and commercial possibilities of motor cars were such bicycle makers as Albert A. Pope, Alexander Winton, and George N. Pierce, and such carriage makers as the Studebaker brothers and William C. Durant. They build the sort of organization necessary for large-scale selling. Among the engineers who recognized the potential of the automobile were Wilfred H. Leland, founder of Cadillac, and Henry Ford. They also realized just how important it would be to make a dependable product with interchangeable parts if motor cars were to be sold in quantity.

Manufacture of automobiles was a complex business; mass production and low prices did not in themselves guarantee success. Since 1900 there have been over 1,500 manufacturers of cars and trucks but less than a dozen have survived. In general, it was those auto manufacturers who concentrated on mass-production, cheaper cars for the general market who survived longest.

The auto industry encouraged innovations in various tributary industries. Because cars ideally required lighter metals, the steel industry developed various alloys. The need for more durable tires encouraged the rubber industry to make better wearing materials; the need for tougher glass stimulated production of shatterproof glass. The call for higher-powered fuel continuously stimulated the petroleum industry to refine ethyl and high-octane gasoline. The earliest automobile fuel was composed of those fractions of crude oil that were too light to be included in kerosene and had previously been considered unsalable. The development of the cracking process in the 1920s was a major improvement in oil refining. Cracking consisted of heating surplus heavier oils under pressure and thereby cracking, or splitting, their large molecules into small ones that form the lighter, more valuable fractions. After suitable chemical treatment, gasoline manufactured by cracking performed better in automobile engines than gasoline derived from straight distillation. In addition, the new industry became a major market for tin, copper, felt, leather, and sundry other products. Perhaps the greatest gains were in road construction. Whereas the states spent a total of $75 million on highway construction in 1918, in 1932 they were spending over $1 billion a year.

The United States' major contribution to automobile manufacture was the system of mass production. In fact, mass production with its special emphasis on standardization and interchangeability of parts was not only suited to the United States but also essential. For, although the American population was large and its potential market considerable, it was also widely dispersed, thus needing such an invention as the automobile with its interchangeable parts. Others had thought of mass assembly production before Ford. In 1900 Wilfred H. Leland of Cadillac Motors demonstrated the perfect interchangeability of parts to his car at the RAC in London when he disassembled three cars, removed eighty-seven parts, replaced them with dealers' stock, then reassembled the cars, and finally drove them for 500 miles without any hitch. However, it was Henry Ford, above all others, who drew together the diverse threads of interchangeable parts, mass production, and cheap, reliable motor cars, to produce a product that changed the world.

The Driving Ambition of Henry Ford

Henry Ford transformed the society into which he was born through an astute mix of pioneer engineering and paternalist management. London *Times* critic John Campbell characterizes Ford thus:

No one better enbodies the contradiction of the American dream than Henry Ford. On the one hand he was the country boy who liked tinkering with farm machines, the democratic genius who popularized a rich man's toy by putting it within the reach of every American, the benevolent employer, and the folksy idealist who used his status as an American hero to preach his personal gospel of self-reliance, fair dealing, and clean living across the nation. On the other hand, it was the mass ownership of motor cars, more than anything else, that destroyed the old rural America he cherished; while his invention of the production line enslaved more thoroughly than ever before all those free Americans to whom he addressed his sermons.

His father, William Ford, was a successful farmer of Scots-Irish descent who ran a profitable farm near Dearborn, Michigan, where Henry Ford was born in July 1863. The farm had its own sawmill, gristmill, and machinery for making homespun wool sheared from its own sheep. Although Henry disliked farm work, he had a special mechanical facility and intuitive logic and at an early age began tinkering with clocks and generally fixing things. According to some, Henry and William were constantly at odds, the son always wanting to work with machines, the father detesting the very mechanization that was transforming farming in the Midwest. By the time Henry was an adolescent, their quarrels were bitter. It is certainly true that at that time Henry Ford had little interest in books and none at all in religion.

In 1891 he started work as an engineer for the Edison Illuminating Company and used his spare time to work on a small motor-driven vehicle he had designed. In 1895 he met his hero, Thomas Edison, who encouraged him to continue his experiments and in 1896 he demonstrated his first car. In order to get it out of his home workshop, he had to demolish a brick wall. It worked and Ford sold it for $200. In 1899, asked by the Edison Company to choose between his job and his obsession for motor cars, he decided to dedicate himself to automobiles full-time.

However, Ford had two false starts before the Ford Motor Company became a viable commercial concern, chiefly because Ford devoted most of his time and energy on the car that was to become the Model T. Neither of his earlier companies, the Detroit Automobile Company and the Henry Ford Automobile Company, survived. These failures attest to Ford's intense difficulties in working in conditions where he lacked full control.

He realised that self-advertisement was essential in any new business and that speed was the best way to attract attention to himself in the new and fast moving world of automobiles. Thus, while he had no interest in speed for its own sake, he knew that breaking speed records was one sure way of achieving celebrity. Thus, when he began to win races at such fashionable tracks as Grosse Pointe, Michigan, where he once attained a speed of seventy miles an hour, he earned the sort of publicity that attracted investors. The Ford Motor Company was formed in June 1903 on money provided by Alexander Y. Malcolmson, a Detroit coal merchant, and John Gray, a Detroit banker, who was able to provide funds of $28,000 in cash. Other stockholders included James Couzens, the coal merchant's secretary who became the business brain of the Ford Motor Company, and two brothers, John F., and Horace E. Dodge, machinists who built engines and chassis for Ford and, later, led their own auto company. This third venture was successful because Ford was kept on the financial rails by accountant James Couzens and was prodded toward ever more efficient production by Harold C. Wills, the true proponent of assembly line production.

In 1903 there were over twenty-five manufacturers of passenger cars and, apart from Ransom E. Olds, none of them sold more than several hundred cars each year. At this time the automobile was still in an experimental stage. There was no standardization of engine, transmission, tools, or process and it was not until 1907 that true interchangeability of parts was demonstrated, even among supposedly identical cars. Nevertheless, public fancy was increasingly taken with the automobile and its various possibilities for transportation and social life. There was a rising public demand for motor cars, even though the majority were too expensive for aspirant middle-class folk.

This was the context in which Henry Ford made a dramatic announcement in 1907. He proclaimed, "I will build a motor car for the great multitude. It will be large enough for the family but small enough for the individual to run and care for. It will be constructed of the best materials, by the best men to be hired, after the simplest designs that modern engineering can devise. But it will be so low in price that no man making a good salary will be unable to own one—and enjoy with his family the blessing of hours of pleasure in God's great open spaces." Ford was certainly correct in thinking that what would sell in huge quantities was not the sort of elaborate, expensive automobiles that most engineers and drivers liked, but something light and reliable, simple and cheap. Cultural historian Warren I. Susman comments in his *History as Culture* (1973) on the significance of Ford's proclamation:

From the vantage point of the time it was issued, this extraordinarily simple statement is breathtaking in its implications. It is, in fact, a prediction of a new social order, an introduction to the world that was to be in the 1920s. It had enormous significance for the individual, the family, the mass society—and perhaps even in a sense proposed a serious redefinition of each. It hinted at a new definition of work and of production. It projected the likelihood of a new life-style. It implied a new kind of possible egalitarianism unheard of in the world's history—and it did all of this not in the name of needs, basic requirements of life, but in terms of possible pleasure: here, indeed, was a consumer vision of the world.

Ford's partners were dissatisfied. Malcolmson wanted Ford to concentrate on the high-priced, six cylinder Model K. The issue was resolved when Ford, backed by James Couzens and the Dodge brothers, bought Malcolmson out for $175,000 in July 1906. This gave Ford control of more than 50 percent of company stock. In time, Ford bought out five of his partners, thereby acquiring financial control of his company. He also redesigned his car and began constructing a plant to house the first complete assembly line.

It was most important that the car should be light and easy to operate and the optimum metal was vanadium steel. No one in America knew how to make vanadium steel and thus Ford brought over a man from England who did. The process required a furnace temperature of 3,000° Fahrenheit, whereas conventional furnaces could reach only 2,700°F. Ford persuaded a steel company to try with an improved furnace and guaranteed it against loss. The trials were successful and the result was steel with a tensile strength of 170,000 pounds (compared with 60,000 or 70,000 pounds in ordinary steels) that could be fashioned into lighter but sturdier parts. Thus vanadium steel was used to make the car stronger and lighter, increasing the ratio of the horsepower to the weight and making it cheaper to run.

The Model T was the first car designed for a mass market and, to ensure its success, Ford found ways to build it cheaply. It was to be "a car for a great multitude," designed to be serviceable and rugged. Its production from 1908 involved a whole series of key decisions on Ford's part. Firstly, Ford created a giant plant, extended over 65 acres in Highland Park, and he tried to cut back on dividends to stockholders in order to plow profits back into new production. Secondly, Ford decided to make only one car: "The way to make automobiles is to make one automobile like another automobile, to make them all alike, to make them come from the factory just alike—just like one pin is like another pin when it comes from the pin factory." In this Ford was following a well-established American tradition of mass production but one that had not, as yet, been applied to automobile manufacture. It entailed a design of car suitable for mass use, rather than one that was suitable for cheap manufacture.

Thirdly, Ford had to find the right techniques for low-cost production. The axis of mass production in Ford's factory was an assembly line, a conveyor belt running the entire length of a long nave along which hundreds of workmen performed specific specialized tasks while the slow moving conveyor belt carried the chassis to and from each workman. Coming in from the sides were feeder belts carrying such parts as carburetors, motor blocks, bolts and screws, windshields, batteries, gasoline tanks, and wheels. The whole process entailed a huge financial commitment because of the number and range of specialist tools required. The idea of continuous movement depended on two principles: bringing the work to the worker and not the worker to the work; and keeping the work waist high so that no one would have to stoop continuously while he was performing delicate tasks. These things were not achieved easily or at once. In fact, it took almost seven years to perfect the system. Thus Ford benefited from the ever better production and marketing techniques introduced by successive generations of salaried managers of the new industries. These included the standardization of processes and products, integration of supply industries, placing assembly plants at strategically dispersed locations, and a continuous production line. Warren Susman concluded in his *History as Culture* (1973), "Never before had such a complex mechanical process been devised or such production been possible. The achievement required a spectacular degree of synchronization, precision, and specialization."

In effect, men, tools, and machines were merged into one gi-

The cheap, black, and ugly Model-T car, based on the principle of interchangeable parts, opened a horizon of mobility for all but the poorest
classes, allowing them the luxury of reliable, personal transport and
opportunities for daily commuting from suburbs to city centers and all
manner of rural recreation. This photo was taken in Oregon in 1921.
(Library of Congress).

gantic machine. Further refinements made it possible to reduce the time required to produce a car. In 1920 a Model T ran off the production line every minute; in 1925, one every ten seconds. Production rose form 39,640 cars in 1911 to 740,770 in 1917.

Ford produced the Model T for almost twenty years, from 1908 to 1927, never changing the basic design, model, or even the body color—black. The Model T was sometimes known as a Tin Lizzie but more often as a "flivver." A flivver was a small and inexpensive automobile, so called because it shook the liver, hence "for the liver" or "f'liver."

> There was a fat man of Fall River,
> Who said as he drove his Ford "flivver,"
> "This bumping and jolting,
> To me is revolting!
> It's hell! but it's good for the liver."

As Ford's production rose, so, too, did sales which climbed steadily from about 12,000 cars in 1909 to over 800,000 in 1917 and by 1918 Ford had 50 percent of the American market. The cheap and dependable Ford Tin Lizzie allowed an artisan living in the inner city to travel to work some miles beyond the outskirts; it enabled farmers to haul light produce to market; and it encouraged families to take day trips and vacations.

Although he solved many problems of production, Ford's methods created new ones. The assembly line created a new sort of work force, one in which the old distinction between highly skilled and manual labor was becoming extinct, since the largest number of employees performed repetitive tasks as machine tenders and assemblers. However, although their work was monotonous, it required alertness, dexterity, and judgment. Thus the degree of mechanization reduced workers to cogs in giant wheels, men who could be quickly trained but who often became dissatisfied at the sheer monotony of their task. Not surprisingly, there was a disturbing, high level of turnover in the labor force.

Mass production depended on "scientific management," a phrase made popular by lawyer Louis D. Brandeis of Boston in 1910. Scientific management was synonymous with the name of Philadelphia engineer Frederick A. W. Taylor. Born into a Quaker family in Germantown in 1856, Taylor was unable to finish his studies at Exeter Academy because of his poor eyesight. He went to work as a laborer for the Midvale Steel Company and rose to become foreman and general technical adviser while he qualified as a mechanical engineer at Stevens Institute of Technology. Taylor defined the basic principles of scientific management thus:

First, the development of a science for each element of a man's work to replace the old rule-of-thumb method; second, the selection and training of workmen to follow the science laid down; third, the payment of extraordinarily high wages to workmen who approach the standard performance set up, and of ordinary wages to those who take more than the standard time allowance; and fourth, the dividing of responsibility between men and management on a basis of scientifically determined function.

To Taylor absolutely nothing was accepted on trust and industrial tradition was to be indicted rather than respected. His "whale of a New England conscience" abhorred waste and compelled him to investigate every accepted method in industry. He astonished even the Germans at the Paris Exhibition of 1900 by the quality of his high-speed lathes as they cut through hard metals with consummate ease. He believed, "The best measure of the value of a tool lies in the exact cutting speed at which it is completely ruined at the end of twenty minutes." Scientific management was also promoted by Henry Lawrence Gantt and Frank B. Gilbreth.

Although Henry Ford allowed only minor variations to his assembly line, his continuous and dramatic reductions in price more than compensated for any public weariness with the traditional design. Thus the Model T cost $950 in 1909, $360 in 1916, and only $290 in 1926. These were marked reductions when we consider the fact of unprecedented inflation caused by World War I and the declining purchasing power of the dollar. In doing this Ford had a definite commercial philosophy. He aimed to reduce the price and thereby increase the number of sales. By improving production efficiency, he could increase his output and thus sell automobiles at ever lower prices, thereby initiating and repeating successive cycles of greater production and lower costs. Salesmen warned him that in his intention to make cars at the cheapest price he was removing exactly the sort of small ornament customers liked, such as the slender yellow line on the bodies. Advised that they wanted a choice of body colors, he was supposed to have replied, "They can have any color they want, so [long as] it's black." As a result of Ford's strategy, ownership of a motor car was to come within the reach, if not the grasp, of numerous Americans. They could each travel as fast as one another. Wealthy patrons with ornamental Packards and Buicks were really little better off than farmers with their Fords.

Sensing and seizing the opportunity for international sales, Ford opened his first factory in Canada in 1904, his first British factory in 1911, and began to diversify his products, building farm tractors in 1916, trucks in 1917, and aircraft in the years 1924–32. By March 1913 the Ford Motor Company had branches in thirty-one American cities and fourteen cities abroad.

In 1914, on the eve of World War I, Henry Ford had been manufacturing more cars than anyone else for almost ten years—and at a price that more people could afford than were any of his competitors—with over half a million Ford cars on the roads—but he was almost unknown as a person. To the public at large his name was the name of a product, not of a man. Then on January 5, 1914, Henry Ford announced in the press that as a means of sharing his profits with his 13,000 employees, he would pay a minimum wage of $5 for an eight-hour day. The announcement completely overshadowed all other national and international news, including the war in Mexico. The *New York Times* suspended its disbelief, exclaiming how "the lowest paid employees, the sweepers, who in New York City may claim from $1.00 to $1.50 a day, are now to receive $5 in Ford's plant." It was, said the *New York Herald,* "an epoch in the world's industrial history." The Detroit *Free Press* brought abolitionist poet John Greenleaf Whittier up-to-date with the pert verse

> Of all glad words
> That now are roared
> The gladdest are these:
> He works for Ford.

However, Ford attached certain social conditions to his minimum wage in which minimum standards of conduct were required of "good workers." John R. Commons reported enthusiastically that Ford was doubling the wages of those "who could pass his sociology examination in the clean and wholesome life." Indeed, Ford established a Sociological Department (subsequently called the Education Department), initially under the control of an Episcopalian minister, to teach workers how to lead an exemplary life, free from tobacco and alcohol. Because such paternalism was suspect to radicals and labor, Ford eventually abandoned the scheme.

The hitherto little known manufacturer from Detroit became the subject of intense press scrutiny. In seven days alone the New York press printed fifty-two columns about him. Thus the public learned how Ford lived modestly, enjoyed skating, and disliked Wall Street; raised pheasants whom he fed on custard; that he placed no special value on a college education, liked to give former prisoners a fresh start, and disapproved of professional charity. Excited headlines were followed by equally heated debate. The Ford idea became as well known as the Ford car. It was a "magnificent act of generosity" (New York *Evening Post*) that would make Ford workers self-respecting and independent; it was a cunning way of stealing an advantage over competitors that would rob workers of their independence as they would be encouraged to spend their money foolishly.

Whatever Ford's real motives for paying $5 a day to men he could have employed for $2, his own preferred explanation that it was "a plain act of social justice" was considered somewhat disingenuous. Nevertheless, Ford's decision expressed what his company needed. If it were to continue to grow, it must have a wider constituency of consumers than those limited few who could afford to buy a car in 1914. New consumers on the scale required could only be created among blue collar workers who must have additional wages if they were to play the new part allotted to them. Henry Ford may have thought he was playing a hunch but in fact Ford the institution had taken over Ford the man.

Mark Sullivan comments on Ford's decision and what it represented. "Never before had the producers of wealth thought of wealth as a thing to be diffused." Previously, men thought of wealth as static, something to be amassed and hoarded and withheld. Thus Woodrow Wilson could not have been more wrong when he observed in 1906, at a time when only the affluent had automobiles, that "nothing has spread socialistic feeling in this country more than the automobile; to the countryman they are a picture of arrogance of wealth, with all its independence and carelessness." Wilson's comment was in tune with the conventional wisdom on cars, that the automobile was a luxury for the wealthy and had little use for ordinary people apart from demonstrating the great gulf between rich and poor. In the long run he and they were proved wrong.

Mark Sullivan expresses the boundless optimism of the progressive generation for a new interpretation of wealth as represented by car production and ownership and its more even distribution throughout society.

The new wealth was not in the form of things, it was in the form of energy, of power of action; it was atoms in motion. Since the new kind of wealth was essentially motion, it did not lend itself to amassing or withholding; it could come into being only through use, and the use of it necessarily enriched the user. The entrepreneurs of the new forms of wealth, the industrial leaders identified with it, could make profit for themselves only insofar as they conferred upon the average man the power inherent in electricity and in the internal combustion engine; they could only enrich themselves by persuading the average man to use the new forms of energy.

Manufacturers wanted as many people as possible to have and use the new forms of energy. This became their dominating motive. Thus Henry Ford, and other manufacturers after him, recognized that they must employ workers not at minimal wages but at higher wages so that they could become maximum consumers of new energy and new products. Thus Ford and others came to think of labor as potential consumers, that workers must be enriched in order that they could consume more. This was a revolutionary concept to a generation brought up on the economics of Adam Smith.

The legend of what Ford was doing for the common man

traveled far and wide. In the 1920s in the very center of social-ism, Communist Russia, what Europeans called "Fordismus" was received as a major contribution to the Marxist revolution by Lenin himself. Indeed, Ford's portrait sometimes hung in Rus-sian factories alongside that of Lenin. In Aldous Huxley's novel, *Brave New World,* the desensitized masses swear by "Our Ford" and worship below a headless cross, decapitated to form a T in honor of the car that changed the world.

However, Ford's revolutionary schemes of $5 a day, the Soci-ological Department, profit sharing, and the projected society of the common man antagonized company stockholders who re-garded them as socialistic. In 1917 they brought and won a spe-cial suit to compel payment of special dividends. This convinced Ford he could only carry out his plans by gaining complete con-trol of his company and thus he bought out all the stockholders. Ford was quite ready to force down the value of his own com-pany's shares in order to do down his partners and acquire sole control as cheaply as possible. Quite simply, he hated banks and simply would not borrow from them even to attain his new goal of complete family ownership. Instead, he raised capital by speeding up production, distributing excess cars on reluctant dealers, and forcing them (and not him) to go to their banks and raise extra money to pay cash for the extra cars, while leaving Ford free. In the 1920s he was master of his own company and such complete family ownership was truly unique for an indus-trial corporation of such wealth and size.

Even more than with the robber barons, like John D. Rocke-feller and Andrew Carnegie, Ford's career suggested that the idea of business success had become keenly identified with the busi-ness of being American. Thus, as the *New York Times* explained, both the man and his achievements seemed the "embodiment of America in an era of industrial revolution." His career had been made possible because of the American system of free enterprise. Ford presented himself as a simple, straightforward sort of fellow who sought neither fortune nor fame but who worked continu-ously for the good of the great multitude of common people. He maintained that his achievement, possible only in America, was the result of his loyalty to proven values, notably thrift, hard work, and self-reliance. Ford's homespun philosophy was adapted from Emerson but twisted to suit his own prejudices. In his own idiosyncratic spelling he declared, "Money the Root of all Eval."

Ford was an eccentric whose personal life was marked by most inconsistent attitudes and behavior. In his private life, Henry was a cheating husband and a specially cruel father to his only son, Edsel. In his professional life, he was arbitrary, jealous, and often crack-brained. During World War I he chartered a so-called "Peace Ship" and planned a transatlantic voyage of freaks and frauds to appeal to European heads of state to end the war but, at the very same time, the Ford Motor Company was a major producer of war materials—as it was to be again in World War II. Prompted by Woodrow Wilson, in 1918 he ran for the Senate and lost in a close contest in which there was considerable poll fraud. He owned a newspaper, the *Dearborn Independent,* for which he employed ghostwriters to provide him with an editorial column that indulged in blatant anti-Semitism. His support for the development of Muscle Shoals, Alabama, to provide cheap fertilizers and hydroelectric power was partly the result of his own greed but partly represented a genuine personal commitment to bring the benefits of industry to the countryside and to decentralize industry. These experiences disillusioned Ford but did not chasten him or teach him to hold his tongue on subjects in which he lacked knowledge and understanding. Yet his genius was such that even when his faults were exposed, his hold on the American imagination remained unbroken.

During World War I the Ford joke became almost as well known at the Ford car and certainly as widely traveled. The Ford joke had no common pattern or viewpoint although each one ended in bathos. Because the Ford car was small, it was supposed to be economical. Thus at a tollgate you could alight, put the car in your pocket, and walk through the toll-gate at the price for pedestrians. The local postman was reportedly dismayed to learn how Ford was going to have all his cars delivered by mail. In time some Ford cars were used so much that they became dilapidated old bangers, hardly distinguishable from scrap metal. A farmer who stripped the old tin roof from his barn and sent it to Ford received a reply, "While your car was an exceptionally bad wreck, we shall be able to complete repairs and return it by the first of the week." A junk dealer watched in astonishment as a customer who arrived at his shop in a motor car towing a dead Ford began to collect up such odds and ends as four feet of bed spring, a fly swatter, the handle of a baby carriage, an old garden hose, and the faceless works of an alarm clock. The driver paid 30 cents for these items. When he left, the junk dealer posted a new sign. Instead of "Junk of All Kinds," it read "Ford Parts and Accessories." Ford cars were also utterly dependable. Thus one man on his deathbed asked to be buried in his Ford because he had "never been in a hole yet which his Ford didn't get him out of." A Cadillac owner always carried a Ford in his tool box "to pull him out when he got stuck in the mud." Of course, Ford had the last laugh for

> Ford has made a million cars
> Out of paint and iron bars. . . .
> Each single car has had one joke
> Cracked by an envy-ridden bloke
> Flung at its fanzied size and jars
> So Ford has sold a million cars.

Road and Highway Construction

An enduring legacy of the automobile revolution was the building of major roads and highways. The extent of surface roads increased from 161,000 miles in 1905 to 521,000 miles in 1925 and 1.52 million miles in 1945.

At first, roads were built by local authorities. Asphalt roads were introduced in New York in the 1870s. In 1891 New Jersey became the first state to enact a law providing state money and offering fund-raising expertise for counties to construct new roads. In 1893 Massachusetts established a state highway commission. The boom in automobiles now made road construction essential. By 1913 all states had adopted similar legislation to Massachusetts. To pay for improved roads and to maintain a check on drivers, New York State introduced a car registration fee in 1904 and in 1919 Oregon introduced a novel, useful tax on gasoline. Yet there was little coordination between states and different decisions and policies among adjacent states were proving a handicap to smooth-running interstate travel. To remedy this situation, Congress passed the Federal Aid Road Act of 1916 that provided federal aid for roads as a national policy to be administered by the Bureau of Public Roads within the Department of Agriculture. The first appropriation was $5 million, based on an estimate of federal aid of $10,000 per mile of road construction, with the states to shoulder all maintenance costs after the roads had been built. However, the act left decisions about the location of roads and the character of improvements to individual states and this led to various shortcomings in what had originally been intended as a national policy of road construction.

A subsequent measure, the Federal Aid Highway Act of 1921, reflected the opinion of lobby groups, such as the Good Roads Movement, that all major centers of population should be linked by a truly federal road system. Accordingly, the new act required the government to distinguish between state and local highways, designating state highways eligible for federal funds, but limited to 7 percent of the total road mileage in the state. The system was further divided between interstate roads that could not exceed three-sevenths of total mileage, with the remainder designated as intercounty roads. Federal aid was limited to 50 percent of the total estimated cost of construction.

The Wright Brothers Learn to Fly

The tragedy of the blind princess Iolanta in a Russian fairy tale is not that she cannot see but that, to protect her, her father, the king, has brought her up without any knowledge of sight. Her attendants tell her that her eyes, which she can feel, are only for crying. When a Moorish physician offers to cure Iolanta's blindness, he warns the king how traumatic the cure must be if it is to be successful. Iolanta must learn she is blind and must want to see. Like everything else in nature, physical sight does not exist in itself. Understanding of her handicap and perception of the world beyond it must precede any attempt to give her sight. There are none so blind as those who will not see. "Before we open innocent, unseeing eyes to the world, her mind must realise this; her soul must want to see and then the desire will awaken her eyes to the light." Iolanta is made to undergo the anguish of realization and the cure succeeds.

The story enshrines two central truths that are appropriate to the early history of manned flight. The first was the need to defy surface possibilities and find the means by which men could fly. It was like a person blind from birth whose understanding of the world is predicated on his blindness and who is suddenly and miraculously given his sight. The experience of a world that had long accepted that man could never fly and then saw flight was similar to this classic example of surprise to the human mind. The second truth is how new sight creates new awareness. The world seen from above was entirely different from the world seen on the ground. It was a matter of proportion and perspective, of being able to see from more than one angle, and of significance.

Without the perception and determination of a tiny minority of gifted inventors at the turn of the century, the airplane would never have been realised. Human flight, an aspiration since the legend of Icarus and Daedalus, still seemed impossible to the majority of people. Those who actually saw the early flights of the pioneer brothers, Orville and Wilbur Wright, could scarcely credit their eyes.

In an article, "Is the Airplane Coming?," for *McClure's* of September 1901, distinguished scientist and mathematician Dr. Simon Newcomb stopped himself short of answering his own question with an absolute "No." Rather, he qualified his "no" in ways meant to carry far greater conviction than the word itself could. "The desire to fly like a bird is inborn in our race, and we can no more be expected to abandon the idea than the ancient mathematician could have been expected to give up the problem of squaring the circle. . . . As the case stands, the first successful flyer will be the handiwork of a watchmaker and will carry nothing heavier than an insect." This attitude, fostered by newspapers and magazines, encouraged the public to remain incredulous of aviation. It simply could not accept flight as among human possibilities. Thus on October 19, 1904, ten months after flight had actually been accomplished, *Puck* printed a stock joke against

Pioneer aviators Orville (left) and Wilbur Wright, the bishop's sons with a mechanical gift with bicycles whose practical skills, symbiotic relationship, and synergy allowed them to transcend an apparently immutable law, that men would never fly across the skies. They had a unique way of imposing a pattern on the laws of nature and in 1903 triumphed with the first manned, powered flight. (Library of Congress).

aviation. "When," inquired his friend (of a putative aviator), more for the sake of asking than for the answer, "will you wing—I believe that is the correct term—your first flight?" "Just as soon," replied the flying-machine inventor, "as I can get the"—and, yet, it has been said that lunatics have no sense of humor—"laws of gravitation repealed."

Among the scientists who attempted, and failed, to make human flight possible was Professor Samuel P. Langley, secretary to the Smithsonian Institution from 1887 onward. In 1896 he twice succeeded in getting an unoccupied motor-driven model airplane, about twenty-six pounds in weight, to fly for about a minute and a half over the Potomac River at Washington. He was encouraged by prominent inventor Alexander Graham Bell and his experiments also attracted the support of the War Department and army who awarded him a subsidy of (initially) $50,000 to build a machine capable of carrying a man. After seven years, Langley and his assistant, Charles M. Manly, were ready for a trial flight with a man-size airplane at Widewater, Virginia, on October 7, 1903. Unfortunately, the Langley airplane, piloted by Manly, tumbled from its catapult car into the Potomac River sixty feet below. Cynics jeered. Langley's misfortune was taken as positive proof that what is is immutable, that man would never fly. The *Washington Post* of October 8, 1903, proclaimed

BUZZARD A WRECK
LANGLEY'S HOPES DASHED
Costly Contrivance Utterly Unable to Take Wing—
The Navigator Escapes with a Ducking and Has the
Shapeless Mass of Steel and Cloth Stored Away.

After a second, and final, failure of the Langley plane to fly on December 8, 1903, the press indulged in vociferous jeering, tossed out with ecstatic arrogance. The *Washington Post*'s editorial concluded, "It is not too much to say that the Langley flying-machine has fulfilled the fondest expectations of its critics." After the mishap, while Langley was looking after Charles M. Manly, a clumsy tugboat crew tore the plane to pieces while grappling for it.

Langley was physically crushed by the tornado of ridicule and his premature death in 1906 was probably hastened by his humiliation. Yet only nine days after Langley's second failure, on December 17, 1903, Orville and Wilbur Wright successfully flew the first powered airplane. Their achievement was the culmination of years of painstaking experiment.

Orville and Wilbur Wright were close brothers, sons of an affluent bishop of the United Brethren church. Wilbur was born on April 16, 1867, and Orville on August 18, 1871. Wilbur's seniority gave him leadership in their joint ventures. He was always disposed to ignore convention and act on his own initiative. Their father encouraged their independence and initiative, even when this meant that Wilbur would not enter the church, as the bishop wanted, and that neither Wilbur nor Orville would follow a family tradition and go to college. They both left high school at seventeen. While Langley was a distinguished scientist, the Wright brothers were obscure practical mechanics. Langley had the support and prestige of the Smithsonian and a government subsidy behind him; to support them, the Wrights had only a bicycle shop, a small manufacturing and repair business, and the casual interest of a few friends. In the 1890s, when the craze for safety bicycles swept across America, they turned themselves into manufacturers, retailers, and repairers of bicycles. Gifted with natural mechanical flair, they created two models, the Wright Special and the Van Cleve. Their bicycle production remained small and was never more than a hundred machines per annum, all sold locally. The Wright Special cost only $18. Yet their little bicycle shop became the laboratory and bank for the new invention of the airplane. As bicycle mechanics they acquired the skill to construct and understand very intricate, lightweight machinery.

In 1896 Wilbur Wright read a newspaper account of how a German engineer, Otto Lilienthal, who had made hundreds of glider flights, had been killed in a glider crash. (A glider was a set of wings on a frame without power.) Orville was convalescing from typhoid and Wilbur waited until he had recovered before discussing flight with him. They read all the works they could find on aviation, including books by the ill-fated Samuel P. Langley, Otto Lilienthal, Louis Pierre Mouillard, and Octave

Chanute (the French immigrant and bridge builder who had laid out the Chicago Stock Yards) and the *Aeronautical Annuals* for 1895–97, published by enthusiast James Means of Boston.

The Wrights distinguished between those aeronautical engineers interested in gliders and those interested in powered machines, and deliberately chose to concentrate on gliding, partly, according to Wilbur Wright, "from impatience at the wasteful extravagance of mounting delicate and costly machinery on wings which no one knew how to manage." Because of their work in the bicycle shop, they were accustomed to test theory by practice and realized that regular practice at flight was essential if man was ever to solve the problems of flight. The problems had remained unsolved precisely because "no one had been able to obtain any adequate practice." Whereas we usually think that the singular achievement of the Wright brothers was the actual invention of the airplane, a separate and equally significant achievement was their mastering the physical act of flying. Without the practical experience of flying a plane, it would not have been possible for the Wrights and their successors to design and build ever more sophisticated planes. Years later, Anne Morrow Lindbergh (wife of the aviator) explained the significance of the physical and mental training of pilots for flying a plane. By implication, she was paying tribute to the way the Wrights set out to solve the problems of aircraft design, production, mechanics, aerodynamics, and navigation:

Since flight is not a natural function of man; since it has been won by centuries of effort; since it has been climbed to arduously, not simply stumbled upon; since it has been slowly built, not suddenly discovered, it cannot be suspended as the word "freedom" is suspended in the mind. It rests, firmly supported, on structure of laws, rules, principles—laws to which plane and man alike must conform. Rules of construction, of performance, of equipment, for one; rules of training, health, experience, skill, and judgment, for the other.

The scientific problem of remaining securely airborne comes from making the center of gravity coincide with the center of pressure. As we have observed, Wilbur had long been interested in Otto Lilienthal's gliders and in 1899 he noted from watching buzzards fly how a successful airplane would need to fly on three axes in order to incline from side to side, to ascend and descend and to steer to left and right, and, perhaps, to perform these maneuvers simultaneously. Thus flight control was of prime importance. In order to achieve it, Wilbur devised gliders that could twist and adjust their wings—something like buzzards. Wilbur began to solve this problem by playing with an empty cardboard box, similar in shape to the biplane glider he was planning, and twisting the box between his hands and distorting its surface. By applying pressure, he could bend the surface of the right side downward, whilst simultaneously bending the surface of the left side upward. Could not the surface of a glider be similarly warped, thereby allowing for lateral balancing according to vertical wind pressure applied to each wing? The central problem that had defeated previous experiments in aviation had been how to keep the airplane on an even keel. In achieving three-axis control, Wilbur made a major contribution to aerodynamics and practical flight. This was done in a series of experiments. Before attempting powered flight, he tried to master gliding flight for which he built three biplane gliders.

In the summer of 1900 the Wrights built their first large glider, using their best ideas and including the principle of wing-warping. The Weather Bureau at Washington advised them that Kitty Hawk in North Carolina, a region of rolling sand dunes, would be ideal for gliding experiments. However, when they arrived there in September 1900 they found that at that season the winds were not strong enough to support a glider carrying a pilot. Thus they simply flew the glider as a kite, manipulating the controls from the ground. This taught them that the various established mathematical tables on which they had based their calculations on wind pressures were faulty. Concerned by the scarcity of true scientific information on the design and construction of airplanes, they built a wind tunnel in their Dayton shop in the winter of 1901–2 to test the operation of about 200 wing and biplane surfaces, thereby solving a series of problems that had eluded trained mathematicians. Thus when they flew the glider again at Kitty Hawk in September and October 1902, it performed nearly 1,000 flights, some of over 600 feet, and all according to calculations.

The Wright's thorough preparation, cautious temperaments, and sound methodological approach laid the basis of their later successes. They avoided wasteful speculation, preferring to move by a series of cautious steps, rather than a few hazardous jumps. Because there were two of them closely attached to, but not utterly dependent upon, one another, they could achieve more than lone inventors and, if, as eventually happened, one died prematurely, there would be no loss to the knowledge already achieved. Beyond their mutual affection, there was a unique mental and intellectual bond. Wilbur was generally reticent with others but loquacious with his brother. They concluded that their lifelong association had helped synchronize their minds so that any events occurring in the vicinity inspired identical reflexes. In any emergency each brother knew what the other would do, without going through any process of knowing, even if one was airborne and the other still on the ground.

The years 1900–3 proved a period of intense research and development in which they moved from kites to gliders. One troublesome early problem was to construct a vertical rudder that could change the direction of the plane without making it lurch dangerously to one side. They solved the problem by connecting the rudder to the lever that controlled the wings. A thrust on the lever caused the wings to warp and the rudder to deflect simultaneously. Having worked out major innovations in aircraft control and assembled a mass of scientific data on construction, they began to build a powered airplane with a total weight of 750 lbs, and carrying a 170 lb, 12 hp gasoline engine. Like Langley before them, the Wrights could find no manufacturer who could make an engine of the power and weight they required. Thus, like Langley, they designed and, with with the help of their assistant, Charles Taylor, built their own in their bicycle shop.

The Wrights' *Flyer I,* subsequently known as the *Kitty Hawk,* was an entirely new biplane with a wing span of 40 feet 4 inches and a wing area of 510 square feet, retaining the front elevator and rear rudder of a glider of 1902. The Taylor engine was a horizontal four-cylinder engine mounted in the center of the lower wing and turning two chain-driven, counter-rotating, pusher propellers. As was the case in the early gliders, the pilot lay prone on the lower wing beside the engine. *Flyer I* was designed to take off from a simple droppable dolly running along a monorail trail extending 60 feet, fly, and then land on a pair of sledlike skids.

Wilbur first tried out *Flyer I* on December 14, 1903, but because he controlled the elevator too closely, the plane plowed into the sand at the end of the launching rail. After the necessary repairs and delays caused by adverse weather, Orville had his turn on December 17, at 10:35 A.M. He achieved a successful takeoff in a wind of 20–22 mph., flew for 12 seconds, attained a height of 120 feet, and landed safely. This was the first successful piloted, powered flight in history. Orville Wright recalled the experience in "How We Made the First Flight" for *Flying* of December 1913.

The course of the flight up and down was exceedingly erratic. The control of the front rudder was difficult. As a result the machine would rise suddenly to about ten feet, and then as suddenly dart for the ground. A sudden dart when a little over 120 feet from the point at which it rose into the air, ended the flight. This flight lasted only 12 seconds, but it was nevertheless the first in the history of the world in which a machine carrying a man had raised itself by its own power into the air in full flight, had sailed forward without reduction of speed, and had finally landed at a point as high as that from which it started.

Wilbur started the fourth and last flight at just 12 o'clock. The first few hundred feet were up and down as before, but by the time three hundred feet had been covered, the machine was under much better control. The course for the next four or five hundred feet had but little undulation. However, when out about eight hundred feet the machine began pitching again, and, in one of its darts downward, struck the ground. The distance over the ground was measured and found to be 852 feet; the time of the flight 59 seconds.

Then they were interrupted. While they were returning the plane to the starting rail, it was overturned by a strong gust of wind and damaged beyond immediate repair. The Wrights dismantled the airplane and packed it up in two boxes and a barrel and returned to Dayton.

The press scoop of the earliest human flight in a powered plane was obtained by reporter H. P. Moore and editor Keville Glennan of the Norfolk *Virginian-Pilot,* who discovered that the Wrights had sent a telegram with the news to their father. From mere snippets of information they constructed a somewhat fanciful story that appeared in the *Virginian-Pilot* of December 18, 1903, under banner headlines:

FLYING MACHINE SOARS 3 MILES IN TEETH
OF HIGH WIND OVER SAND HILLS AND
WAVES AT KITTY HAWK ON CAROLINA COAST
NO BALLOON ATTACHED TO AID IT.

However, very few metropolitan editors showed any interest in the story and those who did use it added facetious science fiction decorations of their own. Thus almost five years elapsed before America was ready to accept that the Wrights had fi.st flown in 1903.

Wilbur and Orville realised that the indifference of the press would work to their advantage. They could beaver away, working to create a larger *Flyer II* with a much improved engine. In the spring of 1904 they rented a 90 acre cow pasture, Huffman Prairie, near Dayton, and there they assembled the new machine and began to fly it. This time the press showed some initial enthusiasm for the venture but when a demonstration flight was postponed on account of adverse weather and mechanical difficulties, journalists and editors lost interest. Nevertheless, when Wilbur made the first full circle in flight on September 20, 1904, his feat was reported by an eyewitness in a small and otherwise obscure magazine of Medina, Ohio, *Gleanings in Bee Culture,* in January 1905 by the editor, A. I. Root, who had traveled to Dayton to see the Wrights fly. On November 9, 1904, Wilbur stayed airborne for over five minutes, making almost four complete circles above the meadow.

Flyer III, incorporating the various improvements from experience with the earlier models, was first flown at Huffman Prairie on June 23, 1905. By October 16 the Wrights had undertaken forty-nine flights altogether in different planes, many of them ranging from 11 miles to 24.5 miles, at an average speed of 38 mph. Most flights were short simply because fuel ran out. By now the Wrights wanted to avoid publicity. They fully realized that accurate reporting would in itself establish their prior claim as true inventors of the first airplane. Indeed, they secured a patent for their airplane on May 22, 1906. Yet they also knew press reports would stimulate additional interest and lead to certain surveillance of their work, and, perhaps, to the theft of their ideas. In order to prevent further military or commercial inspection of their planes, they stopped all flights between between October 16, 1905, and May 6, 1908. Then they returned to Kitty Hawk with the much improved *Flyer III* in order to refresh their skills as pilots.

As the Wrights got to know a small group of journalists assembled to see the miracle of flight, they were invited to attend and report successive flights at Kitty Hawk, and the journalists continued to telegraph their ecstatic stories to metropolitan headquarters. New York *Herald* reporter Byron R. Newton's dispatch in the New York *Herald* of May 14, 1908, concluded triumphantly, "With the ease and swiftness of a huge eagle, the Wright brothers' aeroplane made a flight of three miles at ten o'clock this morning. . . . There is no longer any ground for questioning the performance of the men and their wonderful machine."

Some commentators believed that mankind was on the verge of successful flight and that, had it not been for the Wrights in 1903, some other inventor, American or European, would have succeeded by 1907 or 1908. In fact, no other inventors beside the Wrights gave any indication that they were about to do so. In 1908, after the army invited inventors to bid for airplane construction, only the Wrights submitted a plane. Two other inventors who had entered bids failed to present airplanes for the trials and lost their deposits. France was the only European country with a fair number of people at all interested in flight and its involvement was stimulated by the success of the Wrights. Far more learned and experienced engineers than the Wrights had failed to see what was really needed to make powered flight possible. It was an American achievement, just as the telephone, phonograph, incandescent light bulb, and motion picture of Bell and Edison had been quintessential American inventions.

One of the Wrights' early flights over Fort Myer, Virginia, in July 1909. (Library of Congress).

Aviation

Civil aviation moved through three distinct phases; first, the initial invention of the airplane of 1903–9, and the barnstorming period of 1909–25; second, the widening field of civil aviation of 1925–45, in which modern purpose-built airliners were constructed and airline corporations were established to provide passenger and cargo services; third, the period from the 1950s when jet planes superseded monoplanes, when transatlantic aviation came of age, and when the United States came to dominate civil aviation.

The development of powered airplanes in the period 1903–9 was made possible by the happy convergence of a number of different lines of experimentation and innovation. They included the discovery and tapping of a fuel, petroleum, and finding ways of converting it to energy; the development of lightweight aluminum, precision energy and electrical power. Such things provided materials and methods to build an aviation gasoline engine for powered flight.

In mid-1908 the army agreed to use airplanes if they proved successful in trials, and the Wrights began production under license. They also persuaded European inventors of their entitlement to the claim of inventors of a successful airplane, after a series of public exhibition flights of their new machines in France, all by Wilbur who flew a hundred times there between August and December 1908. Meanwhile, Orville was testing and exhibiting models in the United States, thus enabling the Wrights to win their first contract for a military plane in 1909. Together they dominated the new field of aviation throughout 1909, and built planes for Europe and the United States in 1909 and 1910. However, the Wrights jealously guarded their formula for successful airplane construction and proved intransigent toward suggestions for further modification and improvement. Tragically, Wilbur died of typhoid in 1912. Orville lived until 1948 and during these thirty-six years continued to make significant contributions to aviation.

Nevertheless, other gifted designers seized the initiative and continued to develop airplanes. Among the inventors ardently anxious to see man fly was Alexander Graham Bell. His ideal was an airplane that would not have to land at all but could be tethered aloft like a kite. He was obsessed with the ideas of stability and gentle descent. Encouraged by his wife, Mabel, he concentrated on various experiments with kites, outsize frameworks of numerous tetrahedral cells, in which he was much assisted by Frederick W. ("Casey") Baldwin, a graduate engineer from Toronto. Bell created a circle of aeronautical engineers, including Casey, John McCurdy, Lt. Thomas E. Selfridge of West Point, and Glenn Hammond Curtiss.

Curtiss's father, a harness mender of Hammondsport, New York, had died when Glenn was only six. He had but one sister who went deaf. He was a shy, reticent, even dour, man who found relief in machinery and speed. After opening a bicycle shop, he won every bicycle race in sight for three years. After he lost a race, he turned his attention to motorcycles, both racing and making them, and in 1907 he rode the fastest mile yet traveled by man at 136 miles per hour. In the meantime, he founded his own company, G. H. Curtiss Manufacturing Company. Bell stimulated his interest in aviation and in July 1907 he became the little group's engine expert at the Bells' country estate at Beinn Bhreagh ("Beautiful Mountain"), at Baddock Bay, Nova Scotia. The five men and Mabel Bell formed the Aerial Experiment Association (AEA) on October 1, 1907. Bell was now sixty and his task was to coordinate their efforts and advise on successive improvements in aircraft design. Unlike the Wrights, the AEA welcomed public interest and because Bell was so widely known, they could always command it for demonstrations in 1908. The AEA promoted the aileron, a device used earlier in France, that hinged the tips of upper wings together in such a way as to let them move in opposite directions from one another. The most successful of these early planes was the *June Bugg* of Glenn Curtiss. On July 4, 1908, Curtiss won a prize from the *Scientific American* for the first heavier-than-air flight of more than 1 kilometer (0.6 miles).

For a time the AEA and the Wrights were locked in rival patent claims about ailerons and wing warping, eventually resolved in the AEA's favor. They were also awarded Patent No. 1,011,106 for a flying machine on December 5, 1911. When Thomas Selfridge returned to Washington for army trials of the Wright plane, he volunteered to be Orville Wright's passenger on a required two-man flight. The plane crashed at Fort Myer, Virginia, on September 17, 1908. Orville Wright was badly injured and Thomas Selfridge died of his injuries that night—the first fatality in powered flight. Shaken, the surviving members of the AEA nevertheless concentrated on completing the *Silver Dart* of John McCurdy, flown at Hammondsport in December 1908 and then at Baddock Bay on February 23 and 24, 1909—the first powered flights in Canada. Then they closed down the AEA on March 31, 1909. Glenn Curtiss had just organized his own aircraft company. Curtiss now emerged as the foremost inventor, eclipsing even the Wrights. It was one of his planes, the *Gold Bug,* that won a leading prize in 1914 and it was his aileron, rather than the Wright wing warping, that became the practical standard in the future. He also developed the first successful seaplane, *Flying Fish,* adopted by the U.S. Navy.

Samuel Franklin ("Colonel") Cody, a native of Texas who became a naturalized Briton, was another aviation pioneer. He designed a tri-plane and in 1908 he made the first *official* powered airplane flight at Farnborough, England. Like certain other daring aviators, he gave his life in the cause when he died in an airplane crash near Aldershot in 1913. The first American monoplane was invented by Henry W. Walden in 1909. Elmer A. Sperry invented the gyroscope (1913), thereby showing that special navigation instruments could be designed to work on airplanes.

The development of air travel in North America showed how planes could open up the interior with far greater flexibility than steamboats and railroads. At first, pilots and entrepreneurs were so preoccupied with the challenge of flying coast to coast that they took less interest in overseas flights. The first regular air service in the United States began in Florida in 1914 when pilot Tony Janus established the St. Petersburg-Tampa Airboat Line with one tiny seaplane that carried one passenger at a time across Tampa Bay. On May 15, 1918, the first regular airmail service was inaugurated when two army pilots flew a Curtiss Jenny from Washington, D.C. to New York. In 1919 Eddie Hubbard began flying airmail regularly from Seattle to Vancouver across the Canadian frontier in a single engine seaplane. His first passenger, Bill Boeing, was the man who built the plane. In 1920 Aeromarine Airways in Florida began flying single-engine former navy seaplanes, carrying four passengers at a time between Key West and Havana.

At the outset of World War I, it was becoming clear that the United States was lagging behind Europe in airplane development and construction. Effective military aviation had begun with the navigable military airplane of the Wrights but, thereafter, the initiative passed to Ferdinand von Zeppelin of Germany who produced such planes as the LZ-70 and L3 for the German Navy. Following a report by the Smithsonian Institution in 1915 about the limitations of American production, the government established a National Advisory Committee for Aeronautics, providing special research facilities at Langley Field, Virginia, and stimulating an astonishing record of research, experiment, and design. The U.S. Army used airplanes within its Signal Corps. Although neither army nor navy had combat aircraft, the federal government established an Aircraft Production Board in order to build planes according to Allied designs, and to produce the Liberty Engine. In 1918 the American government placed 1,370 planes at the European front but only 740 actually fought, partly for lack of pilots, partly because they were not needed. At the peak of production it built 150 Liberty Engines per day and had 52,000 by 1918. Furthermore, in 1914 the navy established a training school for aviators at Pensacola, Florida.

It was in World War I that planes first demonstrated their lethal potential. Ace pilots such as Captain Eddie Rickenbacker shot down about three enemy planes for every American plane lost. The early enthusiasm for air travel took a nose dive as aviators began to recognize how political barriers and limitations of human behavior would set frontiers in the sky. Sir Erle Richards, professor of international law at Oxford University, remarked in 1915 how "The practice of the present war seems definitely to have established the right of every state of sovereignty over the air space above its territories."

After the war the government had no use for its apparently surplus planes. Some, amazingly enough, were destroyed outright. Others were used as "barnstormers," offering rides to the general public and thus creating an appetite for civil aviation. A most productive use was for carrying federal mail. In 1918 the Post Office began regular mail flights, extending them across the continental United States in 1920, and introducing night flights in 1921.

The Contribution of the Railroads to
The Revolution in Transportation

Changes brought by airplanes and automobiles did not result in a wholesale reconstruction of an entire society. Even by 1945 airlines and automobiles had not equalled, far less surpassed, railroads in providing convenient transportation across long distances at competitive prices. Although major railroad track construction was complete by 1900, there was still a significant amount of construction afterward, reaching a maximum mileage of 254,251 miles in 1916. Thereafter, the increasing availability of automobiles and the laying of numerous roads for them led to a slight decline in railroad use and the extent of track declined from its peak of 1916 to 234,182 miles in 1945. Some new lines were constructed. The Pacific Coast Extension of the Chicago, Milwaukee, St. Paul and Pacific Railroad was opened on May 19, 1909. The Western Pacific, an extension of the Denver and Rio Grande mainline railroad moving from Denver through Salt Lake City to San Francisco, was completed on August 22, 1910.

In the period 1900–45 engineers sought to reduce distance by constructing special suspension bridges across water and cutting tunnels to eliminate lengthy, time-consuming climbs. Tunnels included the seven-mile Cascade Tunnel in Washington (1929) and the Moffat Tunnel in Colorado (1929) that shortened the route between Denver and Salt Lake City by 173 miles. The Lucin Cut-Off, completed in March 1904, was a new route between Ogden and Lucin, shortening the original journey by 103 miles, in part by a track on a trestle across the Great Salt Lake. Extra railroad bridges were constructed, linking New York City to the mainland and to Long Island, notably the Williamsburg Bridge (1903) and the Hell Gate Bridge (1917), giving the Pennsylvania Railroad access to Long Island.

Between 1900 and 1910 average freight rates remained at 75 cents per ton per mile and were not increased until 1913 when they rose by 5 percent. In the same period passenger rates were 2 cents per person per mile. In 1916 over 77 percent of intercity freight was moved by train. That year 98 percent of all people traveling between cities did so by train.

American railroads traditionally carried more freight than passengers and it was essential for their locomotives and, indeed, all other component parts, to perform well in freight transportation. Not surprisingly, therefore, America led the rest of the world, including Britain, in the development of steam locomotives. By 1900 the American trend was for locomotives of greater efficiency and power, such as the Pacific 4-6-2 (1886) and Atlantic 4-4-2 (1888). The Hiawatha Express, which ran between Chicago and the twin cities, used four streamlined Atlantics in 1935. The first locomotives designed to run regularly at speeds of 100 mph were the "2-8-2" (1897) and "2-10-2" (1903), both produced by Baldwin and known as the *Santa Fe* type. Those suitable for carrying heavy freight, the *Texas* type, were the "2-10-4" type, first produced in 1925.

There were many technological improvements. Mechanical stokers were introduced in 1905 and soon became more important as grates were widened to over 50 feet. In 1938 the Interstate Commerce Commission ruled that all coal-burning passenger engines of over 160,000 pounds and freight engines of over 175,000 pounds must be served by mechanical stokers. In 1925 the General Steel Castings Corporation produced a cast steel engine frame in one piece and most engines were thus produced by 1930. The Delaware and Hudson Railroad began using all-welded boilers in 1934.

Steam locomotive technology focused on articulated locomotives that provided the greatest power on railroad lines with severe curvature and spread their weight out on light track, something they could do because of their two swiveling bogies. The main type of bogies was the Mallet, a four-cylinder compound consisting of a high-pressure engine in fixed rear frame and a low-pressure engine in pivoted front frame. The first Mallet (o-6-6-0) was developed by the Baltimore and Ohio Railroad in 1903. A later model was the Union Pacific "Big Boys" (4-8-8-4).

Twenty-five were built in the World War II years of 1941–44, a peak period of locomotive construction. These locomotives could draw 135,375 lbs at 7,000 horsepower.

From 1926 onward American engineers also developed diesel locomotives. Diesel engines produced about 1.9 times as much work as oil-fired locomotives, giving off less pollution. By the 1930s diesel locomotives were becoming far more common for passenger and freight services, especially after they were widely adopted by the Burlington and Quincy and the Union Pacific Railroad. The Burlington Zephyr of 1934 was the first diesel-electric streamlined locomotive, traveling nonstop between Chicago and Denver at speeds of 77.6 mph. In 1939 General Motors produced the Electro Motive No. 103, a four-unit freight loco, producing 5,400 horsepower, soon the most widely used and most versatile locomotive with the greatest stamina, whatever the distance, altitude, climb, or temperature. In 1941 the Santa Fe Railroad inaugurated the first mainline diesel freight service. Its initial success led to the prompt transfer from steam and oil to diesel drawn locomotives on all railroads.

Despite the considerable advantages of electric power, electrified trains did not penetrate all parts of the United States in the period 1900–45. This was essentially because the large capital costs involved in installing an electrified railroad system could only be recovered if the system was used intensively. Because of the great distances between major centers outside the industrial Northeast, American railroads ran a few larger trains rather than many small ones. Such electrification as was carried out was introduced on suburban lines rather than on interstate lines.

As to passenger travel, the trend at the turn of the century was for higher standards of comfort and safety and greater speeds. Cast-steel bogie-truck frames were introduced in 1903 and quickly became standard for carriages, allowing greater resilience. The Long Island Railroad introduced all-steel passenger cars in 1905 and by 1927 its entire fleet was built completely of steel, providing increased strength and greater security against fire. In 1927 the Chicago, Milwaukee, St. Paul and Pacific Railroad introduced the first air-conditioned carriages that were in regular use by 1930. The first completely air-conditioned train in regular service was by the Baltimore and Ohio on its service between Washington and New York in 1931. To install air-conditioning cost at least $5,000 per passenger car. Nevertheless, the Illinois Central (1932) and Burlington (1934) followed the lead set by the B and O. By 1940 over 12,000 passenger cars were air-conditioned.

Passengers wanted speed as well as comfort and safety, especially on services between the major cities. In 1902 the New York Central and Hudson River Railroad introduced its *Twentieth Century Limited* between New York and Chicago that quickly entered a race with the Pennsylvania Railroad's *Penn Special* as to which could complete the run sooner. Thus the time of the journey was reduced to eighteen hours but later increased to twenty hours. Nevertheless, the competition led to a streamlining in train design that reached a peak in the 1930s. Indeed, in 1938 the New York-Chicago run took only sixteen hours by streamlined train. By 1930 there were more than 15,000 new steam locomotives, costing $765 million. Between 1928 and 1930 over $1.7 billion was spent on about 850,000 freight cars.

In 1929 there were about 20,000 intercity passenger trains in operation. In 1930 the average intercity railroad revenue was 3.25 cents per passenger mile. However, fares were cut in the depression and in 1940 the average fare was 1.90 cents. Commuter fares for regular passengers were lower still. Travel by railroad was far safer than by either automobile or airplane. Fatalities declined from 0.28 per 100 million passenger miles in the 1920s to 0.14 per 100 million passenger miles in the 1930s. After some uncertain years in the 1920s and 1930s, American railways received higher revenues at $4.29 billion in 1940. In 1941 railroad freight traffic reached 475 billion ton-miles, 6 percent above the last record year of 1929 and 17 percent higher than the year of 1918. In 1940, when the extent of railroad tracks was about 233,000 miles, passenger services were running on about three-quarters of the network and railroads carried 65 percent of all commercial intercity passenger traffic.

CHAPTER EIGHT

Words Without Pictures;
Pictures Without Words:
Radio and Movies

·ℱ·

R ADIO BROADCASTING is the transmission and reception of communication signals made up of electromagnetic waves traveling through the air and used in programs broadcast for public information, education, and entertainment. Radio broadcasting added a significant new dimension to modern communication, a breakthrough that went beyond the mass communication of motion pictures and telephone because it combined the sound of one with the direct entertainment of the other and carried them directly into the home. This modern form of communication had considerable potential both as a means of social manipulation and control, and of education, relaying news, ideas, and entertainment from the world outside. Radio was to exercise a profound social force, not least economically, expanding and intensifying the campaign for the consumer market by introducing advertising and all its pressures into the home. Moreover, it was the success of radio broadcasting in the 1930s that provided the model and commercial foundation for the development of television in America after World War II.

However, because it was not until the 1930s that radio enjoyed its golden age of varied programs and widespread popularity and influence, broadcasting in America was a relatively late phenomenon in the early twentieth century. Indeed, the history of radio was neither straightforward nor smooth. Like the origins of the other key technologies of the twentieth century, the invention of radio cannot be attributed to one person nor traced back to a single moment in history. Whereas advances in the automobile and airplane required great practical and mechanical knowledge, the development of radio depended upon considerable scientific knowledge, notably in mathematics and physics. The later technical sophistication of radio was a product of science-based industry and military research.

Wireless Telegraphy

Daniel Czitrom argues in *Media and the American Mind* (1982) that there is a continuous thread of endeavor leading from telegraph to telephone and then to radio, that radio was the product of a concerted technical evolution. Ironically, once electromagnetic telegraphy had been developed in the nineteenth century, various scientists began to look for ways to dispose of the wires. Notably, Benjamin Morse proposed and experimented with conduction through water to extend his system to telegraph land lines. Many were based on the principle of induction, whereby an electric current appears in one circuit when it is placed near another.

In the end, the scientific basis of radio lay in the idea of electromagnetic waves traveling through space as expounded by such university scientists as William Crookes and Clerk Maxwell in Britain, Heinrich Hertz in Germany, and Edouard Branly in France. William Crookes played a crucial role in seeing the need and finding the practical means to meet it, discovering the immense possibilities of "ethereal vibrations or electric rays." Crookes's ideas made a great impact on Guglielmo Marconi in Italy who decided to draw together the ideas of these various scientists and, in particular, find a practical application for the radio waves discovered by Heinrich Hertz. Marconi was also able to draw on the wealth of his affluent family, arouse the interest of the British General Post Office, and in 1897 win industrial backing to establish the Marconi Wireless Telegraph Company. Marconi wanted to achieve wireless communication on land and over water, especially between lighthouses and lightships. The Marconi Wireless Telegraphy Company would come to dominate worldwide wireless technology and business until World War I. Perhaps Marconi's major contribution to the development and emergence of radio broadcasting was his success in increasing the distances and reliability of transmission. The climax of his experiments came in 1902 when Marconi sent signals across the Atlantic. With the later incorporation of British inventor Sir Oliver Lodge's tuning device, Marconi was able to provide perfect wireless connections. Despite the fact that there was considerable speculation in radio in the 1900s, its future practical use remained unrealized until the 1920s. No one foresaw the creation of radio broadcasting networks. Financiers and scientists concentrated on the importance of wireless telegraphy, even calling radio "ethereal telegraphy."

In 1899 Marconi established a highly successful American subsidiary of his company while the United States federal government, newly awake to the naval, military, and commercial possibilities of wireless telegraphy, encouraged competition among American companies. Thus in 1902 Reginald A. Fessenden created the National Electric Signaling Company. Fessenden was the first major experimenter in the United States to work with wireless. He had been first approached by the United States Weather Bureau to apply wireless technology to weather forecasting. Fessenden aimed to improve significantly upon Marconi's achievements by developing a long-range wireless that used continuous waves, rather than Marconi's spark gap technique. In 1903 Fessenden acquired a high-speed generator of alternating currents from General Electric. However, Fessenden's business ventures failed.

In these opening years of commercial wireless another American who challenged Marconi's monopoly was Lee de Forest. Although proving a technical failure during its first trial, the coverage of a yacht race, de Forest's radio system drew enough publicity to attract financial support for the De Forest Wireless Telephone Company of 1902. The company supplied the army,

Enrico Caruso, the most famous tenor of the twentieth century, as Riccardo in Verdi's *Un Ballo in Maschera*. A Neapolitan immigrant, Caruso was not only the Metropolitan Opera's most famous artist but also exerted a decisive influence on the fortunes of phonograph disks. His recording of "Vesti la giubba" from *Pagliacci* was the first to sell a million copies and his vocal bloom, style, and élan set the standard for all tenors who followed him. (Photo by Mishkin, Library of Congress).

navy, and United Fruit Company, which needed to communicate with its plantations. Even so, the company was dissolved in 1907.

Later experimenters wanted to improve transmission, reception, and selectivity of radio waves. The original method of spark gap transmission was crude. It required a large surge of power that fanned out most of the transmitted energy across a broad band and produced a loud crashing noise. The ideal solution was a continuous modulated signal that, among other things, would carry music and speech. An immediate development was the arc generator that produced a rapid series of sparks across a narrower gap. Patented by the Dane Valdemar Poulsen in 1902, arc generators were used extensively in the United States, especially by the navy that employed its generators until World War II. With General Electric, Fessenden had constructed a generator to alternate the radio signals into smooth, continuous waves. Yet it was a colleague, E. F. W. Alexanderson, who actually perfected a high speech alternator in 1909. These gargantuan machines produced very powerful, clear signals. In 1918 a 200 kilowatt alternator was operated in New Brunswick, New Jersey, that provided such effective long-range communication that it was used to announce President Woodrow Wilson's Fourteen Points to the world.

The crucial second generation of radio technology began around 1912 with the beginnings of experimentation into the vacuum tube. In 1904 a Marconi worker, John Ambrose, discovered that a positive plate would attract the negative electrons. Thus scientists now possessed a one-way gate or valve that could transform an alternating current, like a radio wave, into direct current. In the detection of radio waves, a vacuum tube could make very high frequency signals audible. Lee de Forest inserted a third element, a charged grid, into the vacuum that meant the tube functioned as an amplifier. De Forest used his audion early in the century, broadcasting two operas from the Metropolitan Opera in New York in 1910 in which tenor Enrico Caruso sang. That same year AT&T bought some of the rights to the audion and used it to amplify long-distance telephone calls.

The vacuum tube was the essential component necessary for full-scale broadcasting of music and speech that would begin in the 1920s. This was prefigured in 1915 when the U.S. Navy station at Arlington, Virginia, used 500 audions to relay speech and music across to the Eiffel Tower, Paris. Even more critically the audion or triode (three-element vacuum tube) could amplify the reception of radio signals. Since this would allow use of loudspeakers rather than earphones, the incorporation of the audion in the receiver opened up new possibilities for home entertainment.

Simultaneously, the improvement of the actual detection, rather than sound projection, of radio signals was under way. Between 1903 and 1908 Fessenden developed an electrolytic, liquid detector that was more sensitive and used widely until 1913. These devices were superseded by the firm solid state device, the cats whisker, and crystal radio set. Around 1906 Greenleaf W. Pickard had discovered that a crystal of silicon would let electricity flow in only one direction. The cats whisker was the fine, metal point that was necessary to search for the most suitable spot for the best reception. At the same time, H.H.C. Dunwoody discovered that carborundum, a waste product of electric furnaces, worked just as well as the more expensive silicon. Therefore, the principal advantages of the crystal receiver were that it was both cheaper and easier to construct than the other detectors. The incorporation of a couple of vacuum tubes dealt with its major drawback, weak incoming signals. Not surprisingly, crystal sets would be the basis of the public wireless boom of the 1920s.

A final technical perfection of the wireless was the development of syntonic tuning. At an early stage scientists realized that a means of tuning a wireless to a single station so that other stations on nearby frequencies could signal without interference, had to be found. Both Marconi and John Stace Stone in America devised a method of selective tuning that used the principle of resonance whereby the frequency of the receiver matched that of a particular incoming signal.

During this crucial period not only was wireless telegraphy perfected but powerful, established businesses also intervened to protect their monopolies. The visible hand of business management showed its strength as clearly in the invisible world of wireless as it did in the worlds of oil, steel, and finance. Thus

AT&T became involved as much to protect its own industry as to advance wireless telegraphy. Frank Jewett, chief of Alexander Graham Bell's research team, said, "It was clear to the AT and T Co. . . . that full, thorough, and complete understanding of radio must be had at all times if the art of telephony . . . was to be advanced and the money invested in that service safeguarded." Accordingly, in 1913 and 1914 AT&T bought up all available radio patent rights. However, before 1920 the dominant industrial force in radio alone was British Marconi. In 1915 Marconi began negotiations with General Electric eventually to gain exclusive use of the most powerful transmitter of the day, the Alexanderson Alternator.

Radio Waves

Yet, if the technology was largely ready before 1920—for example the crystal set, audion, and syntonic tuning were all workable within a decade after Marconi's first transatlantic transmission—and the industry was highly capitalized, what stalled the appearance and growth of modern, mass radio broadcasting until the late 1920s? In part, it was that, although this was a crucial period of experimentation and technical success, serious squabbles over patent rights tended to distract from the major technical developments and their wider application. It was a characteristic outcome of the way radio—like other inventions—was being discovered almost simultaneously in several different places. Ever the patent rights to the audion were divided. De Forest owned the rights to the third element while Marconi possessed those concerned with the other two. This hindered the mass production of audions for a number of years.

The main factor retarding the spread of radio, though, was that the wireless industry of the time devoted itself primarily to maritime communications. Radio was being immediately applied to shipping. As early as 1899 wireless was used by ships at sea to call for help. In 1909 the crews of eighteen ships owed their lives to radio distress calls. More routinely, radio had tremendous commercial advantages in the dispatching and ordering of goods carried by ships. British Marconi dominated the prewar radio industry because it led in this growing, profitable market. In 1901 Marconi had secured the prestigious contract to equip the Lloyds of London signal installations. The commercial strength of Marconi was such that, for a time, it ordered its shore stations to communicate only with vessels that rented Marconi receiver-transmitters. Thus, when World War I broke out Marconi ran 90 percent of all American-ship-to-shore communication.

As radio was increasingly used to save lives and property at sea, the need to protect vital transmissions from interference became imperative. Both the monopoly of Marconi and the tendency of individual countries to impose their wireless standards and equipment, regardless of possible interference and incompatibility, were seen as dangerously counterproductive. The more farsighted specialists called for international regulation at an international conference on radio, held in Berlin, Germany, in 1903. The resulting protocol called for total cooperation between all wireless systems. A second conference in 1906 introduced SOS as the globally recognized distress signal. The wide-ranging and detailed decisions made at this conference were to take effect from July 1, 1908, but complications in various countries caused a delay. Congress originally refused to ratify the agreements, partly because many congressmen feared that American radio would be subject to foreign control. Eventually, the first Radio Act was passed in 1910. This incorporated much of the 1906 agreements, principally that oceangoing ships carrying more than fifty passengers and steaming between ports that were 200 or more miles apart had to carry radio equipment, with a range of at least 100 miles.

The loss of the *Titanic* off the Newfoundland coast in 1912 highlighted serious shortcomings in wireless legislation. The 705 survivors were picked up by the *Carpathia* and saved, thanks to radio, but the ship that answered the distress signal came from 58 miles away while a much nearer ship failed to give assistance simply because its only radio operator had fallen asleep. A subsequent international conference spurred on the United States to amend its act of 1910. It now stipulated that any ship with fifty or more passengers traveling over whatever distance between ports had to have radio, a secondary power supply, two or more op-

The pioneer stage of radio was much advanced by radio hams, amateur enthusiasts like John Pringle, a fourteen-year-old high school student in Chicago, photographed in 1922 as he listened in to a broadcast from Key West on a set he had partially built himself. (Library of Congress).

erators, and direct communication between the operator and the bridge.

The problem of interference also had a domestic dimension. Reviewing Marconi's achievement in 1902, Ray Stannard Baker projected a future of radio broadcasting in which large organizations and private individuals alike could secure their own personal, private frequencies for radio transmission. This progressive notion soon found support in the emergence of numerous radio hams following the discovery that cheap crystals could be used to detect radio waves. By 1917 over 8,500 amateurs were operating their own transmitting stations. These numerous stations wreaked havoc with military and commercial communications and the government responded to pressure for order and decided to regulate frequencies.

The Radio Act of 1912 divided the wireless spectrum into specific frequencies that were to be used exclusively by certain interests. Since the act did not mention broadcasting, it contributed inadvertently to a new period of confusion in the 1920s. It awarded the secretary of commerce broad, but contradictory, powers to assign wavelengths and time limits to parties but did not allow him to refuse anyone license.

Despite the overwhelming concern for using radio as a means of point-to-point communication, it would be wrong to assume that there were no attempts at public broadcasting before 1920. Determination to publicize their inventions led both Lee de Forest and Fessenden to make the first broadcasts. On Christmas Eve, 1906, Fessenden made the first publicly announced transmission of voice and speech. His initial publicity referred to marine radio operators hearing angels' voices while, six months later, Fessenden distributed cards saying "Did you get my wireless?" Yet this, and the opera broadcasts that de Forest made, were but brief experiments. The firm origins of radio broadcasting lay amongst the large numbers of radio amateurs. By 1915 they had formed a national organization, the Radio Relay League (RRL), and started to publish a magazine, *QST*. Thus technical information was rapidly and successfully cross-fertilized. There were an increasing number of amateurs who began to transmit programs of music, conversation, and news.

Since he aimed for a general audience and used radio waves, rather than cable, to transmit speech and music, Charles D. Herrold was probably the first true broadcaster. Based at the College of Engineering and Wireless in San Jose, California, Herrold started to transmit regular news bulletins and music programs in 1904. After becoming licensed, his station broadcast from the 1915 World

Exposition in San Francisco. During World War I, Herrold was off the air but in 1921 the station restarted as KQW. (It was later known as KCBS of San Francisco.)

Despite such experimentation, the industry saw the future of radio in terms of making greater profits from wireless point-to-point communication. Nevertheless, the commercial manager of American Marconi, David Sarnoff, wrote a memo to his general manager in 1916 suggesting ". . . a plan of development which would make radio a "household utility' in the same sense as the piano or phonograph." He talked of a "Radio Music Box." Although the memo was forgotten, it was of some significance not least because its author would become the president of RCA.

Although all high power commercial stations were commandeered and all amateur and experimental broadcasting prohibited in 1917, World War I somewhat advanced the development of radio. Wireless proved to be useful in combat. The navy depended on its $20 million investment in shore situations. The pressing need for trained operators led to the conscription of amateurs and the setting up of radio schools. Thus the public pool of knowledge about radio grew.

The war put an end to divisive wrangles over patents with the establishment of the first patents' pool. Prior to the war, it was impossible to mass-produce the audion or triode vacuum tubes because of the division of patent rights. However, the navy needed large quantities of vacuum tubes to install in its maritime radio system. Accordingly, the navy now came to an arrangement whereby companies should provide the best possible equipment and the navy would pay for any necessary patent infringement.

Motion Pictures

One of the most potent and enduring myths of the industrial age is the story of Baron Frankenstein creating a man from the limbs and embers of various dead men. However, his handsome creation is not a complete success and turns into a deformed monster. The story is often taken as a metaphor for industrial man creating machines the better to carry out his work but which then turn upon him. Hollywood, the center of American, and, indeed,

In *The Bank* Charlie Chaplin demonstrated his ability to jolt audiences at the beginning of his films by strolling into a bank, turning the vault safe with immaculate precision, and opening it only to remove a mop and pail, thereby disclosing the difference between capital and labor. Chaplin was the preeminent cinema artist of the silent era whose classic comedies mixed social comment, lyricism, and ingenious clowning. (Museum of Modern Art).

world, film production, notably in the heyday of the studio years of 1930–45, has enshrined this myth not only in the creation of beautiful actress Gallateas by Pygmalion directors who breathed life into their perfect statues, but also in the studio system that attempted to raise its players to mythological status. The system was intended to celebrate and perpetuate human perfection and Hollywood was most influential in standardizing elegant fashions of face and form. Thus Hollywood supplied a modern fountain of youth.

From the start Hollywood has been synonymous with both glamor and with commercial vulgarity—a fact that led to critical scrutiny and exposure by perceptive and disillusioned novelists such as F. Scott Fitzgerald in *The Last Tycoon*, Nathanael West in *The Day of the Locust*, and Gore Vidal in *Myra Breckenridge*. The surface glamor of Hollywood has also been a target of criticism by certain Soviet writers who affect to find in the veneer all that is deplorable in the American film industry in particular and in the substance below all that is deplorable in the American dream in general. Thus Soviet critic Albertas Laurinchukas opined in 1967, "All the propaganda of the capitalist world is saturated with a scandalous and piquant, mysterious and glittering, enticing and murderous elixir called Hollywood. . . . Hollywood is the world's largest factory of filth, where there is no room for dreams. People there smile only when the camera lights are turned on."

Yet much of Hollywood epitomizes the more significant aspects of modern American history. The story of movies and Hollywood encompasses some central folklore of American history: competition among inventors as to who can best solve the technical problems of the new machines; the perennial conflicts between entrepreneurs on the inside of a privileged cartel and the outsiders determined to penetrate a monopoly market; the visible hand of marketing to create public appetite for an entirely new product; the managerial revolution of industry that instituted a studio system for economic stability and survival and found its art form bound by commercial needs of economies of scale; and an industry profoundly affected by such economic cycles as the boom of the 1920s and the slump of the 1930s. One of the most lucid and perceptive accounts of motion picture history has been given by Gerald Mast in his *A Short History of the Movies* (1971) and this brief account summarises much of his writing.

The Invention of Motion Pictures

Films were (and remain) dependent on machines created by inventors not interested in making art but rather in making a scientific curiosity work. Cameras to shoot films and projectors to show them were inventions first exploited as novelties and only later integrated as two machines in a whole process of shooting and projecting films. Edison's English associate, William Kennedy Laurie Dickson, wrote about the invention of motion pictures in a pamphlet, *History of the Photographic and Scientific Experiments and Developments Leading up to the Perfection of the Vitascope* (1896). "It is the crown and flower of nineteenth-century magic, the crystallization of eons of groping enchantments. In its wholesome, sunny and accessible laws are possibilities undreamt of by the occult lore of the East; the conservative wisdom of Egypt, the jealous erudition of Babylon, the granded mysteries of Delphic and Eleusinian shrines."

In the period 1850–75, three kinds of mechanical research laid the foundations for the perfection of motion pictures: research into the persistence of vision; still photography; and mechanized entertainment. As we have noted about inventions in other fields, one of the striking facts about the invention of motion pictures is the simultaneity of discovery by different inventors in at least four countries—Britain, France, Germany, and the United States.

Motion pictures are an optical illusion in which viewers think they are seeing continuous, flowing motion. In fact, they are really watching disconnected, still excerpts of the motion that viewers interpret as continuous because of the way the human eye works. Our brains retain the images for a split second longer than our eyes, thus making us unconscious of our eyelids blinking. While the eyelid covers the eyeball, our mind retains the image prior to the blink. Thus our minds blur successive but individual views into a fluid sequence. This is persistence of vision, identified by English scientists Peter Mark Rôget and Sir John Herschel. Motion picture cameras take a series of single, still photographs, or frames, at about the rate of 16 frames per second. Each second contains 16/30ths of a second of exposed action and 14/30ths of a second of darkness between frames. Early mechanical toys exploited the phenomenon of persistence of vision.

In 1834 William George Horner produced the zoetrope, a rotating circular drum with individual images in sequence on a lower level and individual eye slits on an upper level through which the viewer would see painted figures dance. In 1834 Baron Franz von Uchatius started experiments combining these so-called stroboscopic toys with a series of magic lanterns, or slide projectors, lined up so as to cast successive images on a screen, perfected by the projecting phenakistiscope of 1854—an early version of animated cartoons.

Hitherto, the images were drawings—cartoons. There had to be natural pictures—photographs—before there could be moving pictures, a combination of still photographs and stroboscopic toys. Photographs were based on the principle of a completely dark box that lets in light through a tiny hole covered by a lens. The lens projected an inverse image of the view facing it on the wall opposite the lens. What was necessary to make a photograph was a photographic plate to retain the image instead of the wall. In 1839 Frenchman Louis Jacques Mandé Daguerre achieved clear and permanent images, Daguerreotypes, on silvered copperplate, after fifteen minutes' exposure. Successive refinements over the next thirty years reduced the exposure time to a fraction of a second. The breakthrough into genuine motion pictures of continuous action was achieved by English immigrant Eadweard Muybridge. The notorious maverick photographer had achieved a *succès de scandale* by killing his wife's lover and then persuading a jury to acquit him of murder. In 1877 he won a bet for Governor Leland Stanford of California by demonstrating conclusively that a racehorse at full gallop had all four hooves off the ground. Muybridge set twelve cameras in a row along a racetrack. Attached to each camera across the track were twelve strings; the horse raced down the track, tripping the wires, and the photographs recorded the scene.

Thomas Edison's interest in movies was to provide a visual accompaniment to the phonograph he had invented in the 1870s. By 1899 the sales of the spring-motor phonograph amounted to

$500,000, although the mass production of records as disks did not begin until February 1902, after Eldridge Johnson had organized the Victor Talking Machine Company in 1901. Much earlier, Edison conceived the idea of moving, speaking pictures. His initial idea was to etch tiny photographs in the same sort of way that sound was recorded on phonograph cylinders. Thus each cylinder would carry sound and pictures. However, it proved impossible to reduce photographs to the size of pin points. When Edison went to Europe in 1889 he left William Kennedy Laurie Dickson in charge of making filmstrips and improving machinery for reproduction. When Edison returned in October 1889, Dickson, using celluloid film produced by George Eastman of Rochester, New York, had perfected a way of projecting film upon a screen and synchronizing it with sound, the kinetophonograph. Edison's most significant contribution was to perforate the side of the film to facilitate its rolling past the shutter. Dickson also created motion picture studios. Dickson had a small room constructed, protected by black metal plates, and known as the Black Maria, with a roof that could be opened to let in sunshine to light the action and that could be rotated to catch the sun throughout the day.

In order to achieve effective film projection, inventors had to solve two problems: the projector required enough light to make the image clear and the film had to run evenly past the source of light without tearing or catching fire. One of the first successful projectors was achieved by the Lathams of Virginia, former Confederate officer Major Woodville Latham and his sons, Gray and Otway, who perfected a superior camera and projector in 1895 known as the Panoptikon or the Eidologscope. It doubled the size of film shown to about 70 mm. Successful projection depended upon intermittent (rather than continuous) movement of the film so that each frame halted momentarily in front of the light.

Edison had been too mean to extend his patent rights to Europe and his omission allowed brothers Auguste Marie Louis Nicolas Lumière (the elder) and Louis Jean Lumière (the younger) of Lyons to develop a superior, portable camera, operated by a hand crank with which they shot their first film, *Workers Leaving the Lumière Factory* (1895). They made 35 mm the standard width of film, sixteen frames per second the approximate standard speed (until the introduction of sound necessitated a slightly faster pace for better sound production); and they contributed a new name for their invention—cinématographie.

The transformation of small screenings into large screen exposures was the work of little-known inventor and realtor Thomas Armat of Washington. Edison's backers knew that the new invention would appeal to the public if it carried Edison's name. Accordingly, when the Amazing Vitascope was shown to the press on April 3, 1896, it was described as "Thomas A. Edison's latest marvel." It was Thomas Armat who realized that film would run more smoothly with a small loop to relax the film tension immediately before and after it passed across the film gate. William Dickson, by now a renegade associate, developed a camera taking pictures eight times larger than Edison's. He filmed the *Empire State Express* and when his show opened at Hammerstein's Theater on October 12, 1896, the sight of the great train hurtling along was so so realistic that it alarmed some of the audience into stampeding for the exit.

In the United States two new companies challenged Edison's lead. The American Mutoscope and Biograph company was led by William Dickson and made films up on the roof of the Biograph offices near Broadway and 14th Street. The Vitagraph Company was founded by English immigrant J. Stuart Blackton who had also worked as reporter and cartoonist for the *New York World* before pirating Edison's machine. Vitagraph also shot films on the roofs of buildings in Manhattan, including the fictitious *Tearing Down the Spanish Flag* (1898) that they represented as a newsreel recording a historic event in the Spanish-American War.

The rope that held early movies from the abyss of fading audience interest in formula episodes of ordinary life was stage melodrama and farce as practiced by such successful playwrights as David Belasco, Pinero, and Boucicault. In France Georges Méliès proved far more creative, using some of the possibilities of the cinema for visual tricks in such films as *A Trip to the Moon* (1902) where the first spaceship to land on the moon arrives splashing the eye of the man in the moon.

Early films were like staged plays with screenplay, sets, and acting to provide a stationary camera with a single viewpoint, fixed perspective, like one member of a theater audience in the front stalls. However, whereas a stage set is an essential of stage drama because space in a theater is concrete, natural space in film is variable. Although the cinema screen is fixed, the images cast upon it move. Thus in film, it is the single camera shot that is the principal unit of the drama. Individual shots are selected and pieced together to compose longer scenes that can themselves be mixed in a variety of ways. What was essential in the movies was the creation of an intelligible series of images that provide continuity of story, meaning, and emotional momentum.

It was Edison cameraman Edwin S. Porter (who had earlier pretended to be Edison's son in order to get work as a touring projectionist) who first got camera, action, and shots to move freely. In *The Life of an American Fireman* (1903) he moved from the hero outside a blazing house to the family inside to be rescued and back again. In *The Great Train Robbery* (1903) Porter was more imaginative still, enlisting the audience's response to shift its emotional focus on the outlaws' victim by abruptly returning to the telegraph office where the operator lies assaulted, thereby moving backward and changing the spatial focus. Later, more sophisticated directors would build on the technique of elliptical editing to emphasize fluid movement and energy.

The period 1895–1905 was marked by intense commercial competition, indeed, piracy, of invention and even of film strips. For ten years Edison had private detectives scour the country far and wide for any infringement of the Latham loop for which he held the Armat patent. For his part, Armat, now discontented by Edison's appropriation of full credit for an invention he had transformed (and also for doublecrossing him by manufacturing his own projection machine despite an agreement not to do so), brought suit against Edison. Altogether 200 court cases were heard in these years over patent rights and infringements.

In 1902 the first purpose-built motion picture theater opened in Los Angeles, Thomas L. Tally's Electric Theatre. In 1905 the first nickleodeon opened in Pittsburgh, a special theater accompanying film screenings with music played on the piano and charging an entrance fee of 5 cents. By 1910 there were at least 5,000 such movie theaters across the United States. Civic dignitaries were much concerned by low general standards of sanitation in these cinemas and that they were being used for free sex in the back rows. Accidents were common, largely because of overcrowding, and from fires, caused by hazardous machines and inflammable celluloid.

Yet the building of numerous cinemas and their increasing popularity had an immediate and progressive impact on the film industry. The establishment of custom-built movie houses imposed radical shifts in the relationship between producers and exhibitors. To satisfy its clients, a nickelodeon needed to show complete programs of at least six films (each of one reel and lasting for about an hour altogether). There was no point in the cinema owner or manager acquiring films outright. His clients would only want to see a particular movie once or twice. Thus in the movie business the situation was ripe for a middleman to supply films for the theaters, either buying or leasing films from the production companies, and then renting them to the movie theaters. Thus a chain was forged between the first producers, distributors, and exhibitors who comprised the first generation of motion picture moguls.

Once the American film industry had established its three tiers of production, distribution, and exhibition, Thomas Edison realized that it was in his interests to impose order on chaos and the upshot of the early trials and tribulations of the industry was a giant combination of nine leading film companies in 1908—Edison, Biograph, Vitagraph, Essanay, Kalem, Lubin, Selig, Méliès, and Pathé. The giant merger, entitled the Motion Picture Patents Company, acted as an economic pool and agreed to support the interests of the individual companies, pooling their technical resources by sharing patent rights to the various machines, and acting as an oligarchy to exclude all other companies and machines from what was now their business. Thus a distributor who wanted to carry films by the Patents Company—still providing the most superior films—could not carry films produced by any other company. Furthermore, the Patents Company signed an exclusive contract with George Eastman by which Eastman

Innovative director David Wark Griffith intended his monumental epic, *Intolerance,* to extend further the horizons of cinema art while silencing critics who had accused him of racism. The spectacle of such scenes as the storming of the Walls of Babylon (here) was contrasted with the poignancy of intimate moments and Griffith's notable cross editing to achieve frantic climaxes. (Museum of Modern Art).

would supply raw film stock only to the Patents Company, already his largest customer, and, therefore, the one with the greatest commercial hold over him.

This historic agreement of the Motion Picture Patents Company not only ended ten years' internecine competition but also turned American film production into a monopoly of the nine bright shiners. They leased films only to a privileged group of distributors who treated with them and who soon joined forces as the General Film Company. The distributors rented film only to exhibitors who, in exchange for a small licensing fee of $2 per week, agreed to show only Patents Company movies.

Of course, several distributors and exhibitors within the cartel disliked the monopoly in practice, partly because it reduced profits. Within a few months two of the malcontents—William Swanson in Chicago and Carl Laemmle in New York—broke away from the cartel and urged others to become independent. Thus the war of the patents was followed by a war over the trust. Their immediate problem was to find films not made by a company in the Patents monopoly and both Laemmle and Fox turned into producers creating the film companies that are best known as Universal-International and Twentieth-Century Fox. Moreover, Fox sued Patents as a trust in violation of the Sherman Antitrust Act. The established companies, true to their credentials as latterday robber barons, fought back by fielding not only able lawyers but also strong-arm gorillas who were despatched by Patents executive Jeremiah J. Kennedy to vandalise the property of the independents and intimidate their staff.

From the point of view of the federal government, the Patents Company was the sort of relatively small organization that could be prosecuted successfully—unlike larger and more complex trusts. However, the case won by other factors, primarily the multiple and resilient opposition. Laemmle, Fox, and such other independent producer-distributors as Adam Kessel and Charles Bauman, and Edwin S. Porter, flourished, creating, respectively, the Bison Life Motion Picture, and the Rex, companies. They acquired film stock from England and France and encouraged older film companies associated with the cartel to organize separate, independent companies. The outcome of the war over the Motion Picture Patents Company was that the trust was forced to dissolve by the courts and all nine of its constituent companies had expired by 1925 while the independent companies survived. In the process, they carried film production into a new and exciting period of artistic growth.

One of the first big commercial successes of the cinema was French tragedienne Sarah Bernhardt and members of the Comédie Française in *Queen Elizabeth* (1912). It was directed by Louis Mercanton and produced by Film d'Art, a French company formed in 1907 to create a serious cinema using the best creative and interpretative artists. In America it was promoted by Adolph Zukor and its success seemed to show that serious and long films could be popular with the masses. However, *Queen Elizabeth* had more lessons for the fledgling industry. It showed that shots, acting, and perspective must be different on film from stage. Bernhardt's outsize mannerisms were incompatible with the different range and smaller scale of expression required for film. Another lesson was that the camera must vary shots between long-range for public moments and close-ups for private ones.

The directors and studios in the fading trust were adamantly hostile to making longer, so-called, feature films of two hours because they would be far more expensive to produce than programs of short films, requiring a large permanent staff, far more equipment, and extensive marketing. Thus Zukor was drawn into the net of the independents when the Patents Company refused to let him make longer pictures in America on the model of *Queen Elizabeth*.

In fact, it took only a quarter of a century for films to graduate from cheap entertainment to big business in which ever longer pictures required more material, more elaborate production, better actors, and ever more publicity to generate larger profits. The subsequent history of film is concentrated on major talents, whether producers, directors, or actors, and certain films that were crucial in the development of film as art or commerce. The American film industry of the 1910s and 1920s was based on the achievements of three men—D. W. Griffith, Mack Sennett, and Charles Chaplin.

Mack Sennett and Charlie Chaplin

Director, actor, and screenplay writer Mack Sennett first worked for inventor Thomas Edison, the Biograph Company, and director D. W. Griffith, whose techniques of cutting and editing he absorbed and then parodied in a series of comic films for Keystone. Their particular speciality was an ensemble of grotesque policemen, the Keystone cops. The visual art form of one-reel films was eminently suited to the sequence of gags devised by Sennett that made the most of people and cars colliding abruptly with one another.

The essence of Sennett's comedies was to turn human beings into imperfect, mechanical toys at odds with their environment and colliding with falling buildings, motor cars, and custard pies. The effects were achieved partly by precise timing, partly by comic invention, and partly by slow shooting (between eight and twelve frames per second) but fast projection (between sixteen and twenty frames per second) to heighten the overall mechanical effect. Although Sennett began his projects with some semblance of a plot, he was far more dependent on visual gags devised and developed by improvisation on the set. The finished product had little structure or continuity, remaining a sequence of gags brought to an end when the leading characters fell back exhausted and sometimes soaked to the skin. Sennett's first feature film, *Tillie's Punctured Romance* (1914) with the outsize Marie Dressler, the small Charlie Chaplin, and comedienne Mabel Normand was entirely typical of the genre, featuring comic dance routines at a fancy dress ball, a chase by Keystone cops, and a grand finale in which all the principal characters capsize in the Pacific Ocean off Santa Monica. Sennett also exploited cinematic distortion. In *The Surf Girl* (1916) he uses reverse motion to have all the other characters in a crowded swimming pool thrown back out of the water by the great impact of a fat man sliding into it. Slow-motion shooting but fast-forward projection turn the pool into a frenetic water ballet. Sennett appreciated that, since his actors were in almost continuous motion, the camera must provide the audience with a fixed point of view, single point perspective, that would not only offer them some repose but also help reduce the actors to simple physical types.

Comic actor Charlie Chaplin was spotted by Adam Kessel and director Mack Sennett while he was on tour across America with Fred Karno's English Pantomime Troupe. He began work for Keystone in 1913 at a wage of $150 per week. Sennett expected to draw on Chaplin's acrobatic abilities and play his small, lithe gymnast against the outsize Fatty Arbuckle or Marie Dressler. However, Chaplin's natural warmth lent a depth and, sometimes, a pathos that reached further than Sennett's marionettes. He took bowler hat and cane from French comic actor Max Linder, outsize shoes from Ford Sterling, and baggy pants from Fatty Arbuckle and began to create his own highly individual character of the wistful but resourceful tramp. Despite his differences with Sennett's methods, Chaplin's creation was a signal public success, allowing him to leave Sennett in 1915 and accept a contract with Essanay for $1,250 per week to create his own films.

Despite Chaplin's doubts about certain projects, he never doubted himself. His background had seeds of profound tragedy. His father, Charles, a successful songwriter and performer, abandoned his family shortly after young Charles was born in London and his mother, Hannah, slid into madness and was institutionalized from time to time. Charles and his older half brother, Sydney, had a difficult childhood—fatherless, in and out of workhouses, and usually frightened. When Chaplin became affluent, he sent for Sydney who came to Hollywood but failed to match his brother on screen but, instead, became a successful business manager for him behind the scenes.

Chaplin's screen persona was of a vulnerable but resilient outsider—whether immigrant, artisan, or prisoner—attracted by the glamorous veneer of affluent society but disturbed by its superficiality. Yet his short films rarely have a continuous thread. The comic sequences are like separate charms on a bracelet. Chaplin's expansion of a comic sequence from gag to scene in such films as *The Tramp* (1915) and *The Adventurer* (1917) entailed greater consistency of plot and situation and more thorough exploration of characters who are defined by the gags than was the case in Sennett's films. As an escaped prisoner in *The Adventurer* who finds himself at a society reception, his clumsy table manners result in splashes of ice cream falling from a balcony above onto other guests below, down the ladies' décolleté gowns, and expose his social naiveté. Sennett's chases were escapades about the abandon and gaiety of undisciplined movement; Chaplin's chases were designed to maximize his dexterity and show his skill at eluding capture, whether on the escalator in *The Floorwalker* or by roller skates in *The Adventurer*.

Chaplin's special genius lay in his inventive ability to devise comic surprises near the start of his films that jolt the audience, producing effects that are just the opposite of bathos. In *The Adventurer* he first appears, finally digging himself out of imprisonment through a hole in the sand. In *The Immigrant* it seems that all the passengers are seasick and this is why they are leaning over the side of the ship. Not so, Charlie. When the camera pans over to him, it shows that he is leaning over the side to fish.

Chaplin turned physical types into rich comic caricatures, notably his customary heavy villain, Eric Campbell. He used Campbell as an example of outsize boorishness among bullying policemen *(Easy Street)*, lecherous aristocracy *(The Count)*, and inattentive waiters *(The Immigrant)*. In each of these films the tramp is an outsider whose true values are higher than those of his supposed social superiors. Indeed, in Chaplin's films all the parts are subordinate to unfolding the character of the tramp, explaining the qualities that isolate him from other people but which make him superior to those who have compromised their ideals in order to stave off loneliness. To draw out the more wistful side of his character, Chaplin used a usually blonde woman often played by Edna Purviance, as a symbol of natural purity unspoiled by material interests.

Chaplin's shorts also provided biting social comment on such contemporary (and later) issues as poverty, hunger, and crime, not to mention religious hypocrisy and drug addiction. Chaplin shows police corruption in *Police* when his character is persuaded by other policemen to perform his duties honestly so that they can make even more money dishonestly through bribes. The minister who preaches a plangent sermon that persuades Charlie not to steal a man's watch then goes on to pocket it himself. *Easy Street* is deeply pessimistic about society and shows the city as an urban jungle, a hostile place fit only for (and occupied by) parasites and thieves. At the end of the film, when its thieves' kitchen has been transformed into a religious mission with hoodlums and gangsters converted into saints, it is clear that Chaplin is burlesquing religious revivalism.

Chaplin was especially adroit in his use of things, inanimate objects that could be turned into weapon, tool, or even food and frequently served as all three until he had exhausted all the possibilities in any given situation. In *The Pawnshop* he treats an old clock as patient, toy, and jewel. Defeated by the kneading of dough, he runs it through the wringer of a washing machine. Subsequently, he uses the wringer to dry cups and saucers. However, a doughnut that he can just about get his teeth into and eat then breaks a plate that it lands on.

Chaplin's work was known right across America and he was celebrated in countless miniature statues. As English journalist and historian A.J.P. Taylor puts it, he was as timeless as Shakespeare and as great. He worked for four different companies in his first five years and by 1918 was earning $1 million per annum in a contract for the exhibitor and distributor First National Pictures, the start of his career as an independent film producer, producing ever longer and more complex films in the 1920s. Critic Garson Kanin once asked Chaplin how he felt upon his rapid elevation from supporting player to celebrated star, "hailed by film and literary and social critics as a genius in a medium that hadn't yet produced one. Were you surprised?" "Not at all," replied Chaplin. "I always knew I was a poet."

The most influential and charismatic star in the history of Hollywood because he was a dominant creative and interpretive artist for such a long time during the formative years of the American film industry, Chaplin had few peers in the other function of film stars, as a newspaper and magazine subject for gossip and innuendo about his sex life. In short, he became a legend in his own bedtime. The women in Chaplin's life were a reflection of his artistic development. He was married four times—to actresses Mildred Harris, Lita Grey, Paulette Goddard, and, finally, in June 1943, to Eugene O'Neill's daughter, Oona, when she was eighteen and he was fifty-four. The marriage lasted until his death thirty-four years later and they had five daughters and three sons. Eugene O'Neill disapproved of the marriage, partly because of the difference in age and partly because of Chaplin's reputation as a philanderer. In addition to his marriages, Chaplin had close relationships with leading players Mabel Normand, Edna Purviance, Pola Negri, Georgia Hale, Marion Davies, and Virginia Cherrill, and his secretary, May Reeves. In 1943 his former mistress, Joan Barry, turned against him and did everything in her power to undermine his career, including bringing a paternity suit against him. Blood tests proved he was not the father of her child, yet, after a hung jury at the first trial, a second jury found him guilty. Private peccadilloes by Hollywood stars were all part of the entertainment they provided when private lives became public affairs.

Griffith

The cinema artist most responsible for the transformation of motion pictures from a primitive to a finished art form was director David Wark Griffith.

Griffith, who was raised in Kentucky, intended to become a playwright and based his early stage dramas on the lurid melodramas of David Belasco. Years later he found ways of transferring quintessential Belasco trademarks to the screen—highly charged emotional scenes, melodramatic contrasts, and a recurrent, sentimental theme of innocence betrayed. Edwin Porter, now in charge of production at Edison, offered Griffith work as an actor at $5 a day in various rescue and escape movies. It was from Porter that Griffith learned how editing could (and must be) used to shape the emotional momentum of a film. When he moved to another company, Biograph, it was just as Biograph was beginning to make two films a week and required a second director. Griffith was persuaded to take on the job.

He directed more than 150 films over the next five years, providing himself with opportunities to test a variety of new techniques and arrive at a signal conclusion—that it was the dramatic interest of a shot that must determine the camera's relationship to it. This was entirely different from the conventional wisdom that insisted on the full (or far) shot in order to reward the audience with full length view of actors and sets. Instead, Griffith used a wide range of shots including long (or distance) shot, full shot, medium shot (of head and torso), close up, and intense close up (of eyes and mouth). Then he combined them into an integrated sequence that moved freely between the various shots. Thus Griffith broke the stage's inappropriate hold over cinema technique. Yet, in the deeper sense, Griffith's method was truly theatrical. As cinema historian Gerald Mast persuasively explains:

Although a scene on the stage is anchored in immovable space, it really is a series of shifting 'beats,' of emotional pivots and pirouettes, of thrusts and parries, of comings together and splittings apart. Despite the stasis of the setting and the audience's viewing angle, the theatrical scene is not static; it is constantly shifting, changing, and evolving. Griffith translated these stage 'beats' into film terms. When the mood shifted, when the emotions charged, the camera shifted. It caught that intimate moment when a single member of a group made up his mind to take a significant emotional leap; it caught the smallness of a solitary soldier in the midst of a huge army or a vast battlefield. Griffith discovered that the emotional content of a scene, not the location of the scene, determined the correct placement of his camera and the correct moment to cut from one perspective to another.

Moreover, the members of a stage audience continuously alter their focus on a stage play and also shift their emotional perspective of the drama not only as it unfolds but also within individual scenes—not to mention their varying concentration on the play. Griffith found a way to translate these continuous shifts into cinematic terms.

Furthermore, Griffith developed two moving shots, hitherto little used: the pan shot, in which the camera moves from left to right (or the other way round) in order to follow action moving across the screen and emphasize such motion; and the traveling, or tracking, shot that not only accompanies characters or objects as they move but also emphasizes their psychological excitement riding horses, railroad trains, and motor cars. Griffith also made profound advances in editing when he realised that separate locations and events in different times could be linked by cross-cuts (or parallel cuts) either to increase suspense in the case of attacks and chases or to deepen psychological interest, in such an instance as a cross-cut from a soldier killed in battle to his family awaiting the news at home. Both sorts of cuts were intended to (and did) find an appropriate visual expression for inner, and sometimes secret, feelings.

In the 1920s and 1930s modern cinemas, such as the Trans-Lux Theater on 58th Street and Madison Avenue, New York, completed in 1931, offered patrons the luxury and comfort of the best stage theaters and the latest in art deco design. (Library of Congress).

While Griffith was perfecting his craft, studios began using the more reliable electric light for filming, instead of remaining dependent on the alternately harsh and watery, if natural, sunlight. However, it was only Griffith who realized that artificial light must also be varied rather than a constant hard glare if it were to suggest such effects as daylight fading or firelight flickering, or to enhance the emotional impact of a scene. His control of effective tonal lighting achieved perfection in *Broken Blossoms* (1919) in which subtle lighting enhances the film's whole atmosphere and underscores its moral points.

As well as his innovations in technique, Griffith instituted three reforms among his casts. He showed actors how to act for the camera by underplaying, knowing his cameras could capture the most subtle expressions. In *The New York Hat* (1912), based on Anita Loos's first screenplay, he taught Mary Pickford how to show her longing for a stylish hat with which she can attract a man and thus escape the tedium of small town life, only to find later that she becomes a victim of small town moralizing. He chose actors who were physically appropriate for their roles, thereby helping define the system of type casting. Finally, he insisted on rehearsals—something considered a waste of time in a period of silent films when a director could instruct actors through a megaphone while shooting film. Moreover, Griffith started to build a cinema ensemble, of actors used to performing together, using such actors as Mary Pickford, Lillian and Dorothy Gish, Mae Marsh, Lionel Barrymore, Robert Harron, and Donald Crisp who became familiar with one another and with Griffith's intentions.

In these years Griffith took his material from literary classics, blood and thunder romances, and recent novels. He also exposed such contemporary problems as urban squalor and in *The Musketeers of Pig Alley* initiated one of the cinema's most enduring genres—the crime thriller. A special feature of Griffith's movies were chase and rescue episodes in which the audience's excitement was sustained by ever shorter cuts between different locales. Mack Sennett parodied Griffith's rescue films in such comedies as *Barney Oldfield's Race for Life* (1913). Ford Sterling ties Mabel Normand to a railroad track and then actually steals a train, "for the express purpose of running her over," as Gerald Mast puts it.

By 1913 Griffith was ready to make films longer than a single reel. He achieved as much in the development of specified techniques as he was going to and he wanted to make his innovations serve more complex and moral aims, teaching his audiences positive values of fidelity to hearth and home and to social harmony. He also exposed the evils of social disruption, whether the subject was war, sexual license, or the absence of tenderness. Griffith saw the world and its people poised between the positive virtues of gentleness and trust and the destructive vices of violence. He conveyed gentleness by turning the Gibson girl of easel art into a Griffith's girl of motion picture art—incandescent, gentle, and blonde. However, in Griffith's mature films this idealized woman was clearly a figure of fantasy.

Griffith's last film for Biograph, *Judith of Bethulia* (1913), was a transitional work that revealed his dexterity in cross cutting and his new moral emphasis and, in the climactic battle, provided an artistically successful collision of contrary images. When Biograph proposed to control Griffith by turning him into a director of studio production without being able to make his own films, Griffith left the company for Mutual, taking with him his best cameraman, G. W. ("Billy") Bitzer, and all his leading actors. Their first effort for Mutual, *Home Sweet Home* (1914), was Griffith's first attempt to use four separate stories to make a central point about the composer of the famous song, John Howard Payne, being reclaimed by Heaven, despite an earthly life of indulgence and waste, because his song expressed an ideal that had sustained different people through their own lives.

Griffith's contract with Mutual allowed him to make one independent project each year. In 1914 he turned Thomas Dixon's epic novel about the old South in the era of the American Civil War and later into a film, emphasizing the bitter tragedies of Reconstruction. Griffith's father had served in the Confederate army and the director felt keenly about (to him) the injustices of the southern experience. Most controversial was the novel's idealizing of the white terrorist groups generally known as the Ku Klux Klan.

Only Griffith knew what he could accomplish with Dixon's meretricious novel. He had no script and created the work impromptu out of the materials to hand—story, sets, locations, actors, and technicians. He used thousands of people and animals and numerous sets at a hitherto unprecedented cost, for a motion picture, of $125,000. The film took six weeks to rehearse and nine weeks to shoot in a period when other directors made one film every week. When the film opened in Los Angeles on February 8, 1915, the novelist was so struck by Griffith's transformation of his tawdry material that he persuaded the director to use a more epic title than *The Clansman—The Birth of a Nation.*

Griffith prised open *The Clansman* by focusing on the different experiences of a northern family, the Stonemans, and a southern one, the Camerons, through the era of the Civil War until they are united by marriage. This intimate story is set against a larger canvas of set pieces, representing a society torn apart by violence and then brought together again by simple human emotions. The most spectacular scenes never lose their intimate dimension and it was here that Griffith's awesome editing technique came into play. He moved continuously from the general to the specific, alternating close and distant shots and changing angles so as to capture the different views of his characters. Of particular interest at the time was the masking, or irising, effect Griffith used to concentrate attention first on a weeping mother on the brow of a hill surveying the destruction wrought by an invading army in the valley below and then on the entire panoramic scene. The film closed with Griffith's most complex rescue sequence in which the knights of the Ku Klux Klan deliver two groups of victims from death and worse, a masterpiece of editing in response to the rhythmic and emotional needs of the audience.

The film was even more controversial than the novel, partly because more people saw the film than read the book, partly because Griffith's images and cinematography were so potent, and partly because of the increasingly widespread excitement that movies were generating. Praised by President Woodrow Wilson, damned by Progressives and liberals for its racism, the film was banned in certain cities lest it fuel riots of whites against blacks. The crudest scene reviling black citizens during Reconstruction showed how an empty state assembly suddenly became populated by ignorant black assemblymen reclining with bare feet on desks and drinking booze straight from the bottle.

Whatever its political bias, *The Birth of a Nation* was a significant work in the history of the performing arts and one that, like great paintings, touched people's hearts as much as their minds with a clear message despite its richness and complexity. People admired the historical pageant, appreciated Griffith's craft, and were moved by many intimate moments. In short, the film was accessible to everyone on many levels. Yet, as with earlier and later films by Griffith, there was a gulf between the generalizations about love and fidelity and the specific instances intended to illustrate them. Very few people would credit the Ku Klux Klan in any of its forms as the agency best equipped to build a Kingdom of God on earth, a point made somewhat abstrusely at the end of the film.

The controversy over Griffith's treatment of black citizens in *The Birth of a Nation* wounded Griffith deeply and he was determined to redeem himself. Moreover, the huge commercial success of *The Birth of a Nation* allowed Griffith to prepare his own cinematic defense in an even more ambitious and extravagant film, *Intolerance,* made at a cost of $2 million.

There were two principal and two lesser stories to illustrate Griffith's recurrent themes. The main stories were about Belshazzar's Feast, ending in the overthrow and murder of the king of Babylon, and a modern story about an American youth falsely convicted of murder who is eventually saved from the gallows as his son is rescued from an orphanage. The briefer stories were about the crucifixion of Jesus outside Jerusalem and the Massacre of St. Bartholomew's Eve in France. Griffith emphasizes the evil machinations of selfish clerics in Babylon, Judea, and France, whether priests, Pharisees, or ministers, and of busybody social reformers in the United States. All of them use religious differences as a pretext for antisocial actions. All are persuasively caricatured. There are four frenetic climaxes, each of which underscores the others, but only in the modern story does good triumph over evil. Griffith showed his hatred of injustice as much through his cross cutting and composition as the acting styles. The cold factory owner who has had police disperse protesting workers with bullets is shown sitting apart from the mayhem outside the factory gates perfectly still and diminutive in an outsize office.

However, a people being roused by government propaganda

to support American intervention in World War I with all its might and main was not likely to respond to a somewhat complex and unpleasant film preaching pacifist values. *Intolerance* was an unqualified commercial disaster. Its failure left Griffith dependent on other businessmen for the remainder of his career.

Griffith now made a series of comparatively unimaginative, even lugubrious, pictures based on scripts written to a formula but not guaranteed to draw audiences. Two of these were interesting for greater unity, polish, and general skill than his epic masterpieces. *Broken Blossoms* (1919) is a triangle set in the Limehouse district of London. It tells of an unloved girl, Lucy (Lillian Gish), used by her stepfather (Donald Crisp) as a skivvy, who falls in love with a Chinese mystic, Cheng Huan (Richard Barthelmess). Cheng Huan wants to turn her into a princess of flowers at the service of Buddha. In a frantic climax her stepfather beats her most brutally, dragging her from a closet where she hides, turning continuously in a circle of despair close to autism. All three die—Lucy from the assault, the stepfather from retaliation by Cheng Huan, and Huan by suicide. The broken blossoms are a symbol of true love torn apart by violence in low life, exactly the sort of subject that verismo composers were turning into operas. Griffith's special achievement in *Broken Blossoms* was his evocative and masterly use of lighting, from the luminous room of flowers in Cheng Huan's shop to the garish boxing ring. *Way Down East* (1920) is another rescue film notable from the way Griffith intercut most effectively shots of Niagara Falls with scenes of Lillian Gish prone on an ice floe about to be saved by Richard Barthelmess.

Thereafter, Griffith's artistic abilities declined, partly because his technical skills had outrun his ability to move people. But he was also a victim of the change in public taste. Urban cinema audiences in the 1920s craved surface excitement and had no interest in Griffith's moralizing. They wanted to share vicariously in the rise of reel characters from rags to riches and enjoy, at least on screen, the sort of high life Griffith so much disliked. The final failure of his lugubrious diatribe against the national prohibition of alcohol, *The Struggle* (1931), convinced all the studio bosses that Griffith's day was over. He eked out another seventeen years in Los Angeles, excluded from the very industry he had transformed almost single-handedly into a major art form.

The Early Years of Hollywood and the Studio System

The course of the film industry was largely determined by several crucial developments in the 1910s: the move from New York to California; the creation of a first generation of movie moguls; the creation of feature films; the inception of a star system; and the eclipse of the European film industry during World War I.

Southern California became the home of film production by the independents for a variety of reasons. It was far removed from the Trust's wrecking crews in New York and, indeed, the patent laws, and it was close to the Mexican border, whither studios could escape with their property in case of pursuit. Moreover, it had such powerful scenic attractions of mountains, plains, desert, and ocean and an even and reliable supply of sun. The name Hollywood was given to the suburb by an early settler, Mrs. Horace H. Wilcox from Kansas. Cecil B. De Mille was the first producer to film there. He made *The Squaw Man* (1913) in a barn on what is now Hollywood Boulevard. Griffith moved his company to California in three successive winters, 1910, 1911, and 1912, and filmed his masterpieces there. By 1913 most film companies had relocated to Hollywood.

Moreover, the American industry was supported by considerable capital provided by the good offices of the producers who had become even more powerful than the original movie trust: Carl Laemmle, William Fox, Samuel Goldfish, Jesse Lasky, Marcus Loew, Louis B. Mayer, Lewis J. Selznick, and Adolph Zukor. These were the first movie moguls, a term coined by *Time* magazine in 1923, first as "cinemoguls." Some of the movie moguls were Irish Americans, such as Eddie Mannix at MGM and Winfield Sheehan at Fox; some were Greeks, such as the Skouras brothers, also at Fox. However, the majority were Jewish, first- and second-generation immigrants from Russia and Poland.

Ironically, this first generation of movie moguls who shaped the taste of two generations of moviegoers was woefully lacking

One of the most ornate picture palaces was Grauman's Chinese Theater, Wiltshire Boulevard, Los Angeles, a quaint monument to eclectic
Chinoiserie that remains a tourist attraction for its imprints of the hands
and feet of stars along the concrete forecourt and sidewalks. (Library of
Congress).

in education and artistic sensibility. The experiences of the movie
moguls as owners of nickleodeons and amusement arcades had
hardened them to vagaries in public taste and taught them how
to apply salesmanship without discretion or inhibition, whatever
the product. Screenwriter Ben Hecht passed this caustic judg-

ment on the taste of the movie moguls, "He is usually a man who has no taste to be violated or distorted. He admires with his whole soul the drivel his underlings produce in his factory." Their phenomenal commercial success was due to perfect timing. They had begun when American society was becoming increasingly obsessed with movies and American movies were all the rage in Europe. They succeeded because they rode the tiger rather than trying to tame it. Seymour Martin Lipset in *The First New Nation* (1963) explains the chutzpah and resilience of the movie moguls thus:

Since the emphasis is on individual success in the United States, those individuals or groups who feel themselves handicapped and who seek to resolve their consequent doubts about their personal worth are under strong pressure to 'innovate,' that is, to use whatever means they can find to gain recognition. The pressure to innovate may be reflected in efforts which established groups would not make—for example, the development of new and risky industries by those of recent immigrant background and low status who are banned by limited economic resources and social discrimination, from advancing up economic ladders.

Unlike the Patents Company producers, Laemmle, Fox, Goldfish, and Zukor were ready to take the risk of making longer films and made the requisite investment. Thus the movie trust had already lost the war for audiences, who loved longer films before the adverse court decisions of 1915 forced it to dissolve. By 1915 film programs had acquired their definitive form—a major feature film supported either by one or two short films, or a shorter, more cheaply produced film.

The star system of accredited players came into existence about this time. Hitherto, players were not named and those artists who came to be recognized were known either by the names of their characters or by the name of the studio. The independents thought that a better paid film star would be more cost-effective than an unnamed, if cheaper, player. Thus they enticed such leading artists as Florence Lawrence ("the Biograph Girl"), Arthur Johnson, and King Baggott. The success of the star system was such that by 1917 two players, Mary Pickford and Charlie Chaplin, were preeminent and competing with one another to see who could exact the highest fees, each signing contracts for $1 million.

The star system captured public imagination as it was promoted not only in the movies themselves but also from 1912 onward through special movie magazines. The concoction of film publicity turned the artist into a product imbued with certain pronounced personal traits of character in the manner of such ancient deities as Apollo and Aphrodite, and to be worshipped as such. The only living precedent for the publicity and adulation heaped on stars whose incandescent screen presences were the artistic product of costumiers, makeup artists, and lighting technicians was in the rarified world of opera dive, the outsize dandies and dowdies of high fashion.

During World War I studios were marketing artists like exotic perfumes. One of the first products was Theda Bara, the sultry temptress of *A Fool There Was* (1915). Originally Theodosia Goodman of Chicago, her film name was an anagram of Arab Death, and she was presented as an Arabian siren, descendent of the Cleopatras of Egypt, a sexual vampire feeding off men's desires. "Vampire" was shortened to "vamp," thereby providing English with a new word as verb and noun. Her crude version of exoticism was eagerly lapped up by a credulous public.

The most persuasive of the early film stars created character prototypes, copied by less authoritative artists. Mary Pickford's playful little minx was widely imitated, as were romantic leads Richard Barthelmess and Charles Ray, exotic Latins Rudolph Valentino and Ramon Navarro, and cynical European lechers Erich von Stroheim and Adolphe Menjou. Lillian Gish portrayed innocent women ennobled by suffering; Gloria Swanson played resilient women of the world; Douglas Fairbanks, swashbuckling rogues; William S. Hart, cowboy survivors.

World War I killed the European film industry as surely as it annihilated a generation of young soldiers. Ironically, raw film stock was made from exactly the same chemicals needed to make gunpowder. European governments at war chose to make gunpowder to kill people rather than films to entertain them. Nevertheless, the need for entertainment was still there. American movies thus came to dominate European screens during and after the war. When the film industry of Europe recovered years after the war, the role of French, Russian, German, and Swedish directors was to dazzle viewers with all sorts of artistic innovations rather than to challenge the commercial ascendancy of Hollywood.

The first generation of movie moguls expected of the film industry the greatest commercial profits from the greatest number of patrons, something they believed could only be achieved by appealing to the lowest common denominators of taste, a formula imposed on Hollywood in its crucial years and which it has only periodically been able to transcend. If the film industry was to work commercially, it had to appeal to the widest possible audience and, therefore, must appeal and be accessible to blue collar workers across the country from all manner of ethnic groups. The Jewish movie moguls would be much better placed to know what would, and would not, work commercially and artistically, than perhaps any other group of people.

The most successful company of the silent movies was Paramount, created by Adolph Zukor, and producing three kinds of movies: Class A with stage actors and high-class pretensions; Class B with regular screen actors such as Pickford; and Class C, inexpensive, quickly produced feature films. Mary Pickford's films were far more successful than the others and Zukor began concentrating on feature films. He also took over companies owned by Lasky, Selznick, and Porter and a general distributor, Paramount Pictures, that gave its name to the giant combine. Zukor was the most successful of the early moguls not because of economies of scale in production but because of excess, the money to pay for the most popular stars who could command the greatest audiences.

A second amalgamation was Metro-Goldwyn-Mayer (MGM), the creation of Marcus Loew, owner of a chain of cinemas who wanted to make more money by producing films. In 1924 he acquired two unsuccessful production companies, the Metro Picture Company and the Goldwyn Picture Company. Samuel Goldwyn (originally Goldfish) had just left his own company before the amalgamation, and remained deeply resentful of the outcome. Loew installed another theater owner, Louis B. Mayer, as head of production at MGM and Mayer brought with him a young assistant, Irving Thalberg, to oversee actual shooting. Mayer became one of the most hated men in the industry for his megalomania and vindictiveness. After his death, Samuel Goldwyn was supposed to have said, "The reason so many people showed up at his funeral was because they wanted to make sure he was dead." (In fact, very few people went to Mayer's funeral.)

It was Marcus Loew who finally achieved the sort of vertical integration in American motion pictures that French moguls Léon Gaumont and Charles Pathé had previously attained in Europe. MGM shot its pictures in Goldwyn's studios and then distributed its films across Loew's chain of cinemas. Thus Loew controlled all three stages of motion pictures—production, distribution, and exhibition. Zukor took his cue from Loew and insisted on a system of block bookings from theater owners who did business with him. It was all or nothing. If they wanted the best of Mary Pickford, they had to acquire a year's supply of fifty-two programs from Zukor.

Theater owners resented the new Paramount policy. In 1917 several joined a protest group, the First National Exhibitors Circuit, led by W. W. Hodkinson and J. D. Williams. Their aim was to persuade established stars such as Charlie Chaplin to make pictures specially for their theaters and thereby bypass Paramount. By this arrangement film stars acquired financial and artistic independence and the theater owners could exhibit their own popular products. First National was successful and soon ranked third in the world of commercial film.

A fourth power was the United Artists Corporation formed by D. W. Griffith, Charlie Chaplin, Mary Pickford, and Douglas Fairbanks in 1919. While United Artists had neither studios nor theater, it was based on the commercial pull of preeminent cinema artists who were to make their own films and then have them released by the common company. Oscar Price, publicity assistant to Secretary of the Treasury William Gibbs McAdoo, had advised the four artists that they should form a company to capitalize on their talents while they were all together on a tour selling bonds in World War I and it was Price who served as the first president. However, he was succeeded, in turn, by Hiram Abrams, Joseph Schenck, and Al Lichtman. United Arists never achieved its original aim of owning a chain of theaters. Griffith soon left the organization and Chaplin made only seven pictures for release by United Artists over the next thirty years. In 1950 the survivors, Chaplin and Mary Pickford, sold most of their shares to a syndicate.

Movie theaters expanded to become outsize, opulent auditoriums, comfortable with padded chairs, such as the Strand, which was built on Broadway in 1914, and the Vitagraph (later the Criterion), which could seat 2,000 people. Samuel L. ("Roxy") Rothafel conceived of a new cinema house, the Roxy, and went on to acquire and maintain a chain of New York cinemas, such as the Rialto and the Capitol, and culminating in Radio City Music Hall in the Rockefeller Center. Rothafel was concerned to raise the general tone of exhibition and added live symphony orchestras, ballets, and variety acts to the screening of movies, an anachronism that has survived in Radio City Music Hall as a bizarre tourist attraction. Roxy had his ushers dress in much the same colors as the walls and carpets of his theaters. He also decorated the theaters with classical statues and various ornamental flourishes to column, beam, and balcony. In Los Angeles Sid Grauman devised a Chinese theater replete with pagoda roofs and oriental decoration. It was subsequently more famous for its sidewalk with imprints of the hands and feet of famous stars and survived the great days of Hollywood as a tourist attraction in Los Angeles.

CHAPTER NINE

On the Rise:
Architecture and Skyscrapers

·ᴄʒ·

THE DISTINCTIVE skyline of Manhattan with its towering skyscrapers has become a metaphor for modern American cities. The skyscraper itself, a tall building based on a steel frame,
has become the most indigenous form of American architecture.
However, it was the new technology of engineering, based on
improved processes of steel and the construction of bridges, such
as the Brooklyn Bridge, completed in 1883, that made possible
the new form of American architecture.

Offices in tall buildings depended on new means of communication and illumination—the typewriter, telephone, elevator, and
electric light—all of which were invented in the 1870s. In the
1880s progressive architects, enthusiastic about the invention of
the elevator, began experimenting with iron and steel frames beyond ten stories. Thus were skyscrapers built in New York and
Chicago. The skyscraper became the manifestation of the new
urban civilization that had developed by the end of the nineteenth
century. It was a tall structure built of metal as well as stone,
consuming less ground space yet accommodating more people
than the largest stone buildings of the mid-nineteenth century.

The Prudential Building (also known as the Guaranty Building), Buffalo, by Adler and Sullivan (1894–95). This was one of Louis Sullivan's most successful skyscrapers, based on a steel skeleton covered with a sheath of terra cotta fire clay tiles. (Photographed by Jack E. Boucher for the Historic American Buildings Survey in May 1965; Library of Congress).

Louis Sullivan and the Chicago School (1856–1924)

The history of the skyscraper begins in Chicago with the work of the Chicago School of Architects. It was led by Louis Sullivan, and its basic tenet was that a building should express a total cultural purpose. Thus the traditional decoration of city buildings would be abandoned. Sullivan proclaimed that the skyscraper "must be tall, every inch of it tall . . . it must be every inch a proud and soaring thing, rising in sheer exultation that from bottom to top it is a unit without a single dissenting line."

The Wainwright Building in St. Louis, completed in 1891, is an example of Sullivan's main intention for the skyscraper—to emphasize its height. This is achieved by vertical piers rising from the second floor to the ninth. As a concession to traditional architecture, the Wainwright includes a heavy cornice and base, which create a counterpoint to the vertical thrust of the building. The spandrels—the panels below each window—are decorated with terra cotta ornaments. Sullivan was deeply influenced by the work of Henry Hobson Richardson, whose earlier Marshall Field Warehouse of 1887 was a prototype building for the Chicago School. It is a powerful mass, Romanesque in its form but tight and ordered in the same sense that a Renaissance palace was. Sullivan said that it was like "a man that walks on two legs . . . a virile force . . . stone mortar, here, springs into life."

Chicago is rightly regarded as the birthplace of the skyscraper. However, it is ironic that Sullivan's Schlesinger & Mayer Department Store of 1901–4—because of the need to provide large floor spaces for retail selling—was a building with considerable horizontal emphasis in its design. How, then, could a relatively low building with a horizontal emphasis influence the design of skyscrapers, very high buildings? The answer lies in the building's very particular use of building material and the special nature of its construction.

The Carson, Pirie, Scott & Co. Building (as the Schlesinger & Mayer came to be known after a change of ownership) exploited the possibilities of the new steel frames to their fullest with a layered grid pattern that allowed a continuous flow of horizontal space through its large windows and, also, revealed the columns, beams, piers, and spandrels that supported the structure. This was the glass curtain wall—an architectural phenomenon now synonymous with modern skyscraper architecture—in one of its earliest manifestations in an American city. Steel and glass were united with subtle ornamentation to create the building that Louis Sullivan had called for in his work, *Ornament in Architecture* (1892), "well formed and comely in the nude." One of the main tenets of the new architecture, together with the notion that form must follow function, was that ornament, when necessary, should complement, rather than disguise, the structure. Sullivan's department store was completed in 1904 and was the culmination of the first phase in the development of the steel frame first used in Chicago in 1885 in the first prototype skyscraper, the Home Insurance Building by William Le Baron Jenney (1832–1907).

It was, indeed, Louis Sullivan who, more than any other single architect, gave us the basic form of the modern skyscraper and a theory to accompany it. One of his biographers, Robert Twombly, explains that "Sullivan felt you can't look to history for forms, that the skyscraper represented a new American civilization and required a form based on its new function." To Sullivan, building facades were symbols for the life cycle—birth, growth, maturity, decline, death, and renewal. The age of industrialization presented the architect not only with new techniques and materials, as encapsulated in the steel frame, but it confronted them also with a new purpose. The spirit of the age demanded new forms that would signify the achievements and potential of a growing industrial order. For a while Sullivan met this demand and for a while he enjoyed success, but, because he was something more than a rational business architect, his work eventually became unacceptable and then, finally, was ignored. Sullivan was a visionary with a sometimes romantic notion of what his architecture should look like and the place it should occupy in the urban world. For this reason Sullivan (together with his pupil, Frank Lloyd Wright [1867–1959]), was to be the model for Canadian author Ayn Rand's uncompromising but charismatic architect, Howard Roark, in her contentious novel *The Fountainhead* (1943). However, where the fictional titan triumphs, the real

This detail of the Prudential Building shows how clearly architect Louis Sullivan had found a new mode of ornament that was original and fresh and that emphasized the building's soaring height. (Photographed by Jack E. Boucher for the Historic American Buildings Survey in May 1965; Library of Congress).

life titan was punished for his refusal to compromise, and thus Sullivan ended his days unknown and largely unappreciated as an architect.

The son of an Irish father and Swiss mother and born in Boston, Sullivan enjoyed a carefree childhood in a cultured family. He studied for a year at MIT before starting work as a draughtsman for the firm of Frank Furness in Philadelphia. In 1873 he went to live in Chicago where his parents had already settled and there he worked as a draughtsman for William Le Baron Jenney. Like most architects in Chicago, Jenney's firm was engaged to help rebuild the city after the devastating fire of 1871. In 1874 Sullivan decided to leave Chicago and continue his studies for a year at the Ecole des Beaux-Arts in Paris.

On his return to Chicago, Sullivan had a series of jobs until he formed first a friendship and, then, in 1883 a close partnership with engineer Dankmar Adler. The partnership of Sullivan and Adler was a perfect complement of mind and method. Architectural historian and critic Thomas S. Hines comments, "While Adler's contributions lay in the more practical spheres of planning, acoustics, structural engineering and client relations, Sullivan, as designer, gave the buildings their ultimate esthetic identities." The most famous Sullivan-Adler skyscrapers were the Schiller Building (1891–93) and the Stock Exchange (1893–94) in Chicago, the Wainwright Building (1886–91) in St. Louis, and the Prudential (also known as the Guaranty) Building (1894–95) in Buffalo. Architectural historian Paul Goldberger considers the Guaranty Building Sullivan's masterpiece. It stretched to thirteen stories and here, at last, the skyscraper appears a true soaring tower and not a thick cube. The treatment of the top is most graceful, seeming to grow out of the arches that crown each row of vertical windows.

However, there were profound differences in temperament between Sullivan and Adler and this led to the break up of their partnership in 1895, after which Sullivan's fortunes began to fail. Sullivan remained a frustrated genius who felt much pent up frustration, loneliness, and anger in early twentieth-century America. Robert Twombly in his biography Louis Sullivan (1986) deduces from various factors, such as Sullivan's late, short, and unsuccessful marriage, his close friendships with men only, and various themes in the ornaments to his buildings that Sullivan was really homosexual. "Sullivan preferred male to female anatomy as the object of study. . . . Throughout his youth he idolized a series of older men, never women, and at the Sistine Chapel learned from Michelangelo the power and possibility of being male, of being *super* male." Thus, for instance, as we have noticed, Sullivan described Henry Hobson Richardson's Marshall

Field and Company wholesale store, an inspiration for many of his early buildings, as a "virile force," a building with "red blood; a real man, a manly man . . . an entire male."

It is possible Sullivan found architecture a way of partly sublimating his repressed sexuality. In Sullivan's buildings the moldings on columns surge from the base to the apex where they form an arch and run down the next colume to the base. "In a building, ornament represented for him the female, emotional, poetic side of nature, and the mass its male, rational, logical component. He believed both natures should be in balance in a building, as in a person."

After the breakup of his partnership with Adler, Sullivan received fewer commissions, although the high quality of his work remained. Robert Twombly asserts that Sullivan's "genius never failed him. It was not for loss of ability that he got fewer jobs. Sullivan fell from favor because of his assault on the establishment, his lack of institutional support, his standoffish personality, his refusal to compromise, his ill-deserved reputation as an impractical artist, his reluctance to do houses, and because of changing attitudes toward ornament. . . . The result was further withdrawal into himself, so deeply at times that even when he got work, he seemed unable to do it." Yet Sullivan's influence on the so-called Chicago School of Architecture was incalculable.

However, many people did not like the new architectural form of skyscrapers and championed a more derivative architecture, based on older styles—Greek, Roman, and Renaissance—and freely mixing elements from these and other periods. The men and women of the young twentieth century walked in city streets that were sometimes in the shadow of tall modern buildings and sometimes dominated by stirring neoclassical facades. A song of 1908, *In the City Where Nobody Cares,* typified fears that were widely voiced that the growth of urban society had led to the individual becoming less important, a decline of the community spirit, and the dominance of the machine over man. One commentator complained that the skyscraper was "shutting out the light of the heavens and circumscribing the air of the streets, to both of which possessions people are entitled and which in the pursuit of health, happiness and prosperity they should demand."

Probably the most spectacular thing about skyscrapers at the turn of the century was not seeing them rise from the ground; it was seeing the ground below from the new towers on high. Until the creation of skyscrapers, most people lived at, or close to, ground level. Only a few daring balloonists had risen into, and moved across, the air. As skyscrapers rose, people rode ever higher in the elevators and saw the world from above, the world laid flat like a pattern with previously invisible roofs and the ground-plan of the modern American city turned into a map. Hence, people became increasingly aware of a new sort of cityscape—one based on frontage and pattern rather than on perspective and depth. This world below was flat but it contained the movement of people, horses, carriages, and automobiles. If it was seen as a map, it also suggested abstract shapes, and provided the space in which the most progressive European and American art would unfold in the period 1907–20 in the forms of cubism, precision-ism, and synchromism.

American Renaissance in Architecture

Another leading architect of the day was Daniel H. Burnham (1846–1912), who, unlike Sullivan, was a born compromiser. In 1903 Burnham's Flatiron Building was completed in New York City. Its peculiar shape and name were the result of its triangular site that, in turn, is due to the diagonal axis of Broadway as it meets with the horizontal line of 23rd Street and vertical line of Fifth Avenue in Lower Manhattan. The aesthetic success of the Flatiron Building was due more to its remarkable shape and its comparative isolation in the cramped city than to its ornate covering of French Renaissance ornament. This is the key to the essential difference between the new architectural purist, Sullivan, and the compromiser, Burnham, who, above all things, was a businessman and devised an architecture to serve business expectations in a time of industrial and commercial growth.

Burnham's career had begun in the last decades of the nineteenth century in partnership with John Wellborn Root (1850–1891), whose untimely death allowed him to divert the character of their practice from its original emphasis on the new architec-

The Flatiron Building, New York, by Daniel H. Burnham and Company, 1903. In what architectural historian Paul Goldberger calls "a time of intense, almost delirious, growth," it dominated the junction of Broadway and Fifth Avenue that had determined its particular shape. (Library of Congress).

ture to a historicist approach. The classicist architecture of Chicago's World's Columbian Exposition of 1893 that was overseen by Burnham, was emblematic of this change and became a focal point in American architectural ideas. The Flatiron's excessive ornamentation is an example of the eclectic application of classical motifs to modern construction, as was Burnham's Wanamaker Department Store, erected in Philadelphia in 1911, and designed, somewhat inappropriately, to be an imitation of a Renaissance palace.

Burnham had, indeed, moved to the profession of architect from the world of business and it was his business acumen that assured him his position as a leading architect of the day. Louis Sullivan, who was, of course, not an entirely objective critic, was damning in his criticism of Burnham in his *Autobiography:* "During this period there was well under way the formation of mergers, combinations and trusts in the industrial world. The only architect to catch the significance of this movement was Daniel Burnham, for in its tendency towards bigness, organization, delegation and intense commercialism, he sensed the reciprocal workings of his own mind." On the other hand, Sullivan sought an architecture that he considered more democratic and less concerned with historical ornament and less elitist. However, the flowing tide of historicist architecture was irresistible, and it was swelled not only by individual businessmen who wanted suitably grand and inspiring accommodation for themselves and their commercial empires, but also by government—federal, state, and municipal. The sheer scale and quantity of classicist public architecture was daunting, and Daniel Burnham was deeply involved in its creation.

The City Beautiful movement rose out of the public success of the Columbian Exposition and the other great fairs of the epoch: the Trans-Mississippi and International Exposition of Omaha in 1898; the Pan-American of Buffalo in 1901; and the Louisiana Purchase in St. Louis, 1904. The planning of these fairs resulted in spacious, free-flowing and attractive malls that, since they were unrelated to the harsher reality of industrial cities, provided a welcome relief from the raw disorder of urban America. For the Columbian Exposition landscape architect Frederick Law Olmsted Sr., had created a series of lagoons that enhanced the classical architecture of the buildings and the space that surrounded them by reflecting shimmering visions of the gleaming stucco surfaces. This, and the use of electric lights, gave rise to epithets such as the "White City" and the "Magic City." Throughout the nation city governments aspired to emulate the success of the Magic City.

The most important and prestigious City Beautiful commission was for the improvement of Washington, D.C. It was also the only real success of the movement because Washington already had the fundamental potential for becoming a very beautiful city in the late eighteenth-century plan of the French landscape designer and planner, Major Pierre Charles L'Enfant. In 1900, as a result of protests by congressmen and architectural writers, the Senate Parks Commission was created to investigate the possibility of finishing Charles L'Enfant's uncompleted plan.

Under the leadership of Senator James McMillan, the Senate Parks Commission included the famous talents who had helped produce the very successful World's Columbian Exposition of 1893 in Chicago: Daniel Burnham, Charles F. McKim, Frederick Law Olmsted, Jr. (son of Olmsted, Sr., and now in charge of his company), and, later, the sculptor Augustus Saint-Gaudens. This team of prestige architects, artists, and planners first looked to colonial capitals like Annapolis and Williamsburg for their inspiration, then turned their gaze farther afield and even farther back in time to Europe's grand cities, such as Paris, Rome, and London.

The first plan was published in 1902 and covered all the additional land that had become available since L'Enfant's day through the reclamation of the flatlands close to the Potomac. The reclaimed land to the west of the Washington Monument was to be dedicated to a memorial to President Abraham Lincoln, with the two memorials connected by a decorative canal now known as the Reflecting Pool. Circular ponds and gardens were to have been constructed immediately in front of the Washington Monument, thus recreating by illusion L'Enfant's original Presidential House-Washington Monument axis that had been compromised because of fears for the foundations of the projected 600 foot obelisk. However, despite its historicist tone, the McMillan plan was not the simple revival of L'Enfant's intentions, but was, rather, a variation on his original theme, a topographical expansion of the neoclassical plan. The McMillan plan did not receive an immediate and definite response from Congress. Indeed, the plan was never actually implemented as a whole but in a rather piecemeal fashion. Many of its individual elements were realized as they won approval and were built individually. Even a crucial element such as Burnham's new Union Station was only made possible through the architect's personal negotiations with Alexander Cassatt, president of the Pennsylvania Railroad.

Nevertheless, Burnham tried to restore the city's original grand sense of scale by placing major public buildings on the axes where L'Enfant had intended them to be. Thus he moved the Baltimore and Potomac Railroad Depot that had been constructed on the Mall near the Capitol. Burnham's new and monumentally impressive structure—Union Station—was placed in a space of its own on Capitol Hill. Union Station was special amongst all of the great railway stations built during this period: whereas they were all conceived as grand gateways to their cities, only Burnham's design fulfilled its role properly because it had adequate landscaped space around it to accentuate its monumental presence.

In 1910 the creation of the Commission of Fine Arts signaled the beginning of the federal government's commitment to the supervision of the capital's public sculptures and, later, public buildings as well. World War I virtually halted work on the city's improvement and, in fact, created new problems for federal planners by swelling the population to permanently high levels and requiring the provision of housing and office space for war workers. However, the early twenties saw the work resume in earnest. The Lincoln Memorial, with its imposing statue by Daniel Chester French, and the Reflecting Pool were completed as were many of the numerous grand public buildings in white stone for which Washington is renowned throughout the world, such as Cass Gilbert's Treasury Annex. Under the Public Building Act of 1913, the Public Buildings' Commission was instructed to devise standards for public buildings, but not until 1926, following much press agitation over the government's "million dollar rent bill," were moves made to provide permanent accommodation for the expanded civil service ranks. In that year, under a new Public Building Act, some $50 million was appropriated to construct public buildings, and thus the Federal Triangle with its unified group of monumental public buildings came into being and obliterated notorious slum communities with names such as Swamppoodle and Murder Bay.

Daniel Burnham was strong on compromise and on rhetoric to support his views. His most famous line, although one that he never actually uttered,—it was culled from his writings by an assistant—is one of the most famous in American architecture: "Make no little plans; they have no magic to stir men's blood." Yet Burnham's big plans did not make for an architecture that outlasted changes in public taste, and neither did the eclectic style he encouraged, but the style did last long enough to supplant the work of more truly modern architects like Louis Sullivan.

Skyscrapers

Although the nation's capital did not permit construction of tall buildings, so as not to dwarf the Washington Monument and the Capitol, in Chicago and New York the skyline was reaching ever upward and the man on the street was walking along the foot of ever-deepening artificial canyons. In the period from the turn of the century to the outbreak of World War I, it was now New York, rather than Chicago, that led the way in skyscraper construction. In fact, the island of Manhattan with its hard bedrock proved especially suitable for skyscraper construction, although skyscrapers were restricted to two areas, Lower Manhattan and Midtown, because it was only in these areas that the rock formation was solid enough to support such structures. In 1908 Ernest Flagg (1857–1947) saw the realization of his Singer Tower that, at 600 feet, was then taller than any other building in the city by at least 200 feet. However, his design was stylistically confused, with vestiges of French Beaux-Arts ornament and an ornate mansard top to the tower that would have been more suitable on a suburban house. Architectural critic Paul Goldberger has referred to the Singer Tower, with its energy, narrowness, and top-heaviness, as "an eager weed" in New York's skyline. Clearly, Flagg was trying to clothe something dramatically new in an architectural form that was already old. Another example of eclectic architecture was provided by the Metropolitan Life

Tower in New York, constructed in 1909 by Napoleon Le Brun and Sons. They produced a virtual replica of the Campanile in St. Mark's Square, Venice. Yet the Tower was a handsome and effective element on the skyline, rising narrow and free, its profile an easily identifiable symbol. The face of the clock, which was three stories high, enhanced the tower's role as a benign element in the cityscape.

The general obsession of industrial and financial entrepreneurs with height, with owning the *tallest* building, had begun even while the Singer Tower was still only a plan on the drawing board. In 1913 there appeared the skyscraper that was to retain the title for a remarkable seventeen years and today still remains as one of the most beautiful of all skyscrapers. The Woolworth Building by Cass Gilbert (1858–1934) is 792 feet in height and cost some $13.5 million that chain store owner F. W. Woolworth paid in cash. The international retail chain still maintains its offices in the building's gothic splendor that inspired the epithet, "The Cathedral of Commerce." Woolworths were naturally delighted by this flattering name and used it in 1917 as the title of a brochure devoted to the building: "Just as religion monopolized art and architecture during the medieval epoch," wrote the Reverend S. Parker Cadman, "so commerce has engrossed the United States since 1865."

Cadman was not alone in recognizing that commerce had supplanted religion as the major inspiration of prestige architecture in America. Novelist Henry James, too, remarked on this same phenomenon on his return to America from Europe after an absence of twenty years. However, James was not only astonished by this development; he was deeply disturbed. He wrote in *The American Scene* (1907) about his arrival and how from the ship he studied the skyline and saw that "monsters of greed" had transformed Manhattan into "a huge, jagged city." In the space of twenty years not only had the skyscraper been born, but it had quickly "earned" the right to climb higher than church steeples, because it was the new church of a new religion, commerce. The Woolworth Building was designed in the gothic style that has its origins in medieval architecture and Gilbert was successful in exploiting this style to suit a skyscraper. Despite its antiquity, Gothic

The Woolworth Building, New York, by Cass Gilbert (1913). By an adroit mix of modern engineering and Gothic ornament Gilbert achieved a capacious building with an impression of considerable delicacy. The lower building to the left is the old Municipal Building, now demolished. (Library of Congress).

Pennsylvania Railroad Station, New York, by McKim, Mead, and White (1903–10) provided an imperial gateway to the city with a main concourse designed on the lines of the Baths of Caracalla, Rome, and an outer concourse (here) that made full use of modern steel construction while retaining an aura of mystery. (Library of Congress).

architecture can be very much suited to tall buildings because it emphasizes the skeletal nature of a building's structure. Many architects of this period adopted an eclectic approach in their design, borrowing from past styles with varying degrees of both success and failure.

Charles Follen McKim (1847–1909), William Rutherford Mead (1846–1928), and Stanford White (1853–1906) were three architects who championed historicist architecture as taught at the most prestigious architecture school of the day—the Ecole des Beaux-Arts in Paris. Although the term historicist is essentially pejorative, it is used to identify those architects who drew from and imitated various historical styles and ornaments and yet mixed them eclectically. The partnership of McKim, Mead, and White was formed in New York in 1879 and the firm dominated prestige American architecture in the last decades of the nineteenth century. Only McKim had studied at the Beaux-Arts, but the influence of the Ecole in this period was not restricted to the work of its former students. The school's policy had been shaped in the reign of Louis XIV and its aim was to produce French art as a standardized, high quality product that combined ideals of beauty and clear planning with the sort of pragmatic approach we might associate with the civil service. Indeed, its function was similar to that of the conservative National Academy of Design in New York—the promotion of art as an expression of national culture. It may seem strange that an institution devoted to fostering French nationalism should have enjoyed such influence in America, but if we recollect that the United States was dominated by people of European ancestry, then it is easier to understand why the art and the tenets of the European Renaissance were considered suitable for what some commentators have called the American Renaissance. The Ecole des Beaux-Arts enjoyed remarkable influence in America and, indeed, was the model for the embryonic American architectural schools, the first of which was opened at the Massachusetts Institute of Technology in 1866.

McKim, Mead, and White designed New York's original Pennsylvania Station, now demolished, but which was, in its time, a monument to the eclectic architecture of the American Renaissance. Built between 1903 and 1910, it was the epitome of classic, historicist architecture. The exterior and interior of the great ticket hall came straight from the Roman Baths of Caracalla—imperial Rome in twentieth-century America. However, the ticket hall was only the frontage to this enormous railway station. Behind this public place with its ticket counters and information booths decked in Roman trimmings lay the concourse, another huge enclosed space made possible by modern engineering. But this second atrium was not designed as a piece of pseudo-classic architecture. On the contrary, it was all bare steel and glass, more truly suited to the building's modern purpose. Modern architecture was always subservient to historical illusion in buildings of the American Renaissance because the trimmings of classicism hid the structures of modern engineering that actually supported these monumental buildings.

McKim, Mead, and White also turned their hands to the creation of a historicist skyscraper in New York's Municipal Building of 1913. The firm won the commission after a competition and the design was an attempt to fuse Beaux-Arts classicism with the skyscraper. The result is somewhat grandiose with an elaborate top in overdone, wedding-cake style that does not truly complement the building's base and its main shaft. The architect attempted to create a skyscraper that would be a classicizing civic monument like the court houses and banks of the age, but succeeded only in achieving stylistic exaggeration.

While the eclectic style was the order of the day in New York, in Chicago the new architecture of Louis Sullivan and other members of the Chicago School was still enjoying its brief period of dominance in the commercial and industrial field. In 1910 influential architect and theorist Peter Bonnet Wight (1838–1925) published an essay on warehouse architecture, "Utilitarian Architecture in Chicago." Wight had previously been a follower of the conservative English artistic authority John Ruskin, a fact borne out in his Venetian Gothic design of 1863 for the National Academy of Design in New York, but almost half a century later he praised the way in which the Chicago School had elevated function as a primary concern in design.

However, this praise was only for industrial structures. When the new styles were applied to civic or monumental architecture, the critics turned from applause to derision. Their double standards are illustrated in the work of the architect Albert Kahn (1869–1942). Kahn was a strong and innovative industrial designer who, in 1903, created a factory for the Packard Motor Company made of reinforced concrete and steel. The design ensured that, for the first time ever, the entire production process was brought under one roof. He also designed the Ford Motor Company's Highland Avenue Factory in Detroit where the first Model T rolled off the production line in 1913. These successful industrial designs in the idiom of the new architecture were noticed by young European architects destined to introduce modernism into world architecture. In this way architectural critic and historian Lewis Mumford was able to claim in his book, *The Brown Decades* (1931), that the Chicago School was the immediate forerunner of modernism in architecture. However, Albert Kahn never considered his greatest achievements as real architecture. When he designed an administration building for Ford, or office buildings for Fisher and General Motors, or the Detroit Public Library, he and his clients chose eclectic disguise and historicist ornament rather than the unadorned "honesty" of the new architecture.

In *A Concrete Atlantis* Reyner Banham shows how there is a "casual, cultural and conscious connection" between the early industrial and domestic architecture of Walter Gropius and Le Corbusier in Europe and certain American factories and grain elevators built in the period 1900–20. In 1913 Gropius compared American grain elevators to the "work of ancient Egyptians," partly on account of their austerity, partly on account of their monumentality, and partly on account of their economy of space. The development of daylight factories, "multi-story American industrial buildings with exposed concrete frames, filled in only by transparent glazing," was at its height between 1898 and 1917, and the most successful were constructed in only seven years, between 1906 and 1913. The first concrete grain elevator was probably Peavey's folly in Minneapolis (1899) and the most successful was the concrete central elevator in Buffalo (1917) that could hold 4.5 million bushels in its massive cylinders.

Frank Lloyd Wright

America's most famous architect, Frank Lloyd Wright, began his career in Chicago with his own particular idea of what constituted honesty in architecture and a determination to stick by that idea that transformed him into a modern legend. Wright lived from 1867 to 1959 and died within a few weeks of his ninety-second birthday: his working life lasted seventy-two years. However, it is ironic that Wright's importance to the history of American architecture lies not in the fact that he was a representative figure, but in his very uniqueness. In 1903 Wright was given his first major commercial commission by the Larkin Mail Order Company who employed him to design their administration building in Buffalo, New York. The Larkin Building, completed in 1904, is a landmark in modern architecture. Throughout his career Wright sought to rid his buildings of any sense of enclosure. The concept of human life being lived within a closed box was anathema to him—a legacy of his youth in the open spaces of Wisconsin. In designing the Larkin Building, it occurred to him that the four supporting towers need not stand at the corners of any four-sided building. By moving the towers, and using twice as many, the corners of the box could be opened, thus allowing air, light, and people to circulate throughout the building. At the same time the towers were used to provide services such as ventilation, plumbing, and conduits for electrical wiring. The newly positioned towers supported the walls and floors on a cantilever principle that Wright often illustrated with the graphic example of a tray balanced on a waiter's upturned fingers. The fingers are the cantilevers that take the load as they are spread and balance it while the arm acts as the central support. Not only was the cantilever system economical in its use of materials but it was also highly flexible and capable of bearing great shifting loads. The most spectacular proof of this point came in 1923 when Wright's cantilevered Imperial Hotel in Tokyo, Japan, survived an otherwise devastating earthquake without damage.

The Larkin Building was a considerable success as a new and

creative way of organizing space. Yet, for all sense of spatial freedom experienced by those working in it, it was, in fact, the first hermetically sealed, air-conditioned building in the world. Plate glass was used on a large scale to provide maximum natural lighting. Wright himself designed all of the building's metal furniture, an innovation that was not always comfortable as those (including Wright himself) who used it have testified. The Larkin Building went a long way toward being a showcase for Wright's "organic" architecture. It was a subtle unification of inspiring modern form and functional concern, but Wright did not receive another major business commission in America until the mid-1930s. In the realm of business profits, Wright was eclipsed by architects such as Daniel Burnham and McKim, Mead, and White.

The story of Midway Gardens in Chicago illustrates the fact that Wright's architecture was also largely unappreciated by the public during the first three decades of this century. In 1913 he was approached by property speculator Ed Waller, Jr., with the idea of creating a beautiful concert garden in the middle of industrial Chicago. The architecture of the garden's walls and balconies were based on strict geometrical forms and the plans and the building went ahead very quickly. This was the year in which the Armory Show brought the influence of European modernism in the shape of cubism and futurism to America. But Wright was always keen to dissociate himself from others who might be moving in his direction. Clinging defiantly to his individuality, he wrote in his autobiography:

At the time the Midway Gardens were designed, 1913, l-Art Nouveau was dying in France, where it originated, and gasping wherever else it happened to have caught on, and various experiments in the "abstract" in painting and sculpture were being made in Europe, exciting the aesthetic vanguard and insulting the rank and file. But the straight line, itself an abstraction, and the flat plane for its own sake, had characterized my buildings from the first hour I had become building-conscious.

Despite, or perhaps because of, their merit as modernist architecture, Midway Gardens floundered in a mire of financial difficulties and were bought by the Edelweiss Brewing Company:

The Edelweiss tried to "hit them up"—hired someone to come in, paint the concrete, stencil the plain surfaces, add obnoxious features, out of balance, and nasty. The whole effect was cheapened to suit a hearty bourgeois taste. The scheme that had once been integral was now "decorated" in the meanest and worst of the popular sense of the word. Where there had been integral with materials and purpose, here was raw red, dead white, and bad blue paint.

The Midway had sunk to the level of a beer garden and, when struck by national prohibition of alcohol, Wright's once distinguished scheme proved to be beyond salvage, both financially and artistically. Never did it occur to Wright that his progressive design for Midway Gardens might be "insulting to the rank and file" in the same way that, to his mind, the European modernist painters were. His progressive faith in America made it impossible for him to equate himself with Picasso or Marcel Duchamp because they were not American artists and, therefore, could not hold a vision of a harmonious *Usonia.* Wright coined the romantic term *Usonia* as a name for his vision of a perfectable United States. Ultimately, Midway Gardens provided only one consolation for Wright—the demolition expert hired to destroy the complex found it so solidly constructed that it was troublesome to demolish and he lost money on his contract.

Apart from the Imperial Hotel, Tokyo, begun in 1916 and completed in 1922, Midway Gardens was Wright's last public work for twenty-two years. However, it would be untrue to say that these were lean years for Wright. His talent did not find public expression but it continued because, unlike his mentor, Louis Sullivan, he had a rich talent for domestic architecture that sustained him when his modern designs proved too inaccessible for the public and commercial world in America.

Wright's vision of a perfectable architecture and society is perhaps best illustrated in his Taliesin projects. Taliesin I (1911) was his Wisconsin home and studio named after a Welsh Druid poet, a bard who sang the glories of art. It was built on a remote hill and was the logical extension of the Prairie School of Architecture that had begun with Wright's first important commission, the Winslow House of 1893. The Prairie School espoused an integral vision that demanded that building and site should be united

organically, inseparable and complimentary. Writing of Taliesin
I in his autobiography, Wright said, "I knew well that no house
should ever be on a hill or on anything. It should be of the hill.
Belonging to it: hill and house should live together each the hap-
pier for the other." Ironically, for someone who regularly championed the virtues of democracy, Taliesin was conceived as
Wright's court. Away from the constrictions of society (including marriage and family), he could give rein to his free spirit and
devote his life to the pursuit of a greater calling. This was Wright's
conception of democracy for the individual. In reality it meant
that the concept of collective *Usonian* democracy would remain
just that—a concept and nothing more. Wright's separatist outlook in many ways accounted for his success, but also negated
any practical hope of changing the larger society that lay beyond
Taliesin.

The Skyscraper as an Art Form

Wright was most singular among leading American architects in
his theorizing on social issues. The majority of known architects
were content, when able, to create prestige buildings that, in an
age of rapid commercial expansion, were more often than not
commercial structures. The 1920s was a period of unparalleled
economic growth, especially in the huge expansion in mass communications. Cinema, radio, magazines, and newspapers all bur-
geoned in the decade. It is appropriate that one of the most important, and sensational, architectural commissions of the 1920s
was for the design of a newspaper's offices. In 1922 the *Chicago
Daily Tribune* launched a competition to find a design for its new
building, and in so doing switched the focus on skyscraper construction away from New York and back onto Chicago. Feature
stories, headlines, and illustrations about the competition were
published in both the daily and the Sunday editions of the *Tribune,* thus captivating public as well as architectural interest.

   In publicizing the competition for its new premises, the *Chicago Daily Tribune* was not so much drawing attention to architecture as it was increasing its own prestige and bolstering its
own sales. Ambition is one of the nation's major driving forces

and it shows itself most strongly in the world of business. For the corporation, or the individual businessman, the height of ambition could be realized with the lending of a name to a glorious, and preferably monumental, building. The new Tribune Building had to express in a suitable manner all the power and wealth of an influential newspaper.

The competition attracted 281 entries from throughout the world but not all of them were serious designs. Some foreign entrants deliberately chose to ridicule the spirit of the century. One design consisted only of an elongated Doric column that poked fun at American classicism. Another was a skyscraper grown into the form of a plains Indian wearing full ceremonial war bonnet. However, the winning design by John Mead Howells (1868–1959) and Raymond Hood (1881–1934) was serious in its attempt to create a monumental landmark that expressed the vigorous spirit of a successful newspaper. It was completed in Chicago by 1925, but the Tribune Building merely serves to illustrate the fact that American architecture was still dominated by a historicist outlook in the early 1920s. It is worthwhile noting that, in fact, it was only Raymond Hood who designed the Tribune Building— Howells was too busy with work of his own to help create the competition entry.

Like Cass Gilbert's Woolworth Building, the Tribune Building is a gothic cathedral of commerce. The towering mass was decorated with gothic tracery and was capped by structurally superfluous flying buttresses. Just as other commercial architects sought to disguise the modern load-bearing steel frame of their tall buildings, then so, too, did Raymond Hood. Not only was such architecture dishonest in taking its cue from history, but it also failed to express the new geometry of America's industrial design that had been noted and celebrated by, for example, the Precisionist painters Charles Demuth, Charles Sheeler, and Georgia O'Keeffe in their work of the early 1920s.

Strangely though, Hood's winning design was not the most influential piece of architecture to emerge from the Tribune competition. A late entry submitted by the Finnish architect Eliel Saarinen (1873–1950) only just cleared customs in time for it to be rushed into the final stages. It was awarded second prize but many contemporary commentators felt that it should have been the winner. Although it was never built, its influence was immediate—Saarinen was brought from Finland to Detroit where he built and directed the Cranbrook School and, together with his son, Eero (1910–1961), made considerable contributions to American architecture. His Tribune design, although it was only architecture on paper, was a remarkably successful beginning in America. Saarinen conceived his skyscraper not as a mere soaring facade like Raymond Hood, but as a three-dimensional mass. Before 1916 the planner John M. Carrere (1858–1911) had drawn up a scheme that restricted tall buildings in New York City within the limits of a plane that passed at an angle of twenty degrees from the vertical on the opposite sidewalk. The New York zoning law of 1916 reinforced this tendency toward the building of setback skyscrapers that allowed light down into the streets below and regulated the number of occupants possible in any one building. The law was adopted by other cities and Saarinen's design for the Tribune took account of it by expressing the building's height in a series of stepped rectangular masses that, while still ornamented, relied mainly on their very presence for their effect. This cubic approach to the problem of skyscraper design was to influence much city architecture in the twenties and early thirties.

Another important contribution to the development of the American skyscraper in the 1920s came from the drawings of the architect Hugh Ferris (1889–1962). He enjoyed such success as an illustrator in the early twenties that he became a full-time artist who rendered the architectural visions of others onto canvas. In 1929 he published *The Metropolis of Tomorrow*, a book that, with its polemical text and fifty drawings, drew further attention to the idea of skyscrapers as conglomerations of vertical mass tailored to fit the requirements of the 1916 zoning law, rather than decorated icons of the commercial and imperial spirit.

Saarinen, through his never-built Tribune Building, and Ferris, through his drawings, were altering fundamental consideration of the previous historicist outlook on skyscraper design. Their new approach constituted a new style that was a better visual explanation of a society founded on capital and industry. Their

drawings and designs were of buildings for capital and industry
that looked the part without excessive reference to past styles.
The cubic geometry of their designs was in keeping with the
industrial mechanisms that produced the nation's wealth. Moreover, the impersonality of a building with little or no ornament
reflected the impersonality of corporations that were coming to
rely less on individual potentates and more on inconspicuous teams
of trained managers. Finally, these were designs for buildings of
substance—they proclaimed their presence by virtue of their very
mass and they suggested that the corporate edifice, designed in a
modern idiom, was monumental. One instance of Hugh Ferris's
sketches being given practical form is the New York Telephone
Company Building, or Barclay-Vesey Building, of 1926 that replaced outright classicism for a stripped down, almost sleek style.
Lewis Mumford, who greatly disliked skyscrapers and despaired
of their frozen style, saw here the dawn of a new age in skyscraper design.

Skyscraper architects of the 1920s and 1930s took notice of these
new fundamental precepts in design and created works that were
distinctively modern in appearance. Both the Chrysler Building
and the Empire State Building have become modern myths that
are perhaps overcited in architectural history. Nevertheless, although they were deliberately conceived as prestige structures,
they exploited modern methods of construction and design to the
full. Like the Woolworth Building, they were both the tallest in
the world when completed. In 1930 William Van Alen (1883–
1954) secretly constructed a 120 feet spire within the famous crown
of the Chrysler so that it would be topped off at 1,048 feet in
height, thus beating by some 100 feet another New York skyscraper being built by his erstwhile partner, H. Craig Severance.
The decision epitomized the craze for height. The interior was
lavishly decorated in the art deco style that evolved from the
1925 Exposition Internationale des Arts Décoratifs et Industriels
Modernes in Paris and was used extensively in American business architecture of the late twenties. Art Deco, with its sharply
delineated lines and forms and playful reference to historic styles
and motifs, was a corruption of the style of art nouveau that had

been used extensively in French and American ironwork of the late nineteenth century. The Chrysler's gargoyles below the spire were fashioned after the ornaments on the hood of a 1929 Chrysler car. The exterior of the Chrysler is dominated by the art deco stainless steel crown and spire that have become one of the most instantly recognizable emblems in all architecture and express both the absurdity of a commercialized society and the stylistic élan of America in the 1920s. It seems to encapsulate the energy and flamboyance of New York at that time.

The Empire State at 1,250 feet was designed and built within eighteen months. Its construction was a combined feat of personal ambition and regimented team work, completed in 1931. Architectural historian Rem Koolhas, in his book, *Delirious New York* (1978), has charted the history of the Empire State Building and the old Waldorf-Astoria Hotel that was demolished to make way for it. The Waldorf was a successful symbol of the opulence and achievement of the Astor family, but, nevertheless, it was demolished. Koolhas suggests that the Waldorf-Astoria's problem was simply that it was not a skyscraper. Certainly it is true that by the 1920s there had been so many successes in the skyscraper form that only a skyscraper could be a real symbol of social power and modernity in the 1920s. Richmond H. Shreve, one of the Empire State's three chief architects, wrote in 1930:

. . . two million square feet . . . fifty thousand tons of steel . . . rising nearly a quarter of a mile in a brief eighteen months. Stone from Maine and Indiana, steel from Pittsburgh and Elmira, cement from Pennsylvania and New York, timber from Oregon or the Carolinas, brick from the Hudson River Valley or from the clay pits of Connecticut, glass from Ohio, marble from Vermont or Georgia or Italy . . . from all the world must come together and fit together with accuracy of measurement and precision of time.

The architect's catalogue of national and international endeavor is as effective as the very best of press releases in evoking an image of the Empire State as the apotheosis of the commercial spirit. But, like the Chrysler Building's stainless steel spire, the Empire State is simultaneously a sublime and ridiculous symbol.

It does not have as inventive a profile as the Chrysler but is more restrained and just as handsome. The sheer soaring height is sublime with its steel window frames that fit flush with the exterior cladding of polished Indiana limestone. Its setbacks at the twentieth, thirtieth, and sixtieth floors were an optimum interpretation of the 1916 zoning law. It is a most skilful piece of massing. However, one of the ridiculous elements of the building is that, although it was conceived in economic prosperity, it was created in economic depression. Writing in *Architectural Forum* for January 1931, another of the building's architects, William F. Lamb, announced that, "In essence there is a pyramid of non-rentable space [elevator shafts and service ducts] surrounded by a pyramid of rentable space." In fact, it proved extremely difficult to attract tenants in the depression of the 1930s and, for a while at least, the Empire State Building was simply a pyramid of nonrentable space. In a similar vein was the famous mooring mast for airships—a forward-looking but foolish and impractical plan to make the Empire State a symbolic point of entry to Manhattan Island and the nation. The ape, King Kong, Hollywood's tallest, darkest leading man, may have found the mooring mast most useful, but, ironically, it is the mast that prevents the building, in contrast with many other Manhattan skyscrapers, from enjoying the benefits of the latter-day airship—the helicopter.

For many years the tallest building in the world and one of the most elegant of all skyscrapers, the Empire State Building became a symbol, not only of the New York skyline but of tall buildings everywhere and thus entered folklore. It is best seen from afar where its tower seems at once to blend into the skyline and yet command it. At night it remains, even in the late 1980s, the focal point of Midtown Manhattan, eclipsing the higher towers of the World Trade Center built much later in the 1970s.

However, despite their absurdities, both the Empire State and the Chrysler were crucial in helping to rid skyscraper architecture of its historicist element. By 1929, for example, Raymond Hood was able to design another newspaper building, this time for New York's *Daily News,* that displayed a complete rejection of the principles used in the prize-winning Tribune Building. The Daily News Building was a stark and impersonal statement on the role

The Empire State Building, New York, by Shreve, Lamb, and Harmon (1931) contains an impressive art deco lobby of translucent marble. (Observatory Department, Empire State Building, New York).

of commercial design. Gothic tracery was replaced by continuous and cold polished surfaces that were presented in hard-edged geometric forms.

In 1931 Hood went a step further toward an appropriate

expression of the corporate edifice with his design for the publishing firm of McGraw-Hill. The use of glass was emphatic and this rendered the building's corners transparent, thus disclosing the supporting steel skeleton. However, this articulate expression of the curtain wall was not as simple as it first appeared. Each of the building's window shades was colored golden so that, when pulled down, they presented a uniform pattern that contrasted with the supporting skeleton's sheathing of light blue tiles. The tiles were graduated from a darker tone of blue at the base to a lighter one toward the top, blending the skyscraper with its environment. One of Hood's assistants was assigned to check the location of each single tile and was stationed in a building opposite the construction site with a pair of binoculars. Such precise concern with form and color, as opposed to historical allusion and ornament, signified that America's commercial architects were beginning to apply the tenets of modernism to the solution of their design problems. The building was severe, even factory-like, and yet graceful.

Hood was also involved in the design of America's most famous integrated complex of skyscrapers. The Rockefeller Center, completed in 1940, ensured that American architects would never again turn to blatant historicism in skyscraper design and, indeed, heralded the arrival of the slab form—trademark of the modernist skyscrapers of the International Style. For the first time skyscrapers were conceived as a group. Rem Koolhas has called the Rockefeller Center "a masterpiece without a genius." Indeed, it was a remarkable feat of collective design and managerial effort as Raymond Hood suggested when he wrote in *Architectural Forum* in 1932: "It would be impossible to estimate the number of official minds that have engaged in untangling the complexities of the problem; and certainly the number of unofficial minds that have pondered over it is even a more meaningless guess. Architects, builders, engineers, real estate experts, financiers, lawyers—all have contributed something from their experience and even from their imagination." The Rockefeller Center had no single creative genius but it did have a single patron—John D. Rockefeller, Jr. He bravely financed the venture at the height of the Great Depression of the 1930s. However, his courage did

Rockefeller Center, New York, by Benjamin Wistar Morris; Reinhard and Hofmeister; Corbett, Harrison and MacMurray; and Hood and Fouilhoux (1932–40). When the Metropolitan Opera withdrew from a project to provide it with a new home, John D. Rockefeller developed the empty space into the first large-scale project of urban renewal in which a series of, eventually, nineteen high buildings were designed as an integral group dominated by the centerpiece, the RCA Building. The photograph shows the plaza still under construction in 1935 but illuminated at night. (Library of Congress).

have its financial reward. By 1977 Rockefeller Center's 10 million square feet of rentable office space was earning the Rockefeller family some $100 million a year. The fifty-fifth and fifty-sixth floors of the RCA Building, tallest of the nineteen that make up the complex, also provided the Rockefeller family with Room 560, the headquarters of their massive public relations operation. Rockefeller Center quickly, and justifiably, became one of Manhattan's major tourist attractions that in itself greatly enhanced the Rockefeller family's public relations. The Rockefeller Center was a summation of everything architects in the 1920s and 1930s had been striving for—a coherent yet romantic expression of tower design and rational organization of the various components.

The 1930s witnessed Frank Lloyd Wright's return to large-scale commercial architecture with the S. C. Johnson and Son Administration Building in Racine, Wisconsin, where work began in 1936 and was completed in 1939. The Johnson Building was a modern design that did not rely on the straight line or vertical expression for its effect. Its interior is distinguished by the use of tapered columns that resemble elongated mushrooms. Springing from a narrow base, they expand at the capitals into a circular "lily-pad" shape that supports the exposed roof and ceiling made of Pyrex glass tubing. Taken as a whole, the Johnson Building is certainly more than the sum of its parts and is an unparalleled union of function and form, coupled with a highly sensual understanding of the nature of materials. Wright was dismayed by the tall, thrusting buildings that were being created in urban America. He viewed them as corruptions of the work of his master, Louis Sullivan, and he saw the corrupting influence as European, not American: "Yes, now the ideal of an organic architecture, gone abroad, comes back deformed, turned up on the ground edgewise. So it names itself an international style?"

The International Style

The International Style did not, in fact, name itself, but was named by two Americans, Henry Russell Hitchcock and Philip Johnson. These two wrote the catalogue for the eponymous 1932 exhibition at New York's Museum of Modern Art, and the term has

The twin, cascading setbacks of the RCA Building, completed in 1933, show how architect Raymond Hood enhanced light, air, and space around the seventy-story skyscraper, bestowing poetry on the entire complex. (Rockefeller Center Management Corporation, New York).

been used ever since to describe the architecture that came to dominate American cities and provided the majority of prestige structures throughout the world after 1945. Social commentator Tom Wolfe in his somewhat bombastic account of modern architecture in America, *From Bauhaus to Our House* (1981), sides with Frank Lloyd Wright and blames the emergence of the International Style on a left-wing European conspiracy. Wolfe presents his readers with a photograph of a "stately and ruminant" Frank Lloyd Wright circa 1935 with the caption, "He looked into the future of American architecture—and saw Walter Gropius's face. He was not pleased." Walter Gropius (1883–1969) was a founder of the German Bauhaus, at the school of design centered in Weimar that specialized in modernism in architecture, and, when Hitler closed the Bauhaus in 1933, many of its staff and students fled to America. Gropius himself enjoyed a very successful and influential career in America, although it was not until after World War II that large-scale building began again in earnest after the hiatus brought about by the Great Depression of the 1930s.

It is not surprising that Frank Lloyd Wright should find the creations of the International Style distasteful and even distressing. They were all essentially closed boxes, a form that Wright had struggled to eradicate from his own design. The master architect of the box was Ludwig Mies van der Rohe (1886–1969), originally of Aachen, later a Nazi, who was to exercise an influence in America after 1945 that matched that of Wright. Mies had a dictum that was as simple as his Platonic worldview and his buildings—"less is more." His first major commission in America was for the design of the Illinois Institute of Technology (IIT) built in Chicago between 1940 and 1946. The project was a varied one, including classrooms, laboratory buildings, living quarters, subsidiary buildings, and a place of worship. Yet, despite this varied brief, Mies contrived to create a unified complex of 25-foot units applied in a symmetrical grid. Each building's steel frame was clearly articulated on the exterior and provided a visual regularity that was essential to the dignified anonymity of the International Style. The enclosing walls were made of brick, and, more often, glass, and were hung between the supporting

Frank Lloyd Wright, maverick eccentric among twentieth-century architects, as renowned for his private escapades as for his professional work. (1938; Library of Congress).

steel frames. In fact, even although the IIT Complex appeared to be a showpiece for the curtain wall (the distinctive feature of prestige International Style architecture in the postwar years), many of the enclosing walls were supported, rather than suspended.

The IIT complex was a visually attractive expression of the International Style's use of modern materials and avoidances of historicist design. However, the complex was sadly lacking from a functionalist point of view. For instance, the religious building at the IIT had to have the word "Chapel" added to it in order to signify its function. Ironically, the architecture department of IIT, initially located in one of the large campus buildings, was found to be too noisy for the architectural students to work in—they were then relegated to the building's basement. In the end, Mies abandoned the project because the I.I.T. asked him to compromise his sacred principles in favor of functional needs.

The 1930s witnessed both Frank Lloyd Wright's return to commercial design and the creation of his masterwork in domestic architecture—Fallingwater, at Bear Run, Pennsylvania. This is perhaps the most famous house in twentieth-century domestic architecture. The design was unprecedented in being poised over a rocky stream with stark geometric shapes that make no concessions to the natural wilderness that surrounds the house. However, the work is consistent with Wright's Prairie ideal and, with its intersecting and projected planes, suggests spontaneity. Indeed, those working with Wright at the time have said that the design was conceived and sketched with no hesitation whatsoever.

Thus American architecture in the early twentieth century can be divided in a very general manner into two main camps: the new architecture that called for new emphasis on function and included the skyscraper amongst its forms; and historicist architecture that looked to the classic styles of the past as inspiring and appropriate to America's growing commercial empire. Of course, a masterpiece, such as the Woolworth Building, confounds this generalization in the way that generalizations will be confounded, and is testimony to the fact that the new architecture and historicism could not only coexist but could also result in aesthetic and functional success of the highest order. However, whatever the historical trends and their historical significance, the most striking element in prestige American building in the first half of the twentieth century is its vigor and variety that parallel

Darwin D. Martin House, Buffalo, by Frank Lloyd Wright (1904). This Prairie House was famous for Wright's emphasis upon horizontal planes in keeping with the surrounding landscape; his versatile use of interior space; and his general sense of harmony and proportion. In 1967 the house was acquired by the State University of New York at Buffalo as the president's residence. (Photographed by Jack E. Boucher for the Historic American Buildings Survey in May 1965; Library of Congress).

the national culture as expressed in other areas such as literature and painting. Nowhere is the nation's culture expressed more permanently than in its buildings, and much of the architecture of the early twentieth century is a living legacy in the form of working buildings.

CHAPTER TEN

American Art Comes of Age
and Goes to Pieces

·ॐ·

CONFLICT BETWEEN old and new has been part of the very
fabric of America, and the American worlds of art and literature in the twentieth century have been no exception. American painting and American literature, like the nation itself,
underwent great changes in the first half of the twentieth century. New styles were applied and new themes exploited and this
ensured vitality and variety in the visual and the written arts.
Among these was modernism, a usage, mode of expression, or
peculiarity of style or workmanship characteristic of modern times.
Jonathan Swift used the term in 1737; in 1864 Nathaniel Hawthorne referred to "such modernisms as astral lamps." A supporter of modern ways was a modernist. Thus he or she would
pursue modern ways in education, preferring new to older literature, learning modern languages to ancient, science to arts. He
or she would favor modernizing, to make or render modern,
challenge obsolete words, introduce new customs, or remodel an
old building. However, modernism and realism were not mu-
tually exclusive.

World renowned American expatriate Henry James is the writer who enjoyed a legend of being "The Master," an epithet taken from the title of an 1892 collection of his own short stories, *The Lesson of the Master,* and justly acquired as a result of the technical perfection of three novels he completed in the twentieth century: *The Wings of the Dove* (1902), *The Ambassadors* (1903), and *The Golden Bowl* (1904). James's realism hinged on the complex psychology of human motivation rather than ethics or naturalistic representation. Yet ethics and verisimilitude were important to James. Indeed, his highly moral appreciation of character values and his painstaking descriptions of physical reality were crucial in his writing. However, it was in the realm of the mind that James held his interest and his power. He was a detached spectator of life in both an immediately physical and a geographic sense. It would seem that the characters he observed so acutely did his living for him. Many were Americans living and traveling in Europe, detached from their home nation and often adrift in the unfamiliar waters of European society and culture.

After a very successful early period that ended with *The Portrait of a Lady* (1881), James had concentrated on collecting all his fictions and creating several new works in different forms, including four unsuccessful comic dramas. The failure of these stage plays was, in large part, due to the sophistication of James's ideas and written style that did not easily translate into the sort of dramatic form necessary for the theater. Plays must show action and psychology directly and James failed to do this. It has been suggested that his, albeit unsuccessful, experiments in drama profoundly influenced the structure of his later novels with their scenic progression and their fixed, single point of view.

This fixed point of view, the literary equivalent of single point perspective in painting, is a hallmark of almost all of James's fiction in which a single narrator reports observations of characters without ever really interacting with them. In fact, James's narrators are very much like James himself—detached observers of life whose pleasure arrives vicariously through the characters they study so closely. The Master was very much aware of this quality in his narrators because in 1901 he parodied himself in his novel, *The Sacred Fount,* set in the midst of an English weekend party where the perversely inquisitive and opinionated narrator

Henry James by John Singer Sargent (1913). It was inevitable that Sargent, "an American (artist) born in Italy, educated in France, who looks like a German, speaks like an Englishman, and paints like a Spaniard" and master of the surface glamour and inherent superiority of Edwardian high society, should paint Henry James who captured in his novels the shifting quicksands of expatriate society and the paradoxes underlying the surface. (National Portrait Gallery, London).

is given a salutary earful by another character whom he has re-
galed with his bizarre theories concerning relationships between
other fellow guests. However, *The Sacred Fount* is not a simple
parody; firstly, because nothing is simple where James is concerned, and, secondly, because throughout the novel the reader
is never presented with a truth, but is left to conjecture about the
possibilities of truth. We are never told whether the narrator is,
as is suggested by one character, crazy, or whether he has hit the
nail on the head with his strange but uncomfortably plausible
hypothesis. Much of the tension of a James novel arises from the
contrast between surfaces that are deceptive and inner motives
that shift continuously.

The fact that James was capable of self-parody suggests the
self-conscious nature of all of his writing. The technical and stylistic perfection of his later novels is also testimony to their author's acute self-consciousness and thus helps illuminate the single greatest irony regarding Henry James. As well as being
detached from life like his narrators, he was detached, too, from
the art that so absorbed him. His faculties of self-criticism were
so highly developed as to make every single element of his writing a conscious intellectual movement in the orchestration of his
literature. There is something essentially disturbing in the thought
of a man who lived both real life and the life of the imagination
so carefully, but it was through this profoundly cerebral approach to life and literature that James found satisfaction in the
status he achieved as a writer.

Many readers and some critics have reacted strongly against
the self-conscious perfection of James's work, finding it too rich
and too refined to stomach and even, some have argued, too
unreal. However, the obvious quality of James's realistic fiction
earned him a reputation that encouraged disciples. Amongst them
was one of the leading women writers in the history of American
literature, Edith Wharton (1862–1937). She was, like James, an
expatriate—after 1909 she spent most of her life in Paris—and
was also an extremely moral writer. It is a tribute to her skill
that she successfully applied a stable and balanced view to material that could easily have led to sentimentality or moralism.

The House of Mirth (1905) is her most celebrated novel and tells the story of Lily Bart, a twenty-nine-year-old New York beauty who turns her search for a wealthy and respected husband into a career. She denies her true feelings when she marries the man who will secure her status rather than the man whom she loves. Thus she brings about the tragic end of the novel as she suffers through unrequited love, infamy, and, eventually, suicide. *The House of Mirth* displays a moral concern for the actions of characters and a concern for literary realism and fine prose that marks Edith Wharton's debt to James. However, this same novel also displays Wharton's interest in her characters' visible position among their physical environment that contrasted with James's liking for metaphysical investigations into the minds of his characters. Edith Wharton was a writer of the exterior without being merely superficial, while Henry James was a writer of the interior without being claustrophobic.

Other major works of fiction by Edith Wharton include *The Reef* (1912), her most Jamesian novel, that is confined almost entirely to the chateau in France and to the mind of her heroine, Anna Leath; and *Ethan Frome* (1911), a grim story of jealousy and resentment set on a bleak New England farm. *The Age of Innocence* (1920) deals with a young New York socialite, Newland Archer, and his difficult choice between his conventional fiancée, May Welland, and the unconventional object of his desires, Ellen Olenska, alienated wife of a dissolute Polish count. He is called Archer but his fiancée, later, wife, May, is the better shot with bow and arrow. Social convention and May's predatory family make Newland's choice for him, and, as with most Wharton novels, the done thing reigns. *Custom of the Country* (1913) is Wharton's major satire on American society and has an expatriate theme that again brings us to James's work, although it is difficult to imagine Wharton's vulgar and selfish midwestern protagonist, Undine Sprague, inhabiting the rarified pages of a James novel in a major role. In her sojourn through old New York society, the nation of France, and several husbands, Undine is sometimes reminiscent of Sinclair Lewis's social-climbing antihero, George Babbitt.

It is all too easy to praise a modern work and reject a conservative one as an anachronism caught in the web of the past with little relation to American civilization and identity. Yet conservative art inspired by Europe was tremendously popular among all classes and projected a form of civilization that was deeply gratifying—an art of superb craftsmanship suggesting ornament, wealth, and exoticism.

The American Renaissance

Art played a crucial role in promoting nationalism, especially when profound industrial and economic changes were causing wide social dislocation. Cass Gilbert (1859–1934), architect of two state capitols and a series of public buildings, including the Woolworth Building, wrote in the *American Architect* of August 5, 1929, how the state should satisfy man's "natural craving for art," and thereby secure "patriotism and good citizenship." Underlying the cult of nationalism was the genteel tradition and its respect for art and culture as indices of civilization. Charles Eliot Norton, professor of art history at Harvard, claimed that the "highest achievements" in the arts "were not so much the products of solitary individual artists" as the expression of a nation's "faith," "loftiness of spirit," and the "embodiment of its ideals." Vernacular, homespun art was disparaged in favor of the preferred, official art of tradition.

The American Renaissance, first identified in 1880, was at its height in the period 1901–17. Painters and sculptors, architects and craftsmen believed they had captured in the United States the spirit of the Italian Renaissance of 1420–1580. Just as some American robber barons saw themselves as following in the tradition of French and Italian merchant princes not only in commerce but also as patrons of the arts, so did their architects and decorators believe they must aspire to the example of their predecessors in the Renaissance. Sculptor Augustus Saint-Gaudens (1848–1907) declared after the initial planning session for the World's Columbian Exposition for Chicago in 1893, "This is the greatest meeting of artists since the fifteenth century." Artists were also inspired by colonial America and the mingling of Italian techniques and colonial style resulted in such works as Au-gust Saint-Gaudens's bronze *The Puritan* (1887 and 1898) and Daniel Chester French's *The Minute Man* (1871–75).

Paradoxically, despite its European inspiration, the American Renaissance was intensely nationalistic, appropriating the sym-bols, images, and techniques of previous civilizations to create a magnificent pageant in which the United States was the culmi-nation of history for an age that believed in progress. Artists and their patrons conceived a new civilization with public buildings and monuments modeled on the columned temples of Greece and the triumphal arches of Rome, adorned with sculptures and mu-rals depicting heroes in various virtuous endeavors. The Ameri-can Renaissance was also an expression of American imperialism in which architect Stanford White (1853–1906) justified his im-porting of many art treasures to decorate grand houses by say-ing, "In the past, dominant nations had always plundered works of art from their predecessors; . . . America was taking a leading place among nations and had, therefore, the right to obtain art wherever she could."

In art, as in architecture, this was a period of eclecticism in which patrons placed Chinese vases, Gobelin tapestries, Louis XV furniture, Venetian paintings, and polar bear hearthrugs along-side one another in the same room. The mania for collecting was inspired by British and French appropriation and display of Re-naissance art and other major art movements. Moreover, artists and writers justified the new American eclecticism. John La Farge (1835–1910) declared "We are not as they [the Europeans] are—fixed in some tradition; and we can go where we choose—to the greatest influences, if we wish, and still be free for our future."

Nevertheless, American artists prized Europe as the source of Western art. George E. Bissell claimed in *Municipal Affairs* of June 1902 how "From babyhood to decrepit age all [Europeans] revel in art, and this daily contact with the beautiful quietly moulds the character and creates an unerring taste, not only in things artistic, but in the properties of life." Charles Hutchinson of the Art Institute of Chicago said in an address of 1916, "It is not the sole mission of art to amuse or furnish moral instruction. The true mission of ART as Hegel says, is to discover and present

Elie Nadelman, *Dancing Figure* (1916–18) gold leaf on broze, 29½" x 12" x 11½". Polish expatriate sculptor Elie Nadelman (1882–1946) fled to New York in 1914 where his refined works, reducing the human form to a series of elegant curves, won him the patronage of Helena Rubinstein. (Collection of Whitney Museum of American Art, New York).

the ideal." Ideal art was an idealized interpretation of the world that drew upon the past rather than from nature, as the artists of the Italian Renaissance had done. Essentially, the ideal meant images that were noble and beautiful, were universally applicable, and carried the idea of elevated thought and virtue.

In sculpture and painting the human figure, nude or simply clad, was either used to personify such things as Justice, Industry, or the State, or a real person imbued with higher virtues. To emphasize the allegorical nature of their work, artists and sculptors lent their subjects classical garments, shields, wreaths, and wings. In 1912 Abbott Thayer (1849–1921) explained his liberal use of wings on female subjects: "Doubtless my lifelong passion for birds has helped to incline me to work wings into my pictures; but primarily I have put on wings probably more to symbolize an exalted atmosphere (above the realm of genre painting) where one need not explain the action of his figures." In his *Washington Laying Down his Command at the Feet of Columbia,* painted for the Baltimore Courthouse in 1902, Edwin Blashfield (1848–1936) sanctified an event important in the history of Maryland by a mix of historical portraits and allegorical figures.

Since Abraham Lincoln was the greatest hero of the American Civil War, it was not surprising that he became the subject of numerous idealized sculptures by Daniel Chester French in Lincoln, Nebraska (1909–12) and Augustus Saint-Gaudens in Chicago (1887 and 1897–1905), of which the most monumental occupied the Lincoln Memorial in Washington, D.C. (1911–22). It was the creation of architect Henry Bacon (1850–1931), sculptor Daniel Chester French, and mural painter Jules Guerin (1866–1946). The building was planned as a classical temple with thirty-six doric columns, representing the states when Lincoln was president and forty-eight festoons for the number of states in the early twentieth century. Guerin's murals on either side of the statue were to "typify in alleging the principles evident in the life of Lincoln"—Emancipation and Reunion. The outsize sculpture of Lincoln is a hero upon a Roman chair with two sets of fasces.

Artists' search for symbols also led them to the most distinctive form of the American Renaissance, the ideal American woman as virgin, a symbol of Liberty, Justice, and Columbia. They depicted elegant young women glowing with health but unaware of their latent sexuality. The American virgin was discovered in all forms of art from the highbrow of paintings by Thomas Derring (1851–1938) to the lowbrow of the Swift Packing Company's Premium Calendar. The most practiced exponent was Charles Dana Gibson (1867–1944). The typical Gibson girl with full hair, hourglass figure, and fresh gaze was an American icon at the turn of the century. In literature she was a major presence, notably in Henry James's *Daisy Miller* (1879) in which a misunderstanding by an American virgin abroad leads to her death, and *Portrait of a Lady* (1881) in which a misunderstanding by an American virgin abroad leads to her entombment in a loveless marriage and the early death of the man who truly loves her.

John Singer Sargent (1856–1925) was, perhaps, the supreme American artist of the portrait. His formal portraits of Edwardian aristocrats in London record a social type as well as an individual and carry the values of British society with its self-confidence and hauteur at the turn of the century. Social caste and type are implicit in all his portraits, notably those of exquisite, vivacious creatures of fashion, like *Eva and Betty, Daughters of Asher and Mrs. Wertheimer* (1901) and *The Duchess of Portland* (1902), or of imperial proconsuls such as *Sir Frank Swettenham* (1904) and *The Earl of Dalhousie* (1900). His three *Acheson Sisters* of 1902 was not only learned as a variation on the Three Graces but also as a homage to the eighteenth-century artist Joshua Reynolds. Even in an age of tall society women, Sargent's women were impossibly tall. The confidence and charm they and other women sitters exude speak of women who knew they were in charge of fashionable society.

Nevertheless, Sargent delighted in the exotic and bizarre and this element continuously breaks out in his studies of Japanese dancers or of his nieces in Turkish costume. Sargent was also much influenced by the French impressionists of whom Claude Monet became a close friend. Their influence is apparent in all his works. There was no effect of light on form that Sargent could not capture immediately on canvas in a few rapid strokes. In 1907 and 1908 he painted fewer portraits. Sated with worldly success, he wanted to experiment in brilliant landscapes painted in Italy, Spain, and the Alps and the murals for the Boston Public Library and the Boston Museum of Fine Arts that came to dominate his last years.

Although inspired by ancient models and the Italian Renaissance, American sculpture showed far more human personality than its models. During his studies in Paris and a visit to Rome, Augustus Saint-Gaudens (1848–1907), a great sculptor of the age, developed a subtle style of modeling from Renaissance ornamental motifs. While drawing from Greek sculpture, Gaudens gave his creatures a sort of tender personality as if they were not detached gods and goddesses but men and women with their own characters, virtues, and faults. His sculptures avoided the sort of deep hollows of classical statues, preferring low relief to suggest some sort of veil between sculpture and viewer.

Another American sculptor who specialized in public statues of American heroes was Paul Wayland Bartlett (1865–1925). He was disturbed by the poor quality of many public memorials to the Civil War across America. He himself concentrated on heroes before the Civil War, such as *Washington at Valley Forge* (cast 1927) and *Lafayette on Horseback* (1899–1908), exhibited in the Louvre as a gift of the American people to the French people in acknowledgement of Bartholdi's *Statue of Liberty*.

During the American Renaissance the traditional distinctions between decorative art and representative art became blurred. Arthur Mathews (1860–1945) of California and his wife, Lucia, produced exquisite designs in furniture and paintings and often used paintings as decorative elements within their furniture and painted works such as *Sacred and Profane Love* (1915), inspired by a painting of Titian's. In the bust, *La Jeunesse* (c. 1910), Herbert Adams (1856–1945) used polychrome marble for head and shoulders and dark applewood for gown. The mix of materials and colors blurs the distinction between sculpture and decorative art.

Once again mural paintings became a major art form. New buildings, especially public buildings, required the assistance of murals, sculpture, and other decoration to complete the design. Indeed, unity of the arts was necessary to any major architectural plan at the outset. In the *Craftsman* of October 1904 Charles M. Shean, president of the National Society of Mural Painters, predicted how "the future great art of this Republic, so far as it is expressed in painting, will find its complete and full development on the walls of our public buildings . . . and it will be primarily a recording art," in which the subjects should commemorate "the growth of the state from the scattered and struggling colonies of the Atlantic seaboard to the Imperial Republic stretching from ocean to ocean."

Murals by John La Farge, John Singer Sargent, Gari Melchers (1860–1932), and H. Siddons Mowbray (1850–1928) adorned capitols, churches, libraries, and expositions. In 1895 the National Society of Mural Painters was incorporated and served to establish and regulate the new profession and educate the public about civic art. Their subjects ranged from the biblical to the allegorical, to the contribution of arts, science, and technology to the new American world of scientific and social achievement. In his murals at the Iowa Statehouse, Kenyon Cox (1856–1919) charted the progress of civilization while for the supreme court room of the Minnesota State Capitol John La Farge produced four panels inspired by the broad history of law and depicting Confucius, Moses, Socrates, and Count Raymond of Toulouse (whose subject is Adjustment of Conflicting Interests). At the request of Charles McKim, H. Siddons Mowbray decorated the University Club (1904) and J. P. Morgan Library (1905–7) in New York with murals inspired by Pinturicchio's work in the Vatican.

The achievement of the artists of the American Renaissance has been summed up by art historian Richard N. Murray: "Through the use of traditional subjects and stylistic references to the art of the antique and the Italian Renaissance, American artists gave substance to their own contemporary art and set their history into that of the entire range of Western civilization. They remained Americans, yet they were part of the broad flow of art, history, and culture." They established the American Academy in Rome in 1894 to train a second generation of artists, sculptors, and architects in the techniques and sources of ancient and Renaissance art and the principles of coordination. In 1906 the National Academy of Design merged with the Society of American Artists and the National Society of Mural Painters, and together with the National Sculpture Society continued to exert a strong influence in the world of American art until the 1920s. Major collectors, such as John Gellatly and Charles Lang Greer, also contributed to the American Renaissance. In 1929 Gellatly gave his large collection of paintings and sculpture to the National Gallery of Art (now the National Collection of Fine Arts, Smithsonian Institution) to form a basic collection representative of the American Renaissance.

Despite its undoubted achievements, the proponents of the American Renaissance felt it necessary to defend their principles against artists and critics who were now advancing a modern art that more nearly represented contemporary life in the United States. In *The Classic Point of View* (1911) Kenyon Cox expressed the aims of his generation and tried to defend them against modernist attacks.

The Classic Spirit is the disinterested search for perfection; it is the love of clearness and reasonableness and self-control; it is, above all, the love of permanence and continuity. It asks of a work of art, not that it shall be novel or effective, but that it shall be fine and noble. It seeks not merely to express individuality or emotion but to express disciplined emotion and individuality restrained by law. It strives for the essential rather than the accidental, the eternal rather than the momentary. And it loves to steep itself in tradition.

Cox expressed his ideas in *Tradition* (1916) in which a woman in classical clothes, representing art of the past, has given the light from her torch to the lamp of knowledge in the hand of a second woman, Tradition, who is about to pass it to two Titianesque women, representing the art and literature of the future.

Even before World War I the ideas of the American Renaissance were becoming less and less acceptable to a new generation of artists, critics, and patrons. Those who had first established the American Renaissance in the 1870s and 1880s now discovered it was they who were the old guard of tradition. Artists loyal to the American Renaissance greatly disliked and reacted against the new art forms of cubism, expressionism, and the Bauhaus. Such artists created a series of monuments to World War I, the West Virginia State Capitol (1922–32), the outsize presidential heads carved on Mount Rushmore (1927–41), and the National Gallery of Art (1937–41). Some tried to modernize the American Renaissance. Thus we have the stark classicism of Paul Cree, the art deco of Paul Manship (1885–1966), and the regional post office murals of the Works Progress Administration (WPA).

Realism in Literature

Realist writers, such as Theodore Dreiser (1871–1945) and Upton Sinclair (1878–1968), were also making their names in their native United States. After the First International Copyright Act of 1891, which eliminated the competition of a cheap reprint industry based on material from foreign resources, new publishing entrepreneurs, such as Frank Doubleday, began to promote new writers through aggressive salesmanship, including commissioning of articles, advance payment, and ingenious promotion campaigns. Authors welcomed this and saw the new International Copyright law as a sort of American author's declaration of independence from the elitism of the Gilded Age dominated by European taste. Dreiser was a literary pioneer and in many ways bears a parental responsibility for American fiction by Anderson, Fitzgerald, Hemingway, and Lewis in the 1920s, Faulkner, Steinbeck, and Wright in the 1930s, and even the work of novelists of the 1960s and 1970s such as Norman Mailer and Saul Bellow. He was the first major American writer to emerge from the "melting pot"; his father was a German Catholic millhand and Dreiser spent his childhood in poverty moving from one Indiana town to another. This fact makes his achievement all the more remarkable.

Dreiser's childhood was much conditioned by ambivalent feelings toward his unstable father, unswerving devotion to his mother as she moved the family from town to town, and his own intimations of disgrace. While he was growing up his eldest brother, Johann Paul, Jr.,—later the songwriter Paul Dresser—who sometimes sang in blackface, lived with a madam, and was convicted of burglary. Another brother made money by dubious means, including blackmail. Dreiser's sister, Emma, ran away with Hopkins, a married man who had already embezzled money. When

he was twenty Dreiser was discharged from his job as a clerk in
Chicago after "borrowing" money from his employer without
permission in order to buy an overcoat. Dreiser later used these
last two incidents in his novel *Sister Carrie*. Forced to find another job, Dreiser became a journalist and this, coupled with his
discovery of, and enthusiasm for, Balzac, sharpened his skills as
a writer. He also worked for the music publishers who promoted
Paul Dresser's songs. Despite Paul's largess, he was deeply jealous of his brother, the more so when Paul appropriated from
him and, worse, improved upon, the basic idea for his most popular song, "On the Banks of the Wabash."

A combination of passionate integrity, brute determination, and
plain luck led Theodore Dreiser to his huge success, the creation
of an American epic literature in which the environment played
a leading role alongside the protagonist. His characters are deeply
affected by their environment and are treated with a wide-ranging compassion without moral judgement. Dreiser was far less
intellectual than his intellectual influences—Balzac, Tolstoy, Zola,
Spencer, Hardy—but then he did not have to be since he was
able to draw on autobiography and the real-life successes and
failures of his eight brothers and sisters for material.

His first novel, *Sister Carrie* (1900), shows him in full possession of his literary powers, dealing with the pilgrimage of an
eighteen-year-old country girl to Chicago, then later to stardom
on the New York stage, and following the hackneyed scenario
of the Cinderella variation on the Horatio Alger rags-to-riches
tale. However, in Dreiser's naturalistic novels, man is at the mercy
of the external industrial world created by him and his behavior
is largely determined by that environment. Thus *Sister Carrie* opens
with the material circumstances of the heroine made clear in an
inventory of her dress, handbag, and funds and an explanation of
her historical circumstances in August 1889 when she carries the
bloom of youth but also its illusions and ignorance. At first the
novel was considered scandalous not simply because Carrie herself was mercenary but also because it implied that all other people were commodities who could be bought and sold. Moreover,
the other leading character, Hurstwood, loses his footing once
and for all time in complex circumstances when the safe door

Novelist Theodore Dreiser found his material in the varied fortunes of his own large German-American family and the material impact of industrialization and urbanization on the human spirit. (Library of Congress).

closes and turns him into a frantic thief and he elopes with Carrie. This is a world in which the protagonists try and project a desired public image and attract wealth without earning it. Money has become a force in its own right and those who covet worldly success must prostitute their souls to achieve it and remain, like Carrie at the close, unfulfilled. Dreiser's salesmen and factory workers, his images of sweatshops and horsecars were icons of social history. Thus *Sister Carrie* encapsulates humble lives of unbroken drudgery amid West Side apartment blocks and the tawdry restaurants and hotels of old Broadway. A recent biographer, Richard Lingeman, comments, "Dreiser's great strength is his empathy with his characters, which reaches its peak in the final scenes about Hurstwood. In the supreme effort to make believable the climactic downfall of this, the most strongly imagined figure in the book, Dreiser *became* Hurstwood, producing his every thought, his every emotion, from inside himself."

Dreiser's publishers, Doubleday, were somewhat embarrassed by *Sister Carrie* and, indeed, its initial sales were miniscule. Frank Doubleday had taken on the book on the basis of author Frank Norris's enthusiasm and disliked the fact that the libertine heroine not only went unpunished but rose to become a brilliant figure in society. Dreiser survived the stillbirth of *Carrie* by eking out a living working, first, on a railroad construction gang and, then, as a hack journalist. Dreiser almost became Hurstwood, prey to depression. Eventually, he became editor of a popular magazine, *The Delineator,* that he transformed into a comprehensive women's magazine. He was so successful that when, in 1907, a new edition of *Sister Carrie* made the book popular, he found himself too busy, at first, to write more novels.

In *Gerdhardt* (1911), Dreiser turned the structure of *Sister Carrie* inside-out and the protagonist is presented as a saint. Indeed, it was this book that found widespread acceptance and allowed Dreiser to leave editing and hackwork and concentrate on fiction. The result of this new freedom was *The Financier* (1912) and *The Titan* (1914), two novels constituting two-thirds of the "Trilogy of Desire" and completed posthumously in 1947 with the publication of *The Stoic,* providing a persuasive account of the rise and eventual frustration of the unscrupulous and ambitious robber baron, Frank Cowperwood. Much of the Trilogy of Desire can, in fact, be read as a roman à clef since Dreiser based his fictional captain of industry on the infamous Charles T. Yerkes (1837–1905), the Chicago traction magnate.

The last of Dreiser's major novels, and, perhaps, his single most impressive work, is *An American Tragedy* (1925), in which he identifies closely with his brooding and manipulated protagonist, Clyde Griffiths. Clyde's tragedy is the wretched banality of his life and his inability to decide—neither can the reader—whether he is a victim of society or a compos mentis murderer. However, society has no problems making such enormous decisions and summarily executes him for letting his discarded and pregnant girlfriend drown so that he can rise socially through another liaison. Determinism served up in such a deeply concentrated pitch of pessimism and morbidity characterizes many of Dreiser's themes and helps explain the often overwhelming turgidity of his style. It also helps explain why we might see him as the father of the modern American novel with its often profound disaffection and criticism of modern life.

Another master of startling surfaces of paradox, but combined with grotesque elements and ironies of plot, was the popular short story writer O. Henry. When short stories were published in book form, they had rarely sold well. Once periodicals were becoming widely established as the prime means of promoting advertisements, they found short stories of between 4,000 and 12,000 words the ideal art form to set aside their enticing advertising copy. Editors combed the country for talented amateurs who could distill their own experience into an effective story.

O. Henry (pseudonym of William Sidney Porter, 1862–1910), was by far the most popular of these writers. One of the most prolific writers ever, he was born in North Carolina and raised without much schooling by his uncle. After years as a rolling stone, he was charged with embezzlement of funds from a bank in Austin, Texas, when his comic magazine, *The Rolling Stone* of 1894, failed and he fled to New Orleans and Honduras. He returned when his wife was dying and served a long prison term in Columbus, Ohio. It was from here that he began to write again and published his stories of which *Whistling Dick's Christ-*

mas Stocking (1899) was the first. His great success led to a salaried contract with the New York *World*. It was O. Henry who developed a new technique, the surprise or twist ending to pull the rug from under his characters' feet and remove the wool from his readers' eyes. His style is anonymous but his dialogue is authentic and his ability to evoke atmosphere considerable. In his hands the short story developed in America far more quickly at this time than any other kind of fiction, and far more quickly than in Europe. His first collection was *Cabbages and Kings* (1904), set in South America. Tales of New York in *The Four Million* (1906) include his classic stereotypes, while *Heart of the West* (1907) is a western collection and the hero of *The Gentle Grafter* (1908) is a confidence man. Yet, as English literary critic Eric Mottram explains, "the fatalism of his stories penetrated his life as well" and he died a hopeless alcoholic.

Upton Sinclair (1878–1968) was also a realist, but he began his career in the distinctly unrealistic genre of juvenile pulp fiction, and before he was twenty he wrote over two million words a year, the profits enabling him to pay his way through the College of the City of New York. While doing postgraduate work at Columbia University, he wrote six novels, among them, *King Midas* (1901), *The Journal of Arthur Stirling* (1903), and *Manassas* (1904). The tone of these works was evoked by Sinclair himself when he remarked that Jesus, Hamlet, and Shelley shaped his thought and that he was deeply disappointed when the world did not meet him with the love and trust with which he approached it. *The Jungle* (1906), about the scandals in the meat packing industry, marked Sinclair's conversion to socialism and the profits of this novel were invested in his short-lived cooperative writers' colony, the Helicon Home Colony in Englewood, New Jersey, that attracted much vilification in the press. His most audacious public venture was in 1934 when he united large sections of the unemployed and progressive elements into the EPIC (End Poverty in California) League that captured the Democratic machine in the state and very nearly won him the governorship. In 1933 an EPIC supporter became Democratic governor of California.

Sinclair never quite enjoyed the recognition that his ability as both an artist and a social commentator deserved. His various books—over a hundred altogether—have sole by the million and exist in over a thousand translations in fifty languages. His personal papers tip the scales at over eight tons and are lodged at the Lilly Library of the University of Indiana. In nearly all of his novels the polemicist dominates the artist. In *The Jungle,* for example, he weakens the novel's artistic effect by having his protagonist, Jurgis Rudkus, undergo a somewhat incredible, and certainly rather convenient, conversion to socialism. The novels that followed constituted a series of lengthy and often artistically crude assaults on the institutions and mechanisms of capitalist society: Wall Street in 1908 with *The Moneychangers;* war in 1919 with *Jimmie Higgins;* the mining industry in 1917 with *King Coal;* government in *Oil!* of 1927, which concentrates on the corruption of the Harding administration. Sinclair's talent for active debate and reformist agitation was best expressed, not in his novels, but in the series of polemics that he wrote between 1918 and 1927. In 1940 he began his most ambitious project when he published the first part of his eleven-novel roman-fleuve, *World's End,* in which he offered a detailed investigation of the international scene from World War I onward through the life of his protagonist, Lanny Budd. The series, like much of Sinclair's writing, was stylistically undistinguished and somewhat wanting in humor and sex, yet it still enjoyed enormous popularity. This success may be due to the fact that the series surveyed an enormous mass of information in an era that placed great value on the apparent but indisputable reality of factual knowledge.

However, realism, despite its strengths, did not have a monopoly in American literature. While Theodore Dreiser and Upton Sinclair were recreating the world naturalistically in America, and Edith Wharton was doing the same thing in Paris, another expatriate American woman writer was creating a name for herself as an avant-garde leader and an artistic guru. Gertrude Stein (1874–1946) was educated at Radcliffe College and Johns Hopkins University in Baltimore where her primary interests were psychology and medicine. At Harvard she was particularly influenced by the psychologist and philosopher William James (1842–1910), brother of Henry James. The most radical feature of Stein's writing was her stylistic experimentation through which she sought to create a "cubist" literature of prose, independent of meaningful associations and relying merely on "sound-orchestration" for its effect. In a sense, then, Stein's approach to writing was the antithesis of, say, Wharton's realism in which the aim was to arrive at meaning through representation of perceived reality. Stein's desire to abandon meaning in literature may have been born out of a Harvard project on automatic writing and was certainly encouraged by her contact with cubist painters in Paris but there remains no doubt that many of those who enjoy and appreciate her work transgress her own rules in the process of discerning meanings from the jumbled shards of consciousness that fill the page. Books such as *Three Lives* (1909), *Tender Buttons* (1914), and *Geography and Plays* (1922) helped make her name as an unreadable writer. To a large extent she herself was aware of the difficulties presented by her writing, as she suggested in "As Fine as Melanctha," a story from *Three Lives,* "Nobody knows what I am trying to do but I do and I know when I succeed."

Stein's most ambitious literary project was *The Making of Americans,* published in 1925 but written almost twenty years earlier. This was an attempt to write a total history of America by reporting in infinite detail and repetition the history of the Hersland family, and the novel runs to over 900 pages. A young American expatriate writer, Ernest Hemingway, helped type the manuscript of *The Making of Americans.* He was not working as Stein's secretary, but was helping out a friend and mentor. Together with writers like Sherwood Anderson and F. Scott Fitzgerald, Hemingway was a frequent visitor to Stein's salon at 27 rue de Fleurs, Paris, and their somewhat bizarre relationship became one of the more thoroughly discussed in the history of American literature.

Later in her career Stein abandoned her literary experiments and began writing in a more accessible style that, when combined with such public activities as her mothering of American GIs during World War II, made her a public figure. However, in a way, this move to orthodox writing did not represent a complete volte-face since, for all her radicalism, Stein consistently held very conventional views on such a basic issue as nationality. She was perhaps the only modernist to maintain and express deeply patriotic feelings. Similarly, her analysis of human motivation was hardly at the sophisticated level of Freudian theory, despite he'r serious interest in human psychology. Many American authors of this time (and they were not by any means all modernists) were under the influence of Freud and his revolutionary theories on the nature and function of the human psyche. The books written during this last successful and happy period in Gertrude Stein's life include *The Autobiography of Alice B. Toklas* (1933), which ostensibly concerns her lifelong companion but which is, in fact, an autobiographical fragment of Stein's life in Paris. *Lectures in America* of 1935 was the result of a tour completed the previous year. *Everybody's Autobiography* (1937), *Paris, France* (1940), and *Wars I Have Seen* (1945) are all essentially personal, straightforward narratives.

For many reasons—not least for her early experiments in unintelligibility—it is easy to make fun of Gertrude Stein, but still she exerted a strong influence in the history of American literature. The absurdity of her literary experiments had value because it signified a new mode of perceiving the world and recreating it on' paper. Gertrude Stein was a pioneering modernist and in part led the way for Fitzgerald, Hemingway, Sherwood Anderson, and Sinclair Lewis—writers who were deeply critical of the world "fit for heroes" that followed the war and who shared and employed modernist sensibility.

Cubism

While she lived in Paris, Gertrude Stein sponsored and encouraged young painters such as Georges Braque, Pablo Picasso, and Juan Gris who were breaking the laws and traditions of four centuries of Western art with their sensational new style that came to be known as cubism after a derogatory comment made by an art critic, Vauxcelles. Stein exhibited the works of these young *inaccrochables* and thus helped nourish her reputation as an avant-garde leader, while at the same time she relished this visual equivalent of her own linguistic experiments.

The laws of perspective, proportion, and naturalistic representation imply that the artist and the observer are in full control of the world, and that it is a relatively simple process to recreate it and make sense of it. Ever since the Italian Renaissance most painting had followed the convention of a single-point perspective to convey depth, based on the fact that objects seem smaller the farther away they are from the viewer. There had been no more influential means for ordering the illusion of distance on a flat surface, determining the size and position of objects. Although it was persuasive, it was not comprehensive. It presupposed a certain way of looking at things that did not always correspond with the way we really see. In fact, perspective was a form of abstraction, idealizing and simplifying the relationship between eye, brain, and object, turning the onlooker into a stationary, impartial viewer of a unified and stable field. Although perspective in art depends on particular rules, it generalizes about human experiences that have to conform to its scheme.

A new style, cubism, destroyed the illusions of perspective and proportion and presented the world as seen from a myriad of different angles, angles akin to the fractional world that was emerging with the machine. The Cubists took painting far away from the safe conventions of naturalistic representation and revolutionized the way in which artists perceived the world. It was, in fact, a celebration of the machine and the new view of the world from above provided by skyscrapers and airplanes or that of the world in motion provided by automobiles. During a visit to New York in 1915 artist Francis Picabia declared how "upon coming to America it flashed on me that the genius of the modern world is in machinery and that through machinery art ought to find a most vivid expression. . . . I mean simply to work on and on until I attain the pinnacle of mechanical symbolism." Just as new technology was providing people with new ways of seeing the world, it was inevitable that this change would be reflected in artistic styles.

At the turn of the century very few people felt the sort of uncertainties about the machine that later generations were to do. Very few had firsthand experience of the squalor and poverty of urban ghettos that socialist theorists Marx and Engels had protested. For example, the giant Corliss Engine of the Centennial Exhibition outside Philadelphia, which had survived to generate energy for the Pullman works outside Chicago, was taken as a tireless giant slave of steam and steel. In short, as art critic Robert Hughes has observed in his *The Shock of the New* (1981), "The machine meant the conquest of process." This became ever more true as increasing numbers of people were drawn to the new machine-mad environment of industrial cities with their promise of electricity, gas, and running water, as well as public transportation and bourgeois comforts and diversions.

No conventional painting could express the comparatively new public experience of movement, of rapid travel in a machine on wheels. Hughes continues:

For the machine meant the conquest of horizontal space. It also meant a sense of that space which few people had experienced before—the succession and superimposition of views, the unfolding of landscape in flickering surfaces as one was carried swiftly past it, and an exaggerated feeling of relative motion (the poplars nearby seeming to move faster than the church spire across the field) due to parallax. The view from the train was not the view from the horse. It compressed more motifs into the same thing. Conversely, it left less time in which to dwell on any one thing.

As we have already observed, the 1890s and 1900s saw a culmination in the series of inventions that laid the foundations for twentieth-century technology. In addition to their profound social consequences, they amounted to the greatest revision to man's understanding of the world for two centuries as the age of steam passed into the age of electricity. As artists felt they were at the end of one period of history and the beginning of another, art responded to the various accelerated changes in society and celebrated the new by turning its machines into symbols of the new technological age.

The key transitional painting in the move from realism and impressionism to cubism was *Les Desmoiselles d'Avignon* (1906–7) by Pablo Picasso. In fact, it was but one of a series of lesser paintings of 1907 that carry the new design of the human form we recognize as cubist. Picasso was relatively unknown; his colleague, Georges Braque, wholly unknown outside their circle. Their obscurity gave them the freedom and courage to experiment. They knew that our knowledge of objects is based on comprehensive views top and bottom, front and back, and sides. They wanted to compress inspection of objects (which in real life takes time) into one moment, providing a synthesized view. Instead of a one-dimensional representation of reality, they proposed to substitute a multiple view as the most important element in realistic representation. The Cubists were convinced that our memory of something is as significant as the aspect it presents to us at any one moment. Both Picasso and Braque owned African carvings and exploited them (as French imperialists were exploiting equatorial Africa) by adapting their deliberate alterations to the human body and face.

Desmoiselles was painted quickly after numerous sketches and then revised. The influence of Paul Cézanne was tempered by El Greco's compact figure compositions and the angular shapes of his draperies, rocks, and clouds. The three women on the left show the influence of primitive Iberian sculpture and of early Egyptian art, whereas the hatched faces of the women on the right, painted later than the others, inspired by Negro masks, seem barbaric, almost ghoulish, and make the somber faces of the others look dignified, even gentle, by comparison. The painting was originally intended as an allegory of venereal disease, *The Wages of Sin,* in which a sailor carousing in a brothel is reminded by a medical student entering from the left with a human skull that all is vanity. According to Robert Hughes, in its final version the scene becomes the simple parade of prostitutes of the house before a prospective client who selects the one he fancies. In fact, it is the viewer whom Picasso turns into the client who is being stared at by the girls, a sinister variant on a traditional solicitation—"Hello, sailor." Robert Hughes asks, are the women, with their impassive, stonelike, but slightly ironic air, simply indifferent to the client or are they interrogating him? Less, "Hello, sailor!" than "Watch it, sailor!" Despite Picasso's assiduously nurtured public image of inexhaustible virility, the painting is about sexual anxiety. The girls are, if anything, ironic, even judgmental. The violent dislocation of human form implies a recurrent theme of some western artists, fear, terror even, of women. The combination of form and subject greatly disturbed the first

Pablo Picasso, *Les Desmoiselles d'Avignon* (1907) oil on canvas, 8′ x 7′8″. Picasso's inspired mix of African and Iberian art finally broke through the conventional Western art form of representation, based on single-point perspective, to establish a new mode, cubism, that dissected and recreated three-dimensional subjects on a single plane in keeping with the flat surface of a one-dimensional canvas. (Collection, The Museum of Modern Art, New York. Acquired through the Lillie P. Bliss Bequest).

people who saw the painting. Braque found it depressing and ugly. He said Picasso had been "drinking turpentine and spitting fire." Nevertheless, from 1908 he, too, began to develop the new art form of cubism. Picasso had once again demonstrated his uncanny ability to realize form and make the viewer feel the surface shape, weight, and edge of things.

The cubism of Picasso and Braque quickly moved to abstraction, to that point where there were only enough signs of the real world painted in conventional enough terms to supply a new tension between realism and abstraction. Robert Hughes concludes, "As description of a fixed form, they are useless. But as a report on multiple meanings, on process, they are exquisite and inexhaustible: the world is set forth as a field of shifting relationships that includes the onlooker." Once their paintings touched pure abstraction, they retreated and began to glue real objects into their works, using sand, sawdust, iron filings, and oilcloth, turning their paintings into collages. They used such items of modern mass production as newsprint, packaging, and wallpaper. Their associate, Juan Gris, painted such objects, rather than pasting them into his canvases, in order to celebrate the work of mass production. Fernand Léger went so far as to paint his fellow soldiers in the trenches of World War I as if they were automata made up of barrels and tubes, redesigning the human body as if it were put together like the guns of war.

Not only did Picasso bring a completely new fresh vocabulary to easel paintings with his fragmented, distended, and reassembled forms but he was also forging a new sophisticated way of creating a full, expressive picture out of the shallow space of the traditional cubist grid. In his hands and the hands of other artists, cubism destroyed the illusions of perspective and proportion and presented the world as seen from a myriad of different angles, angles akin to the fractional world that was emerging with the machine. The Cubists took painting far away from the safe conventions of naturalistic representation and revolutionized the way in which artists perceived the world.

Modern Art Comes to America

While Gertrude Stein helped effect this revolution in Paris during the first decade of the century, modernist painting was also creating interest in America. Initially, modernism traveled across the Atlantic because of the work of one man, photographer, artistic patron, and collector Alfred Stieglitz (1864–1946). It was Stieglitz who in 1908 gave Auguste Rodin and Henri Matisse their first exhibitions in the New World; in 1908 it was the turn of Henri Rousseau, le douanier; in 1911, Picasso and Paul Cézanne. Stieglitz had an open mind on art and refused to adhere to the fixed categories and classifications of the art world. He judged each painting on its own merit and although he himself was a prize-winning photographer, he eschewed the giving of prizes and any competitive or commercial spirit in art dealing. Indeed, it is easy to understand why Stieglitz was one of the great nurturing figures in American art. His exhibitions at 291—a small gallery named after its approximate location on Manhattan's Fifth Avenue—have become legendary.

It is interesting and somewhat surprising that a photographer should become a champion of modernist painting since, although the camera is a very modern, in the sense of recent, invention, it is capable of creating images that are the ultimate in naturalistic representation and thus deny the tenets of modernism. Many photographers of this period liked to imitate painting in their work by retouching and manipulating their photographs at the laboratory stage. However, Stieglitz preferred a sharp-focus, pictorial approach that he felt realized both the limitations and the possibilities of the medium of photography. His credo was close to that of realism in its search for unadorned pictorial representations of city life. Perhaps it was precisely because the camera had for him filled the role of reporter that he looked to painting as an alternative art form that went beyond realism.

The modernists certainly went beyond realism, and, in the opinion of both the general public and many critics, they also went beyond the artistic pale. Stieglitz's pioneering exhibitions at 291 brought modern painting to America for the first time but they were essentially select and exclusive affairs without much attendant publicity. The average American had to wait until the infamous Armory Show of 1913 before seeing and hearing about the scandalous and fraudulent painters from Europe who could not even reproduce the human form naturalistically on canvas. Indeed, the International Exhibition of Modern Art, held in New York City at the 69th Street Regiment Armory Building between February 15 and March 15, 1913, was a *succès de scandale* rather than a *succès d'estime*. The public was shocked and titilated by the fauve, cubist, and post-impressionist works of the European avant-garde. The cubist room was dubbed, "The Chamber of Horrors," and the International Section proved so controversial that it was shown later in the year in Chicago and Boston.

Even if both popular and critical reaction was for the most part hostile, the Armory Show had everyone talking about modern art. The young Association of American Painters and Sculptors (AAPS) was largely responsible for the show's success. Within fourteen months of their formation, this group, in opposition to the conservative traditions of the National Academy of Design, had pulled off a spectacular coup in organizing the most renowned exhibition in the history of art in America. Under the leadership of the artists Walt Kuhn and Arthur Davies, they attracted massive publicity for modern art that stands as testimony to their energy and organizational ability. At one stage they even investigated the possibility of hiring an electric sign announcing the show in Times Square. Unfortunately, the estimated cost of $900 for six weeks was too much for their tight budget. Nevertheless, they timed and manipulated press releases to gain maximum publicity with masterly precision and produced 50,000 pamphlets for the show along with four pamphlets on modern art in editions of 5,000 copies each. A series of fifty-seven halftone postcards of exhibits was created—the first example of a practice now followed by every art gallery in the world. America knew that modernism existed, but America displayed a distrust of modernism that, although deeply xenophobic, was perfectly understandable.

The American people were essentially wary and suspicious of intellectuals and alien cultures. Many historians have made the point that the period around the turn of the century saw a conflict between the traditional values of rural America and the new values of urban America. Rural America had been the dominant force in the nation's culture during the nineteenth century but now the city had emerged and, in the words of historian William E. Leuchtenburg, "The city represented everything—Europe, Wall Street, religious skepticism, political radicalism, sophistication,

intellectual arrogance—which prewar America most feared."
Modern art was a thing not to be trusted because it was intellectual and international. In the same way that America was to become disillusioned with Woodrow Wilson, precisely because of
his intellectualism and internationalism, the nation was resentful
of modern art. Theodore Roosevelt, always more attuned to public
consciousness than Wilson ever was, was much closer to the feelings of the man in the street when he commented on the Armory
Show: "There are thousands of people who will pay small sums
of money to look at a faked mermaid; and now and then one of
this kind with enough money will buy a cubist picture, or a picture of a misshapen nude woman, repellant from every stand-
point." The equation of modernism with the infamous faked
mermaid of the showman Phineas Barnum is indicative of the
depth of scandalous feeling induced by the show's international
section.

The Armory Show's most discussed and reviled exhibit was
Marcel Duchamp's *Nude Descending a Staircase no 2,* prompting
the *American Art News* magazine to sponsor a competition inviting contestants to spot where the painting's declared subject actually was. The winning entry came in the form of a ditty.

> You've tried to find her,
> And you've looked in vain
> Up the picture and down again,
> You've tried to fashion her of broken bits,
> And you've worked yourself into seventeen fits;
> The reason you've failed to tell you I can,
> It isn't a lady but only a man.

Cartoonist J. F. Griswold provided a version of the painting for
the *Evening Sun:* "The Rude Descending a Staircase (Rush Hour
at the Subway)," In *Everybody's* Julian Street called the painting
"an explosion in a shingle factory."

The critics of the official art world were hardly more enlightened in their reactions to the Armory Show. Cubism was
sometimes described as "insurgency in art" and "bedlam in art"
by conservative critics who compared cubist paintings to prehistoric cave art—a better compliment than they intended and not

so wide of the mark. Royal Cortissoz, an eminent critic of the period, vociferously warned against the invasion of "Ellis Island Art." This analogy with America's feared immigrant processing station is deeply expressive of traditional nativist fears, but the hysterical and reactionary Royal Cortissoz was not typical of critical condemnation of modernism. Kenyon Cox, painter, critic, and leading member of the National Academy of Design, rejected modernism on a rational and intelligent moral basis. His conservatism was very apparent in his article, "The 'Modern' Spirit in Art" that dealt directly with the Armory Show: "I was quoted the other day as having said that the human race is rapidly approaching insanity. I never said it, but if I were convinced that this is really 'modern art' and that these men are representative of our time, I should be constrained to believe it." Cox was fully committed to representative, traditional art, and he was depressed by the move toward abstraction that came with modernism. Behind his conservatism toward modern art lay a conservatism toward life: "Believing as I do, that there are still commandments in art as in morals, and still laws in art as in physics, I have no fear that this kind of art will prevail, or even that it will long endure." Laws in art certainly do exist, as do laws in physics and in morals. However, these laws are not immutable commandments. They must change continuously, adapting to altering conditions of life and new knowledge. The twentieth century has been a century of rapid change and if modernist painting appeared beyond the pale to some people in 1913, it was only because they had not realized the extent to which the parameters of human life were changing. Modern painters were seeking new styles that could help explain a radically changing culture to themselves and that culture's inhabitants.

Poet and eccentric Harvey Kemp visited the new art and wrote a malicious ditty on cubism in which he described being torn between not really liking it and wanting to approve anything that was outrageous.

> I cannot shake their wild control;
> Their colors still go roaring through their soul, . . .
> Strange cubes evolving into half-guessed forms,

Cyclones of green, and purple rainbow-storms,
Thus artists on huge Jupiter might paint
(Or some mad star beyond the earth's constraint) . . .
You go out with a whirlwind in your head
The thing, at least, is not inert and dead;
There's life and motion there, and rending force,
Color-Niagaras thundering on their course,
Power that breaks like a great wave in spray—
And what it means we'll let tomorrow say!

Tomorrow did say. Modernism was to prove a stronger influence on art than the American Renaissance. Cubism was its harbinger.

However, native American artists did not immediately understand or try and imitate the analytic cubist works of Picasso and Braque at the Armory Show. Although many made gestures toward the look of modernism, they did not have any deep sense of the reasons behind cubist art. Nevertheless, their work as individuals suggested that the informal colony of artists was slowly kindling various American styles that would eventually take the form of abstract expressionism in the 1940s.

Amongst the American moderns who were exhibited at the Armory Show and sponsored by Alfred Stieglitz were the following painters who went on to become leading figures in the history of American art: John Marin, Max Weber, Marsden Hartley, Arthur Dove, Stanton MacDonald Wright, and Georgia O'Keeffe.

Stanton MacDonald-Wright (1890–1973) was one of the first American painters who self-consciously set out to develop the modernist themes and styles initiated by European artists such as Paul Cézanne, the Fauves, and the Cubists. Working in Paris with another American, Morgan Russell, he started the self-proclaimed movement known as synchromism. He sought to fuse the tenets of cubism with his concern for light and color, creating often monumental canvases that convey great dynamism in their large and colorful geometric patterns but which failed to develop the really important facet of cubism that was the reorganization of space. MacDonald Wright, in his enthusiasm for the new movement, actually predicted the end of painting and the beginning of a pure, disembodied art of color and light. In fact, he abandoned synchromism in 1920 after having carved himself a niche in history by producing one of the first full-length color motion pictures, and he only returned to color painting in the mid-1950s.

John Marin (1870–1953) was a more typically American painter in that he exploited some facets of cubism in developing his own highly individual style. Many of his technical and stylistic devices grew out of time spent in Europe between 1905 and 1910, although he did not actually come into contact with cubism until his return to Europe and his introduction to Alfred Stieglitz. He worked for the most part in watercolor and used both urban and rural scenes as the points of departure for his largely abstract works. He eschewed proportion and perspective and during the twenties used the cubist "frame within a frame" technique. However, Marin's modern style does not disguise his connection with the American landscape painters and the American scene painters of the nineteenth and twentieth centuries. In *Lower Manhattan* of 1922 he captured the vitality of New York City in a characteristic watercolor. The airy, distorted effects are appropriate enough since his vantage point was the top of the Woolworth Building, then the highest skyscraper in the city. Under Stieglitz's patronage, Marin was one of the first American moderns to attract buyers and his success encouraged other painters to break free of traditional, representative art.

Max Weber (1881–1961) studied and painted in Paris between 1905 and 1909. More than any other American, his work was in close relation to the cubism of Georges Braque and Pablo Picasso but was without the acute self-consciousness of, say, MacDonald Wright's synchromism. Like Braque and Picasso, Weber was very much influenced by African sculpture that he saw while in Paris and many of the figures in his paintings are consequently exotic and angular in appearance. Not only did machines provide new angles and new ways of viewing the world but they also ushered in a new era of improved transport and communication bringing together previously distant cultures. On his return to America, Weber found little professional welcome, apart from the encouragement and exhibitions given him by Stieglitz. Eventually, he

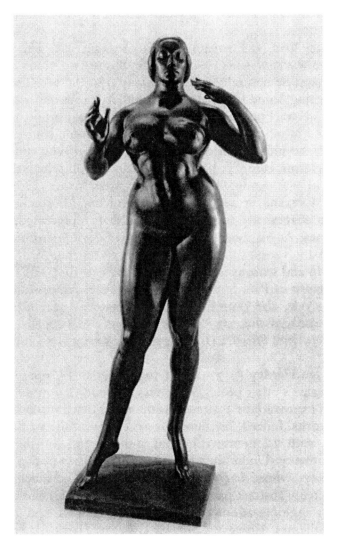

Gaston Lachaise, *Standing Woman* (1912–27) bronze, 70″ x 28″ x 17″. Parisian sculptor Gaston Lachaise emigrated to the United States in 1906 and settled in New York in 1912. There he developed a mature style of heroic women sculptures for which his wife, Isabel Dutaud Nagle, generously provided the model, that deliberately sacrificed anatomical detail to enhance flowing lines and thereby emphasize female sexuality. (Collection of Whitney Museum of American Art, New York).

abandoned his cubist experiments for a more naturalistic, expressionist style.

Arthur Dove (1880–1946) went to Paris in 1907. The art capital of the world was his base while for almost two years he toured France, and he naturally found his way into the Stieglitz coterie on returning home late in 1909; naturally, because he was one of the first abstract painters to emerge from either Europe or America. Like Marin, Dove was inspired by the natural landscape, and the artist he most admired was Paul Cézanne, who, during the late nineteenth century, had created paintings in which the natural world was rendered in almost abstract shapes. Dove went beyond Cézanne in reducing and abstracting the natural landscape to shapes that suggested, rather than represented, objects and scenes. As his work developed, Dove devised abstract forms inspired by various kinds of experience: the music of George Gershwin and various jazz musicians between 1911 and 1920; the photographs of Paul Strand in the early 1920s; nature and reproductive cycle, also during the 1920s. Between 1924 and 1930 he created collages that are "object portraits" of people he knew. *Portrait of Alfred Stieglitz* (1925) contains a camera lens and a clock spring.

Marsden Hartley (1877–1943), too, went to Europe, but, unlike Stieglitz's other protégés, he was influenced more heavily by German expressionist abstractions than by French or Italian modernist works. Indeed, he found the art capital of the world intimidating, with its intense affections and emphasis on the importance of theory. Under the influence of the Russian painter Wassily Kandinsky, whose *Improvisations* are generally considered to be the first truly abstract paintings, Hartley's German paintings consisted of agglomerations of shapes that he saw as equivalents of musical themes. However, like Max Weber, Hartley later moved toward naturalistic representation.

In *Portrait of a German Officer* of 1914 Marsden Hartley displayed his debt to the early German Expressionists. He used many emblems of Prussian militarism, including the iron cross. Later in his career Hartley moved to a more naturalistic, representational painting in such works as *Crow with Ribbons* (1941). The blackness of the bird contrasts sharply with the white cloth and the blood-red background serves to emphasize the pathos of the scene—the crow has become a hunter's trophy.

Georgia O'Keeffe (1887–1986) was a young art teacher from Texas whose drawings were brought to the attention of Stieglitz. He was greatly impressed by their originality and arranged to exhibit them. Her work was abstract in design but always firmly rooted in reality and she was never attracted by cubist dislocations and fragmentations. *Lake George Window*, created in 1929, illustrates these points. Initially, this painting appears to be totally representational, almost photographic. However, closer inspection shows that it lacks detail and comes close to abstract design. O'Keeffe is the finest of all the first generation American modernist painters, a status accounted for by her ability to synthesize most of the progressive tendencies in American painting up to World War II, and by dint of her remarkably long career.

Realism in American Art

Robert Henri (1865–1929) was a leading figure in the battle to establish modern, realist art in New York and the nation. As a student at the Pennsylvania Academy of Fine Arts he was taught by Thomas Anschutz—in turn a prodigy of the famous Thomas Eakins (1844–1916), a pioneer in the development of realism in American painting—and completed his artistic training with study in Paris where he absorbed the influence of the Impressionists. In 1902 Henri began teaching at the New School of Art in New York and it quickly became clear that he had now found his vocation. He established a coterie of students and followers who were urged to paint what they saw around them in the metropolitan atmosphere of the city. His approach was liberal and his enthusiasm boundless, two qualities that accounted for his astonishing success as a teacher. Indeed, the Henri classes came to be looked upon as a symbol of the new ferment in the social and cultural life of the nation. In 1901 he addressed the students of the School of Design for Women, Philadelphia, and advised them as follows:

I do not want to see how skillful you are—I am not interested in your skill. What do you get out of nature? Why do you paint this subject?

What is life to you? What reasons and what principles have you found? What are your deductions? What projections have you made? What excitement, what pleasure do you get out of it? Your skill is the thing of least interest to me.

This plethora of questions highlights Henri's lively approach to his art. It also illustrates just what he meant by an "art for life's sake" that was founded on personal experience and feeling, rather than an "art for art's sake" that was based on intellect and technical proficiency. In retrospect, it seems inevitable that such a forceful teacher would come into conflict with the official art world.

Ironically though, Henri himself experienced little difficulty in gaining acceptance from the academies—his paintings were often not as radical as his theories on painting. In 1907 the jury of the National Academy of Design rejected a number of paintings by Henri's friends and followers. He was so annoyed by the jury's decision that he withdrew his own entry (which had already been accepted) as a protest. The Macbeth Galleries in New York sponsored an exhibition of the rejected painters during the following year. There were eight of them in all, hence the group's name, The Eight. With Henri as their leader, they were: William Glackens, George Luks, John Sloan, Everett Shinn, Maurice Prendergast, Arthur Davies, and Ernest Lawson. Together these painters achieved for American realist painting what Theodore Dreiser, Sinclair Lewis, and Sherwood Anderson, amongst others, realized for the literary world in the early century—an appreciation of naturalistic realism as a worthy and incisive mode of artistic expression.

William Glackens (1870–1938), in common with John Sloan and George Luks, began his career as a newspaper illustrator and then moved to painting. It is fitting and understandable that this group of urban realists should contain several newspaper artists. In newspaper work the daily life of the city was unavoidable in its most attractive and its most distasteful aspects. As we have already observed, several of the most prominent social progressives were journalists and the newspaper artist, before the introduction of inexpensive photographic reproduction, was just as well placed as the journalist to absorb the meaning and significance of the city. Glackens's early work conveys a deep sense of excitement at life in a modern city, particularly with regard to social gatherings—theater and restaurant scenes, for example. However, his later work lacks both his youthful energy and his commitment to urban realism and, as a consequence, looks jaded in comparison. Everett Shinn (1873–1953) was similarly enamored with the world of fashion and theatrical life. George Luks (1866–1933) was first and foremost a portraitist who captured character in his paintings of city people, both affluent and working class. Neither Glackens, Shinn, nor Luks exerted any appreciable influence as individuals. Their importance in the history of American painting lies in their membership of The Eight.

On the other hand, John Sloan (1871–1951) was, artistically speaking, the single most important member of the group. As an individual painter he even eclipsed Henri though he never approached Henri's capacity as a teacher and polemicist for the new realism. In 1904 Sloan moved from Philadelphia to New York and, true to the teachings of Henri, immediately immersed himself in city life. Like Glackens and Luks, Sloan had been trained as a newspaper illustrator, but, unlike them, he did not work rapidly enough for the daily editions of the *Philadelphia Press* and, instead, produced more ambitious work for the Sunday editions and advertisements. This careful approach was later transferred to his painting and it has led at least one art historian to an explanation of his success. Mahonri Sharp Young has written that: "Sloan painted things Henri could not handle, for he had the intensity that Henri lacked. Sloan painted better than he could talk; Henri worse. He took up the city scene where Henri left it off; it didn't mean much to Henri, but it was everything to Sloan." Sloan was truly captivated by the city and his enthusiasm for his work is encapsulated by broad masses of dark and light that lend his paintings a posterlike vigor that is not inappropriate if we consider the nature of his commitment to the tenets of political socialism.

Sloan, an intelligent and sensitive man, had not been unmoved by the ferment and turmoil of the closing decades of the nineteenth century. His political sympathies had always inclined leftward but it was not until 1908 that he became an active member of the Socialist party in those years before World War I when the Socialist party, led by Eugene V. Debs, was a considerable force in national politics. Sloan himself twice ran for elected office but without any hope of winning and on both occasions was "glad to lose," because success would have effectively put an end to his career as a painter.

Nevertheless, cultural historian Robert M. Crunden in his interdisciplinary review of the period 1919–1941, *From Self to Society* (1972), has attributed Sloan with the position of painter of American socialism "in its most attractive guise." It is certainly true that Sloan's work signifies a direct link between progressive painting and the progressive political climate of the period. In Crunden's words:

He illustrated realistic stories about the poor and thus emphasised their importance in a democratic country. He drew topical cartoons that supported strikers or attacked selfish businessmen and exploiters. Perhaps most important, he led the school of American realist painters in their attempt to capture the city for modern art, and leave for dead the old, conventional, academic art that still stressed the painting of antiques, of idealized views, and the sculptural qualities of historical scenes.

Although many of his friends, including Robert Henri, refused to be moved by his support for the Socialist party, Sloan was married to an ardent Socialist. Dolly Sloan was much more active in practical matters than her husband ever was. She sold books and distributed tracts at meetings, collected for various causes, and espoused firm views on issues, such as pacifism, birth control, and woman suffrage. The contrast between Dolly and John Sloan serves to illustrate the shallow level of his commitment to the Socialist creed. Sloan eventually came to feel that his art was being compromised by the religious-like devotion required by Socialism and the matter came to a head with his work for the weekly Socialist magazine, the *Masses*.

The Masses achieved fame in 1912 when it was taken over by the progressive Max Eastman who introduced new and prestigious contributors such as John Reed and the artist Art Young. Sloan was art editor and the magazine's policy was to reproduce drawings that did not compromise with the readership or advertisers, but displayed artistic excellence in their own right. However, propaganda eventually became the central concern of the magazine's editors because of their concern to promote political consciousness, and this demanded an orthodoxy from the illustrators that Sloan, along with others such as the young Stuart Davis, was not prepared to give. In 1916 he resigned.

Sloan was stifled by orthodoxy, even when it happened to concur with his political sympathies, and his final conclusion about painting was, "I don't believe an artist has any duty to society in his work." Indeed, when Sloan returned to painting he found that the city scene had lost much of its attraction for him—he had been spoiled by the self-consciousness that is a constant requirement of all political art. Instead, he turned to figure painting but continued to use social scenes in his drawing and engraving.

While he worked on *The Masses* Sloan had often been in disagreement with Art Young who, as an artist, was fully prepared to conform to the requirements of propaganda and believed that "if we put an ash-can in a drawing," then a contribution was being made toward the realization of a revolution. This was the phrase that gave the name to a group of painters known as the Ash Can School. The Eight and the Ash Can School have frequently been confused, and even thought of as identical, because it was five painters from The Eight who constituted the Ash Can School. Henri, Glackens, Luks, Shinn, and Sloan were rebels in their time who were, as their collective name suggests, subversive in their approach to art.

The art of the remaining three members of The Eight, while not so overtly radical, was still progressive and did not conform to academic expectations. For example, Maurice Prendergast (1859–1924) who, unlike the other members of The Eight, had traveled and painted in Europe and created works that were often merely advanced pastiche of the French Impressionists. His favorite subjects were crowds of people that could be woven into overall visual fabrics that the observer is forced to study as a whole entity. Ernest Lawson (1873–1939) was primarily a landscape painter whose treatment of urban America often served to illuminate the sordid reality of the new world in this time of industrial upheaval. Similarly, Arthur Davies (1862–1928), while being a painter of natural landscapes and nudes, was far from acceptable to the official art world by virtue of his muted colors and rhythmic draughtsmanship.

George Bellows (1882–1925) was a realist painter who was connected with The Eight by virtue of his friendship with Robert Henri rather than by any close artistic ties. Indeed, while The Eight exhibited at the Macbeth Galleries in 1908 in protest at their exclusion from the National Academy of Design, Bellows was enjoying the privilege of being the youngest artist ever elected an associate of the same institution. He became a full member of the Academy in 1913 and in that same year exhibited also at the Armory Show. Despite his membership of the conservative Academy, Bellows was a Socialist and a pacifist and regularly contributed to *The Masses* between 1912 and 1917. His art remained firmly rooted in naturalistic realism thoughout his career and always had a dramatic, journalistic quality about it. His *Dempsey and Firpo* of 1924 was the last of six boxing paintings. Bellows went to the fight, along with a crowd of 90,000, on September 1, 1923, because he had been assigned by the New York *Evening Journal* to make an illustration. He chose the famous episode from the first round in which "Dempsey was knocked through the ropes" by Firpo and "fell in my lap. I cursed him a bit and placed him carefully back in the ring with instructions to be of good cheer." (In fact, Dempsey knocked Firpo out in the second round.)

Not all artists before World War I were optimistic about the machine. Some saw it as threatening, even dehumanizing. The idea that man's inventions could rise against him and eventually destroy him was an essential myth of the early Industrial Revolution given potent form by Mary Shelley in *Frankenstein* (1818). After unsuccessful attempts at Cubism and Fauvism, the French artist Marcel Duchamp (1887–1967), who was an intermittent visitor to the United States, provided the definitive mechano-sexual symbol in his unfinished *The Large Glass,* also known as *The Bride Stripped Bare by Her Bachelors, Even* (1915–23). It was a project in the form of lead painted on glass, for a contraption of unclear purpose, a meta-machine that serves as an allegory of profane love. In the top section a naked Bride continuously undresses while below the Bachelors, made up of empty jackets and uniforms, continuously grind away their unfulfilled frustration.

From 1914 the new machinery was turned upon humanity itself. World War I obliterated faith in technology as a benevolent machine. The myth of a better future disintegrated in shellshock. Both American and European writers and painters moved into a period of irony, protest, and disgust. Any joy in the promise of science and technology, optimism born in the machine age, was cut down by the terrible instruments of war. Not only were people's cherished images of progress shattered but also their words. Language was broken by the terrors of the Somme, the hypocrisy of government propaganda, and the new terrible age of industrialized, mass death. Language could no longer carry its earlier meanings. The war changed words in literature and images in art once and forever.

CHAPTER ELEVEN

Pacific Overtures?
Imperialism and Realpolitik

·ॐ·

O NE OF the clearest signs that the twentieth century would be the American century was the great overseas expansion of the United States. This was not simply a matter of acquiring land, whether as colonies, dependencies, or protectorates, but, also, of expanding commerce and trade and, by so doing, penetrating the economic infrastructure of other societies across the world. Following the emergence of the United States as the world's dominant industrial power, American manufacturers were seeking markets abroad and financiers were beginning to invest capital overseas. "Our industries have expanded to such a point that they will burst their jackets if they cannot find a free outlet to the markets of the world," Woodrow Wilson told the Democratic National Convention of 1912. "Our domestic markets no longer suffice. We need foreign markets."

As early as 1902 Europeans were noticing what they called "the American invasion" of machinery companies, notably in sewing and office machinery, elevators, shoe machinery, printing machinery, pumping machinery, and telephone equipment. In the fields of electrical machinery and chemicals, American companies had rivals among German companies. Almost two-thirds of forty-one companies with mines, plants, or other facilities abroad were in food and machinery. All these had at least two plants abroad and twelve had at least four plants abroad. By 1914 direct American investment abroad equaled 7 percent of the domestic gross national product, exactly the same proportional percentage as in 1966.

Companies expanding overseas followed a similar pattern. First, they created an extensive foreign marketing organization through branch offices. Second, because of tariffs, high costs of transportation, and low cost of labor, they built factories abroad. Then, having achieved integrated production and marketing overseas, they decided to buy raw or partly finished materials locally because they cost less and were obtained more quickly. Thus, in chewing gum, American Chicle, Wrigley's principal competitor, had 3 million acres of land in Mexico where it produced its material, and ran factories in Britain and Canada to make chewing gum.

After 1900 the domestic demand for meat was so great that the great American meat packing firms no longer had sufficient supplies to meet growing foreign demand. Thus leading meat packers Armour and Swift obtained packing plants in Argentina, Brazil, and Uruguay to process meat for Europe. They also acquired necessary shipping and expanded their European branches for distribution. They used the same sort of integrated network to coordinate a flow of meat from Argentina to Europe that they had established twenty years earlier in the United States to connect the western plains with the eastern market.

The United States was acquiring a vested interest in the stability of Europe, Asia, and Latin America—if only to protect its own economy. Thus it would be impossible for the United States to continue its traditional foreign policy of avowed isolation indefinitely. Instead of avoiding entangling alliances, the United States would need to find diplomatic partners. Senator Orville H. Platt of Connecticut remarked in 1893, "A policy of isolation did well enough when we were an embryo nation, but today things are different. We are the most advanced and powerful people on earth, and regard to our future welfare demands an abandonment of the doctrine of isolation." He concluded, "It is to the ocean that our children must look, as they once looked to the boundless West."

Furthermore, advances in communications and transportation were drawing the world more closely together. In particular, advances in shipbuilding, especially of submarines, were dissolving the strategic value of the Atlantic Ocean. Finally, the unification of Germany, followed by its rise as the leading military power in Europe, and the contemporaneous rise of Japan in Asia disturbed the traditional balance of power and was lessening the naval supremacy of Britain upon which American security had largely depended. Thus a pressing reason for expanded foreign policy was the new pressure of power politics as the great nations jostled for imperial, commercial, territorial or strategic supremacy.

In *The Rise of the Trading State* (1985) Richard Rosecrance explains how two major but contradictory processes were developing in the late nineteenth century. The first brought people of different countries closer together. For the new technology of steamships, railways and telegraphs encouraged the development of a truly cosmopolitan network of commerce, an international division of labor based on economic complements of food, raw materials, and industrial products, financed primarily through a system of credit and insurance centered in the City of London. In time, ever more countries were drawn into this network of international commerce and finance. Thus by 1913 the volume of world foreign trade was twenty-five times greater per capita than it had been in 1800. However, the second process divided people rather than bringing them closer together. It amounted to increased tensions and rivalries among the great powers as shown by their scramble for colonies, military alliances, arms races, and a profusion of jingoism, based on propaganda encouraging hatred and fear. This process, too, was aggravated by new technology in which what Richard Rosecrance calls the "firepower revolution" of high-explosive shells, quick-firing artillery, machine guns, mines, and torpedoes was about to render future battlefields more deadly and devastating. Furthermore, the cost of sustaining modern armies and navies (and, subsequently, air forces) would also be devastating economically. Thus, in the words of historian and critic Paul Kennedy, "One trend pressed toward international co-operation and interdependence, while the other pressed toward violence and destruction."

Cultural historian and intellectual Henry Adams urged a new foreign policy for the United States to reflect changed circumstances. He regarded Germany as the principal rival to the United States. In 1906 he declared, "We have got to support France against Germany and fortify the Atlantic system beyond attack; for if Germany breaks down England or France, she becomes the center of a military world, and we are lost. The course of concentration must be decided by force—whether military or industrial matters not much in the end."

Presidents and their advisers certainly realized that America was a world power with crucial economic interests overseas. They wanted a more systematic foreign policy with strategic deployment of military and naval forces to back it up. However, they could not persuade most Americans to accept a more vigorous foreign policy. Presidents could initiate and develop foreign policy but they risked vociferous opposition from Congress, jealous of its rights and committed to the traditional principle of no entangling alliances. Public opinion may not have been informed about all this but it was influenced by other pertinent factors. One was the immigrant tradition. Americans were primarily the descendants of European immigrants or immigrants themselves. Whether they had left Europe specifically to escape military conscription or religious persecution, or, more generally, to participate in the economic opportunities of the American Industrial Revolution, they developed a profound resentment of the Old World. They associated kings, kaisers, and czars with tyranny and absolutism.

What catapulted the United States to the center of the stage of world affairs was its participation in the Spanish-American War of 1898. The Spanish island colony of Cuba in the Caribbean had been in continuous revolt against bad government for several decades. After it could not persuade Spain to moderate its strategy, the United States intervened, partly to protect American business, tobacco, and sugar interests in Cuba, partly because it could no longer tolerate a divisive revolution ninety miles off the coast of Florida, and partly on account of humanitarian motives, because the American Congress and people felt compelled to redress unjust Spanish social policies. President William McKinley proposed intervention in the name of humanity and this was what Congress agreed in the war resolution passed on April 13 and 20, 1898. However, both houses accepted an extra acticle to the war resolution, proposed by Senator Henry M. Teller of Colorado, that stated that the United States had no imperial intentions toward Cuba and that, after peace had been secured, it would leave the island to govern itself. However, expansionists, led by Assistant Secretary of War Theodore Roosevelt and Senator Henry Cabot Lodge of Massachusetts welcomed the war for the opportunity it offered to acquire naval bases in the Pacific and the Caribbean, notably Spain's other possessions, the Philippines and Puerto Rico.

The Spanish war was over on August 12 when McKinley signed a protocol by which Spain was ordered to evacuate Cuba, to cede Puerto Rico and Guam, an island in the Marianas group, to the United States, and to allow America to occupy Manila until a peace treaty had determined the future of the Philippines. The protocol thus set a constitutional precedent for an extension of presidential power.

McKinley was genuinely concerned for the future safety of the Filipinos. He recognized their inexperience in government and also dreaded the predatory intentions of Germany toward the islands. Moreover, he was equally eager to secure extra trade and new trading routes for the United States. Thus, on October 28, from a mixture of interested and disinterested motives, he instructed his peace commission negotiating with Spain in Paris to demand the entire archipelago. The treaty was eventually signed in Paris on December 10, 1898. To compensate Spain, the United States paid $20 million for the Philippines, Puerto Rico, and Guam. When the Senate finally voted on the treaty on February 6, 1899, it was ratified by fifty-seven votes to twenty-seven, only two votes more than the necessary two-thirds.

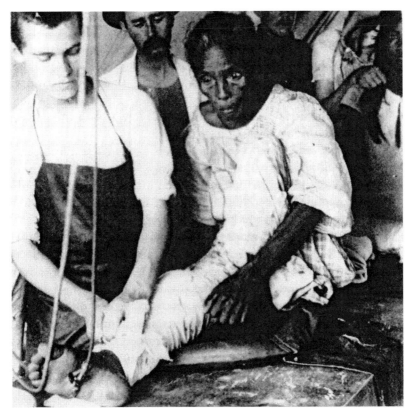

This poignant scene of an old woman being tended in hospital in Manila after being shot through the leg while carrying ammunition to the Filipinos during the uprising of 1899–1901 was, unfortunately, only one early instance illustrating the inhumanity of imperialist and racist wars against subject peoples that were to mar the history of the twentieth century. (Stereograph of 1899 by R. Y. Young; Library of Congress).

The Acquisition of Empire

America and its statesmen now learned that it was far easier to acquire a colonial empire than it was to govern it. Imperialism was to prove a headache, a heartache, and a disappointment. The treaty was followed by a Filipino uprising led by Emilio Aguinaldo that lasted two years and in which more people died than in the war of 1898. It ended with the capture of Aguinaldo on March 27, 1901. The American military government was replaced on March 4, 1901, by a civil commission of four members. William Howard Taft, then a circuit judge, headed the commission to establish a civil government in the Philippines. The average weight of the commissioners was 227 pounds and it was said the natives would find them "an imposing spectacle."

Commercial and naval opinion now believed the Philippines were of no significant value for developing trade with Asia and, besides, they could not be defended from attack. Moreover, public opinion recoiled from the terrible cost in terms of money and human life of subduing the Filipino revolt.

In Cuba General Leonard Wood, as temporary governor-general, devised the future form of the island's relations with the United States. The Platt amendment to an army appropriation bill of March 2, 1901, allowed the president to end the occupation of Cuba after its government agreed to five conditions: never to make a treaty that would impair its independence; never to contract a debt it could not repay; to consent to American rights of intervention to preserve Cuba's independence and stabilize its government; to execute a sanitary program planned during American occupation; and to allow the United States a naval base on the island. In part, this was because American statesmen still distrusted the pretensions of the German kaiser, Wilhelm II.

As to Puerto Rico, the other Caribbean acquisition of 1898, the Foraker Act of April 12, 1900, provided a small amount of self-rule, allowing the islanders to elect a Lower House, while giving the president the right to appoint the governor, the heads of the executive departments, and members of the Upper House. It was revised on March 2, 1917, by the (second) Jones Act that granted citizenship to the islanders and allowed them to elect both chambers of the Assembly.

It seemed that in the Philippines the United States was assuming the sort of position Spain had once occupied in Cuba. McKinley's declared policy to the Philippines was "benevolent assimilation." However, progress was slow. In a series of test cases, the Insular Cases, of May 27, 1901, the Supreme Court declared that the Philippines and Puerto Rico were territories appurtenant but not part of the United States. Thus their peoples were subjects not citizens. The United States could, therefore, both acquire the islands and erect a tariff wall against their crops of sugar and tobacco. Problems of imports and tariffs punctuated the course of the Philippines' progress to independence. On July 1, 1902, Congress passed the Civil Government or First Organic Act for the Philippines. First, it made Filipinos citizens of the Philippine Islands. Second, it established an executive branch of government, comprising a five-man commission, headed by a governor-general, to be appointed by the president of the United States with the consent of the Senate. It provided for a legislature of two chambers, to be established after two years, with the Lower House to be elected by the Christian tribes and the Upper House simply to consist of the commission. William Howard Taft was the first governor-general and his sympathetic nature and proven honesty supposedly did much to win round the Filipinos to American rule. Taft, with well-intentioned racist candor, described the Filipino as "the little brown brother," a remark that drew the riposte from American soldiers who hated their task:

> He may be a brother of Big Bill Taft;
> But he ain't no brother of mine.

The war bred new legends of ugly Americans.

To further the cause of Philippine independence, a later governor-general, Francis Burton Harrison, agreed with Filipino leaders Sergio Osmeña and Manuel Quezon to transfer as much power as possible to Filipino leaders and thus convince Congress that the islands were worthy of, and ready for, full independence. By 1913 four of the nine commissioners, 71 percent of civil servants, 92 percent of teachers, and all governors of the Christian provinces were Filipinos. President Woodrow Wilson agreed in principle with Harrison but the Republicans, who controlled Congress, would not. The compromise between Wilson, Harrison, and Congress took the form of a Second Organic Act for the Philippines, the (first) Jones Act, passed on August 29, 1916. Whilst reserving sovereignty to the United States, the Jones Act created an elected Senate in the Philippine legislature to supersede the commission, eased suffrage requirements, and allowed the governor-general, with the consent of the Philippine Senate, to appoint heads of most executive departments.

In the Hare-Hawes-Cutting Act of December 29, 1932, Congress, much scared by the Japanese invasion of Manchuria and wanting to abandon any problem that could lead to friction, provided for complete independence of the Philippines, after a transitional period of ten years. However, this measure was vetoed on January 13, 1933, by President Herbert Hoover, passed over his veto, and finally rejected by the Filipinos on October 17, 1933, who objected to American military and naval bases on the islands. Advised by President Franklin D. Roosevelt to eliminate the clauses about bases, Congress then provided independence in a revised bill that was passed as the Tydings-McDuffie Act of May 24, 1934, by which the islands were to remain a semiautonomous commonwealth until July 4, 1946, when they would become the Philippine Republic. Ironically, it was selfish, rather than idealistic, Americans who lobbied Congress for Philippine independence. Certain farm and labor blocs believed that, if the Philippines were truly independent, then they could achieve effective barriers against cheap Filipino products and labor.

Americans soon lost their enthusiasm and romance for expansion when they realized that, unlike settlement of the Great American Desert, imperialism overseas did not simply mean driving away the natives and acquiring more free land but, rather, administering established communities. This form of imperialism was welcome to Britain because Britain was primarily a mercantile and shipping nation whose economic interests were served by such acquisitions. Besides, it had a class, composed of merchants and middle-class administration, trained for such work. It was, perhaps, consideration of these factors that led American statesmen to turn increasingly to China, a settled but underdeveloped country with vast untapped resources and a social and economic infrastructure that could be bent to the will of an imperial power, without the hateful chore of territorial occupation.

The Open Door and the Russo-Japanese War

Among the great powers, Britain, France, Germany, Japan, and Russia had all obtained major concessions from China, either in trading rights or leaseholds on ports or strategically placed territory. Thus the empress dowager, Tz'u-hsi, was supposed to have exclaimed of China's predators, "The various powers cast upon us looks of tiger-like voracity, hustling each other in their endeavors to be the first to seize upon our . . . territories." For, China lay like a beached whale. Its defeat by Japan in the First Korean War of 1894 was a clear signal that it could not defend itself against modern armies and navies.

The leading contenders in the projected dismemberment of China were Russia and Japan. Tensions arose between Russia and Japan in competition for Manchuria, a Chinese state north of the Great Wall, comprising the provinces of Heilungkiang, Liaoning, and Jehol. Manchuria was a traditional target of Russian expansion: it provided the most direct route from the west to Vladivostock. The Russians extracted a Chinese concession to build, maintain, and guard a railway across it, the Chinese Eastern Railway, linked with the Trans-Siberian Railway, and they had also wanted to build a second railway to the ice-free ports, Dairen (or Dalny) and Port Arthur, across the Liaotung Peninsula.

Japan also feared Russian penetration of Korea, a country from which it had already exacted special privileges and over which it had gone to war with China in September 1894. When Japan was victorious, it ensured that the Treaty of Shimonoseki of April 17, 1895, awarded it valuable prizes: Formosa (or Taiwan), the Pescadores, Port Arthur, and the Liaotung Peninsula; and Chinese recognition of Korean independence. Unfortunately for Japan, France, Germany, and Russia were so disturbed by its dramatic success in upsetting the balance of power that they put pressure on Japan to forgo one concession—the Liaotung Peninsula, including the harbor and fortress of Port Arthur: these were the keys to northern China. Their pressure and Japan's capitulation lived on in Japanese psychology as the Triple Intervention. The Japanese could certainly accuse the West of hypocrisy for, within five years, Germany had taken Tsingtan, France had secured a lease of Kwangchow Bay, Britain had been granted the lease of Wei-hai-Wei and the New Territories of Hong Kong, and Russia had taken control of the Liaotung Peninsula and Port Arthur. Of all these events the one that most outraged Japan was the Russian acquisition of the very territory it had yielded in 1895. Few doubted that a conflict between Russia and Japan was now inevitable.

Secretary of State John Hay's (1898–1905) strategy in this delicate situation was to try and get all the major powers to agree to peaceful and equitable economic penetration of China in a so-called Open Door policy, announced in a series of unilateral notes—the First Open Door Notes of September 6, 1899, to March 20, 1900, and the Second Open Door Notes of July 3, 1900. In between came a terrifying demonstration, the Boxer uprising of June 13, 1900, in which foreign legations in Beijing were attacked by staunch Chinese nationalists who killed 231 foreigners.

Both the First and Second Open Door Notes represented an American attempt to persuade China to accept the United States as moderator in its relations with other powers. Moreover, both McKinley and Hay hoped that China would, in time, identify its economic interests with those of the United States. The Open Door was also a symbol that the American advocates of expanded markets, commerce, and shipping were gaining ground at the expense of those who wanted outright colonization. In a much-quoted letter to William Howard Taft of December 22, 1910, Theodore Roosevelt advised his successor that the success of the Open Door depended on goodwill among the nations. If one of them chose to defy it, there was little the others could do without going to war. A war over China was outside America's interests and beyond its military capacity. It would be better to reach amicable settlement with Japan by diplomacy. In 1903, when Russia began to invade Manchuria, Roosevelt was furious—but powerless to act.

After due consideration about this unwelcome development, Japan signed an alliance with Britain on January 30, 1902, renewed first in 1905 and then in 1911. For its part, Britain thus gained a counterweight to Russia in the Far East. Japan gained tacit British acceptance of its interests in Korea. Russia and Japan now contested openly for Manchuria and Korea. Japan broke off diplomatic relations on February 6, 1904, and engaged Russian vessels off Seoul on February 8, before formally declaring war on February 10. The London *Times* commented with unwitting irony, how "The Japanese Navy has opened the war by an act of daring which is destined to take a place of honour in naval annals."

As far as American public opinion was concerned, "Gallant Little Japan" was standing up to the ferocious Russian bear. This was certainly Roosevelt's view. Nevertheless, he told Cecil Spring-Rice in a letter of June 13, 1904, that decisive Japanese victory might prejudice the development of American interests in China and eventually lead to a war in Asia between the United States and Japan. Thus he offered to mediate to end the damaging war. Although Japan had scored a series of military and naval victories, both sides were ready for peace by 1905. Russia had been defeated on land and at sea and the Romanovs faced political disruption at home; Japan had overextended itself financially and could not afford to lengthen its lines of transportation and communication any further.

In the Treaty of Portsmouth, New Hampshire, which ended the Russo-Japanese War on September 5, 1905, the Russians agreed to transfer to Japan the lease of the Liaotung Peninsula, including Port Arthur and Dairen, and the branch of the Chinese Eastern Railroad below Changchun (soon renamed the South Manchuria Railroad), as well as the southern half of Sakhalin; and, also, to recognize Japan's "paramount political, military, and economic interests in Korea." Both countries agreed to evacuate all of Manchuria (apart from the areas leased to them) within eighteen months. A side effect of the treaty was to turn Russian interest away from the Far East and back toward the Balkans and conflict with Austria-Hungary.

American planners were much disturbed by their wartime realization that Japan could take enemy strongholds on hostile shores and that, therefore, both the Philippines and Guam could be taken by Japan with small chance of recapture. Indeed, Roosevelt remained apprehensive that Japan might have designs on the Philippines. Accordingly, he had Taft, under cover of a visit to

Manila, visit Tokyo in secret, where he concluded the Taft-Katsura secret agreement of July 27, 1905, by which the United States gave its approval to the idea of Japan's penetration of Korea, in exchange for assurance that Japan would not interfere in the Philippines. Later the two countries, by exchange of notes, reached the Root-Takahira agreement of November 30, 1908, that consolidated American-Japanese friendship. Not only did Japan guarantee not to attack the Philippines but also said it supported the Open Door in China. Roosevelt thus acquiesced in Japanese domination of Korea (which could not be defended) and recognized the special position of Japan in Manchuria (which betrayed the spirit of the Open Door). In short, Roosevelt was conceding Japan's right to expansion.

Russia and Japan were subsequently reconciled and signed a secret convention on July 30, 1907, dividing Manchuria into Russian and Japanese spheres of influence. Japan had consolidated its position in Korea to such an extent that it could dispose of the king and, on August 22, 1910, formally annex the country that it was to rule for the next thirty-five years.

The Open Door policy continued to trouble American statesmen because they were propounding a doctrine that could not be sustained. China's problems with the great powers deepened. On February 12, 1912, the Manchu dynasty was overthrown by insurgents who established a republic of which Yuan Shi Kai was elected president by a National Assembly on February 15. The fledgling republic could not withstand the advances of Japan, determined to turn China into a protectorate.

During World War I Japan took full advantage of Germany's concentration of its forces in Europe to seize the German base of Tsingtan on November 7, 1914, after a siege. The war also provided special opportunities for Japan to exact foreign concessions from China. Instead of concentrating on its footholds in Shantung (newly captured from Germany), southern Manchuria, and inner Mongolia, the Japanese foreign minister, Kato Takaakira, devised a series of Twenty-One Demands presented to Yuan Shih-k'ai on January 18, 1915. Not only did they cover the transfer to Japan of Shantung and various territorial and railroad rights in Manchuria but also insisted that China should employ Japanese

"GOOD OFFICES"

Theodore Roosevelt used his considerable diplomatic skill to achieve the Treaty of Portsmouth, New Hampshire, at the end of the Russo-Japanese War. This cartoon by W. A. Rogers for *Harper's Weekly* of June 24, 1905, shows the modestly clad American president holding apart the two rival emperors. (Library of Congress).

political, military, and financial advisers in government and that China should purchase half of its war material from Japan. On March 13, 1915, Secretary of State William Jennings Bryan (1913–15) protested to Japan. Although Japan abandoned the most outrageous demands on May 9, 1915, by then public opinion in the United States had been thoroughly alienated by Japan's greed.

Nevertheless, China was obliged to sign two treaties: the first conceding the transfer to Japan of German interests in Shandong; the second giving Japan new privileges in southern Manchuria and the eastern part of inner Mongolia. These concessions amounted to four of the five groups of the original demands. Here was a turning point in America's relations with Japan. Japan never recovered the moral prestige that had been its main prize in 1905. In despair, Bryan sent identical notes to Beijing and Tokyo, declaring that the United States could not recognize any agreement "impairing the treaty rights of the United States and its citizens, the political or territorial integrity of the Republic of China, or the international policy relative to China commonly known as the open door." This fooled no one. The Open Door was a piece of rhetoric: however, it could not be maintained without force.

The Big Stick of Theodore Roosevelt

From September 1901 to March 1909 American foreign policy bore the decisive imprint of Theodore Roosevelt. Although TR had the reputation of being a most pugnacious president, his two terms in office were tranquil and he was widely regarded as a supreme diplomat who had negotiated the peaceful resolution of most dangerous disputes. At the same time he had elevated the United States to the position of a leading power in the world, without firing a shot. His aphorism, "Speak Softly and Carry a Big Stock," showed due respect for civilized priorities. It was the availability of power, rather than its use, that made for effective diplomacy. He claimed he was not really an imperialist. "I have as much desire to annex more islands as a boa-constrictor has to swallow a porcupine wrong end to." By his support for a permanent Court of International Justice, his attempt at compul-

sory arbitration between the New World and the Old, his voluminous correspondence with European kings and statesmen, and
his visit to the Panama Canal in November 1906—the first visit
abroad by an incumbent president—he set precedents of initiative
and mobility for the future.

When Wilhelm II of Germany tried to test the new Anglo-
French understanding or Entente Cordiale of April 8, 1904, by
suggesting an international conference on the subject of Morocco's future, Roosevelt could not resist the temptation to get involved. The crisis illustrates the tensions and ill feelings of the
European powers as they aligned themselves in rival blocs of Alliance and Entente. Roosevelt's instructions at the Algeciras Conference on January 16, 1906, to Henry White, his envoy, clearly
indicate that he considered Germany the real threat to peace. Thus
he ordered White to support Britain and France. France wanted
unrestricted control of most of the country, with Spain occupying a smaller zone. American support for France ensured that it
could establish a protectorate over Morocco a few years later.
The General Act of Algeciras was signed on April 7, 1906, and
subsequently ratified by the Senate, on December 12, 1906, where
it met with a barrage of criticism.

Roosevelt was convinced it was essential for the United States
to create a larger navy more appropriate to its newly acquired
territorial responsibilities. The War of 1898 had not only left the
United States with "echoes of glory" but also "a legacy of duty."
Thus he insisted on the building of at least two battleships a year.
Ten battleships and four armored cruisers were added to the fleet
by 1905. In 1907 he secured additional appropriations for building more battleships to compete with Japan. As he repeatedly
claimed, it was only by strength that the United States could
safeguard its interests. "The American people must either build
and maintain an adequate navy or else make up their minds definitely to accept a secondary position in international affairs, not
merely in political, but in commercial, matters. It has been well
said that there is no surer way of courting national disaster than
to be 'opulent, aggressive, and unarmed.' " Roosevelt capped his
achievements and despatched an American fleet of sixteen battleships and 12,000 men on a tour of the world, from December

16, 1907, to February 22, 1909, partly to demonstrate its augmented size and potential and partly to apprise Germany and Japan that America could fight to protect its overseas interests.

The Panama Canal

The sinking of the *Maine* in 1898 had brought to a head public support for an isthmian canal. While McKinley had wanted to mobilize American ships after the sinking of the *Maine* and concentrate a fleet in the Gulf of Mexico, it was not possible to do so immediately. One indispensable battleship, the *Oregon,* was on the wrong side of the continent in the Pacific Ocean off San Francisco. It took seventy-four days for the *Oregon* to make its way down the Pacific coast, around Cape Horn, and up the Atlantic. Journalist Mark Sullivan concludes, "That trip and the emotions it caused, had more to do with American determination to have a Panama Canal than any other cause." The projected canal of the new century would be as significant strategically as the first transcontinental railroad of 1869 had been commercially.

Thus the government began to clear the way for cutting an interoceanic canal. In March 1899 Congress created an Isthmian Canal Commission to inspect routes and draw up plans for construction. Britain was persuaded to abandon its rights to a canal under the Clayton-Bulwer Treaty of 1850 and accept the Hay-Pauncefote Treaty of November 18, 1901, transferring the projected canal to sole American control. The arrangement suited both parties. Britain wanted to withdraw much of its fleet to concentrate it in the North Atlantic against any threat from the rapidly expanding German navy of Kaiser Wilhelm II. Thus, by laying a cornerstone of Anglo-American friendship in the new century, did John Hay achieve his diplomatic memorial.

There were still many hurdles. A political map of the isthmus with its several small republics is rather like the neck of a giraffe with its special markings. Moreover, it was an unstable region. There had been fifty-seven revolutions there in as many years. Roosevelt was to play a decisive part in the next one. After some disagreement over the rival claims of Colombia and Nicaragua as to the optimum canal route, Congress finally chose Colombia in the Hay-Herrán Treaty of January 22, 1903. According to the treaty, the New Panama Canal Company was to sell its property to the United States and Colombia was to grant the United States sole right to cut, operate, and maintain the canal for a hundred years. In exchange for these rights, the United States would pay Colombia $10 million immediately and, from 1912, an annual rental of $250,000.

However, John Hay antagonized the Colombian Senate in the capital, Bogotá, which, from a mix of patriotism and greed, defeated the treaty on August 12, 1903. The most substantive complaint was that the down payment to Colombia was only a quarter of the amount paid to the Panama Canal Company. Roosevelt reacted to the Colombians' request for a higher fee with unbridled fury, calling them the "contemptible creatures in Bogotá" and "foolish and homicidal corruptionists." He was exasperated beyond endurance. At one time he even considered seizing the isthmus.

There was no need. A successful revolution in the province of Panama, organized by engineer Philippe Bunau Varilla, led to the secession of Panama from Colombia and, hence, American negotiations with a new republic. The success of the revolution of November 3, 1903, depended on the cooperation of American forces. Roosevelt had ordered an American ship, the *Nashville*, to the isthmus "to prevent landing of any force, either government or insurgent, at any point within fifty miles of Panama." Three days after the revolution, the United States recognized the new Republic of Panama. Roosevelt's action was so hasty as to invite accusations of collusion. Panama was more than willing to exploit its greatest asset, the canal route.

The new canal treaty with Panama of November 18, 1903, improved on the original terms with Colombia. It granted the United States permanent control of a strip of land five miles wide (instead of three) on each side of the proposed canal and of four minute islands in the Bay of Panama. Within this zone the United States could cut, operate, maintain, and defend a canal. The compensation to Panama was the same as that intended for Colombia: a down payment of $10 million, to be followed by an annual rental of $250,000, originally to begin in 1912 and, later, brought forward to 1908. Moreover, the United States had to guarantee and maintain the independence of the Republic of Panama. Thus Panama became an American protectorate.

Despite widespread suspicion about Roosevelt's part in the revolution, the call for party unity among Republicans was compelling, especially in an election year, and the treaty was ratified by the Senate on February 23, 1904, by sixty-six votes to fourteen. Thus, after much vexation, did Roosevelt acquire the opportunity to cut the canal, one of the most spectacular coups in his entire career. Nevertheless, Roosevelt's usurpation of the national rights of Colombia for the sake of American economic and strategic interests provoked howls of anguish about Yankee imperialism throughout Latin America. Secretary of War Elihu Root's comment on Roosevelt's self-justification before the Cabinet was that he had acted like a man accused of seduction but found guilty of rape.

The cutting of the Panama Canal was a great feat of enterprise that owed much to technical skill, medical knowledge, and individual heroism. In May 1904 Congress established a commission of seven men (five engineers, one naval officer, and one army officer) to organize the cutting of the canal. The forty-mile stretch of the Canal Zone was a damp, tropical jungle, intensely hot, swarming with mosquitoes and a natural home of typhus, dysentry, and yellow fever. Unless these diseases could be controlled, the Americans would never have a real chance of completing and maintaining the canal. Accordingly, Roosevelt was persuaded by a delegation representing the American Medical Association (AMA) and other medical groups to appoint an eighth, subordinate, commissioner in charge of sanitation. This was Colonel William Crawford Gorgas who had exterminated yellow fever in Havana.

Unfortunately, the rest of the commission took no notice of army surgeon Dr. Walter Reed's theory about the stegomyia mosquito transmitting yellow fever or Gorgas's proposed percautions, until the outbreak of an epidemic in November 1904. This led to the wholesale desertion of construction workers and ships' crews. Outraged, Roosevelt eventually dismissed the entire Isthmian Canal Commission. However, he retained Gorgas

The military possibilities of aircraft over land and sea were already being recognized before World War I. This photograph of January 18, 1911, shows the reconnaissance plane, *Ely*, having just taken off from the USS *Pennsylvania*. (Library of Congress).

in order that he could now employ the same progressive methods in Panama as he had in Havana. By September 1905 Gorgas had exterminated the disease.

In time both Roosevelt's administration and public opinion became discouraged by the slow progress of canal construction. It was continuously delayed by emergencies that a cumbersome commission of seven men, restricted by procedure, could not meet.

Thus Roosevelt decided to form a new commission of army and navy officers under the chairmanship of Lieutenant Colonel George W. Goethals and now formally including Gorgas. Gorgas tried to eliminate malaria, propagated by the anopheles mosquito. Gorgas had stagnant waters drained and vegetation cut within a 200-yard radius of human habitation. He encouraged people to keep lizards and spiders that preyed on mosquitoes. Month by month between 1906 and 1913 the proportion of canal workers suffering from malaria fell from 40 percent to 10 percent. However, malaria was not eliminated and Gorgas attributed this to the fact that Goethals, the new chairman, entrusted the sanitation work to laymen without specialist knowledge. Nevertheless, as a result of Gorgas's work, the death rate was only 6 per 1,000 per annum in the canal zone, compared with 14.1 per 1,000 per annum in the United States. More than any other single individual, it was Gorgas who had made possible the Panama Canal.

There remained the problem of reconciling, first, Panama and Colombia and, second, Colombia with the United States. Despite continuous efforts by a series of statesmen, the tool for this, the Treaty of Bogotá of April 6, 1914, was not ratified by the Senate until April 20, 1921. In the final version, the United States granted Colombia compensation of $25 million and certain rights in the Canal Zone, but refrained from any apology. In return, Colombia recognized Panama. There was also a dispute about tolls since President William Howard Taft proposed to give American ships passing through the canal a rebate, until diplomatic pressure from European nations persuaded both him and Congress otherwise. The Panama Canal was formally opened to commercial ships on August 15, 1914.

Latin America and the Caribbean

With the removal of Spain and the part withdrawal of Britain from the Caribbean, the United States soon announced its role of preserving stability in a region essential to its own security. The most pressing problem was intervention by European powers in Latin America.

When, first, Britain and Germany and, later, Italy mounted a blockade of Venezuela in 1902 to force the government to repay its debts, Roosevelt did nothing. After all, he had written to the German ambassador, Speck von Sternberg, on July 12, 1901, "If any South American state misbehaves toward any European country, let the European country spank it." When all parties to the dispute agreed to settle according to arbitration, the crisis dissolved without the United States having to take action. However, the Roosevelt corollary to the Monroe Doctrine of 1904 was shaped by the Venezuelan debts crisis.

Roosevelt recognized that American public opinion disliked the principle and practice of European powers sending troops to Latin American countries to collect debts. This resolve was strengthened by a ruling of the Hague Court on February 22, 1904, that European powers had the right to use force to collect bad debts. Roosevelt's preferred alternative was for the United States to collect and redistribute revenues from unstable Caribbean republics. Accordingly, in his message of December 6, 1904, he emphasized that the United States had no intention of acquiring new territory in the Western Hemisphere. However, it was interested in the stability and prosperity of neighbor states. Thus "chronic wrongdoing, or an impotence which results in a general loosing of the ties of civilized society, many in America, as elsewhere, ultimately require intervention by some civilized nation, and in the Western Hemisphere the adherence of the United States to the Monroe Doctrine may force the United States, however reluctantly, in flagrant cases of wrongdoing and impotence, to the exercise of an international police power."

In the light of his pronouncement, in 1905 Roosevelt undertook to settle controversies about the $40 million debts of the impoverished Dominican Republic. He established a special financial agency that deprived European holders of defaulted Dominican bonds of any excuse for action by their government in violation of the Monroe Doctrine and, moreover, declared $20 million of claims to be unjustifiable. The financial agency reorganized the Customs Service and this yielded enough revenue for the government to repay foreign debts and fulfill its domestic expenses.

In comparison with his impetuous chief, Secretary of State Elihu

Root (1905–09) acted on the assumption that his main duty was "to keep the country out of trouble." He was a skilled diplomat whose experience as secretary of war had taught him the problems of military organization and colonial administration. Unlike John Hay, he was on good terms with both the Senate and Latin American ministers whom he treated as equals.

Whereas Roosevelt had never been much interested in trade and investment and paid little attention to those who were, both President William Howard Taft and his secretary of state, Philander C. Knox (1909–13), identified American foreign policy more closely with the interests of the business community. Historian Richard W. Leopold characterizes Knox as a "lazy, testy, and supercilious" secretary, whose "brusqueness antagonized the sensitive Latins," and who "lacked the patience and attention to detail so essential in international relations." Whether the State Department encouraged American investment abroad to build up political power, or extended political power to safeguard the trade and investment it had encouraged, the upshot was that the politics, economics, and societies of other countries were disturbed. For example, in 1908 80 percent of Mexico's railroads and almost 50 percent of its total wealth were owned by American citizens. In times of crisis they would seek the protection of their investment by their government.

Philander C. Knox wanted to extend Roosevelt's policies for Latin American debts by creating special debt funds in the United States in order to give no excuse for European military intervention. Accordingly, in 1911 he negotiated the Knox-Castrillo Convention of June 6, 1911, with Nicaragua, by which Nicaragua agreed to refund its debts. However, the Senate refused to ratify either treaty. In the meantime, the administration had encouraged New York bankers to make a loan to the government in Nicaragua in expectation of Senate approval. Thus, after the Nicaraguan government of Adolfo Diaz fell to revolution on July 29, 1912, the administration ordered 2,400 sailors and marines to occupy the country on September 19 to save the bankers from loss. Taft's critics accused him of indulging in "dollar diplomacy." Investment abroad, they said, was exploitation of backward nations and protected by armed might.

Woodrow Wilson was far more committed than any previous American statesman to intervention abroad in pursuit of moral principles. In a speech on Latin American relations at Mobile, Alabama, of October 27, 1913, he declared that it was the duty of the United States to demonstrate that its professions of friendship were true and based on the ethics and principles of friendship and honor:

We must show ourselves friends by comprehending their interest whether it squares with our own interest or not. It is a very perilous thing to determine the foreign policy of a nation in terms of material interest. It is not only unfair to those with whom you are dealing, but it is degrading as regards your own actions. . . . We dare not turn from the principle that morality and not expediency is the thing that must guide us and that we will never condone iniquity because it is most convenient to do so.

However, in practice, the foreign policy of Woodrow Wilson and his first secretary of state, William Jennings Bryan, differed very little from that of Roosevelt and Taft. When it came to the tropics, Bryan played orange to Wilson's lemon. Wilson might try and justify his intervention in the Caribbean or Latin America according to moral principles but the consequence was much the same as before—an extension of America's economic and political power. When Latins were told by Americans to accept United States involvement in their countries, because "You know it makes sense," they were supposed to reply, "But dollars for you."

Until the world war, the greatest controversy about Wilson's foreign policy was his refusal to recognize governments he regarded as morally tainted. Thus Wilson condemned revolutions in Cuba, Equador, Haiti, and the Dominican Republic, as well as Russia by withholding recognition on the grounds of unconstitutionality. "I am going to teach the South American republics to elect good men," he boasted. Congress gave tacit approval to his policy. But Wilson's morality fell victim to reality in the aftermath of the Mexican revolution.

On May 25, 1911, a Mexican revolution led by Francisco Madero toppled the corrupt dictatorship of Porfiro Diaz but fueled a cauldron of political instability and terrorist violence. A second revolution of February 18, 1913, led to the overthrow and murder of Madero, his brother Gustavo, and the vice-president, Piño Suarez, and established Victoriano Huerta as president. Huerta sought American recognition. Wilson was not ready to recognize Huerta's government because he thought recognition would be interpreted as approval of the violence by which Huerta had come to power. Thus, in a State Department announcement of November 24, 1915, Wilson withheld recognition. This was a clear breach of America's regular policy since the United States had, in the past, always recognized established governments *de facto*. Wilson hoped that his new policy would undermine Huerta and persuade him to hold free elections and thereby establish a constitutional government. At best, Wilson scored a limited success. His opposition to Huerta did, indeed, render the position of the new president untenable and led to the establishment of a third new government under Venustiano Carranza. However, this was after a further complicating incident.

Wilson chose a petty incident, the mistaken arrest of eight American sailors from the *Dolphin* at Tampico on April 9, 1914, to justify American intervention in Mexico. Their commanding officer, Rear Admiral Henry T. Mayo, insisted on the sailors' release, and a full apology and a formal salute to the American flag from Mexico. Huerta refused and Wilson, with the support of Congress, ordered a blockade of the Mexican coast on April 20, 1914. In addition, American sailors and marines, acting on Wilson's orders, captured the port of Vera Cruz with a loss of four dead and twenty wounded, while the Mexican casualties were in hundreds. Wilson's final decision to use 6,700 troops to capture Vera Cruz came when he learned from Mayo that a German ship with war supplies, which could be used by Mexico against the United States, was about to enter the harbor. A nasty incident was defused by an offer of mediation from the ABC powers (Argentina, Brazil, and Chile). The crisis was then resolved at a conference at Niagara Falls, meeting from May 20. Besieged by the constitutionalists, Huerta abdicated on July 15 and, on August 20, Carranza entered Mexico City in triumph.

Even the new Carranza government in Mexico incurred Wilson's displeasure. Carranza was challenged by one of his former

With his sights perhaps already set on the presidency, Franklin Delano Roosevelt served Woodrow Wilson as assistant secretary of the navy—the same cabinet position that his distant cousin, TR, had first held and, like cousin Ted, he was, from the first, generally regarded as a "big navy man." (1913; Library of Congress).

generals Francisco ("Pancho") Villa, who began a civil insurrection against him on September 23, 1914. Between January and April 1915 another commander, Alvaro Obregón, led the Carranzistas to victory against Villa who was driven ever northward with his army. Wilson was advised to recognize Carranza, which he did on October 19, 1915, and the next day he imposed an embargo on the export of arms that would discriminate against

Villa. Villa retaliated by trying to divide Wilson and Carranza.
On March 9, 1916, Villa led a band of 1,500 Mexican revolution-
aries across the border and into New Mexico where they attacked the town of Columbus and an adjacent camp of the Thir-
teenth U.S. Cavalry, killing nine civilians and eight soldiers. The
cavalry pursued the bandits fifteen miles into Mexico and killed
120 of them.

The outrage was a climax to years of disorder along the border. Wilson reported to the Senate how, over the previous three
years, seventy-six Americans had been killed in Mexico and another thirty-six had been killed by Mexicans on American soil.
Wilson hoped that Carranza would be able to subdue these vicious bandit gangs but he was unable to. In response to deep
public outrage, Wilson agreed to a punitive expedition of 6,000
under the command of Brigadier General John J. Pershing. Its
task was to invade Mexico on March 15, 1916, and try and capture Pancho Villa and bring him back to stand trial in the United
States. This was apparently with the prior agreement of Carranza.

However, Pershing's force was quite inadequate for such a
guerrilla campaign. Villa simply divided his forces into small
groups and they hid in the wooded ravines away from Pershing's
slow moving army. Carranza now complained about the abuse
of Mexico's sovereignty and, on June 16, his general in the north,
Jacinto Trevino, ordered Pershing to advance no farther. On June
21 Mexican and American troops clashed near Carrizal and twelve
Americans were killed and twenty-three captured. On June 28
Carranza, now in a conciliatory move, had them released and
assured Wilson he would do everything he could to prevent future raids on American soil. Pershing withdrew his forces. Now
faced with the imminent prospect of intervention in World War
I, Wilson decided to cut his losses with Mexico. Acting on the
advice of Secretary of State Robert Lansing (1915–20), he formally recognized the Carranza government on March 13, 1917.

Despite its problems with Mexico, the supremacy of the United
States in the Western Hemisphere was total and assured. American forces intervened in trouble spots in defense of American

property and lives. The usual reason given was to maintain law and order.

Cuba became the first American protectorate. By a treaty of May 22, 1903, the United States obtained the right to intervention to preserve Cuban independence and governmental stability. The agreement was put to the test on September 28, 1906, when President Tomas Estrada Palma resigned in the face of rebellion and the Cuban Congress could not decide on a successor. The island was soon plunged into chaos. Theodore Roosevelt dispatched his secretary of war, William Howard Taft, to Havana and subsequently carried out his advice to assume temporary control. The second American military occupation of Cuba ended on January 28, 1909, with the inauguration of President José Miguel Gomez, and by March 31 all American troops had withdrawn. In May 1912 another uprising in Cuba threatened the Gomez administration. In the summer of 1914 President William Howard Taft, greatly concerned about the safety of American property, sent eight battleships and 2,000 marines to occupy the ports of Guantanamo, Cuero, and Nipe Bay. The rebellion collapsed with the sudden death of the leader and in August American forces withdrew.

On July 27, 1915, a revolution in Haiti, led by Dr. Rosalvo Bobo, succeeded in overthrowing President Vilbrun Guillaume Sam who was hounded from his refuge in the French Legation, where he was tortured, killed, and mutilated on July 28, 1915. From the harbor of Port-au-Prince Rear Admiral William B. Caperton of the *U.S. Washington* sent a force to restore order. On September 16 he signed a treaty with the new president, Sudre Dartiguenave, providing for American supervision of the island's finances. By withholding funds for public services, Caperton obliged the Haitian Senate to ratify the treaty. American occupation of Haiti continued until August 1934 and American military staff supervised construction of roads and sanitation programs but remained unpopular.

In addition to widespread use of force to protect its interests, the United States continued to acquire extra territories and rights. On February 18, 1916, the Senate ratified a treaty with Nicaragua by which the United States, for $3 million, acquired two naval bases and the right to build a canal across Nicaragua. On August 4, 1916, Secretary of State Robert Lansing and the Danish minister, Constantin Brun, signed a treaty for the purchase of the Danish West Indies by the United States for $25 million. On September 7 it was ratified by the Senate and the United States took possession on March 31, 1917.

From a mixture of commercial and disinterested motives, the United States actively sought to promote greater cooperation both among Latin republics and between them and America. Roosevelt's second secretary of state, Elihu Root, made a goodwill tour of seven Latin American countries in 1906 and Taft's secretary, Knox, visited ten Caribbean islands in 1912. Their aim of emphasizing American goodwill was complemented by a series of conferences. International conferences of American states were held in Mexico City (1901–2), Rio de Janeiro (1906), Buenos Aires (1910), and another was planned for Santiago, Chile, (1914) but postponed on account of World War I. Moreover, Root persuaded eighteen Latin American countries to participate in the Hague conference of 1907. In 1914 Wilson and his adviser, Colonel Edward House of Texas, went further and devised a Pan American Pact, based on four points about territorial integrity, boundary disputes, arbitration, and an arms embargo. This, too, foundered on the adversary seas of the world war.

Arbitration Proceedings

Although the years up to World War I were remarkable for the creation of peace societies and studies of the causes of the war, little real progress was made to preserve peace. In the first ten years of the century American public opinion clung, unrealistically, to the very noncommittal attitude of which Roosevelt and his successors complained. Despite the ephemeral enthusiasm for the Open Door, the Panama Canal, and the Treaty of Portsmouth, public opinion was indifferent to what was happening outside the United States. With the passing of time, this indifference increased rather than lessened.

This indifference showed itself in renewed opposition to a big navy. Roosevelt had succeeded in transforming the navy into an effective fighting force in the face of continuous opposition. Taft had to fight the same battle in Congress that reflected public insistence that the United States should take the lead in reducing armaments. The upshot was a compromise whereby the program of building two battle ships a year was continued at a cost of maintaining other units in the fleet.

Many thought that great wars, like those of the French Revolution and Napoleonic periods, were a thing of the past. It was almost a century since the whole of Europe had been enveloped in such wars and some thought it would be too expensive and destructive to wage modern warfare. At worst, wars would be brief. Moreover, Americans counted on insulation from war by the isolation of the Western Hemisphere by the Atlantic and Pacific Oceans. They did not consider the economic interdependence of the great powers.

McKinley, Roosevelt, Taft, and Wilson all tried to persuade the Senate of the need for treaties creating diplomatic machinery for the peaceful resolution of disputes. Here was an embryonic idea of a concert of nations and an early form of collective security. Both were anathema to the Senate. However, while the United States showed new willingness to take part in international diplomacy, it steadily refused to make any binding commitments that might reduce its freedom of action. The First Hague Conference of 1899 was the idea of Czar Nicholas II of Russia, who was more anxious to ease Russia's difficulties than he was to minimize the risk of war by reducing armaments. Nevertheless, twenty-six countries in all, sent delegations. McKinley sent a distinguished delegation, including veteran diplomat Andrew D. White and naval historian Alfred Mahan, but they were instructed by Hay to avoid commitments on armies and navies. Instead, they were to promote a plan for an international court, to which would be submitted all disputes that conventional diplomacy could not resolve. The conference yielded no tangible results and all but one of the various declarations of July 29, 1899, concentrated on humanizing, rather than eliminating war. The exception was the Convention for the Pacific Settlement of International Disputes that created a Permanent Court of Arbitration, a system of nominated jurists whose services could be called upon. The Second Hague Conference of June 15, 1907, was attended by forty-four nations and, before it adjourned on October 18, had adopted twenty-one understandings in all. Mr. Dooley described them as decisions about "how future wars shud be conducted in th' best inthrests iv peace."

What he could not achieve with multilateral treaties, Roosevelt tried to do with bilateral arrangements. Roosevelt had Hay sign eleven bilateral conventions with five major powers between November 1, 1904, and February 11, 1905, by which they agreed to submit disputes to arbitration. However, the Senate substituted the word "treaty" for "special agreement" in each document, thereby ensuring its own rights to approve or veto any ruling by arbitration. In Roosevelt's opinion, this undermined the whole point of arbitration. By 1908 both Roosevelt and the Senate were ready to compromise and the Senate approved all but three of twenty-four bilateral treaties, signed by Root between February 10, 1908, and January 23, 1909, by which all disputes, except those involving the vital interests, independence, and honor of the signatories, would go to arbitration.

When Secretary of State Knox tried to extend the scope of arbitration by treaties with Britain and France on August 3, 1911, removing the categories of exemptions and creating a joint commission of inquiry, he had to negotiate a series of reservations with the Senate before they were approved on March 7, 1912. Like Roosevelt in 1905, Taft refused to accept the reservations because he thought they were no advance on the Root conventions of 1908–9.

Wilson continued the policies. Between August 7, 1913, and October 13, 1914, Bryan concluded thirty bilateral Treaties for the Advancement of Peace by which signatories agreed to refer disputes to a permanent commission that would have a year to investigate the facts, during which neither side would begin hostilities. This was the original "cooling off period." While many first and second rank powers signed, Germany, Japan, Columbia, and Mexico did not. Because of the great prestige of the first Wilson administration, Bryan succeeded in persuading the Senate to ratify twenty of these treaties. However, only ten commissions were actually established and none ever investigated a dispute.

Among those who deluded themselves into thinking that a simple international and social mechanism could solve the problem of war and peace was the usually hardheaded Andrew Carnegie. Carnegie reserved his grandest and most grandiose scheme for the cause of universal peace. When it went awry, the result broke his heart. For years he had served as president of the Peace Society of New York and eagerly responded to a suggestion by Andrew D. White that he endow a Temple of Peace at The Hague where nations could take their disputes. Moreover, in 1910 he created a board of carefully selected trustees, including President William Howard Taft and Elihu Root, who served as secretary, to form the Carnegie Endowment for International Peace and to which he gave $10 million to be used "for the abolition of international war, the foulest blot upon our civilization." When war broke out in summer 1914, Carnegie broke off work on his autobiography with the words "The world convulsed by war as never before. Men slaying each other like wild beasts."

CHAPTER TWELVE

It's a Long Way to Tipperary: America and World War I

·ჯ·

THE ASSASSINATION of Franz Ferdinand, heir to the Austro-Hungarian throne, by a Serbian nationalist in Sarajevo, the capital of Bosnia, on Sunday, June 28, 1914, led to a great war because the incident and its sequels touched upon the most sensitive nerve ends of the great powers. On July 7 Austria-Hungary decided on war and delivered a stern ultimatum to Serbia on July 23 but was rather surprised to receive a somewhat conciliatory reply on July 27. Nevertheless, Austria-Hungary declared war on Serbia on July 28. Russia mobilized its troops to defend its little ally, Serbia, (July 30) and thereby incurred the hostility of Germany, anxious to support Austria-Hungary, by declaring war, first on Russia (August 1) and then on France (August 3). Disturbed by Germany's silence about the neutrality of Belgium, Britain declared war on Germany (August 4). Turkey, convinced Germany would win, signed an alliance with Germany against Russia on August 2, 1914. This quite unnecessary intervention was to bring down the Ottoman Empire, just as Austria-Hungary's petulant decision to pose as a great power

Soissons, France, devastated by German bombardment. (From the *Chicago Daily News* of January 14, 1915).

by declaring war had produced a crisis fateful for the world and mortal to itself.

Technically speaking, the war was not really caused by the dangerous system of antagonistic alliances since none of the countries acted within the letter of their agreements. Germany, pivot of the Triple Alliance, was pledged to go to war if Russia attacked Austria-Hungary but actually declared war before this happened. France, pivot of the Triple Entente, was pledged to attack Germany if Germany went to war against Russia. Instead, it went to war rather than yield to a German demand for unconditional neutrality. Fundamentally, the war was caused by disruption to the balance of power, following Russia's defeat by Japan. Both France and Russia chafed at Germany's determination to dominate Europe, something it could have better achieved by years of peace rather than years of war. Yet this option was foreclosed by the aggressive habits of German diplomacy in the various international crises to 1914, and the aggressive outlook of the people as cultivated by the rulers, especially Kaiser Wilhelm II and his chancellor, Theobold Bethmann-Hollweg. Ironically, the leading participants needed one another even more in peace. Germany was Russia's leading trading partner. Britain was Germany's chief market. Yet, oblivious of economic need, militarists on both sides perfected plans to damage their political enemy and thereby destroy the very economies that actually sustained their own peoples.

The war produced an initial surge of patriotic enthusiasm in the various countries. For contemporaries in Europe, it was the Great War of 1914–18; in American propaganda of 1917, the Great Crusade. The phrase First World War was coined by military correspondent C. à C. Repington in November 1918 and soon afterward it became for Americans World War I. It was truly global, extending to twenty-seven countries in five continents, and bringing revolution to four great powers and widespread economic and social dislocation to most of the others. There now began an age of destruction and warfare, revolutions and dictatorships, that lasted for thirty-five years in Europe and subsequently spread to the other continents.

Military Stalemate and American Neutrality

At the beginning of World War I Americans tried to persuade themselves that they had little concern with the tragedy. On December 8, 1914, Wilson himself declared that it was "a war with which we have nothing to do, whose causes cannot touch us." Nevertheless, as historian Foster Rhea Dulles explains, "The United States was to find itself in a position where the policy it followed—whether of intervention or non intervention—was to have a decisive effect in determining both the outcome of war and the kind of world in which twentieth century man was to live."

At first Wilson resented the war and tried to forget about it. He regarded it as a relapse into barbarism, something shameful to the world and personally odious to him. One of his biographers, William E. Dodd, explains that "It was his dread of being diverted from his main business, his dread of becoming entangled in the meshes of European powers that lent so much earnestness to his repeated announcements of American neutrality." Wilson's complacency was also broken by a personal tragedy, the death of his wife, Ellen Axson Wilson, on August 6, 1914. When he most needed the self-effacing and steadying support of this tender woman, he faced a void.

Wilson's main proclamation of neutrality of August 19, 1914, told the American people "We must be impartial in thought as well as in action. The United States must be neutral in fact as well as in name." Thus Americans must on no account enlist in the army of a belligerent or any armed vessel to be used in the war. For their part, belligerent nations must respect America's neutrality and not allow their ships to make war in American waters or use American ports as part of their naval strategy. Furthermore, Wilson spoke to Congress on December 8, 1914, with his customary high-handed petulance against preparedness. To prepare for war "would mean merely that we had lost our self-possession, that we had been thrown off our balance by a war with which we have nothing to do, whose causes cannot touch us."

However, behind the scenes it was different. When Brand Whitlock, American minister to Belgium, told Wilson that "in my heart there is no such thing as neutrality, I am heart and soul for the Allies," Wilson agreed. "So am I," he said, "no decent man could be anything else." Joseph Tumulty, his campaign manager, recorded in his *Woodrow Wilson as I Knew Him* (1921), how the president had told him that he would never "take any action to embarrass England when she is fighting for her life and the life of the world. . . . England is fighting our fight." Nevertheless, Wilson knew that a policy of open partiality would divide Americans at home. Furthermore, he thought America had a moral duty to remain at peace so that it could exercise its full weight in the interests of peace and justice at the opportune moment.

History is rich in ironies and Wilson was to become enmeshed in the device of his own ideals. Hence, as journalist Mark Sullivan puts it:

Yet it came to be that the war was Wilson's greatest responsibility; and, later, that Wilson was, in the whole world, the figure about whom the war raged and the peace swirled. For some five years, 1914–1919, the history of the United States, as respects the Great War, was mainly the history of Woodrow Wilson's mind. For the last two years, 1917–1919, the history of the whole world was the history of Wilson's mind. And the results of Wilson's acts lay upon the world for more than a decade after the end of the war. For at least nine years after his death (in 1924) the world was racked by ideas that Wilson had introduced; steps that he had taken or attempted continued to be the concern of statesmen, the preoccupation of nations and of peoples.

The supreme irony was that the war in which Wilson would intervene as a test of his statesmanship would destroy him and his statecraft.

At the outset both sides expected a great naval battle between Britain and Germany in the Atlantic and a military battle between the continental Allies and Germany on land. People expected quick and decisive victories that would bring hostilities to a speedy conclusion. There was almost no recognition of the economic interdependence of the nations of the world and the part the disruption of war would play in their futures. Thus Sir Edward Grey, British foreign secretary, told the House of Commons on August 3, 1914, the day before Britain declared war, "If we are engaged in war, we shall suffer but little more than we shall suffer if we stand aside." All this began to change irrevocably in the last months of 1914.

The essence of German strategy in 1914 was, first, to make a swift attack on France before it had mobilized and, then, to concentrate huge forces on Russia. Since the Franco-German frontier was heavily fortified, Germany could only achieve a quick, decisive victory by marching its troops through Belgium, in violation of a treaty of 1839 guaranteeing its territorial integrity. It was the threat of this action, necessary from a purely military point of view, that had brought Britain into the war and the action itself that began the process of alienating the United States from Germany.

Before the war Americans thought highly of Germany. The basis of their appreciation was knowledge of the industrious, efficient, and friendly German-Americans, more sizable in numbers than any other ethnic group from the immigrants of the nineteenth century. Certain German words, such as "Prosit," "Gesundheit," and "Gemütlichkeit," were then part of the pattern of everyday speech. German music was played everywhere and many of the traditions around Christmas had come from Germany. It was from Germany, rather than Britain, that America took its standards of education, especially in higher education. Hitherto, German militarism had been a subject of ridicule. However, Americans looked on the German invasion of Belgium as a big dog pouncing on a little one and took the side of the underdog. Germany's callous scorn for the treaty of 1839 was summed up by a remark by the German chancellor, Bethmann-Hollweg, to the British ambassador in Berlin, Sir Edward Goschen, on August 4. Outraged at Britain's declaration of war, he declared, "Just for a scrap of paper Great Britain is going to make war on a kindred nation." His angry candor was to cost Germany dear since the crucial phrase, "scrap of paper," was to be turned into effective propaganda by the Allies.

Moreover, traditional American regard for Germany could not survive the battery of such news headlines provided by the New York *Tribune* as

GERMANS PREPARE TO HURL FULL FORCE ON
  CONFIDENT BELGIANS   (August 16, 1914)
GERMANS EXACT FIFTY MILLION DOLLARS FROM
  BRUSSELS AND LIEGE   (August 22)
GERMANS SACK LOUVAIN—WOMEN AND CLERGY SHOT
                    (August 29)

Mark Sullivan recalls "Louvain was the climax of Belgium, and Belgium the precipitant of American opinion." Edward S. Martin, editor of *Life,* agreed. In the issue of January 7, 1915, he observed, "For us the great, clear issue of this war is Belgium. If we see anything right at all in this matter, Belgium is a martyr to civilization, sister to all who love liberty or law; assailed, polluted, trampled in the mire, heel-marked in her breast, tattered, homeless." The German word for frightfulness, "Schrecklichkeit," was applied by their enemies to their means of making French and Belgian civilians truly docile, extermination by shell attacks on their cities. Thus, in its issue of June 10, 1915, *Life* carried this dialogue between two Southerners:

> "Dem Englishmen has got a gun dat'll kill you at five miles."
> "Huh! Dey ain't got nothin' on dem Jummans. W'y, man, wid deir guns, all dey ask to kill you is yo' address!"

The same humanitarian zeal that had characterized some American imperialists in Latin America was turned to constructive acts toward Belgium by Americans at home and abroad. In the hectic days at the beginning of the war millionaire engineer Herbert Hoover had helped arrange for the exodus of Americans from London. His initiative prompted Walter Hines Page, American ambassador in London, to persuade him to find ways of feeding Belgium, an industrial country that usually imported 80 percent of its food, and now finding its regular supplies exhausted, its supply routes cut off, and facing famine within days. Within three months, Hoover had organized a team of volunteers into a special Commission for Relief in Belgium with a fleet of thirty-five ships moving supplies of food valued at $5 million per month from the United States, Canada, and Argentina across the Atlantic and distributing it in Belgium.

For the first three years of the war there was to be military stalemate following the German invasion of northern France. When France won the battle of the Marne on September 6, 1914, it could not exploit its victory and expel Germany from its soil. In their retreat from the Marne the weary Germans stumbled on a tactical discovery that shaped the course of the war, that men in trenches with machine guns could resist all but the most overwhelming odds. They dug themselves in and so did the British and French. By November 1914 there was a line of trenches extending from Switzerland to the English Channel. Siege warfare replaced conventional battles. The *New York Times* published an account, taken from the *Times* of London of December 18, 1914, of how these protectve trenches, five feet deep and two feet wide,

. . . curl and twist about in a maddening manner to make them safer from shell-fire. Little caves are scooped in the walls of the trenches, where the men live about four to a hole, and slightly bigger dug-outs where two officers live. All the soil is clay, stickier and greasier than one could believe possible. It's like almost solid paint, and the least rain makes the sides of the trenches slimy, and the bottom a perfect sea of mud—pulls the heels off your boots almost. One feels like Gulliver walking along a Liliputian town all the time. The front line of trenches— the firing-line—have scientific loopholes and look-out places in them for seeing and firing from, and a dropping fire goes on from both sides all day long, but is very harmless. . . .

The first attempt at trench warefare was the first battle of Ypres of October 12–November 11, 1914, in which every day new forces replaced those at the front line until both sides were exhausted. When one side broke the other's line, new troops would fill the breach. Moreover, the toll in human life was astonishingly high. By the end of the year one man in every ten of the British Expeditionary Force had been killed and three-quarters of these died at Ypres. Of the others, half were wounded.

This was far from the British fantasy of war, their first eleven playing cricket against the Germans' first eleven. Accordingly, in July 1915 Kitchener (secretary of war) and Haig (commander in chief) tried to break the German line in a tremendous joint assault with the French at the Somme. This was intended as a knockout blow. The Germans replied with their machine guns and the prolonged slaughter lasted until November by which time Britain had lost 420,000 men, France 194,000, and Germany 465,000. Although the term body count was not known in 1915, here was the first time that governments used the tactic of measuring military success by counting human corpses in terms more appropriate to real estate.

The hopelessness of the situation by which millions of young men would be led to slaughter in the trenches for no tangible gain horrified Americans and Europeans. Edwin Dwight's verse, *Victory,* published in *Life* magazine on April 8, 1915, parodied the cycle of advance and retreat:

> Five hundred miles of Germans,
> Five hundred miles of French,
> And English, Scotch and Irish men
> All fighting for a trench;
>
> And when the trench is taken
> And many thousands slain,
> The losers, with more slaughter,
> Retake the trench again.

Nor did the war go well for the Allies on the eastern front where things were more mobile. On October 28, 1914, two German cruisers entered the Black Sea and bombarded Odessa, effectively closing the Straits. Thus Russia could not nourish its armies without extra supplies from western Europe. By December 18 Russia's supplies of munitions were exhausted. It was now on the defensive and simply hoped that it could prevent invasion while Britain and France won the war on the western front.

Not surprisingly, Americans consoled themselves with the conviction that they were well out of Europe. The Chicago *Herald* remarked more directly, "Peace-loving citizens of this country will now rise up and tender a hearty vote of thanks to Columbus for having discovered America." "This European war," opined the *Buffalo Courier,* "suggests that maybe the white man's burden is the white man himself."

Dismayed by their adverse fortunes, Britain, France, and Russia had now committed themselves to the outright destruction of Germany as a great power. They soon realized they would require some material aid from the United States and to do this they needed effective propaganda. Thus fifty-three British authors, acting as "press agents," pitted their wits against twenty-two heads of German universities, while forty-five British artists and critics were arrayed against ninety-six German professors. In

A French prisoner of war exhibited in Berlin. (From the *Chicago Daily News* of January 14, 1915).

the war of words Britain enjoyed singular advantages. Britain had cut the only German cable to the United States, thus reducing German contact to the still imperfect new invention of wireless and the slow and haphazard mail that Britain could (and did) intercept. Moreover, Allied propaganda was more adroit than German propaganda. Accordingly, the news America received about the war was colored by its route from London and Paris or outright censorship. Most significant of all, the English language united American and British culture through a complex web of sentiment, literature, and institutions and it was this common denominator that eclipsed all things German. Not only Shakespeare and Wordsworth but also the war poets Wilfred Owen and Rupert Brooke became part of the heritage of all English-speaking nations.

Stories of atrocities were used to send a thrill of horror through America. Allied propaganda alleged that Germans had mutilated Belgian nuns and babies, and had crucified Canadian soldiers by sticking bayonets through their hands and feet. A more gross story took advantage of the fact that Germans made use of dead horses and that in German the word "Kadaver" is used for the bodies of dead animals. It was said that the German quest for efficiency was so grotesque that they scavenged battlefields for corpses, then bundled them into bales and had them shipped back to Germany to be treated chemically and made into lubricating oil, fertilizer, and soap. In World War II such atrocities were to become reality, though they suspended all belief. In World War I they were still gruesome fiction. Press censorship actually encouraged a proliferation of sensational stories since any story about the war was good copy. Indeed, the press reached its zenith of influence during the war. Newspapers were the only source of news and their circulation rose with every calamity. In time, the German ambassador in Washington advised the German chancellor in Berlin that German propaganda might just as well be abandoned for all the good it was doing.

One cartoon in *Life* hinted that a major reason for America not intervening directly was the immense profits it accrued through neutrality and by manufacturing supplies for the Allies. Indeed, the Allies bought vast quantities of munitions. Britain controlled the sea and its ships and those of its Allies could move across the Atlantic unhindered until German submarines took action. Germany was also entitled to buy munitions but, unlike Britain, it could not take them home. German merchant shipping was almost completely paralyzed while British shipping carried on imperturbably, confident of Britain's naval and commercial dominance at sea.

The Tide Turns Against Germany

Strictly speaking, there was no such thing as "international law" and the "law of the sea" was no more than the code of practice of the dominant naval power, currently Britain. As a belligerent, Britain was not interested in protecting neutral rights and began to violate them. It declared contraband thirty-two raw materials that could be used by Germany, including copper, rubber, gasoline, cotton, and, also, food. It seized ship after ship carrying them from the United States to other neutral countries. Moreover, Britain drew up a blacklist of some eighty American companies whom it suspected of trading with Germany, which they were perfectly entitled to do. Next, it prevented these companies from trading with neutral countries. American exporters who wanted to do business with European neutrals had to beg permission of the British Embassy in Washington. Before permission was granted, they had to submit a list of their foreign customers that was sent to London and made available to their British competitors. Secretary of the Interior Franklin K. Lane remarked on May 29, 1915, "England is playing a . . . high game, violating international law every day." Britain's arguments rested on the quicksand nature of international laws on contraband and blockade and the precedent set by the United States during the Civil War. Moreover, Britain paid for cargoes seized on their way to Germany, thus reducing the commercial arguments against its quasi-legal or illegal actions.

Wilson made a series of protests to Britain that were effectively parried by the British government and the American ambassador in London, Walter Hines Page, who believed absolutely in the Allied cause. The most singular example of his acting in the interests of Britain came when Britain notified America that it would seize the *Dacia,* on the grounds that here was a German vessel interned in America whose transfer to American ownership could not be recognized by Britain. The incident was widely regarded as a test of American nerve. Page cunningly defused the situation by persuading British Foreign Secretary Sir Edward Grey to have the French seize the ship instead. While the claims and counterclaims of Britain and Germany confused Americans, there remained a fundamental distinction between their naval tactics. Britain seized ships; Germany sank them and their American passengers.

Disputes between America and Germany arose when Germany declared on February 16, 1915, that the very nature of its submarines made it impossible to disembark passengers and crew before sinking enemy ships or to seize neutral vessels carrying contraband and take them to port. Furthermore, Germany had declared twelve days earlier that all waters surrounding the British Isles were now a war zone in which enemy and neutral ships alike might be sunk. Wilson now warned Germany that the United States would hold it to "a strict accountability" if its submarines destroyed American ships and American lives. On May 10, 1915, he went further, declaring that America was a nation "too proud to fight" and so sure of its course that "it does not need to convince others by force that it is right." Nevertheless, it would consider the use of force if others disregarded its neutral rights.

The sinking of the *Lusitania* off the Irish coast by the submarine *Unterseeboot 20* on May 7, 1915, with the loss of 128 American lives among 1,198 people who were drowned, put Wilson's policy of neutrality to its first major test. The United States required Germany to repudiate the submarine attack that it considered to be in clear violation of the code of modern warfare. Germany curtly refused on the grounds that the *Lusitania* had been carrying contraband cargo. Wilson despatched a second note that was so stern that William Jennings Bryan resigned as secretary of state in protest. He did not think American citizens could travel on ships carrying contraband in the Atlantic and expect to remain immune from the war. Sooner or later Wilson's insistence on America's rights would lead the United States into war. Bryan's preferred solution was to renounce responsibility for Americans who risked their lives by traveling on belligerent ships. He said, "Germany has a right to prevent contraband from going to the Allies, and a ship carrying contraband should not rely upon passengers to prevent her from attack—it would be like putting women and children in front of an enemy."

Public opinion sided with Wilson, rather than Bryan. If anything, Wilson was criticized after the *Lusitania* affair for being too lenient toward Germany. Not since the sinking of the *Maine* in 1898 had an event so stirred the country with a mix of horror and rage and public anger was exacerbated by the bombastic response of the German-American press. Dr. Bernhard Dernburg, head of the German Red Cross in America, declared with pompous insensitivity, "The death of the Americans might have been avoided if our warning had been heeded; we put in advertisements and were careful to put them next to the announcements of the Cunard Line's sailing dates; anybody can commit suicide if he wants to." As the *Nation* of May 13, 1915, put it, by the sinking of the *Lusitania,* Germany "has affronted the moral sense of the world and sacrificed her standing among the nations."

At one point Herbert Hoover went to Berlin to protest the submarines' sinking of ships of the Belgian Relief Commission. When he was assured by a German naval official that it would not happen again, Hoover, who was not convinced, replied with a parable. "There was a man once who was annoyed by a snarling dog. He went to see the owner and asked him to muzzle the dog. 'There is no need of that,' said the owner, 'the dog will never bite you.' 'Maybe,' said the first man. 'You know the dog will not bite me. I know the dog will not bite me. But does the dog know?' "

Submarine warfare continued to take its terrible toll. On March 24, 1916, a French ship, the *Sussex,* was sunk in the English Channel and several Americans were seriously injured. This time the American protest of April 18, 1916, amounted to an ultimatum. Unless Germany discontinued submarine warfare against ships carrying passengers and freight, the United States would break off diplomatic relations. On May 4, 1916, Germany undertook not to sink merchant ships without warning and without saving human lives. This is sometimes known as the *Sussex* pledge. However, in return, Germany expected the United States to insist that Britain fulfill America's other standards of international law affecting neutral rights. Otherwise, Germany reserved "complete liberty of decision." The State Department flatly refused to accept the condition about British policy toward neutrals. Nevertheless, for nine months, from May 4, 1916, until

January 31, 1917, Germany sank no ships in violation of the American code. Thus it seemed Wilson had scored a considerable diplomatic victory in the most trying circumstances possible.

Throughout the first three years of the war, there was no coordinated military or naval strategy by the Entente powers. Indeed, their mutual competitiveness over possible colonies aroused deep mutual suspicions. In March and April 1915 the Entente powers, in a series of secret notes, agreed that Russia should take Constantinople and the Straits. In return, Britain would take part of Persia (Iran) and France would acquire Syria, Cilicia, and Palestine. The bargain was less cynical than it was made to seem by the Bolsheviks when they published the correspondence in 1918. There were strong (but not permanent) strategic and military arguments for the division. In 1916 the Allies went further and agreed to partitions of Syria (to France), Mesopotamia (to Britain), and Armenia and Kurdistan (to Russia). By the notorious and secret treaty of London of April 26, 1915, Italy agreed to make war against Austria-Hungary, in exchange for the promise of land in the Tyrol and Dalmatia—acquisitions it had earlier been refused by Germany. What the Allies really wanted, of course, was American intervention.

Various factors combined to draw the United States closer to war on the side of Britain and France. For one thing, American trade with Germany and Austria had dwindled whereas the United States was providing the Allies with vital economic aid, food, and munitions. Between 1914 and 1916 the total value of exports to the Allies rose from $824.86 million to $3.21 billion. The sale of American munitions alone to the Allies increased in value from $40 million in 1914 to $1.29 billion in 1916. This substantive increase in foreign trade rescued America from an economic depression. Within a year the fabric of commercial life was so interwoven with the economy of the Allies that any disruption would have seriously damaged American business.

However, the Allies could not continue to pay indefinitely without some system of credits or loans. On October 15, 1915, Britain and France secured a loan of $500 million from a consortium of American bankers led by the House of Morgan. This was only half the sum they really wanted. At the urging of Secretary of State Robert Lansing and Secretary of the Treasury William Gibbs McAdoo, Wilson tacitly approved the loan, despite the State Department's original advice of 1914 that credits were "inconsistent with the spirit of neutrality." By the time the United States had entered the war it had loaned $2 billion to the Allies, as compared with only $27 million to the Central powers. Thus America now had a clear financial stake in an Allied victory.

However, commercial support was a different proposition from armed intervention. Despite the *Lusitania,* progressive journalist Walter Lippmann told a British socialist, Alfred Zimmern, in a letter of June 7, 1915, "The feeling against war in this country is a great deal deeper than you would imagine by reading editorials." This was partly on account of repugnance to war, partly because of a fear that American nationalism would be strained by fighting a country to which German-Americans were attached, and partly because of "general international irresponsibility and shallowness of feeling." In 1915 only Americans on the Atlantic seaboard would have supported outright intervention in the war. In the West and Midwest news of the *Lusitania* caused a temporary sensation but did not move public opinion. Among the educational and political establishment, led by President Emeritus Charles W. Eliot of Harvard, Vice-President Thomas R. Marshall, and former president, Theodore Roosevelt, opinion was firmly in favor of the Allies.

The war stirred rather different loyalties among the Irish, Italian, Polish, Russian, Hungarian, and German ethnic groups, who began to take sides in foreign language newspapers. The New York *Sun* satirized the competing voices thus:

> The barber to the right of me was
>   hoching for the Kaiser.
> The barber to the left of me was
>   hacking for the Czar.
> A gentleman from Greece was shearing
>   off my fleece,
> While very near a swarth Italian
>   stropped his scimitar.
> And when presently discussion, polyglot
>   and fervid,

> On political conditions burst about
>   my chair,
> I left the place unshaven—I
>   hope I'm not a craven,
> But I sort of like to wear a head beneath
>   my hair!

The claims and counterclaims gave rise to the term "hyphenated Americans." This led, in turn, to doubts among "average Americans" as to whether they existed at all. Was the United States really a nation or just an international rooming house? Thus nativists found yet another argument for the restriction of immigration and used Theodore Roosevelt's phrase "hundred percent American" to describe the ideal citizen.

In Congress opponents of intervention found common cause in the Gore-McLemore Resolution of February 22, 1916, following Bryan's advice and warning American citizens they must not travel on the vessels of belligerent nations. In practice, this would have meant on mainly British vessels since there were no German merchant ships on the seas. The speaker, Champ Clark, warned Wilson that the motion would pass by a majority of two to one. This was the last thing Wilson wanted and he wrote an open letter to Senator William Stone of Missouri, chairman of the Senate Committee on Foreign Relations, against it. As a result, the House decided to "table" the resolution, consigning it to political oblivion, by 275 votes to 135.

Pacifists argued for American mediation between the belligerents. Their leading spokesman was William Jennings Bryan. In November 1915 Hungarian pacifist Rosika Schwimmer persuaded car manufacturer Henry Ford to try and mediate in the war. Ford's prestige was such that it seemed he could accomplish anything he chose. On December 4, 1915, they sailed as delegates to neutral capitals of Europe, traveling on a so-called "peace ship," the *Oscar II,* and they tried to enlist the support of congressmen, state governors, and other public figures including Bryan, Jane Addams of Hull House, and Margaret Wilson, the president's daughter, all of whom declined. Instead, a miscellaneous collection of gatecrashers turned the peace ship into a carnival of parasites, cranks, and clowns. It achieved nothing.

Preparedness and the Election of 1916

Wilson and his supporters began to promote preparedness and campaign for a better army and navy. In 1914 there were only 92,710 men authorized for the regular army and nearly half of them were abroad. Of the remaining 53,022 nearly half were used to man the coast and the other 24,602 were the only truly mobile army, a smaller number than at any time since the American Civil War. The organized militia, usually called the national guard, comprised another 27,410 men. This inadequacy was exposed by Frederick Louis Huidekoper in *The Military Unpreparedness of the United States* (1915). In the army the leading advocate of preparedness was General Leonard Wood who campaigned tirelessly for greater appropriations and created summer camps to train young men for five weeks at a time.

In December 1915 Wilson advised Congress to raise the standing army to 141,843 with a reserve of 400,000 volunteers to be trained for two months a year for three years. The National Defense Act thus increased the regular army, and integrated the national guard into the National Defense system and created an officers' reserve corps. The Naval Appropriation Act authorized the construction of new cruisers and battleships. The United States Shipping Board appropriated $50 million to buy and construct merchant ships. Moreover, Congress established a Council for National Defense to coordinate industry and resources. However, in touring the country during the election campaign to rouse public support for his policy, Wilson maintained, as at Cleveland on January 29, 1916, "You may count upon my heart and resolution to keep you out of the war." Theodore Roosevelt characterized the opponents of the arms trade and a big navy as a "flapdoodle pacifist and mollycoddle outfit." Roosevelt was outraged by the way Wilson kept shifting his ground on the subject of preparedness, and, it must be admitted, by the way Wilson was appropriating his own politics. However, Wilson knew that public opinion cared more about feeling than argument and his well-paced, dexterous speeches made precisely the impression that he intended. If he wanted to be reelected in 1916 he had to speak for preparedness but against intervention.

Wilson's renomination at the Democratic National Convention in St. Louis was a foregone conclusion. However, the campaign slogan, "He kept us out of war," was forced upon him and his allies by Joseph Tumulty and the convention chairman, Governor Martin Glynn of New York. Nevertheless, it became the most potent slogan of the entire campaign and was decisive in Wilson's eventual victory. While he and his aides emphasized the past tense, there was no doubt the slogan was widely interpreted as a pledge, almost a contract: elect me and you will be kept out of war.

At their convention in Chicago the Republicans nominated Charles Evans Hughes, a former Progressive governor of New York, and at that time an associate justice of the Supreme Court. Not only was he a candidate of proven ability and great integrity but he was also uncontroversial, having taken no part in the Republican schism of 1912. Hughes was unfairly smeared as Charles ("E-vasion") Hughes and with deliberately appealing to the hyphenated vote of Irish- and German-Americans, those ethnic groups opposed to Britain whose size was such that they might determine the outcome of the election. Hence, according to critics, a vote for Hughes would be a vote for the kaiser. Roosevelt had hoped for the Republican nomination which he was denied, partly because of the divisions of 1912, partly because his bellicose attitude to Germany would have discredited Republican criticism of Wilson's foreign policies. Yet, when it was offered him, TR turned down the Progressive nomination.

Wilson realized he would need to court the Progressive vote. He did so by nominating Progressives George Rublee to the Federal Trade Commission and Louis D. Brandeis, a Boston lawyer, to the Supreme Court. However, this was a most controversial move because Brandeis was a Jew, a critic of big business, and an advocate of organized labor. Moreover, it was an open secret that former president William Howard Taft coveted the seat since Yale University Law School was too small for him.

Furthermore, in order to make doubly sure of Progressive support, Wilson began to cultivate the editors of the main Progressive journal, the *New Republic,* funded by the wealthy Straight family, and led by Herbert Croly, Walter Weyl, and Walter Lippmann. Wilson did this firstly through his intermediary, Colonel Edward House, and then by select personal interviews. During the campaign Wilson was perfectly candid to Walter Lippmann about the high risk of war. Thus Lippmann advised his colleagues, "What we're electing is a war president—not the man who kept us out of war." Nevertheless, Wilson was much taken with the *New Republic's* scheme of April 1916 for an international union of liberal peoples united in collective action against aggressor states. This was the embryo of the League of Nations.

According to later tallies, Wilson took 9,127,695 votes (49.4 percent of the total) and Hughes had 8,533,507 (46.2 percent). Thus Wilson had 30 states and 277 votes in the electoral college and Hughes had 18 states and 254 votes in the electoral college.

Nevertheless, the outcome of the election was in doubt for several days. First returns from the eastern states suggested Hughes had won. However, the next day it became clear that Wilson was taking normally Republican states west of the Mississippi as well as the South. (Only twice since 1916—in 1948 and 1960—has the result of a presidential election not been known on the same day.) One pivotal state was California, which Hughes lost by the narrow margin of 3,773 votes, whereas the Republican candidate for the Senate, Hiram W. Johnson, carried it by the much larger margin of 296,815 votes. This astonishing disparity between presidential and senatorial results aroused widespread comment. The reason was that the Republican party in California was torn by factions. In California the electors were voting on the issue of Progressive politics, rather than foreign policy, and this factor aided Johnson but harmed Hughes. In the recriminations that followed the election, the Republicans came to recognize that their factionalism had lost them the presidency yet again.

To many Irish- and German-Americans the principal issue was Wilson's policy in the war. Much as German-Americans resented Wilson and what he stood for, they disliked TR even more on account of his exaggerated denunciation of hyphenated-Ameri-

In 1917 silent screen star Douglas Fairbanks, (Sr.), invites Americans to buy war bonds and support American intervention in World War I on the side of Britain and France. He stands in front of the Federal Building, New York, astride the pedestal statue of George Washington, the president who had warned against entangling alliances. (Library of Congress).

cans. Thus when Hughes won the Republican nomination, they praised his platform of "straight and honest" neutrality throughout the German-language press. German-Americans divided their support fairly evenly between Wilson and Hughes. While Hughes carried the German vote in Oregon, Minnesota, and Illinois, Wilson took such traditional German centers as Milwaukee and St. Louis and much of the German-American vote in Maryland and Ohio.

However, the Irish, infuriated by Wilson's partiality to Britain in the war and over the abortive Easter Rising, deserted him entirely. After one of Irish spokesman Jeremiah O'Leary's denunciations of Wilson for his Anglophile policies, Wilson wrote with his customary disdain, "I should feel deeply mortified to have you or anybody like you vote for me. Since you have access to many disloyal Americans and I have not, I will ask you to convey this message to them." Not surprisingly, Wilson failed to take any state in which the Irish vote was strong, including such traditionally Democratic cities as New York, Boston, and Chicago. Wilson was somewhat compensated for the Irish defection from the Democratic standard by the votes he picked up from those ethnic groups whose countries had been overrun by the Central powers. Thus Polish-Americans, who had opposed Wilson in 1912, voted for him in large numbers in 1916.

American Intervention

Wilson realized that his earlier pronouncements on holding Germany to "strict accountability" would inevitably draw America into war once Germany resumed unrestricted submarine warfare. Rather than accede to the inevitable, he decided to instigate peace negotiations through his adviser, Colonel Edward M. House. On December 18, 1916, Wilson appealed for an end to hostilities. Much to the dismay of his advisers, who favored the Allies, House was an incurable meddler who divided where he meant to unite. He held out the hope of war before Grey and peace before Wilson and achieved neither.

Negotiations broke down on an inescapable fact. What was compromise for one side was defeat to the other. Without defeat in the field, compromise was impossible. Coming to terms without victory would have been an open admission of governmental failure, that countless sons killed at the front had died in vain. Nevertheless, to entice Wilson, the Allies were ready to present themselves as champions of self-determination for Italians, Slavs, and Turks. Thus did they change their original war aims to a commitment to revise the maps of central Europe and the Near East.

Wilson himself suggested the guidelines for a future peace in a major public address, the "peace without victory" speech of January 22, 1917, before the Senate. He said the new world order should be based neither on military power nor entangling alliances but, rather, on the democratic principles of self-government, freedom of the seas, and limitations of armaments—all principles that he ascribed to the United States. He also committed himself to the principle of collective security through an international agency in which the United States would play a pivotal role. "In every discussion that must end this war, it is taken for granted that the peace must be followed by some definite concert of power which will make it impossible that any such catastrophe should ever overwhelm us again. It is inconceivable that the people of the United States should play no part in that great enterprise."

Germany could only be defeated by the intervention of the United States and this finally occurred on account of Germany's own folly. German strategy was to cut off Britain's supply of arms and food in an attempt to force the country to submit before American forces intervened. On January 31, 1917, Germany announced through its ambassador to the United States, Count Johann von Bernstorff, that it would begin unrestricted submarine warfare on February 1: "All sea traffic will be stopped with every available weapon and without further notice." However (and the exception made the announcement more intolerable than an absolute embargo), the United States would be allowed to send one passenger ship to Falmouth, England, once a week, provided it were marked with three alternating stripes in white and red, always followed a specified course, and arrived at Falmouth on a Sunday and departed on Wednesday. Journalist John

Bach McMaster ridiculed the German injunctions as requiring the passenger steamship to be painted like a zebra or a barber's pole and flying a flag like a kitchen tablecloth.

The German policy of unrestricted submarine warfare was spectacularly successful. In February 1917 Germany sank 536,000 tons of shipping; in March 603,000 tons; in April 1.25 million tons. The American naval headquarters advised Walter Hines Page on June 25, 1917, how "ships are being sunk faster than they can be replaced by the building facilities of the world. This means simply that the enemy is winning the war. There is no mystery about that. The submarines are rapidly cutting the Allies' lines of communication. When they are cut or sufficiently interfered with, we must accept the enemy's terms." At the time the British government did not dare reveal the gravity of the situation with only three weeks' supply of food in hand.

The rate of sinking was more than twice the rate of construction. In 1917 German submarines destroyed 6.61 million tons altogether, whereas total naval construction in Allied and neutral countries throughout the world was only 2.70 million tons. However, the real damage was even worse because submarines incapacitated many ships that were left afloat but so badly damaged that they had to be put out of commission. Moreover, the rate of accident at sea was higher than in peacetime. Ships were poorly manned, moved without lights, and had to take chances, unnecessary in peace. Because of submarines, ships moved more cautiously, and, therefore, slowly, and thus services were much reduced. The upshot was that the effective paralysis of Allied shipping was in sight.

Public opinion demanded a positive response from Wilson in defense of American rights and Wilson reacted on February 4 by breaking off diplomatic relations with Germany, in part to demonstrate that he had meant what he had said at the time of the sinking of the *Sussex* in 1916, and in part to retain public credibility. However, Wilson resisted the advice of his more impatient cabinet colleagues to arm merchant ships until February 26 when he asked Congress for the necessary authorization and an appropriation of $100 million to carry it out. Thus roused, the House passed the enabling legislation to arm merchant ships by 403 votes to 13. In the Senate 11 senators, led by La Follette, opposed the measure and delayed it until the end of the session on March 4, 1917, after which it would lapse. On March 3 a majority of 75 senators, anxious to have the bill passed, published a protest denouncing the recalcitrant 11. Their statement, and indeed the entire incident, gave Wilson an opportunity to turn his anger from Germany to the 11 senators, denouncing them as "a little group of willful men" who held up action by the overwhelming majority of Congress and thereby "rendered the great government of the United States helpless and contemptible." Accordingly, supported by Attorney General Thomas Watt Gregory, Wilson took the law into his own hands and, using a piracy statute of 1819, he announced on March 9 that merchant ships were being armed at his command.

There was widespread discussion on the propriety of such action. However, the State Department rallied public opinion on February 24 by publishing a note, the so-called Zimmermann telegram, that it had intercepted. This was a note from the German foreign minister in Berlin to the German minister in Mexico, proposing a German-Mexican alliance that might also include Japan, should the United States go to war against Germany. In return for its support, Germany promised Mexico the recovery of Texas, New Mexico, and Arizona.

Other events played a part in America's conversion to intervention. In Russia the abdication of the czar, Nicholas II, on March 15, 1917, and the advent of a republican government under Kerensky in Petrograd seemed to transform the war into a clear conflict between democracy and autocracy. Nevertheless, it made German victory more likely.

Wilson now decided that he must take America into the war, partly to protect its rights at sea, and partly to ensure that his grand design could be realized. However, he needed a particular incident to justify intervention. On March 12, 1917, a German submarine sank the unarmed American merchant ship, *Algonquin*. On March 18 German submarines sank three other ships (the *City of Memphis,* the *Illinois,* and the *Vigilancia*).

Wilson now faced the difficult task of appearing before a somewhat reluctant Congress and persuading it to declare war on Germany on April 2, 1917. This required the subtlest as well as the most emotive speech of his career. In order to anticipate ethnic divisions in the United States, he concentrated on distinguishing between the German government and the German people. One he equated with "Prussian autocracy," "dynasties," and "autocratic governments backed by organized force which is controlled wholly by their will, not by the will of their people." The other aroused feelings of "sympathy and friendship" and to whom Americans were "sincere friends." At the same time, he gave concrete assurance that the United States sought "no indemnities," and "no material compensation" and had "no selfish ends to serve." He crowned his subtle dialectic with a masterstroke, declaring the path America must follow, "God helping her, she can do no other." This was a paraphrase of Martin Luther's famous declaration "Ich kann nich anders" at the start of the Reformation. Thus, in Wilson's rhetoric, America's intervention was in the spirit of a religious crusade, to restore freedom to the German people. On April 4 the Senate approved the war resolution by 82 votes to 6 and the House did so on April 6 by 373 votes to 50. The joint congressional declaration of war was signed by Wilson that very day, April 6. It was Good Friday.

In the last resort the United States went to war over unrestricted submarine warfare because Wilson's policy on this subject, formulated according to his rigid, narrow morality, left him no option but to prove himself. Growing economic trade with the Allies, increasing sympathy for their cause, and deepening conviction that the defeat of Germany was in the national interest—all these factors drove the policy on neutral rights to a single inevitable conclusion.

Many Progressives now favored intervention, genuinely believing that the war was a crusade for international liberty and justice. They included Charles A. Beard, Albert J. Beveridge, John Dewey, Felix Frankfurter, Harold Ickes, and Stanley King. The editorials of the *New Republic* by Walter Lippmann and Herbert Croly showed utter faith in Wilson's ideals, declaring that "the liberal peoples of the world are united in a common cause." Nevertheless, staunch Progressives from the West and Midwest were resolutely opposed to intervention. Represented by Senators Robert La Follette of Wisconsin and George W. Norris of Nebraska, their isolationism was deep-rooted and arguments in favor of America taking up arms in defense of democracy allowed them to reply that to so do would imperil democracy as yet unfulfilled at home. La Follette, in particular, argued that American intervention would be a denial of everything the United States supposedly stood for. On April 4, 1917, he asked the Senate, "Are we seizing upon this war to consolidate and extend an imperial policy?"

Congressional opponents of intervention bitterly assailed Wilson and the interventionists for maneuvering the United States into a false position in order to benefit bankers and arms manufacturers. They vehemently denied that any American interests were in any danger from Germany and rigorously asserted traditional isolationist beliefs that involvement in a European war would result in the needless and useless sacrifice of young American lives.

Between the two opposing progressive camps lay a school of thought that accepted a war between the United States and Germany to protect American shipping but opposed entering the European theater. Congressman Irvine Lenroot of Wisconsin spoke for this bloc. Senator William E. Borah of Idaho propounded national rights but opposed Wilson's internationalism. After the declaration of war, he introduced a resolution reaffirming the traditional foreign policies of Washington, Jefferson, and Monroe. "I join no crusade," he maintained. "I seek or accept no alliance; I obligate this government to no other power. I make war alone for my countrymen and their rights, for my country and its honor."

The evidence we have of outright opposition to war is scant but some historians conclude it was simmering underneath a facade of patriotic conformity. In August 1917, for example, Oklahoma had a Green Corn Rebellion of protest against the war from tenant farmers, Indians, and blacks who burned bridges and cut pipelines in protest. There were occasional protest marches by blacks in New York and other cities.

Unlike European socialists, the Socialist party of America staunchly opposed the war and American intervention, on the grounds that it was a struggle of competing capitalist orders. On April 7, 1917, the day after the declaration of war, the Socialists adopted a resolution, subsequently overwhelmingly ratified by a party referendum, that "We brand the declaration of war by our government as a crime against the people of the United States." They advocated "continuous, active and public opposition to the war, through demonstrations, mass petitions, and all other means within our power." They opposed conscription and war loans and proposed propaganda campaigns against military instruction in schools.

Before the war the peace movement had been educational and legalistic. By 1917, when the more established peace societies, such as the Carnegie Endowment, were converted to intervention, many Progressives were in the process of founding new organizations. The war was a threat to their values, their belief in progress, and their concept of a world in which problems could be solved. They saw the war as a social problem as much as an international one. The new pacifists included socialists, social workers, social gospel clergymen, and feminists as well as people with religious scruples about fighting. Several new societies, the Women's Peace Party, the American Fellowship of Reconciliation, the American Union Against Militarism, and the People's Council of America for Peace and Democracy, were expressions of this new phenomenon. What the members shared was a distinct view of the war and a predilection to make that view a fundamental principle. Moreover, the struggle against economic privilege within all nations at war was recognized by pacifists everywhere who thus became conscious of common international bonds and objectives. The American Union Against Militarism (AUAM) grew out of a series of meetings at Henry Street Settlement House in New York arranged by the founder of the House, Lillian Wald, at the start of the war. By 1917, when it was formally organized, the American Union had 1,500 members who published 600,000 pieces of literature and spent $35,000. It circularized civic groups, trade unions, and Granges (farmers' unions), lobbied congressmen, and organized mass meetings in the principal industrial cities.

Although the United States's official language was English, it remained a deeply Germanic country. Not only had more German immigrants entered America in the nineteenth century than from any other ethnic group but they had also sown certain deep traditions in the New World—devotion to family and church, love of scholarship and debate—that were more Germanic than British. Hence, to German-Americans, American intervention was nothing short of a catastrophe, especially since it provoked a final nativist crusade to eliminate every last vestige of German culture in the United States. However, despite intense provocation, most German-Americans loyally accepted the decision to intervene and supported the war effort, as did all but the most extreme Anglophobes among Irish-Americans. Only such extremists as Jeremiah O'Leary of the American Truth Society continued to denounce Britain and rejoice in British setbacks. It was for expressing such opinions that the *Gaelic-American, Irish-World,* and *Freeman's Journal* were all barred from federal mails in 1918.

However, on the whole, public opinion was now ready to persuade itself that here was a war radically different from imperial wars of the past. This was going to be a war to make the world safe for democracy and a war to end all wars. Thus for many Americans the war became sublimated into a great crusade. Complete victory over Prussian militarism would achieve an enduring and just peace. The Progressives' traditional confidence in the inevitability of social progress was now being transferred to the sphere of international affairs. Many years later Protestant theologian Reinhold Niebuhr observed in *The Irony of American History* (1952), "the fact is that every nation is caught in the moral paradox of refusing to go to war unless it can be proved that the national interest is imperilled, and in continuing in the war only by proving that something much more than the national interest is at stake."

Mobilizing an Army

The war brought about something close to a revolution in the organization of government. "It is not an army that we must shape and train for war," said Wilson, "it is a nation." For those historians who see the period 1870–1920 as a search for order,

World War I was the event that brought the federal government's hitherto fumbling control of industry, business, agriculture, and politics together in a cohesive achievement.

Wilson accepted military conscription as a terrible necessity. Indeed, he had already approved draft legislation secretly devised by Secretary of War Newton D. Baker on lines suggested by Generals Leonard Wood, Hugh Scott, and Tasker Bliss, and Judge Advocate General Enoch H. Crowder. They proposed a procedure that would be least offensive and would actually look like volunteering, even, in Baker's own words, like men "going to the polls to vote." Thus, men of draft age would register in their local precinct and local civilians (sheriffs and governors, rather than army officers) would choose those to be selected for, and those to be exempted from, military service. To create the necessary machinery would take at least two months and thus, before Congress had passed the Draft Act, Baker, Crowder, and their particular official, Major Hugh S. Johnson, had the Government Printing Office print over 10 million blank draft forms.

In Congress the debate over conscription divided the parties. Opponents of the draft said it would "Prussianize America," that "conscription is another name for slavery," and would "destroy democracy at home." The dispute was satirized by cartoonist J. N. Darling in the Des Moines *Register* of April 11, 1917, in a drawing where a volunteer fireman (Congress) on duty at a blazing house throws the children (sound measures such as expert military advice) out of the window and then dutifully carries a feather bed (volunteer army) down the ladder.

Moreover, passage of the draft legislation was delayed by Roosevelt's allies in Congress who much favored a bill allowing the creation of volunteer units. Wilson was obliged to accept the bill but he refused Roosevelt's request to raise a volunteer unit, despite the pleas of Marshall Joffre and Prime Minister Clemenceau who knew that Roosevelt's presence in France would boost Allied morale.

The draft bill passed and was signed by Wilson on May 18, 1917. It required all men between twenty-one and thirty to register with a draft board on June 5, 1917. (Subsequently, the age limit was widened from eighteen to forty-five). The penalty for evasion was one year's imprisonment. Those exempt from service were federal, state, and local government officials, aliens, felons, ministers, and munitions workers. Those selected for actual service were chosen by lottery drawn in the Senate Office Building on July 20, 1917. Newton D. Baker first drew a capsule from a board—it was number 258. Thus, every man assigned the number 258 in each of the 4,500 local boards was obliged to take a medical examination as the next stage in the process. Only 70 percent were found medically fit to serve. According to Leonard P. Ayres in "The War with Germany, a Statistical Study," the three drafts altogether drew 23,908,576 men in the United States and another 325,445 in the territories, 44 percent of the adult male population, at a cost of $30 million. However, only 6,373,414 went into service.

There was a boom in weddings among men who thought marriage would prove a shelter from the draft. Draft boards also granted exemption to 56,830 members of religious sects opposed to military service, such as the Quakers, Brethren, Mennonites, and others. More troublesome to the board was a class of conscientious objectors moved by ethical, but not religious, scruples. Nevertheless, an Executive Order of March 20, 1918, recognized this other category of objectors, about 3,900 in all, and arranged for them to engage in noncombatant service, provided they could satisfy a Board of Inquiry of the sincerity of their beliefs.

The draft set a precedent beyond enforced military service. It signaled a new form of government activity—an immense, carefully orchestrated publicity campaign—supported by secret and elaborate preparations, to anticipate and nullify any opposition and make public opinion receptive to government plans.

To train and discipline the draftees, sixteen army camps were created under canvas in the South and another sixteen cantonments established in the North, each with a capacity for 40,000 to 50,000 men. This was a prodigious feat to achieve in three months since a typical cantonment required 1,200 buildings on a camp site of 5,000 to 11,000 acres with rifle range and drill grounds on another 2,000 acres, and, linking all the sites, 25 miles of hard roads. The cantonments used 450 million feet of board lumber,

140,000 wooden doors, 721,000 cots, and 54,000 toilet bowls. Each cantonment cost, on average, $8 million; each camp, $1.9 million. The entire project of construction was second only to the Panama Canal.

All camps provided a sixteen-week period of preliminary training for forty hours a week. Here was the staple of folk legend. In *Oh! How I hate to get up in the morning* Irving Berlin, who was a sergeant at Camp Upton, New York, as well as a prodigious songwriter, delighted draftees because his song emphasized again and again that the army bugle blew at 5:45 AM, turning the rhythm of reveille into a repeated protest, "I can't get 'em up, / I can't get 'em up."

In *Nineteen Nineteen* novelist John Dos Passos summed up his view of the physical and mental humiliation of the soldiers in the biography of Joe Doe:

> Naked he went into the army;
>   they weighed you, measured you, looked
> for flat feet, squeezed your penis to
> see if you had clap, looked up your
> anus to see if you had piles, counted
> your teeth, made you cough, listened to your
> heart and lungs, made you read the letters on
> the card, charted your urine and your
> intelligence,
>   gave you a service record for a future
> (imperishable soul)
>   and an identification tag stamped with
> your serial number to hang around your
> neck, issued O.D. regulation equipment, a
> condiment can and a copy of the articles of
> war.
>   Atten'SHUN suck in your gut you c——r
> wipe that smile off your face eyes right
> wattja tink dis is a choich-social?
> For-war-D'ARCH.

In its preparations the government looked to wars of the future as well as the present. On July 14, 1917, the House voted appropriations of $640 million for the creation of an air fleet and on October 4 the War Department announced that contracts had been awarded for building 20,000 airplanes.

In June 1917 Wilson appointed General John J. Pershing commander of the American Expeditionary Force, in preference to Wood, whom he distrusted as a friend of TR's. In all, 2,086,000 men served in the European theaters. Their contribution was decisive.

Like friends and foes alike, American troops experienced shell shock, battle fatigue, and tuberculosis, arising from the poison gas, and the cold, wet, and filth of the trenches. More than 50,000 Americans died in France, compared with 3 million British, French, and Russian soldiers in all theaters. The scourge of venereal disease infected about one man in every five. Unlike earlier Progressives, the military authorities could not attribute it to drunkenness or alcohol abuse. For a time they pretended the problem did not exist, despite rudimentary medical control of official French brothels. In the end, the Allies agreed that free treatment of venereal disease was the only way of protecting society.

Military experiences of venereal disease abroad helped provoke a concerted, but small-scale, preventative campaign at home. In 1918 the Chamberlain-Kahn Act appropriated $4 million for the establishment of a Division of Venereal Diseases in the United States Public Health Service. By 1931 850 clinics had been founded and were using the Salvarsan method of treatment, a partial but inconclusive success. The death rate from syphilis and its related diseases was at its highest during the 1920s. In 1910 it was 13.5 per 100,000 people, rising to a peak of 19.1 in 1917. In 1920 it was 16.5; in 1930 it was 15.7; and by 1940 it had fallen to 14.4.

The most potent description of the experience of American servicemen in Europe comes from the lost generation of war novelists, including not only Ernest Hemingway and John Dos Passos but also Thomas Boyd, E. E. Cummings, and Charles Yale Harrison; from the British point of view, Wilfred Owen, Siegfried Sassoon and Rupert Brooke; and from the German point of view, Erich Maria Remarque; and from the Hungarian, Andreas Latzko. They expressed horror at useless slaughter and the degradation of military life, outrage at the abuse of words by

An American marine receives first aid in the trenches on March 22, 1918. (National Archives).

government propaganda, and their disillusion captured the imagination of a whole generation. The vicious nether world of the trenches was vividly evoked.

Through the Wheat (1923) by Thomas Boyd is dominated by

sardonic grim invective. Private Hicks longs to leave the dull routine of his desk job in the army for the excitement of the front. Once there, he passes through pained disillusion to complete and utter desolation. Finally his inner self is extinguished: "The action seemed to draw his feet from the earth. No longer did anything matter, neither the bayonets, the bullets, the barbed wire, the dead nor the living. The soul of Hicks was numb." One of the central images of the book is of soldiers mercilessly forced to cross and, thereby, defile a wheat field, a symbol of nature, unaware of what they do. Thomas Boyd suggests that war deprives life of sanctity, and death of dignity, when corpses are consigned to derelict entombment:

Before they were dumped into their temporary graves their pockets were searched and the contents placed in little piles on the ground. Some of the bodies were unrecognizable although the men had seen them and talked with them the day before. One or two of the bodies looked as if life had fled them peacefully. The uniforms were unspotted with blood, the faces were calm. But some of the faces were distorted. The lips rose from the teeth and made them look like fangs. One body, on which the skin looked like liver, had been struck lifeless a few days earlier. It stunk terrifically.

Charles Yale Harrison is obsessed by hatred of the army in his story of a Canadian regiment's experiences, *Generals Die in Bed* (1928). Of all the novelists, he has perhaps the most heightened sense of terror, particularly in the scene in which the hero cruelly stabs a young German assailant with his bayonet during a trench fight. Harrison's climax is not in the presentation of the psychological numbness of the soldier but the wreaking of vengeance on the defeated Germans. A brigadier general incites his men to merciless slaughter by charging them to remember the torpedoing of a hospital ship by the "Huns." Shortly afterwards, the hero, who has been wounded and taken away from the fighting, learns that the torpedoed ship was really carrying ammunition, not wounded men.

Other writers take as their theme the responsibility of the individual for acts of violence that cannot be imputed to statesmen. William March in *Company K* presents the conflict of wills between a brutalized sergeant and terrified privates. He describes the petty revenges men inflict on one another when their nerves are shattered by constant exposure to horror. In *Mattock* (1927) James Stevens describes a callow and provincial private, brought up to be a "Christian American Soldier," whose every effort to do right ends badly, but who survives all scrapes to return to his deadening provincial background in the Midwest. He is the perpetual moaner, the soldier always out of step, of whom an ironic twist makes a temporary hero and then a coward. Here is a man who learns nothing by his experience but reverts to type.

Mobilizing Industry

The history of modern warfare has largely been the history of supply and demand. What tipped the scales of war decisively in favor of the Allies in World War I was the intervention of the United States with its vast industry and agriculture that could supply arms, material, and food to Europe. To coordinate its supplies the federal government regulated various means of communication and transportation—telephones, telegraphs, railroads—certain basic industries, such as coal mines, and restricted freedom of speech. Thus in the first six months of the war the United States took back rights and freedoms it had taken the individual centuries of struggle to obtain.

In a memorandum of April 7, 1916, Secretary of War Newton D. Baker advised Wilson, "The European War has brought into sharp relief the fact that under modern conditions a great war involves . . . such an organization of the industrial and commercial, financial and social resources of the nation as will enable them to be mobilized both to support the military arm and to continue the life of the nation during the struggle." Furthermore, Baker told a conference of editors on May 25, 1917, how "War is no longer Samson with his shield and spear and sword, and David with his sling; . . . it is the conflict of smokestacks now, the combat of the driving wheel and the engine." To win the war the whole of society, and not just its army, had to be turned into a cohesive, efficient machine.

Woodrow Wilson retired more into himself. As James Kerney explains in *The Political Education of Woodrow Wilson* (1926),

"Wilson took personal command of the government. He isolated himself still further, remaining much in his private apartments and seeing few people." In this way, he thought he could function better. Wilson disliked exuberance, pomposity, crudeness, and assertiveness in others. He liked qualities he thought of as feminine—sensitivity, delicacy, insight, and intuition—and he expected these of his closest associates. He found them in three trusted executives, Secretary of War Newton D. Baker, Bernard Baruch, chairman of the War Industries Board, and George Creel, chairman of the Committee of Public Information. Wilson conducted the war through these men who had the rare talents of being able to stimulate, entertain, and propitiate him.

Bernard Baruch's task at the War Industries Board (WIB) was to coordinate the different component parts of American industry for war as surely as Henry Ford in his automobile factories. Accordingly, Baruch carefully selected an elite of professionals and businessmen who had risen on account of their imagination, flexibility, and forcefulness, including Charles M. Schwab of U.S. Steel, Alexander Legge of International Harvester, Robert S. Lovett of Union Pacific, and Samuel M. Vauclain of Baldwin Locomotive Works.

Baruch organized the WIB in eleven sections, or divisions, to administer such things as requirements, finished products, facilities, and price fixing and particular products such as steel, chemicals, textiles, explosives, and building materials. The WIB had the power to regulate what industry produced and for whom. When it discovered that 8,000 tons of steel per annum were used for corsets, it discontinued corset manufacturing so that the steel could be put to more essential use.

Moreover, it assisted industrialists in converting their factories to wartime production of such things as masks and belts for the army medical corps. Thus shirtwaist factories turned to signal flags, radiator factories to guns, automobile factories to airplane parts, and piano factories into airplane wings. Building materials became so scarce that those who wanted to construct barns or houses had to get a certificate of necessity from a neighborhood committee. The conservation division of the WIB set itself the task of eliminating waste by persuading manufacturers to standardize their products. Thus 232 different kinds of buggy wheels were reduced to 4 and 287 styles and sizes of auto tires were reduced to 9. Shoe colors were reduced to 3 (black, white, and tan) and 150 different colors of typewriter ribbon were reduced to 5. The length of upper shoes was reduced to spare more leather for soldiers' boots. These changes, trivial in themselves, had a profound and permanent impact on fashion. Never again would women's dresses skirt the ground. Petticoats disappeared. Hats became smaller. A few women cut their hair although the bob cut was not generally established until the 1920s.

Railroads in World War I

The problem of domestic transportation for military supplies and personnel and for goods forced Wilson and the federal government to pursue a policy of temporary nationalization of the railroads—precisely the sort of federal intervention the Progressives had resisted earlier. As Europe required ever-greater supplies, American railroads carried ever more military supplies and food to the Atlantic coast. Thus by 1916 the rail ton-mileage was 30 percent higher than the previous year and in 1917 it was another 43 percent higher. The Army Appropriation Act, passed on August 29, 1916, had a provision to create a Council of National Defense "for the coordination of industries and resources for the national security and welfare." It agreed that the American Railroad Association, now comprised of eighteen railroad managers, should establish a special committee on military transportation, led by Daniel Willard, president of the Baltimore and Ohio Railroad. Their principal problem was the shortage of railroad cars to cope with expanded demand. By March 31, 1917, the railroads had 145,000 fewer cars than they needed, and by November, 158,000 fewer cars. To compound their problems, as many as 3,400 locomotives already ordered had been delayed in production because of priority given to engines needed in Europe.

Threatened with railroad paralysis, caused by lack of locomotives, freight cars, and fuel as well as escalating costs, Wilson took control of the railroads by proclamation at noon on December 28, 1917. Wilson's son-in-law and secretary of the treasury,

William Gibbs McAdoo, noted for his proven experience, was appointed director general of railroads. Wilson upheld the property rights of the owners in a subsequent Railroad Control Act of March 21, 1918, that declared the companies would receive adequate compensation based on average annual earnings in 1914–17. Congress also provided a revolving fund of $500 million to pay for federal operations.

McAdoo took advice from Alfred Holland Smith, president of the New York Central and a close personal friend, and concentrated on three things—rates, wages, and equipment. He divided the entire network into three regions (eastern, southern, and western), placed stringent controls over freight to ensure it always went by the fastest route, and ordered the building of 1,930 locomotives and 100,000 cars at a cost of $380 million. Unnecessary passenger traffic was discouraged, unprofitable or duplicate passenger services were eliminated, time-tables were rationalized, and, to save food, dining facilities were reduced. Thus 67 million passenger-train miles were eliminated in 1918, a reduction of one-tenth of the 1917 passenger services. Railroads made economies by taking Pullman cars off trains, as sleeping car and passenger service was curtailed. Assistant Railroad Director Walter D. Hines estimated that this resulted in an annual saving of $95,000. Despite such economies, American railroads had 8 percent more passenger traffic in 1918 than the year before. This was despite fare increases for passengers of 18 percent from June 25, 1918. At the same time freight rates rose by 28 percent.

Moreover, wages were to be increased from May 25, 1918. Until this time 51 percent of railroad workers earned only $75 per month. Individual increases were according to a sliding scale to favor workers previously disadvantaged. All workers who had previously earned $46 a month were to receive an increase of $20 (an increase of 43 percent). Passenger train brake men, who had earlier received $85 a month were awarded another $34 (an increase of 40 percent) while the very few who had earned $250 a month received no increase at all. Women were to be paid the same rates as men. Thus average annual wages rose from $1,004 in 1917 to $1,485 in 1919.

The whole wartime arrangement, while essential to help win the war and, in the case of pay rises, no more than individual workers deserved, was most costly. Thus total operating expenses (including rentals to the railroads) for the twenty-six months of federal control from January 1, 1918, to March 1, 1920, cost over $900 million, plus another $200 million subsequently paid to the railroad companies as compensation for their claims that rolling stock had not been maintained. Undermaintenance was partly the fault of Walker D. Hines who succeeded McAdoo as director in January 1919. Heedless of the wartime changes it had done so much to achieve, the federal government in 1919 and 1920 proceeded to return those sections of the economy it had appropriated and regulated during the war to the private sector.

On February 28, 1920, President Woodrow Wilson signed the Esch-Cummins Railroad bill, returning the railroads to private control from March 1. The various clauses of the act were based on the idea of genuine competition between the railroads under the supervision of the ICC, with a guaranteed net income in each rate-making group equal to 5.5 percent on the value of roads within the group. It allowed consolidation of railroad lines and created a Railroad Labor Board to settle labor disputes. Existing rates, wages, and government rents would continue until September 1 and the roads were allowed ten years to refund their indebtedness to the government.

Though the government had only the best of traditional intentions toward the railroads, the change was premature and not in the railroads' best economic interests. The net gains from passengers and freight were such that the railroads could not afford to repay the government. Rather than modernize their equipment and improve their services, the railroads preferred to blame the government, first for controlling them in the war and then for abandoning them to the competitive market afterward. Moreover, the stronger railroads were unwilling to merge their interests with the weaker ones in the interests of the industry as a whole. Nevertheless, the new Railroad Labor Board ended a damaging labor dispute in the summer of 1920 by awarding pay rises of an average of 22 percent.

Social Consequences

The start of wartime industrial and commercial expansion was especially significant for one ethnic group, black Americans. Whites were being drawn increasingly into the armed services and newly created war industries. However, the war prevented European immigrants from coming to America and taking their place as laborers. Thus from 1915 onward agents for northern employers began recruiting black labor from the South. However, at least four times as many blacks went North because of word of mouth than did so at the prompting of labor agents. The exodus was mainly spontaneous and largely unorganized; whatever the personal motives for individual moves, the collective motive was bad political and social treatment in the South. The Great Migration was facilitated by railroad transportation and continued after the war was over. In sum, the South lost 323,000 black citizens in the 1910s and 615,000 in the 1920s—about 8.2 percent of its black population.

At the outset, white attitudes to the migration were somewhat ambivalent in both North and South. As time went on, they became alarmist: northerners resented another ethnic disruption following in the wake of the new immigration; southerners did not want to lose their ready supply of cheap labor. Some southern communities passed laws to prevent blacks leaving. This happened in Montgomery, Savannah, Greenville, and elsewhere. Charleston editor William Watts Ball commented ruefully in 1923, "We have plenty of Southerners whose disposition is identical with that of the ancient Egyptians—they would chase the Negroes to the Red Sea to bring them back." However, nothing could reverse the tide.

In the North black migrants were condemned by circumstances to a life in squalid tenement ghettos, the urban equivalents of what the South had called the "black belt." Inevitably, they faced resentment and hostility from white workers who feared for their livelihood. In 1917 there were race riots in towns and on army bases.

The war was also pivotal for women, coming at a time when

political success was almost in the grasp of suffragists. For one thing, women took the place of men drafted into the services. They became telegraph messengers, elevator operators, streetcar conductors, and worked as full operatives in munitions factories and railroad works. Their numbers expanded in professions traditional to women such as nurses, stenographers, and clerks. Industry hired 40,000 more women than before. Full employment increased the average real income of blue-collar workers by 20 percent.

The government launched a propaganda campaign to encourage shipyard workers, now exempted from the draft, to build a "Bridge to France" as "Two to one; two to one," the ratio by which America was losing the submarine race to Germany, was transformed into the slogan of the campaign. Since shipyards had neither the capacity nor men for a program of such magnitude, engineers decided to use parts prefabricated in distant factories and delivered to, and assembled at, the yards. In 1918, 85 percent of ship hulls were being manufactured in distant steel works.

In 1917 and 1918 the government increased the number of shipyard workers from 50,000 to 350,000 and built 341 shipyards with a total of 1,284 launching ways. July 4, 1918, was celebrated by launching 95 ships. In all that year, 533 ships of a total of 3,030,406 tons were completed. Hog Island in the Delaware River was transformed into the biggest shipyard in the world—846 acres with 250 buildings and 80 miles of railroad tracks and employing 34,049 workers.

These services, important in themselves, would have been wasted without major revisions to Allied strategy. Rear Admiral William S. Sims argued against traditional British tactics in submarine warfare, trying to patrol large areas of the Atlantic and thus failing to provide ships with adequate cover. Sims persuaded British Prime Minister Lloyd George to institute a system of convoys, fleets of merchant ships protected by destroyers. The first convoy left Gibraltar on May 10, 1917. Whereas before convoys started a quarter of ships were lost, after the system was introduced, fewer than 1 percent of ships were lost from all causes. The number of ships requiring convoy was about 140 each week.

As a result of all these measures, German submarine warfare

became much less effective. In the six months from February to July 1917 German submarines sank 640,000 tons of shipping per month; in the six months from August 1917 to January 1918 it was an average of 300,000 tons; and from February 1918 to the Armistice it was 200,000 tons per month.

Food and Drink

Europe needed grain as well as arms. Herbert Hoover was the obvious candidate to take on the domestic administration of food. This entailed management of crops so as to feed not only the newly expanded army and the civilian population at home but also the Allies' armies and their civilians abroad.

Hoover's task was nothing less than to make food go round three times as far as in peacetime, whether by increased production, increased saving, or better distribution, or a combination of all three. He had an uncanny ability to absorb specialist knowledge about sources and distribution and to manipulate the supply to meet the needs of 300 million people around the world. As a result of Hoover's herculean efforts, the amount of bread produced rose from 3.32 million metric tons before the war to 10.56 million metric tons in 1918–19, and the amount of meats and fats rose from 645,000 metric tons before the war to 2.36 million metric tons in 1918–19.

In order to get the best balance of food supplies between America and Europe, Hoover knew he had to modify the dietary habits of 120 million Americans and, in particular, their tendency to waste food. He realized this could be best done by persuasion. He had the power to take away business licenses of any manufacturers and dealers whose business was worth $100,000 per annum and who indulged in war profiteering. He rarely imposed this penalty, preferring to make violators pay a contribution to the Red Cross in lieu of a fine. On January 26, 1918, Hoover published a timetable of voluntary denial: wheatless Mondays and Wednesdays, meatless Tuesdays, and porkless Thursdays and Saturdays. On May 26 he set a weekly ration of two pounds of meat per person. There were also heatless days when fuel administrator Harry A. Garfield decided to have towns reduce their consumption of electric power. Daylight saving time was introduced across the country.

Moreover, Hoover took dealers into his confidence by inviting them to conferences, engaging their sympathy, and ensuring their cooperation. To economize with food became the smart thing to do and established a vogue. However, the results were sometimes ridiculous rather than sublime. Assistant Secretary of the Navy Franklin D. Roosevelt and his wife, Eleanor, tried to comply with Hoover's campaign to save food. Their conservation program was complimented by the Food Administration as "a model for other large households." The *New York Times* of July 27, 1917, reported how "Mrs. Roosevelt does the shopping, the cooks see that there is no food wasted, the laundress is sparing in her use of soap, each servant has a watchful eye for evidence of shortcoming on the part of others; and all are encouraged to make helpful suggestions in the use of 'left overs.' " The account made Eleanor ridiculous across Washington, especially her reported remark, "Making ten servants help me do my saving has not only been possible but highly profitable."

What was necessary for food was also necessary for drink. American intervention in the war was also the decisive factor in the introduction of national prohibition. As Charles Merz, *New Republic* journalist and later pioneer historian of the wet (opposition to prohibition) cause, explains, "The war did three things for prohibition. It centralized authority in Washington; it stressed the importance of saving food; and it outlawed all things German."

The prohibition movement gained momentum with the rationing of foodstuffs at the expense of brewing and distilling. Drys (proponents of prohibition) argued that, while the United States was assenting to voluntary rationing to provide Europe with grain, it was subversive of the war effort to liquidate crops and turn them into alcohol. They advised the administration to keep alcohol from army camps and shipyards. Secretary of the Navy Josephus Daniels was a confirmed dry and, as early as April 5, 1914, had forbidden the use of alcohol in the navy. In June 1917 he extended the compass of prohibition and ended the practice of distributing sailors going on shore leave with contraceptives. He did not want a profusion of seamen on shore. Congress then designated dry and decent zones around military camps. Moreover, Woodrow Wilson was persuaded by Herbert Hoover to reduce the alcoholic content of beer to 2.75 percent by weight in a proclamation on December 8, 1917. (Previously, the percentage had been three or four times higher.) Wilson also limited the amount of food that could be used in brewing to 70 percent of what it had been in 1916. Furthermore, the Agricultural Appropriations Act of 1917 banned the use of foods in beer, wine, and spirits. Wartime prohibition thus passed Congress to take effect on July 1, 1919, unless the armed forces had been demobilized by then.

The final resort of the drys, the Eighteenth Amendment, obliged Congress to pass national prohibition while, paradoxically, evading its own responsibility. Yale professor Irving Fisher said a constitutional amendment would be the best means of reconciling wet and dry points of view, "on the theory that it did not really enact prohibition, but merely submitted it to the States."

In the course of the debates in Congress the wets (opponents of prohibition) tried to buy time. Thirty-six of the forty-eight states would have to ratify the measure before it became part of the Constitution and wets counted on controlling thirteen state legislatures. Thus wets argued for an unprecedented time limit of six years for ratification. Drys compromised at seven in exchange for another wet proposal, that the liquor trade should have a year to wind up its affairs. In so doing, drys were inadvertently confirming a temporary legitimacy on the liquor industry. The amendment passed the Senate by 65 votes to 20 in August 1917 and the House by 282 to 128 in December. Compared with the first attempt at national prohibition in 1914, the drys had gained 85 votes in the House. Of these 39 were Republican votes from midwestern congressmen promoted by the Anti-Saloon League to oust wet Democrats in the elections of 1914 and 1916.

The Eighteenth Amendment banned the "manufacture, sale or transportation of intoxicating liquors" in the United States and empowered Congress and the states "to enforce this article by appropriate legislation." It did not prohibit buying and drinking alcohol nor did it explicitly proscribe possession of alcohol and its domestic manufacture. Thus it was the trade rather than the article itself that was beyond the pale. Those who could afford to stock up in advance or continue to buy later on were not breaking the law by doing so.

The Anti-Saloon League and its allies were past masters at lobbying state legislatures and swinging crucial votes, for it was in the state capitals they had first sharpened their wits. The wets who had insisted on a time limit for ratification by the states were mistaken if they thought that thirteen wet states could hold out even after wartime hysteria had evaporated. The case for ratification was presented to state legislatures by men who claimed the support of millions of voters. Forty-six state legislatures ratified the amendment. Again and again prohibitionists used a basic appeal put forward in the Senate by William Kenyon of Iowa, "If liquor is a bad thing for the boys in the trenches, why is it a good thing for those at home? When they are willing to die for us, should we not be willing to go dry for them?"

The debate was of crucial concern to German-Americans and their interest was ruthlessly exploited by both dry and wet sides in different ways. Brewers and German-Americans had already linked forces with results fatal for both. By 1914 the National German-American Alliance, organized by Dr. Charles John Hexamer in 1901 to spread German culture, had more than 2 million members. In the states where it was at its strongest—New York and Pennsylvania in the East and Ohio, Wisconsin, Indiana, Illinois, and Iowa in the Midwest—drys were unable to secure statewide prohibition before the war because beer gardens were a focal point of German culture and it seemed to German-Americans that a prohibition of alcohol was a persecution of their ethnic heritage. From 1913 onward, the Alliance, supported by liquor interests, began to lobby Congress and the administration in competition with prohibitionists.

All the wartime efforts of the German Alliance to counter adverse publicity were turned against it by its enemies. Its ill-judged indictments of England were construed as disloyalty to America. On November 9, 1917, league counsel Wayne Wheeler told the *New York Times*, "The liquor traffic aids those forces in this country whose loyalty is called into question at this hour. The liquor traffic is the strong financial supporter of the German-American Alliance. The purpose of this Alliance is to secure German solidarity for the promotion of German ideals and German Kultur and oppose any restriction of the liquor traffic."

Clergymen had made hatred of all things German fashionable, describing the kaiser as the "beast of Berlin" or the "werewolf of Potsdam." Ardent prohibitionist Rev. Dr. Billy Sunday spoke for many when he told the House, "Thou knowest, O Lord, that no nation so infamous, vile, greedy, sensuous, bloodthirsty ever disgraced the pages of history." All manner of people and things German were subject to censure. Conductor Karl Muck was taken into custody as an enemy alien. The mayor of East Orange, New Jersey, forbade violinist Fritz Kreisler from playing in concert. Instead of banning sauerkraut, it was renamed liberty cabbage. Americans also lost their sense of proportion as regards German measles (renamed liberty measles), and dachshunds (renamed liberty pups). According to Mark Sullivan, Cincinnati banned pretzels from free lunch counters in its saloons. In this context Wayne Wheeler was able to enlist Theodore Roosevelt's opposition to the German-American Alliance and, because of his prestige, ensure support throughout the country. On April 11, 1918, the Alliance voted to disband. In the Midwest German disappeared as a second language of official communication.

Mobilizing Public Opinion

The American people would cooperate in the war effort if they knew what was expected of them. It was essential for government to stay in touch with the people. On August 29, 1916, Congress established an official Council of National Defense, consisting of six cabinet officers, the secretaries of war, navy, interior, agriculture, commerce, and labor, and an advisory commission of civilians. The advisory commission included business leaders familiar with nationwide companies, such as Walter S. Gifford of the American Telephone and Telegraph Company, Julius Rosenwald of Sears Roebuck, and Daniel Willard of the Baltimore and Ohio Railroad. The commission established 184,000 local councils across the country to execute its provisions and report back on the needs of particular communities.

On the eve of the war declaration, Wilson had pondered whether a nation such as the United States could participate in the Great War without becoming brutalized by it. He confided his doubts to Frank Cobb, editor of the *New York World,* who recalled their conversation:

He said that when a war got going it was just war and there weren't two kinds of it. It required illiberalism at home to reinforce the men at the front. We couldn't fight Germany and maintain the ideals of Government that all thinking men shared. . . . "Once lead this people into war," he said, "and they'll forget there ever was such a thing as tolerance. To fight you must be brutal and ruthless, and the spirit of ruthless brutality will enter into the very fibre of our national life, infecting Congress, the courts, the policeman on the beat, the man in the street." . . . He said a nation couldn't put its strength into a war and keep its head level; it had never been done.

Accordingly, the government sought to protect its war plans by ensuring cooperation and loyalty by law. On June 15, 1917, Congress passed the first Espionage Act, which forbade obstruction of the draft and insubordination in the services. It provided penalties of up to twenty years in prison and a fine of $10,000. On May 16, 1918, the Sedition Act forbade writing or printing any "disloyal, profane, scurrilous or abusive language intended to cause contempt, scorn, contumely or disrepute as regards the form of government of the United States, or the Constitution or the flag." It specifically warned against obstruction in the sale of war bonds, inciting insubordination in the services, and attempts to discourage recruiting. The Trading-with-the-Enemy Act of October 1917 allowed the federal government to censor the foreign language press.

Thus domestic support for American involvement in the "war to make the world safe for democracy" was based on a paradox. To set Europe free, the United States had to be restricted. Freedom of speech, conscientious objection, and radical dissent were suppressed as much as possible. Methods of suppression received the tacit approbation of the public and enthusiastic execution by people in authority. Wilson's fear for freedom came true. One induced conscientious objector of the Doukhobortii sect refused to perform any military service and even to put on military uniform because he believed these things were forbidden in the Bible. He was imprisoned at Alcatraz under grueling conditions and was later transferred to Fort Leavenworth where he died of pneumonia. When his widow came to take away the body she found it dressed in uniform. Rose Pastor Stokes was sentenced to ten years' imprisonment for having written to the Kansas City *Star* that "the Government is for the profiteers" and, when Wilson realized that the editor responsible for publishing her article had not even been indicted, the president wanted him imprisoned, too.

The newly created Committee on Public Information began as a simple clearing house for everyday information about government activities but was developed out of all recognition by its chairman, George Creel, into something far more formidable and sinister.

As he became ever more confident, Creel increased the scope of CPI activities, creating a Division of Pictorial Publicity under Charles Dana Gibson that drew on the myriad talents of painters, illustrators, cartoonists, and sculptors. Among those artists who designed war posters were Howard Chandler Christy (Win the War—Buy a Bond), Edward Hopper (Smash the Hun), and James Montgomery Flagg (Tell That to the Marines).

In addition, Creel organized a motion picture division to boost morale and, during movie intermissions, had special orators speak on a subject of current interest or propaganda. These speakers, both amateur and professional, numbered perhaps 75,000 altogether and were known as 4 Minute Men. In four minutes they exhorted the public to buy bonds, support the draft, and help conserve food in a series of well-mounted campaigns or drives. Altogether, they made 7.55 million speeches in movie houses, schools, churches, synagogues, and camps to an aggregate audience of 314.54 million people. The most successful was a French priest, Captain Paul Perigard, a hero of Verdun.

Moreover, Creel's impetuous behavior was to stir up future trouble for Wilson in Congress. Creel ridiculed congressmen critical of Wilson in a way that increased tensions between Republicans and Democrats. He boasted how he never lost an opportunity to hold Senators Hiram Johnson of California and James Reed of Missouri up to ridicule and contempt. However, he reserved his most deadly salvo for Senator Henry Cabot Lodge, crediting him with ignorance rather than dishonesty. "The Lodge mind [is] like the soil of New England—highly cultivated, but naturally sterile. An exceedingly dull man and a very vain one—deadly combination—his vanity fosters his ignorance by persistent refusal to confess it." Later, Lodge would repay Wilson for Creel's gratuitous insult.

The Cost

As we may infer, the mobilization of all sectors of society required organization on an unprecedented scale. The cost was colossal. How was the money raised? Two-thirds of the cost of the war was financed by loans; the other third by taxation. At the outset, there was not enough money in the Treasury to finance the war. Accordingly, on April 24, 1917, Congress authorized the Treasury to borrow $5 billion in bonds. As secretary of the treasury, William Gibbs McAdoo decided to raise the money through banks whom he expected to give their services to the country and by a great drive to sell Liberty Bonds across the nation, many in small denominations so that all classes of society could take part. The first Liberty Loan drive exceeded $3 billion, 50 percent more than was required. By the end of the war $21 billion altogether had been raised by the sale of government bonds. War Savings Stamps were promoted by the slogan "Lick the stamps and lick the Kaiser."

To raise additional revenue, the principle of progressive taxation was applied to all existing taxation. Income tax was raised from 1 percent on everything over the first $3,000 to 2 percent on everything over $1,000. In 1916 surtaxes were 1 percent on incomes over $20,000 and 13 percent on incomes over $2 million. Thereafter, a surtax of 1 percent was imposed on incomes over $5,000 and 50 percent on incomes over $2 million. Public opinion was scandalized by the great profits by firms manufacturing and selling war material. Accordingly, in response to public disquiet, the Revenue Act of 1917 taxed their profits at rates ranging from 20 percent to 60 percent. Progressives led by La Follette found these rates inadequate and wanted them increased. Corporation income was taxed at 6 percent and there were also taxes on excess profits.

The sum total of these various measures was as follows: during the war the federal debt rose from $1 billion in 1916 to $25.6 billion in 1920. The amount raised by taxes increased from $788 million in 1916 to over $5 billion in 1919. The federal deficit was $853 million in 1917, $9 billion in 1918, and $13 billion in 1919.

The war accelerated economic changes within the United States. During wartime inflation the purchasing power of the dollar fell from 100 to 45. A new poor, dislocated from its previous social position, confronted a "new rich." Those living on fixed incomes, such as the returns from bonds, mortgages and rents, and who had previously been affluent, now shared a new poverty with those living on fixed salaries—such as government officials and teachers. Between 1916 and 1919 salaried workers lost 22 percent of their purchasing power. The new rich, who profited from inflation, were those with investments in land, shares in corporations and industry, and even artisans whose wages had risen, too. It was estimated that the war created 42,000 new millionaires while the number of people earning between $30,000 and $40,000 tripled. With their lapse from social position because of their fall in fortune, the former rich were no longer the guardians of morals, the arbiters of taste. Reduction in the real income of intellectuals, such as university faculty, was a contributory cause of intellectual alienation from contemporary society and their questioning of its basic assumptions. The moral license of the Jazz Age began with the shifting economic fortunes of classes in the war.

CHAPTER THIRTEEN

The Lost Peace: The Eclipse
of Woodrow Wilson

·ॐ·

THE OMENS for an Allied victory were not good in 1917. Britain was being starved of food by submarines that were also destroying its ships. The French army launched an assault on the western front that failed and this led to mutinies in the army. The Russian armies were disintegrating with desertions and mutinies. In the fall, Austria and Germany launched a major offensive against Italy. In October the Bolshevik Revolution, led by Lenin and Trotsky, felled the Kerensky government and, intent on wide social reform, they prepared to treat with Germany.

As committed Marxists, the Bolsheviks also wanted to show that the war for democracy was really a capitalist contest for spoils. Thus they hoped to turn the Allied peoples against their governments. The revelations embarrassed these governments. For Wilson, they were a calamity, ridiculing his rhetoric, his intentions, and his integrity. Although Wilson tried to forestall publication of the secret treaties in America, pacifist Oswald Garrison Villard printed the complete texts in the *New York Evening Post.* Wilson could but hold his ground, insisting he would not be bound by secret treaties.

The Fourteen Points

In the war of propaganda Wilson's strategy was to drive a wedge, first, between the German government and the German people and, then, between Germany and its allies, especially Austria-Hungary, in such statements as "The military masters of Germany who proved also to be the masters of Austria-Hungary"; "Austria is at their mercy." To the smaller states he held out the special promise of independence in such statements as "We shall hope to secure for the peoples of the Balkan peninsula and for the people of the Turkish Empire the right and opportunity to make their own lives safe . . . from the dictation of foreign courts" (December 4, 1917).

George Creel set himself the task of giving these speeches truly universal circulation. A Foreign Mail Press Bureau, directed by Ernest Poole, despatched printed material every week. Wilson's official speeches were carried on the wireless and soon translated and transmitted across the world. Movie houses everywhere showed films about America's war effort. Consequently, two decades before the cult of personality became a device of propaganda associated with Hitler and Stalin, there was a Creel phenomenon, the cult of Wilson. The cult of Wilson was not only evident everywhere in western Europe with posters, postcards, and photographs, but also in Italy and Russia. It spread in the East as far as China, where Creel claimed an edition of Wilson's speeches had become a best-seller, and in the West to the Peruvian Andes. Creel's agent in Copenhagen reported back, "I have seen a new understanding of President Wilson come into the minds of the Danes so that they placed him on a plane beside their greatest national heroes; I have known them to cut out the photographs of him sent out by us which appeared in Danish papers and place them in a sort of family shrine."

Creel's agent in Russia, Edgar G. Sisson, persuaded Creel, and through him, Wilson, that if the president's messages were to be truly effective in Germany and Russia they must be translated and distributed to ordinary people in a short and accessible form. Accordingly, with the help of his intermediary, Colonel Edward

The Big Four in Paris in 1919: Lloyd George of Britain, Orlando of Italy, Clemenceau of France, and Woodrow Wilson of the United States. John Dos Passos observed in *U.S.A.* how they were four old men, shuffling out the pack. (Library of Congress).

House, Wilson restated his war aims and peace terms in a condensed form, the Fourteen Points. Wilson had already prepared himself for this.

While Walter Lippmann was working in the War Department as an aide to Secretary Newton D. Baker, he and House conceived the idea of a research body to gather political, cultural, and geographical information about Europe and its colonies that the administration could use at the end of the war. The organization, known as the Inquiry, was headed by Sidney E. Mezes with Lippmann as executive secretary. His task was to collate and edit the work completed in secret by about 125 specialists and scholars. Lippmann recognized that the government would require much more information about the rest of the world if it were to translate ideals into politics.

For three weeks in December 1917 Sidney Mezes, Walter Lippmann, and others tried to coordinate the specific interests of the movements of national liberation with the provisions of the secret treaties, providing House with a special document, "The War Aims and Peace Terms it Suggests" on December 22, 1917. It was later revised in consultation with Wilson and House, anxious to reveal their "New Diplomacy" to Congress. Thus, in their final version, the Fourteen Points were the work of Wilson, House, Lippmann, and Mezes. They had to reconcile complex and contradictory interests, to boost public morale and satisfy national aspirations.

The first five points, and the last, were devised by Wilson and covered general principles: open diplomacy; freedom of the seas; lower tariffs; disarmament; the rights of colonial peoples; and the League of Nations. These points aroused widespread public enthusiasm. The remaining territorial points were more crucial to the belligerents. Point Six recommended a liberal policy to revolutionary Russia to allow its political development without outside interference. Point Seven recommended the evacuation and restoration of Belgium. Point Eight was about the restoration of Alsace-Lorraine to France. Point Nine disposed of Italy's exaggerated claims to the Austrian Tyrol, Trieste, and the Dalmatian coast, recommending that Italian frontiers should be fixed "along clearly recognizable lines."

Point Ten called for internal (or federal) autonomy within the Austro-Hungarian Empire for nationalist groups. (Only later did Wilson agree to the dissolution of the empire, a concession Lippmann subsequently said had installed weak states in Central Europe, destroying the balance of power, and opening the way for Hitler.) On Point Eleven, about the Balkans, Wilson revised the specific recommendations of the Inquiry toward Serbia and Bulgaria. Wilson merely wanted it stated that Serbia must have access to the sea, with frontiers based on national, economic, and historic rights.

Point Twelve proposed the security of Turkey and guaranteed autonomy to its subject peoples. As to Point Thirteen, about Poland, the Inquiry wanted a revived Polish state attached to a democratic Russia or Austria-Hungary. Wilson was not content with this and insisted on an independent Poland to include those territories inhabited by "indisputably Polish populations" but with access to the sea through lands predominantly German.

Wilson delivered the Fourteen Points in a speech to Congress of January 8, 1918, aimed not only at the United States but also the world outside, especially Germany and Russia. They were now intended partly as basis for peace negotiation, and partly as Wilson's promise of how he himself would shape the peace. Wilson was not surprised by the ominous silence of the Allied governments to his momentous speech. His tactic was to excite their peoples to put pressure on their governments. Throughout 1918, in a series of speeches, he went on to amplify the Fourteen Points with various particulars and principles.

The Fourteen Points also proved a most successful strategy among new immigrants. They eagerly seized upon the doctrine of self-determination and converted it into a way of turning the war into a crusade for national liberation. Thus American of Czech, Polish, and South Slav origins set aside previous differences and worked in concert for the restoration of Poland and the creation of Czechoslovakia, Yugoslavia, and Albania.

The Armistice of 1918

Meanwhile, in 1918, Germany seemed to be on the point of winning the war in Europe only to have victory snatched from the jaws of defeat by the United States. First, the Bolsheviks treated with Germany at Brest-Litovsk on March 3, 1918, yielding up the Baltic provinces and the Ukraine. Germany could now transfer troops to the western front from which they launched a great offensive on March 21, 1918. First the British and then the French were driven back with appalling loss of life. In this crisis Georges Clemenceau, the French prime minister, proved himself of indomitable will and persuaded the Americans and the British, who, apart from Lloyd George, were most reluctant, to accept a unified command of their forces under General Ferdinand Foch, now declared supreme commander of the Allied armies in April 1918. The arrival of about 750,000 extra American troops that spring provided the Allies with enough extra forces to mount a counteroffensive on the highway from Château-Thierry to Soissons on July 18. It was complemented by a second, British, offensive on August 9 that breached the Hindenburg line where the Germans had been entrenched since 1914. At this late stage in the war the Allies were able to make effective use of armored tractors—tanks—to puncture the German lines.

Despite these advances in the West, the war might have still continued indefinitely on the western front had not the central powers begun to crumble in the East. Turkey was eliminated by Allenby at the battle of Megiddo on September 19. Bulgaria signed an armistice on September 29. The Allies could now break into central Europe. The German commander, Ludendorff, advised the reluctant German government he could not spare forces to protect central Europe without losing the West and persuaded them to seek an armistice so that he could regroup and consolidate his shattered forces.

After the new German chancellor, Prince Max of Baden, began negotiations for an armistice on October 3, Wilson pushed the Germans back from one position to another in a series of exchanges. They had to evacuate Belgium, give up submarine warfare, agree to the Fourteen Points, and negotiate military terms of the armistice with Foch. Moreover, they had to accept the principle of democratic control in the German government. Not until they had agreed to all of these did Wilson turn over the correspondence to the Allies. He was at the zenith of his power. By his stand on democratic principles, Wilson undoubtedly contributed to the fall of the kaiser, who first fled to Holland and then abdicated on November 9. This was on the advice of his cabinet, now faced with wide social unrest and a naval mutiny at Kiel.

Since the Allies had not defined their war aims, they had only themselves to blame if Wilson decided for them. The Allies jibbed especially at two of the Fourteen Points. They reserved complete freedom of interpretation about freedom of the seas (Point Two) and they insisted on reparations from Germany for damage to their civilian populations as well as the restoration of French territory (Point Eight).

In September 1918 Lippmann was assigned to Colonel Edward House's staff in Paris at the time House was explaining Woodrow Wilson's Fourteen Points to the Allies in order to get them accepted. This required a close definition of the meaning of the Points that House sought in turn from Lippmann and from Frank Cobb, editor of the New York *World,* on October 25. House demanded the qualifications within twenty-four hours. Lippmann prepared memoranda on thirteen of the Points, and Cobb provided a memorandum on the last. The definitions accepted by Wilson as well as House were thus largely the work of Walter Lippmann. Lippmann tried to reconcile the Fourteen Points not only with the secret discussions of the Allies before and during the war but also with the secret discussions taking place at the end of the war. In order to justify these discussions in view of Point One, which called for "open covenants openly arrived at," Lippmann provided a somewhat sophistical distinction. Confidential negotiations were permissible so long as their final outcome was made public. The difficulties with some of the other points were not solved. They were postponed in the hope that the League of Nations would do something about them once it was in session. Thus, the final days of war were a muddle of confusion and haste in which the Fourteen Points and the terms of armistice got hopelessly tangled. Nevertheless, the Allies reviewed and grudgingly accepted the spirit of the Fourteen Points on November 4.

The Ottoman government signed an armistice with Britain on October 30; the Austro-Hungarian high command did so with Italy on November 3; and a German delegation signed with the Allied forces on November 11. Thus the Great War came to an end. The Ottoman and Hapsburg Empires had already ceased to exist.

Mark Sullivan recorded the joy of New York as the news of the Armistice broke there:

Lights sprang out on the Statue of Liberty. Air-raid sirens blared. Noise increased, multiplied, travelled along the water-front; ships and tugs tied down their whistles, lit all their lights, ran up flags; sailors tossed calcium-burning flares on the dark water. Munitions factories across the Hudson took up the chorus. Newsboys were crying themselves hoarse as far as the Bronx. Minute by minute the wave of clangor deepened over the city. No one could sleep. . . .

The early morning sun found Fifth Avenue a solid mass of people, cheering, waving flags, milling about in ecstasy. Autoists, caught in the mob, sounded horns in continuous din, back-fired intentionally with terrific clatter.

As if to parody the cruel deaths in the trenches an epidemic of influenza followed the war. In the United States it appeared first in Boston, Philadelphia, and New York, with deaths rising slowly throughout the war until the fall of 1918 when there were, on average, 175 deaths a day. By October thirty-six states were affected; almost a quarter of the population fell ill and of every 1,000 sick, 19 died. The total number of deaths in the United States was between 400,000 and 500,000. Most of them were between the ages of twenty and forty. The young and old escaped. The highest death rate was in Baltimore where the weather was too cold for burial services and, as a result, a plague from the accumulated corpses was a real possibility. In early 1919 the pandemic vanished but it left its victims prone to tuberculosis and cardiac illnesses. The epidemic was taken by some as a symbol of an old society passing away.

The end of the war was also followed by the death of the first of the political titans, Theodore Roosevelt. When his son Quentin, a pilot, was shot down and killed behind enemy lines in 1918, TR lost his will to live and declined into invalidism. On January 5, 1919, he died at Sagamore Hill, Massachusetts. He was buried with the utmost simplicity at Oyster Bay on January 9. However, in New York the day was marked by complete silence. As the casket was lowered into the grave every streetcar, subway train, and factory stopped in tribute. In Washington Congress and (for the first time) the Supreme Court adjourned for the day. On his deathbed TR told his sister, Corinne, how he wished that he might have died for his country, like Quentin. Corinne answered that most people would be willing, in times of peril, to die for their country. "The difference, Theodore, between you and the majority of us is that you not only are willing and anxious to *die* for your country but that you *live* for your country every day of your life."

The financial cost of World War I on all sides was put at $337.94 billion by Professor E. L. Bogert of the department of economics of the University of Illinois in a postwar investigation he made for the Carnegie Endowment for International Peace. Direct costs were $186 billion and indirect costs $151 billion. The total loss of life was 9,998,771, more than twice the estimated loss in all other wars from Napoleon onward. Moreover, the price might in future, said the report, include "the very breakdown of modern economic society." Indeed, the balance of power was shifting irrevocably. All the old ambitions of monarchical and republican Europe became trivial in comparison with the impending struggle between the two world powers, Russia and the United States, at first unconscious but fundamentally implacable rivals. As English historian A.J.P. Taylor suggests in his *The Struggle for Mastery in Europe* (1954), "This was more than a rivalry of Power; it was a rivalry of idealism. . . . Universal revolution on the one side and the Fourteen Points on the other presented Utopian programmes for achieving permanent peace. . . . Europe was superseded; and in January 1918 there began a competition between communism and liberalism which has lasted to the present day."

World War I developed no American military and naval heroes to compare with those of the American Civil or Spanish-American Wars. There was much contemporary discussion as to why. The common explanation was psychological. World War I was not fought through to a decisive military finish. Just as the United States was stoking its most intense fighting emotions Germany surrendered and, incidentally, aborted the patriotic emotions of the United States and, indirectly, led to national sentiments developing even darker undercurrents than jingoism in the course of the 1920s.

The Tragedy of Woodrow Wilson

At the peak of his fame Woodrow Wilson enjoyed a prestige throughout the world unknown to any other American president. During his two visits to Paris of the winter of 1918–19 and the summer of 1919, Europeans looked to Wilson as a deliverer and redeemer. Everywhere he went he was feted on a scale unknown since Napoleon. Delegations of Swedes, Poles, Albanians, Iraquis, and Ukrainians, among others, waited for him at his house in Paris or in the Crillon Hotel, where he held court, to plead their cause. "The mass of European peasantry, shopkeepers, and day laborers looked forward to his arrival as men looked in mediaeval times to the second coming of Christ," observed William E. Dodd. Yet the hero of 1918 was to leave office in 1921, his health broken, his party crushed, and his great dream in fragments.

Wilson made the achievement of world peace by collective security the cornerstone of his foreign policy. Though he failed in his lifetime to convince the United States, his ideal shaped the perception of two generations across the world as to what was necessary, possible, and desirable for the concert of nations.

The war had changed the world. The number of separate nations in Europe in 1914 was seventeen; in 1919 it was twenty-six. Four great powers—Russia, Germany, Austria-Hungary, and Turkey—and some lesser powers, would endure political revolutions. But the traditional territorial aspirations of the nations remained much as before. Wilson himself revered William Gladstone as "the greatest statesman that ever lived" and his own program of political freedom, self-determination, and free trade was within the nineteenth-century Liberal tradition of the great British prime minister. Wilson's cardinal weakness was his moral intensity that would not brook criticism or opposition and this, and political and medical misfortune, were to destroy his hopes. In his mammoth trilogy, U.S.A., novelist John Dos Passos places his biography of Woodrow Wilson dead center. He agreed with much of the war historians' later revisionist critiques of the president, whom he regarded as a supreme, tragic, and impotent, hero—a patrician politician who had betrayed his own liberalism by going to war in the first place and then betrayed his professional integrity by compromising the spirit and letter of the Fourteen Points. The promise of self-determination excited dreams among peoples all over the world that no statesman or conference could fulfill.

Whatever his errors, Wilson was fighting for a great ideal, a wider horizon of peace and justice than anyone else. It was certainly more enlightened than many of the philosophies of the twentieth-century statesmen he had to deal with. The Fourteen Points became the belated basis of a provisional agreement for peace between the Allies and Germany by the time of the Armistice on November 11, 1918. However, they were not a solid basis for lasting peace. Not only were they subject to somewhat different and conflicting interpretations but they were also undermined by secret wartime treaties between the belligerents and additional requests, such as for reparations from Germany. Moreover, their letter was too simplistic for the ethnic, religious, territorial, and political complexities of Europe and the spirit behind them was tarnished by four years of bitter hostilities. The French prime minister, Clemenceau, was supposed to have remarked, "Mr. Wilson bores me with his Fourteen Points. Why God Almighty has only ten!"

Paris Conference of 1919

The Peace Conference at Paris had first opened on January 12, 1919, with delegates from twenty-seven countries. The chief task of negotiations was undertaken by a Council of Ten and, when this proved too cumbersome, by a Council of Four: David Lloyd George of Britain; Georges Clemenceau of France; Vittorio Orlando of Italy; and Woodrow Wilson.

Against advice and precedent Wilson had gone to Paris himself at the head of the American delegation. He was accompanied by Secretary of State Robert Lansing; his personal adviser, Colonel Edward House; the permanent military representative on the Supreme War Council, General Tasker Bliss; and a retired diplomat, Henry White. The only Republican, White, was of no significance in his party. Although the Senate would have to ratify the treaty, Wilson had not asked it to endorse the Fourteen Points and did not appoint a senator to the delegation. The exclusion of leading senators affronted prominent Republicans and stored up trouble for the future.

At the end of October 1918 Wilson had made an unnecessary appeal to the American electorate for a vote of confidence on his foreign policy in the midterm elections. Republicans across the country, who had supported the administration loyally in the war, were cut by Wilson's request which was interpreted as downright ingratitude and this made it easy for Republican leaders to foment public distaste. On November 5 the polls returned a Republican majority in Congress of 240 to 190 in the House and of 49 to 47 in the Senate. Theodore Roosevelt could, therefore, claim with much justification on November 26, 1918, "Our allies and our enemies and Mr. Wilson himself should all understand that Mr. Wilson has no authority whatever to speak for the American people at this time. His leadership has just been emphatically repudiated by them."

Yet in Europe, at the height of his international reputation, Wilson convinced himself he could bring peace without victory. But the crowds acclaiming him in London, Paris, and elsewhere, wanted a settlement in the interests of their own nations. Those who hated Germany forced their leaders into extreme positions. David Lloyd George had just won a British general election with the greatest majority of seats ever after a campaign of vicious slogans, including, albeit against his will, "Hang the Kaiser" and "Make Germany pay until the pips squeak." Georges Clemenceau, the French premier, had won a vote of confidence of fourfifths of the French chamber. "He had one interest, France," writes historian William E. Leuchtenburg, "and one concern, that Germany must never march again." He was seventy-eight and recalled the humiliating defeat of the Franco-Prussian War and the loss of Alsace-Lorraine as well as the cruelty of the recent conflict. Determined that Germany should never again be able to threaten France, he was reluctantly persuaded to abandon an original intention of dismembering the country even though Germany had now become a republic. The German republic was proclaimed in November 1918. Two months later a national assembly met at Weimar, a city associated with German culture, especially Goethe and Schiller, to devise a new constitution and arrange elections. Thus in January 1919 was created the Weimar Republic that would survive until the Third Reich of 1933.

Whereas Lloyd George was prepared for some moderation toward the new German republic, the discourtesy of the German foreign secretary, Count Ulrich von Brockdorff-Rantzau, hardened not only his resolve but also that of Woodrow Wilson.

Treaty of Versailles

The Treaty of Versailles with Germany was not only harsh but added insult to injury. As he had intended, Clemenceau secured the reduction of the German army to a maximum of 100,000 men without heavy artillery and without an air-force. Ironically, because it was to be a force of men on long service, it turned out to be capable of providing the nucleus for a rapidly trained conscript army. To compensate France for wartime devastation to its own industry, the mining reserves of the Saar valley were placed under international control. After fifteen years the people there would decide on their future affiliation—whether to France or Germany—by a plebiscite. As a safety precaution, the right bank of the Rhine was to be demilitarized. The left bank and its bridges and bridgeheads of Cologne, Coblenz, and Mainz on the right were to suffer an army of occupation for fifteen years that Germany had to maintain. Poland, which had disappeared as an independent state in the 1790s when it was partitioned by Russia, Austria, and Prussia, was revived as a nation state according to the Wilsonian principle of the self-determination of nations. But, contrary to the self-determination of nations, Germans were placed under Polish rule in Silesia and a corridor giving Poland access to the sea at Danzig (now Gdansk) separated East Prussia from Germany. On the insistence of Lloyd George, Danzig became a free city under the Polish Customs Union.

South Africa and Australia were not prepared to give up the German colonies they had acquired in the war, South-West Africa and New Guinea. Thus they defied Wilson and, for the sake of appearances, the term "mandates" was used to cover the acquisitions. Britain took German East Africa and some other territory in West Africa. Japan was granted formal entitlement to Shandong in China.

Germany was forced to pay an immediate indemnity to the Allies of $5 billion and to agree to pay further reparations of an unspecified amount to be decided later. Moreover, the Treaty of Versailles in its "war guilt" clause pronounced Germany the sole cause of the war. Wilson could hardly repudiate the war guilt clause since his own wartime rhetoric had done so much to incriminate the kaiser and the whole German establishment. Rather than assent to the treaty, the German cabinet of Philipp Scheidemann resigned on June 23, 1919. "L'heure du lourd règlement de comptes est venue," "The hour has come for the serious settlement of debts." declared Clemenceau in the Hall of Mirrors at Versailles on June 28, 1919; and five years after the assassination of Franz Ferdinand at Sarajevo, the event that had precipitated the war, peace with Germany was signed.

Thereafter, the Conference turned to peace treaties with the other defeated powers, each named after a Parisian suburb. Treaties were concluded with Austria at St. Germain on September 10, 1919, with Bulgaria at Neuilly on November 27, 1919, with Hungary at Trianon on June 4, 1920, and with Turkey at Sèvres on August 10, 1920. The United States negotiated in all but the Treaty of Sèvres, but only the Treaty of Versailles was submitted to the Senate. British and French troops occupied Constantinople and the other territories of Turkey were in upheaval. Wilson disapproved of the secret agreements about Turkey but, since the United States had never declared war on Turkey, he could hardly justify interfering. Since the Hapsburg Empire had disintegrated, the task of drawing frontiers of the succession states was left to experts of the various foreign offices. In some cases self-determination could not be applied evenly to two or three different ethnic groups living in the same territory. If they sought it, they were living in a world of ecstatic words conjured up by Wilson.

Wilson's reputation as a peacemaker was undermined by the way the Paris settlement clearly violated the Fourteen Points. The treaties were not open covenants openly arrived at but bargains

The official composite portrait of the *Signing of the Treaty of Versailles* in the palace's famous Hall of Mirrors by Sir William Orpen. The German envoys cower before the triumphal trio of Wilson, Clemenceau, and Lloyd George. (Imperial War Museum, London).

negotiated behind closed doors. The most persistent difficulties arose out of conflicts between the Points and the Allies' secret wartime agreements. For instance, by the notorious Treaty of London of 1915, Italy had been promised the Southern Tyrol,

Istria, and the northern part of Dalmatia as its price for joining the Allies. Fiume (later Trieste) was not part of the deal because it was assumed to be Hungary's natural seaport. But at the end of the war Hungary was disrupted by the union of its subordinate kingdom of Croatia with Serbia to constitute the new state of Yugoslavia. Both Yugoslavia and Italy vied with one another over Fiume. Wilson was not party to the Treaty of London but Lloyd George and Clemenceau were. If the Italians insisted that Britain and France should abide by the treaty, they could not claim Fiume. However, if they abandoned the treaty and claimed Fiume on the basis of national origins (since the town itself, if not the district, had an Italian majority), they could not logically claim other land where the inhabitants were not of Italian origin. Thus they would have to give up northern Dalmatia. Wilson was adamant; enraged, Orlando withdrew from Paris. Thus the question of Fiume was left unresolved until January 1924 when Italy and Yugoslavia agreed on a compromise by which Italy took Fiume and Yugoslavia took most of Dalmatia.

Given such flouting of the principle of the self-determination of nations as resulted from turning over the Austrian Tyrol to Italy, putting Germans under Polish control in Silesia, and placing Chinese under Japanese control in Shandong, it was not difficult for Wilson's enemies in the United States to rouse opposition to the Democrats from German-Americans and other American ethnic groups. In April 1919 Wilson was ill with influenza and it was at this time he gave in to the demands of others on the Rhineland, the Saar, Fiume, and Shandong.

Conferences are a matter of trade and barter and Wilson was not a wheeler-dealer—it was contrary to his open nature. Journalist William Allen White recalled how "Time and again, at Paris, he came out of the Council of Ten realizing belatedly and freely admitting in private that he had agreed to something too hastily. . . . His advisers sat silently aghast as he bartered away things which they knew were dear to him, in ignorance of the play or the board." In private Wilson admitted to Geroge Creel that too much was expected of him, partly because of the great success of Creel's publicity, partly because "People will endure their tyrants for years, but they tear their deliverers to pieces if a millennium is not created immediately. Yet these ancient wrongs, these present unhappinesses, are not to be remedied in a day or with a wave of the hand. What I seem to see—I hope I am wrong—is a tragedy of disappointment." Moreover, during this period also Wilson's friendship with Colonel House ended in a rift.

Wilson hoped that inequities of the settlements especially concerning the "successor" states would be reconsidered by the League of Nations, his mechanism to keep the peace.

Wilson mistakenly thought the Allies would oppose the League of Nations and was somewhat surprised that the British Foreign Office had anticipated him and had already drawn up a draft scheme. It provided the basis for the League Covenant and was duly written into the Treaty of Versailles before anything else. The Covenant of the League of Nations gave every member an equal vote in the Assembly while the United States, Britain, France, Italy, and Japan and four other countries elected for a limited period would constitute the Council, an executive body. League members were pledged to "respect and preserve as against external aggression the territorial integrity and existing political independence of all members"; to submit to arbitration all disputes and to refrain from hostilities until after a "cooling-off period" of three months after the arbiters investigating disputes had made their decision; and, if recommended by the League Council, to impose military, naval, and economic sanctions on nations disregarding the Covenant. The Council had jurisdiction over the former colonies of Germany and Turkey as mandates, over conditions of labor, traffic in women and children, arms and munitions, drugs and the control of health. The Covenant accepted "the validity of . . . regional understandings like the Monroe Doctrine." There would also be a permanent secretariat of which the first secretary was Sir Eric Drummond and the second, Joseph Avenol.

The rapid agreement on the Covenant obscured fundamental differences between the Anglo-Saxon and Latin contingents. The United States and, to a lesser extent, Britain, wanted the League to become a tool for conciliation, eliminating international hostility. France wanted to use the League to perpetuate its wartime alliance and, hence, achieve security against Germany. The conference missed the opportunity to bring about financial stability. Britain should have suggested the cancellation of debts between the Allies, including Russia, while the United States was still in the flood of enthusiasm. By the time common sense prevailed, a great opportunity had passed by. What financiers were reluctant to accept was that European nations were no longer good debtors now that the fulcrum of international finance, sanctity of contract, had been broken by the war.

When the terms of the peace treaties were published, the editors of the *New Republic* forsook Wilson. The *New Republic*'s attack of May 17 was headed "Is it Peace?" The editorial by Lippmann declared, "We do not see how this treaty is anything but the prelude to quarrels in a deeply divided and hideously embittered Europe." The following week, under the title "This is not peace," the editors recommended that America should withdraw from commitments to Europe. Thus Article Ten of the League Covenant about collective security was the hardest for them to accept. Undoubtedly, the most bitter draught of all for the liberals to swallow was the fact that Wilson's failure was theirs also, especially since it was America's inexpertise and ignorance that were under attack. They found it easier to blame Wilson than accept their own complicity.

The conference broke up. "I think I did as well as might be expected," observed Lloyd George somewhat wrily later, "—seated as I was between Jesus Christ and Napoleon Bonaparte." However, as far as Clemenceau was concerned, Wilson simply talked like Jesus Christ but acted like Lloyd George.

There remained the problem of Communist Russia. Alarmed by uprisings that left Communists briefly in control of Berlin, Munich, and Budapest, Britain and France sent troops to seize Russia's ports and aid the counter-revolutionary White insurgents. Wilson was persuaded by diplomat William C. Bullitt to see what could be obtained from Lenin. He returned from a diplomatic mission to Moscow with a promise that Russia would pay its war debts, and offer concessions to the West in exchange for recognition of the Bolshevik government. However, by now, Wilson had been persuaded by the Allies to withhold recognition.

Wilson's decision to press ahead with intervention against the Bolsheviks stirred the liberals against him even further. Moreover, the administration misrepresented the extent of American support for the Whites. In his *Liberalism in America* (1919) Harold Stearns said that the liberals were as guilty as Wilson. Seduced by the prospect of power, they had suspended their powers of judgment. By removing the moral foundations of action, they had demeaned pragmatism and turned it into expediency. The substitution of method for moral values was the "technique of liberal failure—the method of compromise . . . whereby one hopes to control events by abandoning oneself to them."

The United States and the League

Wilson's greatest diplomatic coup and most costly political mistake had come when the Paris Conference decided, on January 25, 1919, to make the League of Nations an integral part of the Treaty of Versailles. Repudiating objections by more than a third of the American Senate to the constitution of the League until after peace was signed, Wilson said in New York on March 4, 1919, on the eve of his second visit to Europe, that there were "so many threads of the treaty tied to the covenant that you cannot dissect the covenant from the treaty without destroying the whole vital structure."

Wilson had dramatized his defiance but, in doing so, he was revealing his strategy in advance. This was giving hostages to fortune and was far removed from the dexterity of Wilson in his former days of supreme self-control. His arrogant retort encouraged defiance among his foes who now determined to resist the whole treaty. So long as the League remained a generalization, it was taken as a worthy part of America's postwar aims. Wilson's defiance made people aware for the first time that here was a most controversial subject. Wilson captured public attention for the Republican senators who found an audience eager to listen to their interpretation that, by joining the League, America would give up part of its sovereignty. They sowed doubt on fertile soil. For now, with all passion spent, there was a slump in patriotic idealism.

Wilson also learnt that almost every immigrant group within the United States found fault with the treaties. German-Americans resented the way they had been treated in the war, and blamed Wilson for American intervention and the notorious war guilt clause. Irish-Americans resented Wilson's reluctance to apply his own doctrine of self-determination to Ireland and his open distaste for Irish extremists. They thought Article 4 of the League Covenant might mean that Irish-American soldiers might be drafted and sent to Britain to help Britain extinguish Irish patriots in a revolt. Immigrants of Italian, Polish, and Czech origins chafed because the Big Three had curtailed their national aspirations for additional territories.

When Woodrow Wilson called Congress into special session in June 1919 to debate the treaty, he encountered ugly resistance. Because they had won the midterm elections the Republicans had been able to place one of Wilson's most bitter critics, Henry Cabot Lodge of Massachusetts, in the chair of the Senate Foreign Relations Committee. The prospect for the treaty was bleak. Lodge led a group of Republicans jealous of the president's prerogative in foreign affairs, determined on complete American independence from Europe, and anxious to resist the Democrats' intention of fighting the 1920 elections as the party that had led America through a victorious war to a conclusive peace.

Some historians believe that all available evidence suggests that in early 1919, despite widespread criticism, the majority of Americans were ready to approve the Treaty of Versailles and accept American membership of the League of Nations. The evidence is the accounts and opinions published in newspapers, especially of polls, and resolutions passed by thirty-two state legislatures, labor unions, women's groups, farm organizations, and professional societies. Even Wilson's most bitter critics, Lodge and Borah, conceded this. Such was Wilson's prestige and such was public support for the League that the Senate would probably have to accede to the treaty, despite the opposition of numerous isolationists within it.

Opinion in the Senate was divided into four schools of thought. Firstly, there were those who would accept the treaty without change. Later called the Non-Reservationists, this group com-

prised forty Democrats and one Republican, Porter J. Mc-
Cumber of North Dakota. It was led by Gilbert B. Hitchcock of
Nebraska, chairman of the Senate Foreign Relations Committee
in 1918. Secondly there were those who would accept the treaty
with minor alterations. These Mild Reservationists consisted of
thirteen Republicans headed by Frank B. Kellogg of Minnesota,
later secretary of state. Thirdly were those who would accept the
treaty with major amendments. These Strong Reservationists
consisted of twenty-one Republicans and four Democrats. Led
by Henry Cabot Lodge, they included Warren Gamaliel Harding
of Ohio, subsequently Wilson's successor as president. Fourthly
were the Irreconcilables, consisting initially of fourteen Republicans and three Democrats, including the Republicans William E.
Borah of Idaho, Philander C. Knox of Pennsylvania (Taft's secretary of state), Frank B. Brandegee of Connecticut, and Hiram
W. Johnson of California, the Democrat James A. Reed of Missouri, and the Progressive Robert La Follette of Wisconsin.

The treaty went for examination to the Senate Foreign Relations Committee. Walter Lippmann cooperated with the Irreconcilables, feeding them information he had gained at the Inquiry
and in Paris, that proved most embarrassing to Wilson. When
Wilson appeared before the committee, he was asked why he had
not insisted that the Allies repudiate the secret treaties before taking America into the war. Wilson answered that he did not know
about the treaties until he was in Paris in December 1918. This
was disingenuous bluff. As we have seen, in December 1917
Lippmann had been assigned the task of reconciling Wilson's
principles with the aims of the treaties in order to provide the
draft that became the Fourteen Points.

When William C. Bullitt appeared before the committee, he
had his revenge on Wilson for rejecting the Russian overtures.
With ill-concealed glee he revealed the bitter truth of the political
maneuvers behind the scenes at Paris. He recalled Robert Lansing's private remarks to him that the treaty was a disaster and
the League useless. When Bullitt had finished his testimony, Wilson looked as unscrupulous as Lloyd George and not nearly so
accomplished.

Wilson was unable to counter the personal and political resis-

Human tragedy is often attended by farce. Indian chief Lemuel Occum Fielding, known as "the last of the Mohicans," with his son and daughter in Washington on November 17, 1920, to offer an Indian tea remedy to Woodrow Wilson following his debilitating stroke and, also, to press their claim for land in Norwich, Connecticut. As Indian intellectual Arthur C. Parker observed, you "have to play Indian to be Indian." (Library of Congress).

tance to his proposals, yet he was unwilling to accept more than mild amendments to his grand design. Thus he embarked on a speaking tour of the United States on September 4, 1919. This fateful tour was a forlorn attempt to appeal to the conscience of ordinary Americans across the country. But Wilson could make little headway against popular isolationism and intolerance. The Irreconcilables followed him wherever he spoke. They countered his conviction that, "I can predict with absolute certainty that within another generation there will be another world war if the nations of the world do not concert the method by which to prevent it," with ridicule.

Wilson had little remaining strength to continue the struggle. On September 25, 1919, he collapsed at Pueblo, Colorado, and returned to Washington. On October 4 he was found half conscious on the bathroom floor, having suffered a second stroke. Thereafter, he was too ill even to be shaved. His second wife, Edith, and doctor kept all visitors from him, except for Joseph Tumulty who had to avoid exciting him. George Creel recalled later, "At sight of me he gestured pathetically, a tragic sweep of the hand that took in the whole of his helpless, wasted body, and great tears filled his eyes."

In the face of repeated assertions from Mrs. Wilson and Tumulty that Wilson was not disabled, the Senate despatched a "smelling committee," led by Senator Albert W. Fall of New Mexico, to ascertain the facts for themselves. On a second occasion Wilson exerted maximum effort to appear cogent and in control for half an hour before them. However, in a bitter rage he dismissed Secretary of State Robert Lansing on February 7, 1920, when he learned Lansing had been calling cabinet meetings without him.

Cut off from his allies and friends by his illness, Wilson nevertheless insisted on controlling a battle he could not even fight. As the historian of the League of Nations, F. P. Walters, puts it, "A difficult situation was thus converted into irretrievable defeat." To meet Wilson's arguments, Lodge and the Senate Foreign Relations Committee had reduced their numerous early criticisms to fourteen reservations by November 6, 1919. The most significant was about Article 10—by which the putative signatories agreed to respect and preserve the territorial integrity and political independence of all members of the League. The United States, they argued, could accept no such obligation without the specific assent of Congress for each and every instance. Two other reservations would have given the United States exclusive authority over the tariff and immigration. On November 19, 1919, the Treaty of Versailles was defeated in the Senate both *with* Lodge's reservations (which Wilson wanted his supporters to suppress) and *without* (which the Irreconcilables resisted). Thus ratification was denied in a paradoxical situation. Those voting against any Covenant at all were at one with those who voted for the Covenant as it stood. To both sides it was a case of all or nothing.

Whereas the Senate Democrats, led by Senator Gilbert Hitchcock, were willing to pay the Republican price for ratification and compromise, Wilson was not. He maintained that, if the reservations were accepted, one or other of the foreign powers would have refused ratification in turn. Britain, for instance, could have objected to a reservation in favor of Irish independence. And the United States would not want to be obligated by decisions in a council where the British Empire had six votes against its one. Latin American countries might object to United States' reluctance to relinquish its prerogatives in the Monroe Doctrine. It is probable the other signatories would have preferred even qualified American adherence to the League rather than its total abstention from it. This was certainly true of Britain and France. More important was Wilson's rejection of Lodge's reservation to Article 10. The United States could not send troops abroad without the approval of Congress, anyway, so the objection was not necessary. But underlying the semantic dispute was a chasm of different assumptions. Those Americans who favored supporting the League perhaps did so without fully understanding the implication of collective security. For membership of the League would involve a clear break with the prevailing myth of American isolation that had really outlasted the substance of policy. It meant that America would assume new responsibilities. Most Americans still thought they could maintain national security without making external commitments. For the ultimate weapon of the League against aggression would have to be an international force—an army. Most Americans could not accept this. The United States was not ready psychologically.

Yet a majority of Republicans and Democrats in the Senate still favored the ideal of membership of the League and blamed both Wilson and Lodge for their obduracy. When the next session opened in January 1920 attempts were made at the compromise. At a final vote on March 19, 1920, there was a substantial majority for ratification of the treaty with reservations but seven votes less than the necessary two-thirds. The thirty-five votes against the forty-nine in favor included twenty-three of Wilson's loyal followers agreeing with twelve Irreconcilables in accordance with the president's wishes. As Senator Frank Brandegee put it to Lodge, "We can always depend on Mr. Wilson. He never has failed us."

Labor Problems

Another casualty of the period was organized labor that found itself a victim of wartime hysteria, federal legislation by way of the Espionage Act (1917) and Sedition Act (1918), and deep nativist fears aroused by the Bolshevik Revolution in Russia. Moreover, suppression of protest against the war provided a convenient cover for the suppression of radicals with whom critics of the war were identified. Labor agitation could be crushed not because it was radical but because it was, supposedly, unpatriotic. As Henry F. May explains in *The End of American Innocence* (1960), "Enemies of the war were often in fact, and were always believed to be, opponents of the dominant American civilization on other counts." "You can't even collect your thoughts without getting arrested for unlawful assemblage," Max Eastman, editor of the *Masses,* told an audience in July 1917. "They give you ninety days for quoting the Declaration of Independence, six months for quoting the Bible, and pretty soon somebody is going to get a life sentence for quoting Woodrow Wilson in the wrong connection."

Under the new laws 1,532 people were arrested for disloyal statements, 65 for threatening the president, and 10 for sabotage. Here was the real beginning of the Great Red Scare. William Haywood and 94 other members of the IWW were tried and sentenced to prison as was Socialist leader Eugene V. Debs, who was brought to trial for a speech at Canton, Ohio, in which he had declared, "The master class has always declared the war, and the subject class has always fought the battles. The master class has had all to gain and nothing to lose, while the subject class has had nothing to gain and all to lose—especially their lives." Debs was found guilty and sentenced to twenty years' imprisonment. George W. Anderson, a federal judge from Boston, later declared that 90 percent of the pro-German plots were fictions and this was also the opinion of Alice Roosevelt Longworth.

The *Masses* had opposed any American involvement from the outset. Max Eastman attributed the war to capitalist greed in a contest for territory and markets. Ironically, in September 1914, he believed the disruption of war would hasten class conflict. In the same issue John Reed echoed Eastman's views and described the conflict as a "Traders' War." The *Masses'* long record of hostility to militarism brought it into direct conflict with Wilson's administration and the entire editorial board was charged with conspiracy to obstruct the draft.

The Climax of the Great Red Scare

Union no-strike pledges and government propaganda appealing to patriotism did not pacify a large body of the nation's industrial work force. According to some estimates, the cost of living rose by 51.7 percent in the period 1917–20. Moreover, at the same time, labor shortages had provided workers with the opportunity to attack the managerial efforts to undermine their control in the workplace. Although the number of workers organized in unions doubled from about 2.5 million in 1916 to about 5 million in 1920, the disputes that were erupting in industry involved much more than simply the right to form a union. A whole range of questions were being asked about managerial prerogatives, work rules, speed-ups, pay systems, and the operation of industries. For a brief moment in the aftermath of the war, they brought the various struggles of skilled and unskilled workers closer together than at any other time in American history.

Organized labor was angry. It felt its role in American society had been legitimized by its fullhearted part in the war effort, the *de facto* recognition of AFL unions during the war, and the unprecedented federal intervention in labor matters by the president who had, for example, set hours and working conditions in certain industries such as lumber. However, it was greatly disturbed by massive postwar inflation and the government's inability, or reluctance, to deal with it.

In 1919, working-class militancy reached previously unknown heights. Over 4 million workers, representing a remarkable 22 percent of the workforce, took part in various strikes and lockouts across the country. The dramatic industrial battles of the period 1919–22 represented a critical watershed for working-class radicalism in the United States. Across the country, workers demanded increased wages, shorter hours, union recognition, and rights of collective bargaining.

The long series of postwar strikes and lockouts began with a strike by harbor workers in New York on January 9, 1919, and continued with a strike of 35,000 dress and waist makers who wanted a 15-percent–wage increase and a forty-four–hour week. On March 12, 4,500 employees of the Public Service Railway Co., which ran through 141 towns and cities in New Jersey, walked out, forcing the company to close down its services. On April 11 Director General Frank T. Hines of the railroads (still under federal control) acceded to wage demands totaling $65 million, rather than face a strike of railway workers. On July 17, 30,000 cigar workers in New York went on strike. On August 7 New England railroad shopmen walked out, causing the cancellation of 102 passenger trains. And so on.

Perhaps the most radical mass strike involving AFL unions took place in Seattle. On January 21, 1919, 35,000 shipyard workers stopped work in protest over an unfair wage rate and appealed to the Seattle Central Labor Council to call a general strike. Within two weeks, 110 local unions had voted to support the call, well aware that they risked expulsion from their various internationals. A General Strike Committee was created to run the strike and to continue to provide the city with such essential services as garbage collection and hospital laundry. The distinctly syndicalist emphasis of the strike was made clear in the committee's official declaration:

Labor will not only SHUT DOWN the industries, but Labor will REOPEN, under the management of the appropriate trades, such activities as are needed to preserve public health and public peace. If the strike continues, Labor may feel led to avoid public suffering by reopening more and more activities
UNDER ITS OWN MANAGEMENT
And that is why we say that we are starting on a road that leads—NO ONE KNOWS WHERE!

However, once the strikers had committed themselves to the mass strike, they had to face the prospect either of provoking military confrontation if their actions turned revolutionary, or of giving in. The General Strike Committee, under heavy pressure from the international officials of the various AFL unions, finally voted to call off the strike on February 11, 1919. Nevertheless, the new unionism of workers was more militant than any for several decades; even so, it stepped back from the edge of revolution.

The most serious and damaging dispute was the steel strike, beginning on September 22, after U.S. Steel, led by Judge Elbert H. Gary, refused to accept the formation of a new union of steel workers organized by the radical wing of the AFL. On the first day, union leaders claimed how 279,000 out of 350,000 workers had quit. For their part, the companies said no more than 20 percent were on strike. In fact, strike solidarity varied from place to place. Most workers in Chicago stayed out; most workers in Pittsburgh continued to work. The strike was punctuated by violent clashes. Five men were killed at New Castle, Pennsylvania. On September 23 two strikers were killed and fifty wounded by mill guards at a Buffalo plant. The strike widened. When the Bethlehem Steel Company rejected union demands, a further strike was called and about a quarter of the workers came out. At Chicago the Jones and Laughlin plants had to close down. By late September it was the biggest strike the country had yet seen. Under the leadership of syndicalist William Z. Foster, the steelworkers attempted to force the giant corporations to end the tyranny of company towns, and, also, recognize their right to organize in labor unions. The brutal conflict finally ended in defeat for the strikers who gave in on January 8, 1920, and left behind a number of profound lessons for the labor movement to consider.

The vast powers of repression wielded by the corporations once again proved lethal to the militant industrial unionism of the steelworkers. A report by the Interchurch Commission concluded:

The United States Steel Corporation was too big to be beaten by 300,000 working men. It had too large a cash surplus, too many allies among other businesses, too much support from government officers, local and national, too strong influence with social institutions such as the press and the pulpit, it spread too much of the earth—still retaining absolutely centralized control—to be defeated by widely scattered workers of many minds, many fears, varying states of pocketbook and under comparatively improvised leadership.

Although William Foster was adept and dedicated, the many minds and ethnic prejudices of workers remained vulnerable targets for manipulation by the employers.

The end of the war had also unleashed a particularly virulent wave of nativism and xenophobia that shattered the country's radical groups and completed the liquidation of most of the radical leaders begun in 1917. On February 4, 1919, the Senate, stirred by a declaration from Senator William King of Utah that the Bolsheviks were working to overthrow capitalistic governments, appointed a committee to investigate Bolshevik activities in the United States. On February 11 the Department of Justice had fifty-three Communists deported at Ellis Island. On March 10 the Supreme Court sustained the wartime conviction of Eugene V. Debs for violating the Espionage Act in his speech of June 16, 1918, and gave him a new sentence of ten years' imprisonment. Debs replied that the judges were "begowned, bewhiskered, bepowdered old fossils who have never decided anything." On March 12, 1919, Debs, in a farewell speech at Cleveland, added insult to injury when he referred to Lenin and Trotsky as the "foremost statesmen of the age." (While he was still in prison he ran as presidential candidate for the fifth time in the election of 1920, receiving his highest total of popular votes, 919,799, but only 3.4 percent of the vote—less than in 1912.)

This was the climax of the Great Red Scare.

On April 30, 1919, what was alleged to be a nationwide plot to assassinate various public officials on May Day was thwarted by the discovery of sixteen packets containing bombs in the New York General Post Office. In addition, another thirty-four time bombs, intended for celebrities such as Justice Oliver Wendell Holmes, Secretary of Labor William B. Wilson, and Attorney General A. Mitchell Palmer, were seized. Four hundred soldiers, sailors, and marines raided the office of the New York *Call,* a socialist newspaper, on May 1, beat up several journalists, and damaged the plant.

Conservatives blamed the Communist International, created in 1918 to promote world revolution. They believed random bomb attacks were a prelude to a Communist uprising. The climax of terrorist activities came on June 2, 1919, when Attorney General A. Mitchell Palmer's Washington home on R Street was badly damaged by a bomb thrown by an unknown man who was killed in the explosion. "Go to sleep," Eleanor Roosevelt, living across the street, told her son, James, "It's only a little bomb." The same day the homes of Mayor Davis of Cleveland, Justice Albert F. Hayden of Roxbury, Massachusetts, and Judge G. C. Nott of New York were also damaged by bombs. However, the worst bomb outrage of all took place in Wall Street on September 16, 1920, before the Subtreasury and Assay Office, when a stationary horse-drawn wagon exploded, killing thirty-eight passersby immediately, and injuring hundreds of others, including people at windows six stories above the ground. The damage to property was variously estimated at between $500,000 and $2.5 million. It was widely assumed that the explosion was the work of radical terrorists but the criminals were never traced and no one was indicted.

When 1,117 men of the Boston police went on strike on September 9, 1919, to protest their commissioner's refusal to allow them to join the AFL, they turned a volatile atmosphere into a hysterical one. Of all wage earners the police had most cause for complaint. Their salaries had risen little in the war, especially when compared with inflation. The police decided to form unions in the belief that thus could they improve their lot. The Democratic mayor, Andrew Peters, called out the Boston companies of state troops to maintain order and put a stop to widespread looting. Governor Calvin Coolidge of Massachusetts issued an edict on September 11, calling on citizens to uphold law and order. The next day new men, many of them war veterans, were appointed to the places of the striking police. At this point Samuel Gompers of the AFL pleaded that the defeated strikers be allowed to return to their jobs, only to receive in reply Coolidge's famous telegram: "There is no right to strike against the public safety by anybody, any time, anywhere." For this Coolidge was congratulated by Woodrow Wilson and became a national hero.

However, the public found its savior from the Great Red Scare in Attorney General A. Mitchell Palmer, a man of exaggerated presidential ambition. Declaring that it had discovered a revolutionary plot, the Department of Justice began a systematic nationwide raid on Reds, and arrested over 200 people in New York. Legend has it that Palmer's kangaroo courts served over 5,000 arrest warrants and deportation orders in thirty-three cities across the country. On December 21 alone the United States had 249 radicals deported to Russia in the *Buford*.

In the Southwest, the Great Red Scare struck directly at the remnants of grassroots socialism that had endured the war. Kansas and Oklahoma legislators joined Arkansas in passing so-called red flag laws to prohibit any public display of radical sympathy. Governor J.B.A. Robertson of Oklahoma was prophetic when he warned striking telephone workers that "The Ku Klux Klan will have to come back unless there is a change for the better." In Washington State lumberjacks included several committed IWW activists who wanted better hours and conditions for timber workers and wanted them to be paid in federal money, rather than in company scrip. Against them were ranged the combined forces of the Employers Association and their tools, the Loyal Legion of Loggers and Lumbermen, a mix of veterans and workers who raided IWW meeting places to beat up and lynch the organizers. The worst incident occurred at Centralia on Armistice Day 1919 where a veterans' parade was diverted to attack a Wobblies hall and captured Wesley Everest, who was shielding an IWW secretary, Britt Smith. Everest was mutilated, castrated with a razor, and hanged from a bridge. At the inquest the coroner simply recorded that he had broken out of jail and committed suicide.

The public had become so intolerant that it even accepted the expulsion of duly elected legislators. On November 10, 1919, the House of Representatives voted by 309 to 1 to unseat Socialist representative Victor L. Berger of Milwaukee. On January 7, 1920, the New York State Legislature refused to admit five Socialists elected from New York City, despite the protest of Governor Al Smith who opposed the political suppression of legally elected representatives of a duly constituted party.

Big Bill Haywood was also imprisoned by Judge Landis for his alleged subversive activities during the Great Red Scare. During a brief period out on bail, he fled the country and went to live in Moscow. His health already broken, he could not adjust to the new, and foreign, workers' republic and died within two years. He was cremated and his ashes were interned below the walls of the Kremlin. John Reed also died in Russia of typhus in 1920 at the age of thirty-two. Reed had visited Russia in fall 1917 to report on the revolution. His *Ten Days That Shook The World* (1919), written after his return to America in 1918, was his account of the Bolsheviks' seizure of power. An exciting and vivid narrative, filled with heroes of the revolution, it was also a testament to Reed's own conversion to communism. He was not merely a witness but also a participant and addressed the Third Congress of Soviets and went on patrols with the Red Guards.

The internecine quarrels of radicals themselves accelerated the demise of their associations. In summer 1919 moderates within the Socialist party expelled the most left-wing members who were demanding that the party be reconstituted along Leninist lines. Between 1919 and 1928, the Socialist party declined from 118,000 members to 7,793, and shifted emphasis from a predominantly working-class, pragmatic, political party to a party of middle-class intellectuals. The expelled left-wingers regrouped and re-emerged later as the Communist party of America, but they, too, remained plagued by factional disputes and erratic policy changes.

For its part, the AFL desperately tried to court management by suppressing local militancy and sponsoring anti-Bolshevik rallies. However, once the economy had slipped into a severe depression in 1921–22, when unemployment rose to 19.5 percent, employers found conditions conducive for implementing the so-called American Plan, the plan to abolish union shops in many industries. Several huge industrial conflicts, involving 400,000 railway workers, 600,000 coal miners, and 60,000 textile workers, were fought and lost by labor as a preface to the Jazz Age.

During and after World War I, the coalition of governmental and corporate forces finally purged the labor movement of its most radical activists. The Wobblies were smashed; the Socialist party defeated; and the Communists scattered into competing factions. Although a strong protest movement managed to win the aging Debs's release from jail in 1921, as a result of the clemency of President Warren Harding, the heart of American radicalism had been torn out.

A ludicrous postscript to World War I was provided by Henry Ford who brought a $1 million libel suit against the *Chicago Tribune* for having called him "an anarchist." The case opened at Mount Clemens, Michigan, on May 12, 1919, and, much to his irritation, Ford was cross-examined, a process that revealed the woeful state of his general knowledge. Asked to define his theory of government, Ford declared, "It's a long subject." He admitted he knew little about history. "I live in the present," he said tersely. He agreed he knew nothing about the causes of the wars of 1812 and 1898, nor did he know why the United States maintained troops in Puerto Rico. "I haven't been very much interested in armies," said the promoter of the Peace Ship. Yet his interest in newspapers extended no further than a daily reading of their headlines. Provoked beyond endurance, he delivered his most memorable statement ever. "History is bunk!" he exclaimed, a rejoinder with which many of the postwar lost generation of writers would come to agree. If history was bunk, then World War I was a bugger.

Aftermath

An immediate political outcome within the United States of the debate on war and peace was the defeat of the Democratic candidate, Governor James B. Cox of Ohio, in the presidential election of 1920 and the victory of the Republican senator from Ohio, Warren G. Harding, by the largest majority to that time. These nominees provided the choice but the main issue was the foreign policy of Woodrow Wilson, by now a somewhat prone protagonist. At the Republican National Convention in Chicago Lodge called, "Mr. Wilson and his dynasty . . . must be driven from all control, from all influence on the Government of the United States." Republican speakers were instructed to caricature the Peace Conference as a poker game with Lloyd George calling, "I'll bet you Fiume," and Wilson replying, "I'll raise you Alsace." Chauncey M. Depew made a sarcastic speech parodying the participants in Paris. In this interpretation the European ministers flattered Wilson and, in exchange for their support of the League, "a heaven on earth," of which he would be "the recording angel," he gave them territorial concessions, until the Italian, Sonnino, insisted on Fiume as his price. The president resisted for "it so happened that nobody there had ever heard of Fiume. Nobody knew where Fiume was, whether one of the Sandwich Islands or a fixed star."

Gradually, events at home began to displace foreign affairs from the front pages of the press. The social harmony of wartime America came to an abrupt end in 1919 with such things as unprecedented inflation, labor disputes, and race riots. Underlying public unease lay fears of Bolshevik, terrorist conspiracy. Returning soldiers and civilians alike were disabused of their faith in progress and were openly skeptical of the League of Nations. Among Wilson's last words on the subject, as reported by Joseph Tumulty in his *Woodrow Wilson as I Knew Him* (1921), were that America had renounced a "fruitful leadership for a barren independence. The people will have to learn now by bitter experience just what they have lost. . . . We had a chance to gain the leadership of the world. We have lost it, and soon we shall be witnessing the tragedy of it all."

The second titan now passed from the political scene. Woodrow Wilson eked out his broken old age until his death in February 3, 1924, in a house on S Street in Washington, where he remained an object of curiosity, coming out occasionally with his lean, wizened face smiling mechanically to onlookers but always with the left side averted. Yet, despite alternating bouts of irascibility and gentleness, he managed to move discreetly in public and not embarrass his successors. William Allen White remarked of his dignified and courteous performance in this last act that he "had never seen before so inspiring a spectacle, so triumphant a climax to a bitter tragedy."

The other titans of American industry and the arts were also passing from the scene and into legend just as the political achievements of the Progressive Era were passing into history. In the very different, more flexible, atmosphere of the 1920s urban society would find new icons among the creative heroes of the lost generation while the sterile landscape of federal politics awaited transformation in the 1930s during the Olympian rule of Franklin Delano Roosevelt.

Sources

·❦·

A NY HISTORIAN who attempts a comprehensive account of a
country over a period of twenty or more years immediately
puts himself in the debt of others. If he is to be alert in his scholarship, there must be something of Rossini's thieving magpie in
his nature. Notwithstanding original research into such papers as
those of the NAACP in the Library of Congress, Walter Lippmann
at Yale, Jane Adams at Swarthmore College, and other primary
sources, mainly in the Library of Congress—all of which were
scrutinized for this volume—the historian will undoubtedly seek
interpretations and essential facts from numerous secondary works.

He or she is likely to be moved and captured by a select few.
In my case, such writers as Alfred Dupont Chandler, Jr., on industrial corporations and their management; Milton Friedman on
economics; William Leuchtenburg on political and social history;
Alan Kraut on immigration; C. Vann Woodward on the South;
Arthur S. Link on Woodrow Wilson; and Gerald Mast on motion pictures, have all had a profound influence on me. Their
very different histories are judiciously written and persuasively
argued and their facts and ideas are represented, and acknowl-

edged, in this work. Similarly, a series of social historians, beginning with Mark Sullivan for the early century provide us with numerous anecdotes, much wit, and a sense of the thrust of popular and cultural history not readily available in more specific political or economic histories.

The following bibliography is, like the book itself, intended as a basic guide for anyone new to the history of the United States in the period. It does not include every book or article mentioned in the text but, rather a representative selection of those that we might expect to find in a good university library.

Statistics provided in this book on population, immigration, agricultural and industrial production, and election returns are usually taken from the United States Bureau of the Census, *Historical Statistics of the United States,* 2 vols. (Washington, D. C. 1975). A useful abridged version of the bicentennial edition is Ben J. Wattenberg (ed.), *The Statistical History of the United States from Colonial Times to the Present* (New York, 1976). I have taken supplementary factual or statistical information from Richard B. Morris and Jeffrey B. Morris (eds.), *Encyclopedia of American History* (6th ed. New York, London, et al., 1982). The bibliography is arranged in subsections by chapter with principal texts placed first in each subsection, and the whole preceded by a list of general works.

Bibliography

·ᢒ·

GENERAL

Arthur S. Link and William B. Catton, *American Epoch: A History of the United States*, vol. 1, *1900–1936* (New York, 1986).

Mark Sullivan, *Our Times: The United States 1900–1925*, 6 vols. (New York and London, 1925–1935).

Frederick Lewis Allen, *The Big Change: America Transforms Itself 1900–1950* (New York, 1952).

Otis L. Graham, *The Great Campaigns: Reform and War in America, 1900–1928* (Englewood Cliffs, N.J., 1971).

Richard Hofstadter, *The Age of Reform: From Bryan to F.D.R.* (New York, 1955).

Eric F. Goldman, *Rendezvous with Destiny: A History of Modern American Reform* (New York, 1956; first published 1952).

Paul T. David, *Party Strength in the United States, 1872–1970). (Charlottesville, Va., 1972).*

Walter Dean Burnham, *Critical Elections and the Mainsprings of American Politics* (New York, 1970).

George M. Marsden, *Fundamentalism and American Culture: The Shaping of Twentieth Century Evangelism 1870–1925* (New York and Oxford, 1980).

Milton Friedman and Anna Jacobson Schwartz, *A Monetary History of the United States 1867–1960* (Princeton, N.J., 1963).

Chapter 1

INVENTIONS

John W. Oliver, *History of American Technology* (New York, 1956).

Robert Higgs, "American Inventiveness, 1870–1920," *Journal of Political Economy*, 742 (May/June 1971).

L. Sprague deCamp, *The Heroic Age of American Invention* (Garden City, N.Y., 1961).

Bruce Norman, *The Inventing of America* (New York, 1976).

Roger Burlingame, *Engines of Democracy: Inventions and Society in Mature America* (Salem, N.H., 1976; first published 1940).

Waldemar B. Kaempffert, *A Popular History of American Invention* (New York, 1924).

Robert E. Conot, *A Streak of Luck—Edison* (New York, 1979).

Robert V. Bruce, *Bell: Alexander Graham Bell and the Conquest of Solitude* (Boston, 1973).

Henry G. Prout, *A Life of George Westinghouse* (New York, 1972; first published 1921).

Mitchell A. Wilson, *American Science and Invention, A Pictorial History* (New York, 1960).

Siegfried Giedion, *Mechanization Takes Command* (New York, 1969; first published 1948).

INDUSTRY

Samuel Haber, *Efficiency and Uplift; Scientific Management in the Progressive Era, 1890–1920* (Chicago, 1973).

Robert Higgs, *The Transformation of the American Economy, 1865–1914: An Essay in Interpretation* (New York, 1971).

Thomas C. Cochrane and William Miller, *The Age of Enterprise: A Social History of Industrial America* (New York, 1942; revised 1961).

David A. Hounshell, *From the American System to Mass Production 1800–1932: The Development of Manufacturing Technology in the United States* (Baltimore, 1984).

Victor S. Clark, *History of Manufactures in the United States 1607–1928*, vol. 3, *1893–1928* (New York, 1949; first published 1929).

Alfred Dupont Chandler, Jr., *The Visible Hand: The Managerial Revolution in American Business* (Cambridge, Mass., 1977).

——, "The Beginnings of 'Big Business' in American Industry," *Business History Review*, 33 (Spring 1959).

George H. Evans, Jr., *Business Incorporation in the United States, 1800–1943* (New York, 1948).

Sidney Fine, *Laissez-Faire and the General Welfare State: A Study of Conflict in American Thought, 1865–1901* (Ann Arbor, Mich., 1964; first published 1956).

Richard Hofstadter, *Social Darwinism in American Thought, 1860–1915* (Boston, 1955; first published Philadelphia and London, 1955).

Vincent Carosso, *The Morgans: Private International Bankers 1854–1913* (Cambridge, Mass., 1987).

Chapter 2

PROGRESSIVISM

J. A. Thompson, *Progressivism* (British Association of American Studies Pamphlet, Cambridge, England 1979).

Arthur S. Link and Richard L. McCormick, *Progressivism* (Arlington Heights, Ill., 1983).

William M. Leary, Jr., and Arthur S. Link, compilers, *The Progressive Era and the Great War, 1896–1920* (Arlington Heights, Ill., 1978).

Lewis L. Gould, editor, *The Progressive Era* (Syracuse, N.Y., 1974).

Lewis J. Gould, *Reform and Regulation: American Politics from Roosevelt to Wilson* (New York, 1986; first published 1977).

E. E. Schattschneider, *The Semi-Sovereign People: A Realist's View of Democracy in America* (New York, 1960).

William H. Harbaugh, "The Republican Party, 1892–1932," in Arthur Schlesinger, Jr., editor, *History of U.S. Political Parties*, 4 vols. (New York, 1973), 3, pp. 2069–2125.

Robert H. Wiebe, *The Search for Order, 1877–1920* (Chicago, New York, and London, 1967).

Richard M. Abrams, *Issues of the Populist and Progressive Eras, 1892–1912* (New York, 1969).

Benjamin P. DeWitt, *The Progressive Movement: A Non-Partisan Comprehensive Discussion of Current Tendencies in American Politics* (New York, 1915).

Richard L. Watson, Jr., *The Development of National Power: The United States, 1900–19* (Boston, 1976).

Jerome M. Clubb, "Party Coalitions in the Early Twentieth Century," in Seymour M. Lipset, editor, *Emerging Coalitions in American Politics* (San Francisco, 1978), pp. 61–79.

Howard W. Allen and Jerome Clubb, "Progressive Reform and the Political System," *Pacific Northwest Quarterly*, 65 (1974), 130–45.

Richard L. McCormick, "The Discovery That Business Corrupts Politics: A Reappraisal of the Origins of Progressivism," *American Historical Review*, 86 (1981), 242–74.

PROGRESSIVISM AND SOCIAL REFORM

Lincoln Steffens, *The Shame of the Cities* (New York, 1904).

Upton Sinclair, *The Jungle* (New York, 1905).

Robert H. Bremner, *From the Depths: The Discovery of Poverty in the United States* (New York, 1956).

Roy Lubove, *The Progressives and the Slums: Tenement House Reform in New York City, 1890–1917* (Pittsburgh, 1962).

John D. Buenker, *Urban Liberalism and Progressive Reform* (New York, 1978; first published 1973).

Charles H. Hopkins, *The Rise of the Social Gospel in American Protestantism, 1865–1915* (New Haven, Conn., 1940).

Henry F. May, *Protestant Churches and Industrial America* (New York, 1949).

Paul McBride, *Culture Clash: Immigrants and Reformers, 1880–1920* (San Francisco, 1975).

Paul Boyer, *Urban Masses and Moral Order in America, 1820–1920* (Cambridge, Mass., 1978).

Lillian Wald, *The House on Henry Street* (New York, 1969; first published 1915).

Jane Addams, *Twenty years at Hull House* (New York, 1961; first published 1910).

Allen F. Davis, *American Heroine: The Life and Legend of Jane Addams* (New York, 1973).

——, *Spearheads for Reform: The Social Settlements and the Progressive Movement 1890–1914* (New York, 1967).

Roy Lubove, *The Professional Altruist: The Emergence of Social Work as a Career, 1880–1930* (Cambridge, Mass., 1965).

PROGRESSIVISM AND BUSINESS

Robert H. Wiebe, *Businessmen and Reform: A Study of the Progressive Movement* (Cambridge, Mass., 1962).

Gabriel Kolko, *The Triumph of Conservatism: A Reinterpretation of American History 1900–1916* (New York, 1963).

James Weinstein, *The Corporate Ideal in the Liberal State, 1900–1918* (Boston, 1968).

Thomas K. McGraw, *Prohphets of Regulation: Charles Francis Adams, Louis D. Brandeis, James M. Landis, Alfred E. Kahn* (Cambridge, Mass., 1984).

Melvin I. Urofsky, *Big Steel and the Wilson Administration: A Study in Business-Government Relations* (Columbus, Ohio, 1969).

Robert H. Wiebe, "The House of Morgan and the Executive," *American Historical Review*, 65 (1959), 49–60.

PROGRESSIVISM AND THE CITIES

Martin J. Schiesl, *The Politics of Efficiency: Municipal Administration and Reform in America, 1880–1920* (Berkeley, Ca., 1977).

Zane Miller, *Boss Cox's Cincinnati: Urban Politics in the Progressive Era* (New York, 1968).

Melvin G. Holli, *Reform in Detroit: Hazen S. Pingree and Urban Politics* (New York, 1969).

James B. Crooks, *Politics and Progress: The Rise of Urban Progressivism in Baltimore, 1895–1914* (Baton Rouge, La., 1968).

Russel B. Nye, *Midwestern Progressive Politics: A Historical Study of its Origin and Development, 1870–1958* (East Lansing, Mich., 1959).

Sheldon Hackney, *Populism to Progressivism in Alabama* (Princeton, N.J., 1969).

Samuel P. Hays, "The Politics of Reform in Municipal Government in the Progressive Era," *Pacific Northwest Quarterly,* 55 (1964), 1957–69.

J. Joseph Huthmacher, "Urban Liberalism and the Age of Reform," *Mississippi Valley Historical Review,* 49 (1952), 231–41.

James Weinstein, "Organized Business and the City Commission and Manager Movements," *Journal of Southern History,* 28 (1962), 166–82.

Bradley R. Rice, *Progressive Cities: The Commission Government Movement in America 1901–1920* (Austin, Tex., 1977).

PROGRESSIVISM AND THE STATES

Richard L. McCormick, *From Realignment to Reform: Political Change in New York State, 1893–1910* (Ithaca, N.Y., 1981).

Richard M. Abrams, *Conservatism in a Progressive Era: Massachusetts Politics, 1900–1912* (Cambridge, Mass., 1964).

Charles McCarthy, *The Wisconsin Idea* (New York, 1912).

David P. Thelen, *The New Citizenship: Origins of Progressivism in Wisconsin, 1885–1900* (Columbia, Mo., 1972).

Herbert F. Margulies, *The Decline of the Progressive Movement in Wisconsin, 1890–1920* (Madison, Wis., 1968).

Robert Sherman La Forte, *Leaders of Reform: Progressive Republicans in Kansas 1900–1916* (Lawrence, Kans., 1974).

Robert W. Cherry, *Populism, Progressivism, and the Transformation of Nebraska Politics, 1885–1915* (Lincoln, Nebr., 1981).

Carl H. Chrislock, *The Progressive Era in Minnesota, 1899–1918* (St. Paul, Minn., 1971).

George E. Mowry, *The California Progressives* (Berkeley, Ca., 1951).

Kevin Starr, *California in the Progressive Era* (New York, 1986).

Michael Rogin, "Progressivism and the California Electorate," *Journal of American History,* 55 (1968), 297–314.

LEADING PROGRESSIVES

David P. Thelen, *Robert M. La Follette and the Insurgent Spirit* (Madison, Wis., 1986; first published 1976).

Richard Lowitt, *George W. Norris: the Making of a Progressive 1861 to 1912* (Westport, Conn., 1983; first published 1963).

Alfred Lief, *Democracy's Norris: The Biography of a Lonely Crusade* (New York, 1939).

Robert F. Wesser, *Charles Evans Hughes: Politics and Reform in New York, 1905–1910* (Ithaca, N.Y., 1967).

Spencer C. Olin, Jr., *California's Prodigal Sons: Hiram Johnson and the Progressives, 1911–1917* (Berkeley, Ca., 1968).

Herbert F. Margulies, *Senator Lenroot of Wisconsin* (Columbia, Mo., 1977).

Elting E. Morison, *Turmoil and Tradition: A Study of the Life and Times of Henry L. Stimson* (Boston, 1960).

Charles B. Forcey, *The Crossroads of Liberalism: Croly, Weyl, Lippmann and the Progressive Era, 1900–25* (New York, 1961).

Ronald Steel, *Walter Lippmann and the American Century* (New York, 1980).

ARTICLES ON PROGRESSIVISM

Louis Galambos, "The Emerging Organizational Synthesis in Modern American History," *Business History Review*, 44 (1970), 279–90.

William T. Kerr, Jr., "The Progressives of Washington, 1910–12," *Pacific Northwest Quarterly*, 55 (1964), 16–27.

Richard B. Sherman, "The Status Revolution and Massachusetts Progressive Leadership," *Political Science Quarterly*, 78 (1963), 61–65.

Jack Tager, "Progressives, Conservatives and the Theory of the Status Revolution," *Mid-America*, 48 (1966), 162–75.

David P. Thelen, "Social Tensions and the Origins of Progressivism," *Journal of American History*, 56 (1969), 323–41.

Forest A. Walker, "Compulsory Health Insurance: 'The Next Great Step in Social Legislation,' " *Journal of American History*, 56 (1969), 290–304.

Larry J. Easterling, "Senator Joseph R. Bristow and the Seventeenth Amendment," *Kansas Historical Quarterly*, 41 (1975), 488–511.

Roger E. Wyman, "Middle-Class Voters and Progressive Reform: The Conflict of Class and Culture," *American Political Science Review*, 68 (1974), 488–504.

Peter G. Filene, "An Obituary for the Progressive Movement," *American Quarterly*, 22 (1970), 20–34.

PROGRESSIVISM AND FEDERAL POLITICS

John Morton Blum, *The Progressive Presidents: Theodore Roosevelt, Woodrow Wilson, Franklin D. Roosevelt, and Lyndon Johnson* (New York, 1980).

John Milton Cooper, Jr., *The Warrior and the Priest: Woodrow Wilson and Theodore Roosevelt* (Cambridge, Mass., 1983).

George Juergens, *News From the White House: The Presidential Press Relationship in the Progressive Era* (Chicago, 1981).

Frederic Austin Ogg, *National Progress, 1907–1917* (New York, 1918).

THEODORE ROOSEVELT

George E. Mowry, *The Era of Theodore Roosevelt and the Birth of Modern America, 1900–1912* (New York, 1962; first published 1958).

John Morton Blum, *The Republican Roosevelt* (Cambridge, Mass., 1954).

William H. Harburgh, *The Life and Times of Theodore Roosevelt* (New York, revised 1975; first published 1961).

Theodore Roosevelt, *Autobiography* (New York, 1913).

Edmund Morris, *The Rise of Theodore Roosevelt* (New York, 1979).

Daniel H. Burton, *Theodore Roosevelt* (New York, 1972).

G. Wallace Chessman, *Theodore Roosevelt and the Politics of Power* (Boston, 1969).

Joseph Bishop, *Theodore Roosevelt and His Time* (New York, 1920).

Henry F. Pringle, *Theodore Roosevelt: A Biography* (New York, 1956).

Carlton Putnam, *Theodore Roosevelt: A Biography* (New York, 1958).

Jacob A. Riis, *Theodore Roosevelt the Citizen* (New York, 1904).

Edward Wagenknecht, *The Seven Worlds of Theodore Roosevelt* (New York, 1958).

Owen Wister, *Roosevelt: The Story of a Friendship* (New York, 1930).

Archibald W. Butt, *The Letters of Archie Butt, Personal Aide to President Roosevelt* (Garden City, N.Y., 1924).

Fred S. Wood, editor, *Roosevelt as We Knew Him: Personal Recollections of 150 Friends* (Philadelphia, 1927).

Alice Roosevelt Longworth, *Crowded Hours* (New York, 1933).

PROGRESSIVE CRUSADES

Paul R. Cutright, *Theodore Roosevelt, the Making of a Conservationist* (Urbana, Ill., 1985).

Gifford Pinchot, *The Fight for Conservation* (New York, 1910).

Martin L. Fausold, *Gifford Pinchot: Bull Moose Progressive* (Syracuse, N.Y., 1973; first published 1961).

Alpheus T. Mason, *Bureaucracy Convicts Itself: The Ballinger-Pinchot Controversy of 1910* (New York, 1941).

Samuel P. Hays, *Conservation and the Gospel of Efficiency* (Cambridge, Mass., 1959).

Louis Filler, *Appointment at Armageddon: Muckraking and Progressivism in the American Tradition* (Westport, Conn., 1976).

Joseph Kenkel, *Progressives and Protection: The Search for a Tariff Policy* (Lanham, Md., 1983).

James H. Timberlake, *Prohibition and the Progressive Movement 1900–1920* (New York, 1970; first published Cambridge, Mass., 1963).

WILLIAM HOWARD TAFT

Henry F. Pringle, *The Life and Times of William Howard Taft*, 2 vols., (New York, 1939).

Paola Enrico Coletta, *The Presidency of William Howard Taft* (Lawrence, Kans., 1973).

Donald Anderson, *William Howard Taft: A Conservative's Conception of the Presidency* (Ithaca, N.Y., 1973).

Judith Icke Anderson, *William Howard Taft: An Intimate History* (New York, 1981).

William Manners, *TR and Will: A Friendship that Split the Republican Party* (New York, 1969).

William Howard Taft, *The President and His Powers* (New York, 1967; first published 1916, also published as *The Chief Magistrate and His Powers*).

Stanley Solvick, "William Howard Taft and the Payne-Aldrich Tariff," *Mississippi Valley Historical Review*, 50 (1963), 424–42; "The Pre-Presidential Political and Economic Thought of William Howard Taft," *Northwest Ohio Quarterly*, 43 (1971), 87–97.

Lewis J. Gould, "Western Range Senators and the Payne Aldrich Tariff," *Pacific Northwest Quarterly*, 64 (1973), 49–56.

David W. Detzer, "Business Reformers and Tariff Revision: The Payne-Aldrich Tariff of 1909," *The Historian*, 35 (1973), 196–204.

Claude Barfield, " 'Our Share of the Booty': The Democratic Party, Cannonism and the Payne Aldrich Tariff," *Journal of American History*, 57 (1970), 308–23.

John D. Baker, "The Character of the Congressional Revolution of 1910," *Journal of American History*, 60 (1973), 679–91.

Chapter 3

INSURGENCY AND THE INSURGENTS

Kenneth W. Hechler, *Insurgency: Personalities and Politics of the Taft Era* (New York, 1970; first published 1940).

James Holt, *Congressional Insurgents and the Party System, 1909–1916* (Cambridge, Mass., 1967).

David P. Thelen, *Robert M. La Follette and the Insurgent Spirit* (Madison, Wis., 1986; first published 1976).

Richard Lowitt, *George W. Norris: The Making of a Progressive, 1861–1912* (Syracuse, N.Y., 1980; first published 1963).

John Braeman, *Albert Beveridge: American Nationalist* (Chicago, 1971).

Thomas Richard Ross, *Jonathan Prentis Dolliver: A Study in Political Integrity and Independence* (Iowa City, Iowa, 1958).

CONSERVATIVE REPUBLICANS

Horace Samuel Merrill, *The Republican Command, 1897–1913* (Lexington, Ky., 1971).

Norman M. Wilensky, *Conservatives in the Progressive Era: The Taft Republicans of 1912* (Gainesville, Fla., 1965).

Blair Bolles, *Tyrant from Illinois: Uncle Joe Cannon's Experiment with Personal Power* (New York, 1951).

Nathaniel W. Stephenson, *Nelson W. Aldrich: A Leader in American Politics* (Port Washington, N.Y., 1971; first published 1930).

L. Ethan Ellis, *Reciprocity 1911: A Study in Canadian-American Relations* (New Haven, Conn., 1939).

John Braeman, *Albert J. Beveridge: American Nationalist* (Chicago, 1971).

1912

John Allen Gable, *The Bull Moose Years: Theodore Roosevelt and the Progressive Party* (Port Washington, N.Y., 1978).

William Manners, *TR and Will: A Friendship that Split the Republican Party* (New York, 1969).

Theodore Roosevelt, *The New Nationalism,* with introduction and notes by William E. Leuchtenburg (Englewood Cliffs, N.J., 1961).

Herbert Croly, *The Promise of American Life* (New York, 1909).

Woodrow Wilson, *The New Freedom,* with introduction and notes by William E. Leuchtenburg (Englewood Cliffs, N.J., 1961).

James C. German, "Taft, Roosevelt and United States Steel," *The Historian,* 34 (1972), 598–613.

Lewis J. Gould, "Theodore Roosevelt, William Howard Taft, and the Disputed Delegates in 1912: Texas as a Test Case," *Southwestern Historical Quarterly,* 80 (1976), 33–56.

WOODROW WILSON

Arthur S. Link, *Woodrow Wilson and the Progressive Era, 1910–1917* (New York, 1963; first published 1954).

——, *The Road to the White House* (Princeton, N.J., 1947).

——, *The New Freedom* (Princeton, N.J., 1956).

——, *Confusions and Crises* (Princeton, N.J., 1964).

——, *Campaigns for Progressivism and Peace* (Princeton, N.J., 1965).

——, *The Higher Realism of Woodrow Wilson* (Nashville, Tenn., 1971).

——, *The Papers of Woodrow Wilson* (Princeton, N.J., 1966).

Edwin A. Weinstein, *Woodrow Wilson: A Medical and Psychological Biography* (Princeton, N.J., 1981).

Herbert Bell, *Woodrow Wilson and the People* (Hamden, Conn., 1968).

David H. Hirst, *Woodrow Wilson, Reform Governor* (Princeton, N.J., 1965).

John Morton Blum, *Joe Tumulty and the Wilson Era* (Boston, 1951).

Joe Tumulty, *Woodrow Wilson as I Knew Him* (Garden City, N.Y., 1921).

David D. Anderson, *Woodrow Wilson* (Boston, 1978).

Edmund Ions, *Woodrow Wilson* (London, 1972).

Paul M. Angle, *Crossroads: 1913* (Chicago, 1963).

James Kerney, *The Political Education of Woodrow Wilson* (New York, 1926).

Charles Sheridan Jones, *President Wilson, The Man and His Message* (London, 1918).

Arthur Douglas Howden Smith, *Mr. House of Texas* (New York, 1940).

Hugh Hale Bellot, *Woodrow Wilson* (London, 1955).

Tom Shachtman, *Edith and Woodrow* (New York, 1981).

John J. Broesamle, *William Gibbs McAdoo: A Passion for Change, 1863–1917* (Port Washington, N.Y., 1973).

Henry Parker Willis, *The Federal Reserve* (New York, 1917).

Paul M. Warburg, *The Federal Reserve System: Its Origin and Growth*, 2 vols. (New York, 1930).

Frank Burdick, "Woodrow Wilson and the Underwood Tariff," *Mid-America*, 50 (1968), 272–90.

Richard M. Abrams, "Woodrow Wilson and the Southern Congressman, 1913–1916," *Journal of Southern History*, 22 (1956), 417–37.

BRYAN

Louis W. Koenig, *Bryan: A Political Biography of William Jennings Bryan* (New York, 1971).

Chapter 4

IMMIGRATION

Alan M. Kraut, *The Huddled Masses: The Immigrant in American Society, 1880–1921* (Arlington, Heights, Ill., 1982).

Oscar Handlin, *The Uprooted* (Boston, 1951).

Maldwyn Allen Jones, *American Immigration* (Chicago, 1960).

——, *Destination America: 1815–1914* (New York and London, 1976).

P. A. M. Taylor, *The Distant Magnet* (New York, 1971).

Richard L. Ehrlich, *Immigrants in Industrial America, 1850–1920* (Charlottesville, Va., 1977).

Thomas J. Archdeacon, *Becoming American: An Ethnic History* (New York, 1983).

Maxine Schwartz Seller, *To Seek America* (Englewood Cliffs, N.J., 1977).

Leonard Dinnerstein and David Reimers, *Ethnic Americans: A History of Immigration and Assimilation* (New York, 1975).

Marcus Lee Hansen, "The History of American Immigration as a Field for Research," *American Historical Review*, 32 (1926–27), 500–518.

Rudolph Vecoli, "Ethnicity: A Neglected Dimension of American History," in Herbert Bass, editor, *The State of American History* (Chicago, 1970).

——, "Contadini in Chicago: A Critique of *The Uprooted*," *Journal of American History*, 51 (December 1964).

Herbert Gutman, "Labor History and the 'Sartre Question,'" *Humanities*, 1 (September/October 1980).

ITALIAN IMMIGRATION

Joseph Lopreato, *Italian Americans* (New York, 1970).
Erik Amfitheatrof, *Children of Columbus* (New York, 1972).
Alexander De Corde, *Half Bitter, Half Sweet: An Excursion into Italian-American History* (New York, 1971).
Robert Foerster, *Italian Emigration of Our Times* (Cambridge, Mass., 1968; first published 1919).
John H. Mariano, *The Italian Contribution to American Democracy* (Boston, 1975; first published 1924).
Edward Banfield, *The Moral Basis of a Backward Society* (New York, 1958).
Richard Gambino, *Blood of My Blood* (New York, 1975).
John W. Briggs, *An Italian Passage: Immigrants to Three American Cities, 1890–1930* (New Haven, Conn., 1978).
Virginia Yans-McLaughlin, *Family and Community: Italian Immigrants in Buffalo, 1880–1930* (Ithaca, N.Y., 1977).

JEWISH IMMIGRATION

Moses Rischin, *The Promised City: New York's Jews 1870–1914* (Cambridge, Mass., 1962).
Ronald Sanders, *The Downtown Jews* (New York, 1969).
Arthus S. Goren, *New York Jews and the Quest for Community: the Kehillah Experiment: 1908–1922* (New York, 1970).
Irving Howe, *World of Our Fathers* (New York, 1976).
Aude Manners, *Poor Cousins* (New York, 1972).

POLISH IMMIGRATION

Paul Fox, *The Poles in America* (New York, 1970; first published 1922).
W. I. Thomas and F. Znaniecki, *The Polish Peasant in Europe and America*, 2 vols. (New York, 1958).
Joseph Wytranal, *America's Polish Heritage: A Social History of the Poles in America* (Detroit, 1961).
——, *The Poles in America* (Minneapolis, 1969).
Helen Znanieckia Lopata, *Polish Americans: Status and Competition in an Ethnic Community* (Englewood Cliffs, N.J., 1976).

SLAVIC IMMIGRATION

Emily Balch, *Our Slavic Fellow Citizens* (New York, 1969; first published 1910).
Wasyl Halich, *Ukranians in the United States* (Chicago, 1970; first published 1937).

Emil Lengyel, *Americans from Hungary* (Philadelphia, 1975; first published 1948).
George J. Prpic, *Croatian Immigrants in America* (New York, 1971).
Jerome Davis, *The Russian Immigrant* (New York, 1969; first published 1922).

GREEK IMMIGRATION

Theodore Saloutos, *The Greeks in the United States* (Cambridge, Mass., 1963).
Charles C. Moskos, Jr., *Greek Americans: Struggle and Success* (Englewood Cliffs, N.J., 1980).

ARMENIAN IMMIGRATION

Aram Yeretizian, *A History of Armenian Immigration with Special Reference to Los Angeles* (San Francisco, 1974).
Michael J. Arlen, *Passage to Ararat* (New York, 1975).

ARAB IMMIGRATION

Habib Ibrahim Katibah, *Arab-Speaking Americans* (New York, 1946).

IMMIGRATION FROM THE ORIENT

Jack Chen, *The Chinese of America* (San Francisco, 1980).
Betty Lee Sung, *Mountain of Gold* (New York, 1967).
Mary B. Coolidge, *Chinese Immigration* (New York, 1969; first published 1909).
Stanford M. Lyman, *Chinatown, USA* (New York, 1965).
Yamamoto Ichihashi, *Japanese in the United States* (Stanford, 1969; first published 1932).
Harry Kitano, *Japanese Americans: The Evolution of a Subculture* (Englewood Cliffs, N.J., 1969).
William Petersen, *Japanese Americans: Oppression and Success* (New York, 1971).

IMMIGRATION FROM THE WESTERN HEMISPHERE

Marcus Lee Hansen, *The Mingling of the Canadian and American Peoples* (New Haven, Conn., 1970; first published 1940).
Maurice Violette, *The Franco Americans* (New York, 1976).
Rodolfo Acuna, *Occupied America: The Chicano Struggle toward Liberation* (San Francisco, 1972).
Matt S. Meier and Feliciano Rivera, *The Chicanos: A History of Mexican Americans* (New York, 1972).

RECEPTION, INTEGRATION, AND IDENTITY

William Tefft and Thomas Dunne, *Ellis Island* (New York, 1971).
David M. Brownstone, Irene M. Franck, and Douglas L. Brownstone, *Island of Hope, Island of Tears* (New York, 1979).

Thomas Monroe Pitkin, *Keepers of the Gate: A History of Ellis Island* (New York, 1975).

Josef Barton, *Peasants and Strangers: Italians, Rumanians and Slovaks in an American City, 1890–1950* (Cambridge, Mass., 1975).

Thomas Kessner, *The Golden Door: Italian and Jewish Immigrant Mobility in New York City, 1880–1915* (New York, 1977).

Edward P. Hutchinson, *Immigrants and their Children, 1850–1915* (New York, 1976; first published 1956).

Ivan H. Light, *Ethnic Enterprise in America: Business and Welfare among the Chinese, Japanese and Blacks* (Berkeley, Ca., 1972).

Charles H. Mindell and Robert W. Haberstein, editors, *Ethnic Families in America: Patterns and Variations* (New York, 1976).

Vladimir Nahirny, *Language Loyalty in the United States* (The Hague, 1966).

Isaac Metzker, editor, *A Bintel Brief* (New York, 1971).

Abraham Cahan, *The Education of Abraham Cahan* (Philadelphia, 1969).

Irving Howe and Kenneth Libo, *How We Lived: A Documentary History of Immigrant Jews in America, 1880–1930* (New York, 1979).

Humbert S. Nelli, *From Immigrants to Ethnics: the Italian Americans* (Oxford and New York, 1983).

Richard M. Linkh, *American Catholicism and European Immigrants, 1900–1924* (Staten Island, N.Y., 1925).

Milton M. Gordon, *Assimilation in American Life: The Role of Race, Religion and National Origins* (New York, 1964).

Horace M. Kallen, *Culture and Democracy in the United States* (New York, 1924).

Will Herberg, *Protestant, Catholic, and Jew* (New York, 1960; first published 1955).

Stanley Feldstein and Lawrence Costello, editors, *The Ordeal of Assimilation: A Documentary History of the White Working Class, 1930s to the 1970s* (Garden City, N.Y., 1974).

Salvatore La Gumina and Frank J. Cavaioli, editors, *The Ethnic Dimension in American Society* (Boston, 1974).

NATIVISM AND IMMIGRATION RESTRICTION

John Higham, *Strangers in the Land: Patterns of American Nativism, 1860–1925* (New Brunswick, N.J., 1955).

——, *Send These to Me: Jews and Other Immigrants in Urban America* (New York, 1975).

Franz Boas, *Race and the Democratic Society* (New York, 1945).

Marion T. Bennett, *American Immigration Policies: A History* (Washington, D.C., 1963).

Robert A. Divine, *American Immigration Policy, 1924–1952* (New Haven, Conn., 1972; first published 1957).

Leonard Dinnerstein, David Reimers, James M. Berquist et al., "A Reexamination of a Classic Work in American Jewish History: John Higham's *Strangers in the Land,*" *American Jewish History,* 76 (December 1986), 103–226.

AMERICAN INDIANS

David Murray, *Modern Indians* (British Association for American Studies: South Shields, Tyne and Wear, and Cambridge, 1982).

Francis Paul Prucha, *A Bibliographical Guide to the History of Indian-White Relations in the United States* (Chicago and London, 1977).

George P. Murdock and Timothy J. O'Leary, *Ethnographic Bibliography of North America* (New Haven, Conn., 1975).

Murray L. Wax, *Indian Americans: Unity and Diversity* (Englewood Cliffs, N.J., 1971).

Alvin M. Josephy, *The Indian Heritage of America* (New York, 1971).

Angie Debo, *A History of the Indians of the United States* (Norman, Okla., 1971).

Darcy McNickle, *Native American Tribalism: Indian Survivals and Renewals* (New York, 1973).

Sar A. Levitan and B. Hetrick, *Big Brother's Indian Programs—with Reservations* (New York, 1971).

Alan L. Sonkin, *The Urban American Indian* (Lexington, Mass., 1978).

Jack O. Waddell and O. M. Watson, editors, *The American Indian in Urban Society* (Boston, 1971).

Hazel W. Hertzberg, *The Search for an American Indian Identity: Modern Pan-Indian Movements* (Syracuse, N.Y., 1971).

M. Gidley, photographs by E. H. Latham, *With One Sky Above Us: Life on an Indian Reservation at the Turn of the Century* (New York and Exeter, 1979).

Jeanne Guillemin, *Urban Renegades: The Cultural Strategy of American Indians* (New York, 1975).

James F. Downs, *The Navajo* (New York, 1972).

Bruce Johansen and Roberto Maestas, *Wasi'chu: The Continuous Indian Wars* (New York and London, 1979).

Elizabeth S. Grobsmith, *Lakota of the Rosebud: A Contemporary Ethnography* (New York, 1981).

Karen I. Blu, *The Lumbee Problem: The Making of an American Indian People* (Cambridge, 1980).

Edmund Wilson, *Apologies to the Iroquois* (London, 1960).

Malcolm McFee, *Modern Blackfeet: Montanans on a Reservation* (New York, 1972).

Ethel Nurge, editor, *The Modern Sioux: Social Systems and Reservation Culture* (Lincoln, Nebr., 1970).

PUBLIC SCHOOLS

Colin Greer, *The Great School Legend: A Revisionist Interpretation of American Public Education* (New York, 1972).

Diane Ravitch, *The Great School Wars: New York City, 1805–1973: A History of the Public Schools as Battlefields of Social Change* (New York, 1974).

Lawrence A. Cremin, *The Transformation of the School: Progressiveness in American Education, 1876–1957* (New York, 1961).

David Tyack, *The One Best System: A History of American Urban Education* (Cambridge, Mass., 1974).

Robert Carlson, *The Quest for Conformity: Americanization through Education* (New York, 1975).

Chapter 5

LABOR

James R. Green, *The World of the Worker* (New York, 1980).

John R. Commons, et al., *History of Labor in the United States,* 4 vols. (New York, 1918–1935).

Sanford Cohen, *Labor in the United States* (Columbus, Ohio, 1960).

Melvyn Dubofsky, *Industrialism and the American Worker, 1865–1920* (New York, 1975).

David Brody, *Workers in Industrial America: Essays on the Twentieth Century Struggle* (New York, 1980).

Richard Edwards, *Contested Terrain* (New York, 1979).

Jeremy Brecher, *Strike!* (Boston, 1979).

Robert D. Parmet, *Labor and Immigration in Industrial America* (Boston, 1981).

Edwin Fenton, *Immigrants and Unions: A Case Study: Italians and American Labor* (New York, 1975).

Victor Greene, *The Slavic Community on Strike: Immigrant Labor in Pennsylvania Anthracite* (South Bend, Ind., 1968).

Gerald Rosenblum, *Immigrant Workers: Their Impact on American Labor Radicalism* (New York, 1973).

Mark Riisler, *By the Sweat of Their Brows: Mexican Immigrant Labor in the United States, 1900–1940* (Westport, Conn., 1976).

Cletus E. Daniel, *Bitter Harvest: A History of California Farmworkers, 1870–1941* (Ithaca, N.Y., 1981).

Roy Lubove, *The Struggle for Social Security, 1900–1935* (Cambridge, Mass., 1968).

Don Divance Lescohier, *Working Conditions,* vol. 3 of *The History of Labor in the U.S., 1896–1932* (New York, 1935).

LABOR UNIONS

Irwin Yellowitz, *Industrialization and the American Labor Movement, 1900–1950* (Port Washington, N.Y. and London, 1977).

Marc Karson, *American Labor Unions and Politics, 1900–1918* (Carbondale, Ill., 1958).

Bernard Mandel, *Samuel Gompers: A Biography* (Yellow Springs, Ohio, 1963).

Milton J. Nadwonny, *Scientific Management and the Unions, 1900–1932: A Historical Analysis* (Cambridge, Mass., 1955).

Irwin Yellowitz, *Labor and the Progressive Movement in New York State, 1897–1916* (Ithaca, N.Y., 1965).

Jonathan Dembo, *Unions and Politics in Washington State, 1885–1935* (New York and London, 1983).

David Montgomery, "The 'New Unionism' and the Transformation of Workers' Consciousness in America, 1909–22," *Journal of Social History*, 7 (Summer 1974).

RADICAL MOVEMENTS

Melvyn Dubofsky, *We Shall Be All: A History of the I.W.W.* (Chicago, 1969).

Nick Salvatore, *Eugene V. Debs: Citizen and Socialist* (Urbana, Ill., 1982).

Ray Ginger, *The Bending Cross—A Biography of Eugene Victor Debs* (New Brunswick, N.J., 1949).

James R. Green, *Grass Roots Socialism: Radical Movements in the Southwest, 1895–1943* (Baton Rouge, La., 1978).

John H. M. Laslett, *Labor and the Left* (New York, 1970).

James Weinstein, *The Decline of Socialism in America 1912–1915* (New Brunswick, N.J., 1984; first published 1967).

John Laslett and Seymour Martin Lipsett, editors, *Failure of a Dream? Essays in the History of American Socialism* (New York, 1974).

Robert Justin Goldstein, *Political Repression in Modern America* (Cambridge, Mass., 1978).

Irving Howe and Lewis Coser, *The American Communist Party: A Critical History* (New York, 1974; first published 1957).

Gregory R. Woirol, "Observing the I.W.W. in California, May–July 1914," *Labor History*, 25 (Summer 1984).

THE NEW SOUTH

C. Vann Woodward, *Origins of the New South, 1877–1913* (Baton Rouge, La., 1951).

George B. Tindall, *The Emergence of the New South, 1913–1945* (Baton Rouge, La., 1967).

J. Morgan Kousser, *The Shaping of Southern Politics: Suffrage Restriction and the Establishment of the One-Party South, 1880–1910* (New Haven, Conn., 1974).

Sheldon Hackney, *Populism to Progressivism in Alabama* (Princeton, N.J., 1969).

Dewey W. Grantham, *Southern Progressivism: The Reconciliation of Progress and Tradition* (Knoxville, Tenn., 1983).

Lewis J. Gould, *Progressives and Prohibitionists: Texas Democrats in the Wilson Era* (Austin, Tex., 1973).

Evan Anders, *Boss Rule in South Texas: The Progressive Era* (Austin, Tex., 1982).

Anne Firor Scott, "A Progressive Wind from the South, 1906–1913," *Journal of Southern History*, 29 (1963), 53–70.

BLACK AMERICA IN THE PROGRESSIVE ERA

Rayford Logan, *The Betrayal of the Negro: from Rutherford B. Hayes to Woodrow Wilson* (Toronto, 1969; first published as *The Negro in American Life and Thought: The Nadir 1877–1901,* New York, 1954).

Ray Stannard Baker, *Following the Color Line: An Account of Negro Citizenship in the American Democracy* (New York 1964; first published 1908).

August Meier, *Negro Thought in America 1880–1915* (Ann Arbor, Mich., 1963).

W.E.B. DuBois, *The Souls of Black Folk* (New York, 1961; first published 1903).

——, edited by Herbert Aptheker, *Against Racism: Unpublished Essays, Papers, Addresses 1887–1961* (Amherst, Mass., 1985).

Elliot M. Rudwick, *W.E.B. DuBois: A Study in Minority Group Leadership* (Philadelphia, 1960).

Seth M. Scheiner, "President Theodore Roosevelt and the Negro, 1901–1908," *Journal of Negro History,* 47 (July 1962), 169.

Arthur S. Link, "The Negro as a Factor in the Campaign of 1912," *Journal of Negro History,* 32 (January 1947), 81.

Chapter 6

THE NEW WOMAN

Carl N. Degler, *At Odds: Women and the Family from the Revolution to the Present* (New York, 1980).

Carol Hymowitz, *A History of Women in America* (New York, 1978).

Eleanor Flexner, *Century of Struggle* (Cambridge, Mass., 1959).

Michael Gordon, *The American Family; in Social and Historical Perspective* (New York, 1931).

WOMEN'S LEGAL AND POLITICAL STATUS

Bertha A. Rembaugh, *The Political Status of Woman in the United States* (New York, 1911).

Elizabeth Cady Stanton and Susan B. Anthony, *History of Woman Suffrage,* 6 vols. (New York and Rochester, 1881–1922).

Jennie Wilson, *The Legal and Political Status of Women in the United States* (New York, 1911).

Aileen Kraditor, *The Ideas of the Woman Suffrage Movement, 1890–1920* (New York, 1965).

Robert J. Lifton, editor, *The Women in America* (Boston, 1967).

William L. O'Neill, *Divorce in the Progressive Era* (New Haven, 1967).

——, *Everyone Was Brave* (Chicago, 1969).

Jack S. Blocker, "The Politics of Reform: Populists, Prohibitionists and Woman Suffrage, 1891–1892," *The Historian*, 34 (May 1971), 130–145.

James R. McGovern, "The American Woman's Pre-World War I Freedom in Manners and Morals," *Journal of American History*, 55 (1968), 315–18.

WOMEN CHANGING PLACES

Sheila M. Rothman, *Woman's Proper Place: A History of Changing Ideals and Practices 1870 to the Present* (New York, 1978).

Mary Ryan, *Womanhood in America: From Colonial Times to the Present* (New York, 1975).

Ann Firor Scott, *The American Woman, Who Was She?* (Englewood Cliffs, N.J., 1971).

——, *The Southern Lady: From Pedestal to Politics, 1830–1930* (Chicago, 1970).

Carroll Smith-Rosenberg, *Disorderly Conduct: Visions of Gender in Victorian America* (New York, 1985).

Robert Smuts, *Women and Work in America* (New York, 1959).

June Sochen, *Movers and Shakers* (New York, 1973).

——, *The New Woman in Greenwich Village, 1910–1920* (New York, 1972).

Meredith Tax, *The Rising of the Woman: Feminists, Solidarity, and Class Conflict, 1880–1917* (New York, 1980).

Karen J. Blair, *The Club Woman as Feminist: True Womanhood Redefined, 1868–1914* (New York, 1980).

Sophonisba Breckinridge, *Women in the Twentieth Century* (New York, 1933).

Marie Jo Buhle, *Women and American Socialism, 1870–1920* (Urbana, Ill., 1981).

Beverly Cassara, editor, *American Women: The Changing Image* (Boston, 1962).

William H. Chafe, *Women and Equality* (New York, 1977).

Susan Strasser, *Never Done: A History of American Housework* (New York, 1982).

Alice Kessler-Harris, *Out to Work: A History of Wage-Earning Women in the United States* (New York and Oxford, 1982).

Ruth Schwartz Cowan, *More Work For Mother: The Ironies of Household Technology from the Open Hearth to the Microwave* (New York, 1983).

Cecyle S. Needle, *America's Immigrant Women* (Boston, 1975).

Charlotte Baum et al., *The Jewish Woman in America* (New York, 1976).

Leslie Woodsock Tentler, *Wage-Earning Woman: Industrial Work and Family Life in the United States, 1900–1930* (New York, 1979).

MARGARET SANGER AND THE CAMPAIGN FOR BIRTH CONTROL

Emily Taft Douglas, *Margaret Sanger: Pioneer of the Future* (New York, 1970).

David M. Kennedy, *Birth Control in America: The Career of Margaret Sanger* (New Haven, Conn., 1970).

Lawrence Lader, *The Margaret Sanger Story and the Fight for Birth Control* (Garden City, N.Y., 1955).

Margaret Sanger, *Woman and the New Race* (New York, 1920).

Linda Gordon, *Woman's Body, Woman's Right: A Social History of Birth Control in America* (New York, 1976).
Gerda Lerner, *The Female Experience: An American Documentary* (Indianapolis, 1977).
Donald K. Pickens, *Eugenics and the Progressives* (Nashville, Tenn., 1968).

Chapter 7

REVOLUTIONS IN TRANSPORTATION

Robert Lacey, *Ford* (New York and London, 1986).
Keith Sward, *The Legend of Henry Ford* (New York, 1968).
James J. Flink, *The Car Culture* (Cambridge, Mass., 1975).
———, *America Adopts the Automobile, 1895–1910* (Cambridge, Mass., 1970).

RAILROADS

John Stover, *The Life and Decline of the American Railroad* (New York, 1970).
Alfred Dupont Chandler, Jr., *The Railroads, Pioneers in Modern Management* (New York, 1979).
Albro Martin, *Enterprise Denied: Origins of the Decline of American Railroads, 1897–1917* (New York, 1971).
Gabriel Kolko, *Railroads and Regulations, 1877–1916* (Princeton, N.J., 1965).
K. Austin Kerr, *American Railroad Politics 1914–1920* (Pittsburgh, 1968).

Chapter 8

RADIO

Erik Barnouw, *A Tower in Babel: A History of Broadcasting in the United States* (Volume 1, to 1933) (New York, 1966).
Richard Levinson and William Link, *Stay Tuned* (New York, 1983).
Christopher Sterling and John M. Kitros, *Stay Tuned* (New York, 1978).

HOLLYWOOD AND THE MOVIES

Gerald Mast, *A Short History of the Movies* (revised edition New York, 1986; first published 1971).
Paul Michael, editor, *The American Movies Reference Book: The Sound Era* (Englewood Cliffs, N.J., 1970).
Larry May, *Screening Out the Past: The Birth of Mass Culture and the Motion Picture Industry* (first published 1980; revised Chicago, 1983).
Kevin Brownlow, *The Parade's Gone By* (New York, 1968).

Robert Sklar, *Movie-Made America: A Cultural History of American Movies* (New York, 1975).

Eugene Rosow, *Born to Lose: The Gangster Film in America* (New York, 1978).

Raymond Lee and B. C. Van Hecke, *Gangsters and Hoodlums: The Underworld in the Cinema* (New York, 1971).

James Agee, "Comedy's Greatest Era," in Agee, *Agee on Film* (Boston, 1964), pp. 2–19.

DIRECTORS, MOGULS, AND STARS

Andrew Sarris, *The American Cinema: Directors and Directions, 1929–1968* (New York, 1968).

Iris Barry and Eileen Bowser, *D. W. Griffith: American Film Master* (New York, 1965).

Lillian Gish, *The Movies, Mr. Griffith, and Me* (Englewood Cliffs, N.J., 1969).

Charlie Chaplin, *My Autobiography* (New York, 1964).

David Robinson, *Chaplin: His Life and Art* (New York, 1985).

Isabel Quigley, *Charlie Chaplin: Early Comedies* (New York, 1968).

Mack Sennett, *King of Comedy* (New York, 1954).

Rudi Blesh, *Keaton* (New York, 1966).

Stephen Farber and Marc Green, *Hollywood Dynasties* (New York, 1984).

Philip French, *The Movie Moguls: An Informal History of the Hollywood Tycoons* (Harmondsworth, Middlesex, 1971; first published London, 1969).

Chapter 9

ARCHITECTURE AND SKYSCRAPERS

Marcus Whiffen and Frederick Koeper, *American Architecture, 1606–1976*, 2 vols. (Cambridge, Mass., 1981), 2.

Paul Goldberger, *The Skyscraper* (New York, 1982).

Wayne Andrews, *Architecture, Ambition and Americans: A Social History of American Architecture* (revised edition, New York, 1978; first published 1955).

Sam Bass Warner, Jr., *The Urban Wilderness: A History of the American City* (New York, 1972).

Frederick Gutheim and Wilcomb E. Washburn, *The Federal City: Plans and Realities*, published in cooperation with the National Capital Planning Commission by the Smithsonian Institution Press (Washington, D.C., 1976).

Blake McKelvey, *American Urbanization: A Comparative History* (Glenview, Ill., 1973).

Lewis Mumford, *Sticks and Stones: A Study of American Architecture and Civilization* (revised edition, New York, 1955).

Robert W. Rydell, *All the World's a Fair: Visions of Empire at American International Expositions, 1876–1916* (Chicago, 1984).

Chapter 10

PAINTING AND SCULPTURE

Barbara Rose, *American Art since 1900* (New York, 1967).

Robert E. Hughes, *The Shock of the New Art and the Century of Change* (New York and London, 1981).

Milton Brown, *American Painting from the Armory Show to the Depression* (Princeton, N.J., 1955).

Daniel Mendelowitz, *A History of American Art* (New York, 1970).

Holger Cahill and Alfred Barr, Jr., *Art in America in Modern Times* (New York, 1934).

Thomas Craven, *Modern Art: The Men, the Movements, the Meaning* (New York, 1934).

John I. H. Baur, *Revolution and Tradition in Modern American Art* (Cambridge, Mass., 1951).

Lloyd Goodrich, *American Art of Our Century* (New York, 1961).

Oliver W. Larkin, *Art and Life in America* (New York, 1949).

William Innes Homer, *Alfred Stieglitz and the American Avant-Garde* (Boston, 1977).

Richard McLanathan, *The American Tradition in the Arts* (New York, 1968).

Mary Ann Tigle and Elizabeth Ewing Lang, *Art America* (New York, 1977).

Eugene Neuhaus, *The History and Ideals of American Art* (Stanford, 1931).

Royal Cortissoz, *American Artists* (New York, 1923).

Robert B. Harshe, "Art and American Life," An Address in *National Education Association: Addresses and Proceedings* (Salt Lake City, 1913), pp. 581–86.

Chapter 11

IMPERIALISM AND REALPOLITIK

Richard W. Leopold, *The Growth of American Foreign Policy* (Cambridge, Mass., 1961).

Foster Rhea Dulles, *America's Rise to World Power 1898–1954* (New York, 1955).

William Appleman Williams, *The Roots of the Modern American Empire* (New York, 1969).

George F. Kennan, *American Diplomacy 1900–1950* (Chicago, 1985; first published 1951).

Robert Osgood, *Ideals and Self-Interest in America's Foreign Relations* (Chicago, 1953).

Frank Merli and Theodore A. Wilson, editors, *Makers of American Diplomacy* (New York, 1974).

Richard D. Challener, *Admirals, Generals, and American Foreign Policy, 1889–1914* (Princeton, N.J., 1973).

Goran Rystad, *Ambiguous Imperialism: American Foreign Policy and Domestic Politics at the Turn of the Century* (Esselte Studium, Lund, Sweden, 1975).
James A. Field, Jr., "American Imperialism," *American Historical Review*, 83 (1976), 644–68.

ECONOMIC EXPANSION

Emily Rosenberg, *Spreading the American Dream: American Economic and Cultural Expansion 1890–1945* (New York, 1982).
Mira Wilkins, *The Emergence of the Multinational Enterprise: American Business Abroad from the Colonial Era to 1914* (Cambridge, Mass., 1970).
William H. Becker, *The Dynamics of Business-Government Relations: Industry and Exports 1893 to 1921* (Chicago, 1982).
Robert B. Davies, *Peacefully Working to Conquer the World: Singer Sewing Machines in Foreign Markets 1854–1920* (Salem, N.H., 1976).

RACIAL ATTITUDES

Rubin F. Weston, *Racism in United States Imperialism: The Influence of Racial Assumptions on American Foreign Policy 1893–1946* (Columbia, S.C., 1972).
Willard B. Gatewood, Jr., *Black Americans and the White Man's Burden 1898–1903* (Champaign, Ill., 1975).
Robert W. Rydell, *All the World's a Fair: Visions of Empire at American International Expositions, 1876–1916* (Chicago, 1984).

THE PHILIPPINES

Peter Stanley, *A Nation in the Making: The Philippines and the United States 1899–1921* (Cambridge, Mass., 1974).
Stuart C. Miller, *"Benevolent Assimilation" The American Conquest of the Philippines 1899–1903* (New Haven, Conn., 1982).
Glenn A. May, *Social Engineering in the Philippines: The Aims, Execution, and Impact of America's Colonial Policy 1900–1913* (Westport, Conn., 1980).
John M. Gates, *Schoolbooks and Krags: The United States Army in the Philippines 1898–1902* (Westport, Conn., 1973).
Richard Hofstadter, "Cuba, the Philippines, and Manifest Destiny," in Hofstadter, *The Paranoid Style in American Politics and other Essays* (New York and London, 1966).

ROOSEVELT'S FOREIGN POLICY

Howard K. Beale, *Theodore Roosevelt and the Rise of America to World Power* (Baltimore, 1984; first published 1956).

Frederick W. Marks III, *Velvet on Iron: The Diplomacy of Theodore Roosevelt* (Lincoln, Nebr., 1979).

Richard A. Collin, *Theodore Roosevelt, Culture, Diplomacy, and Expansion: A New View of American Imperialism* (Baton Rouge, La., 1985).

Gordon C. O'Gara, *Theodore Roosevelt and the Rise of the Modern Navy* (New York, 1969).

Raymond A. Esthus, *Theodore Roosevelt and the International Rivalries* (Waltham, Mass., 1970).

FOREIGN POLICY UNDER TAFT

Walter Vinton Scholes, *The Foreign Policies of the Taft Administration* (Columbia, Mo., 1970).

William Howard Taft, *The United States and Peace* (New York, 1973; first published 1914).

Ralph Eldon Minger, *William Howard Taft and United States Foreign Policy: The Apprenticeship Years, 1900–1908* (Urbana, Ill., 1975).

RELATIONS WITH LATIN AMERICA

Samuel F. Bemis, *The Latin American Policy of the United States* (New York, 1943).

Walter LaFeber, *Inevitable Revolutions: The United States in Central America* (New York, 1983).

Lester D. Langley, *Struggle for the American Mediterranean* (Athens, Ga., 1976).

Dana G. Munro, *Intervention and Dollar Diplomacy in the Caribbean, 1900–1921* (Westport, Conn., 1964).

Lester D. Langley, *The Banana Wars: An Inner History of American Empire 1900–1934* (Lexington, Ky., 1983).

Ramon Ruiz, *Cuba: The Making of a Revolution* (New York, 1970; first published 1968).

David Healy, *The United States in Cuba, 1898–1902: Generals, Politicians, and the Search for Policy* (Madison, Wis., 1963).

THE PANAMA CANAL

David McCullogh, *The Path between the Seas: The Creation of the Panama Canal 1870–1914* (New York, 1978).

Walter LaFeber, *The Panama Canal: The Crisis in Historical Perspective* (New York and Oxford, 1979).

RELATIONS WITH MEXICO

Karl M. Schmitt, *Mexico and the United States, 1821–1973: Conflict and Coexistence* (New York, 1974).

Josefina Vazquez and Lorenzo Meyer, *The United States and Mexico* (Chicago, 1985).

P. Edward Haley, *Revolution and Intervention: the Diplomacy of Taft and Wilson with Mexico 1910–1917* (Cambridge, Mass., 1970).

RELATIONS WITH CHINA

Akira Iriye, *Across the Pacific: An Inner History of American-East Asia Relations* (New York, 1967).

Warren I. Cohen, *America's Response to China, An Interpretive History of Sino-American Relations* (second edition, New York, 1980; first published 1971).

Paul A. Varg, *The Making of a Myth: The United States and China 1897–1912* (Westport, Conn., 1980; first published 1968).

Michael Hunt, *The Making of a Special Relationship: The United States and China to 1914* (New York, 1983).

Jerry Israel, *Progressivism and the Open Door: America and China 1905–1921* (Pittsburgh, 1971).

Robert McClellan, *The Heathen Chinese: A Study of American Attitudes toward China, 1890–1905* (Columbus, Ohio, 1971).

RELATIONS WITH JAPAN

Akira Iriye, *Pacific Estrangement: Japanese and American Expansion 1897–1911* (Cambridge, Mass., 1972).

Raymond A. Esthus, *Theodore Roosevelt and Japan* (Seattle, 1966).

Thomas A. Bailey, *Theodore Roosevelt and the Japanese-American Crisis* (Gloucester, Mass., 1964).

Charles E. Neu, *The Troubled Encounter: The United States and Japan* (Melbourne, Fla., 1979; first published 1975).

———, *An Uncertain Friendship: Theodore Roosevelt and Japan 1906–1909* (Cambridge, Mass., 1967).

WILSON'S FOREIGN POLICIES

Harley Notter, *The Origins of the Foreign Policy of Woodrow Wilson* (New York, 1965; first published 1937).

Arthur Link, *Wilson the Diplomatist* (Princeton, N.J., 1957).

———, *Woodrow Wilson: Revolution, War and Peace* (Arlington Heights, Ill., 1979).

———, editor, *Woodrow Wilson and a Revolutionary World 1913–1921* (Chapel Hill, N.C., 1982).

Lloyd C. Gardner, *Safe for Democracy: The Anglo-American Response to Revolution, 1913–1923* (New York and Oxford, 1984).

Jeffrey J. Safford, *Wilsonian Maritime Diplomacy* (New Brunswick, N.J., 1978).

George Sylvester Viereck, editor, *As They Saw Us* (New York, 1929).

——, *The Strangest Friendship in History: Woodrow Wilson and Colonel House* (New York, 1932).

Sigmund Freud and William C. Bullitt, *Woodrow Wilson: A Psychological Study* (London, 1967).

Edwin A. Weinstein, *Woodrow Wilson: A Medical and Psychological Biography* (Princeton, N.J., 1981).

Kendrick A. Clements, *William Jennings Bryan: Missionary Isolationist* (Knoxville, Tenn., 1982).

Chapter 12

WORLD WAR I

Bernadotte Schmitt and Harole E. Wedeler, *The World in the Crucible, 1914–1919* (New York, 1984).

A.J.P. Taylor, *The Struggle for Mastery in Europe, 1848–1918* (Oxford and New York, 1954).

Frederick Paxson, *American Democracy and the World War*, 3 vols. (Totowa, N.J., 1986; first published 1936–48).

Ellis W. Hawley, *The Great War and the Search for a Modern Order* (New York, 1979).

Manfred Jonas, *The United States and Germany: A Diplomatic History* (Ithaca, N.Y., 1985).

Daniel M. Smith, *The Great Departure: The United States and World War I 1914–1920* (New York, 1965).

Robert H. Ferrell, *Woodrow Wilson and World War I 1917–1921* (New York, 1986).

NEUTRALITY

Patrick Devlin, *Too Proud to Fight: Woodrow Wilson's Neutrality* (New York and Oxford, 1975).

Marion Siney, *The Allied Blockade of Germany 1914–1916* (Ann Arbor, Mich., 1957).

Thomas A. Bailey and Paul B. Ryan, *The Lusitania Disaster: An Episode in Modern Warfare and Diplomacy* (New York, 1975).

Barbara Tuchman, *The Zimmermann Telegram* (New York, 1985; first published 1966).

Edward Buehrig, "Wilson's Neutrality Re-Examined," *World Politics,* 3 (October 1950), 1–19.

Bernadotte Schmitt, "American Neutrality, 1914–1917," *Journal of Modern History,* 8 (June 1936), 200–211.

Paul Birdsall, "Neutrality and Economic Pressures, 1914–1917," *Science and Society,* 3 (Spring 1939), 217–28.

Harold Synett, "The Business Press and American Neutrality, 1914–1917," *Mississippi Valley Historical Review*, 32 (September 1945), 215–30.
Daniel Smith, "Robert Lansing and the Formulation of American Neutrality Policies, 1914–1915," *Mississippi Valley Historical Review*, 43 (June 1956), 59–81.

INTERVENTION

Ross Gregory, *The Origins of American Intervention in the First World War* (New York, 1972).
D. F. Fleming, "Our Entry into the World War in 1917," *World Politics*, 11 (February 1940), 75–86.
Richard Leopold, "The Problem of American Intervention in 1917: An Historical Prospect," *World Politics*, 11 (April 1950), 404–25.
Walter Millis, "Will We Stay Out of the Next War?: How We Entered the Last One," *New Republic*, 83 (July 31, 1935), 323–27.
H. Schuyler Foster, Jr., "How America Became Belligerent," *American Journal of Sociology*, 40 (January 1935), 464–75.

MOBILIZATION

J. G. Harbord, *The American Army in France, 1917–1918* (Boston, 1936).
Russell F. Weigley, *The American Way of War: A History of United States Military Strategy and Policy* (New York, 1973).
——, *History of the United States Army* (New York, 1967).
Bernard Baruch, *American Industry in War* (New York, 1941).
Valerie Jean Connor, *The National War Labor Board: Stability, Social Justice, and the Voluntary State in World War I* (Chapel Hill, N.C., 1983).
Robert D. Cuff, *The War Industries Board: Business-Government Relations during World War I* (Baltimore, 1973).
Charles Gilbert, *American Financing of World War I* (Westport, Conn., 1970).
John F. McClymer, *War and Welfare: Social Engineering in America 1880–1925* (Westport, Conn., 1980).
Stephen L. Vaughn, *Holding Fast the Inner Lines: Democracy, Nationalism, and the Committee on Public Information* (Chapel Hill, N.C., 1980).
Paul A. Koistinen, "The 'Industrial-Military Complex' in Historical Perspective: World War I," *Business History Review*, 41 (1967), 378–403.

THE HOME FRONT

David M. Kennedy, *Over Here: The First World War and American Society* (New York and Oxford, 1980).
Edward R. Ellis, *Echoes of Distant Thunder: Life in the United States 1914–1918* (New York, 1975).

Maurine W. Greenwald, *Women, War, and Work: The Impact of World War I on Women Workers in the United States* (Westport, Conn., 1980).

Barbara J. Steinson, *American Women's Activism in World War I* (New York, 1981).

Michael T. Isenberg, *War on Films: The American Cinema and World War I 1914–1941* (Cranbury, N.J., 1981).

Frederick C. Luebke, *Bonds of Loyalty: German-Americans and World War I* (DeKalb, Ill., 1974).

Alfred W. Crosby, Jr., *Epidemic and Peace, 1918* (Westport, Conn., 1976).

Frederick Paxson, "The American War Government 1917–1918," *American Historical Review*, 26 (October 1920), 54–76.

Sidney Kaplan, "Social Engineers as Saviors: Effects of World War I on some American Liberals," *Journal of the History of Ideas*, 17 (June 1956), 347–69.

Allen F. Davis, "Welfare, Reform, and World War I," *American Quarterly*, 19 (1967), 516–33.

WARTIME POLITICS

Seward W. Livermore, *Politics is Adjourned* (Seattle, 1966), second, paperback edition entitled *Woodrow Wilson and the War Congress 1916–1918* (Seattle, 1968).

S. D. Lovell, *The Presidential Election of 1916* (Carbondale, Ill., 1980).

David Sarasohn, "The Election of 1916: Realigning the Rockies," *Western Historical Quarterly*, 11 (1980), 285–305.

David Burner, "The Breakup of the Wilson Coalition of 1916," *Mid-America*, 45 (1963), 18–35.

Selig Adler, "The Congressional Election of 1918," *South Atlantic Quarterly*, 36 (October 1937), 447–65.

Seward W. Livermore, "The Sectional Issue in the 1918 Congressional Election," *Mississippi Valley Historical Review*, 35 (June 1948), 29–60.

BLACK AMERICA IN WARTIME

Florette Henri, *Black Migration: Movement North 1900–1920* (Garden City, N.Y., 1975).

Arthur E. Barbeau and Florette Henri, *The Unknown Soldiers: Black American Troops in World War I* (Philadelphia, 1974).

Marvin E. Fletcher, *The Black Soldier and Officer in the United States Army 1891–1917* (Columbia, Mo., 1974).

Robert V. Haynes, *A Night of Violence: The Houston Riot of 1917* (Baton Rouge, La., 1976).

Elliot M. Rudwick, *Race Riot at East St. Louis, July 2, 1917* (Carbondale, Ill., 1964).

William M. Tuttle, *Race Riot: Chicago in the Red Summer of 1919* (New York, 1970).

Chapter 13

DISSENT IN WARTIME

Charles Chatfield, *For Peace and Justice: Pacifism in America 1914–1941* (Knoxville, Tenn., 1971).

C. Roland Marchand, *The American Peace Movement and Social Reform, 1898–1918* (Princeton, N.J., 1972).

Charles DeBenedetti, *Peace Heroes in Twentieth Century America* (Bloomington, Ind., 1986).

——, *The Peace Reform in American History* (Bloomington, Ind., 1980).

Paul L. Murphy, *World War I and the Origin of Civil Liberties in the United States* (New York, 1980).

H. C. Peterson and Gilbert Fitt, *Opponents of War 1917–1918* (Westport, Conn., 1986; first published 1957).

Charles Stewart, "Prussianizing Wisconsin," *Atlantic Monthly*, 123 (January 1919), 99–105.

THE GREAT RED SCARE

Robert Murray, *Red Scare: A Study in National Hysteria 1919–1920* (Westport, Conn., 1980; first published 1955).

William Preston, *Aliens and Dissenters: Federal Suppression of Radicals, 1903–1933* (Cambridge, Mass., 1963).

Stanley Cohen, *A. Mitchell Palmer, Politician* (New York, 1977; first published 1963).

George Mowny, "The First World War and American Democracy," in Jesse Clarkson and Thomas Cochran, editors, *War as a Social Institution* (New York, 1941).

John Blum, "Nativism, Anti-Radicalism, and the Foreign Scare 1917–1920," *Midwest Journal*, 3 (Winter 1950–51).

Robert Warth, "The Palmer Raids," *South Atlantic Quarterly*, 48 (January 1949), 1–23.

Nelson Van Thalen, "The Bolsheviki and the Orange Growers," *Pacific Historical Review*, 22 (August 1953), 39–50.

RELATIONS WITH SOVIET RUSSIA

Peter G. Filene, *Americans and the Soviet Experiment 1917–1933* (Cambridge, Mass., 1967).

John L. Gaddis, *Russia, the Soviet Union and the United States: An Interpretive History* (New York, 1978).

Beatrice Farnsworth, *William C. Bullitt and the Soviet Union* (Bloomington, Ind., 1967).

George F. Kennan, *Soviet American Relations, 1917–1920* (Princeton, N.J., 1956).
——, *Soviet Foreign Policy, 1917–1941* (Princeton, N.J., 1960).
Christopher Lasch, *The American Liberals and the Russian Revolution* (New York, 1962).
John Thompson, *Russia, Bolshevism, and the Versailles Peace* (Princeton, N.J., 1967; first published 1966).
Betty M. Untenberger, editor, *American Intervention in the Russian Civil War* (Lexington, Mass., 1969).

THE PARIS PEACE CONFERENCE AND THE TREATY OF VERSAILLES

Ray Stannard Baker, *Woodrow Wilson and World Settlement* 3 vols. (Garden City, N.Y., 1922–1923).
Thomas Bailey, *Woodrow Wilson and the Lost Peace* (New York, 1944); *Woodrow Wilson and the Great Betrayal* (New York, 1945); published jointly as *Wilson and the Peacemakers* (New York, 1947).
Paul Birdsall, *Versailles Twenty Years After* (Hamden, Conn., 1962; first published 1941).
Inga Flota, *Colonel House in Paris: A Study of American Policy at the Paris Peace Conference 1919* (Princeton, N.J., 1980; first published 1973).
Herbert Hoover, *The Ordeal of Woodrow Wilson* (New York, 1958).
Keith Nelson, *Victors Divided: America and the Allies in Germany, 1918–1923* (Berkeley, Ca., 1973).
R. C. Binkley, "Ten Years of Peace Conference History," *Journal of Modern History*, 1 (December 1929), 607–29.
Paul Birdsall, "The Second Decade of Peace Conference History," *Journal of Modern History*, 11 (September 1939), 362–78.

AMERICAN CONTROVERSY OVER THE LEAGUE

Denna F. Fleming, *The United States and the League of Nations 1918–1920* (New York and London, 1932).
Ralph A. Stone, *The Irreconcilables: The Fight Against the League of Nations* (New York, 1970, 1973).
——, *Wilson and the League of Nations: Why America's Rejection?* (Melbourne, Fla., 1978).
William C. Widenor, *Henry Cabot Lodge and the Search for an American Foreign Policy* (Berkeley, Ca., 1980).
John Garraty, *Henry Cabot Lodge* (New York, 1965; first published 1953).
Karl Schriftgiesser, *The Gentleman from Massachusetts: Henry Cabot Lodge* (Boston, 1944).
Selig Adler, "The War-Guilt Question and American Disillusionment, 1919–1928," *Journal of Modern History*, 23 (March 1951), 1–28.

AFTERMATH

Paul Fussell, *The Great War and the Modern Memory* (New York and Oxford, 1975).

Stuart I. Rochester, *American Liberal Disillusionment in the Wake of World War I* (University Park, Pa., 1977).

Stephen R. Ward, editor, *The War Generation: Veterans of the First World War* (Milwood, N.Y., 1975).

Stanley Cooperman, *World War I and the American Novel* (Baltimore, 1967).

Index

⟨ornament⟩